A HIS   O

RUSSIA,
CENTRAL ASIA AND
MONGOLIA

THE BLACKWELL HISTORY OF THE WORLD (HOTW)

General Editor: **R. I. Moore**

Published

A History of Middle and South America
Peter Bakewell, Emory University

A History of India
Burton Stein, Late of SOAS

A History of Russia, Central Asia and Mongolia
David Christian, Macquarie University

In Preparation

A History of the Mediterranean
World
David Abulafia,
University of Cambridge

The Birth of the Modern World
C. A. Bayly, University of Cambridge

The Origins of Human Societies
Peter Bogucki, Princeton University

A History of Australia, New Zealand
and the Pacific
Donald Denoon,
Australian National University

A History of Africa
Paul Lovejoy, Toronto University

Elements of World History
R. I. Moore, University of Newcastle

A History of the Islamic World
David Morgan, SOAS

A History of the
Ancient Mediterranean
Ian Morris, Stanford University

A History of South-East Asia
Anthony Reid,
Australian National University

A History of China
Morris Rossabi, Columbia University

The Early Modern World
Sanjay Subrahmanyam,
University of Delhi and Ecole des
hautes études en Sciences Sociales, Paris

A History of Japan
Conrad Totman, Yale University

The Beginnings of Civilization
Robert Wenke,
University of Washington

A HISTORY OF
RUSSIA,
CENTRAL ASIA
AND MONGOLIA

*VOLUME I: INNER EURASIA FROM
PREHISTORY TO THE MONGOL EMPIRE*

DAVID CHRISTIAN

First published 1998

Reprinted 2000

Blackwell Publishers Ltd
108 Cowley Road
Oxford OX4 1JF
UK

Blackwell Publishers Inc.
350 Main Street
Malden, Massachusetts 02148
USA

British Library Cataloguing in Publication Data

A CIP catalogue record for this book is available from the British Library.

Library of Congress Cataloging-in-Publication Data has been applied for

ISBN 0–631–18321–3 (hdbk)
ISBN 0–631–20814–3 (pbk)

Typeset in 10 on 12 pt Plantin by Newgen Imaging Systems (P) Ltd, India
Printed in Great Britain by TJ International, Padstow, Cornwall

This book is printed on acid-free paper

CONTENTS

PLATES

FIGURES

Maps

TABLES

SERIES EDITOR'S PREFACE

THERE is nothing new in the attempt to understand history as a whole. To know how humanity began and how it has come to its present condition is one of the oldest and most universal of human needs, expressed in the religious and philosophical systems of every civilization. But only in the last few decades has it begun to appear both necessary and possible to meet that need by means of a rational and systematic appraisal of current knowledge. History claimed its independence as a field of scholarship with its own subject matter and its own rules and methods, not simply a branch of literature, rhetoric, law, philosophy or religion, in the second half of the nineteenth century. World History has begun to do so only in the second half of the twentieth. Its emergence has been delayed on the one hand by simple ignorance – for the history of enormous stretches of space and time has been known not at all, or so patchily and superficially as not to be worth revisiting – and on the other by the lack of a widely acceptable basis upon which to organize and discuss what is nevertheless the enormous and enormously diverse knowledge that we have.

Both obstacles are now being rapidly overcome. There is almost no part of the world or period of its history that is not the subject of vigorous and sophisticated investigation by archaeologists and historians. It is truer than it has ever been that knowledge is growing and perspectives changing and multiplying more quickly than it is possible to assimilate and record them in synthetic form. Nevertheless the attempt to grasp the human past as a whole can and must be made. Facing a common future of headlong and potentially catastrophic transformation, the world needs its common history. Since we no longer believe that a complete or definitive account is ultimately attainable by the mere accumulation of knowledge we are free to offer the best we can manage at the moment. Since we no longer suppose that it is our business as historians to detect or proclaim "The End of History" in the fruition of any grand design, human or divine, there is no single path to trace, or golden key to turn. There is also a growing wealth of ways in which world history can be written. The oldest and simplest view, that world history is best understood as the history of contacts between peoples previously isolated from one another, from which (some think) all change arises, is now seen to be capable of application since the earliest times. An influential alternative focuses upon the tendency of economic exchanges to create self-sufficient but ever expand-ing "worlds" which sustain successive systems of power and culture. Others seek to understand the differences between societies and cultures, and there-fore the particular character of each, by comparing the ways in which they have developed their values, social relationships and structures of power. The rapidly developing field of ecological history returns to a very ancient tradi-tion of seeing interaction with the physical environment, and with other animals, at the centre of the human predicament, while insisting that its understanding demands an approach which is culturally, chronologically and geographically comprehensive.

The Blackwell History of the World does not seek to embody any of these approaches, but to support them all, as it will use them all, by providing a modern, comprehensive and accessible account of the entire human past. Its plan is that of a barrel, in which the indispensable narratives of very long term regional development are bound together by global surveys of the inter-action between regions at particular times, and of the great transformations which they have experienced in common, or visited upon one another. Each volume, of course, reflects the idiosyncrasies of its sources and its subjects, as well as the judgement and experience of its author, but in combination they offer a framework in which the history of every part of the world can be viewed, and a basis upon which most aspects of human activity can be com-pared. A frame imparts perspective. Comparison implies respect for differ-ence. That is the beginning of what the past has to offer the future.

R. I. Moore

SERIES EDITOR'S ACKNOWLEDGEMENTS

The Editor is grateful to all of the contributors to the Blackwell History of the World for advice and assistance on the design and contents of the series as a whole as well as on individual volumes. Both Editor and Contributors wish to place on record their immense debt, individually and collectively, to John Davey, formerly of Blackwell Publishers. The series would not have been initiated without his vision and enthusiasm, and could not have been realised without his energy, skill and diplomacy.

ACKNOWLEDGEMENTS

IN working on this book during seven years I have accumulated many debts, and I can formally thank only a small number of those who helped me. I hope those I don't mention will forgive my negligence but know that I am grateful all the same.

My greatest debt is to Bob Moore, who first suggested that I attempt a coherent history of Russia and Central Asia. He did so after reading a study I had written on the vodka trade in which he (rightly) detected an enthusiasm for world history. Bob even supported me when I decided that Mongolia and Sinking had to be included as well; and when I panicked at the size of the task I had taken on, his steady insistence on the importance of large, synoptic histories meant a tremendous amount to me. As editors, John Davey and Tessa Harvey have maintained just the balance of pressure and encouragement that a writer needs; their energy and their faith in the 'Blackwell History of the World' and this particular volume augur well for the success of the entire series.

My main institutional debt is to Macquarie University, where I have taught Russian and World History for twenty years. I was granted several periods of Study Leave and two research grants while working on this book, and this allowed me to travel extensively in Inner Eurasia. I am also extremely grateful to the Australian Research Council, which helped fund three research trips. Colleagues in Macquarie's History Department provided a friendly and stimulating atmosphere, and didn't flinch as I drifted into Central Asian and Mongolian history, World History, and eventually even 'Big History'.

Intellectual support is doubly necessary for those attempting large synoptic histories such as this in a discipline in which synthesis is still regarded as an inferior skill to primary research. So I am extremely grateful for the many bibliographical suggestions, friendly criticisms and interested questions I received from specialists in fields in which I was a beginner. Jonathan Shepard helped me with sources on the early history of Rus'. Adeeb Khalid and Wynne Russell gave me a lot of bibliographical advice at a very early stage. At a later stage, I benefited from the advice, suggestions and criticisms of members of Indiana University's superb Department of Central Eurasian Studies and Research Institute for Inner Asian Studies, including Aleksandr Naymark, Denis Sinor, Devin Deweese, Yuri and Ludmilla Bregel and Christopher

Beckwith. Members of the small community of Australasian Slavists have encouraged me in what may have seemed at first a crazy project. They include Linda Bowman, Stephen Wheatcroft, Harry Rigby, Liz Waters, Graeme Gill, Stephen Fortescue and John Miller. Members of the recently formed Australasian Society for Inner Asian Studies have also been extremely supportive. Colin Mackerras, Lewis Mayo, Shahram Akbarzadeh, Bill Maley, Ian Bedford, Bill Leadbetter, John Perkins, Craig Benjamin, Sam Lieu, Alison Betts and Seven Helms have all read or commented on pieces of work generated while writing this volume. Stephen Wheatcroft first encouraged me to attempt a formal defence of the notion of 'Inner Eurasia', and Jerry Bentley published the paper that emerged from this attempt, while Bill Leadbetter alerted me to the crudity of some of my early attempts to generalize about the Scythian world. Amongst the growing community of 'World Historians', Jerry Bentley and Terry Burke have been extremely encouraging at different stages of my writing, as have Joop Goudsblom and Fred Spier. Alev Guven taught me basic Turkish, and Archie Brown kindly invited me for a brief but productive visit to St Anthony's college. In 1997, George Brooks and David Ransel invited me to spend a very useful and enjoyable month in Bloomington, Indiana. Carole Menzies, Librarian of the Slavonic Reading Room of the Bodleian Library, helped me trace some obscure references during two brief research trips to Oxford; Slavists who have worked in the Bodleian will know what a pleasure it is to work in Carole's fiefdom. I am extremely grateful to Helen Rappaport for her painstaking copy editing of a difficult manuscript.

I also want to thank the many people in the former Soviet Union and Mongolia who treated me with such hospitality during my travels. They include Dmitrii, Katya and Vera Shivdkovskii, Irina Dolina, Natasha Skorobogatykh, Valerii Nikolayev, Valya and Sasha Pavlenko, Marat Durdiyev and Mayya Erina.

With a project such as this, the conventional caution (that no one mentioned here can be held reponsible for the inadquacies of my work) deserves particular emphasis. Some colleagues warned me that I was attempting an impossible task, and specialists will be aware of advice I should have taken but did not take or failed to seek out.

Finally, writing a large book on a complex topic can be lonely work. My mother, Carol, is a writer and she was also my first teacher. I hope she will accept this as a gift to her and to my father, John, who would have loved to see this book if he had lived long enough. I also know that I would not have enjoyed working on this volume so much, and could not have completed it without the support of Chardi, Joshua and Emily. This book owes much more than they realize to their love and companionship.

David Christian
February 1998

INTRODUCTION

> As a great yurt are the heavens
> Covering the steppe in all directions
> On the plain of Ch'ih-le
> Under the mountains of Yin
>
> Blue, blue is the sky
> Vast, vast is the steppe
> Here the grass bends with the breeze
> Here are the cattle and sheep
>
> Hsien-pi[1]

DEFINING INNER EURASIA

This is the first volume of a two-part history of Russia and the lands of what I will call 'Inner Eurasia'. This volume surveys the prehistory and history of this huge and distinctive region up to the time of the Mongol empire, in the thirteenth century of the contemporary era.

Though designed to stand on its own, when taken with the second volume it will offer a unified history, from prehistory to the present day, of the lands that lie at the heart of the Eurasian landmass. Inner Eurasia includes most of the former Soviet Union – Russia, Ukraine, Belarus, Moldova, and the Baltic states – as well as Russia's huge territories in Siberia. It also includes Russia's former empire in Central Asia, as well as China's central Asian empire, within the modern provinces of Sinkiang and Kansu. Finally, it includes Mongolia, both the parts within modern China, and those within the Mongolian People's Republic. I have not discussed the ecologically distinctive highlands of the Caucasus and Tibet, though one could make a case for their inclusion.

Inner Eurasia is one of two distinct regions that make up the Eurasian landmass. 'Outer Eurasia', its logical complement, includes several well-watered coastal sub-continents that lie in a great arc from Europe, to the Middle East, to India, and to South and East Asia. Dense populations emerged first in Outer Eurasia; so, too, did the world's first urban, literate civilizations. Dazzled by these rich and complex societies, and absorbed in the vast amount of written documentation they generated, historians have neglected

Map 0.1 Inner Eurasia and Outer Eurasia.

the drier, and more sparsely populated heartland of Eurasia. Both the 'logo-centrism' (the bias towards literate sources and literate societies) and the 'agrocentrism' (the bias towards agrarian, urban civilizations) of modern historiography have focused historical research overwhelmingly on the lands of Outer Eurasia. These two volumes are about what the geographer, H. J. Mackinder, called the 'heartland'. Dominating the heartland is a vast, arid plain, the largest plain in the world. Mackinder called this the 'Great Lowland'.[2] My central theme is the colonization and settlement of Inner Eurasia by our own species of large mammal over a period of 100,000 years.

I would have preferred to use an existing historical label for this region, but reluctantly decided that none are quite right. Mackinder's phrase, the 'heartland', is tempting, but linked to claims for the geo-political significance of this region that I do not accept. Even more tempting is the term, 'Central Eurasia' (or 'Inner Asia'), as used by Denis Sinor. For some periods, 'Central' and 'Inner Eurasia' cover much the same ground. Despite this, I have reluctantly decided not to use the term, 'Central Eurasia'. There are two main reasons. First, Sinor uses it primarily in a cultural sense, to define the region dominated, at any particular period, by non-agrarian peoples. This means that the borders of 'Central Eurasia' are cultural rather than ecological or geographical, and that they are, therefore, mobile. Indeed, Sinor argues that Central Eurasia has steadily contracted in recent centuries. Such a category makes it difficult to explore how ecology has shaped agrarian as well as pastoralist societies, and also shaped their long-term relationship. Second, the phrase 'Central Eurasia' is often used as a synonym for 'Inner Asia', which has linked it closely with the study of peoples speaking Altaic languages. This anchors it too firmly to language rather than ecology or geography.[3]

While many fine histories have been written about parts of this huge territory, it is not usual to treat it as a single historical unit.[4] This is largely because the various regions of Inner Eurasia vary greatly in their linguistic, ecological and cultural traditions, so that each has attracted its own body of specialists – Mongolists, Iranologists, specialists in pastoralism, in Chaghatai Turkic, in Siberian shamanism. In addition, written sources are extremely sparse, especially for the steppe regions, so that specialists have to tease information from difficult, obscure and prejudiced written sources, or rely on archaeology or linguistic studies for much of what they say. These difficulties have generated some astonishingly erudite scholarship. But they have also discouraged attempts at synthesis. So the attempt to write a unified history of Inner Eurasia requires some justification.[5]

I have tried to write a coherent history of this region for two reasons. First, I believe it is useful in principle for historians to look at the past from unfamiliar perspectives. While the large-scale perspective may miss details and nuances that are important on a more conventional scale, it may also reveal larger patterns that other approaches miss. For example, it provides the history of modern Russia with an ecological and historical context absent from many standard histories of Russia. It also highlights large-scale patterns of interaction between pastoralist and farming societies from North China to the Balkans.

The second reason for trying to see the history of Inner Eurasia whole is that Inner Eurasia is in fact a coherent historical region.[6] Despite its ecological and cultural variety, there is an underlying unity to the geography, and consequently, to the history of Inner Eurasia. This means that it is impossible fully to understand the history of parts of this region without seeing them in their larger context. There is no need to state such a hypothesis dogmatically. There are good reasons why historians have treated Russia or Central Asia or Mongolia or Siberia as coherent regions with coherent histories. I will claim merely that it may also be fruitful to think of 'Inner Eurasia' as historians already think of 'Europe', or 'Africa' or 'India'. I will argue that there is an ecological unity to Inner Eurasia that has shaped the history, the lifeways, and the politics of the region. Even where we cannot identify political, ideological or economic links between different parts of Inner Eurasia, their societies faced similar ecological, political and military challenges, and responded in similar ways.

For these reasons, I will argue that the history of Inner Eurasia is different from that of Outer Eurasia. To state the central claim baldly, it is that the relative ecological difficulties of Inner Eurasia required of the peoples that settled it strategies of ecological, economic, political and military mobilization that were subtly but significantly different from those of Outer Eurasia. These shaped all features of Inner Eurasian history, from the Stone Age to the twentieth century.

Finally, I will argue that the history of Inner Eurasia is *important*. It is important in its own right, and because of the scale and distinctiveness of the societies that occupied it. But what happened in inner Eurasia also had a profound effect on what happened in Outer Eurasia. This is palpably true of the twentieth century, when Inner Eurasia was dominated by one of the world's two superpowers, the USSR. However, it has also been true in much earlier periods as well. For several millennia, the histories of China, India, Persia, Mesopotamia and Europe were affected militarily, politically, commercially and culturally by the distinctive societies Of Inner Eurasia. Inner Eurasian peoples also carried ideas, goods and traditions between the various regions of Outer Eurasia, which explains why Eurasian history has retained a certain unity despite the many differences between its various regions. Writers such as the Greek historian, Herodotus, or the Han historian, Ssu-ma Ch'ien, were merely the first to write about the historical importance of inner Eurasian history; but archaeology shows that the region's importance extended deep into prehistory.

THEMES AND APPROACHES

The past is an entire Universe, and our attempts to grasp it are childishly inadequate. Nevertheless, we have to try. A volume covering as large a territory and as large a period of time as this, must select ruthlessly, and the knowledge and expertise needed to do the job completely are beyond the abilities of any one author, certainly *this* author, a specialist in Russian history by training.

Though I have tried to suggest some novel perspectives, I make no claim to offer information that will be new to specialists, nor can I do justice to the vast amount of primary research available.[7] Particularly in Inner Asian history, the task of handling the primary sources is exceptionally difficult. They are scarce, difficult to interpret, and in a wide variety of often obscure languages. This is a job for the specialist, not the synthesizer. So is the interpretation of archaeological or linguistic evidence. As a result, I have had to rely largely on secondary works produced by specialists. I have concentrated mainly on more recent works, as well as modern editions of some of the more familiar primary sources. I have also used some of the vast and impressive monographic literature on each of the many areas this volume discusses, though specialists will easily note volumes that should have been used but were not, or volumes that should not have been used but were. At best, a volume like this can synthesize the better general studies of each area, try not to ignore too many detailed studies, and try not to add too many new inaccuracies.

However, on the large scale of these volumes, nuance is often less important than trend. I hope that the risk of missing nuances or misreading details is offset by a breadth of view that allows the presentation of a clear story, and may sometimes reveal trends and regularities that even the specialists have missed.

I focus on several related themes. The first concerns the distinctive features of Inner Eurasia as a unit of world history. 'Inner Eurasia' is the sort of historical object that only large-scale studies can bring into focus. However, an awareness of the distinctive features of the region should also affect more detailed studies of the region's history. The second group of themes turns on the complex dialectic between lifeways and social and political structures. How did the distinctive lifeways of Inner Eurasia shape the larger social and political units that often appear to dominate history? How, in turn, did the history of these large units help preserve or transform lifeways? What links households, tribes and villages, to states and empires in this region? This is the same dialectic that interested Marx as he constructed his concept of 'modes of production'. What is the relationship between the technologies people use to sustain life (Marx's 'forces of production') and the social and ideological structures within which individual human beings act ('social relations')? So, though this volume is a social history, it is not just that. It explores the links between the dominant themes of social history and those of a more traditional historiography that focused on state structures.

These central themes can be summarized in a single, major question: how did the ecological conditions of Inner Eurasia affect the relationship between lifeways and social structures, and the ways both lifeways and social structures evolved in this region?

THE ARGUMENT

This first volume covers 100,000 years of human history, while the second volume will cover a mere 800 years. The first volume describes the migrations by which Inner Eurasia was first settled by members of our species. It then deals with the distinctive lifeways that evolved in Inner Eurasia during the neolithic period. Finally, it describes the equally distinctive ways in which state-like structures evolved in Inner Eurasia.

Our species evolved in the warm climates of Africa's savanna lands. This meant that certain social and technological adaptations were necessary before early humans could settle colder regions of the world. The most accessible regions of inner Eurasia were arid, and had less abundant vegetation than the better-watered sub-continents that surround it to the west, south and east. The crucial adaptations necessary for colonizing this cold, dry, heartland, were the control of fire, and a concentration on hunting rather than gathering as the main source of foodstuffs, clothing and protection from the elements. For all these reasons, Inner Eurasia was settled later than Outer Eurasia, and by communities that exploited animals more than plants. The history of Inner Eurasia was distinctive, therefore, even in the palaeolithic era.

There may have been occasional forays into Inner Eurasia by early species of hominid, but the first durable settlement was achieved by Neanderthal humans during the last ice age, from *c*.100,000 years ago. However, even Neanderthal colonization of Inner Eurasia was tentative, and confined to the benign southern borderlands. From *c*.35,000 years ago, Neanderthal settlers were replaced by fully modern humans, whose technologies and lifeways were more complex and adapted more precisely to the region's harsh environments. During the Upper Palaeolithic, from *c*.40,000 to 10,000 years ago, there emerged a wide range of lifeways, some of which were remarkably modern. Equipped with more varied technologies, and with a fully developed capacity for speech and language, modern humans colonized even northern regions of ice-age Inner Eurasia, such as Siberia. From there, some of them colonized the Americas.

The last stage of the ice ages ended about 10–12,000 years ago, in a period of unusually rapid warming. As climates warmed, huge woodlands spread across the northern half of Inner Eurasia, while the steppelands contracted southwards. Changes in climate and ecology demanded new technologies and new lifeways. In a period of forced experimentation there emerged new hunter-gatherer lifeways adapted to the expanding forest lands, to the tundra and Arctic coasts, and to the steppelands of the south. Eventually, there appeared lifeways based on the domestication of plants and animals. In a few regions of Eurasia, these lifeways stimulated population growth and the emergence of the populous agrarian communities which have dominated much of the world's history ever since.

In Inner Eurasia, farming societies of the early neolithic spread slowly and with difficulty. They appeared first in the oases of southern Central Asia and then in the wooded steppes of modern Moldova and Ukraine. But for several millennia, farming societies were confined to these border regions of Inner Eurasia. In the steppes, there appeared lifeways based on the domestication of animals rather than plants. Pastoralism (in particular *horse* pastoralism) became the dominant lifeway of the Inner Eurasian neolithic, as farming was the dominant lifeway of the Outer Eurasian neolithic. In the forest lands north of the steppes, forest lifeways, only slightly different from those of the upper palaeolithic, survived until the twentieth century.

Pastoralism is the dominant lifeway described in this volume, and it gives to the history of Inner Eurasia its distinctive flavour throughout the neolithic era. However, pastoralist lifeways never existed in isolation.[8] On the contrary, the history of Inner Eurasia during the neolithic era is, above all, a history of relations between pastoralists and other communities, living from farming or the foraging lifeways of the forests. It is also a history of relations with the powerful agrarian societies that emerged in Outer Eurasia.

The powerful social structures we usually think of as 'states' were a product of these difficult relationships. Inner Eurasia was not an area of 'pristine' state formation. States appeared here as pastoralist societies engaged with the agrarian societies along the southern borders of Inner Eurasia. And when states appeared in Inner Eurasia, they took forms so distinctive that many historians have doubted whether we should even call them states. They operated according to different principles from the great states of Outer Eurasia, and their histories are also quite different. So, the era of 'state-formation' is also distinctive in Inner Eurasia.[9]

However, the demographic weight of Outer Eurasia eventually told. Though the states of Inner Eurasia had a huge impact on neighbouring societies of Outer Eurasia, the influence of Outer Eurasia on them was even greater. Inner Eurasian states formed largely in response to commercial and military pressures and opportunities generated in Outer Eurasia. Their evolution also depended to a large extent on commercial and ideological developments in Outer Eurasia. As a result, Inner Eurasian history was dominated by a large frontier zone along its southern fringes. It was in this zone that Inner Eurasian societies directly encountered the armies, the technologies, the ideas, the religions, the trade goods and the populations of Outer Eurasia. This frontier zone became the dynamo of Inner Eurasian history, and the repercussions of events in this zone rippled deep into remoter regions of Inner Eurasia.

This volume ends in the thirteenth century of the modern era. Two contradictory developments mark the transition to a new era. The spectacular rise of the Mongol empire in the thirteenth century seemed to demonstrate that pastoralist lifeways, despite their demographic disadvantages, could still match the military power of the agrarian world. In retrospect, it is clear that this was an illusion. Eventually, the pastoralist lifeways of Inner Eurasia would succumb to the persistent demographic, technological, economic and cultural pressure of Outer Eurasia. What sealed their fate was the persistent expansionism of China, and the emergence within Inner Eurasia itself of powerful and expansionist agrarian states in Central Asia and then in Rus', Lithuania and Muscovy. The second volume will describe the prolonged and often desperate conflict between agrarian, pastoralist and hunter gatherer lifeways as Muscovite and Chinese expansionism cut into the steppelands and woodlands of Inner Eurasia like the blades of a vast pair of shears. The final sections will discuss the impact of capitalism on Inner Eurasian lifeways, and the extraordinary Inner Eurasian backlash against capitalism known as 'Communism'.

A NOTE ON DATING AND SPELLING

Dates up to c.10,000 years ago will be referred to as 'BP' ('Before the Present'). For dates after 10,000 years ago (that is to say, most dates after chapter 2), I will use the convention of 'BCE' ('Before the Common Era' or before 2000 years ago) and 'CE' ('Common Era', or since 2000 years ago).

Spelling and terminology present severe problems in a volume such as this which covers many different lands and periods. In choosing among a variety of possible spellings for names, places and technicalities, I have aimed at consistency and readability rather than linguistic precision. For the most part, I have adopted the spellings used in the *Cambridge History of Early Inner Asia*. For some modern place names, I have used spellings in the *Times Atlas of the World* (1994 edn).

NOTES

1 From a sixth-century Chinese version of a poem of the pastoralist Hsien-pi, who lived in Mongolia and north-west China; Jagchid and Hyer, *Mongolia's Culture and Society*, p. 10.

2 Mackinder, *Democratic Ideals and Reality*, pp. 73–4 and 'The geographical pivot of history', *Geographical Journal*, (1904), 23:421–37.

3 See Mackinder, *Democratic Ideals and Reality*, and Sinor 'Central Eurasia'.

4 Among the few attempts at synthesis are Grousset's *Empire of the Steppes*, which was first published in 1939 and is now dated; and the *Cambridge History of Early Inner Asia [CHEIA]*, which is a collective work and does not aim at a unified account of its subject.

5 There are good brief discussions of these difficulties and of the main types of written sources on Inner Asia, in Sinor, *Inner Asia: History, Civilization, Languages*, chs 5–9, and also in Sinor, 'Central Eurasia'.

6 I argue this in Christian, ' "Inner Eurasia" as a Unit of World History'.

7 A glance at Sinor, *Introduction à l'étude de l'Eurasie Centrale*, or Bregel, *Bibliography of Islamic Central Asia*, suggests the amount of material available on Inner and Central Asia alone.

8 This is the central argument of A. M. Khazanov's fundamental study of pastoralism: *Nomads and the Outside World*.

9 See Christian, 'State formation in the steppes'.

FURTHER READING

'Inner Eurasia' is not a standard object of historical enquiry, so there are few general histories that cover the same ground as this study. Closest of all is the *Cambridge History of Early Inner Asia*, referred to in notes as CHEIA, edited by a modern pioneer of Inner Asian studies, Denis Sinor. Sinor's definition of 'Central Eurasia' or 'Inner Asia' is close to the notion of 'Inner Eurasia', as adopted in this volume, but not close enough to have provided a better label. (See Sinor, 'Central Eurasia'.) However, the *Cambridge History* consists of a number of separate essays by different specialists, while this volume attempts a unified interpretation of 'Inner Eurasian' history. Nevertheless, the *Cambridge History* is an essential reference work, and contains invaluable bibliographies. Sinor, *Inner Asia: history, civilization, languages: a syllabus*, though slightly dated, still offers the best short introduction to Inner Asian studies, and contains useful short bibliographies and discussions of sources. There is a valuable collection of Sinor's essays in *Inner Asia and its Contacts with Medieval Europe*. The idea of 'Inner Eurasia' owes something to the work of Mackinder (*Democratic Ideals and Reality*), who pointed out the fundamental topographical and climatic differences between Inner and Outer Eurasia. My own essay, 'Inner Eurasia', attempts to define this region as a historical entity.

There are several general histories that cover much, if not all, the ground covered in this volume. The best known history of the Eurasian steppes, Grousset's *Empire of the Steppes*, appeared in 1939 and is now dated, but still worth reading. Of the same vintage is Teggart, *Rome and China*, which looks for correlations between events at both ends of the Eurasian steppes, and McGovern, *The Early Empires of Central Asia*, which concentrates on the Hsiung-nu and the Huns. An even older work, Huntington's *Pulse of Asia*, offered a climatic explanation of pastoralist migrations which influenced the work of Arnold Toynbee. More recent histories of the Eurasian steppes are Klyashtornyi and Sultanov, *Kazakhstan*; Kürsat-Ahlers, *Zür frühen Staatenbildung* (which uses the theories of Norbert Elias); and Kwanten, *Imperial Nomads: A History of Central Asia, 500–1500*. Golden's *Introduction to the History of the Turkic Peoples* is very up to date, but ranges more widely than its title suggests. Khazanov's fundamental study of pastoralism, *Nomads and the Outside World*, ranges over large periods of time, though it is not, strictly, a history of pastoralism. Its analysis of the close links between pastoralist and agrarian societies means that no future history of Inner Eurasia will be able to focus just on the pastoralist world. Barfield's *The Nomadic Alternative* is a fine textbook account of nomadic pastoralism. Typical of modern approaches to pastoralism in Inner Eurasia are the essays in the collections edited by Gary Seaman: *Rulers from the Steppe, Ecology and Empire*, and *Foundations of Empire*. There are also many good short and up-to-date essays on topics covered in this volume in the Unesco *History of Humanity*, of which three volumes have appeared covering all periods up to the seventh century CE.

There are several large-scale histories of significant parts of Inner Eurasia. On the eastern region, the pioneering studies of Owen Lattimore are now dated in some respects, but still well worth reading. See, in particular, *Inner Asian Frontiers of China*, and *Studies in Frontier History*. Important recent studies of the Mongolian frontier are Barfield, *Perilous Frontier*, and Jagchid and Symons, *Peace, War, and Trade along the Great Wall*. Jagchid and Hyer, *Mongolia's Culture and Society* is also wide-ranging in its coverage, but more sociological and ethnological in its approach. On the central region and the Iranian borderlands, the pioneering studies of Barthold, in particular, his *Turkestan down to the Mongol Invasion*, are still of great value. There is a ten-volume Soviet edition of his collected works: *Akademik V. V. Bartol'd: Sochineniya*. More recently, Richard Frye has written several general histories of the region, including *The History of Ancient Iran, The Heritage of Persia, The Golden Age of Persia*, and *The Heritage of Central Asia*. Hambly *Zentralasien* (available in English as *Central Asia*) is also valuable. Altheim's *Attila und die Hunnen* is dated in some respects, and eccentric in some of its ideas, but much wider in scope than its title suggests. An influential survey history in Russian by a Central Asian historian is Gafurov, *Tadzhiki*. This contains an extensive bibliography, and the 1989 edition includes a long essay by Litvinskii adding new references and describing recent research. A vital recent source is the *History of the Civilizations of Central Asia* (referred to in notes as HCCA) of which three volumes are now available. See also, the *Cambridge History of Iran*. Modern studies of western Inner Eurasia tend to focus either on the early history and prehistory of Rus', or on the Balkan borderlands. Broadest in their scope are Vernadsky's volumes on *Ancient Russia, Kievan Russia*, and *The Origins of Russia* (still very worth reading today, though dated in some respects), and Dolukhanov's recent study of the *Early Slavs*, which includes valuable chapters on the prehistory of western Inner Eurasia. The multi-volume Soviet history, *Ocherki istorii SSSR*, can still be useful, although its approach and some of its information is now severely dated. Sinor, *Introduction à l'étude de l'Eurasia Centrale*, is a superb guide to sources on the languages and history of Inner Asia published before 1961. A very brief guide to sources, including some sources published up to 1969, is available in Sinor, 'Central Eurasia', and further guides are available in Sinor, *Inner Asia*. Bregel, *Bibliography of Islamic Central Asia*, surveys literature on the pre-Islamic period. Moravcsik, *Byzantinoturcica*, is an invaluable handbook on the peoples of the Byzantine borders, and the sources on them.

PART I

The Geography and Ecology of Inner Eurasia

[1] THE GEOGRAPHY AND ECOLOGY OF INNER EURASIA

INNER EURASIA: DEFINITIONS

What are the borders between Inner and Outer Eurasia? In some areas it is easy to identify them. Elsewhere it is more difficult.

Along the southern rim of 'Inner Eurasia', mountain chains provide a natural border. A few natural gateways breach this border through the Balkans, the Caucasus, Persia, Afghanistan and northern China. To the east and west, ecology rather than topography defines the borders of 'Inner Eurasia'. However, it does so without much precision. Do Hungary, Romania and Poland belong within Inner Eurasia? Does Manchuria or the Ordos region in the great loop of the Yellow River? There is no need to attempt a definitive answer to such questions. We can simply describe such regions as borderlands. They belong sometimes to Outer Eurasia and sometimes to Inner Eurasia. However, for most purposes Manchuria will not be included within Inner Eurasia. Nor will Tibet or the Caucasus mountains, regions whose ecology is quite different from that of the Inner Eurasian plains. Nor will eastern Europe west of the Pripyat marshes. To the west of the Pripyat marshes there is great variety in relief, geology, vegetation, climate. To the east there is uniformity of landforms and also of climates. As a distinguished historical geographer has written:

> The climatic frontier between the maritime and continental climates, however imprecise it may be, must fall in this very same zone.... The great east–west trending vegetation and soil belts, themselves a product of physiographic and climatic uniformity, come to a halt in this zone to give way, westwards, to a fine-grained pattern in which, everywhere, local variations in bedrock, drift, aspect, slope and height are reflected in vegetation and soil.[1]

In the far north, the tundra and the Arctic ocean offer borders as clear as the mountain ranges to the south.

One advantage of using the terminology of 'Inner' and 'Outer' Eurasia is that it bypasses the ancient, but misleading and Eurocentric distinction between Europe and Asia. Geographers of the classical world first distinguished between Asia and Europe, placing the border at the Bosporus or, further north, at the River Tanais, the modern Don.[2] Once geographers in the Mediterranean world began to understand that the Don was no barrier at all, the distinction between Europe and Asia was so deeply rooted that geographers simply looked for a new border. Eventually, most came to accept the proposal of an eighteenth-century Russian geographer and historian, V. N. Tatishchev, who placed the border at the Urals mountains.[3] Remarkably, this entirely artificial division has survived in historical writing to the present day.

Yet there have been dissenting voices. In Russian geographical thought there were many attempts to define a distinctive geographical region that was Russia's natural homeland. Most interesting for our purposes is the group of émigré Russian geographers and historians known as the 'Eurasianists'. The Eurasianists argued, on geographical and cultural grounds, for the unity and coherence of what they called 'Eurasia'.[4] By this, they meant a region similar to what I have called 'Inner Eurasia'. Here, I have rejected the term, 'Eurasia', because it belongs more logically to the entire Eurasian land mass.

Within the borders of Inner Eurasia, there has existed an immense variety of climates, landscapes, lifeways, languages and religions. Nevertheless, the entire region can usefully be treated as a single, coherent unit of historical analysis. The geography and ecology of the region have shaped its history from prehistory to the present. They have done so by posing distinctive problems that demanded distinctive solutions.

DOMINANT FEATURES OF THE GEOGRAPHY OF INNER EURASIA

PHYSICAL GEOGRAPHY

Inner Eurasia's geographical coherence appears most clearly on a physical map of the world. Its dominant geographical feature is a vast plain, the largest unified area of flatlands in the world. What the great Russian historian, Klyuchevskii, wrote of his homeland is true of most of Inner Eurasia: 'Monotony is the chief characteristic of [Russia's] surface: one form of relief dominates almost her whole extent.'[5] Though several mountain ranges exist within Inner Eurasia, particularly in Eastern Siberia, Mongolia and Sinkiang, and though much of Eastern Siberia, like Mongolia, is really a large, elevated, tableland, none of these regions present significant barriers to movement.

The Inner Eurasian flatlands assembled over vast epochs through the collision and fusing of different portions of continental crust. The most important event in the geological history of the plain was the joining of two large sheets of continental crust, or 'cratons', the Siberian and Russian 'platforms', during the 'Permian' epoch, about 250 million years ago. This process left the Urals mountains as still visible scars of what geologists call a 'suture'.

The flatness of the Inner Eurasian plains had immense political, cultural and military consequences. While land armies dominated warfare, natural features such as mountains or seas were the main barriers to military expansion. Just as the English Channel explains why Britain is a natural political unit, so the absence of such barriers helps explain the size of the cultural, commercial and political units that eventually appeared in Inner Eurasia. Successful armies, such as the Mongol armies that drove through the steppes from the east, or the Muscovite forces that drove through seventeenth-century Siberia, met no serious physical barriers to their movement until they reached the western, southern or eastern borderlands of Inner Eurasia. Inner Eurasia is therefore a natural unit of military history. That is why it was also a natural unit of political history, and that is why, during the last two millennia, there have appeared in Inner Eurasia some of the largest land empires ever created. Flatness also explains why networks formed from trade, ideas, religions and tribal migrations have linked different regions of Inner Eurasia over huge distances since prehistoric times. The great Inner Eurasian empires formed from societies that already shared much with each other culturally, commercially and politically.

ECOLOGY

Three main features define Inner Eurasia ecologically. These are: (1) interiority; (2) northerliness; and (3) continentality.

First of all, Inner Eurasia is inner. It is remote from the sea to the west, south and east, and its long northern coastline is frozen for most of the year. So interiority has meant aridity. Even rain-bearing winds from the Atlantic lose much of their moisture before they enter western Inner Eurasia. South of the forest zone, average annual rainfall today is less than 250 mm, and in most of Central Asia, Chinese Sinkiang and Mongolia, average precipitation varies from 250–500 mm. This is too dry to support farming without irrigation. North of these regions and east of the Urals there are few regions that enjoy more than 500 mm a year, and these lie along the western edges of the Russian plain. In contrast, most of Europe, the northern Mediterranean, India, South-East Asia and China enjoy more than 500 mm of rainfall a year. The relative aridity of Inner Eurasia had profound ecological consequences, for the amount of rainfall (more strictly, the ratio of rainfall to evaporation, the 'effective moisture') is a crucial determinant of the amount of vegetation and therefore of potential food production. In the northern tundra and forest lands of Inner Eurasia, coldness compensates for lack of rainfall by reducing evaporation, so that here, aridity poses fewer problems than further south.[6]

Second, Inner Eurasia is northerly. St Petersburg lies close to the 60° parallel, along with Stockholm and Oslo. Anchorage, the capital of Alaska, lies only two degrees farther north than St Petersburg. The southern parts of Inner Eurasia, between 50° and 40°, lie in the same latitudes as the northern Mediterranean and Central Europe, but, with less rainfall, and more extreme climates, they are largely regions of steppe and cold desert. Though these were the first parts of Inner Eurasia to be settled in prehistoric times, even these lands lie north of the latitudes in which the first civilizations emerged in Egypt, Mesopotamia, Northern India, and China.

Northern latitudes mean colder average temperatures and less sunlight. Latitude affects average atmospheric temperature, which, all else being equal,

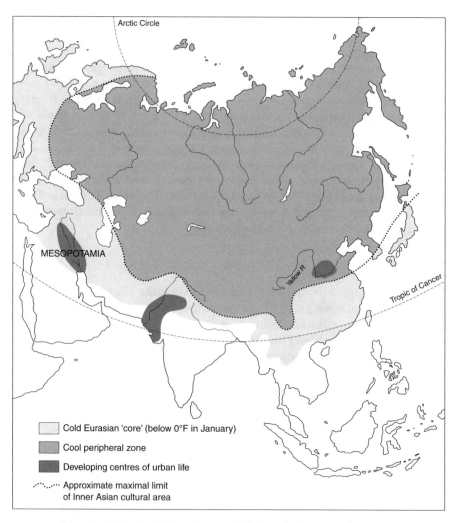

Map 1.1 The 'cold Eurasian core' (below 0 degrees in January).

decreases by about 0.5°C for every degree of increase in latitude. There is an important sense in which Inner Eurasia is *colder* than Outer Eurasia, so that, as one writer has said: 'Winter is the dominant season in Central Eurasia.' This is how Mackinder put it:

There is one striking physical circumstance which knits [the Heartland] graphically together; the whole of it, even to the brink of the Persian Mountains overlooking torrid Mesopotamia, lies under snow in the winter-time. The line indicative of an *average* freezing temperature for the whole month of January passes from the North Cape of Norway southward, just within the "Guard" of islands along the Norwegian shore, past Denmark, across mid-Germany to the Alps, and from the Alps eastward along the Balkan range. The Bay of Odessa and the Sea of Azof are frozen over annually, and also the greater part of the

Baltic Sea. At mid-winter, as seen from the moon, a vast white shield would reveal the Heartland in its largest meaning.

To make things worse, in much of Inner Eurasia, aridity and cold conspire together, for limited cloud cover deprives the land of much needed insulation during the winter nights.[7]

Latitude also determines the total amount of light that falls on a given area. As sunlight is the main source of new energy in the biosphere, the amount of sunlight reaching any particular region is a fundamental measure of its capacity to sustain life. The energy of sunlight is captured through photosynthesis, which sustains the plants (the 'primary producers') which stand at the base of most food-chains. Primary producers account for about 99 per cent of all organic matter. All else being equal, the amount of sunlight determines the amount of vegetation which, in turn, limits the size of animal and human populations.

Latitude also affects rainfall. Warm equatorial winds carry moisture upwards, which they shed as they travel north and south away from the equator. Eventually, having shed most of their rain, they descend at around the 30° parallel, creating most of the world's desert lands. In Inner Eurasia, the mountain rim to the south exacerbates this effect, for the mountains push rain-bearing clouds high and squeeze out any moisture they still contain. As a result, along the southernmost parts of Inner Eurasia there lies a chain of interconnected deserts and arid steppelands.

The flatness and size of Inner Eurasia explain a third main feature: the continentality of its climates. In coastal regions, seas moderate temperature changes, for the sea warms and cools more slowly than the land. On the other hand, large land masses allow more extreme fluctuations of temperature and more severe climates; and Inner Eurasia lies at the heart of the largest land mass in the world. In Inner Eurasia, the prevailing westerlies have lost their moderating influence by the time they reach the Urals. So, the further east one travels, the more severe the contrast between summer and winter climates. Dryness and extremes of temperature both increase towards the east, so the diagonal line from north-west to south-east, which delimits the region where growing seasons are less than 90 days long, also marks off a good half of Inner Eurasia whose climate is either Arctic or sub-Arctic.[8] Where the growing season is less than 90 days, serious agriculture is hardly possible. (Coastal regions on the Pacific constitute a partial exception.)

The most favourable climates in Inner Eurasia can be found south of the western part of this line. Moving east, the pasturelands become more arid, and farming more difficult, which creates an important climatic and ecological gradient from west to east. To the south of the eastern half of this line, climates are semi-arid or arid, with limited rainfall, warm summers and very cold winters. Mongolia has particularly harsh winters, with temperatures dropping below freezing for as much as six months each year. The extreme cold of this region is exacerbated by a relatively stable winter high pressure zone over Mongolia. In fact, the climates of the eastern half of Inner Eurasia are the most continental of all the earth's climates.

Continentality means that temperatures move through huge arcs from summer to winter, and sometimes within a single day. The Franciscan Monk, John of Plano Carpini, described the weather he saw in travelling through Kazakhstan and Mongolia in the middle of the thirteenth century:

> The weather there is astonishingly irregular, for in the middle of summer, . . . there is fierce thunder and lightning which cause the death of many men, and at the same time there are very heavy falls of snow. There are also hurricanes of bitterly cold winds, so violent that at times men can ride on horseback only with great effort. When we were before the [camp of the emperor and his chief men] we lay prostrate on account of the force of the wind and we could scarcely see owing to the great clouds of dust. There it never rains in the winter, but often in the summer, though it is so little that sometimes the dust and the roots of the grass are hardly moistened. Very heavy hail also often falls there. . . . Then also in summer there is suddenly great heat, and suddenly extreme cold. In winter in some parts there are heavy falls of snow, in others however but slight.[9]

THE IMPACT OF GEOGRAPHY

Aridity, northerly latitudes and continental climates combined to create a harsh environment for human settlement. 'Primary productivity', or the amount of solar energy stored in plants, was highest in the forest lands that dominated the cold, northern half of Inner Eurasia.[10] It was much lower in the steppelands and desertlands of the southern half, where most of the populations of Inner Eurasia lived from c.4000 BCE to the time of Chinggis Khan. As a result, the more densely settled regions of Inner Eurasia were characterized by low ecological productivity and a shortage of easily accessible food energy. Even in the south, there are exceptions – ecological 'hot spots', in which moderate climates, good soils and good supplies of rain or river water make for productive agriculture. The most important large area of this kind lay west of the Urals. With this important exception, none of these 'hot spots' falsify the generalization that the most accessible parts of Inner Eurasia are more impoverished ecologically than most parts of Outer Eurasia.

The differential in average natural productivity between Inner and Outer Eurasia has been of immense and enduring significance. As this volume will show, it has shaped the history of Inner Eurasia in profound ways and over long periods.

The most obvious consequence of Inner Eurasia's harsh ecology was low population density. Until recently, most of Inner Eurasia lacked the dense populations that underpinned the urban civilizations of Outer Eurasia. In the early 1980s, the population density of the entire Soviet Union was no more than about 12 people/k^2. In the most populated regions, west of the Urals, it was c.50 people/k^2, in contrast with 229 for the UK and 182 for modern India.[11] Along the northern borders of China, the demographic contrast is particularly striking. In 1940, Owen Lattimore estimated that China within the Great Wall had a population of 400–500 million living in an area of approximately one and a half million square miles, while the Inner

Eurasian borderlands of China beyond the Great Wall (including Tibet) had a population of only 1/10th as much, in an area twice the size of China.[12] Much of the history of Inner Eurasia turned on the contrasting population densities within and beyond its borders.

Low population densities might simply have ensured that Inner Eurasia remained marginal to the dominant regions of world history, a sort of Eurasian equivalent of the North American plains. However, Inner Eurasia's centrality in the Eurasian landmass ensured it a more prominent historical role. What happened in Inner Eurasia affected Outer Eurasia because most of the land routes connecting the various civilizations of Outer Eurasia passed through Inner Eurasia. As a result, the history of this region had a considerable impact on the rhythms of Outer Eurasian history. The trade routes that passed through the Inner Eurasian borderlands flourished best when controlled by large Inner Eurasian empires, though trade also boomed when Outer Eurasian empires from Persia or China controlled large stretches of the trade routes. The emergence of the first extensive steppe empires coincided with the first appearance of a flourishing trade route across Inner Eurasia, dominated by the power of Han China and the pastoral nomadic Hsiung-nu. As McNeill has shown, these links also laid the foundations for a unified Eurasian epidemiological system.[13] The Türk empire of the sixth century CE created political links across Eurasia for a second time, while the Mongol empire of the thirteenth century created a third economic, cultural and epidemiological system embracing much of the Eurasian land mass.[14] The exchanges made possible by the creation of the Mongol empire stimulated economic and cultural development through-out Eurasia, and may have contributed significantly to the rise of European capitalism.

Inner Eurasian societies impinged on the civilizations of Outer Eurasia in other ways. Though they usually lacked the resources to conquer the civiliza-tions of Outer Eurasia, Inner Eurasian armies could be very powerful, and they often probed for weak spots in the sedentary lands. Sometimes they found them. When they did, they exacted tributes, and sometimes sup-planted Outer Eurasian ruling classes.

For several millennia, then, the centrality of Inner Eurasia ensured it a strategic role in the history of the Old World, and helped shape the history of the emerging Eurasian world-system. So, despite its small populations, Inner Eurasia has not been a region 'without history', in Eric Wolf's phrase.[15]

Relations with Outer Eurasia also had a profound impact on the societies of Inner Eurasia. Outer Eurasian trade goods, technologies, lifeways, migrants, religions and armies all shaped the societies of Inner Eurasia. Given the lim-ited natural and demographic resources of Inner Eurasia, responding to the challenges of Outer Eurasia usually required an intensified mobilizational effort, whether for war or trade. Whether they wished it or not, the peoples of the southern half of Inner Eurasia were fated not to live in a historical backwater, despite their limited natural resources.

It is this combination of ecological poverty and engagement with more powerful neighbours in Outer Eurasia that has done most to shape Inner

Eurasian history. This conclusion suggests an abstract way of defining what is distinctive about the history of Inner Eurasia. *The societies that did most to shape the history of Inner Eurasia did so because they evolved successful ways of concentrating or mobilizing the scarce human and material resources of a region of relatively low natural productivity.*

Pressure to mobilize the scarce resources of a difficult environment stimulated the evolution of distinctive ecological adaptations, around each of which there emerged distinctive lifeways and distinctive social structures. In the era covered by this volume, two adaptations have been dominant: hunting in the palaeolithic era, and pastoralism in the neolithic era. In the modern era, Inner Eurasian societies adopted the agrarian and then the industrial lifeways of Outer Eurasia. However, even these evolved in distinctive forms that reflected the particular ecological features of Inner Eurasia.

REGIONS WITHIN INNER EURASIA

Though there is a larger unity to the lands of Inner Eurasia, they are also very diverse in their ecologies, their lifeways and their cultures. Inner Eurasia forms a huge rectangle, whose major axis runs east and west. Its grain runs roughly horizontally, along lines of latitude, though for some geographical features, such as average temperatures, the grain is skewed, dropping south as you move east. If you travel along the major axis of Inner Eurasia (which is the experience of those travelling on the trans-Siberian railway), you encounter similar types of vegetation and climate. To see different ecological zones, you must travel north and south.

Vegetation lies at the base of the food-chain. Four main ecological belts are worth noting in Inner Eurasia. Moving from north to south, these are: the tundra, the northern forests, the steppelands, and the deserts.

ECOLOGICAL ZONES

1 THE TUNDRA

Along much of the northern coast of Inner Eurasia, tundra extends up to 200 miles south of the Arctic shore, though in the east it extends much further south. Average daytime temperatures in this region rise above $-10°C$ for only half the year. Frost-free days last only during the short summers of about two and a half months, and snow covers the ground for almost 250 days in the year. The tundra is so cold that the sub-soil itself is frozen all year around in 'permafrost', which sometimes reaches to a great depth. With so much moisture locked up in permafrost or snow, little is available to support plant life, so the tundra is a sort of frozen desert. Its vegetation consists of hardy mosses, lichens, sedges and low-growing trees and shrubs. These ancient forms of vegetation support small populations of rodents, foxes, a few species of birds, and some larger animals such as wolves and reindeer. On the coasts, there are whales, walrus and seals. Though occupied by

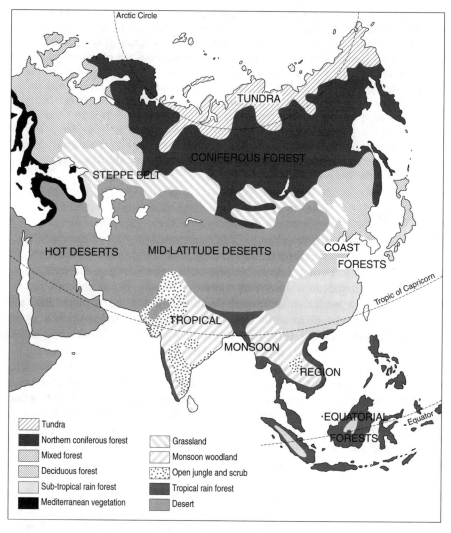

Map 1.2 Ecological zones of Inner Eurasia.

human populations for at least 20,000 years, the tundra's limited resources have never supported dense populations of animals or of humans, and this zone has played a secondary role in the history of Inner Eurasia until very recent times.

The following account, written by a missionary, who lived in Nizhnekolymsk on the Kolyma river, just south of 70°, in about 1850, gives some idea of living conditions in the Siberian far north. Cold was by no means the only hazard in this region. Permafrost meant that when the top few inches of the soil melted in the short summers, it could not drain away. This created ideal conditions for the breeding of insects.

Winter, with all its blizzards, accompanied by unrelieved dampness, and at the same time unrelieved deep cold (a most unfavourable combination), lasts nine months. Then come two and a half months of just dampness, like a bath, with thick marshy emanations; in the air there is a ubiquitous fog of minute blood-thirsty insects, for such are midges and gnats there. From these insects the native has no peace, inside or out, day or night. Furthermore, in summer the sun does not set, which is very picturesque to see described, but is extremely tedious to experience in fact. Average temperature for the year is $-10°C$, and it is below $-37°C$ in December and January. In winter it is cold, damp and gloomy, and the sun does not rise. Vegetation is poor. You do not even find fir and pine; birch has become a dwarf, alder a low-growing shrub, the majestic Siberian cedar has also turned into a dwarf.[16]

2 THE FOREST

Below the tundra lie the woodlands. The most northerly part of the woodlands consists of a huge conifer forest, the so-called *taiga*, that stretches from Scandinavia to the Bering Sea. Below the coniferous forest, in the west, there lies a zone of mixed deciduous and conferous forests. Below that, in the far west, there lies a wedge of temperate deciduous forest that reaches into the western parts of the plain from Europe and extends, narrowing to a point towards the east, until it vanishes near the suture line of the Urals. Taken together, these zones make up the largest area of tree cover in the world.

The great forests of Inner Eurasia appeared at the end of the last ice age, from c.10,000 years ago. Since then, the forests, and the rivers that track through them, have provided resources of many different kinds, including fish and flesh, furs and materials. However, their soils are usually thin and acidic podzols, as forest cover prevents evaporation, so that rainfall drains through the soil, leaching away nutrients. This explains in part why farming developed late in the forest zones, and often used the trees themselves as fertilizer. Swidden farmers cleared areas in the forests and burnt down the trees, then planted seed in the ash. Once they had exhausted its fertility, they moved on. East of the Urals, most post-glacial communities of the woodlands survived without any form of farming or gardening, exploiting the region's animal and plant resources. They herded and hunted reindeer, as well as deer and bear and even tigers in Manchuria and the Far East. They also hunted the region's sable, fox, ermine, marten and squirrels for their valuable furs, which could be worn, or traded to the lands south of the forests. The vast river systems of Siberia pro-vided the main form of communication through the *taiga*. Though most of the major rivers headed north, their tributaries, joined by short portages, provided the routes from the Urals to the Pacific along which Muscovite traders and sol-diers travelled as they took control of Siberia in the seventeenth century.

The German traveller, Baron Haxthausen, who travelled in European Russia in the 1840s, offers a vivid description of the wooded north as he trav-elled to the north of Vologda through the *taiga*:

At the river Sukhona commence those forests which stretch out hence into immeasurable regions. Throughout the whole district as far as Veliki Ustiug, the immense forests come down close to the river, on both sides of the Sukhona; but wherever the bank is not too deep and the soil is fertile there lie on either side of the river villages, generally four to six close together. The forest is partially cleared in these places and the land is excellently cultivated.[17]

As the historian, Klyuchevskii, wrote in the late nineteenth century, the woodlands, both coniferous and deciduous, were the historic heartland for the cultures of Muscovy and Russia:

> Even in the seventeenth century, for a Western European travelling from Smolensk to Moscow, Muscovy appeared an endless forest, in which towns and hamlets were simply larger or smaller clearings. Even today [the late nineteenth century] a broad horizon fringed by a bluish band of forest, is the most familiar landscape of central Russia. The woods offered much to the Russian people, economically, politically and even morally. They built their houses of pine and oak; they heated them with birch and aspen wood, and lit them with birch tapers; they wore boots (*lapti*) made from the bark of lime trees; and they made their domestic utensils of wood or bark. The forests provided a safe refuge from external enemies, taking the place of mountains and fortresses. The state itself, whose predecessor [Rus'] had failed because it was too close to the steppes, could flourish only...under the protection of the forests.[18]

To the lands further south, the resources of the forest lands were of great commercial importance. However, with this exception, the forest lands were almost as marginal to the history of Inner Eurasia as the tundra, until the emergence of Rus' and the exploitation of Siberia's vast mineral and timber resources in recent centuries. Though we will try not to neglect the indigenous societies of the Inner Eurasian forest belt, their history will not loom as large in this volume as that of the southern, non-forested, half of Inner Eurasia.

3 THE STEPPES

The third belt consists of the arid steppelands. Though connected, the steppes divide into three main zones. The western steppes extend from Hungary through southern Ukraine, north of the Black Sea, and to the gap between the Urals and the Caspian Sea. The central steppes include northern Kazakhstan, and extend southwards into southern Central Asia, where they merge into desert. The Zungar gap, between the Altai and T'ien Shan mountain ranges, leads into the eastern steppes of northern Sinkiang and Mongolia. These reach along the northern fringes of the Gobi desert to the Khingan mountains on the western borders of Manchuria.

The Inner Eurasian steppes are part of a vast belt of desert and steppe that reaches from north-west Africa right across the centre of the Old World to Manchuria in the east. In Central Asia, fingers of steppe reach deep into Afghanistan and Iran, so that along this border, the ecological frontier with Outer Eurasia is less precise than along the north Chinese or Eastern European borders. Grasslands often lie in transitional regions between temperate forests and desert lands, where there is enough rainfall to support

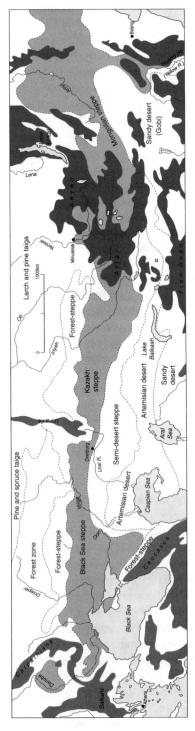

Map 1.3 Steppelands of Inner Eurasia

grasses, but not enough to support trees and forests. Average precipitation in the steppelands varies from 250–500 mm. Rainfall is higher near the coasts, in the far west and in Manchuria; and it is lowest in Mongolia and Sinkiang.[19]

Grasslands offer little direct nourishment to humans, who are incapable of digesting cellulose. Nor could they be farmed on a large-scale before the nineteenth century, even though their soils were often rich chernozems, formed from the composting of steppeland grasses over thousands of years. Farming was difficult in the steppes because the turf was thick and tough, and rainfall was erratic. As a result, until very recently, the steppes have been exploited indirectly, by communities that hunted or herded herbivores that could convert the steppe grasses into meat, blood, sinews, hide, and traction energy. For communities of hunters or pastoralists, the steppes allowed great freedom of movement, almost as much as the sea did to seagoing societies.

Nineteenth-century travellers south of a line from Kiev through Tula, Riazan', Kazan' and Ufa, found themselves in a transitional region of wooded steppes. This extended south to Kishinev, Saratov and the southern tip of the Urals. Haxthausen first saw the wooded steppes from the Kremlin of Nizhnii Novgorod on the high left bank of the Volga.

There is a splendid view of the two rivers [the Oka and the Volga] at their points of junction, the town, and several villages lying on the rivers' banks. But behind this beautiful foreground an immense, flat, wooded plain shuts in the horizon. This is the general character of the scenery in Russia: in the foreground are pretty, often picturesque and even idyllic views, but the background is boundless, flat and wild, the cultivated country forming a mere oasis.[20]

As he travelled through this transitional region, Haxthausen found that:

the steppe becomes gradually perceptible by the forests appearing more and more in isolated patches and the grass plains growing larger in extent. All at once the wood ceases, not a bush is anywhere to be seen and the steppe stretches out in immensity before us.[21]

For European travellers heading further south, the steppelands appeared either exotic or monotonous. Here is an idyllic description of the steppelands south of Voronezh from the memoirs of an Englishman, Edward Clarke, who travelled there in 1800:

The whole of the immense plains were enamelled with the greatest variety of flowers imaginable . . . the earth seemed covered with the richest and most beautiful blossoms, fragrant, aromatic and, in many instances, entirely new to the eye of a British traveller. Even during the heat of the day, refreshing breezes wafted a thousand odours and all the air was perfumed. The skylark was in full song and various insects with painted wings either filled the air or were seen crouching in the blossoms. Advancing nearer to the Don, turtle doves as tame as domestic pigeons flew about our carriage.[22]

Haxthausen was less impressed by the steppes:

> On the evening of the 21st of July we took our departure from Kharkov (towards Ekaterinoslaf), and on awakening in the morning found ourselves in a genuine steppe country, extending as far as the horizon on every side, and for many hours nothing but steppe – at that time of the year anything but beautiful! The soil was dry, and of a blackish-grey colour, the grass parched, with here and there gigantic weeds, generally in the form of bushes, thistles, and *burian* (the best material for firewood in the Steppe), likewise completely dried up. Of trees or forest no trace was to be seen: here and there in the hollows were tall green reeds and willow-bushes. The small rivers glided slowly down between sandy banks. The Steppes I saw were everywhere undulating, like the waves of a sea suddenly arrested in their motion.[23]

4 THE DESERTS

South of the steppes, in Central Asia and Sinkiang, the steppelands give way to arid lands and eventually to desert. In the west are the Ust Urt, Karakum and Kyzylkum deserts of Turkmenistan and Uzbekistan. Divided from them by the Pamirs is the terrible Taklamakan desert of southern Sinkiang. In the seventh century CE, the Chinese pilgrim, Hsüan-tsang, gave a description of the desert east of Khotan, which the twentieth-century traveller, Sven Hedin found to be remarkably accurate even today. East of Khotan, Hsüan-tsang entered the 'Great Flowing Sand'.

> As the sand is in constant motion it is collected and dispersed by the wind. As there are no tracks for travellers many go astray; on every side is a great vast space with nothing to go by, so travellers pile up bones left behind to be marks; there is neither water nor vegetation and there is much hot wind; when the wind blows men and animals lose their senses and become unwell. One constantly hears singing and whistling, and sometimes wailing; while looking and listening one becomes stupified, and consequently there is frequent loss of life, and so these phenomena are caused by demons and sprites.[24]

North and East of the T'ien Shan and Ch'i-lien Shan mountains is the Gobi, which extends from north-eastern Sinkiang into southern Mongolia and Chinese Inner Mongolia. Despite its fearsome reputation, there is grassland in much of the Gobi, so it has always supported small populations of pastoralists. The same is true of much of the Karakum desert in modern Turkmenistan. A modern archaeologist describes this as:

> a mosaic of moving barchan dunes, stable dunes, scattered *takyri* [clay pans formed by standing water], salt flats, and isolated wells stretching out from the foothill plains of the Kopet Dag and Paropamisus mountains. White saxaul (*Halaxyon pesicum*), ephedra (*Ephedra strobilacea*), and *Eremosparton* are shrubby tree species found in the desert. Traditionally, the desert saxaul is collected for firewood.... The desert, except for the barchan dunes, is covered by spring vegetation following the slightest precipitation. The thin growth of annual vegetation provides fodder for herders and nomads but forces a high degree of mobility. In spring, areas of the Kara Kum may appear carpeted with

red with blossoms of the annual poppy (*Papaveaceae*), which has been collected for its medicinal properties.[25]

A common feature of most of the Inner Eurasian desert lands is that rivers drain into them from the mountains on their borders, creating fertile oases. As a result, the many oases of Central Asia and Sinkiang supported small pockets of dense settlement sustained by irrigation agriculture and trade. Here, there emerged societies quite different from those of the steppelands. Their cultures reflected a complex symbiosis between the strict demands of irrigation agriculture, and the cultural, commercial and military pressures of pastoral nomads to their north, and agrarian empires to their south and east. They were the main stopping points along the Silk Roads, and the foundation for the many small trading city-states that flourished from Kansu to the Black Sea from the second millennium BCE.

THE BORDERLANDS

The southern borderlands of 'Inner Eurasia' included not just the narrow strip of oasis city-states, but also the deserts and steppes that surrounded them. It was in this larger borderland region that relations between the agrarian civilizations of Outer Eurasia and the very different societies of Inner Eurasia were at their most intense. The two worlds probed each other's strengths and weaknesses along this historical, ecological and geological fault line.

As a result, the southern edge of Inner Eurasia provided most of the dynamism of Inner Eurasian history from prehistory to the present. Shocks from the frontier zone were transmitted with diminishing intensity to the zones of the interior, which were less influenced by Outer Eurasia, and whose lifeways were more distinctly 'Inner Eurasian'. So, for some purposes, it is helpful to think of Inner Eurasia as a series of concentric arcs, each shaped by the nearness of Outer Eurasian influences. The zones of densest population and of most intense historical change were those closest to the borders with Outer Eurasia. Moving away from the frontier, populations and communities become smaller and more dispersed, lifeways more distinctively Inner Eurasian, the level of mobilization and of involvement in the broader currents of Inner Eurasian history less intense. Communities in the remote inner arcs were human reservoirs, supplying slaves or material tributes for those closer to Inner Eurasia. In this way, there emerged a geographically distributed hierarchy in the history of Inner Eurasia which explains why so much of the history that follows will focus on the arcs closest to Outer Eurasia.

Seen in this light, the oddity of Inner Eurasian history is that a very unstable frontier of ecological and political conflict dominated its history for several millennia. In the recent history of North America, or Australia, such ecological and cultural frontier zones were so unstable that they lasted only for a century or two. In Inner Eurasia, the complexity of inter-ecological frontier conflicts shaped the entire history of the region, not just one brief phase of its history. The paradoxical question arises: why was the instability of the frontier so stable a feature of the borderlands? And the answer, surely, is that the ecological divide between Inner and Outer Eurasia was so fundamental that it allowed no one type of society a decisive military, demographic or cultural advantage until the modern era.

CULTURAL ZONES

However, the pressure of Outer Eurasian civilization was constant and inescapable, and in recent millennia it led to the appearance of distinctive cultural zones within Inner Eurasia.

In ancient times, the most important gateways into Inner Eurasia were through the northern and north western borders of China; across the Central Asian borders with Iran and Afghanistan, and through the passes of the Caucasus (the Darial pass, and the coastal route through Darband); and through the passage between the Black Sea and the Carpathians that leads from the Balkans. These points of entry shaped the cultural geography of Inner Eurasia by channelling particular Outer Eurasian influences to particular regions of Inner Eurasia. There was a neat symmetry about the impact of cultural influences from Outer Eurasia. This is worth noting early on, as it persisted throughout the period of human settlement of Inner Eurasia. There emerged four main 'cultural' zones within Inner Eurasia, distinguished by the nature and direction of the main cultural influences that acted on them. Three were dominated by the major 'gateways' onto the plain, while the fourth, which included the northern arcs of Inner Eurasia, was distinguished by the absence of strong influences from Outer Eurasia. Conveniently, we can label these zones the western, southern, eastern and northern cultural zones. They took the form of segments slicing across the arcs of Inner Eurasia's ecology.

The western segment includes the lands west of the Urals and the Caspian sea. The most powerful external influences came from the Mediterranean and Mesopotamian lands to the south-west and, more recently, from the European lands to the west. The southern region includes Central Asia and Kazakhstan. These are regions in which the main outside influences, from palaeolithic times to the present day, came from the south or south-east, from Iran, Afghanistan and India. For most purposes, the Tarim basin, now the southern part of Sinkiang, can also be included in this zone, though Sinkiang was also subject to powerful influences from China. It therefore belongs partially to the third zone, the eastern segment. Moving east, the influence of China rose steadily. The Chinese sphere of influence included Zungaria, Kansu and Mongolia, and occasionally parts of southern and eastern Siberia.

The northern zone includes the northern tundra and much of the woodland zone, from Scandinavia in the west to the Bering Straits in the north-east. Here, the impact of Outer Eurasia was limited until recent centuries. Though colonized late in palaeolithic times, the highly specialized adaptations required to settle it insulated the far north from developments further south until the present day. The great historical importance of this region derives from the fact that the Americas were settled from here, by peoples who took with them the ecological, and cultural adaptations of north-east Siberia, and perhaps, also, its languages.

NOTES

1 Parker, *Historical Geography*, p. 28.
2 As Sinor points out, even Herodotus realized how artificial this division was, and wondered 'why three names...should ever have been given to a tract of land which is in reality one'; *CHEIA*, p. 2, citing Herodotus, *Histories*, IV, 45.
3 Bassin, 'Russia between Europe and Asia', pp. 2–3, 6.
4 Attempts to see Inner Eurasia whole are surveyed in Hauner, *What is Asia to Us?*; for an introduction to the ideas of the 'Eurasianists', see Bassin, 'Russia between Europe and Asia', pp. 13–17; there is a translated collection of Trubetzkoy's writings in N. S. Trubetzkoy, *The Legacy of Genghis Khan*.
5 Klyuchevskii, *Sochineniya v 9-ti tomakh*, 1:64–5.
6 R. N. Taaffe, 'The geographical setting', in *CHEIA* (pp. 19–40), pp. 28, 35; and see Sinor, *Inner Asia: History, Civilization, Languages* p. 8.
7 Mackinder, *Democratic Ideals*, p. 110; Sinor, *Inner Asia*, p. 9.
8 *Macquarie Atlas*, 69; sub-arctic climates are characterized by 'light precipitation; short cool summers, long very cold winters', ibid., p. 68; north-east Siberia is one of the coldest regions on the planet; mean January temperatures in Verkhoyansk are −59°, and can drop to −100°; Taaffe, 'The geographical setting', in *CHEIA*, pp. 25–6.
9 Dawson, *Mission to Asia*, pp. 5–6.
10 Coniferous forests generate $c.300,000$ kg/km^2 per annum of plant production, and mixed or broad-leaf forests generate between 500,000 and 560,000; while dry steppe lands generate as little as 50,000; Dolukhanov, *Ecology and Economy*, p. 6.
11 Dolukhanov, *Early Slavs*, p. 18.
12 Lattimore, *Inner Asian Frontiers of China*, p. 12.
13 See Frank and Gills, *The World System: From Five Hundred Years to Five Thousand*; and see McNeill, *Plagues and Peoples*.
14 On the second unification, see Beckwith, *The Tibetan Empire*; on the Mongol 'world system', see Abu-Lughod, *Before European Hegemony*.
15 An allusion to Eric Wolf's superb, *Europe and the People Without History*.
16 Cited in Armstrong, *Russian Settlement in the North*, p. 8.
17 Haxthausen, *The Russian Empire*, 1:190–1.
18 Klyuchevskii, *Sochineniya v 9-ti tomakh*, 1:83.
19 Taaffe, 'The Geographic Setting', in *CHEIA*, p. 35.
20 Haxthausen, *The Russian Empire*, 2:223.
21 Haxthausen, *The Russian Empire*, 2:70.
22 Clarke, *Travels in Russia*, p. 47; these lands are also described very beautifully in the novels of Mikhail Sholokhov, such as *Quiet Flows the Don*, and *The Don Flows Down to the Sea*.
23 Haxthausen, *The Russian Empire*, 1:415.
24 Watters, *On Yuan Chwang's Travels*, 2:303–4; Marco Polo's description is similar.
25 Hiebert, *Origins of the Bronze Age Civilization*, p. 8.

FURTHER READING

Taafe, 'The geographical setting', in Sinor, ed., *Cambridge History of Early Inner Asia*, is a good introduction to the geography of Inner Eurasia. Christian, 'Inner Eurasia', argues for the geographical and historical unity of the entire region. Good surveys of the geography of parts of Inner Eurasia can be found in Parker, *Historical Geography*, Forsyth, *History of the Peoples of*

Siberia, Dolukhanov, *Early Slavs*, Hambly, *Central Asia*, Introduction, and in essays by Lattimore. Hauner, *What is Asia to Us?*, discusses early attempts to define a coherent region at the heart of the Eurasian landmass, while Trubetzkoy, *The Legacy of Genghis Khan*, offers a sample of the thinking of the 'Eurasianists'.

For the literate societies of Outer Eurasia, the lands of Inner Eurasia were an exotic 'other' world. This unbalanced relationship generated a huge travel literature dating back to the first millennium. This literature begins with accounts of the campaigns of Cyrus, Darius and Alexander, and continues with the writings of Herodotus, Chang Ch'ien, Hsüan-tsang, Zemarkhos, the great Islamic geographers, the many Outer Eurasians who travelled in the Mongol Empire, from Juvaini to Friar William of Rubruck and Marco Polo, and modern writers such as Haxthausen or Pallas or Aurel Stein.

PART II

Prehistory: 100,000–1000 BCE

[2] FIRST SETTLERS:
THE OLD STONE AGE

AVOIDING INNER EURASIA

The history of Inner Eurasia was distinctive from the moment the first humans tried to enter the region. The archaeological record suggests that the first would-be colonists found Inner Eurasia almost uninhabitable. So Inner Eurasia was settled much later than Outer Eurasia. Its settlement required the development of new technologies and new lifeways. While early hominids in Africa and Outer Eurasia seem to have relied on a mixed diet of plant and animal foods, the first settlers in Inner Eurasia found that its harsh conditions forced them to rely more on animal-based foods. In short, they had to become specialist hunters.

HUMAN EVOLUTION AND THE ICE AGES

There is now overwhelming evidence that humans evolved in Africa. Human genetic material differs from that of modern chimps by only $c.1.6$ per cent. This suggests that the evolutionary lines leading to modern humans and chimps began to diverge only 6–8 million years ago. For the last 4 million years, anthropologists can document human evolution from fossil remains.

Humans evolved during a period of exceptional climatic variability, caused by changes in the earth's orbit and tilt, and by an arrangement of the earth's landmasses that locked up vast ice sheets over the north and south poles. In the last 800,000 years, there have been eight periods of exceptionally cold climates. Each lasted approximately 100,000 years, with occasional periods of extreme cold. Between the ice ages there were warmer periods known as 'interglacials' that lasted between 10,000 and 20,000 years. During the ice ages, the most typical climates have been colder, and more arid than those of recent millennia, for we live, today, in an interglacial period. During the ice ages, forests shrank while savanna and steppelands expanded. Huge amounts of water were locked up in polar ice caps, so that sea levels dropped and the area of dry land increased. In higher latitudes huge glaciers formed, particularly over North America, Scandinavia and north-western Russia. To the south of the ice sheets there were cold steppelands which have no exact counterpart in the modern world.

Table 2.1   Temperature fluctuations during the Palaeolithic

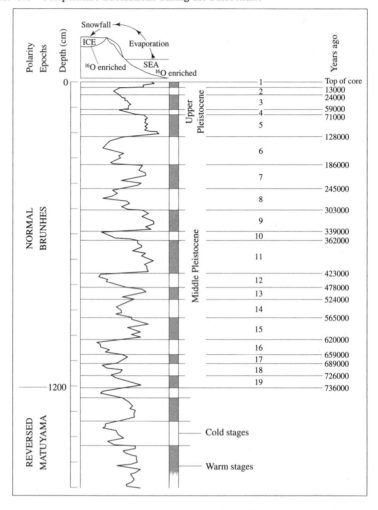

Source: Gamble, *Timewalkers*, p. 43.

As climates changed, animals and plants had to adapt, so that evolution itself speeded up. Our own species, like many other species of the modern world, is a product of this period of accelerated evolutionary change. As the forests of East Africa contracted, tree-dwelling species such as primates adapted to more open spaces. This may explain why the earliest ancestors of modern humans were bipedal primates, the so-called *Australopithecines*, for bipedalism is a more efficient way of covering large distances than the knuckle-walking characteristic of woodland great apes today. It was bipedalism that first distinguished the hominid evolutionary line from the lines leading to modern chimpanzees.

However, the most striking feature of hominid evolution has been the evolution of exceptionally large brains. Brains are costly organs to maintain, which is why so few species have specialized in them. The human brain takes up 20 per cent of the energy needed to support a human body, but accounts for only 3 per cent of body weight. The infants of large-brained species also tend to be more helpless at birth, as they rely less on instinct and more on learning, so they require an exceptional amount of parenting. Nevertheless, a species able to pay the high metabolic and social price for a large brain was likely to do well, particularly in an era of rapid ecological and climatic change. The primate line in general had shown an increasing ability to pay this price, for primate brains had steadily increased in proportion to body size. Large brains may have evolved as part of a larger package of changes caused by a process known to biologists as 'neoteny'. Neotenous species preserve many of the infantile features of the species from which they have evolved. Thus, modern humans have the flat faces and relative hairlessness that characterize modern chimps only during their youth. Most important of all, modern humans maintain the rate of brain growth typical of juvenile chimps, but sustain these rates for longer periods. This means that they grow larger brains, and can learn effectively for longer periods, though they also need more parental support while young. Presumably human males and other close relatives had to take an increasing share in the work of parenting, as human infants became more and more helpless. This may be the main reason why modern humans are social animals. Or perhaps it was the other way around. Some specialists have argued that hominids exploited the many advantages of living in groups, and it was the complex calculus of group dynamics that required the evolution of large brains.[1]

The first species classified within our own genus, *Homo*, evolved about 2.5 million years ago. It is known as *Homo habilis*. While the brains of *Australopithecines* averaged *c*.400 cc, which is close to the size of modern chimp brains, *habilis* brains ranged from 600–800 cc. The brains of *Homo erectus*, whose oldest remains date to just under 2 million years ago, ranged from 850 cc to more than 1000 cc, while the brains of modern humans average *c*.1400 cc.[2]

THE EARLY SETTLEMENT OF EURASIA

Large brains meant greater behavioural flexibility and an ability to adapt to a wider range of environments. They made possible the migrations that eventually spread modern hominids around the entire planet. *Homo erectus* was the first human species to migrate from Africa into Eurasia. They did so at least one, and perhaps 2 million years ago.[2]

Homo erectus settled in many different parts of Outer Eurasia. Here, they could often find relatively benign climates, and savanna lands similar to those in which they had evolved. There are traces of early settlement in parts of western and central Europe, the Middle East, the Indian sub-continent, South-East Asia and China. In Europe, the earliest evidence of human colonization comes from Italy in about 730,000 BP ('Before Present').

By 350,000 BP, early humans had settled in most parts of western, central and southern Europe.[3]

However, early humans found it more difficult to settle Inner Eurasia. Evidence of settlement before c.100,000 years ago is thin and often unreliable. Further, even the most trustworthy evidence of early settlement in Inner Eurasia suggests that it was small-scale, confined to the southernmost rim, and occurred only during the warm interglacials.

Soviet archaeologists devoted much attention to the palaeolithic era, and excavated some 700 palaeolithic sites in Inner Eurasia.[4] Some of these excavations prompted claims for very early settlement. At the Altai mountain site of Ulalinka, A. P. Okladnikov, the pioneer of Siberian and Mongolian prehistoric studies, has found crude pebble tools in layers he dates to almost 1.5 million years old. In 1983, at Diring-Ur'akh, on the Lena river, c. 140 km north of Yakutsk, Yu. A. Mochanov, one of the pioneers of Eastern Siberian archaeology, also claimed to have found human artefacts 1.5–2 million years old. These dates are so old that, if upheld, they would require a revision of some basic ideas about early human migrations. However, in both cases, there are doubts about the dating procedures used (which rely on dating the layers in which artefacts were found), and it is not even certain that the objects themselves are human artefacts. As a result, most Soviet and western archaeologists prefer much later dates for these sites.[5]

Claims that there were early humans in Siberia 200,000 or 300,000 years ago should be taken more seriously. Sites along the river Angara have been tentatively dated to 200,000 years BP. But even here, the dating is suspect.[6] Besides, even if we take such claims seriously, the number of early palaeolithic finds in Mongolia and southern Siberia is much smaller than the number from regions further south such as northern China or the northern parts of the Indian sub-continent.[7] Even in the more benign ecological environments west of the Urals, there is little evidence of settlement before c.120,000 years ago. The contrast with western and central Europe is striking. As John Hoffecker writes: 'It is now apparent that the paleolithic record of the European USSR is profoundly different from that of western and central Europe, and the Near East.'[8]

The best evidence for early human colonization of Inner Eurasia comes, as one might expect, from the southern borderlands. In 1991, a *Homo erectus* jaw was found in Georgia. There have also been finds of Oldowan-type tools in the Caucasus, in layers perhaps 750,000 years old, and of later Acheulian-type tools; while finds in southern Tajikistan may be equally old, though most palaeolithic finds even in this region date from after 250,000 BP. On the border between Tajikistan and Afghanistan, the earliest finds of stone tools occur in thin layers of soils between thicker layers of loess. Loess formed mainly during the colder phases of the ice ages, so this suggests that populations left the region during the colder, drier glacial periods that dominated most of the palaeolithic era.[9]

All in all, the existing evidence suggests that before 100,000 years ago, there were, at best, occasional attempts to settle the more hospitable parts of Inner Eurasia along its southern fringes, and even then only during

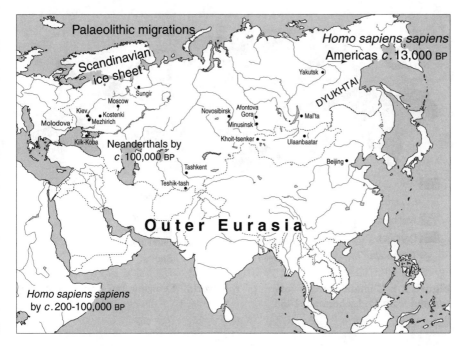

Map 2.1 Paleolithic migrations into Inner Eurasia.

interglacials. For most of the early and middle Palaeolithic era, human colonization of Inner Eurasia was insignificant and occasional.

WHY WAS IT DIFFICULT TO SETTLE INNER EURASIA?

The long, cold, arid winters of the periglacial steppes posed two distinctive problems for early humans. The first was how to keep warm. *Homo erectus* may have used fire even a million years ago. Presumably their ability to scavenge animal carcasses meant that they could also use skins or furs for warmth. However, there are no signs of hearths before about 200,000 BP. This suggests that early humans used fire opportunistically, and had not yet domesticated it enough to survive the harsh winters of ice age Inner Eurasia.[10]

Even trickier was the problem of getting food during the long winters. It was not that Inner Eurasia lacked sources of food. The problem was that the food was of the wrong kind and it was not always available. Humans could not exploit the abundant grasses of the steppes, and most of the edible plants died off in winter. So, for long periods of each year, it was necessary to rely mainly on meat. Meat was available in abundance, for, unlike the tundra landscapes of the far north, those of the ice age steppes were in lower latitudes and enjoyed more sunlight. Their grasslands supported huge populations of herbivores that could convert grass into edible flesh and blood, while the aridity of the cold steppes ensured that winter snow cover

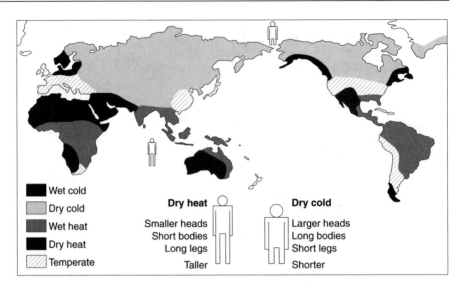

Figure 2.1 Climatic 'stress zones' of the world. Drawing by Annick Paterson, adapted from D. Lieberman, 1984.

was shallow enough to let herbivores feed throughout the winters. Indeed, it is likely that the ice age steppes supported a greater variety and quantity of herbivores than the modern steppes of Inner Eurasia. Species identified by modern archaeologists include reindeer and other types of deer including ibex, saiga antelopes, chamois and giant deer, as well as horse, bison, aurochs, boar, musk-ox, moose and, of course, woolly rhinoceros and mammoth.[11]

Until the 1960s, it was widely believed that early humans were natural hunters, so that it should have been all too easy to exploit the abundant game of the Inner Eurasian steppes. However, studies since the 1960s have shown that amongst modern foraging communities in temperate regions, hunting is usually a less important source of food than the gathering of plant foods. The meat secured by hunting (usually by males) can only provide occasional feasts. The staple foods are usually plants gathered mainly by women. Only in higher latitudes does hunting become the main source of foodstuffs in foraging societies, and such societies have only evolved recently, and rely on extremely complex technological and organizational systems to ensure the success of their hunters.[12] Recent archaeological research suggests that the earliest human societies also relied primarily on plant-based foods. They certainly used meat, for cut marks on animal bones from early palaeolithic sites show evidence of butchering from at least 1.5 to 2 million years ago.[13] However, where hominids butchered meat they usually did so after other carnivores had eaten their fill, or they used the meat from animals that died of natural causes. This suggests an opportunistic and occasional use of animal-based foods, rather than the ability to hunt systematically and reliably enough to depend primarily on animal-based foods. All in all, there is no hard evidence that any early palaeolithic communities could depend on hunting for long periods of time, nor that they needed to as long as they remained in temperate latitudes. Hunting as a distinctive lifeway probably evolved only in the last 500,000 or 200,000 years.[14]

These conclusions highlight the intrinsic difficulties of hunting as the basis of subsistence. Hunting is a more difficult, dangerous and unreliable lifeway than gathering. Animals, unlike plants, can evade predators, and may even fight back. Hunters must also cover more ground than gatherers, for they occupy a higher position on the food chain. This generalization reflects the ecological principle that $c.90$ per cent of all food energy is lost at each level of the food-chain. This means that a given amount of sunlight can support approximately ten times fewer carnivores than herbivores.

Settling Inner Eurasia meant overcoming these difficulties. Systematic and reliable hunting methods meant more than the evolution of new technologies. They also demanded new ways of thinking and even new social structures. Lewis Binford has shown that these different strategies can be observed amongst modern foraging communities. He has identified two fundamentally different subsistence strategies. Under 'forager/gatherer' strategies, which are more typical of temperate or tropical environments, most of the diet comes from plant foods. Foragers set out each day to collect food which they bring back to a home base. Bands change home bases frequently as they follow seasonal changes in food resources, however, there is no period of the year in which no plant foods are available. Often there is a division of labour under which women concentrate on the more reliable plant foods, while men concentrate on hunting. In contrast, under 'hunter/collector' strategies, such as those of many modern Arctic peoples, food comes mainly from animals. Parties of (mainly male) hunters leave camps with very specific goals in mind, based on intimate knowledge of their intended prey. They may be away for days or weeks at a time, and will often store their kill at special storage sites, from which they will bring food back to a base camp when it is needed. As a result, they move their base camps less often than in forager societies, but they range more widely, their movements are more carefully planned, and so are their methods of storage.[15]

The fundamental difference between the two strategies is in the degree of planning. Hunters have to plan in advance and in great detail. They need reliable information about the movements and habits of animal prey over large areas, which can be secured only by maintaining regular contacts with neighbouring groups. Finally, they need reliable methods of storage to tide them over in periods of shortage. Where plant foods cannot provide a dietary safety net, planning has to be precise and detailed. It appears in the choice of hunting gear, in the selection of routes and prey, in the choice of companions and timing, in the maintenance of communications with neighbours, and in the methods of storage. Failure at any point can be fatal for the entire group.[16]

Hunting strategies also imply greater social complexity. The regular exchange of information, and sometimes of material goods, both within and between groups scattered over large distances is critical. This increases the importance of symbolic exchanges of both goods and information, and makes it necessary to clarify group identities. Internally, groups may split for long periods as hunting parties travel over great distances. Such differences may have sharpened the division of labour by gender as systematic hunting took males away from base camps for longer periods. All in all, each group had to exist and survive in several distinct configurations.

For these reasons, Clive Gamble has argued that the difficulties of settling the Eurasian heartland arose less from the technological than from the social and organizational features of early human communities.

> What is lacking [amongst early Palaeolithic communities] is any indication for such modern practices as detailed planning, widespread contacts, or elaborate social display. There is no physical evidence for storage, raw materials all come from within a radius of 50 km., and usually less than 5 km. of the sites where they were used, and any form of art, ornament, jewellery, or decoration is entirely absent.[17]

All in all, the challenge of settling Inner Eurasia seems to have been beyond the technological and social capacities of most *Homo erectus*.

NEANDERTHAL COLONISTS: *100,000–40,000* BP

GEOGRAPHY AND CHRONOLOGY OF NEANDERTHAL SETTLEMENT

The first signs of systematic and durable colonization of parts of Inner Eurasia appear after the beginning of the last ice age, about 120,000 years ago. Though Neanderthals settled only the southern borderlands of Inner Eurasia, their appearance is still an event of great significance in human history for never before had humans established durable colonies beyond the customary ecological range of primates.

Evidence for the colonization of Inner Eurasia during the first half of the last ice age consists either of human remains or of the stone artefacts classified by archaeologists as 'Mousterian', after a site in SW France. The main feature of Mousterian stone tools was the use of flakes and scrapers struck from prepared cores, rather than the heavier hand-axes more typical of the earlier palaeolithic. In Inner Eurasia, the human remains of this period belong exclusively to the early human species known today as '*Homo sapiens Neanderthalis*'. As a result, it is customary (though not entirely accurate) to assume that Mousterian artefacts imply the presence of Neanderthals. This assumption explains why there have been claims for Mousterian finds from regions such as Mongolia, in which there is no direct evidence of a Neanderthal presence.[18]

Neanderthal remains appear mainly in caves, in North Africa, Europe, and the Middle East. The major Inner Eurasian sites are at Teshik-Tash in modern Uzbekistan, in the Caucasus, in Crimea, and at Molodova on the River Dniester. In other words, they fall in a narrow strip from Central Asia to south-west Ukraine. This is not surprising, for of all regions of Inner Eurasia, this is the one whose climate and ecology are most benign.

The earliest evidence of Neanderthal presence in Inner Eurasia dates from *c.*90–80,000 BP, during the early stages of the last ice age, when climates were still quite favourable. During the colder period after 75,000 BP, there may have been times when there was no settlement at all in Inner Eurasia. However, there seems to have been a second wave of settlement after c.65,000 BP.[19] During the earlier phase, Neanderthal colonization was confined to the wide river valleys carved out by melt water from northern glaciers in the south western plains and plateaux of modern Ukraine. These sometimes formed long chains of lakes where there was abundant and varied game. Only later did Neanderthals begin to colonize the more seasonal environments of the steppelands between the great rivers, or the mountain regions in the Caucasus, Crimea and Central Asia. Sites as far north as Volgograd, or Khotylevo on the River Desna were probably occupied during warmer periods.[20]

If we accept the speculative estimate that there may have been about 1 million humans and Neanderthals 100,000 years ago, and no more than 2 million 30,000 years ago, and if we assume that most humans lived in Africa and Outer Eurasia, then we can perhaps guess that Inner Eurasian populations were no more than a few tens of thousands, rising, at most, to about 100,000. This thin, uneven and sporadic pattern of settlement suggests that core Neanderthal populations, whose origins lay perhaps in the Middle East, colonized the marginal environments of south-west Inner Eurasia only in more favourable periods.[21] Perhaps they did so under demographic pressure from the modern humans who began to colonize the Middle East during the early stages of the last ice age.

NEANDERTHAL PHYSIOLOGY, TECHNOLOGY AND SOCIAL STRUCTURE

This pattern of settlement suggests that Neanderthal communities overcame some, but not all, of the difficulties faced by prospective colonists of Inner Eurasia. How did they do so? Did their successes and their limitations reflect their biology, their technologies or their social structures?

Neanderthals evolved from archaic forms of *Homo erectus* somewhere in central or western Eurasia from c.250,000 BP. Though classified, like ourselves, as *Homo sapiens*, recent research has shown that they were less like modern humans than was once thought. They had brains as large, and perhaps even larger, than those of modern humans. However, it seems likely that they could not communicate information as fluently as modern humans for they lacked a modern vocal apparatus. In an important, if not conclusive, study, Philip Lieberman concludes from an analysis of Neanderthal skulls, that:

> classic Neanderthal hominids appear to be deficient with respect to their linguistic and cognitive ability. At minimum their speech communications would be nasalized and more susceptible to perceptual errors: they probably communicated vocally at extremely slow rates and were unable to comprehend complex sentences. They may also have been deficient in cognitive tasks that involve rule-governed logic.[22]

Neanderthal anatomy suggests adaptations for cold and for strength rather than for enhanced ability to communicate. Their relatively squat physiognomy

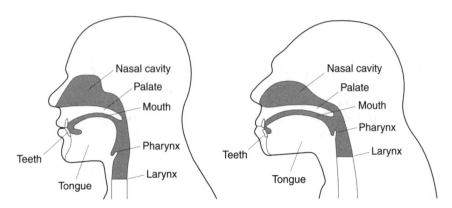

Figure 2.2 Neanderthal and modern vocal apparatus. Drawing by Annick Petersen, reproduced from Christopher Stringer and Clive Gamble *In Search of the Neanderthals* (London: Thames and Hudson, 1993).

may be an adaptation to cold, for smaller, rounder bodies preserve heat better than tall, thin bodies. Their skeletons suggest exceptional muscular strength, and their strong jaws and teeth may often have been used to grip.

Neanderthals clearly hunted. Indeed, throughout their range, they seem to have relied mainly on animal foods. The presence of mammoth bones at many Neanderthal sites shows that they hunted, or at least scavenged even these giant creatures. They also hunted other large species, including bison, horses and particularly deer – red deer or reindeer. The cave sites of Teshik-Tash in Southern Uzbekistan, and Ogzi-Kichik in Tajikistan, contain the bones of mountain goat, turtle, rhinoceros, wild horse, leopard, brown bear, hyena and many smaller animals and birds.[23]

But Neanderthal hunting methods seem to have been less systematic than those of modern hunter/collectors. The evidence of animal bones suggests that Neanderthals relied on scavenging as much as on deliberate hunting, for most bones come from animals that were small, young, old or injured, rather than from fully fit adults. There is no sign that Neanderthals used snares, spear-throwers, or bows and arrows. On the contrary, the evidence both of Neanderthal anatomy and their surviving stone implements suggests that Neanderthal hunting was a dangerous and bloody business, relying less on careful planning than on chance encounters with weak or isolated prey, who were dispatched in single combat by hunters of great strength and courage. Most Neanderthal stone tools were hand-held and there is little sign of hafting, or of any forms of leverage, or of the use of effective projectiles. Their massive bone structure and the appearance of stress fractures hints at a violent form of hunting in which the hunter stabbed repeatedly with hand-held spears. This was still a precariously opportunistic technology to survive by in such a harsh environment.[24]

These conclusions about Neanderthal subsistence methods fit what we know or can infer of Neanderthal social structure. In thinking of social structures, it is helpful to think of several distinct scales or levels, all of which exist

Table 2.2 Levels of social organization in human societies

Level 7	*The modern global system*: (6 billion +); embraces all world societies in hierarchy of influence, wealth, power
Level 6	*World systems and empires*: (100,000s–millions); embrace large regions linked culturally, economically and sometimes politically
Level 5	*States/cities/supra-tribal associations*: (1000s–100,000s +); large, economically and militarily powerful systems, with state or near-state structures
Level 4	*Cultures/tribes/town + surrounding villages*: (500–1000s); linked reproductive groups, sometimes with single leadership
Level 3	*Reproductive groups/clusters of villages*: (50–500); related local groups whose members often intermarry, and share a loose sense of kinship and culture
Level 2	*Local or subsistence groups/villages/bands/camping groups*: 8–50 people; several parental groups that travel or live close together
Level 1	*Parental Groups*: 2–8 people; mother + children, often with father, sharing a dwelling

in modern society, while only the smaller ones existed in the earliest human societies.

The smallest group, which exists in all primate societies, is the parental group. This consists of a mother and one or more young children. Often, but not always, the parental group also includes the father and older siblings. The second level is that of the local or subsistence group. This consists of several related parental groups that normally travel together. It corresponds to the 'band' of anthropological theory and might include anything from five or ten to 50 or 60 people. We can assume the existence of parental groups amongst Neanderthals, while evidence from Neanderthal home sites also demonstrates the importance of subsistence groups. Many cave sites were occupied for long periods, which suggests that they functioned as long-term winter camps, to which groups may have returned many times, perhaps over thousands of years. Caves sometimes contain hearths, and inside some caves there seem to have been special tent-like structures.[25] On the steppes, where there were few caves, Neanderthals seem to have constructed rudimentary tents or windbreaks, perhaps by stretching skins over structures made from mammoth bones.[26]

What is missing is any clear evidence for the next level of complexity, which Robin Dennell refers to as the 'reproductive group'.

> This comprises a set of subsistence groups within which the members of any one unit will tend to find a mating partner; it is, in effect, the regional breeding population that ensures the long term viability of each subsistence group. Since it functions both by encounters between and within groups, it also serves as an information network that can provide each subsistence group with knowledge about their neighbours and their regional – as opposed to local – environment.[27]

We can assume that such groups existed, for bands would have been too small to survive and reproduce alone. However, there is no sign that relations with other subsistence groups led to regular systematic exchanges of goods, or information. Neanderthal sites offer little evidence for the symbols of identity that usually mark the existence of regular social contacts at this level.

There is little sign of a developed capacity to handle symbols: no sign of art work, or jewellery, or ritual centres or complex forms of communication. It seems that the important groups of Neanderthal society were the subsistence groups rather than the reproductive groups.

> Group self-sufficiency in all things (food, mates, raw materials) was their basic strategy rather than using the alliances that could be built, through negotiation, to extend the length of occupation in a region now subject to difficult climatic conditions.[28]

We should not exaggerate these limitations. Neanderthals could probably communicate with each other, and some Neanderthal burials hint at the existence of a limited ritual life. At Teshik-Tash, near the upper reaches of the Amu Darya, an 8- or 9-year old Neanderthal boy was buried in a grave in which the horns of mountain goat had been placed, apparently with some care. In the Tajik cave site of Ogzi-Kichik, there was an oval arrangement of stones, with a set of ibex horns at one end in what appears to have been a shrine of some kind.[29]

Nevertheless, despite these intriguing hints, the symbolic world of Neanderthals seems to have been much less elaborate than that of modern hunters. Indeed, their social relations seem to have been as direct and uncomplicated as their methods of hunting. That may be why, though they settled parts of south-west Inner Eurasia periodically for perhaps 50,000 years, they did so only in small numbers, and probably left as climates deteriorated. As late as 40,000 years ago, most of Inner Eurasia remained beyond the zone of human settlement.

MODERN HUMANS SETTLE INNER EURASIA: 40,000–10,000 BP

THE 'REVOLUTION OF THE UPPER PALAEOLITHIC'

The 'Upper Palaeolithic', during the last 30,000 years of the last ice age, is a period of fundamental change. Neanderthal humans disappear, leaving a world inhabited by only one human species, our own. There is a sharp change in the variety and complexity of technologies and lifeways, and humans begin to colonize much larger areas of the earth. Though spread over many thousands of years, the 'Revolution of the Upper Palaeolithic' was as radical a turning point in human history as the more familiar transitions of the neolithic and industrial revolutions.

These revolutionary changes are particularly sharply defined in Inner Eurasia. They are apparent, (1) in the artefacts that survive from this period; (2) in the new geography of settlement; and finally, (3) in the surviving human remains.

Though typically Mousterian objects survive as late as 30,000 years ago, most tools made after 40,000 BP are smaller, more precisely adapted to specific functions, and made from a greater variety of raw materials. In place of the hand-held axes and choppers typical of the earlier palaeolithic, or

Table 2.3 The revolution of the Upper Paleolithic

Years ago

80,000	70,000	60,000	50,000	40,000	30,000	20,000	10,000	

| | Middle Paleolithic | | | Early \| Upper Paleolithic | | Late upper Paleo-lithic | |

Life at the fireside: the technology of survival

LAST GLACIAL MAXIMUM

- Art
- Bone tools
- Blade technology
- Ceramic technology
- Body ornament
- Artifact styles
- Built hearths
- Structured living space and windbreaks
- Cave 'burials'
- Open site burials
- Storage pits
- Huts
- Microliths

Life on the land: regional exchange

LAST GLACIAL MAXIMUM

- Quarries
- Regional art
- Long-distance exchange of raw materials
- Chains of connection
- Long-term occupation of harsh environments
- Social storage

Expansion into new habitats and the rise of complex behaviour

LAST GLACIAL MAXIMUM

- Sea voyaging
- Colonization of boreal forest
- High mountains
- Deep deserts
- Tropical rain forests
- Small islands

- Spoken language
- Increased forward planning

Source: Gamble, *Timewalkers*, p. 160.

the large flake blades of the Mousterian, there appears a multitude of tiny, delicate blades struck from larger cores. Many seem designed to be hafted onto handles or shafts for use as spears or knives. Over time, there appeared special tools used to exploit particular food resources, such as birds, acorns, or sea mammals. From about 20,000 BP we find evidence of even more complex hunting equipment, including the earliest bows and arrows, spear-throwers, snares and nets.[30] Hooks, needles, punches, awls, hide-burnishers also appear. The choice of materials now includes ivory, bone, shell, antler and wood, as well as stone. Upper palaeolithic tool-makers also selected their raw materials more carefully than their Neanderthal predecessors. At Kostenki on the Don, there are tools made from flints that came from 130 kilometres away.[31]

Dwellings and clothing also became more specialized. In place of the simple windbreaks or caves of the middle palaeolithic, there appear complex and durable structures, carefully designed and laid out. Some of the clothing of this period seems to have been especially tailored for Arctic conditions. At Sungir, near Vladimir in Russia, there is a burial dating from c.23,000 BP, containing the remains of two boys who wore clothing covered with thousands of ivory beads. The position of the beads suggests that the clothes were carefully made and well-fitting.[32]

Equally striking is the fact that not all artefacts of the upper palaeolithic are strictly utilitarian. For the first time there appears in the archaeological record clear evidence of 'art'. This takes a great variety of forms, from clothing, to body ornaments and body painting, to cave paintings, to carved geometric patterns on tools, to the arrangement of buildings. In art, as in technology, there are signs of rapid evolution during the upper palaeolithic. Most 'art' objects found before 25,000 BP consist of simple ornaments, many with geometric designs. After 25,000 BP, the range increases. There appear many figurines, such as the famous Venus figures of c.22–24,000 BP. Inhabitants of the Mezin site, in European Russia, made musical instruments.[33] In Ukraine, archaeologists have found beads and pendants shaped by drilling holes through shells or the teeth of foxes or wolves. Ochre was used as personal decoration. Siberian sites are particularly rich in paintings and ornaments. On the Upper Lena, near Verkholensk, there are near life-size rock paintings of animals, including horses. The Malaya Siya site in western Siberia contains art of various kinds, including sculptures in bone and stone of animals such as mammoth, as well as wall-carvings and engravings. It also includes a strange object that some have interpreted as a form of calendar. Equally striking are the ivory carvings of Mal'ta, which depict animals, including mammoth, and also human figures, some similar to the Venus figurines of Ukraine and Europe.[34] In the Khoit-Senker cave, 90 km south of Khobdo in western Mongolia, there are cave paintings of many different animals, including antelopes, goats and sheep, horse, camel and birds. In their subject matter (animals alone), the paintings of western Mongolia show remarkable similarities with the cave paintings of south-western Europe.[35] Artistic creativity is also apparent in the design of upper palaeolithic tools. Bone artefacts, in particular, are often carved with geometric or naturalistic designs in a way that has no precedent in the middle palaeolithic.[36] The sheer variety of upper palaeolithic artefacts also suggests that their design reflects artistic as well as utilitarian choices.

With more reliable, more varied and less risky hunting techniques, warmer clothing, and a greater array of constructional methods available to them, humans of the upper palaeolithic managed to settle much more of Inner Eurasia than their Neanderthal predecessors. From Ukraine there is abundant evidence of sustained settlement of the ice age steppes, mainly along major river systems. Settlement at the Kostenki sites on the River Don date from as early as 35,000 BP, but there are many upper palaeolithic sites along the Dnieper from c.25,000 BP, as well as on the Dniester. There were also settlements further north. The Byzovaya site, which was occupied between 25,000 and 20,000 BP, lies in the Pechora basin, just 100 km south of the Arctic Ocean and at 65° north. Its inhabitants used mammoth probably both for food and construction, while the nearby site of Medvezhya Cave, contains mainly the remains of reindeer.[37]

For the first time, there is also clear evidence for the colonization of Siberia. The Malaya Siya site near Lake Baikal is one of the oldest Siberian sites, dating perhaps from 35,000 years ago. There are signs here of the hunting of mammoth, horse, reindeer and other large herbivores.[38] From about 20,000 BP, there appear more modern and more distinctive traditions in western Siberia. At the Afontova Gora site near Krasnoyarsk, people lived in easily portable tents, and wore distinctive styles of clothes, including light caftans, fur boots, and short trousers. The main animal remains here are of reindeer.[39] This is also true of the Mal'ta site, near Lake Baikal, which dates from c.14,000 BP. It included dwellings partly dug into the ground, made from a framework of large animal bones and reindeer antlers covered with skins or sods. This may have been a winter gathering place for quite large groups. The people of Mal'ta pursued mammoth, as well as woolly rhinoceros, reindeer and many smaller animals. They were also able tailors, making clothing sewn in double layers to shield them from Arctic winds.[40]

There was settlement even in eastern Siberia. This area is of peculiar interest for it was from here that Inner Eurasian peoples began to colonize the Americas sometime late in the upper palaeolithic. The best known east Siberian sites belong to the 'Dyukhtai' culture. These are named after a site in the Middle Aldan Valley, north and east of Lake Baikal that dates from c.18,000 BP. Y. A. Mochanov, the Soviet archaeologist who has done most work on the Dyukhtai culture, dates the earliest 'proto-Dyukhtai' site, at Evanzhtsy, to 35,000 years BP, but most specialists prefer later dates, and some doubt if any eastern Siberian dates are older than 20,000 years. The Dyukhtai culture shows many similarities with the earliest archaeological evidence from North America, so it is likely that this constituted a core area for the first wave of colonization of ice age North America. Low sea levels during the later ice age would have permitted migrants to travel across a dry Beringian strait.[41]

Differences in the style of stone artefacts in eastern and western Siberia suggests that the two regions were colonized from different zones.[42] The dividing line is the watershed of the Lena and Yenisei rivers. Eastern Siberia was probably colonized from the south, from upper palaeolithic populations of Mongolia or China, while western Siberia may have been colonized from populations of western Inner Eurasia.

All in all, humans managed to settle most of the environments of ice age Inner Eurasia during the upper palaeolithic, with the sole exception of the Arctic shores. It is a reasonable assumption that the increasing number of settlement sites from the upper palaeolithic, and their wider dispersion, implies a substantial increase in Inner Eurasian populations. If we accept that world populations in 10,000 BP were about 10 millions, and assume that Inner Eurasian populations were still much less dense than those of Africa and Outer Eurasia, it follows that the population of Inner Eurasia may have grown from several tens of thousands to several hundred thousands, perhaps to half a million.

The third striking feature of the evidence from the upper palaeolithic is that all human remains now belong to our own species. We know of no Neanderthal remains anywhere after about 30,000 BP, though this does not mean that small refuge populations did not survive. One region where they may have survived quite late is Central Asia, where the remains of most upper palaeolithic sites are still Mousterian.[43] With this (speculative) exception, the human remains of upper palaeolithic Inner Eurasia all belong to our own species, *Homo sapiens sapiens*. From 40,000 years ago, the human history of Inner Eurasia, like that of the rest of our planet, is a history of just one species, our own.

EXPLAINING THE UPPER PALAEOLITHIC

It is tempting to argue that these changes reflect the appearance of modern humans, who brought with them a higher level of technological and artistic creativity. However, this argument runs into some chronological difficulties. Currently, there are two major theories about the emergence of modern humans. The first, and probably the dominant theory at present, argues that modern humans evolved in Africa between 100,000 and 200,000 years ago. At some time after 100,000 BP, groups of modern humans began to migrate out of Africa into Eurasia and Australasia, eventually replacing existing populations of early humans. The alternative theory argues that modern humans are descended from many regional populations of late *Homo erectus*, who maintained just enough genetic contact to remain a single species for the best part of a million years.[44] Whatever theory one adopts, it is clear that modern humans used very ancient technologies for a long time. There is no automatic correlation here between genetic and cultural change. In areas such as the Middle East, which were inhabited both by Neanderthals and modern humans early in the last ice age, the cultural remains of the two species are indistinguishable.

Climatic change may explain some of the differences. During the second half of the last ice age, climates gradually deteriorated. Temperatures fell steadily between 60,000 and 40,000 BP, before stabilizing for another 10,000 years. Then they began to fall once again, reaching the coldest phase (the 'late glacial maximum') between 20,000 and 16,000 years ago. West of the Urals, the Scandinavian ice sheet reached 52°N. during the glacial maximum, and average annual temperatures were between 7° and 10° lower than today. The zone of permafrost may have reached as far south as modern Rostov. (In Siberia, there was not enough moisture to form large ice sheets.) Throughout Inner Eurasia, cold average temperatures reflected the harshness of the winters, for the climates of the brief summer seasons could be relatively benign.[45]

We have seen already that Neanderthal colonization of south-west Inner Eurasia may have declined in colder periods. Presumably, they found it harder and harder to adapt during the second half of the ice age. This might suggest why the latest evidence for Neanderthal populations comes from warmer regions such as south-west France or, perhaps, Central Asia.

While climatic change may explain why Neanderthals left Inner Eurasia, it does not, in itself, explain why modern humans replaced them. Nor does it explain why modern humans evolved increasingly varied technologies in the process. Contemporary archaeologists are inclined to explain such changes in social rather than intellectual or technological terms.[46] Clearly, over some 50,000 or more years, modern humans slowly developed strategies that were beyond the grasp of Neanderthals. Perhaps most important of all, they developed richer and more complex forms of communication which enabled them to exchange the technological, ecological and geographical information needed to survive and flourish in the deteriorating conditions of the upper palaeolithic.

Modern humans have much greater vocal flexibility than Neanderthals and they also have the mental structures necessary to exploit these abilities. These gifts allowed modern humans to evolve a rich and flexible spoken language, which increased the ability to communicate and store information. It even increased the ability of humans to manage their internal psychic world, for words provide a way of labelling objects within our memory, which allows us to manipulate the contents of our minds and to think more effectively. Language helps us communicate with ourselves as much as with others, which is why recent linguistic theories suggest that language is the key to the human capacity for self-awareness or conscious action.[47]

The hunting methods of the upper palaeolithic were closer to those of modern hunters than to those of the early palaeolithic. The preparation of more and more specialized hunting tools already suggests an increase in planning and cooperation. A narrowing of the range of prey species suggests increased specialization, greater knowledge of particular species, and an ability to take even healthy animals more or less at will. In late upper palaeolithic Ukraine, for example, hunting was highly seasonable. Mammoth and fur-bearing animals were hunted in winter, reindeer in the spring, and waterfowl in the summer. North of the Black Sea, organized groups of hunters drove herds of bison to their death.[48]

More complex hunting techniques almost certainly imply the existence of higher levels of social organization. Like modern hunters, upper palaeolithic communities seem to have included stable core groups from which hunting parties regularly split off. The best studied region of upper palaeolithic Inner

Eurasia is in modern Ukraine. Here, Olga Soffer has studied about 29 major late upper palaeolithic sites near Kiev.[49] Many have mammoth bones and pits for the storage of frozen meat. Linked to these are other, less permanent, sites, on high ground, away from the river valleys. These were probably temporary hunting camps. The earliest mammoth bone dwellings appear at Kostenki 11 on the Don, where they date from *c*.20,000 BP. Similar dwellings spread widely in the Dnieper basin, at sites such as Mezhirich, Mezin and Dobranichevka, usually near river valleys. At the spectacular site of Mezhirich on the River Dnieper, there are large concentrations of mammoth bones, along with carefully prepared hearths and many bone or ivory ornaments. Mammoth bones provided a scaffolding over dwellings partly dug into the ground, and covered over with skins. There were about five dwellings, each about 80 m² in area, and each housing up to ten people. The builders used mammoth bones not just for scaffolding, but also as 'tent pegs', in preference to wood, which rots more easily. They forced them deep into the ground and cut sockets into which they inserted wooden poles. They also used mammoth bones as fuel, after splintering them.[50] These settlements were probably winter camps for groups of perhaps 30 people, who may have occupied them for as long as nine months each year.

The relative permanence of these settlements is reflected in the care with which they were built. At the Kostenki 21 site, there were several dwellings along 200 m of the Don river shore, set 10–15 m apart. One dwelling, near marshland, had an area paved with limestone slabs to avoid the damp. There are also objects which seem to have ritual importance, such as the two musk-ox skulls found at Kostenki. Perhaps these were the site of annual gatherings or of ritual activities affirming the unity of related groups.[51]

The inhabitants of these ice age villages lived off frozen stocks of meat kept in storage pits, and thawed out by fire. The meat, most of which came from gregarious herbivores, was hunted in summer and autumn, when the animals were at their fittest. Each year, some of the inhabitants moved out to more temporary summer camps for the hunting season. On returning, they stored meat in pits whose depth suggests they were dug from the top layer of permafrost as it thawed during the brief summers.[52]

Storage may have led to minor inequalities in access to resources, and perhaps to other forms of hierarchy. At some sites, there are central storage pits, which appear to offer equal access to all inhabitants. At Dobranichevka, each dwelling has a circle of two to four storage pits around it. However, at the Mezin site, most of the storage pits appear around a single dwelling which also contains art objects, jewellery and shells whose origin is some 800 km to the south. 'Since . . . this dwelling was neither a special purpose structure . . . nor occupied by a greater number of people, the concentration suggests not only higher status for its residents but also their ability to control considerably greater amounts of surplus.'[53] If, as modern analogies suggest, hunting was mainly a male activity, then it is entirely possible that there emerged gender inequalities in access to basic resources, including food.[54]

Meat was not the only stored resource in these communities. Their inhabitants also harvested fur-bearing animals and made jewellery from exotic materials. The importance of buildings and objects of symbolic significance suggests that influence and power could also be accumulated and stored. Olga Soffer has argued that rhythmic elements in the design of the Mezhirich buildings, such as the systematic stacking of mandible bones chin side up, then chin side down, suggest that these were early examples of monumental architecture.[55] If so, they may imply the emergence of 'big men', who used kinship, gift-giving and personal influence to mobilize the labour and wealth of their neighbours. Certainly, someone had to mobilize the very considerable amount of labour needed to build such structures. Finally, the burials at the Sungir site near Vladimir suggest a degree of status differentiation even before the last glacial maximum. Buried with the boys were spears of mammoth ivory, weapons of stone and ivory, and animal carvings.[56] The youth of the boys shows that status could be inherited in this community, and that points to a structure of ranked families or clans.

Relations between groups became more complex and extensive. Upper palaeolithic communities exchanged goods over large areas. Amber beads, shells and furs are the main 'imported' objects found at Ukrainian sites. These almost certainly reached the region through systems of exchange rather than through special expeditions. Some amber had come from as far as 700 km away.[57] Such exchanges imply more regular and systematic contacts between local groups. They hint at increased geographical knowledge, and a capacity to exploit larger and more varied territories. They suggest that the 'reproductive' group became more significant in the upper palaeolithic.

The scale of such exchanges shows the growing importance of even higher levels of complexity, perhaps involving relations between different reproductive networks, and loosely analogous to tribal networks of the modern world. Some upper palaeolithic art objects suggest the existence of vast networks of contact and exchange. This is true, for example, of the Venus figurines which appear from the Pyrenees to the Don at about the late glacial maximum, or the even more astonishing similarities between the cave paintings of south-west Europe and western Mongolia.[58] Indeed, the most likely explanation for the proliferation of art objects in this period is that it reflects increased exchanges of marriage partners, information, gifts and perhaps ritual knowledge, all of which would have enhanced the importance of ornamentation that gave a sense of identity to local and regional groups. Ornamentation and decoration provided ways of storing information in the external world, like stone age hard disks. They reflect an intellectual strategy that our own species has developed to a high degree, of expanding the capacity of our brains to store and process information by 'extruding our minds...into the surrounding world'.[59] So, the rich symbolic world that appears in the upper palaeolithic is probably the outer sign of an increasingly rich, complex and perhaps even hierarchical social world. Presumably, like modern small-scale communities, upper palaeolithic societies were structured mainly according to gender and kinship. While gender shaped the division of labour within each group, a sense of kinship extending beyond the band would have helped groups exchange marriage partners, information and gifts in networks reaching over vast areas.

Under the difficult conditions of the late ice age, widespread links between different groups provided insurance in bad times, and information about techniques and resources. As one archaeologist has put it, such exchange networks would have been 'as necessary for a successful long term adaptation as skin clothing and other technological items that kept out the cold'.[60] Though rare on the iceage steppes, contacts between groups would have been vital, and shared symbols would have been necessary to ensure their success. These same contacts may explain the emergence of limited forms of gender and social hierarchy, as they enhanced the political leverage of those individuals with the best external contacts.

Increasing exchanges between different groups allowed modern humans to deal with the harsh environments of Inner Eurasia not as individuals or as bands, but with the collective knowledge of many different groups scattered over large areas. This, in turn, explains the accelerating technological virtuosity of the upper palaeolithic, and the ability to colonize areas of Inner Eurasia that had previously resisted colonization. The successful colonization of most regions of Inner Eurasia during the upper palaeolithic was a spectacular sign of our species' increasing technological and social virtuosity.

NOTES

1 Foley, *Humans before Humanity*, pp. 165–71.
2 Recent finds are pushing these dates back; Stringer and Gamble, *In Search of the Neanderthals*, p. 64, refer to a recent discovery in Georgia, in the Caucasus, that may be of a 1.6 million year old *Homo erectus*; new dating techniques also suggest that some *erectus* skulls from SE Asia are almost 1.8 million years old; Roger Lewin, 'Human origins: the challenge of Java's skulls', *New Scientist*, (1994), 1924: 36–40.
3 Gamble, *Palaeolithic Settlement*, pp. 155, 177; and Stringer and Gamble, *In Search of the Neanderthals*, pp. 64–5.
4 Masson and Taylor, 'Introduction', *Antiquity*, vol. 63, p. 782.
5 V. A. Ranov, D. Dorj and Lü Zun-E 'Lower palaeolithic cultures', in *HCCA* (pp. 45–63), 1:57; and see Larichev, Khol'ushkin and Laricheva, 'Lower and middle paleolithic of northern Asia', pp. 422–3, 425.
6 Larichev, Khol'ushkin and Laricheva, 'Lower and middle paleolithic of north Asia', pp. 421, 428.
7 Ranov, Dorj and Lü, 'Lower palaeolithic cultures' in *HCCA*, 1:60.
8 Hoffecker, 'Early upper palaeolithic sites of the European USSR,' p. 237; and see Dolukhanov, *Early Slavs*, p. 198; Champion, et al., *Prehistoric Europe*, p. 43; Soffer, 'The middle to upper palaeolithic transition', p. 721.
9 Ranov, Dorj and Lü, 'Lower palaeolithic cultures' in *HCCA*, 1:48–9; Dolukhanov, *Early Slavs*, pp. 26–8.
10 Goudsblom, *Fire and Civilization*, p. 17; Gamble, *Timewalkers*, pp. 138–9.
11 Klein, 'Late pleistocene hunters', in *Cambridge Encyclopedia of Archaeology* (pp. 87–95), p. 92; Straus, 'Hunting in late upper palaeolithic Western Europe', in Nitecki and Nitecki, *Evolution* (pp. 147–76) p. 150.
12 See the table in Lee, 'What hunters do for a living, or, how to make out on scarce resources', in Lee and DeVore, *Man the Hunter*, pp. 30–48.

13 Nitecki and Nitecki, *Evolution of human hunting*, p. 4, and R. G. Klein 'Reconstructing how early people exploited animals', in ibid. (pp. 11–45), p. 19.

14 Klein, 'Reconstructing how early people exploited animals: problems and prospects', in Nitecki and Nitecki, *Evolution of Human Hunting*, p. 17; and L. R. Binford, 'Were there elephant hunters at Torralba?', in ibid. (pp. 47–105), p. 47.

15 Based on Champion, et al., *Prehistoric Europe*, pp. 67–8.

16 Champion, et al., *Prehistoric Europe*, p. 68.

17 Gamble, *Timewalkers*, p. 139.

18 See, e.g., Novgorodova, *Drevnyaya Mongoliya*, pp. 31–2, for claims of Mousterian finds in the Mongolian Altai in the 1980s; see also Chang, *Archaeology of Ancient China*, 3rd edn, pp. 60–61.

19 Gamble, *Palaeolithic Settlement*, p. 161; Soffer, 'The middle to upper palaeolithic transition', p. 722.

20 Stringer and Gamble, *In Search of the Neanderthals*, p. 80; Dolukhanov, *Early Slavs*, p. 33.

21 Estimates of world population from Fagan, *People of the Earth*, 7th edn, p. 206; and see Stringer and Gamble, *In Search of the Neanderthals*, p. 81.

22 Lieberman, 'The origins of some aspects of human language and cognition', in Mellars and Stringer, eds, *The Human Revolution*, p. 391.

23 Stringer and Gamble, *In Search of the Neanderthals*, pp. 50, 161; Dennell, *Economic Prehistory*, p. 78; B. Allchin, 'Middle Palaeolithic culture' in *HCCA* (pp. 65–88), 1:86.

24 Stringer and Gamble, *In Search of the Neanderthals*, pp. 161–4; Dennell, *Economic Prehistory*, p. 74.

25 Allchin, 'Middle Palaeolithic culture' in *HCCA*, 1:87; Klein, *Ice Age Hunters*, pp. 68–9; Praslov, 'Late palaeolithic adaptations', p. 784; examples can be found at the Molodova I and V sites, and the caves of Chokurcha and Kiik-koba.

26 Klein, *Ice Age Hunters*, p. 69; Fagan, *Journey*, p. 83; Freeman, 'Development of human culture', in *Cambridge Encyclopedia of Archaeology* (pp. 79–86), p. 84; Soffer, 'The middle to upper palaeolithic transition', p. 736.

27 Dennell, *Economic Prehistory*, p. 14.

28 Stringer and Gamble, *In Search of the Neanderthals*, p. 212.

29 Masson and Sarianidi, *Central Asia*, p. 22; the Teshik-tash site was the first to prove human occupation of Central Asia in the middle palaeolithic; on Ogzi-kichik, see Allchin, 'Middle Palaeolithic culture' in *HCCA*, 86.

30 Dennell, *Economic Prehistory*, pp. 88–9. However, the bow and arrow probably appear only towards the end of the late palaeolithic. 'The oldest direct evidence for their presence, wooden arrow shafts from north German sites, comes from the very end of the Pleistocene, 11,000–10,000 years ago.' Klein, 'Late pleistocene hunters,' p. 90. Fagan, *People*, 7th edn, 209, argues that there is evidence of bows in Europe by 15,000 BP.

31 Klein, 'Late pleistocene hunters,' p. 89; and see Stringer and Gamble, *In Search of the Neanderthals*, p. 208.

32 Klein, *Ice Age Hunters*, p. 110; and Soffer, 'Middle to upper palaeolithic transition', p. 736.

33 Dennell, *Economic Prehistory*, p. 92; Hoffecker, 'Early upper palaeolithic sites', pp. 263–4.

34 Fagan, *Journey*, p. 194; and see Okladnikov, 'Inner Asia at the dawn of History' in *CHEIA* (pp. 41–96), p. 56; Larichev, Khol'ushkin and Laricheva, 'The upper palaeolithic of northern Asia', pp. 369–71.

35 Okladnikov, 'Inner Asia at the dawn of history', in *CHEIA*, pp. 56–7; see detailed description in Novgorodova, *Drevnyaya Mongoliya*, pp. 37–48; and A. P. Derevyanko and Lü Zun-E, 'Upper Palaeolithic Cultures', in *HCCA* (pp. 89–108), 1:102.

36 Klein, 'Later Pleistocene hunters', p. 88.

37 Dennell, *Economic Prehistory*, p. 91; Hoffecker, 'Early upper palaeolithic sites', pp. 241, 254; Velichko and Kurenkova, 'Environmental conditions and human occupation of northern Eurasia during the late Valdai', in Gamble and Soffer, eds, *The World at 18,000 BP*, 1:260.

38 Velichko and Kurenkova, 'Environmental conditions and human occupation of northern Eurasia during the late Valdai', in Gamble and Soffer, eds, *The World at 18,000 BP*, 1:258.

39 Okladnikov, 'Inner Asia at the dawn of History' in *CHEIA*, pp. 93–4; Velichko and Kurenkova, 'Environmental conditions and human occupation of northern Eurasia during the late Valdai', in Gamble and Soffer, eds, *The World at 18,000 BP*, 1:261; on the Afontova Gora site, see Abramova, *Paleolit Eniseya. Afontovskaya kul'tura*.

40 Okladnikov, 'Inner Asia at the dawn of History' in *CHEIA*, pp. 56, 93; on other sites of the 'Mal'ta' tradition, see Larichev, Khol'ushkin and Laricheva, 'The upper palaeolithic of northern Asia', pp. 373–87.

41 R. E. Morlan, 'The Pleistocene archaeology of Beringia', in Nitecki and Nitecki, *Evolution of Human Hunting* (pp. 267–307), pp. 273, 277, 296.

42 Larichev, Khol'ushkin and Laricheva, 'The upper palaeolithic of northern Asia', p. 365.

43 Derevyanko and Lü, 'Upper Palaeolithic cultures' in *HCCA*, 1:89.

44 For accounts of this controversy, see Fagan, *The Voyage from Eden*; Stringer and Gamble, *In Search of the Neanderthals*; Foley and Lee, *Humans before Humanity*; Gamble, *Timewalkers*; Leakey, *The Origin of Humankind*.

45 On the permafrost limit, Dolukhanov, *Early Slavs*, p. 14; Soffer, 'The middle to upper palaeolithic transition', p. 721; and see the map in ibid. on p. 720.

46 See, for example, the recent work of Clive Gamble.

47 McCrone, *The Ape that Spoke*; Dennett, *Kinds of Minds*, p. 155 and passim.

48 V. N. Stanko, 'The Palaeoecological Situation in the Black Sea steppe in the late Palaeolithic', *Antiquity*, (1989), 63:787–9, 788; and see Soffer, 'The middle to upper palaeolithic transition', pp. 726, 733.

49 The following discussion is based on Olga Soffer, 'Patterns of intensification'.

50 Z. A. Abramova, 'Two Models of cultural adaptation', *Antiquity*, (1989), 63:789–91, p. 789.

51 Fagan, *Journey*, p. 186; Praslov, 'Late palaeolithic adaptations', p. 786.

52 Soffer, 'Patterns of intensification', p. 243; and 'Storage, sedentism and the Eurasian palaeolithic record', p. 726.

53 Soffer, 'Storage, sedentism and the Eurasian palaeolithic record', p. 727.

54 As suggested in Ehrenburg, *Women in Prehistory*, p. 43.

55 Soffer, 'Patterns of intensification', p. 245, and pictures, pp. 246–7.

56 Soffer, 'Patterns of intensification', p. 259; Gamble, *Palaeolithic Settlement*, p. 188.

57 Stringer and Gamble, *In Search of the Neanderthals*, p. 208; Soffer, 'Patterns of intensification', p. 254.

58 Champion, et al., *Prehistoric Europe*, p. 81; in fact, similar figures have been found in Siberia, at the sites of Mal'ta and Buret'; see Okladnikov, 'Inner Asia at the dawn of History' in *CHEIA*, p. 56. Gamble, *Palaeolithic Settlement*, p. 326

shows the distribution of finds of Venus figurines; and see Stringer and Gamble, *In Search of the Neanderthals*, p. 210.

59 Dennett, *Kinds of Minds*, p. 134.
60 Champion, et al., *Prehistoric Europe*, p. 86.

FURTHER READING

There is an introduction to the prehistory of Inner Eurasia by a pioneering Soviet archaelogist, Okladnikov, in *CHEIA*. There are many good introductions to human evolution, beginning with the *Cambridge Encyclopedia of Human Evolution*, or Foley, *Humans before Humanity*. On Neanderthals, see Stringer and Gamble, *In Search of the Neanderthals*. Clive Gamble's study of *The Palaeolithic Settlement of Europe*, and a more general work, *Timewalkers*, are both general surveys of the palaeolithic. Nitecki and Nitecki, *The Evolution of Human Hunting*, shows that modern hunting strategies evolved only during the later stages of the palaeolithic. Olga Soffer has specialized in the prehistory of the western regions, in *The Upper Palaeolithic of the Central Russian Plains* and other studies, including *The Pleistocene Old World*, and (with Gamble) *The World in 18,000 BP*, vol. 1, High Latitudes. Slightly older is Klein, *Ice-Age Hunters*. On the upper palaeolithic, see Mellars and Stringer, *The Human Revolution*, and Soffer, 'The Middle to Upper Palaeolithic Transition'. Dolukhanov's *Early Slavs* summarizes much recent research, and eclipses earlier studies by Gimbutas, Sulimirski and Klein. Soviet work is summarized in *Paleolit SSSR*.

[3]   *HUNTERS AND GATHERERS*
AFTER THE ICE AGE

THE coldest period of the last ice age lasted from *c*.20,000 to 18,000 years ago. After that climates began to warm. The ice sheets that covered much of north-western Inner Eurasia and pockets of Central Asia and eastern Siberia retreated almost entirely between 18,000 and 16,000 years ago. Then they advanced once more almost to their maximum extent by 15,000 years ago, after which there followed a slower retreat, with occasional rapid advances. By *c*.12,000 years ago, average temperatures were similar to those of today. Geologists mark the beginning of the interglacial period in which we live now from this time. The whole period is known in the geological time-scale as the 'Holocene'. During the Holocene, climates have remained unstable, with periods both warmer and cooler than those of today. Most significant of all these periods is the long period of warmer and wetter climates, between 6000 and 2500 BCE (8000–4500 BP), known as the 'Climatic Optimum'.[1] But there has been no return to ice age conditions (see table 4.3).

The climatic changes at the end of the ice age have been the most important single factor shaping human history since that time. The agrarian and industrial civilizations that have dominated the modern history of our species could not have been created under ice age conditions. Yet the impact of climatic change was different in Inner and Outer Eurasia. In Inner Eurasia, societies of hunters and gatherers, using technologies and living in communities similar in many ways to those of the upper palaeolithic, survived much longer than in most of Outer Eurasia. Indeed, some 'foraging' societies survived as late as the twentieth century. For this reason, this chapter will break the chronological organization of the rest of this book, and describe postglacial hunter-gatherer societies of Inner Eurasia throughout the Holocene era, including those of recent times.

THE END OF THE ICE AGES

THE ECOLOGICAL IMPACT OF GLOBAL WARMING

As average temperatures rose, the ice sheets that covered Scandinavia and much of north-west Russia retreated. Communities used to cold conditions found new lands opening up as they followed the ice sheets northward in Europe and north-western Inner Eurasia. These changes created the coastal tundra landscapes along the northern fringe of Inner Eurasia. Though similar in some ways to the periglacial steppes, modern tundra landscapes are more northerly, and therefore less productive ecologically.

Just south of the tundra, warmer conditions and increased rainfall made possible the growth of trees in what had been periglacial steppes. Trees spread first along the river valleys, and then filled the spaces between, creating the vast forest lands that dominate the northern half of Inner Eurasia today. West of the Urals, as in Europe, the forests were largely deciduous. Conifers dominated the *taiga* of Siberia. During the 'Climatic Optimum', deciduous forests probably spread over much of what is today steppeland.[2] South of the forests post-glacial conditions were arid but warmer. Here there appeared the grass steppes and desert lands typical of the southern half of Inner Eurasia in modern times.

As climates and vegetation changed, so did the animal life of Inner Eurasia. Many large herbivores moved north and eventually died out as their range narrowed, and the hunting techniques of upper palaeolithic populations improved. Extinct species included woolly rhinoceros, steppe bison, giant deer, reindeer, arctic fox, lion and hyena. The mammoth, the musk-ox, the woolly rhino and the Giant Irish Elk were all extinct by the end of the last ice age. The latest find of a frozen mammoth, in north-eastern Siberia, dates to *c*.11,500 years ago.

However, other species multiplied. Along the northern and far eastern coasts of Siberia, fish and sea mammals were available. In the tundra lands just south of the Arctic Sea, many species of deer flourished. In the newly formed forests, which were too cluttered for the large herbivore species of the ice ages, smaller species flourished, including rabbits, rodents of various kinds, and fur-bearing animals such as fox and beaver. Berries and nuts were also abundant. Rivers were free of ice for much longer periods so that fishing became an important source of foodstuffs throughout Inner Eurasia. Rivers and coastal regions also attracted sea mammals and birds. In the steppelands, new species such as aurochs and horse appeared, and river and lake fishing became easier and more productive.

Human communities throughout the world had to adapt to changing ecological conditions. They did so by experimenting with new foodstuffs, and new techniques for hunting, fishing and gathering the foods and materials they needed to survive.

THE STEPPES AND WOODED STEPPES

In the steppes and wooded steppes that appeared south of the spreading woodlands of the early Holocene, foraging lifeways survived for several thousand years. However, at some time during the Climatic Optimum, they vanished, giving way to neolithic lifeways of various kinds.

In the southern Urals region steppe and forest zones overlap. Here, post-glacial communities hunted herbivores such as horse and elk. As climates warmed, migrants entering the Urals region from the south began to use advanced forms of net fishing, though they also hunted. In the Yangelsk and Romanovka cultures, there are signs of sedentary fishing communities as early as 9000 BCE. Their inhabitants went out on long hunting and fishing expeditions, and used huge fishing nets that suggest highly organized methods of fishing.[3]

In Ukraine there are more than 300 sites dating to between 9000 and 6000 BCE. In the Pontic and Volga steppes, most base camps were along rivers or lakes. Cemeteries in the Dnieper valley suggest that here, too, there were reasonably permanent fishing villages. The fact that some individuals were killed with arrows suggests the possibility of conflict over fishing rights.[4]

In southern Central Asia, the Hissar cultures, whose remains have been found along the mountain rim from the Amu Darya to Lake Issyk-kul', are dated from the seventh to the fifth millennia BCE. Most sites appear to have been seasonal camps of hunters following hoofed animals. There are early signs, here, of influences from the neolithic world, but only in the form of domesticated goat and cattle.[5] From the seventh millennium, there is also evidence of settlement in the flatlands of Central Asia and of early forms of domestication. The clearest evidence for the domestication of goats comes from Gari-kamarban cave east of the Caspian Sea, and dates from the seventh millennium. In the regions east of the Caspian Sea, which were both warmer and wetter than today during the Climatic Optimum, post-glacial communities hunted onager, gazelle, goat and sheep, as well as water fowl. They also fished in the Caspian Sea and along the now vanished Uzboi river, which flowed into the Caspian Sea, probably until the second millennium BCE, when it began to flow north into the Aral Sea.[6]

The Kelteminar culture of Central Asia flourished between the sixth and fourth millennia. It was identified through aerial surveys conducted by Tolstov in the 1930s.[7] Its stone and bone tools show an economy based mainly on hunting and fishing. Most of its hundreds of sites suggest a nomadic lifeway, though along the River Uzboi there is evidence of denser settlement. At the classic site of Djanbas, in Khorezm, people lived in a large, circular, frame shelter over 400 m^2.[8] Elsewhere, they lived in domed mud-huts half buried in the ground. The presence of bones of camel, cattle and horses, as well as pottery, suggests neolithic influences.

In the eastern steppes, from Sinkiang to eastern Mongolia, there emerged post-glacial communities similar to those of Central Asia. Eventually, though, in the east as in Central Asia, hunter-gatherer communities came under the influence of emerging neolithic cultures to their south. There are considerable post-glacial remains in Mongolia, mainly in the form of deli- cately worked blades or arrowheads. There are also cave paintings from Arshan-khad in the northern Kentei mountains that probably belong to this period. They show clear continuity with the upper palaeolithic of Mongolia, suggesting that during the early Holocene conditions changed less here than in other regions of Inner Eurasia, allowing greater continuity in lifeways.[9]

After c.6000 BCE, hunter-gatherer lifeways began to vanish from the steppes, until by c.1000 BCE they had all but disappeared. However, there

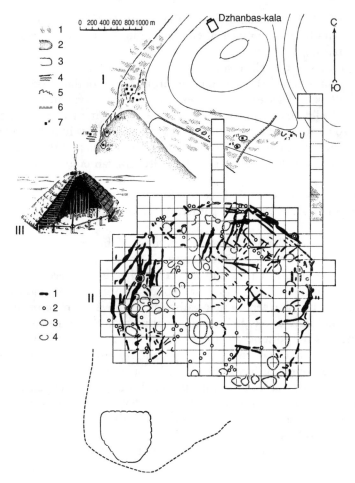

Figure 3.1 Kelteminar site, reproduced from S. P. Tolstov *Po drevnim del'tam Oksa i Yaksarta* (Moscow: Izd-vo vostochnoi literatury, 1962).

was no simple 'wave of advance' of neolithic technologies. Neolithic penetration of the Inner Eurasian steppes and wooded steppes was a slower and more complex process than in western Europe or the Balkans. Here, communities of hunters and gatherers lived near communities of farmers for hundreds, and perhaps thousands of years. Marek Zvelebil has offered a simple, but useful, model of the way these relationships evolved.[10] He suggests that agriculture advanced in three phases. The first phase was that of 'availability': 'farming is known to the foraging groups in question and some exchange of materials and information goes on between farming and foraging settlements, yet farming is not adopted by the hunter-gatherer societies.' The second phase is that of 'substitution'. This ends either when some hunter-gatherers begin to engage in some farming, or when farmers move into the lands previously used by hunter-gatherers. Ecological competition finally ends with the third phase, that of 'consolidation', when farming becomes the dominant adaptation of whole communities and the former ecological frontier disappears. Now, traditional hunter-gatherer technologies survive only as a supplement to farming.[11]

These processes are clearest of all in evidence from Ukraine. Some Ukrainian communities show influences from the neolithic world from as early as 6000 BCE. In eastern Europe, there is early evidence of partially domesticated wild boars and aurochs, the ancestors of modern pig and cattle. There is also clear evidence of sedentary or semi-sedentary hunting and gathering societies from the region between the Carpathians and the Dnieper by c.6000 BCE. These belong to the so-called Grebenikian culture. Its members lived in both dug-out and above-ground huts in small camps up to 20 m wide located in river valleys. They lived by hunting deer, boar, aurochs, small mammals and birds, as well as by gathering plants and molluscs, and catching fish.[12]

During the sixth millennium BCE, communities of the Bug-Dniester cultures replaced those of the Grebenikian culture. These used a wider range of resources, including wild pigs and elk. Though the later evolution of the Bug-Dniester culture takes us into the neolithic world, it shows how blurred the line could be between hunter-gathering cultures with some neolithic techniques, and fully developed neolithic cultures. In the earliest sites of this culture, there is no pottery, but there are bones of domesticated cattle and pigs, as well as evidence of the harvesting and grinding of wild grains. There are also large amounts of fish remains, which suggests that here, as in many other parts of Inner Eurasia, fishing sustained a high level of sedentism. In later sites of this culture, from c.5000 BCE, pottery appears, as well as farming, but farming remained less important than fishing and the hunting of aurochs, deer and boar.[13]

In areas such as western Ukraine, where hunter-gatherer and farming communities lived together from very early times, the differences between agricultural and hunter-gatherer populations were often ethnic and presumably linguistic, showing up in the archaeological record in distinctive skeletal remains.[14] As neolithic influences entered south-west Ukraine from the nearby Cris/Koros culture in what is now southern Moldavia, between 6000 and 4500 BCE, there emerged complex patterns of mutual influence and even symbiosis. While farmers settled fertile intermontane depressions, hunting and gathering communities preferred river valleys.[15]

THE FOREST ZONE

In the early Holocene, the forest zones were probably easier to exploit than the steppelands, though their exploitation required new technologies to take smaller prey such as rabbits or birds or fur-bearing animals. As a result, it seems likely that in the mesolithic era, between c.10,000 and 6000 BCE, the demographic centre of gravity of Inner Eurasia shifted temporarily into the forest zone. The clearest sign is the apparent reduction in the size of cultural areas within the forest zone, which suggests increasing population density. Forest lifeways also became more varied and more complex than those of the upper palaeolithic. Finally, in the woodlands, there appear many relatively sedentary communities of 'intensive foragers', a clear sign that exploitable resources were abundant. As a modern researcher has concluded, in the immediate post-glacial era,

> The most stable forms of economy emerged within the boreal zones; they depended mainly on the exploitation of the natural resources of river valleys and lake basins....The [foraging] cultures of the steppe zone and mountain slopes were less stable.[16]

The success of forest adaptations, as well as their remoteness from the neolithic societies of Outer Eurasia, explains why some survived to the present day.

We know most about the forest societies of northern Russia, Belarus, and the Baltic shores. As the ice sheets retreated, the Baltic region acquired a varied and abundant ecology of forests, rivers and seashores. The earliest post-glacial sites appeared on lake or sea shores and showed the influence of the north European 'Maglemosian' cultures. Settlements were small, except in one or two coastal sites. Gathered plants, fish and shellfish were important in the diet, but so were elk, wild pig, red deer, water fowl and, along the coasts, seals. Inhabiting these sites were small, nomadic groups. As they adapted to the changing ecologies of the early Holocene, their lifeways became more specialized and less nomadic, and they developed rich technologies designed for trapping, fishing, hunting and the taking of sea mammals such as seal. To travel and fish, they used dugout canoes. Some settlements were very large. Archaeologists have found year-round sites in which as many as 100 people may have lived. Some sites were occupied continuously from c.3000 to 1500 BCE. The appearance of pottery in this region from c.4000 BCE may hint at immigration from farming communities further south. If so, it suggests that here, as in the tundra, neolithic immigrants often abandoned their lifeways and took up hunting and gathering lifeways that were more effective in the forest zone.[17]

East of the Urals, there is more continuity with the upper palaeolithic in settlement patterns and technologies. The clearest break occurs in regions whose palaeolithic ancestors had depended on the hunting of large herbivores. In southern Siberia, the semi-sedentary late palaeolithic culture of Mal'ta, with its semi-dug-out dwellings, simply vanished at the end of the palaeolithic. In its place, there appear highly mobile groups, living in skin or bark tents. However, there may also have been communities of intensive foragers and fishers in the region. These show similarities with contemporary cultures of the southern Urals, and illustrate the more general trend of many post-glacial communities from the hunting of large, ice age animals, to the taking of fish, smaller animals and plants. This transition is quite clear in sites between the Yenisei and Angara rivers.[18]

In eastern Siberia, in the post-glacial era as in the upper palaeolithic, the main influences came from the south, and also, perhaps, from the Americas. In Kamchatka, archaeologists have found arrow heads dating to about 8000 BCE, and similar to those of North America. There are other signs of contact between north-east Siberia and the Americas in this period, probably mainly through the Aleutian Islands.[19]

THE TUNDRA

Modern tundra landscapes emerged only at the end of the ice age, and adapting to them meant developing new skills. It is tempting to assume that upper palaeolithic hunters pursued large herbivores north into the emerging tundra regions of northern Siberia. However, the earliest evidence for the systematic exploitation of sea mammals that is characteristic of all Arctic cultures today, dates to the second millennium BCE. In 1975, on Wrangel Island, the Soviet researcher, N. N. Dikov, found evidence of some of the earliest sea-hunting Arctic societies. As the implements found here are very similar to those found from Alaska right across to Greenland, it seems clear that lifeways based on whaling and fishing spread rapidly throughout the arctic lands of north-east Siberia and North America from about the second millennium.[20]

A site at Ust-bel'sk in Chukotka, from the second millennium BCE, gives some idea of the lifeways of peoples who lived mainly by hunting deer, as well as by fishing. The Ust-Bel'sk site lies where the Belaya river enters the Anadyr river, at a point where herds of deer have crossed the river for thousands of years. Indeed Chukots and Yukagirs were still hunting them there in the nineteenth century. Here, archaeologists have found burial mounds in which corpses were accompanied with gifts of food and equipment such as arrows. The presence of harpoons suggests contacts with sea-hunters of the Arctic shore. Some of the corpses were sprinkled with ochre.[21]

On the Pegtymel' river, c.60 km from the Arctic Ocean, Soviet archaeologists have discovered cliff paintings which give the first detailed pictures of the life of deer-hunting peoples of the Arctic about three thousand years ago.[22] Here, too, hunters caught deer as they crossed the river. However, their equipment also includes implements made of walrus which suggests that the same people also hunted along the sea shores further north. Many of the drawings show hunters in boats that look like modern kayaks. They are spearing deer as they swim across the river, while other, larger, boats prevent deer from escaping. One drawing shows hunters on skis pursuing deer in winter, with hunting dogs. Some also show whale hunters in larger boats, presumably in the open sea.

The Pegtymel' petroglyphs hint at the religious life of these Arctic communities of the second millennium, for many include strange, apparently female, figures with mushrooms on or in place of their heads. The mushrooms seem to represent the fly-agaric or death's head mushroom, *Amanita muscaria*. These pictures almost certainly represent shamanistic activities, for the Chukot still use hallucinatory mushrooms, and their mythology claims that those who eat mushrooms often see mushroom guides in semi-human form, who lead them away to fantastic lands. The link with shamanism is clear from the fact that several figures are dancing, and holding either drums or rattles. The Soviet archaeologist, Dikov, suggests that the female figures may

Plate 3.1 Mushroom heads, reproduced from N. N. Dikov *Istoriya Chukotki s drevneishikh vremen do nashikh dnei* (Moscow: Mysl', 1989).

represent a mistress of the deer, a powerful figure common in the mythology of other Arctic peoples.[23]

Reindeer-herding is an even more recent development in the tundra regions of Siberia, and its emergence shows how, eventually, neolithic technologies began to influence even the remote communities of the far north. The Soviet specialist, Vainshtein has argued that reindeer-herding originated amongst peoples ancestral to the modern Samoyed, who were influenced by horse-pastoralists of the steppes during the second or first millennium BCE. As they were squeezed north by steppeland pastoralists, reindeer became the only animals suited for a pastoral lifeway. While their original role may have been mainly to supply meat, by the first millennium BCE, there is already evidence of harnesses and the use of reindeer for transportation. From the Samoyed, forms of reindeer-herding then spread to other peoples of northern Eurasia. From about 1000 CE, Turkic-speaking communities in Siberia learned techniques of reindeer-herding from peoples to their north, but added elements from their own traditions of horse-rearing, such as the milking of does and the riding of deer.[24] It was hard to keep large herds of reindeer in the far north, so that even those communities that herded reindeer used them mainly for transport, while they depended for subsistence on hunting and fishing. Only in the eighteenth century, under the more settled conditions created by Russian colonization and increased trade, did reindeer-herding become the basic form of subsistence amongst many Siberian communities.[25]

If Vainshtein's reconstruction is accurate, it shows how easily peoples familiar with the agricultural and pastoralist lifeways of the neolithic era abandoned those methods once they entered the tundra lands of northern Inner Eurasia. That, in turn, shows how well tundra lifeways were adapted to the harsh conditions of the far north.

HUNTER-GATHERERS OF THE MODERN ERA

By the second millennium of the modern era, neolithic lifeways and technologies were already affecting most of Inner Eurasia. However, their impact was least felt in the forest and tundra lands of Siberia. So, when fur traders from Volga Bulgharia or Novgorod headed into Siberia a thousand years ago, or Russian colonists travelled east in the seventeenth century, they entered a world still dominated by hunting and gathering lifeways.

The rest of this chapter will describe some of these modern hunter-gatherer lifeways, using evidence from more recent times, in the hope of conveying something of the lifeways of this world in an even earlier period. Of course, we must do this with caution, certain that the match between modern Siberia and the early post-glacial world is not perfect. Nevertheless, recent accounts can at least guide our attempts to imagine the lifeways of an earlier era of Inner Eurasian history. As much as possible, this account relies on descriptions of forest lifestyles at the moment when they first came into close contact with Russian colonizers. These show the great variety of technologies, lifeways, languages and beliefs that existed in the forests or tundra of Siberia.

Officially, the Soviet government recognized some 35 native Siberian languages. In reality, many of these groups included several, mutually unintelligible, dialects. This means that there were really far more Siberian languages even in the twentieth century, perhaps as many as 120.[26] Like America or Australia before European colonization, the hunter-gatherer peoples of Siberia consisted of many small peoples speaking different languages and living different lifeways. The following section offers impressionistic sketches of the lifeways of four Siberian groups of communities.

THE KHANTY AND MANSI OF WESTERN SIBERIA

Archaeological evidence suggests the presence of quite homogenous cultures from the River Volga, and across the Urals into western Siberia, between the seventh and fourth millennia BCE. Their homogeneity suggests that they belonged to closely related cultures and most linguists believe that they spoke related languages ancestral to those of the modern Uralic group, which includes Finnish, Hungarian and the Samoyedic languages. From the sixth to the fourth millennium, groups speaking languages ancestral to Samoyedic drifted north. From the third or second millennium, groups speaking languages ancestral to modern Finnic drifted west. Amongst those who remained in the region were those who spoke languages of the Ugric group, which includes modern Hungarian.[27]

When Russian colonizers first moved east of the Urals in the late sixteenth and the seventeenth centuries of the modern era, the main speakers of Ugric languages they met were the Khanty (Ostyaks) and Mansi (Voguls). These were by no means the first contacts of the Khanty and Mansi with agrarian communities. Medieval Russian sources refer to Khanty and Mansi living west of the Urals as the 'Yugra'.[28] Our earliest descriptions of these communities come from Arabic traders who engaged in 'silent trade' with them. The tenth-century Central Asian scholar al-Biruni (b. 973), described the 'silent trade' conducted between Islamic traders and the 'Yugra'.

> The most distant point, where they [the people of the seventh climate] live together is the country Iura [i.e. country of the Yugra]. ... [Travellers proceed] on wooden sleighs, in which they load supplies and which are drawn either by themselves or by dogs; and [they] also [travel] on other [sliding devices], made from bone, which they attach to their feet and with the help of which they cover great distances in short periods. Because of their wildness and timidity, the inhabitants of Iura trade in the following manner; they place their goods down in some place and leave them there.[29]

Sometime in the fourteenth century, under pressure from the principality of Moscow, members of both groups living west of the Urals crossed to the eastern side where they settled amongst related clans. In the sixteenth century, the territories of the Khanty and Mansi extended from the Urals, to about 400 miles east of the River Ob. Their total population was probably no more than about 16,000 people, while Muscovy already had a population of some 10 millions.[30] This is a reminder of the vast demographic gulf that has existed since late neolithic times between hunter-gatherer and farming societies.

According to seventeenth-century accounts, both Khanty and Mansi communities lived mainly from hunting and fishing. They ate fish and flesh raw, smoked or boiled. On hunting trips they carried their meat dried or powdered. Most communities ate few plants, except for gathered berries, wild fruit and nuts, and some roots. They stored wild honey for winter. Like most hunter gatherers, they freely borrowed techniques from neighbouring peoples, including forms of domestication. Some of the northern clans kept herds of reindeer, in imitation of the neighbouring Samoyed, while some southern clans grew barley and kept domesticated cattle and horses.

Reindeer skins and elk-skins, as well as furs provided most of their outer garments. Some clans also used the skins of birds and fish. Southern clans made clothes from vegetable fibres, using simple looms. Most communities decorated their clothes, containers and sometimes even themselves with elaborate patterns and tattoos. In winter, they travelled on skis. They also travelled the rivers of western Siberia, using dug-outs, or canoes made from wooden frames and covered with birch bark.

In 1675, an envoy of Tsar Aleksei Mikhailovich described the lifeways of the Khanty (Ostyaks), after crossing their lands on a trip to China.

> All the Ostyaks catch great quantities of fish. Some eat it raw, others dry it and boil it, but they know neither salt nor bread, nothing but fish and a white root *susak*, of which they collect a supply in summer, dry it, and eat it in winter. Bread they cannot eat; or if any do eat their fill of it, they die. Their dwellings are yourts [tents]; and they catch fish not merely for the sake of food, but to make themselves clothing out of the skins – also boots and hats, sewing them with sinews of the fish. They make use of the lightest possible boats, built out of wood, holding five or six men, and even more. They always carry with them bows and arrows, to be ready to fight at any moment. Wives they have in plenty – as many as they wish, so many do they keep.[31]

This last remark suggests the existence of a clear gender hierarchy, though it is also possible the Muscovite aristocrat was projecting the steep gender hierarchies of Muscovy on to the Siberian societies he visited.

Most Khanty and Mansi lived in semi-permanent winter camps, in huts made with branches and covered with earth. In summer they travelled to less permanent hunting and fishing grounds, where they lived in simpler, lighter dwellings covered in birch bark. Though they had a sense of common identity, the Khanty and Mansi lived in separate clans, headed by chiefs. Justice between individuals was primarily a matter of blood-feuds. Occasionally powerful chieftains united several clans into a larger nation. More commonly, clans engaged in conflict with each other, and with other neighbouring peoples. Their military skills made them formidable opponents even for early colonizers from Moscow or Novgorod, for they used longbows, as well as iron spears, armour and helmets which they forged themselves. The more warlike communities lived in forts protected by walls and earthen ramparts, and were ruled by powerful kings who 'were surrounded by a certain degree of wealth and barbaric splendour, including silver ornaments and vessels and large quantities of sable, fox and other furs.'[32]

SAMOYEDS OF THE NORTH-WEST TUNDRA

Along the Arctic shores north of the Khanty, from north-west of the Urals and as Far East as the Yenisei, lived the reindeer-herding Samoyeds. If the lifeways of the Khanty and Mansi are typical of the *taiga*, those of the Samoyed typify the lifeways of the northern *taiga*, the tundra and the Arctic coasts.

The Samoyed include at least three distinct peoples, the Nganasan, the Enets and the Nenets.[33] In the remote past, Samoyedic peoples probably lived further south, where some may have herded horse and cattle. When Muscovites encountered them in the seventeenth century, some of the southern clans lived as fishers and hunters, like the Khanty. However, most lived mainly from reindeer, both wild and domesticated. They used domestic reindeer to pull the sledges, which were their main means of transport. They used dogs (from which the modern Samoyed breeds originate) to control their herds of reindeer. They also took fish, seals and walrus from the Arctic sea. Reindeer skins provided the main items of clothing and housing. Samoyeds lived in wigwams covered with skins, which could be up to 9 metres wide, and were carried on sledges.

The Samoyeds were more nomadic than the Khanty or Mansi, moving frequently from place to place. Their clans lacked permanent leaders, though they often chose temporary leaders during conflicts with each other or with other peoples. Like most small-scale societies, their wars required elaborate ritual preparations, and contained ritual elements that minimized casualties on either side. Individual clans enjoyed rights to hunting grounds, and clan membership governed rules of marriage and blood-vengeance.

The Samoyeds had shamans, and sacrificed reindeer on religious occasions such as burials. At special natural churches they placed figures representing gods, as well as the remains of sacrificed animals.

TUNGUZ OF NORTHERN SIBERIA

In the seventeenth century, the Tunguz (Ewenki or Ewen), occupied a vast territory between the Yenisei and Lena rivers and further east. Their language, Ewenki, is related to modern Manchurian. In the seventeenth century, they probably numbered about 36,000 people.

Though they lived mainly in the forests, the extreme temperatures of the eastern Siberian taiga may explain why their lives were similar to those of the Samoyeds. They were nomadic, living in wigwams covered with reindeer skins or birch bark, and with internal hearths. They made clothing mainly from elk or reindeer skins. The Tunguz kept herds of domesticated reindeer, using them as pack animals, and also for their milk. They also rode them with special saddles, but rarely used them for food. Instead, they hunted wild reindeer and elk, and most of their food came from the meat and fat of these hunted animals.

Their communities were extremely simple. For much of the year, they lived in small camping groups of one or two families. However, in summer, groups came together in clan gatherings of ten or twelve tents. Each clan had its own hunting grounds, though clans often shared their territories. Individuals found marriage partners from other clans within larger tribal groupings. Clans and tribes did not have permanent leaders, though they often chose temporary leaders at clan meetings, particularly before they fought other clans. Conflicts arose less over property claims, than over accusations of sorcery, or abductions of women or children, or in fulfilment of the demands of blood-vengeance. On such occasions, men would set out in small war-parties, wearing armour made from bone plates, and carrying bows and arrows, as well as swords and simple spears made from knives mounted on shafts. They would often raid enemy camps or ambush enemy hunting parties. Sometimes, there would be conflicts between two war-parties, which might be decided by single combat between two individuals. Occasionally, shamans would mediate conflicts before they led to bloodshed.

The various clans of Tunguz spread over such a huge area that, like the Khanty and Mansi, different clans often took on the cultural attributes of neighbours. In the far north, some Tunguz lived in the tundra, where they used sleds like Samoyeds. On the Sea of Okhotsk, Tunguzic peoples known as Lamuts lived semi-sedentary lives based on fishing and the hunting of seals and walrus, like neighbouring Korak peoples. In the steppes south-east of Lake Baikal, Tunguz influenced by Mongol traditions reared cattle and rode horses. They lived in yurts and even dressed like their Mongol neighbours.

YUGIT OF NORTH-EASTERN SIBERIA

Chukotka, in the far north-east of Siberia, is the most remote region of Inner Eurasia. It is similar ecologically and culturally to Alaska. It is also the most sparsely populated part of Siberia. Of a total native population of about 220,000 in all of seventeenth-century Siberia, the various peoples of the far north-east and Far East accounted for only about 40,000. None of the inhabitants of the region worked metals so that, strictly speaking, they still belonged to the stone age.

The most distinctive of all the peoples of this region were the Siberian Yugit. Like most tribal names of Siberia, this means 'people'. The Yugit travelled freely across the Bering Straits to Alaska and the Aleutians, where there lived closely related people. They lived mainly by hunting sea-mammals of the Arctic, including whales, in particular the Greenland whale. The Yugit hunted from boats made of simple wood frames, covered with walrus hide. Their weapons were spears and bone-tipped harpoons. Whole communities cooperated in the hunt, and they divided the catch evenly.

Yugit culture depended almost entirely on objects made from sea animals. They ate their flesh and blubber both raw and cooked. They also stored seal and whale meat. Blubber supplied fuel for lamps and heating. The Yugit made many utensils from bone or whale baleen, and used seal skins for clothing, boat-making and tents. In summer, they lived in tents covered with reindeer or seal skins. In winter, they lived in semi-subterranean igloos, with frames of stone or the large bones of whales, and coverings of earth and snow.

The religion of the Yugit also turned on the business of catching sea-mammals. They believed in many different spirits, of whom the most important were the goddess of the sea, and her assistant, the grampus. They performed religious ceremonies to ensure success at the beginning of the hunting season. At these festivals, they told stories, danced, and held feasts at which they 'fed' the whales they hoped to catch.

RELIGIONS AND COSMOLOGIES OF SIBERIA

Accounts of the forest and tundra societies of Siberia offer tantalizing insights into the spiritual as well as the material world of ancient Inner Eurasia.

Indeed, the spiritual world of Siberian communities has been studied very closely in modern times, in the belief that it may preserve something of the spiritual world of the prehistoric era in general.

Writing on the cosmologies and religions of Inner Eurasia has been dominated by the notion of 'shamanism'. The term entered the literature through a hostile reference in the autobiography of the seventeenth-century Russian priest and exile, Avvakum. In this passage, Avvakum described how a Russian officer forced a Tunguz from a settlement near modern Chita to *shamanit'*, or tell their fortune. He then offers one of the earliest recorded accounts of a shamanic trance:

> in the evening that wizard...brought a live sheep and began to work magic over it: he rolled it to and fro for a long space and then he twisted its head and flung it away. Then he began to jump and dance, and invoke devils, and, giving great screams the while, he flung himself upon the earth, and foamed at the mouth; the devils were pressing him, and he asked them: 'Will the expedition prosper?' And the devils said: 'It will return with much booty, having gained a great victory.'[34]

Avvakum, regarding the shaman as a representative of the devil, prayed that God would destroy the entire expedition, to disprove the devil's prophecies. When all but one of the expedition's members were killed, the pious Avvakum took this as a sign that his prayers had been heard.

This is the earliest account of shamanic activities in Siberia, but there are many earlier accounts from the Inner Eurasian steppes of activities such as healing or cursing, the control of the weather, or soothsaying. Herodotus described the activities of Scythian soothsayers and medicine men or 'enarei' (IV:67–8) in the fifth century BCE, while the Byzantine writer, Menander Protector, described the purification rituals of the Türk, in the sixth century CE. The Mongols used similar purification rituals in the thirteenth century. Both Turks and Mongols used special stones to control the weather.[35] There are later accounts of shamanic activities in the writings of Islamic geographers and historians, and these, like Avvakum's account, or Herodotus' description of Scythian priests, stress the soothsaying role of shamans or priests. In the earliest Islamic description, the twelfth-century Islamic geographer, al-Marwazi, described a Kirghiz shaman:

> Among the Kirkhiz is a man, a commoner, called *faghinun*, who is summoned on a fixed day every year; about him there gather singers and players and so forth, who begin drinking and feasting. When the company is well away, this man faints and falls as if in a fit; he is asked about all the events that are going to happen in the coming year, and he gives information whether (crops) will be plentiful or scarce, whether there will be rain or drought, and so forth, and they believe that what he says is true.[36]

Another early description, from the Indian historian, Juzjani, describes the shamanic powers of Chinggis Khan. He was, according to Juzjani:

> an adept in magic and deception, and some of the devils were his friends. Every now and again he used to fall into a trance, and in that state of insensibility all

Plate 3.2 Seventeenth-century colour woodcut of a Lapp shaman and his world, reproduced by courtesy of The British Library (Add. Ms 5253, folio 7).

sorts of things used to proceed from his tongue, and that state of trance used to be similar to that which had happened to him at the outset of his rise, and the devils who had power over him foretold his victories. The tunic and clothes which he had on and wore on the first occasion were placed in a trunk and he was wont to take them about with him. Whenever this inspiration came over him, every circumstance – victories, undertakings, the appearance of enemies, the defeat and reduction of countries – anything which he might desire, would all be uttered by his tongue. A person used to take the whole down in writing and enclose it in a bag and place a seal upon it, and when Chingiz Khan came to his senses again, they used to read his utterances over to him one by one; and according to these he would act, and more or less, indeed, the whole used to come true.[37]

By the nineteenth century, the Tunguz word, 'shaman', had established itself as a general term for the religious specialists of Siberian societies. By the twentieth century the word, 'shamanism', was being used to describe the religious practices of palaeolithic and hunter-gatherer societies throughout the world, from Siberia to Australia. As a result, much effort has been devoted to understanding the general features of shamanism.

Shamanism reflects a set of beliefs common to most pre-modern societies. Archaeological evidence, combined with modern anthropological and historical studies, suggest that most human communities before the modern era have experienced the universe as a place full of spirits. They saw conscious intent where modern science sees 'natural' forces. So, they filled the universe with spirits, whose forms, powers and needs varied from community to community. As a result, the details of the spirit world – its personalities, geography, history, and social rules – vary greatly from society to society.

For those who experienced the world in this way, dealing with the spirit world was like dealing with people. The weather, disease, animals, and the many dark forces that threaten human life, all had to be approached like people, to be negotiated with, tricked, fought, or pleaded with, but never manipulated as passive objects, in the manner of modern science. In such a world, there is no room for the assumption, natural to modern science, that humans stand quite apart from nature. On the contrary, individuals and whole communities have often experienced natural forces, or animals, as close relations, closer, in many instances, than other humans. This view is the basis of what is often described as 'totemism'.

In these ways, shamanism reflects the logic of small-scale societies. Ever since Durkheim, anthropologists have assumed that in some sense religion projects the structures of human society onto the wider cosmos. Those who lived in small-scale communities perceived a spirit world similar to their own, in which contacts, negotiations and conflicts were personal, direct, face-to-face. The gods of this world, like its humans, lived in small, non-bureaucratic communities of individuals, and followed similar rules of mutual support and retaliation. There was little room in such a world for the steep hierarchies of gender and status that characterized the universal religions of Outer Eurasia, so that both shamans and spirits could have varied lineages and were as often female as male. Shamans were specialists in the direct, personal negotiations familiar to all foraging societies, and negotiated with the spirit world just as clan leaders might negotiate with other human communities. Shamans bargained for the right to kill prey animals, for fertility, success in war, and freedom from disease. In return, they promised gifts to the gods, usually in the form of sacrifice. Sometimes during these negotiations, they had to give up the lives and souls of humans, and this made them powerful and dangerous figures. When negotiating, shamans used all the methods of tribal diplomacy from gift-giving, to threats, to pleas, to promises of marriage. They treated the spirit world according to the same rules of reciprocity that applied in the human world.

The Khanty and Mansi believed that natural phenomena such as rivers, trees, animals, thunder, all had their own spirits. They treated these spirits as they might treat potential kin, offering them gifts, asking for help, and even intermarrying with them, thereby creating links between particular clans and particular totem animals, such as beaver or elk.

> Effigies of spirits were kept in sanctuaries in the forest where from time to time all the men of the clan congregated for such special ritual ceremonies as averting epidemic diseases or preparing to go to war. The tribal priests or shamans presided over religious rites in these sacred places, sacrificing horses, reindeer or other animals under a tree and smearing the mouths of the spirit effigies with blood to 'feed' them. In early times human beings were sometimes sacrificed in this way. Sacrificial rites were also performed in cemeteries, where the dead were laid to rest in wooden boxes on the ground, accompanied by weapons, implements, spoons and sometimes silver vessels for use in the next world.[38]

The Khanty and Mansi treated bears with particular reverence. Usually, they avoided killing them. Occasionally, they killed bear and feasted on their meat, but only after elaborate rituals to propitiate the bear spirit. As late as the twentieth century, Khanty and Mansi villages still held bear festivals. These included dances, mimed accounts of the bear hunt, the reciting of poetry to the sound of stringed instruments similar to harps or psalteries, and a feast at which the dead bear was the special guest.

Dealing with the spirit world required an understanding of its geography, as did dealings with the profane world. The Tunguz believed in the existence of three distinct realms, linked by a river. The upper world was inhabited by a supreme god and a retinue of lesser gods. The lower world contained the spirits of the dead, while humans lived in the middle world. A similar belief in three realms was widespread in Siberia, though the link between the worlds was more often thought of as a tree, a pillar or a mountain. However, in societies closer to Outer Eurasia, and with more elaborate political structures, this cosmic map often became more elaborate, with each of the three worlds being subdivided in turn, like the complex bureaucratic structures of neighbouring states.[39]

The cosmos of the Tunguz was crammed with spirits, amongst whom an important role was played by 'masters' of different regions, including the

Plate 3.3 A shamanic battle, as depicted on rock carvings from Vitlycke in Scandinavia. An enormous snake coils towards a man with his arms in the air. This image has been interpreted as a sacrifice scene, depicting priest and cult animal and the battle between Thor and the serpent Midgard (© Werner Forman Archive).

forests, mountains, rivers and different species of animals and fish.[40] Tunguz shamans were believed to be able to mediate and negotiate with these spirits, and could ask their spirit allies for help in curing disease or in war or when hunting. The role of shamans could be vital in conflicts with neighbouring communities. Piers Vitebsky cites a description of a magical battle between Tunguz clans.[41] This began, when the shaman of one clan sent a worm to destroy a member of another clan. Once past the spirit guards of the neighbouring clan (a line defended by spirit guardians including a reindeer), it buried itself in the entrails of an individual who became extremely sick as a result. The shaman of the second clan sent goose and snipe spirits to extract the worm, and an owl spirit to deposit the worm, safely, in the underworld. He then sent a spirit pike to carry off the soul of a member of the enemy clan, and shored up his own clan's spirit defences.

Shamans negotiated with the spirit world by mastering states of trance, which allowed them to voyage into the other world. (This is why Mircea Eliade's classic study of shamanism is sub-titled: *Archaic Techniques of Ecstasy.*) To enter the trance state, they danced, used drums or other musical instruments, and sometimes drugs. Tunguz shamans contacted their helper spirits by wearing costumes representing their helpers (usually these were animals or birds), and by dancing and singing themselves into trances. The skills of blacksmiths were often regarded as analogous to those of shamans, and shamans often wore beautifully wrought metal objects, usually representing animals or birds, as part of their costume.[42]

Shamans did not always choose to be shamans. Often, they felt the role had been forced on them as a result of particular, usually near-death, experiences. In addition, though, most shamans also underwent long training with older masters before becoming true shamans.

The famous Yakut shaman Tüspüt (that is, 'fallen from the sky') had been ill at the age of twenty; he began to sing, and felt better. When Sieroszewski met him, he was sixty and displayed tireless energy. 'If necessary, he can drum, dance, jump all night.' In addition, he was a man who had travelled; he had even worked in the Siberian gold mines. But he needed to shamanize; if he went for a long time without doing so, he did not feel well.[43]

There has been much debate about the origins of shamanism. Eliade's study, *Shamanism: Archaic Techniques of Ecstasy*, which appeared in the 1950s, argued that, though the details of shamanic practice might differ, there remained an essential core of beliefs and practices that had its roots in the religious world depicted in upper palaeolithic cave paintings.[44] The most powerful argument in support of this conclusion is the fact that phenomena similar to Siberian shamanism appear to be present in most small-scale societies, particularly those that practised hunting:

It is evident that shamanism is deeply anchored in the old hunting cultures with their individualism, animal-spirit beliefs and hunting symbolism. In one or another form the shamanistic practices occur in all recent marginal hunting cultures, and particularly there.[45]

Nevertheless, the forms and practices of modern shamanism vary so greatly, and there is so little direct evidence of shamanism before modern times, that some writers have argued that shamanism is a recent phenomenon, created by the impact of colonizing societies on hunter-gatherer societies. In Siberia, it has long been clear that shamanic rituals were shaped by influences from the South, particularly from Buddhism. Even the Tunguzic word, 'shaman', may be of Indian origin, related to the Pali *samana*. If so, it probably reached Siberia through the Tocharian and Chinese languages and arrived carrying a heavy freight of Buddhist belief and ritual. Many Siberian spirit names come from Manchurian or Mongol sources, and the costumes, drums and paintings of Tunguz shamans show similar influences. The Manchu themselves claimed that shamanism appeared in the eleventh century, one more piece of evidence for Shirokogoroff's theory that shamanism spread recently, with the spread of Buddhism. Even Eliade conceded that: 'Ethnologically, all the cultures of the nomads are to be regarded as tributaries of the discoveries made by the agricultural and urban civilizations; ... And this radiation, begun in prehistory, continues down to our day.'[46]

There is no need to take extreme positions in this debate. We have already seen evidence, reaching back into the palaeolithic era, that practices similar to those of modern shamanism, have ancient roots. However, it is also true that, as lifeways and social structures changed, so did views of the Universe. Small-scale societies, in particular, were influenced by the appearance of societies whose lifeways, scale and social structures were very different from their own. It is not just that they felt the influence of other religions; the very structure of their cosmos changed. In larger communities, many human contacts were indirect, and all contacts were affected by the emergence of hierarchies of rank, wealth and power.[47] The spirit world, too, acquired ranks of gender and status, official rituals, and bureaucratic rules of diplomacy, so that relations with it became more formal and indirect, less personal and intimate. In larger societies, there emerged religious specialists who mediated less directly with the spirit world, knowing all too well the great distance between themselves and the ruling spirits of the other world. These, we commonly describe as 'priests'. One of the central themes of religious life in Inner Eurasia, where small-scale communities co-existed with much larger communities for long periods, is the complex balance between the lesser and greater gods, and the shamans and priests who specialized in dealing with them.

In the larger, more hierarchical communities of the neolithic world, emerging chiefs and rulers often saw shamans as threats, because of their privileged access to the spiritual world. Inevitably, emerging political leaders competed with shamans for the power and prestige that could be gained through contact with the spirit world.[48] Religions became, increasingly, 'ethnic' religions, tied closely to the fate of a particular political or ethnic grouping.[49] Where shamans survived, they often did so on the fringes of larger communities. Eventually, as state-like structures appeared, shamans were often supplanted by priests, whose claims on access to the supernatural were less exclusive, and who could therefore cooperate more easily with secular powers. Nevertheless, shamanism retains a powerful appeal to the modern day, for what it offers to small communities is a direct, personal and intimate contact with the spirit world that many other forms of religious belief have lost.

The protean nature of shamanism illustrates the variety and flexibility of the hunter-gatherer societies of Inner Eurasia. Our evidence only offers blurred glimpses into their lifeways and world views, and this makes it hard to do them justice. Later chapters will concentrate on larger scale societies, whose impact on their neighbours was more extensive, and for which we have better documentation. But we must remember that, despite the small scale, and the limited impact on other societies of the hunter-gatherer communities of Inner Eurasia, they were extremely successful. They survived for many millennia, in some of the harshest environments in the world. Their history was the history of most of the northern half of Eurasia until about 300 years ago. It is by no means certain that modern industrialized societies will prove as durable as this.

NOTES

1 On climatic changes at the beginning of the Holocene, see Soffer, *The Upper Palaeolithic*, pp. 32, 234, and Van Andel, 'Living in the last high glacial – on the interdisciplinary challenge', in Soffer and Gamble, *The World at 18,000 BP* (pp. 24–38), 1:34–5, for slightly different chronologies; on climatic change in the Holocene in eastern Europe, P. M. Dolukhanov, 'The late mesolithic and transition to food production in Eastern Europe', in Zvelebil, ed., *Hunters in Transition* (pp. 109–20) p. 110; on the 'climatic optimum', Dolukhanov, *Early Slavs*, pp. 48–50.

2 Dolukhanov, *Early Slavs*, p. 50.

3 Matyushin, 'Mesolithic and Neolithic', pp. 137, 140.

4 Mallory, *In Search of the Indo-Europeans*, p. 188; and see Dolukhanov, *Early Slavs*, pp. 58ff, on mesolithic Ukraine.

5 Dolukhanov, 'Foragers and farmers in west-central Asia', in Zvelebil, ed., *Hunters in Transition* (pp. 121–32) p. 124; and Ligabue and Salvatori, eds, *Bactria*, pp. 56–7.

6 Masson and Sarianidi, *Central Asia*, p. 29; on the history of the Uzboi, see Tolstov, *Po drevnim del'tam*, pp. 17–26; and see L. T. Yablonsky, 'The material culture of the Saka and historical reconstruction' in Davis-Kimball, ed., *Nomads* (pp. 201–38), p. 223.

7 V. Sarianidi, 'Food-producing and other neolithic communities in Khorasan and Transoxania' in *HCCA* (pp. 109–26), 1:121–4; Ligabue and Salvatori, eds, *Bactria*, p. 58.

8 See reconstruction in Tolstov, *Po drevnim del'tam*, opposite p. 30, and description, p. 30.

9 Chang, *Archaeology of Ancient China*, 3rd edn, p. 206; A. P. Derevyanko and D. Dorj, 'Neolithic tribes in northern parts of Central Asia', in *HCCA* (pp. 169–89), 1:170–2; see Novgorodova, *Drevnyaya Mongoliya*, pp. 48–54 on the Arshan-khad paintings.

10 The phrase, 'wave of advance', belongs to A. J. Ammerman and L. L. Cavalli-Sforza; on it, see Zvelebil, 'Mesolithic prelude and neolithic revolution', in *Cambridge Encyclopedia of Archaeology* (pp. 5–15), pp. 9–13 and Renfrew, *Archaeology and Language*, pp. 126–9.

11 Zvelebil, 'Mesolithic Prelude', pp. 12–13.

12 Kozlowski and Kozlowski, 'Foragers of central Europe', pp. 99, 101.

13 Gimbutas, *Civilization of the Goddess*, pp. 47, 449.

14 Vencl, 'The Role of hunting-gathering populations', stresses the skeletal differences in eastern European populations.

15 Dolukhanov, 'The late mesolithic and the transition to food', in Zvelebil, ed., *Hunters in Transition* pp. 112–13.

16 Kol'tsov, ed., *Mezolit SSSR*, p. 7.

17 Dolukhanov, 'The late mesolithic and transition to food production in Eastern Europe', in Zvelebil, ed., *Hunters in Transition*, pp. 115–16; Dolukhanov, *Early Slavs*, pp. 53–8; Dolukhanov, *Ecology and Economy*, pp. 179, 196.

18 Okladnikov, 'Inner Asia at the dawn of history', in *CHEIA*, p. 60; Matyushin, 'Mesolithic and Neolithic,' p. 148.

19 Okladnikov, 'Inner Asia at the dawn of history', in *CHEIA*, p. 63.

20 Dikov, *Istoriya Chukotki*, pp. 27–30, 45.

21 Ibid., pp. 31–3.
22 Ibid., pp. 35ff.
23 Ibid., pp. 39–42.
24 Vainshtein, *Nomads of South Siberia*, pp. 131–6.
25 Khazanov, *Nomads*, pp. 112–13.
26 Forsyth, *History of the Peoples of Siberia*, p. 10.
27 P. B. Golden, 'Peoples of the Russian forest belt', in *CHEIA* (pp. 229–55), pp. 231–2; there is less disagreement about the location of the 'Uralic' homeland than about the hypothetical 'Indo-European' homeland; indeed, the presence in Uralic languages of early Indo-European loanwords, has been used as a sort of 'anchor' to locate the Indo-European homeland; see Mallory, *In Search of the Indo-Europeans*, pp. 148–9.
28 Janet Martin, *Treasure of the Land of Darkness*, p. 204.
29 Cited in ibid., p. 21.
30 Forsyth, *History of the Peoples of Siberia*, p. 11; see Martin, *Treasure of the Land of Darkness*, p. 204, on the migration across the Urals.
31 Armstrong, *Russian Settlement in the North*, p. 36.
32 Forsyth, *History of the Peoples of Siberia*, p. 11; most of the previous paragraph is based on ibid., pp. 10–16.
33 The following paragraphs are based on Forsyth, *History of the Peoples of Siberia*, pp. 16–19, 48–55 and 69–75.
34 Zenkovsky, *Medieval Russia's Epics*, pp. 422–3; Vitebsky, *The Shaman*, p. 130, argues that Avvakum was the first to use the term, 'shaman' in Russian; the best general survey of the literature on Siberian shamanism is Humphrey, 'Theories of North Asian Shamanism', in Gellner, ed., *Soviet and Western Anthropology*, pp. 243–54.
35 Boyle, *Mongol world Empire*, XXII, p. 183; Dawson, *Mission to Asia*, pp. 80, 198; Rashid al-Din, *Successors of Genghis Khan*, pp. 36–7.
36 Cited in Boyle, *The Mongol World Empire 1206–1370*, p. 180.
37 Cited in ibid., p. 181.
38 Forsyth, *History of the Peoples of Siberia*, p. 15.
39 Vitebsky, *The Shaman*, p. 17.
40 Forsyth, *History of the Peoples of Siberia*, pp. 51–2.
41 Vitebsky, *The Shaman*, pp. 112–13.
42 Forsyth, *History of the Peoples of Siberia*, pp. 51–2.
43 Eliade, *Shamanism*, pp. 27–8.
44 Ibid., p. 504.
45 A. Hultkrantz, 'Ecological and phenomenological aspects of shamanism', in Diószegi and Hoppál, eds, *Shamanism in Siberia* (pp. 27–58), p. 51; and see Vitebsky, *The Shaman*, p. 30.
46 Eliade, *Shamanism*, pp. 495–501; there is a powerful, but restrained critique of the 'essentialism' of writers such as Eliade, in the Introduction to Thomas and Humphrey, *Shamanism*.
47 On the political dimension of shamanism, neglected in much of the literature, see Thomas and Humphrey, eds, *Shamanism, History and the State*.
48 Hamayon, 'Stakes of the Game: Life and Death in Siberian Shamanism', p. 81; Thomas and Humphrey, eds, *Shamanism, History and the State*, p. 11.
49 There is a good discussion of 'ethnic' religions of the Inner Eurasian steppes in Khazanov, 'The spread of world religions', particularly pp. 12–13.

FURTHER READING

On the end of the last ice age, see Soffer and Gamble, *The World at 18,000 BP*, and Dolukhanov, *Early Slavs*. Soviet work on the mesolithic era is summarized in *CHEIA*; Kol'tsov, ed., *Mezolit SSSR*; Tolstov, *Po drevnim del'tam*; and Dolukhanov, *Early Slavs*. On the mesolithic, see also, Zvelebil, *Hunters in Transition*; *HCCA*, vol. 1; Chang, *Archaeology of Ancient China*; and Novgorodova, *Drevnyaya Mongoliya*. The best introduction to the history of Siberia is Forsyth, *A History of the Peoples of Siberia*, which has been used extensively in this chapter. There are many good studies of shamanism. Eliade, *Shamanism*, is a classic, but it should be supplemented with more recent studies, such as Humphrey, 'Theories of north Asian shamanism', in Gellner, ed., *Soviet and Western Anthropology*; Thomas and Humphrey, *Shamanism, History and the State*; and Vitebsky, *The Shaman*.

[4] *The Neolithic Revolution: Seventh to Third Millennia BCE*

> What a versatile machine this is that can convert grass
> into clothing and butter and fuel and tent hide!
> *Vikram Seth on the yaks of Tibet,*
> *From Heaven's Lake: Travels through Sinking and Tibet,* p. 107

ARCHAEOLOGISTS first used the term, 'neolithic' (or 'new stone age'), to describe a particular type of smoothly polished stone tool whose appearance is now dated to the end of the last ice-age, from about 8000 BCE. In the 1930s, the Australian archaeologist, V. G. Childe, argued that the appearance of neolithic tools signalled profound changes in human lifeways. They marked the first appearance of societies capable of domesticating plants and animals. Unlike hunter-gatherer lifeways, those of the neolithic encouraged population growth, so they introduced a new dynamism into human history. While foraging lifeways could support population densities of approximately one person to every ten square kilometres, even the earliest forms of farming could support as many as 50 people from a similar area. As Colin Renfrew points out, this huge difference in population densities is probably the main explanation – more important even than disease or war – for the eventual displacement of foraging communities by farmers, wherever the ecology suited early forms of farming.[1] As farming communities expanded they surrounded and eventually supplanted local populations of hunter-gatherers. In the course of several thousand years, agricultural communities came to dominate those parts of Outer Eurasia most suitable for early neolithic types of farming.

The demographic dynamism of the neolithic revolution prepared the way for a second transition, which Childe called the 'urban' revolution. This began in Mesopotamia towards the end of the fourth millennium BCE. It created the urbanized agrarian societies that have dominated world history during the last 5,000 years.

Though some of Childe's ideas have come in for rough treatment over the years, the central notion of a 'neolithic revolution' has survived. However, it can be extended to Inner Eurasia only after some modifications. There was a neolithic revolution in Inner Eurasia, but it took quite distinctive forms. Here, early forms of agriculture spread very slowly, and only into a few

Table 4.1 Chart of the neolithic and Bronze ages in Inner Eurasia

= migratory waves

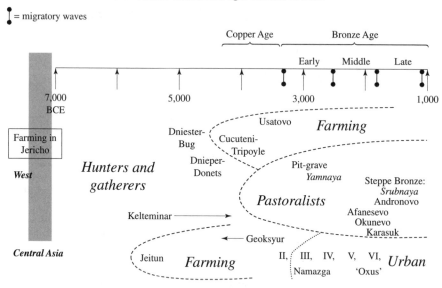

ecologically favoured regions. The neolithic revolution began to have a more profound impact only after the appearance of the distinctive neolithic life-ways known as 'pastoralism', from c.4000 BCE, and the historical impact of pastoralist societies was very different from that of farming societies.

Whereas agriculture exploits domesticated plants, pastoralism exploits domesticated animals. Its importance in Inner Eurasia reflects the general principle that the harsher ecologies of Inner Eurasia forced human populations to move higher up the food-chain, to live off animal-based foods rather than plant-based foods. So, just as in the palaeolithic era Inner Eurasian life-ways were dominated by hunting rather than gathering, in the neolithic era, they came to be dominated by pastoralism rather than by farming. Pastoralist lifeways set the history of Inner Eurasia off on a very different trajectory from that of Outer Eurasia.

EARLY AGRICULTURAL COMMUNITIES OF INNER EURASIA

CENTRAL ASIA

In Inner Eurasia, the earliest agricultural communities appeared in the southern borderlands of modern Turkmenistan sometime during the Seventh millennium BCE, about 2,000 years after the earliest agricultural communities of Mesopotamia. Their appearance may have been encouraged by the warmer and wetter climates of the 'Climatic Optimum', from c.6000–2500 BCE.[2]

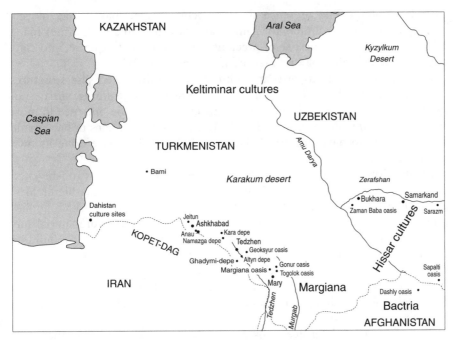

Map 4.1 The neolithic and Bronze ages in Central Asia.

The twenty or so sites of the so-called 'Jeitun' culture lie on a strip almost 700 km long, along the narrow plateau at the foothills of the Kopet Dag and the edge of the Karakum desert, from Bami in the west to Ghadymi in the east.[3] There may also have been some early sites further east, in the waters of the Tedzhen terminal fan.

The village of Jeitun lies today in the Karakum desert, 30 km north of modern Ashkhabad.

> The settlement itself once stood at the top of a sandy hill on the southern edge of the Karakum Desert. Houses here were constructed of clay bricks, heavily tempered with chaff straw. The walls inside were daubed with a clay-and-water solution and were sometimes painted red or black. The floor in such houses was, as a rule, covered with lime plaster 1.0–1.5 cm. thick and painted the same colour as the walls. Sometimes the floor was nothing but a hard beaten surface with ashes spread on top.[4]

The thirty or so houses of Jeitun were rectangular or nearly square, and built to a standard plan with a single room. Few had doors, which suggests that their entrances were covered with mats or hides. Most had large, well-planned fireplaces of a similar design, and placed to the right of the doorway. Opposite the hearths there was often a low niche, sometimes painted black or red, which may have had a ceremonial function. The Jeitun villagers made unsophisticated pottery. Few of their pots show signs of charring, which suggests that cooking was done by placing heated stones in containers, rather than by boiling. The presence of small, cone-shaped baked clay objects which are probably counters for games, and of ornaments or figurines made of bone, sea shells, stones, semi-precious stones such as turquoise, and clay, suggests the existence of a rich leisure and ceremonial life.[5]

Most houses had courtyards and outhouses, and there were also structures for storing grain above the ground. The absence of large storage areas suggests that most households were self-sufficient, as does the presence in most houses of a complete inventory of tools. Each household seems to have made its own tools, to have processed skins and hides and to have done its own woodwork and food-processing.[6]

Most Jeitun settlements include about 30 dwellings and probably had up to 200 inhabitants.[7] There is little sign of gender or status hierarchies. However, there are some signs of public ceremonial buildings, which implies a limited degree of communal organization and the existence of material surpluses. In the middle of the Pessejik-depe site near Jeitun there is a building much larger than those surrounding it, with huge walls, a large fireplace, and traces of mural paintings which may depict snow leopards, and are reminiscent of the nearly contemporaneous frescos of Çatal Hüyük in Anatolia. It contains few ordinary household goods, and was probably a communal centre.[8]

The absence of defensive walls around Jeitun villages suggests that their inhabitants had little to fear from outside. This may reflect the low populations and abundant resources of a frontier region. Indeed, we know from rises in the level of the Caspian Sea that between 6000 and c.2500 BCE climates were quite warm and rainfall was quite abundant during the 'Climatic Optimum', so that the areas of farmable land were probably greater than today. During this period the now vanished Uzboi river linked the Amu Darya river to the Caspian Sea, and the Kyzylkum and Karakum deserts were probably covered with steppe. In hilly regions, there may have been extensive woodlands.[9]

Despite these benign conditions, agriculture at the base of the Kopet Dag was impossible without irrigation. However, irrigation was relatively easy because of the regular, predictable, and usually gentle flow of rivers descending from the mountains. Jeitun's position far out on the alluvial fan, where water flowed more slowly, and the land was flatter, eased the job of digging irrigation channels. Small communities in this region did not have to build the complicated systems of wells and underground channels typical much later of parts of Iran, Arabia and North Africa, or parts of Sinkiang, such as the Turfan oasis. It was usually enough to build simple dams that could divert water into nearby fields and keep it there long enough to water young crops. Like Egypt, the borderlands of Central Asia also enjoyed predictable water supplies. Low rainfall freed farmers from the danger of unseasonal falls; while the thawing of ice high in the mountains meant that rivers were fullest in summer, precisely when water was most needed.[10]

Lattimore's account of irrigation practices in the Tarim basin in modern times applies to much of the southern borderland of western Central Asia in the early neolithic.

> In a typical oasis on the rim of the Taklamakan the conditions that encourage a very early practice of agriculture are unmistakable. A river comes down from high mountains that store ice and snow. It breaks through a lower, desert barrier range and enters flat country. Here it tends naturally to break up into several channels and in the season of high water it spills over into lakes and marshes.[11]

Jungly growths of bushes and thick reed marshes appeared in the delta regions of the Tarim basin, but once these had been cleared by fire or axes, the fertile, loess-bearing soils brought down by the rivers could be worked and even irrigated with nothing more complex than a crude hoe.

Jeitun farmers harvested their crops with sickles made from flint blades that probably fitted into bone handles. The other main farming tools were digging sticks. This was a typical early neolithic technology, dependent almost entirely on the power of human labour. Domesticated livestock was important, but only as a source of food. In the early Jeitun period domesticated goats and sheep provided most of the meat in the diet. By the end of the sixth millennium, there were probably domesticated cattle as well.[12]

There are indirect signs that the Jeitun people spoke early forms of Dravidian.[13] However, there are even stronger signs of Mesopotamian influences. These include the paintings on the walls and floors, the use of game counters, and the many small figurines of baked clay, all of which are reminiscent of societies such as Jericho in the eighth or seventh millennia. Most important of all, the Jeitun villagers used grains and domestic animals first domesticated in the Middle East, as well as Mesopotamian techniques of irrigation agriculture.[14] These facts make it hard to resist the conclusion that the Jeitun settlers were descended from Mesopotamian migrants driven from their homelands by growing populations in the core areas of the Mesopotamian neolithic.

However, it would be wrong to conclude that they simply replaced earlier hunter-gatherer populations. On the contrary, Jeitun farmers clearly borrowed techniques from their foraging neighbours. Bones from gazelle, onager, wild pig and sheep are present in early settlements, along with the remains of fur-bearing animals such as fox, cat and wolf. Indeed, gazelle and onager provided up to 25 per cent of all meat in the diet. Much of the tool kit is also geared to hunting and to the use of animal skins.[15] In a pattern that was to become characteristic of the early neolithic in Inner Eurasia, farmers settled amongst hunters and gatherers, establishing stable long-term relationships in which each community could borrow from the other, while each remained in its own ecological niche. The first farming cultures of southern Central Asia 'for a long time formed a peninsula in a sea of cultures in which there were food-extracting economies.'[16] They were not isolated, but formed part of regional systems that linked hunters and gatherers with early neolithic farmers in relatively stable relationships of material, cultural and probably human exchanges.

Between the fifth and the third millennia, farming populations expanded in southern Central Asia. At first, they extended higher up the rivers of the

Piedmont and into the Murgab valley. In the fourth millennium, farming spread to regions in which water supply was more uneven, and required more complicated irrigation techniques. In the Geoksur oasis, in the Tedzhen delta, there has been found an entire artificially constructed reservoir.[17] Increased populations and more extensive settlement imply improved farming techniques, and probably more complex forms of social organization, particularly in order to manage irrigation systems. The site of Sarazm in the upper Zerafshan valley, shows the presence of agricultural communities very similar to those of the Geoksyur oasis by the late fourth millennium.[18]

Early sites of the Tedzhen delta are similar to those of the Jeitun culture, though the importance of hunting declines, and that of domestic livestock increases. Woollen cloths largely replaced animal skins for clothing. There appear examples of sophisticated metalwork, as well as precious stones such as lapis lazuli, which must have been obtained through trade with communities in the Pamirs. In some regions, there began to appear larger communities, each with clusters of smaller settlements nearby. In the Geoksyur oasis, most burials appear to have taken place in the central settlement of the oasis, which suggests the emergence of a hierarchy of settlements.[19] Within some settlements, there appear larger houses which hint at growing economic differences.

Despite these changes, the Geoksyur delta remained a world of simple, relatively egalitarian farmers.

> There is no evidence … that these tiny villages had accumulated wealth enough to tempt invaders. The material excavated here shows that they were a series of ordinary sedentary agricultural villages with a crude set of equipment typical of rural settlers. In fact, apart from the modestly decorated pottery, small clay figurines and domestic implements there is nothing of any value at these sites, the only luxury items being a few ornaments made of carnelian, turquoise, agate and azurite.[20]

Until the second half of the fourth millennium, southern Central Asia remained firmly within the village world of the early neolithic.

Settlement in the Geoksyur oasis died out by early in the third millennium, perhaps because water supplies became less reliable, or perhaps because increased population was leading to salinization, deforestation, and increased mud-flows. Here as in Mesopotamia, cultures dependent on irrigation were peculiarly subject to ecological disasters, and the Geoksyur communities may have been too simple to undertake the complex organizational tasks needed to maintain the irrigation systems on which they depended.[21]

UKRAINE AND THE NORTH CAUCASUS

The second major area of Inner Eurasia to be settled by early neolithic farmers was in the far west, in the wooded steppes of modern Moldova and Ukraine. Here, settlement began towards the end of the sixth millennium, more than a millennium later than in southern Central Asia, and after agriculture had already spread into the Balkans and parts of Eastern Europe.

Here, too, agriculture almost certainly appeared through migration. Driven by population pressure in the Mediterranean world, and drawn by

Map 4.2 The neolithic and Bronze ages in western Inner Eurasia.

the new opportunities created as climates warmed from *c.*5500 BCE, neolithic populations from the Balkans began to spread north into Eastern Europe in the sixth millennium. Many belonged to the so-called 'Linear Pottery' (or *Bandkeramik*) culture. Populations representing this culture began to colonize the Middle Danube from *c.*5300 BCE. They settled in small communities of 40–60 people, living in rectangular timber and thatch houses which probably housed livestock as well as people. They cultivated barley, einkorn, emmer wheat and flax, using hoes. Some of their farming techniques were surprisingly modern. They used systems of rotation and fallowing, and sometimes grew hedges to mark off fields and to keep in domestic animals. Cattle and livestock played an important role in this system of agriculture.[22] By *c.*4500 BCE similar communities had spread over much of central and western Europe. By *c.*3500 BCE, farming populations probably outnumbered hunter-gatherer communities in most of Europe, except in the far north.

However, in the western borderlands of Inner Eurasia, there was no such 'wave of advance' except in the wooded steppelands of Moldova and parts of Central Ukraine. Early farmers in Moldova and Ukraine avoided the steppelands with their erratic rainfall, and tough turfs, as well as the wooded lands further north, for neither region suited the farming techniques of the early neolithic.[23] As a result, from the fourth millennium BCE to the first millennium CE, the ecological history of western Inner Eurasia was quite different from that of central and western Europe. By at least the fourth millennium BCE, there had emerged a frontier between the farming regions of western

(a)

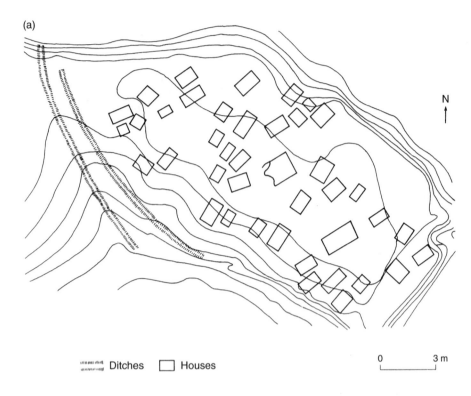

N
↑

▦ Ditches   ☐ Houses

0   3 m

(b)

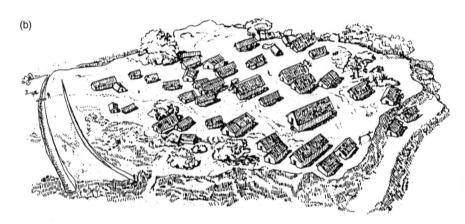

Figure 4.1 Tripolye culture: Kolomiyshchina village, fourth millennium BCE, reproduced from Marija Gimbutas *The Civilization of the Goddess: The World of Old Europe* (New York: Harper & Row, 1991). Reprinted by permission of Harper-Collins Publishers Inc., (© 1991 Marija Gimbutas). Photograph: The Bodleian Library.

and central Europe and the foraging regions of Scandinavia and western Inner Eurasia. This frontier ran from eastern Poland, along the Western Bug, bulged eastwards around the forest-steppelands of central Ukraine and ran west and south towards the Danube.[24]

The hunting and gathering communities of the Bug-Dniester culture first encountered farming cultures from the nearby Cris/Koros culture of what is now southern Moldova, perhaps as early as the sixth millennium BC. Their arrival did not necessarily lead to conflict, for farmers preferred the choice loess soils of flat terraces near rivers, along the Prut, Dniester, and later the Dnieper and its tributaries, while hunters and gatherers preferred regions with more ecological variety.[25] As in Central Asia, early farming communities probably had much to learn from local populations as they adapted techniques first developed in the Mediterranean climates of the Balkans to the colder, more forested lands further north.

Towards the end of the fifth millennium, there began to appear in parts of Moldova and Ukraine areas of denser settlement, and here, at least, hunting-gathering communities may have been forced to move or to take up farming themselves. The Dnieper-Donets cultures of the fifth millennium, may be an example of a hunter-gatherer culture in the early stages of a transition to agriculture. This culture is known from some 200 settlement sites, and many more cemeteries, as well as by the presence of pottery.[26] Though quite sedentary, this was still a transitional economy, relying mainly on hunting and fishing, though its people also kept domestic cattle and pigs and grew barley. Early in the fourth millennium, communities of the Dnieper-Donets shifted eastward away from the wooded steppes into the Azov and Crimean steppes.[27]

They were probably driven east by the spread of the first true farming communities, which belonged to what is known as the Cucuteni-Tripolye cultures. These were first discovered in the late nineteenth century by the Ukrainian archaeologist, V. V. Chvoika, who excavated the site of Tripolye, which is within the boundaries of modern Kiev. Cucuteni-Tripolye communities spread into the wooded steppes of Ukraine from the Dniester-Bug region during the late fifth millennium, reaching the middle Dnieper at least by c.4000 BCE. The human remains of the Cucuteni-Tripolye culture show the continued importance of migrations from the Mediterranean.[28] Recently, it has been suggested that the slow migration of such populations, as a result of over population in the Anatolian homelands of their ancestors, may explain the spread of the Indo-European languages during the neolithic.[29] If this is true, then the farming communities of the Cucuteni-Tripolye cultures probably spoke Indo-European languages; but, as we will see, there are alternative theories that derive the Indo-European languages from the post-glacial indigenes of Inner Eurasia.

In Ukraine, there are some 1000 sites belonging to the Cucuteni-Tripolye culture.[30] Most are on loess soil plateaus, overlooking river valleys. Early sites show the influence of Linear Pottery cultures, and their people still depended largely on hunting. Most early sites have no more than about 20 dwellings. However settlements expanded quite rapidly. By 4000 BCE, some settlements had up to 100 dwellings, and later in the fourth millennium there appeared settlements with as many as 2000 houses. The site of Tallyanky, between the Bug and Dnieper rivers measured 3.5 by 1.5 km, and may have had 10,000 inhabitants.[31] Despite its size, this was not a true town, but a collection of roughly similar farming households. Still, it may have acted as a regional centre, for plots of Tripolye settlements show a regular pattern of larger settlements surrounded by smaller villages.

Like the type-sites of Cucuteni on the Prut and Tripolye on the Dnieper, in some of the larger sites, such as Kolomyishchina, houses stood in a series of concentric circles, with ditches around the entire settlement, which suggests a pattern of slow expansion around an initial nucleus.

> At Vladimirovka on the Bug the largest village known [in this region] contained as many as two hundred houses in five concentric circles. Their sites are represented by platforms of baked clay resulting from the burning and collapse of walls and floors. Post-holes for timber frames define rectangular floors varying between 7 × 4 metres and 27 × 6.5 metres. The walls were of wattle and clay or of compacted earth, coloured over, and the roofs probably of thatch. A middle-sized house contained two separate rooms, each with a clay oven 2 metres square, set against the wall, while the largest known house at Vladimirovka contained five rooms, four with one oven and the fifth with two.[32]

The density of settlement in this region at the height of the Cucuteni-Tripolye culture was remarkable. Unlike southern Central Asia, with its scattered oases, this was a world of rainfall agriculture, with relatively even settlement over quite large areas.

Many Tripolye sites contain remarkable models of houses, some with little figures inside doing household tasks such as baking. This has helped archaeologists to reconstruct the life of Tripolye villagers. Villagers grew wheat, barley and millet, and also peas, grapes, plums and apricots. Their livestock included cattle, goats, sheep and pigs. Villagers worked the land with stone or bone hoes and digging sticks, though it is possible that some later Tripolye farmers also used ploughs pulled by cattle. Hunting of animal such as deer, boar and wild cattle always remained important. As in Central Asia, livestock played a peculiarly important role. The presence of copper implements and ornaments shows that Tripolye settlements took part in trade networks that extended at least as far as the Balkans, the source of most metal ores in this period.[33]

Until the middle of the fourth millennium, the farming lands of Ukraine, like southern Central Asia, remained a frontier zone, where resources were abundant, hierarchies of wealth and power were of little importance, and there was little reason for conflicts between communities. Though houses vary in size in some of the larger settlements, there are no clear signs of the emergence of power centres. Even the temples of the region are not strikingly different from ordinary dwellings, and there is no clear evidence for the existence of chiefly dwellings. Marija Gimbutas has argued that gender relations were also probably egalitarian in this world.[34]

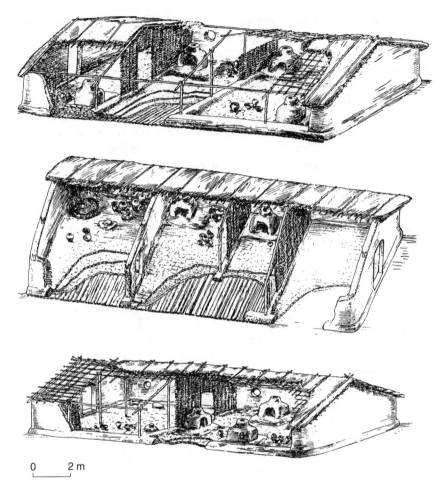

0   2 m

Figure 4.2 Tripolye culture: reconstruction of houses from near Kolomiyshchina village, fourth millennium BCE. Reproduced from Marija Gimbutas *The Civilization of the Goddess: The World of Old Europe* (New York: Harper & Row, 1991). Reprinted by permission of Harper-Collins Publishers Inc. (*c.*1991 Marija Gimbutas). Photograph: The Bodleian Library.

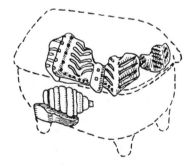

Figure 4.3 Tripolye culture: pottery models of houses. Drawing by Margaret E. Scott, reproduced from E. D. Phillips *The Royal Hordes* (London: Thames and Hudson, 1965).

However, in the fourth millennium, evidence accumulates of growing pressure on resources. One sign is the appearance of very large settlements. The other is the appearance of defensive walls and weapons in later Tripolye settlements. Late Tripolye burials also show the appearance of steep social hierarchies. Though we cannot be certain, these signs may reflect the appearance of powerful pastoralist communities in the steppelands east of the Tripolye communities. The Usatovo culture, which flourished from the Dniester to the Danube from c.3500–3000 BCE, owed much to the Tripolye culture, but the role of horse-breeding and of warfare is greater here.[35] Eventually, the appearance of powerful pastoralist communities further east checked the expansion of agriculture in this region. For several millennia, agriculturalists would remain confined to the wooded steppes of their early settlements, and subject to the exactions of pastoralist communities of the steppes. Not until the first millennium of the modern era would agricultural communities begin once more to expand rapidly within western Inner Eurasia.

OTHER REGIONS OF EARLY FARMING

Small agricultural communities also appeared in other 'hot spots' in Inner Eurasia.

The first Neolithic communities of the Caucasus belonged to the Shulaveri-Shomutepe culture. This flourished in the sixth and fifth millennia in the steppelands north of the Caucasus mountains, and in mountain valleys further south. Its people grew crops and kept livestock (cattle, sheep, goat and pigs). They lived mainly in round clay buildings with small domes, clustered together in small groups and surrounded by walls. They made their tools of bone and stone, and also made simple pottery containers, which show clear links with Mesopotamian cultures such as Tell Hassuna and Tell Halaf. In its later stages, the sites of this culture contain some of the earliest metal implements found in the Caucasus.[36]

In the far east, as in the western and central borderlands, agriculture spread from a core area (the Huang He valley) into neighbouring regions of Inner Eurasia, where it was confined in regional pockets for several millennia. In the steppelands from Sinkiang to eastern Mongolia, communities of hunters and gatherers adopted the ceramic technologies and sometimes even the farming methods of the emerging neolithic cultures of north China. As farming communities spread from Mesopotamia into southern Central Asia, so, here, they spread from the Huang He valley into the north Chinese borderlands, exploiting the more benign climates of the 'Climatic Optimum'.[37]

In Kansu, the earliest evidence of farming communities similar in their technology to the Yang-shao communities of the Huang He valley, dates from the fifth millennium, from the same period as the Tripolye communities of Ukraine.[38] Here, as in the Tripolye region, agricultural communities probably survived in localized hot spots into the modern era. Mongolian scholars have recently found signs of early farming even deep inside Mongolia. The earliest evidence of hoe agriculture here does not occur before the late third millennium, when climates may have been more benign than those of today.

The typical site of this phase is the Tamtsak-bulak site in north-eastern Mongolia, excavated by Okladnikov. The site contains agricultural implements, such as pestles for grinding grain and millstones, as well as hoes, and millet was the primary grain. However, the population still depended largely on hunting, fishing and cattle-breeding. The inhabitants lived in rectangular semi-subterranean dwellings, apparently with no doors, so that people had to enter and leave by the smoke-hole. To have supported permanent settlements as large as those of Tamtsak-bulak, agriculture must have been reasonably reliable. There are also several neolithic sites in the Gobi, some discovered as early as the 1920s by the American archaeologists, Andrews and Nelson, along the beds of rivers that no longer exist.[39]

In southern Siberia, the earliest evidence of farming comes from the Minusinsk basin, which had been an ecological 'hot spot' even in the upper palaeolithic.[40] However, such communities were rare. Indeed, throughout Inner Eurasia, farming communities remained rare and precarious before the first millennium of the modern era.

THE ORIGINS OF INNER EURASIAN PASTORALISM

While lifeways based on the domestication of plants made only limited headway in Inner Eurasia, from the fourth millennium BCE, lifeways based on the domestication of animals began to spread more rapidly. As a result, the neolithic revolution first conquered Inner Eurasia as a technology of pastoralism rather than a technology of farming. This difference was to shape Inner Eurasian history, and its relations with the agrarian societies of Outer Eurasia for several thousand years. Indeed, the contrast between pastoralist Inner Eurasia and agricultural Outer Eurasia was to become one of the enduring features of Eurasian history.

PRECONDITIONS: THE 'SECONDARY PRODUCTS REVOLUTION'

The origins of pastoralism remain a hotly debated topic in modern anthropology. We can eliminate some confusion by concentrating on the wider phenomenon of pastoralism rather than on 'pastoral nomadism'. Lawrence Krader has defined pastoralists as: 'those who are dependent chiefly on their herds of domestic stock for subsistence'.[41] As this simple definition suggests, pastoralism depends on methods of livestock management that are productive enough to form the basis for an entire lifeway. Andrew Sherratt has argued convincingly that such techniques did not appear before the fifth millennium. They emerged as part of the package of technological changes that he has dubbed the 'secondary products revolution'.[42]

By 6000 BCE, sheep, goats and cattle had all been domesticated. Despite this, there is no evidence that any early neolithic communities would have fitted Krader's definition of pastoralism. This is almost certainly because they exploited their animals inefficiently. Treating them as little more than a store of meat, they harvested their animals only once, when they slaughtered them. The 'secondary products revolution' introduced a series of new techniques that made it possible to exploit domestic livestock more intensively. In effect, it allowed multiple harvesting of their produce.

The techniques pioneered during the 'secondary products' revolution mark, in Sherratt's phrase, a 'second generation' of neolithic technologies which extended the geographic range of the neolithic.[43] There were two main types of innovation. First, new techniques made it possible to exploit the traction power of large livestock, either by riding them or by using them to draw wagons, chariots or ploughs. At present, the earliest evidence for horse riding comes from the Srednyi Stog communities of eastern Ukraine, and dates to *c.*4000 BCE, though it is also possible that horses were domesticated further east, at sites such as Boatai in northern Kazakhstan, at about the same time.[44] At the Srednyi Stog site of Dereivka, archaeologists have found a male horse which had probably been ritually slaughtered. With it were two pieces of antler bone which appear to be the cheekpieces of a simple bit. Recent research has also shown that the teeth of this animal are worn in ways usually associated with the use of bits.[45] The fact that an astonishing 68 per cent of the bones at this site belong to horses also indicates that horses were ridden in Dereivka, for, as Gimbutas has argued, it is hard to imagine how herds this large could have been managed except from horseback.[46] Dromedaries (one-humped camels) were first domesticated in Arabia, probably during the third millennium, while in Central Asia, pictures of Bactrian (two-humped) camels with nose rings and pulling carts also appear from the third millennium.[47] Bactrian camels were probably domesticated in the Kopet Dag region, certainly by 2500 BCE and maybe in the fourth millennium BCE, but they were probably fewer in number and less important than dromedaries in Arabia, for in Central Asia they competed with other domesticated species, and were used mainly as draught animals.[48] The earliest evidence for the use of wagons drawn by horse or oxen comes from the late fourth millennium, from the Pontic steppes and Sumer. The earliest evidence for animal-drawn ploughs or 'ards' appears in plough marks found across Europe from the late fourth millennium, while the earliest pictures of ploughs date from the middle of the third millennium.[49]

Second, there appeared techniques that made it possible to use the blood, milk and hair of livestock, both large and small, without slaughtering them. Evidence of milking may date from the fifth millennium, but the first clear evidence for the evolution of wool-bearing sheep and the widespread use of wool, appears in the third millennium BCE.[50] It is not clear how frequently pastoralists used the blood of live horses, but the practice was common in later periods. In the thirteenth century of the modern era, Marco Polo noted that, on long journeys, Mongols could live on the blood of their horses (which they took by piercing their veins), as well as on balls of dried milk.[51]

Exploitation of the milk, fibres, and traction power of living animals significantly increased the productivity of domestic livestock. For the first time, it was possible to produce from domesticated livestock most of the food, clothing, shelter and traction power needed for survival. This made it possible to colonize large areas of grassland unsuitable for early forms of agriculture, but suitable for grazing. It is no accident, then, that extensive colonization of the Inner Eurasian steppes began with the spread of the 'secondary products revolution' after c.4000 BCE.[52]

EARLIEST PHASES OF INNER EURASIAN PASTORALISM:
THE FOURTH MILLENNIUM

Over time, the techniques of the 'secondary products' revolution were integrated into the distinctive lifeways known today as 'pastoralism'. These are lifeways in which most members of society depended primarily on the exploitation of domesticated livestock. Unfortunately, the available evidence allows us only a very obscure glimpse of the early history of pastoralist lifeways.

By the fourth millennium, the southern half of Inner Eurasia included many hunting and gathering societies and a few farming societies that kept domesticated herbivores as livestock. Pastoralism probably emerged from a technological division of labour between these two types of communities. Both in southern Central Asia and the wooded steppes of Ukraine, complex hunting and gathering communities lived near neolithic communities, with which they exchanged goods and technologies. However, the first clear evidence of pastoralist cultures appears in the western steppes, from c.4000 BCE. This is hardly surprising, for, on average, the western steppes offer a much more benign ecology to pastoralists than the steppes of Kazakhstan or Mongolia. Rainfall is higher and the western steppes are criss-crossed by river systems.

The most important steppeland communities of the fourth millennium belong to the Srednyi Stog-Khvalynsk cultures of Ukraine and Southern Russia. They date from the early fourth millennium, and may have survived as late as the early third millennium.[53] The Srednyi Stog-Khvalynsk cultures were neighbours to the Tripolye communities of western Ukraine, and successors to the hunter-gatherer Dnieper-Don cultures. Their anthropological remains are similar to those of the Dnieper-Don cultures, but very different from those of the Tripolye cultures.[54] This suggests that pastoralist lifeways appeared in the steppes not as a result of migrations from neolithic communities, but through adaptations to neolithic technologies by complex hunter-gatherer communities such as those of the Dnieper-Don culture, which occupied lands that were difficult to farm.

Srednyi Stog communities occupied the lower and middle Dnieper, and also reached east into the steppelands and along the lower Donets. Stockbreeding and agriculture were both important in the Srednyi Stog culture, as were fishing and hunting. The presence of pigs, and of grinding implements, shows the continued importance of agriculture. However, the appearance of the first steppeland burial mounds or *kurgany* from the middle of the fourth millennium, the decline in the number of settlement sites, and the evidence of early forms of horse riding, show that the people of the

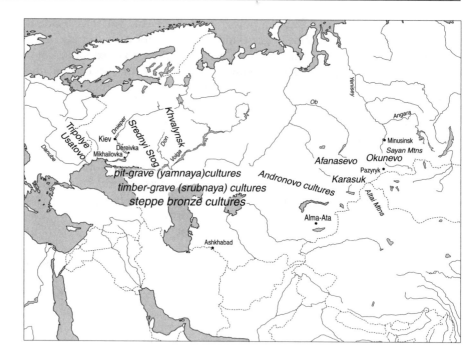

Map 4.3 The pastoralist neolithic.

Srednyi Stog culture were more mobile than the farmers of the Tripolye culture. Presumably some members of each community, or perhaps all members of some communities, went on periodic migrations into the steppes with their herds. Fighting from horseback also seems to have been important, for many *kurgany* include remains of horses and weaponry, though there is as yet no sign of the composite bows that were to make the pastoralists of the first millennium so dangerous in warfare. The appearance of *kurgany* in the fourth millennium also suggests an increase in the numbers living in the steppes.[55]

There seems to have been plenty of contact between pastoralist and agricultural communities in the western steppes. The nature of the goods they exchanged suggests contacts at all social levels, perhaps involving regular visits by pastoralists to farming settlements of the Tripolye culture. In short, we can see the emergence of a new type of regional system that was to prove very durable in Inner Eurasia, and linked pastoralists and farming communities. However, the increasing size of Tripolye settlements, and the appearance of fortifications in both regions suggests that these contacts were warlike. This makes sense, for the warlike remains in some early *kurgany* suggest that early communities of pastoralists posed a much greater threat to agricultural villages than their hunter-gatherer predecessors. The horse-head sceptres which show up west of the Dnieper, on Tripolye sites, and even in Romania, suggest the appearance of pastoralist raiding parties in the far west of Inner Eurasia.[56]

Of the more than 100 settlement or burial sites of the Srednyi Stog culture, the most famous is Dereivka, which was excavated by Dmitri Telegin. As we have seen, this site has yielded some of the earliest evidence of horse riding. Here:

> An area of over 2000 square metres was apparently bordered by some form of fence which enclosed several houses, work places and areas of ritual activity. The houses were slightly sunk into the ground, rectangular in shape, with the largest measuring 13 by 6 metres. Hearths were found within them. Scattered about the site were various activity areas including a place for repairing fish gear and processing one's catch, a potter's workshop, and a place where bones were worked into tools.[57]

Stone and bone were used for most tools. Average ages at death were *c.*27 years, though women were more likely than men to live into their forties.[58]

Further east, there appeared the so-called Khvalynsk culture, named after a site on the middle Volga. This is so similar to the Srednyi Stog culture that most archaeologists group the cultures together. However, there are hints of greater mobility in the Khvalynsk culture, for most of its sites are cemeteries rather than settlements.[59] Such evidence suggests that by 3000 BCE, there lived in the western steppes groups of pastoralists so mobile that we can refer to them as pastoral nomads.[60]

Recent excavations in Kazakhstan suggest that horse riding and pastoralism spread rapidly to the central steppes. The crucial site is Boatai in Petropavlovsk *oblast*. Here there was a settlement of semi-subterranean dwellings with wooden roofs daubed with clay, and dating from the fourth or third millennia BCE.[61] Remarkably, 99 per cent of the animal bones it contains are of horses. Some of the bone artefacts appear to have been cheek pieces, which suggests that at least some of the horses were domesticated and ridden. Here, we seem to have evidence of a community that depended almost entirely on its herds of horses.

All in all, the archaeological evidence suggests that by 3000 BCE, and perhaps even earlier, there had emerged in the steppes of Inner Eurasia the distinctive types of pastoralism that were to dominate the region's history for several millennia. Here, the horse was already becoming the animal of prestige in many regions, though sheep, goats and cattle could also play a vital role.[62] The leading role of the horse is the main feature that distinguishes Inner Eurasian pastoralism from forms of pastoralism dominated by camels, cattle or smaller livestock. Above all, it is the use of horses for transportation and warfare that explains why Inner Eurasian pastoralism proved the most mobile and the most militaristic of all major forms of pastoralism.

THE NATURE AND IMPACT OF INNER EURASIAN PASTORALISM

The emergence and spread of pastoralism had a profound impact on the history of Inner Eurasia, and also, indirectly, of Outer Eurasia. Our knowledge of the very earliest forms of pastoralism is scanty, and modern analogies must be used with caution. Nevertheless, to make sense of the early evidence, we have no choice but to make cautious use of what is known of more modern forms of pastoralism.[63]

Three features of the pastoralist societies of Inner Eurasia help explain their impact: (1) their mobility; (2) their military virtuosity; and (3) their capacity for rapid mobilization.

The mobility of pastoralist societies reflects their dependence on animal-based foods. While agriculturalists rely on domesticated plants, pastoralists rely on domesticated animals. As a result, pastoralists, like carnivores in general, occupy a higher position on the food chain. All else being equal, this means they must exploit larger areas of land than agriculturalists to secure the same amount of food, clothing and other necessities. So pastoralism is a more extensive lifeway than farming. However, the larger the terrain used to support a group, the harder it is to exploit that terrain while remaining in one place. So, basic ecological principles imply a strong tendency within pastoralist lifeways towards nomadism. As a recent study puts it: 'The greater the degree of pastoralism, the stronger the tendency towards nomadism.'[64] A modern Turkic nomad interviewed by the same author commented: 'The more animals you have, the further you have to move.'[65]

Nomadism has further consequences. It means that pastoralist societies occupy and can influence very large territories. This is particularly true of the horse pastoralism that emerged in the Inner Eurasian steppes, for this was the most mobile of all major forms of pastoralism. So, it is no accident that, with the appearance of pastoralist societies there appear large areas which share similar cultural, ecological and even linguistic features. By the late fourth millennium, there is already evidence of large culture zones reaching from Eastern Europe to the western borders of Mongolia.[66] Perhaps the most striking sign of mobility is the fact that by the third millennium, most pastoralists in this huge region spoke related languages ancestral to modern Indo-European languages. The remarkable mobility and range of pastoralist societies explain, in part, why so many linguists have argued that the Indo-European languages began their astonishing expansionist career not amongst Anatolian farmers, but amongst early pastoralists from Inner Eurasia.[67] Such theories imply that the Indo-European languages evolved not in neolithic Anatolia, but amongst the foraging communities of the Don-Dnieper cultures, who took up stock-breeding and began to exploit the Pontic and Caspian steppelands.

Nomadism also subjects pastoralist communities to strict rules of portability. If you are constantly on the move, you cannot afford to accumulate large material surpluses. Such rules limit variations in accumulated material goods between pastoralist households (though they may also encourage a taste for portable goods of high value such as silks or jewellery). So, by and large, nomadism implies a high degree of self-sufficiency and inhibits the appearance of an extensive division of labour. Inequalities of wealth and rank certainly exist, and have probably existed in most pastoralist societies, but except in periods of military conquest they are normally too slight to generate the stable, hereditary hierarchies that are usually implied by use of the term, 'class'. This is one of the reasons why most modern analyses of pastoralist societies avoid the Marxist terminology of class.[68] Inequalities of gender have also existed in pastoralist societies, but they seem to have been softened by the absence of steep hierarchies of wealth in most communities, and also by the requirement that women acquire most of the skills of men, including, often, their military skills.

The second main feature of pastoralist societies is their military virtuosity. For ecological reasons, pastoralist communities are usually more volatile than agricultural communities in their economics, their demography, and their politics. While the basic resource of an agricultural household is normally a fixed plot of land, the basic resource of a pastoralist household is a mobile herd of livestock. Though harvests may vary in size, under normal conditions the size of landholdings changes slowly. On the other hand, herds of livestock can multiply several times within a few years, or they can vanish within weeks due to disease, climatic disasters, or theft. As a result, pastoralists are constantly juggling varying amounts of human labour, varying herd sizes, and varying amounts and grades of pastureland. The human demography of pastoralism exacerbates this instability. Pastoralism lacks the cultural checks to population growth common in hunter-gatherer societies. The use of animal traction power makes it easy to transport infants; while the needs of defence and the possibility of selling livestock and craft products make it easier to use their labour. In arid environments that can support only limited populations, such demographic behaviour inevitably leads to periodic over-population, even at population densities that are low by the standards of the agricultural world.

The instability of pastoralist life affects each household and each group. It inhibits the formation of stable class structures and creates a sort of equality of uncertainty.[69] Instability encourages a wariness and competitiveness analogous to that of capitalist society. Faced with chronic insecurity, pastoralists can rarely afford to stick rigidly to traditional territories or migration routes. Often, they will have to stray onto the pastures of neighbours in order to maintain their herds. In this way, the inherent instability of pastoralist lifeways leads to a constant jostling for pasturelands and inhibits the emergence of a strong sense of individual or even collective property in land. Jostling for land, and uncertainty about ownership lead to frequent raiding and sometimes large-scale warfare.

Raiding, in turn, encourages the cultivation of military skills, particularly, but not exclusively, amongst males. Military skills were particularly well developed among the horse-riding pastoralists of Inner Eurasia. Thus, the Chinese historian, Ssu-ma Ch'ien, who wrote at the end of the second century BCE, reported that amongst the Hsiung-nu:

> The little boys start out by learning to ride sheep and shoot birds and rats with a bow and arrow, and when they get a little older they shoot foxes and hares, which are used for food. Thus all the young men are able to use a bow and act as armed cavalry in time of war. It is their custom to herd their flocks in times of peace and make their living by hunting, but in periods of crisis they take up arms and go off on plundering and marauding expeditions.[70]

Pastoralist lifeways also provide a superb training in many of the skills of warfare. Managing large animals is a more strenuous and a more dangerous activity than managing plants, which are more passive than animals, and less likely to fight back. So pastoralist lifeways prepare much better than farming lifeways for the physical violence of warfare. This lifelong training is usually enhanced and intensified in the hunt, an activity typical of most pastoralist lifeways, and often used systematically as a training for war. As Walter Goldschmidt has argued, other aspects of pastoral nomadic lifeways also hone military skills.[71] The movement of large herds of animals provides training in the logistical skills of warfare, the capacity to navigate through unfamiliar country and to do so in formation with others. Finally, the complex scheduling of pastoralist migrations requires a capacity to coordinate movements over large areas.

Third, pastoralist societies have a remarkable capacity to mobilize rapidly in a crisis. Localized raiding may pit individuals or small groups against each other. However, large-scale raiding requires the formation of alliances that link the basic cells of pastoralist societies into large military and political alliances that can, on occasions, form vast empires. When this happens, slight inequalities in wealth, ability, or status are rapidly magnified, until there emerge steep hierarchies that have often been treated as evidence that true classes existed in pastoralist society. It is no accident that the best known attempt to prove the existence of pastoralist 'feudalism', that of Vladimirtsov, took its evidence mainly from the Mongol empire.[72]

How do such social hierarchies emerge in times of stress or conflict? A highly simplified model of pastoralist social structures in Inner Eurasia may help to understand these processes. At the simplest level of pastoralist society is the parental group (level 1). This consists of a mother and children, and often also a father. Usually, the parental group occupies a single dwelling, whether mobile (a yurt or wagon) or permanent. When nomadizing, pastoralists normally travel in small groups of related parental groups, known in Turkic languages as *auls*. We can call these 'camping' groups (level 2). They are analogous to the 'subsistence' groups of foraging communities, or what Khazanov calls the 'primary kin group'. Camping groups may consist of anything from 8–50 individuals. Modern studies suggest that their composition is highly unstable and can change from season to season or year to year as a result of changing fortunes or family conflicts.[73] Nevertheless, for much of the time, camping groups function as total societies, fulfilling educational, medical, economic, judicial and even military functions normally assumed today by the state. Camping groups are linked into wider networks of between 50 and several hundred people, which we can call 'reproductive' groups (level 3). Reproductive groups meet periodically, usually at winter camps, and heads of households or clan leaders may take collective decisions about migration routes, or internal and external conflicts. In normal times, most marriages probably take place within reproductive groups of this kind, so they also provided the basic framework for lineage systems and family networks.[74]

Table 4.2 Levels of social organization in pastoralist societies

Level 6	*Pastoralist states/empires*: 100,000s–millions; stable political structures formed by distribution of prestige goods acquired from agricultural regions; destruction of tribal ties; bureaucratization
Level 5	*Supra-tribal associations*: 1000s–100,000s; alliances of tribes, usually for military emergencies, temporary, supra-tribal leaders
Level 4	*Tribes*: 500–1000s; alliances of clans, often for military defence; loose leadership structures
Level 3	*Reproductive groups*: 50–500; related camping groups that meet periodically; led by individuals or heads of households; control over migration routes, disputes, etc.
Level 2	*Camping groups*: 8–50 people; Several related parental groups that travel together, highly unstable
Level 1	*Parental groups*: 2–8 people; mother + children, sometimes with father, sharing a dwelling (yurt, wagon)

Face-to-face relations and kinship ties, both biological and symbolic, provide the basic structures of these three levels of social organization. All three are essential to the normal functioning of pastoralist societies.

Above the reproductive group, other levels of organization may appear, particularly in times of crisis. These are not necessary for the normal functioning of pastoralist communities and usually exist in latent forms, ready to be mobilized when needed.[75] For present purposes, it is sufficient to distinguish three such levels. The fourth level I will call the 'tribe' (level 4). This is an alliance of several reproductive groups linked by kinship or other ties, and including up to a few thousand people. It may have strong leaders, or may be organized by meetings of clan heads. However, its members will usually think of themselves as linked by ties of lineage and kinship, and will usually enjoy a collective claim to particular lands.[76] At the next level, tribes may ally under a single leader (level 5), usually in times of warfare, and according to principles that anthropologists describe as 'segmentary opposition'.[77] Such supra-tribal associations may include tens of thousands, even hundreds of thousands of pastoralists, and they can often field large and powerful armies. Leadership may be provided by linked chiefly families, and the power of individual leaders is usually confined to particular emergencies. At this level, the sense of kinship is usually too tenuous to have real meaning, but it may well be retained in symbolic forms.

The highest level of all in pastoralist societies is the pastoralist state or empire (level 6). This level of organization emerged only amongst the horse pastoralists of Inner Eurasia.[78] Leaders at this level manage to form more durable political structures by locking regional groupings into long-lasting alliances. Sometimes they destroy regional tribal structures and replace them with new, and more centralized structures. The presence of mechanisms that prevent fissioning along tribal lines allows us to regard these as true states rather than 'chiefdoms' for, as Service has argued, the true state is a mechanism designed precisely to prevent splitting along segmentary lines.[79] However, creating pastoralist states was extremely difficult, and there is no firm evidence for their existence before the first millennium BCE.

Tribal and supra-tribal associations emerged more easily and much earlier, for they are a response to the chronic instability of the pastoralist world. They form when local groups face threats to their pasture lands from other pastoralists or from neighbouring agricultural states.[80] Faced with such threats, clans join related clans and tribes join related tribes. Intensified jostling is most likely when pastures are already overpopulated, for then even minor changes in migration routes can cause conflicts over large areas of steppe through a sort of domino effect. As a result, periods of intensified instability and increased mobility, leading to the creation of higher levels of organization, seem to occur with a certain regularity.

These fluctuations in levels of mobilization give us some clues when it comes to interpreting the complex archaeological evidence left behind by pastoralists. They can best be understood through a simple, but elegant model proposed by a Soviet archaeologist, Pletneva, that captures well the unstable dynamics of Inner Eurasian pastoralism. Pletneva's model describes three distinct phases of pastoralist mobilization. The first phase is one of pure nomadism.[81] During such phases, whole communities may move in search of new pastures, usually in response to ecological disasters or military defeat. Some households may be forced out of the steppes altogether. Generally, this is a phase of great social, ethnic and linguistic confusion, and also of more or less continuous military emergency, that encourages the appearance of larger social and political groupings. Mobility ensures that pastoralists in this phase of military mobilization are unlikely to leave extensive archaeological remains, though they may leave evidence of widespread disruption, and they may also leave enduring memories of past unity and glory in epic verse. As alliances form, camping and reproductive groups may dissolve into larger groups that are more powerful and better organized. Strong leaders appear from leading families, often according to the rules that Joseph Fletcher described as 'blood tanistry': 'the principle of succession that the most talented male member of the royal clan should inherit the throne, commonly by murder and war'.[82] Such leaders preside over large tribal or supra-tribal armies of pastoralists. However, these large groups are inherently unstable. Their very size threatens to destroy the pastures through which they travel. Besides, the initial goal of their migrations is usually to defend old pastures or find new pastures in which it is possible to resume more stable kinds of pastoralism.

Pletneva's second phase is one of semi-nomadism.[83] As warfare and evictions reduce pressure on existing pastures, pastoralists begin once more to travel in camping groups along more or less regular migration routes. They demobilize. Tribal and supra-tribal structures lose their political significance, though they may survive in the historical memory, in epic poetry, and in a widespread sense of shared identity analogous to modern forms of ethnicity. This explains why, despite their highly segmented social structures, pastoralists often retain a strong sense of belonging to wider communities.

Pletneva's third stage is characterized by sedentism. Loss of livestock or pastures may force some pastoralists to engage in agriculture or trade, and some may begin to form more permanent settlements. Recent research has shown that small agricultural communities probably existed within most pastoralist steppe cultures, either as tribute-paying farmers or where pastoralists supplemented pastoralism with part-time farming of some kind. Such communities may well have satisfied the significant but limited dietary needs of pastoralist communities for some agricultural produce.[84] In periods of warmer and wetter climates, agriculture may spread more widely in lands once suited only to pastoralism. Whole towns may appear in the steppes, often clustering around the winter camps of regional leaders, which are usually in more fertile regions at the edge of the true steppes. Modern examples, from Turkey to the suburbs of Ulaanbaatar, show how, as pastoralists settle down, their tents become more permanent, acquire add-on rooms, and turn into houses, while their camps turn into villages or suburbs.[85] As pastoralists sedentize, they may integrate into the political and economic structures of the agricultural world. However, if demographic, political or climatic conditions change, they may once again begin to nomadize. If they do so, they may have to enter the first, highly nomadic phase, until they can establish new migration routes.

As early as the fourth millennium, there are hints of a longer periodicity to the pattern of mobilization in the Inner Eurasian steppes. Observers of pastoralist societies have noted such cycles ever since the time of Ibn Khaldun, but modern anthropologists have tended to treat such 'migrationist' theories with suspicion, perhaps because too much has been claimed for them. However, as Cribb notes, there is no reason to doubt the existence of large waves of migration in pastoralist regions: 'migratory episodes [such as the Turkic incursions of the eleventh and twelfth centuries] are not illusions but real events which are likely to have archaeological correlates.'[86]

The archaeological evidence suggests that there were periods of widespread disruption in the steppes from at least the second half of the fourth millennium, and perhaps earlier.[87] Among early mobile pastoralists, whose horse-riding skills and equipment remained rudimentary, these migrations were probably slow and stately affairs.[88] In the historic period, the nature of these rhythms can be seen clearly. First there are periods of large-scale mobilization, such as that of the Mongols under Chinggis Khan, in which pastoralists over large areas of steppe are swept up in large-scale military migrations. These were followed by longer periods, sometimes centuries long, in which the consequences of the initial migrations were slowly worked through right across the Inner Eurasian steppelands. During these periods, most pastoralists lived as semi-nomads, while some became sedentary.

What governed these rhythms is unclear. Perhaps they reflect a pastoralist version of the Malthusian cycles that historians such as Ladurie have described in the history of agrarian regions. Or perhaps they are linked to climatic changes. At present, our knowledge of the demographic and climatic history of Inner Eurasia is too crude to test such theories with any rigour. However, impressionistic evidence does suggest that periods of pastoralist mobilization were most likely in cooler and drier periods, when agriculture became unusually difficult in the steppes, and even pastoralism could no longer support large populations. This can be seen by comparing the chart of climatic change during the Holocene with table 4.4, which lists what seem to

Table 4.3 Fluctuations of temperature and rainfall during the Holocene

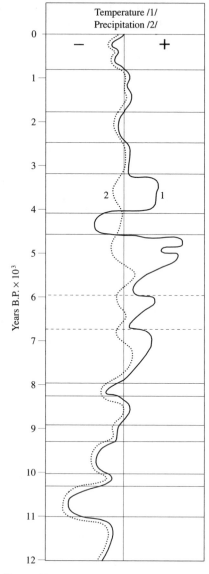

Source: Dolukhanov *Early Slavs*, p. 48.

have been the main periods of widespread mobilization in the steppes of Inner Eurasia.

This simple model may help make sense of the history of Inner Eurasia during the many centuries in which the rhythms of its history were dominated by the rhythms of pastoralist societies. If pastoralist lifeways did indeed emerge in fourth-millennium Ukraine and spread into the steppelands of

Table 4.4 Migratory cycles in the steppes: 3400 BCE–1200 CE

Date	Evidence of Migrations
c.3400–3200 BCE	Archaeological evidence of invasions
c.2600–2400 BCE	Archaeological evidence of invasions
c.1800–1600 BCE	Invasions of northern India? Chariots/Wagons?
c.1100–900 BCE	Invasions of Iran, Mesopotamia and the Balkans; creation of the Scythian Culture Zone
c.200–0 BCE	The Hsiung-nu Empire; migrations south and west
c.500–600 CE	Turkic Empires; migrations south and west
c.1200–1300 CE	The Mongol Empire

Russia and then Kazakhstan, we can presume that early pastoralists soon occupied most of the best pasture lands in these regions. On the model of pastoralist societies offered here, we should expect that jostling for position would have led to larger migratory movements. It is not surprising, therefore, that there are many hints of large migratory movements late in the fourth millennium. These suggest a return to the first of Pletneva's three phases, that of generalized warlike migrations over large areas. The fact that this was a period of drier climates, in which the area of high quality pasture land may have been shrinking, could explain the timing of these movements.

E. N. Chernykh, a specialist in the early history of metals in the former Soviet Union, has shown that a stable zone of trade in copper ores and goods, the 'Carpatho-Balkan' metallurgical province, collapsed late in the fourth millennium, under the pressure of massive, warlike migrations of pastoralist communities.[89] Pletneva's model suggests that during this phase pastoralists may have been organized in large tribal associations under powerful leaders. Despite frequent local conflicts, the similarity of the cultures of different pastoralist groups suggests frequent exchanges and, perhaps, a widespread sense of identity over large areas of the Inner Eurasian steppes.

These early migratory waves, which probably destroyed many of the neolithic cultures around the Black Sea, may represent the first great migrations of Indo-European language-speakers. The linguist, Harmatta, has drawn a picture of widespread migratory movements of pastoralists, using ox-drawn carts and led by powerful tribal leaders.[90] Chernykh has argued that the large number of ornamental metal goods found in steppeland burials in the late fourth millennium also indicates the appearance of aristocratic groups in the steppes led by powerful redistributive chiefs.[91]

In the course of these movements, pastoralists whose linguistic origins lay in the Russian steppes, occupied much previously unsettled land in the central steppes, and probably expelled the hunting and gathering populations that previously occupied these lands. They also began to exert considerable demographic and military pressure on neighbouring agrarian populations of Ukraine and the Balkans' as powerful chieftains sought valued goods with which to build up their own power.

By 3000 BCE, many of the patterns that were to dominate Inner Eurasian history for several millennia were already in existence. There had emerged several regional systems of interaction between hunter gatherers, farmers and horse pastoralists. The many links between different pastoralist communities ensured that these were joined into a larger, Inner Eurasian system, in which pastoralists played a role similar to that played by merchants in Outer Eurasia, by linking regional systems into a larger network stretching across much of the Eurasian landmass. Finally, in periods of widespread migrations, Inner Eurasian pastoralists invaded parts of Outer Eurasia from Mesopotamia to northern India and perhaps even northern China.

NOTES

1 Renfrew, *Archaeology and Language*, p. 125.
2 Dolukhanov, *Early Slavs*, p. 48.
3 Masson and Sarianidi, *Central Asia*, p. 42; and V. Sarianidi 'Food-producing and other neolithic communities, in Khorasan and Transoxania', *HCCA*, 1:115–16; recent work has shown the links of the Jeitun culture with sites on the Iranian plateau, and this suggests that its origins may date back to the middle of the seventh millennium. Kohl, ed., *Bronze Age Civilization*, p. xiv.
4 Masson and Sarianidi, *Central Asia*, p. 36.
5 Ibid., pp. 37, 40, 42; V. Sarianidi 'Food-producing and other neolithic communities' *HCCA*, 1:119.
6 Ibid. pp. 38, 44–5.
7 Dolukhanov, 'Foragers and farmers in west-Central Asia', p. 129.
8 V. Sarianidi 'Food-producing and other neolithic communities' *HCCA*, 1:118.
9 Dolukhanov, 'Foragers and farmers in west-Central Asia', pp. 123, 126.
10 Dolukhanov, 'Ecological prerequisites for early farming', in Kohl, ed., *Bronze Age Civilization* (pp. 359–85), pp. 372–5; Lattimore, *Inner Asian Frontiers of China*, pp. 155–7.
11 Lattimore, *Inner Asian Frontiers of China*, p. 155.
12 Masson and Sarianidi, *Central Asia*, pp. 41, 43–4.
13 J. Harmatta, 'The Emergence of the Indo-Iranians: the Indo-Iranian languages', *HCCA* (pp. 357–78), 1:371 and 375. Harmatta argues (p. 375) that the land of 'Harali' in a Sumerian hymn on trade with Tilmun, may well have been the Kopet Dag region, and that the name may be Dravidian.
14 Masson and Sarianidi, *Central Asia*, p. 45; Sarianidi, 'Food-producing and other neolithic communities', *HCCA*, 1:116 and 121.
15 Masson and Sarianidi, *Central Asia*, p. 44; Dolukhanov, 'Foragers and farmers in west-Central Asia', p. 129.
16 Khazanov, *Nomads*, p. 90; and see Dolukhanov, 'Foragers and farmers in west-Central Asia', p. 121.
17 V. M. Masson, 'The Bronze Age in Khorasan and Transoxania', *HCCA* (pp. 225–45), 1:228.
18 Ibid., 1:232, and A. I. Isakov, 'L'établissement de la culture paléoagricole dans la vallée du Zerafshan', in *L'Asie Centrale et ses rapports avec les civilisations orientales*, pp. 119–20; Isakov, 'Sarazm: an agricultural center'; and see L. P'yankova, 'Central Asia in the Bronze Age: Sedentary and nomadic cultures', *Antiquity*, (1994), 68:355–72, p. 355.

19 Masson and Sarianidi, *Central Asia*, p. 71; however, Kohl has argued that this may have been an old pattern in southern Central Asia, that first appears in the Jeitun culture. Kohl, ed., *Bronze Age Civilization*, p. xvi; see also Masson 'The Bronze Age in Khorasan and Transoxania', *HCCA*, 1:228 and Masson and Sarianidi, *Central Asia*, pp. 66–7.

20 Masson and Sarianidi, *Central Asia*, pp. 68–9.

21 This is the suggestion of Hiebert, *Origins*, p. 168; and see Dolukhanov, 'Ecological Prerequisites', pp. 378–80, and P'yankova, 'Central Asia in the Bronze Age', *Antiquity*, (1994), 68:355.

22 Fagan, *People of the Earth*, pp. 336–7.

23 McNeill, *Europe's Steppe Frontier*, p. 4.

24 Dolukhanov, *Early Slavs*, p. 199.

25 Fagan, *People of the Earth*, 7th edn, p. 335; Dolukhanov, 'Mesolithic and Neolithic', pp. 112–13.

26 Mallory, *In Search of the Indo-Europeans*, pp. 190–1; see map in Gimbutas, *Civilization of the Goddess*, p. 112, and see p. 460.

27 Their main site here was the Mariupol cemetery; Telegin, *Dereivka*, p. 1.

28 Telegin, *Dereivka*, p. 3; Dolukhanov, *Early Slavs*, p. 65.

29 This theory of the origins of Indo-European languages has been defended by the Soviet archaeologists, Gamkrelidze and Ivanov, and the British archaeologist, Colin Renfrew. For a summary, see Renfrew, *Archaeology and Language*, and his later essay, 'Before Babel'.

30 Mallory, *In Search of the Indo-Europeans*, p. 196.

31 Gimbutas, *Civilization of the Goddess*, p. 105, and see map, p. 102. Catal Huyuk in the seventh millennium, had *c.*7000 people; ibid., p. 17.

32 Phillips, *The Royal Hordes*, pp. 19–20.

33 Chernykh, *Ancient Metallurgy*, pp. 36–40; and see Dolukhanov, 'Mesolithic and Neolithic', p. 113.

34 Gimbutas, *Civilization of the Goddess*, pp. 324, 328–31.

35 Mallory, *In Search of the Indo-Europeans*, pp. 237–8; Dolukhanov, *Early Slavs*, p. 92.

36 Chernykh, *Ancient Metallurgy*, pp. 32–4.

37 Chang, *Archaeology of Ancient China*, 3rd edn, pp. 206–7.

38 Ibid., p. 398.

39 Novgorodova, *Drevnyaya Mongoliya*, p. 56, and see pp. 63–6; A. P. Derevyanko and D. Dorj, 'Neolithic tribes in northern parts of Central Asia', *HCCA* (pp. 169–89), 1:174–5, 180–1.

40 Okladnikov, 'Inner Asia at the dawn of history', in *CHEIA*, p. 70; Forsyth, *History of the Peoples of Siberia*, pp. 22–3.

41 Cited in Cribb, *Nomads*, p. 17, from Krader, 'Ecology of nomadic pastoralism', p. 499; Ekvall has described herds as 'fields on the hoof', cited Cribb, p. 34; the most important survey is Khazanov, *Nomads and the Outside World*; however I differ from him in using the term, 'pastoralism', rather than 'nomadism', to stress reliance on livestock rather than mobility as the central feature of their life-ways, and in emphasizing the importance of the 'secondary products revolution'; for a survey of the origins of pastoralism, see Ibid., pp. 85–9; there is a good general survey of pastoralism in Barfield, *The Nomadic Alternative*.

42 Sherratt 'Plough and pastoralism', pp. 261–305.

43 Ibid., p. 263.

44 Anthony and Brown, 'The origins of horseback riding', pp. 22–3; and Dolukhanov, *Early Slavs*, p. 70.

45 Anthony and Brown, 'The origins of horseback riding', pp. 45–7.
46 Cited in Barclay, *The Role of the Horse*, p. 14.
47 Sherratt, 'Plough and pastoralism', p. 275; Bulliet, *The Camel and the Wheel*, p. 56; Kuz'mina, *Drevneishye skotovody*, p. 36.
48 Bulliett, *The Camel and the Wheel*, pp. 148–53, and see V. M. Masson, 'The decline of the Bronze Age civilization and movements of the tribes', *HCCA* (pp. 337–56), 1:347 for the earlier date.
49 Sherratt, 'Plough and pastoralism', pp. 263–4, 270; and see Piggott, *The Earliest Wheeled Transport*, p. 35.
50 See E. J. W. Barber, 'Problems and methods of reconstructing prehistoric steppeland cloth and clothing', in Seaman, ed., *Foundations of Empire* (pp. 134–42), pp. 136–7.
51 Barclay, *Role of the Horse*, p. 99; and see Khazanov, *Nomads*, p. 53.
52 Dergachev, 'Neolithic and Bronze Age cultural communities', p. 796.
53 Ibid., p. 794. Chernykh dates them a millennium earlier than Dergachev. See Diagram in Chernykh, *Ancient Metallurgy*, p. 13.
54 Telegin, *Dereivka*, p. 129.
55 Dergachev, 'Neolithic and Bronze Age cultural communities', p. 796; on the importance of agriculture, see Mallory, *In Search of the Indo-Europeans*, p. 199.
56 Mallory, *In Search of the Indo-Europeans*, pp. 201, 234–6.
57 Ibid., p. 198.
58 Ibid., p. 202.
59 Chernykh, *Ancient Metallurgy*, p. 44; Mallory, *In Search of the Indo-Europeans*, pp. 206–7.
60 Khazanov dates the origins of true nomadic pastoralism to the first millennium BCE, though he concedes that there were some mobile pastoralists, who conducted large-scale migrations even in the third millennium; *Nomads*, pp. 92–4; however, as argued here, the evidence of steppe burials, and recent evidence of early horse riding both suggest that mobile pastoralism was considerably older.
61 Derevyanko and Dorj, 'Neolithic tribes in northern parts of Central Asia' *HCCA*, 1:185.
62 On the importance of 'key animals', see Barfield, *The Nomadic Alternative*, pp. 9–11.
63 Khazanov, *Nomads*, p. 7, makes the same point.
64 Cribb, *Nomads*, p. 16.
65 Ibid.
66 Mallory, *In Search of the Indo-Europeans*, p. 226, and Gryaznov, *Ancient Civilization of Southern Siberia*, p. 51.
67 See, for example, Mallory, *In Search of the Indo-Europeans*, p. 262 and passim for a recent discussion of such theories; the fact that early Indo-European languages contain many terms linked to pastoralism gives added support to such theories; see also Renfrew, *Archeology and Language*.
68 See the fine survey of Marxist discussions of this issue in Ernest Gellner's preface to Khazanov, *Nomads and the Outside World*, and see Khazanov's discussion on pp. 152–64.
69 Gellner puts it well: 'Nomadic societies know a certain equality (or at any rate a precariousness of fortune precluding stable and internalised inequality)', foreword to Khazanov, *Nomads*, p. xi; Cribb, *Nomads*, p. 18 and passim regards instability as one of the central features of pastoralism.

70 The 110th chapter of the *Shih chi* is on the Hsiung-nu. See Ssu-ma Ch'ien, *Records*, 2:155.
71 Goldschmidt, 'A general model for pastoral social systems'.
72 See Gellner's foreword to Khazanov, *Nomads*, pp. xv, xxiii.
73 Khazanov, *Nomads*, p. 128; Cribb, *Nomads*, p. 45.
74 Cribb, *Nomads*, p. 49; reproductive groups are similar, but not identical, to Khazanov's 'communities of the second order'. Khazanov, *Nomads*, pp. 132–3.
75 Khazanov, *Nomads*, p. 148.
76 For a fuller and more nuanced discussion of the various uses and meanings of the word, 'tribe', in pastoralist societies, see Khazanov, *Nomads*, pp. 149–52.
77 'In any serious dispute between members of different minimal lineages, all outside groups more closely related to one contestant than the other take the side of their nearer kinsmen, and the issue is then joined between the highest order lineages thus involved.' Sahlins, *Tribesmen*, pp. 50–1.
78 Barfield, *The Nomadic Alternative*, p. 17.
79 Cohen and Service, *Origins of the State*, p. 4.
80 Khazanov, *Nomads*, pp. 148–9, lists some of the relevant factors.
81 Pletneva, *Kochevniki srednevekov'ya*, passim and summary, p. 145; ch. 1 refers to a *tabornyi* or 'camping' phase; Cribb borrows Ingold's term, 'untied' pastoralism to describe this phase, *Nomads*, p. 18.
82 Fletcher, 'Turco-Mongolian monarchic tradition in the Ottoman empire', pp. 236–51; see also Fletcher, 'Blood Tanistry'.
83 Cribb, *Nomads*, p. 18, describes this as 'tied' pastoralism.
84 Khazanov, *Nomads*, pp. 69–84 has stressed the importance of this need, but di Cosmo, 'Ancient Inner Asian nomads', pp. 1113–14, argues that demand was probably limited to what could be produced by casual agriculture or the presence of small agricultural communities in the steppe.
85 Cribb, *Nomads*, p. 161.
86 Cribb, *Nomads*, p. 58, and Khazanov, *Nomads*, p. 94.
87 See Chernykh, *Ancient Metallurgy*, pp. 302–7.
88 Khazanov, *Nomads*, p. 94.
89 Chernykh, *Ancient Metallurgy*, p. 52.
90 J. Harmatta, 'The Emergence of the Indo-Iranians: the Indo-Iranian languages', in *HCCA*, 1:367–8; Chernykh, *Ancient Metallurgy*, p. 304; there are hints of even earlier migrations, in the mid-fifth millennium, Gimbutas, *Civilization of the Goddess*, pp. 361ff.
91 Chernykh, *Ancient Metallurgy*, pp. 159, 163.

FURTHER READING

On the earliest farming societies of Central Asia, see *HCCA*, vol. 1; Masson and Sarianidi, *Central Asia* (which is still valuable though showing its age); and Kohl, *Bronze Age Civilization*. On the western region, see Gimbutas, *Civilization of the Goddess*, and the more popular account in Phillips, *The Royal Hordes*. On the 'secondary products revolution', the crucial essay is Sherratt, 'Plough and pastoralism'. There is a large literature on the early history of pastoralism. Khazanov, *Nomads and the Outside World*, Barfield, *The Nomadic Alternative*, and Cribb, *Nomads in Archaeology* offer good introductions. *HCCA*, volume 1, surveys the archaeology of early pastoralism. So does Mallory, *In Search of the Indo-Europeans*, which also offers a good introduction to the complex linguistic problem of the relationship between pastoralism and the spread of the

Indo-European languages. Gimbutas, *Civilization of the Goddess*; and Renfrew, *Archaeology and Language*, take opposing sides in this debate. Telegin, *Dereivka*; Anthony, 'The origins of horse-back riding'; and Dolukhanov, *Early Slavs*, survey the earliest evidence of horse riding. Pletneva, *Kochevniki srevnevekov'ya*, offers a valuable model of the way pastoralist communities evolve; while Goldschmidt, 'A general model', explores some social, technological and psychological aspects of pastoralism. Chernykh, *Ancient Metallurgy*, focuses on changing technologies, while Sahlins, *Tribesmen*, is a general introduction to tribal social structures. On the eastern region, see Chang, *Archaeology of Ancient China*, and Novgorodova, *Drevnyaya Mongoliya*.

[5] *The Bronze Age: 3000–1000 BCE*

T<small>HE</small> migratory wave of the late fourth millennium coincides with the beginning of the Bronze Age. The tradition of dating whole archaeological eras by the types of objects that dominate their archaeological record goes back to the nineteenth century, when, in the absence of modern dating techniques, archaeologists could offer only relative dates based on the types of objects they found in successive layers of archaeological excavations. By convention, the Bronze Age refers to the third and second millennia BCE. Bronze technology was not the most significant aspect of Bronze Age history, either in Outer Eurasia or Inner Eurasia, but the terminology remains useful just because it is so widely used. The most important features of the Inner Eurasian 'Bronze Age' were: the development of pastoralist lifeways and their expansion to the central and eastern steppes; the emergence of flourishing towns and cities in the oases of southern Central Asia; and the evolution of durable relations of exchange and symbiosis between these very different worlds.

Pastoralism in the Third and Second Millennia BCE

T<small>HE THIRD MILLENNIUM</small>: SHIFTING EASTWARDS

Soviet archaeologists conventionally dated the early Bronze Age from the late fourth millennium to *c.*2500 BCE; the middle Bronze Age to about 1800 BCE; and the Late Bronze Age to the end of the second millennium. Conveniently, this scheme coincides with what appear to have been three great migratory waves in the steppes. The first occurred late in the fourth millennium, the second in the middle of the third millennium, and the third quite early in the second millennium. Climatically, the early Bronze Age coincides with the last phase of the Climatic Optimum, while the middle Bronze Age appears to coincide with a period of rapid cooling, and the late Bronze Age with a final few centuries of unusually warm, wet climates. It is tempting to see correlations between these various changes, but at present our evidence is too thin to allow any certainty on the matter.

In the western steppes, the pit-grave (*yamnaya*) group of pastoralist cultures flourished late in the second half of the fourth millennium and for much of the third millennium. They extended for some 3000 kilometres, from the Bug and Dniester rivers in the west, to the Ural river. Similarities in pottery styles have convinced most archaeologists that they are direct descendents of the Sredny Stog and Khvalynsk cultures.[1]

As the name suggests, most evidence for the pit-grave cultures comes from burials; indeed, their main distinguishing feature is the use of shafts or pits (*yama* in Russian) for burials. The few settlements that have been excavated were probably temporary encampments rather than permanent villages.[2] In the Volga region there are hardly any settlements. Even further west, there are fewer settlements than in the fourth millennium. The most important exception to this rule is the large, and later fortified, settlement of Mikhaylovka which eventually covered some 1.5 hectares. Here, querns and flint sickle blades show the importance of agriculture. However, most pit-grave groups depended primarily on stock-breeding. Some sites are in the deep steppe, in regions whose soils were inappropriate for agriculture, while the animal remains in many burials consist mainly of sheep and goats, the animals most suited to nomadic pastoralism.[3] A study of some 800 Bronze Age graves from the open steppes of south Ukraine and Russia, from *c*.3000–1000 BCE has shown that throughout this period whole families lived in the steppes, depending mainly on domesticated animals. Such groups must have been nomadic, for modern ethnographic evidence suggests that to find enough pasture in dry regions such as the lower Volga steppelands, even small groups of pastoralists have to keep on the move.[4]

The archaeological evidence even allows us to glimpse distinct varieties of pastoralism by the third millennium BCE. Sheep and goats were important in the steppes north of the Black Sea and along the lower Volga, whereas cattle and pigs were more common in the foothills of the northern Caucasus, where pastoralism has usually been less nomadic. Horses were more common in the feathergrass steppes of the Don. Forms of agriculture combined with stockbreeding persisted along the lower Dnieper.[5]

The pit-grave cultures contain the first definite evidence for the use of wheeled vehicles on the steppe. Many pit-grave burials include wheels, and some include complete wagons, both two-wheeled and four-wheeled. They were almost certainly pulled by oxen, as early breeds of horses were probably too weak to pull them. However, there is also evidence of horse riding.[6] The presence of weapons such as arrowheads, daggers, axes and maces shows the importance of raiding and warfare. Even more striking is the fact that so many goods found in kurgans seems to have come from elsewhere. According to Chernykh, as much as 60 per cent of the metal goods made in agricultural metal-working zones in the middle Bronze Age ended up in pastoralist kurgans. As most of these goods seem to have been made for ornamental rather than utilitarian functions, their movement into the steppes suggests that they were used by pastoralist chiefs who built up their power by acquiring and redistributing prestige goods produced mainly in agrarian communities. Such evidence shows that pastoralists, farmers and artisans of the western area already formed part of a single regional system of exchanges, that Chernykh has called the 'Circumpontic metallurgical province'. This survived until c.1800 BCE.[7]

During the early and middle Bronze Age, pastoralist lifeways spread in south Siberia and the Central Asiatic steppes.[8] It is tempting to suppose that these movements reflect over-population in the western steppes, or perhaps the impact of cooler, drier climates in the middle of the third millennium.

The first major pastoralist culture of the central steppes is known as the 'Afanasevo' culture, after the site of Afanasyeva Gora, first excavated in 1920. Afanasevo sites extend from the Hangai mountains in Mongolia to the Yenisei, and from the southern Urals to parts of modern Kazakhstan. However, the most important area is the Minusinsk basin, near modern Krasnoyarsk. Most archaeologists date the Afanasevo culture to the mid-third millennium, though some radiocarbon dates suggest it appeared even before 3000 BCE.[9]

Most Afanasevo sites are burials, though at least ten are also settlements. The small number of burials at any one site suggests that people lived in small groups of perhaps only a few families. The shortage of settlement sites suggests that these were mobile pastoralists, with some sedentary populations scattered amongst them, though hunting was also important.[10] The Afanasevans used wheeled vehicles, for more than 100 carts or wagons have been found in burials from east of the Urals dated to before 2200 BCE.[11] The Afanasevo culture is the earliest Copper and Bronze Age culture of the Central Asian steppes. Its inhabitants could not cast metal, but they used native ores from shallow open shafts in the Altai and Kalbin hills, beating them with stone hammers and smelting them in primitive furnaces. There emerged in this period a distinct metal-mining and working tradition in the Altai mountains, whose remains include copper needles and knives, as well as silver, gold and meteorite iron ornaments.[12]

The people of the Afanasevo culture were almost certainly of Europoid origin, and their cultural remains show close similarities with those of the 'pit-grave' cultures of the western steppes. As in the pit-grave cultures, people were buried with flexed legs, ochre is present, and grave-goods include livestock, as well as ceramics. Both its human remains and its artefacts tempt us to see the Afanasevo culture as the product of migrations from further west, combined, perhaps, with the assimilation of local hunter-gatherer populations. So does the fact that most Inner Eurasian pastoralists of the first millennium BCE spoke Indo-European languages.[13]

Such hints confirm the impression of an expanding zone of pastoralism, originating in the west, and dominating the western and central steppes by c.2000 BCE. Mallory concludes that: 'the evidence is slowly accumulating to support the existence of a vast extension of material culture, economy, ritual behaviour and physical type from the Pontic-Caspian eastwards to the Yenisei by about 3000 BC.'[14]

All in all, it seems that by the middle of the third millennium, we are already dealing with a single expanding zone of pastoralist lifeways, whose different archaeological 'cultures' reflect only minor regional differences.

The size of this zone reflects the high mobility of pastoralist cultures, and the amount of technological, cultural and economic exchange that went on between different pastoralist regions.

THE SECOND MILLENNIUM: THE 'STEPPE BRONZE' CULTURES

The many signs of turbulence early in the second millennium allow us to speak with some confidence of a period of large-scale migrations in this period. One of the clearest signs is the appearance of many fortified settlements in the steppes. Indeed most early settlements of the second millennium 'Andronovo' culture had at least rudimentary earthen defences.[15] Evidence of pastoralist incursions appears from Mesopotamia, where there appear new peoples such as the Hyksos, to North India, where the Harappan civilization collapses, and perhaps even to China, where it is possible that pastoralist barbarians destroyed the Hsia dynasty some time between 1800 and 1600 BCE. The scale of the migrations of the early second millennium, and the uniformity of the steppe bronze cultures that appeared in their wake in the western and central steppes, suggest the possibility that there took place large-scale conquests, organized, presumably, by tribal or supra-tribal alliances of pastoralists.

Archaeological, linguistic and mythological research all suggest that the Central Asian steppes, in which many of these migrations originated, were the linguistic homeland of the Indo-Iranian branch of the Indo-European languages.[16] Both linguistic and mythological evidence suggest that the Aryan invaders of India came from a land of pastoralists with some agriculture, who reared cattle, horses and camel. They also took with them knowledge of a new weapon, the horse-drawn chariot. The elaborate horse burials of the Sintashta culture, near modern Magnitogorsk, with their carefully arranged horse burials, show the ritual importance of horses in the pastoralist cultures of the Kazakh steppes. Recent evidence shows that they also contained some of the earliest known light carts or 'chariots', dating from c.2000 BCE.[17] Memories of such chariot burials were apparently carried south into India for chariots are described in the 'Rig Veda', where they were used either for the hurling of spears, or in ritual races. Indeed, it is probable that migrants from the steppe early in the second millennium introduced both the horse and the chariot into India. The same cultural complex also travelled eastwards, for horse riding, chariots and perhaps even horse burials entered the eastern steppes and China during the second millennium.[18] However, though chariots transformed warfare in much of Outer Eurasia in the second millennia, and their introduction made the sedentary world familiar for the first time with the use and management of horses, they probably vanished from the steppes after c.1500 BCE, to be replaced by horse-riding archers using short compound bows.[19]

Metallurgical techniques also spread widely early in the second millennium. Chernykh has shown that there appeared a group of new 'metallurgical provinces' after c.1800 BCE. These expanded northwards into parts of Siberia

Table 5.1 Chart of Central Asian dates in the Bronze Age

	Bactrian Desert Oasis tradition	Margiana Desert Oasis tradition	Eastern Kopet Dag tradition	Central Kopet Dag tradition	Western Kopet Dag tradition
— 1500 BC					
	Molali Period	Takhirbai Period	?	Late Namazga VI	Anau IV A
— 1700 BC					
	BMAC*	BMAC	BMAC burials	Namazga VI	
— 1900 BC					
	—	Late Namazga V	Altyn depe (Exc 1), 0–2	Late Namazga V	Anau III
— 2200 BC					
	—	—	Altyn depe (Exc 1), 3–8	Namazga IV–V	
— 2700 BC					
	—	Geoksyur campsites	Geoksyur	Namazga III–IV	
— 3500 BC					
	—	—	Ilgynly I, II	Namazga II, Namazga I	Anau II Anau Ia, Ib
— 5500 BC					

*BMAC = Bactria-Margiana Archaeological Complex.
Source: Hiebert *Origins of the Bronze Age Oasis Civilization in Central Asia*, p. 166.

(where they brought forest-dwelling communities within the metal-using zone for the first time), southwards into Central Asia, and also eastwards to include much of Kazakhstan as well as the Mongolian steppes and even parts of north China. There is strong evidence that bronze casting techniques developed independently in China, so that these new 'metallurgical' provinces may reflect a merging of the metallurgical traditions of China and the far west. There also appeared new metallurgical centres in eastern Kazakhstan and the Altai, where there were rich and accessible deposits of tin and copper.[20]

The end of this period of large-scale migrations is reflected in the western and central steppes by the appearance of more open, less well defended settlements of the so-called 'steppe bronze' cultures. The best-known 'cultures' of this period are the Andronovo communities of the central steppes and the Srubnaya (timber-grave) cultures west of the Ural river.[21] The cultures of the western and central steppelands are so similar that some researchers regard them as parts of a single complex of cultures reaching from Ukraine to east Kazakhstan.

The most striking feature of these cultures is that, unlike most steppe cultures of the third millennium, steppe bronze communities were largely sedentary. There appear large areas dominated by a sedentary pastoralism, similar, perhaps, to that of the Sredny Stog culture, or even to modern

Cossack communities. Archaeologically, the clearest sign of increasing sedentism is the increase in the number of settlement sites which resemble villages rather than pastoralist campsites. At least 150 Andronovo villages have been excavated.[22] As Khazanov has argued, this change may reflect the warmer and wetter climates of the later second millennium, which made agriculture more viable in the steppes.[23]

The steppe bronze cultures embrace a large region including forest-steppelands from Ukraine to the Yenisei and steppelands further south as far as the Pamirs in modern Tajikistan. Most steppe bronze communities lived mainly from domesticated animals. Evidence of the importance of milk in the diet, and the remains of animal bones and animal-handling implements all show that these were, first and foremost, pastoralist cultures, however sedentary.[24] However, agriculture assumed greater importance on the partially forested fringes of the steppes, while sheep pastoralism was more important in the steppes, the semi-desert, and mountainous regions.[25] Andronovo settlements had large herds of horses and bred hardy sheep that could forage beneath the snow when necessary, and produced fine quality wools. Settlements on the open steppes used water from wells. Some may have practised a form of transhumance, for steppe bronze sites have also been found high in the T'ien Shan and Pamir mountains.[26] Kuz'mina has suggested that it may have been normal amongst most Andronovo communities for shepherds to nomadize with the village's livestock during the summer, while most of the village remained at home to tend crops. The migration routes of Andronovo shepherds can still be traced today, and modern migration routes usually follow them, for they run between sources of water or places where wells could be dug.[27]

There are clear signs of social hierarchies in the steppe bronze cultures. In many Andronovo sites there appear elaborate burials of single individuals in impressive *kurgany* whose construction must have involved the organized activities of entire tribes. Presumably, these were the tombs of important chiefs or war leaders. Occasionally, wives may have been buried with husbands, certainly amongst chiefly families.[28]

Most steppe bronze settlements were small (10–20 houses). The houses were mainly built of wood, though in the deep steppe they also used stone. Particularly in the earlier steppe bronze settlements, they were usually rectangular, and often partially sunk in the ground up to 1 or 1.5 metres. The houses themselves were large, as livestock were kept in them in winter, and many contain internal storage pits. The houses are more like the dwellings described in the early Indo-Iranian epics such as the Vedas, than the small brick and stone structures of southern Central Asia.[29] This supports the notion that during the turbulent early part of the second millennium, migrants from Andronovo populations may have migrated south and formed the Indo-Iranian speaking populations of northern India and Iran. However, in later settlements many houses are round, originating, perhaps, in the temporary huts of steppe bronze shepherds. The similarities in construction between these oval or circular dwellings, and later yurts suggests that the mobile dwellings of later cultures may have evolved as steppe bronze societies became more mobile again towards the end of the second millennium. Andronovo pastoralists also began to use dwellings on carts like the Scythic cultures of the first millennium.[30]

Movements of steppe bronze peoples can often be traced through their characteristic hand made ceramics, fired on open fires and decorated with stamps or geometric patterns of lines. These show that steppe bronze communities began to settle in the agricultural regions of southern Central Asia. There are steppe bronze settlements in the Khorezm region, and around the delta of the Syr Darya. These belong to the Tazabagyab culture, and are probably the earliest agricultural or pastoralist cultures of ancient Khorezm. Some of these settlements may have used simple forms of irrigation.[31] Steppe bronze sites also appear further south, along the Zerafshan, and even in Turkmenistan. In the hilly southern rim of Central Asia, and particularly in the mountainous region that stretches from the Middle Amu Darya to Ferghana, pastoralists and farming communities often merged.[32]

PASTORALISM IN THE EASTERN STEPPES

At some time in the second millennium, pastoralism began to spread in the eastern steppes. At present, our understanding of the chronology of these processes is sketchy. There is no doubt that Central Asian pastoralists played an important role in the evolution of pastoralism in the eastern steppes. There is some evidence for migrations, perhaps as early as the third millennium, from the central steppes into the steppes north of the T'ien Shan mountains. These hint at the possibility that the central steppes were already densely populated, perhaps even *over*-populated, by the second millennium. In recent years, more than 100 Caucasoid corpses have been discovered in Sinkiang, including the astonishing mummies now shown in the Urumchi museum. The oldest of these corpses date from as early as 2000 BCE, and they suggest that most of the population of Sinkiang at this period were of western origin.[33] Further east, though most physical remains are east Asian, the cultural and material remains from the second millennium show signs of strong influences from the central steppes.

However, China also played an important role in the evolution of pastoralism in the eastern steppes. North of the main zones of irrigated agriculture in the valleys of the Huang He and its tributaries, there were large communities of agricultural barbarians at least as early as the Shang dynasty (eighteenth to twelfth centuries BCE?). Powerful agricultural barbarian states such as those of the various 'Ti' tribes continued to play an active role in north Chinese political history even during much of the first millennium.[34]

Pastoralism evolved in the eastern steppes only after a prolonged period in which early agricultural communities lived, like those of the Tripolye farmers, amidst communities of hunters and gatherers. In the more favourable climates that prevailed during the middle and later centuries of the second millennium, the early forms of pastoralism in the eastern steppes were probably quite sedentary, like the steppe bronze cultures further west. As Lattimore suggested, pressure from the expanding populations of Chinese agriculturalists probably forced marginal farmers into arid lands whose aridity and poor soils forced them to specialize in stock-breeding.[35] In this way, the pressure of growing agricultural populations in the Chinese heartland was felt deep in the steppes, even though many elements in the pastoralist lifeways of the east may have been imported from the central steppes.[36]

The first evidence of such processes appears on the borders between the central and eastern steppes early in the second millennium. Here, there appeared pastoralist cultures which show strong influences from both Central Asia and China. They also show a capacity to resist migratory pressures from the west. Indeed, for the first time, there appear migratory countercurrents in the steppes, moving from east to west. These presumably reflect the powerful military and demographic pressure exerted by an expanding Shang China. Signs of growing influence from the east first appear in southern Siberia, in the so-called 'Okunev' culture, which in some areas replaced the Afanasevo culture early in the second millennium. Anthropologically, the Okunev people are east Asian rather than Europoid.[37] Okunev settlements seem to have been larger than Afanasevo settlements, and the wealth of some tombs suggests the emergence of powerful regional chiefs. Gryaznov writes:

> we can observe a distinct rise in the standard of living, shown by the fact that the occupants of the tombs were frequently clad in richly embroidered garments, from which there survive, in addition to the sable teeth... small beads of soft stone, white, brown and black in colour, and a variety of plaques and ornaments.[38]

Oxen were used to draw carts, as is shown on a stone carving. Cast metal implements appear for the first time, some of them apparently weapons.[39] The art work of this culture is magnificent. It includes many carved stone stelae with figures half human and half animal.

One of the most intriguing hints of the growing importance of pastoralism in the eastern steppes appears in what archaeologists refer to as the 'Seima-Turbino' complex of sites. These provide the first, shadowy, evidence of warlike migrations of eastern pastoralists towards the west. Seima-Turbino sites appear right across northern Eurasia, from western Mongolia to Finland and the Carpathians and date to the middle of the second millennium. They appear to be the remains of small groups of metal-workers and mounted warriors, who invaded westwards from the Altai region, right across to Moldova, but remained north of the main steppe bronze centres. Their burials show a warrior culture, whose members used bone armour and bronze weapons, as well as two-wheeled chariots. As they moved west, they probably incorporated people from the Siberian forest communities they conquered. Pictures on ornaments show warriors travelling by river, and also by ski, while being towed by horses.[40] Here are the very earliest known precursors of the great Mongol invasions of the thirteenth century ce. However, their invasion route, north of the steppes, suggests they were not yet strong enough to challenge the steppe bronze societies of the steppelands.

The Karasuk cultures of the thirteenth to tenth centuries reflect even more strongly the pressure on the central steppes of an emerging east Asian pastoralism, with an expansionist dynamic of its own. Eventually, sites of the Karasuk culture replaced Andronovo sites in many areas of southern Siberia and northern Central Asia. Sites with similar features can be found from the Volga to Khorezm to Anyang in China.[41]

Despite many similarities to the Andronovo cultures, particularly in pottery and ornamentation, the Karasuk culture has distinctive features, including a very high standard of bronze metallurgy. Livestock was extremely important, and Gryaznov suggests that Karasuk lifeways may have been more mobile than those of the Andronovo culture.[42] However, some Karasuk communities retained a semi-sedentary way of life, for in the Minusinsk region some large dugout dwellings have been found:

> The houses in...winter settlements looked from the outside like earthen mounds; but under the mounds were spacious rectangular structures with an area of 100 or 200 square metres, sunk into the ground to a depth of 1 1/2 metres or so. The domed or pyramidal roof was covered with a thick layer of earth from the excavation of the house, and in the middle was an aperture to admit light and let out smoke from the fire. This chimney was probably used as an entrance to the house when the ground was frozen hard, although there was also an entrance on one side of the mound. We can deduce the structure of these Karasuk dwellings from the analogy of the underground houses of similar size and type belonging to the Palaeo-Asiatic tribes, which had an entrance through the chimney, using a ladder in the form of a tree-trunk with notches cut in it.[43]

Objects in these houses show a world of largely self-sufficient families who cast their own bronze, carved bone tools, made yarn from vegetable fibres, and wove cloth to make clothing, as well as making their own pottery. It seems likely that such people lived a semi-nomadic life, planting crops around their winter settlements while they left for summer camps, then returning to harvest their crops in the autumn.[44]

The appearance, during the second millennium, of regions of pastoralism in the western Mongolian steppes began a process that was to be completed only during the first millennium, when pastoralism eliminated the remaining farming populations of the eastern steppes.

URBANIZATION IN CENTRAL ASIA: THE 'OXUS' CIVILIZATION

THE THIRD MILLENNIUM: URBANIZATION ALONG THE KOPET DAG

As pastoralism spread through the steppes, in southern Central Asia there appeared Inner Eurasia's first urban civilizations. By the end of the fourth millennium, there already existed in the region of the Jeitun cultures and along the Tedzhen delta, farming communities large enough to be regarded as small towns. During the third millennium BCE, some expanded into small cities, first along the foothills of the Kopet Dag, and then in irrigated oases of the southern Central Asian plain.

Absolute dating is extremely tricky in the Central Asian Bronze Age. Russian specialists date the townships of the Namazga IV period roughly to the period from 2800–2200 BCE, the first cities of the Namazga V period to c.2300–1800 BCE; and the Namazga VI period to the remainder of the second millennium. On the other hand, the American archaeologist, Philip Kohl has argued that the Namazga V and VI periods are up to 500 years earlier than these dates. However, there is general agreement about relative dates, and increased use of radiocarbon dating techniques may resolve these differences in the near future. The following account adopts the dating of the most recent study of the region, by Hiebert, which gives dates similar to those of Kohl.[45]

By the early Bronze Age, Kara-depe ('black hill'), which lies near the site of Namazga-depe in the foothills of the Kopet Dag, was already more than a small village. It may have had between 1000 and 1600 inhabitants, living no longer in the single-roomed houses typical of most of the fourth millennium, but in multi-roomed houses with inner courtyards, separated by narrow laneways.[46] Houses had several different living- and work-rooms, as well as courtyards, kitchens and storage areas. This suggests that they were occupied by large families, or perhaps by families and their employees or servants. There were also large squares which may have been used for public ceremonies or assemblies.

The early Bronze Age is associated with the Namazga IV period, which Kohl dates to the first half of the third millennium.[47] Painted ceramics similar to those of the Near East are typical of the Namazga IV period, and the use of the potter's wheel also spreads in this period, and shows the emergence of a division of labour extensive enough to support classes of specialists. Along the Kopet Dag, in regions based on rainfall farming, there appeared several large settlements with populations of up to 6–7000 people. The best known sites here are Altyn in the south-east, Namazga, and Anau, which is near modern Ashkhabad. These settlements had monumental religious architecture and some of the earliest fortifications to appear in this region. At Altyn-depe, there were large defensive walls and a fortified entrance. There also appear cylinder seals, similar to those of the Indus valley cultures, which suggests the importance of both trade and some degree of accounting or even literacy. In some sites of this period there are intriguing symbols carved on to figurines, which suggest early forms of writing. For the first time we have clear evidence of significant social, economic, and perhaps political differentiation.[48]

True cities, with substantial monumental buildings and an extensive division of labour, first appear in Central Asia in the middle Bronze Age, in the Namazga V period.[49] The ruins of Namazga extend over 170 acres. Most of the houses had as many as 9–12 rooms, and courtyards. There are some signs of a system of water supply to the individual dwellings. One large building appears to be a temple. In what appears to be a suburb of artisans, people worked bronze, gold, silver, and even brass, and also made pottery. Metal-workers in Namazga made weapons and implements of many kinds, including spears, knives, daggers, awls, adzes, as well as many types of jewellery including mirrors, bracelets and pendants.[50]

Altyn-depe, in the Tedzhen delta, is the second major site from this period. It covers about 114 acres. The earliest signs of settlement at Altyn-depe date from the fourth millennium. In the third millennium, the settlement grew into a true city, with distinct artisan quarters, cluttered up with the kilns of potters. There is also a suburb whose inhabitants, judging by their graves, were much wealthier. Figurines contained in burials suggest that their occupants may have been warlords, while other burials may be of priests or priestesses.[51] In Altyn-depe, there is a large tower, built from half a million bricks. Outside it there were dwellings which may have belonged to priests and their families. In the middle of the third millennium a huge monumental gateway was erected. It was 15 metres wide, and divided into two alleys, the narrower one for pedestrians, and a wider one paved with stones for carts and wheeled traffic.[52]

With its variegated population of 6–7000 people, Altyn-depe presumably had a hinterland of smaller communities around it. Namazga certainly had such a hinterland, which suggests that such sites represent the appearance of rudimentary city-states, perhaps with Altyn-depe and Namazga-depe forming rival power centres. However, there is no evidence for the existence of secular rulers or a secular palace at either town. Towns such as Namazga and Altyn-depe lived from the products of local agriculture. Nearby villages grew wheat, barley, chick-peas and even grapes. Altyn-depe's inhabitants made much use of animals, both domestic and hunted, the latter including onager, Persian gazelle and wild goat.[53] They also used cattle to pull ploughs, and certainly used domestic animals to pull carts, as models have been found of camels or horses harnessed to carts. Presumably local villages exchanged foodstuffs for artisan products from the towns, as well as paying tributes of some kind.

Trade was already an important part of the economy of mid-Bronze Age cities. The domestication of camels and the use of animal-drawn carts encouraged long-distance trade. Traders may well have travelled this far from Sumer or Babylon.[54] Relations with Harappa seem to have been particularly close, as Harappan objects appear in Altyn-depe and there was a late third-millennium Harappan city, perhaps a trading outpost, on the banks of the Amu Darya at Shortugai in northern Afghanistan.[55]

Central Asian cities also traded with pastoralist communities to their north, and stimulated urbanization in other parts of Central Asia. The clearest signs appear in the Zamanbabin culture of the Zaravshan valley during the late third or early second millennium. Exchanges of pastoralist products against urban craft goods may have stimulated these exchanges, or it may have been the deposits of tin in the Ferghana valley that attracted traders from the Kopet Dag towards this region. However, it is clear that the emerging proto-towns of the Zerafshan and Ferghana valleys felt the influence of the steppelands as well as the urban centres to their south.[56]

THE SECOND MILLENNIUM AND THE 'OXUS' CIVILIZATION

Recent research has shown that in the late Bronze Age urbanization shifted eastwards into the oases of the Central Asian plains. Here, in lands that previously had supported only simple forms of irrigation and small village communities, there occurred an astonishing urban bloom at the end of the third millennium, in the Margiana oasis, further east in oases fed by the Amu Darya in northern Bactria and southern Tajikistan, and also along the Zerafshan valley. In these regions there emerged a distinctive oasis culture many of whose features have survived to the present day.[57] Though work here was pioneered by the Soviet archaeologists, Sarianidi and Masson, under perestroika and during the post-Soviet era, it has benefited from international cooperation. Sadly, many of its artefacts and sites have been destroyed during the prolonged civil war in Afghanistan.

The older urban centres, such as Altyn-depe and Namazga-depe, declined early in the second millennium, like many of the older cities of Sumer.[58] It may be that their collapse reflects over-population in a region not suited to intensive farming. However, not far to the east, along the Murgab river and the middle Amu Darya, new urban communities were built between c.2200 and 2000 BCE, and it is tempting to suppose that these were founded by communities from the older urban centres, who were forced to migrate because of population pressure in the Kopet Dag cities.[59] In Margiana, where now there is desert, there are some 150 sites dating from the second millennium. Indeed, the region around modern Mary (Merv) became the main centre of urban development in southern Central Asia in this period, and the real heart of the 'Oxus' civilization.[60] It may be that the same climatic changes that encouraged an increase in farming in the 'Steppe Bronze' cultures, also encouraged the establishment of towns in areas previously too arid to support them.

The earliest settlement levels in Margiana (corresponding to Namazga V), contain many objects that suggest they were settled by populations from the Kopet Dag region who adapted to the very different environments of the Margiana oasis. However, the iconography of sites from the first third of the second millennium (Namazga level VI), is very different, and suggests either the appearance of new cultural influences, or the symbolic efforts of an emerging state structure. These later sites have several distinctive features, including a tradition of unpainted ceramics, an entirely new iconography often appearing on small stone objects or cylinder seals, the systematic use of seals for the control of trade and tribute, and new settlement patterns based around large fortified centres described by the Soviet archaeologist, Tolstov, as *qala*.[61]

The *qala* have no prototypes in earlier sites of southern Central Asia and should be thought of as an adaptation to the particular conditions of a region of irrigated oases surrounded by regions best suited to pastoralism and trade. They were large, well fortified areas, covering several hectares. Like medieval European castles, they had thick walls with crenellations and bastions. They contained dense settlements within and unfortified villages outside. At their

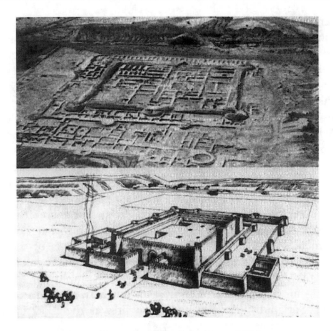

Plate 5.1 Reconstruction of a *qala*: Togolok 21, *c.*2000 BCE, reproduced from *Antiquity*, vol. 68, no. 259, June 1994.

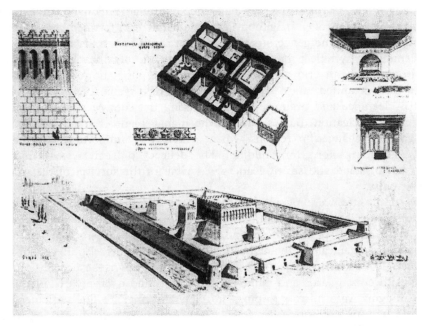

Plate 5.2 Reconstruction of a *qala*: Teshik Kala, *c.*600 BCE. Reproduced from *Antiquity*, vol. 68, no. 259, June 1994.

centre, there were usually separate fortified areas which were probably royal palaces, similar to the 'Arks' of later Central Asian settlements such as Bukhara.[62] Within some of the larger *qala*, such as those of Togolok, there were temples as large as any contemporary temples of Iran or Mesopotamia. The layout of these temples, with their gypsum-plastered white ritual rooms in which hallucinogenic drinks were made, their secret fire altars, and their courtyards surrounded with corridors, survived for over a millennium in Central Asia, and shows clear links with Vedic and later Zoroastrian practices.[63] Some of the larger buildings within the *qala* may have acted as trade centres or caravanserai. They certainly provided refuge for the herds of local pastoralists, some of whom may have lived in the oasis during the winter, but nomadized in the surrounding desert lands in spring.[64] But they also provided refuge for travellers and traders from elsewhere, for the oases depended on exchange systems to supply important raw materials including stone and metals. The most important Bronze Age sites of the Margiana oasis are Kelleli (the earliest), Gonur (the largest), and Togolok.[65] Further west, along the Amu Darya in Bactria, the most important fortified sites of this kind, at Sapalli and Dashly (in northern Afghanistan), appear slightly later. Sarianidi has described these sites as the 'Bactrian-Margiana Archaeological Complex' (BMAC).

In regions such as the Margiana oasis, the *qala* rather than the town was to become the typical form of settlement. Lamberg-Karlovsky has suggested that *qalas* represented a distinctive type of settlement, neither town nor city, and a distinctive style of rule, which he calls the 'khanate'.[66] If later analogies are any guide, city leaders may have ruled through regional landlords or *dihqans*, who controlled neighbouring settlements from fortified *qala* of their own. The rapid emergence of such a pattern at the beginning of the second millennium may reflect the growing complexity and organizational demands of irrigation in an arid area of rapidly growing populations. As irrigation networks expanded, they demanded increasing organization, during the initial clearance and drainage of land, during the construction and maintenance of irrigation ditches, and in the management of water rights and of goods exchanges in regions which lacked many important raw materials, including stone for building. The delicacy of such systems meant that having good and strong leaders was vital for the survival of the whole community.[67]

Bactrian sites were planned and fortified, like those of Margiana, but were perhaps less inegalitarian. Crafts were of a high level, and there appear the first signs of spoked wheels and horse riding. 'The pastoral/agricultural economy is organically combined with a developed commerce.... Exceptionally numerous are metallic objects, including notably weapons – especially battle-axes with cross-guards and tanged spearheads – and a variety of toilet articles, ranging from mirrors to pins, bracelets and rings.'[68] The settlement of Sapalli had at its centre a carefully designed fortress with mud-brick walls and towers. In its centre was a large, open square, with dwellings and workshops along its sides, each with hearths of a uniform design. Perhaps 230–50 people lived in the fortress.[69]

Remarkably, despite their contacts with Mesopotamia and northern India, the cities and forts of the Oxus culture seem not to have developed a fully literate culture, and this explains, in part, why all knowledge of them vanished until the twentieth century.[70]

PATTERNS OF EXCHANGE AND TRADE: A FIRST WORLD SYSTEM?

It is all too easy to think of the pastoralist world of the steppes and the urban world of southern Central Asia as distinct universes. In fact, there was a natural symbiosis between the two worlds. The oasis cities depended on neighbouring pastoralists for some of their supplies of food, and on networks of trade for many of their raw materials.[71] On the other hand, pastoralists controlled the lands through which their trade goods passed, and found in the oasis cities a useful source of agricultural produce and urban manufactures, as well as a link to the trade networks of Outer Eurasia. During the later Bronze Age, these links created a distinctively Inner Eurasian network of technological, symbolic and economic exchanges. As Frank and Gills have argued, this network, in its turn, became attached during the second millennium, to an emerging 'world-system' that joined Inner and Outer Eurasia, by merging regional networks in Mesopotamia and Egypt, northern India, and China. Central Asia was the key to this early 'world-system', which created a tenuous unity between all the major cultural and economic networks of the Eurasian landmass.[72]

In several late third millennium sites in Iran and northern India there appear complexes of objects made from copper, steatite and alabaster, which are clearly of Central Asian origin. These show that the cities of Margiana were actively involved in widespread networks of exchange. Their trade networks even reached as far as China (or at least Sinkiang), for the earliest finds of silk outside of China occur at Sapalli, in northern Bactria, early in the second millennium. The building of *qala* may also suggest the growing importance of trade, for they functioned, in part, as fortified caravanserais.[73] Indeed, as Tosi has argued, the difficult ecology of Central Asia meant that no flourishing culture could exist here unless it depended heavily on trade: 'International trade was to bring the Central Asian oases political stability and continuity of wealth, which would otherwise have been impossible. Agriculture was a dead end as far as economic development was concerned and the expansion of mercantile activities opened the road to a resolution of the looming conflict between increasingly incompatible strategies of primary production.'[74]

At the focal point of an emerging 'world-system', the cities of the 'Oxus civilization' were exposed to influences from an astonishingly wide range of different sources. There seems little doubt that they were founded by migrants from the towns of the Kopet Dag.[75] However, the new symbols that appear early in the second millennium suggest that many other influences

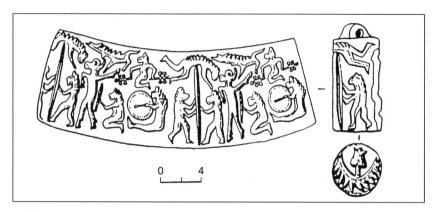

Figure 5.1 Margiana cylinder seal representing shamanic ritual, reproduced from *Antiquity* vol. 68, no. 259, June 1994.

were also at work. Phillipe Amiet has stressed the importance of cultural links with Mesopotamia, in particular, with Elam. He has argued that Margiana was a frontier zone in which Elamite traders exchanged goods with the steppes. Other writers have stressed the importance of Vedic or Avestan symbolism, which suggests close contacts with the emerging Indo-Iranian speaking diaspora of northern India and Iran. However, it is also possible to interpret some of the iconography of the many decorated seals, ceramics and metal ornaments of the Oxus civilization as signs of powerful influences from the steppes.[76] Direct evidence for contacts with pastoral nomads of the steppe bronze cultures appears in the presence of vessels manufactured by pastoral nomads in the *qala* of Gonur and Togolok. The use of hallucogenic substances similar to Vedic 'soma' or Zoroastrian 'haoma', in the temples of the Oxus *qala* can also be interpreted as evidence of shamanistic influences from the steppes.[77] These ritual substances were based on species of the ephedra plant, whose pith was crushed up and mixed with water or milk.[78] A fascinating cylindrical seal from the Togolok site shows acrobats wearing monkey masks and dancing to the beat of a drum. Indeed, Francfort has suggested that shamanistic influences may have been more important than those from the Middle East in the iconography of the Oxus civilization.[79] Sarianidi has argued that Zoroastrianism itself emerged in Margiana through a synthesis of the religions of steppe pastoralists and local urban communities with extensive contacts in Mesopotamia and northern India. If, as Boyce argues, Zoroaster lived in Central Asia some time between 1400 and 1000 BCE, there may have been a direct link between the religious traditions of Margiana in the second millennium, and the reformed religion of Zoroaster.[80] These different interpretations of the culture of the Oxus civilization are not mutually exclusive. On the contrary, they highlight the syncretic quality of the Oxus civilization as the focus of Eurasia-wide systems of intellectual and commercial exchanges.

The syncretism of the Oxus civilization was ecological as well as commercial and symbolic, for its *qala* were surrounded by pastoralists. There are many *kurgany* near settlements along the middle Amu Darya, south of modern Dushanbe, and these clearly belonged to pastoralist communities.[81] The interweaving of pastoralist and agricultural lifeways was particularly complex in the Ferghana valley. Here, some 80 sites are known from the so-called Chust culture, which dates from the end of the second millennium and the early first millennium. These sites appear in 15 distinct clusters, most of which seem to have been fortified clan settlements or towns, some with central citadels. Pottery designs suggest that the inhabitants were descendants of steppe pastoralists.[82] In the Khorezm delta, as we have seen, the earliest evidence of irrigation farming and pastoralism appears in the Andronovo communities of the Tazabagyab culture. In the Bronze Age, as in modern times, some oasis farmers engaged in semi-nomadic livestock herding, sending pastoralist shepherds out on summer migrations with their livestock. Such communities may even have founded settlements out in the desert as temporary summer camps.[83] Neighbouring communities of this kind could often form close ties based on exchanges of goods and services, of language, of culture, and even, if they intermarried, of kinship.

In these different ways, the populations of the steppes and the cities merged their religions, their lifeways and even their genes. Eventually, the Iranian languages of the steppe peoples began to displace the original languages of the Oxus cities, just as Turkic languages began to replace Iranian languages late in the first millennium of the modern era. Neither Outer Eurasian nor Inner Eurasian, the world of southern Central Asia was to remain what it became in the late Bronze Age, the main link between the different worlds of China, India, Mesopotamia and Inner Eurasia. If there was, as Frank and Gills have suggested, a 'world-system' of the second millennium BCE, the cities of Central Asia were its hub. They linked China, India and Mesopotamia, and they also linked the pastoralist and woodland cultures of Inner Eurasia to the agrarian cultures of Outer Eurasia.

NOTES

1 Mallory, *In Search of the Indo-Europeans*, pp. 210–11. Dergachev dates the pit-grave culture to a slightly later period, arguing that it arose between the twenty-seventh and twenty-fifth centuries BCE from the Volga to the Dnieper, then spread to the eastern Carpathians between the twenty-fifth and eighteenth centuries BCE. Dergachev, 'Neolithic and Bronze Age Cultural Communities', p. 796.
2 Shilov, 'Origins of migration and animal husbandry', p. 122.
3 Mallory, *In Search of the Indo-Europeans*, pp. 211–13.
4 Shilov, 'Origins of migration and animal husbandry', pp. 120–3.
5 Ibid., p. 124.
6 Mallory, *In Search of the Indo-Europeans*, p. 213; see also Piggott, *The Earliest Wheeled Transport*, pp. 54–60.
7 Chernykh, *Ancient Metallurgy*, pp. 55, 159, 165.
8 Dergachev, 'Neolithic and Bronze Age cultural Communities', p. 798; the best general study of the archaeology of southern Siberia, though slightly dated

(particularly on the origins of pastoral nomadism), is Gryaznov, *The Ancient Civilization of Southern Siberia.*

9   Mallory, *In Search of the Indo-Europeans*, p. 225; but Dergachev, 'Neolithic and Bronze Age cultural Communities', p. 798, dates it to the second half of the third millennium; see also Okladnikov, 'Inner Asia at the dawn of history', in *CHEIA*, p. 83.

10 Chernykh, *Ancient Metallurgy*, p. 183; however, Gryaznov writes that 'They lived a sedentary life in small settlements of up to ten families.' Gryaznov, *Ancient Civilization of Southern Siberia*, p. 49, though he admits that 'We know nothing about the type of house they lived in', Ibid.; see also Gryaznov, *Ancient Civilization of Southern Siberia*, p. 48; and Mallory, *In Search of the Indo-Europeans*, p. 223.

11 Anthony and Vinogradov, 'Birth of the chariot', p. 38.

12 Okladnikov, 'Inner Asia at the dawn of history' in *CHEIA*, pp. 80, 83.

13 Mallory, *In Search of the Indo-Europeans*, 223–5; Mallory, 'Speculations on the Xinjiang Mummies', p. 379; V. V. Volkov, 'Early nomads of Mongolia', in Davis-Kimball, ed., *Nomads* (pp. 319–33), p. 320.

14 Mallory, *In Search of the Indo-Europeans*, p. 226.

15 Kuz'mina, *Drevneishye skotovody*, p. 44; Dergachev, 'Neolithic and Bronze cultural Communities', p. 799; Chernykh, *Ancient Metallurgy*, p. 305.

16 Kuz'mina, *Drevneishye skotovody*, p. 37.

17 Anthony and Vinogradov, 'Birth of the Chariot', p. 36; on Sintashta, see V. M. Masson, 'The decline of the Bronze Age civilization and movements of the tribes', *HCCA*, 1:347–8; and Mallory, *In Search of the Indo-Europeans*, p. 347; on the linguistic and mythological evidence, Kuz'mina, *Drevneishye skotovody*, pp. 28–9.

18 Masson, 'The decline of the Bronze Age Civilization', *HCCA*, 1:347; and see Victor Mair, 'Prehistoric Caucasoid Corpses of the Tarim Basin', p. 283; and Chang, *Archaeology of Ancient China*, 3rd edn, p. 279: 'The horse-drawn chariot is the only Shan – late Shang – innovation that may have originated in the Near East, where an almost identical complex of chariot parts occurs archaeologically centuries earlier.'

19 Anthony and Vinogradov, 'Birth of the chariot', p. 40.

20 Chernykh, *Ancient Metallurgy*, pp. 200, 305; see also Chang, *Archaeology of Ancient China*, 3rd edn, p. 279.

21 See Dergachev, 'Neolithic and Bronze Age cultural Communities', p. 799.

22 Kuz'mina, *Drevneishye skotovody*, p. 43.

23 Khazanov, *Nomads*, p. 95.

24 Kuz'mina, *Drevneishye skotovody*, p. 32.

25 Dergachev, 'Neolithic and Bronze Age cultural Communities', p. 800.

26 Masson 'The decline of the Bronze Age Civilization', *HCCA*, 1:348.

27 Kuz'mina, *Drevneishye skotovody*, pp. 29–30, 38–9; Andronovo communities were expert well-makers; see Ibid., pictures after p. 48.

28 Gryaznov, *Ancient Civilization of Southern Siberia*, pp. 93–4; Kuz'mina, *Drevneishye skotovody*, p. 97 suggests that these were the tombs of warrior-elites, ancestors of the Indian *kshatriya* caste.

29 Kuz'mina, *Drevneishye skotovody*, pp. 43–5; Mallory, *In Search of the Indo-Europeans*, pp. 228–9.

30 Kuz'mina, *Drevneishye skotovody*, pp. 40–1, 48.

31 Tolstov, *Po drevnim del'tam*, pp. 47, 52, 74ff; P'yankova, 'Central Asia in the Bronze Age', p. 368.

32 Masson, 'The decline of the Bronze Age Civilization', *HCCA*, 1:350.

33 Victor Mair, 'Prehistoric Caucasoid corpses of the Tarim Basin', pp. 289, 303.

34 Prusek, *Chinese Statelets*, pp. 212–13; the Ti had few horses and fought on foot and were probably descendants of neolithic farmers of the North Ordos.

35 Lattimore, *Inner Asian Frontiers of China*, pp. 277–8; and see Derevyanko and Dorj, 'Neolithic tribes in northern parts of Central Asia' in *HCCA*, 1:180–1.

36 Chang, *Archaeology of Ancient China*, 3rd edn, p. 396.

37 Gryaznov, *Ancient Civilization of Southern Siberia*, p. 51; the Okunevo culture was 'genetically unrelated' to the Afanasevan culture according to Mallory, *In Search of the Indo-Europeans*, p. 263.

38 Gryaznov, *Ancient Civilization of Southern Siberia*, p. 61; other objects included knuckle bones which may have been used in games. Ibid.

39 Okladnikov, 'Inner Asia at the dawn of history', in *CHEIA*, p. 81; Gryaznov, *Ancient Civilization of Southern Siberia*, p. 61.

40 Chernykh, *Ancient Metallurgy*, pp. 215–32.

41 A. Askarov, V. Volkov and N. Ser-Odjav, 'Pastoral and nomadic tribes at the beginning of the first millennuim BC', *HCCA* (pp. 459–72), 1:460; and see Tolstov, *Po drevnim del'tam*, pp. 64 and 71, on Karasuk-type finds in Khorezm.

42 Gryaznov, *Ancient Civilization of Southern Siberia*, pp. 84–5, 97–8.

43 Ibid., p. 104.

44 Askarov, Volkov and Ser-Odjav, 'Pastoral and nomadic tribes', in *HCCA*, 1:461; Gryaznov, *Ancient Civilization of Southern Siberia*, p. 104.

45 Hiebert, *Origins*, e.g. p. 166; see also P'yankova, 'Central Asia in the Bronze Age', p. 355.

46 The following description is from Masson and Sarianidi, *Central Asia*, pp. 77, 80; on the evolution to multi-roomed houses, P'yankova, 'Central Asia in the Bronze Age', p. 359.

47 Kohl, ed., *Bronze Age Civilization*, p. xxxi.

48 Dolukhanov, 'Foragers and farmers in west-central Asia,' p. 130; P'yankova, 'Central Asia in the Bronze Age', p. 359; Hiebert, *Origins*, p. 171.

49 Kohl, ed., *Bronze Age Civilization*, p. xxxi; V. M. Masson 'The Bronze Age in Khorasan and Transoxania in *HCCA*, 1:237, Masson also accepts the earlier date of 2300 BC for Namazga V.

50 Masson and Sarianidi, *Central Asia*, pp. 112–14, 120.

51 Masson, 'The Bronze Age', *HCCA*, 1:231; there is a good description of the site in Chernykh, *Ancient Metallurgy*, pp. 172–4.

52 Masson, 'The Bronze Age', in *HCCA*, 1:233; Masson and Sarianidi, *Central Asia*, p. 116; on the 'ziggurat', see V. M. Masson, 'Altyn-depe during the Aneolithic period', in Kohl, ed., *Bronze Age Civilization*, pp. 63–95; however, J.-L. Huot, 'Les ziggurats mésopotamiennes et l'Asie Centrale', rejects Masson's suggestion that these were like ziggurats, as they are too early and too small; see *L'Asie Centrale et ses rapports*, Paris, 1988, pp. 37–42.

53 Chernykh, *Ancient Metallurgy*, p. 174; Masson and Sarianidi, *Central Asia*, p. 119; Masson, 'The Bronze Age', in *HCCA*, 1:240.

54 Masson and Sarianidi, *Central Asia*, p. 125; and *HCCA*, 1:244–5.

55 Masson, 'The Bronze Age', in *HCCA*, 1:242; on its date, see Ligabue and Salvatori, eds, *Bactria*, p. 65.

56 Masson, 'The Bronze Age', in *HCCA*, 1:244–5; on the Zamanbabin culture, Masson and Sarianidi, *Central Asia*, p. 125.

57 See the series of articles in *Antiquity*, vol. 68, no. 259 (June 1994); Ligabue, and Salvatori, eds, *Bactria*; and works of Sarianidi, such as *Drevnosti stran Margush*, or *Drevnii Merv*.

58 Dating remains controversial. Kohl dates the Namazga VI period from *c.*2100 BCE (Kohl, ed., *Bronze Age Civilization*, p. xxix), while Masson and Sarianidi, *Central Asia*, date it to the early or even middle second millennium; P'yankova, 'Central Asia in the Bronze Age', p. 355, gives sixteenth to tenth centuries for Namazga VI and 2300–1850 BCE for Namazga V, but adds that 'Western European and American archaeologists tend to push back these dates for the Namazga V and VI periods by some 500 years; however, there is general agreement about the relative internal chronology in Central Asia based on the ceramics'. Hiebert, *Origins*, p. 374, gives 2200–2000 for Namazga V and 2000–1750 for Namazga VI.

59 Dates from C. C. Lamberg-Karlovsky, 'Bronze Age khanates of Central Asia', p. 398; and see Hiebert, *Origins*, pp. 172–5.

60 Masson 'The decline of the Bronze Age Civilization', *HCCA*, 1:340; P'yankova, 'Central Asia in the Bronze Age', p. 359 and see map p. 373.

61 See Lamberg-Karlovsky, 'The Oxus Civilization', p. 353; there is a map of sites on p. 356 and illustrations on p. 357 show clearly the sharp change from painted to non-painted ceramics.

62 Lamberg-Karlovsky, 'Bronze Age khanates', p. 400; P'yankova, 'Central Asia in the Bronze Age', p. 363.

63 V. Sarianidi, 'Temples of Bronze Age Margiana', *Antiquity*, 68 (1994):388–97; pp. 395–6.

64 Hiebert, *Origins*, pp. 134–5; C. C. Lamberg-Karlovsky, 'The Bronze Age of Bactria', in Ligabue and Salvatori, eds, *Bactria* (pp. 13–21), p. 20.

65 P'yankova, 'Central Asia in the Bronze Age', p. 361.

66 Lamberg-Karlovsky, 'The Bronze Age *khanates*'; and see Hiebert, *Origins*, p. 176.

67 K. M. Moore, N. F. Miller, F. T. Hiebert and R. H. Meadow, 'Agriculture and herding in the early oasis settlements of the Oxus Civilization', *Antiquity*, 68 (1994):418–27; p. 420.

68 Masson, 'The decline of the Bronze Age Civilization', in *HCCA*, 1:343; and see Kohl, 'The ancient economy', in Rowlands, et al., *Centre and Periphery*, p. 19.

69 Masson 'The decline of the Bronze Age Civilization', *HCCA*, 1:343.

70 Hiebert, *Origins*, p. 12.

71 Moore, Miller, Hiebert, Meadow, 'Agriculture and herding', p. 426.

72 Frank and Gills, *World System*, p. 84.

73 Ligabue and Salvatori, eds, *Bactria*, p. 20; F. T. Hiebert, 'Production evidence for the origins of the Oxus Civilization', *Antiquity*, 68(1994):372–87; p. 376; Lamberg-Karlovsky, 'The Oxus Civilization', p. 354; on finds of silk, see Ligabue and Salvatori, eds, *Bactria*, p. 71.

74 Ligabue and Salvatori, eds, *Bactria*, p. 71.

75 Masson, 'The decline of the Bronze Age Civlization', in *HCCA*, 1:243.

76 H.-P. Francfort, 'The Central Asian dimension of the symbolic system in Bactria and Margiana', pp. 406–18; Amiet, 'Elam and Bactria', in Ligabue and Salvatori, eds, *Bactria* (pp. 125–40), p. 137; and see Sarianidi, 'Aegean-Anatolian motifs', on parallels with the Aegean world.

77 Sarianidi, 'Temples of Bronze Age Margiana', pp. 388–97; V. Sarianidi 'New discoveries at ancient Gonur', in *Ancient Civilizations from Scythia to Siberia*, 2(3) (1995):289–310; pp. 302, 310; and P'yankova, 'Central Asia in the Bronze Age', *Antiquity*, p. 356.

78 Boyce, *History*, 1:157–8.
79 Francfort, 'The Central Asian dimension', p. 415, which also reproduces the Togolok seal, and stresses the role of shamanism; Sarianidi, 'Temples of Bronze Age Margiana', p. 394.
80 Boyce, *History*, 1:189–90; and see Sarianidi, 'Temples of Bronze Age Margiana', pp. 302, 310.
81 On these, see B. A. Litvinsky and L. T. P'yankova 'Pastoral tribes of the Bronze Age in the Oxus Valley, (Bactria)', in *HCCA*, 1:379–94.
82 A. Askarov, 'The beginning of the Iron Age in Transoxania', in *HCCA* (pp. 441–58), 1:447–51.
83 Moore, Miller, Hiebert, Meadow, 'Agriculture and herding', p. 426; P'yankova, 'Central Asia in the Bronze Age', p. 365; Tolstov, *Po drevnim del'tam*, p. 52.

FURTHER READING

On Central Asia in the Bronze Age, *HCCA* volume 1 is now fundamental. Masson and Sarianidi, *Central Asia*, is still useful, though Kohl, *The Bronze Age Civilization of Central Asia*, and *L'Asie Centrale*, and Hiebert, *Origins of the Bronze Age Oasis Civlization* are much more up to date. There are valuable essays in Ligabue, ed., *Bactria*, and in *Antiquity*, vol. 68, no. 259 (1994). On the steppe lands, see *HCCA*, volume 1; Mallory, *In Search of the Indo-Europeans*; Gryaznov, *The Ancient Civilization of Southern Siberia*; Kuz'mina, *Drevneyshie skotovody*; Tolstov, *Po drevnim del'tam*; and the special issue of *Antiquity* on steppe archaeology, vol. 63, no. 241 (1989). On the eastern region, the basic introductory survey is Chang, *Archaeology of Ancient China*; but see also Novgorodova, *Drevnyaya Mongoliya*; and Prusek, *Chinese Statelets*. Chernykh, *Ancient Metallurgy*, is valuable on the spread of metalworking technologies. Piggot, *The Earliest Wheeled Transport*, and Anthony, 'Birth of the chariot', are on early chariots. The *Journal of Indo-European Studies* (1995), vol. 23, nos 3 and 4 is devoted to evidence of Indo-European migrations into the eastern steppes. Frank and Gills, *The World System*, discuss the possibility that there existed a Bronze Age 'world system', focused on Bactria. Rowlands, et al., *Centre and Periphery*, also discuss early systems of long-distance trade and exchange.

PART III

The Scythic and Hunnic Eras:
1000 BCE–500 CE

[6] THE 'SCYTHIC' ERA: 1000–200 BCE

D<small>URING</small> the first millennium BCE, written sources on Inner Eurasian history become available for the first time. The earliest written sources, like most later sources until recent centuries, were produced in the literate cultures of Outer Eurasia. The very earliest are probably the eighth-century Assyrian accounts that describe invasions of pastoralists called 'Gimmirai' (Cimmerians) from the Caucasus. Later sources include chronicles, travel itineraries, official histories such as those of the Han dynasty, and unofficial studies such as Herodotus' *Histories*, the best single source on Inner Eurasian societies during the first millennium BCE. The quality of these sources varies greatly, but all of them, to a greater or lesser extent, portray pastoralists as barbarians and outsiders. Despite this, written sources of the first millennium allow us, for the first time, to name individual leaders and even whole peoples, to date particular events, and to describe aspects of Inner Eurasian lifeways that archaeological evidence alone cannot capture. As a result, our picture of Inner Eurasian societies becomes richer and more sharply focused.

However, the limitations of the written evidence mean that archaeological evidence remains vital. Fortunately, it is peculiarly rich. In the early eighteenth century, well-organized groups or artels of grave robbers (*bugrovshchviki*) looted thousands of the kurgans dotted throughout the Inner Eurasian steppes. Some of their finds were acquired by the eighteenth-century Russian industrialist, N. Demidov, who founded the metalworks of the Ural mountains. In 1715, Demidov, gave a collection of Scythian objects to Peter the Great, who was so impressed that he issued a decree giving official protection to such archaeological finds. This event marks the beginning of the rich Russian and Soviet tradition of Scythian studies, and indeed of Russian archaeological studies in general.[1]

Paradoxically, the increasing quantity and quality of the evidence available for the first millennium BCE creates new problems for the historian. In particular, it becomes hard to know if we are seeing new phenomena, or simply seeing older patterns with a new clarity. These difficulties are particularly acute when dealing with pastoralist societies. The archaeological evidence suggests that steppe societies became more nomadic from the end of the second millennium, though there were always some groups of sedentary pastoralists on the borders of the steppes, particularly along the Syr Darya. Both archaeological and written evidence also suggest that steppe societies became more organized politically and militarily during the first millennium. But how great was the change? It has often been argued that these changes mark the first emergence of the militarized horse pastoralism that was to become typical of the Inner Eurasian steppes.[2] Earlier chapters have given some reasons for rejecting strong versions of this hypothesis. However, it is clear that the nature of Inner Eurasian pastoralism did change significantly at the end of the second millennium. In particular, there spread throughout the steppes a series of artistic, technological and military changes that created a surprisingly homogenous steppe culture. This culture is best known through Herodotus' accounts of Scythic societies of the Pontic steppes, but its elements could be found throughout the Inner Eurasian steppes. The spread of this 'Scythic' culture complex also affected the more sedentary lands south of the steppes. Here, increased urbanization reflects an intensification in commercial, political and military contacts between pastoralist and agrarian societies.

THE 'SCYTHIC' ERA

THE 'SCYTHIC' CULTURE COMPLEX

Late in the second millennium or early in the first millennium, there are many signs of increasing mobility in the steppes. If there was a single epicentre to these changes, it probably lay in central or eastern Kazakhstan and south Siberia, for sources from the west, south and east all seem to portray movements away from this point.[3]

We do not know precisely why mobility increased in this period. Some researchers have stressed the role of climatic changes. The cooler and drier climates that dominated much of the first millennium probably made farming harder in the lands of the steppe bronze cultures. Pastoralists reacted by grazing their herds over larger areas and becoming more nomadic, or by engaging in irrigation farming, or by seeking new pasturelands in better watered lands further south.[4] If modern analogies are any guide, such changes would have intensified conflicts over pasture lands, and encouraged the formation of larger tribal alliances. In this way, cooler and more arid climates may explain the emergence of more mobile, more warlike, and more 'statelike' groups of pastoralists.

Alternatively, as a previous chapter has suggested, an increase in mobility may reflect long-term cycles leading to periodic overpopulation, with, or without the intervention of climatic change. As human and animal populations rose during the second millennium, they would have increased conflicts over pasture lands. The rapid urbanization of Central Asia in the first millennium suggests that there was also overpopulation in neighbouring agrarian regions, though here it could be accommodated by expanding irrigation networks and urban settlements. This may explain why rising mobility in the steppes was accompanied by rapid urbanization in southern Central Asia, Khorezm, along the Black Sea and in Sinkiang.

Increasing mobility in the steppes and rapid urbanization to the south may also reflect an intensification of trans-ecological trade with Outer Eurasia. It has been suggested, for example, that the spread of chariot warfare in China and Mesopotamia created a demand for steppeland horses in numbers that could only be satisfied by importing horses from the steppes. But intensified urbanization in northern China, Central Asia, and the Mediterranean world, may also have increased the demand for horses, leather and other goods from the steppes. An increase in the demand for horses would have encouraged pastoralists to expand their herds and compete for more pasture lands. Pastoralists with large herds would have used larger areas, which meant looking after their herds from horseback, following them on long migrations and, when necessary, fighting for new pasture lands.[5] Intensified exchanges with agricultural regions would also have increased the resources available to regional tribal leaders, and enhanced their political and economic power.

Finally, there may be technological explanations for increasing mobility and conflict in the steppes. Particularly important is the appearance of small but powerful and accurate compound bows that could be fired from horseback. Compound bows combine several different materials, including wood, horn and sinews, which give them added strength and flexibility. They appear from as early as the third millennium in Mesopotamia and Inner Eurasia. However, the smaller and more efficient compound bows used by the Scythians and shaped like Cupid's bow are known only from the ninth century BCE. Though small enough to be used from horseback (c.1.25 m), they had a remarkable draw length which gave them great power and accuracy. As a result, they greatly enhanced the effectiveness of mounted archers and led to the emergence of a more mobile, expansionistic and militaristic style of pastoralism. Indeed, Pulleyblank has argued that it was the power of its mounted archers that really distinguishes the 'classic' horse nomadism of Inner Eurasia, and allowed the formation of steppe empires as powerful in their way as the agrarian empires emerging in Outer Eurasia.[6] All these scenarios are plausible, but at present the evidence is too imprecise to test any of them rigorously.

Whatever the cause, there was clearly a sort of phase change in the steppes late in the second millennium or early in the first millennium, and this entailed widespread warlike migrations over large areas of Inner Eurasia. Increased mobility helped establish a unified zone of mobile pastoralism, with a relatively homogenous culture. Elements of this culture were shared not only by peoples speaking ancient forms of Iranian, but also by groups speaking ancient forms of Turkic and Mongolian, while its symbolism may derive, at least in part from the traditions of the forest world. Watson describes these cultures as 'Scythic'. Many artistic motifs spread from the steppes and the Altai into the Ordos region of northern China. Other elements of the Scythic culture, such as three-sided arrows and compound

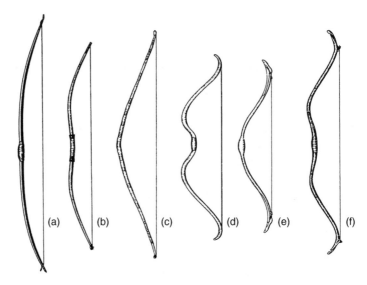

Figure 6.1 Types of bows, reproduced from *Scientific American*, June 1991 (© Hank Iken).

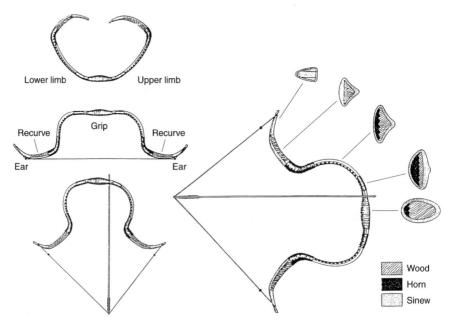

Figure 6.2 Evolution of compound bows, reproduced from *Scientific American*, June 1991 (© Hank Iken).

bows, may have travelled in the opposite direction. Watson has suggested that the diagnostic features of 'Scythic' culture were:

1   the adoption of iron metallurgy;
2   the use of the *akinakes*, a short sword, of specific design and systematic development;
3   the customary conservative use of certain artistic motifs, particularly the stag and the animal combat, all of which are combined with
4   the pastoral nomadic life and a patriarchal, little centralized social organization.

We could add to this list (5) the use of improved compound bows; (6) the widespread use of bronze cauldrons; (7) the making of 'deer stones' (*olenniye kamni*); and, perhaps most important of all, (8) the appearance for the first time in the steppes, of complex horse harness, which suggests a qualitative improvement in techniques of riding.[7]

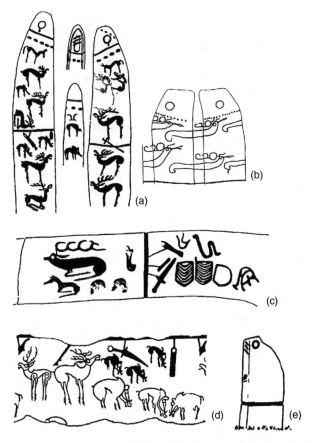

Figure 6.3 'Deer stones', reproduced from Jeannine Davis-Kimball, V. A. Bashilov et al., *Nomads of the Eurasian Steppes in the Early Iron Age* (Center for the Study of Eurasian Nomads, Berkeley, Cal.: Zinat Press, 1995).

It is possible that many of the pastoralists who shared in this culture had a loose sense of ethnic ties, at least within the proto-Iranian speaking zone, which reached from the Danube to the T'ien Shan mountains. According to Quintus Curtius, a 'Saka' ambassador told Alexander in c.328: 'we touch upon Bactra, except that the river Tanais [Syr Darya or Don?] is between us. Beyond the Tanais we inhabit lands extending to Thrace, and report says that the Macedonians border upon Thrace. Consider whether you wish enemies or friends to be neighbours to your empire.'[8] If, as seems likely, Alexander had already encountered Scythian armies on the Danube, the threat must have seemed real enough.

MILITARIZATION AND MOBILIZATION IN THE STEPPES

The impact of these mobile and expansionist pastoralist cultures was felt from China to Central Asia to the Caucasus and the Balkans.

Early in the first millennium, there appeared mobile, and warlike pastoralists on the northern Chinese borders, with close links to the central steppes. They bred small, tough, Przhevalski horses, and used Bactrian camels, particularly in or near the Gobi desert. The first literary evidence of mobile pastoralists on China's north eastern borders dates from the invasion of north China, in c.823 BCE, by a people known as the Hsien-yün. These were mounted, warlike nomads, who probably originated in western Mongolia or the Altai region. Pastoralist cavalry armies may have caused the fall of the Western Chou dynasty in 771 BC. From the eighth century, signs of mounted nomadism with strong 'Scythic' influences spread right along the northern frontier zones of China. By the fifth century, Chinese historians began to refer to a distinctive group of northern barbarians, the 'Hu', who fought from horseback. By 600 BCE, mobile pastoralism dominated the steppes of eastern Mongolia and by 400 BCE, it probably dominated much of the Ordos region as well.[9] In both areas, pastoralists probably squeezed out small farming populations that had lived there since neolithic times. However, some farming communities clearly survived and, though small in numbers, and using primitive agricultural methods, they provided their pastoralist overlords with agricultural goods and artisan products such as pottery.[10]

The horse-riding 'Hu' barbarians of the fourth century posed so great a military threat to states of north China that in 307 BCE a Chao ruler, Wu-ling, made his armies abandon their chariots and adopt not just the barbarian style of cavalry warfare and archery, but also their clothing, including the use of trousers, rather than tunics. This led to something of a revolution in Chinese military methods on the northern frontiers. Indeed, the adoption of more mobile, steppe methods of warfare may have helped the creation of a unified Chinese state in the late third century under the Ch'in.[11] Intensified wall-building in the third century was also a response to the threat posed by northern pastoralists. By the third century BCE, we know of at least three large and powerful supra-tribal federations north of the Chinese heartlands: the Hsiung-nu in the Ordos region, the Yüeh-chih in the Tun-huang region

Plate 6.1 Ordos bronzes with 'Scythian' designs. Private collection.

to the west, and the Tung-hu (or 'eastern barbarians') in eastern Mongolia and along the borders with Manchuria.

The 'Scythic' cultures of the Mongolian steppes were probably transmitted from western Mongolia. The 'slab-grave' cultures, which extend from eastern Mongolia to the lakes region of western Mongolia, are contemporaneous with the Scythic cultures of the central and western steppes, and show strong Scythic influences. 'Their graves contain beautiful bronze objects and iron articles.... The Scythian-type bronze pots, axes, daggers, arrowheads, bronze and iron horse's bits from the stone-slab graves of Mongolia bear a striking resemblance to similar articles found in the graves of the region beyond the Baikal and in Ordos.'[12] Yet their graves also contain goods from the Mediterranean, India and China, which provides a striking indication of the extent of cultural and material exchanges in the steppes by 1000 BCE. Clearly, relations between China and the steppe were shaped as much by peaceful as by warlike exchanges. Most human remains of the slab-grave burials are East Asian, but towards the west some show a strong admixture of Europoid types.[13]

In some parts of Central Asia, there emerged powerful pastoralist leaders who managed to form relatively stable alliances between smaller tribal groups. This, in turn, enabled them to mobilize large armies and significant material resources. The huge tomb of Arzhan in Tuva, which dates from the eighth century, lies close to the likely epicentre of these migratory movements, and represents one of the earliest expressions of an evolving Scythian/Saka culture. It shows how much wealth powerful steppe leaders could mobilize, even early in the first millennium. The tomb included seventy chambers arranged like the spokes of a wheel, and contained about 160 saddle horses under a mound 120 metres wide.[14] At the centre were buried a man and a woman, who wore furs and elaborate decorations. They clearly ruled a large and powerful tribal confederation. Subordinate princes or nobles

Plate 6.2 Tagisken 'mausoleum', reproduced from V. M. Masson and V. I. Sarianidi *Central Asia* (London: Thames and Hudson, 1972).

were buried to their south, west and north. The objects in this vast burial mound contain the main elements of Scythian culture, including Scythian weaponry, horse harness and ornamentation in the Scythian animal style. This is the earliest large tomb to contain these elements, which suggests that Herodotus was right in claiming that Scythic cultures spread westwards from Central Asia.[15] The populations ruled by such leaders were mobile pastoralists, though in mountainous regions they probably had permanent winter settlements, whose dwellings are illustrated in the Boyar rock carvings in modern Tuva.[16]

There are also signs of political and military mobilization amongst more sedentary groups of pastoralists, whose lifeways were probably similar to the steppe bronze cultures of the late Bronze Age. Achaemenid armies in Central Asia encountered several groups known as 'Saka', all of whom wore the strange pointed caps that appear on Achaemenid carvings and described by Herodotus (7:64). Most could field large armies, and some dominated large territories. An inscription from the time of Darius I listed three main groups of Saka: (1) the *Haumavarga*, who lived in Ferghana and were becoming sedentary; (2) the *Tigraxauda*, who lived in Sogdia (the valleys of the Zerafshan and Kashka Darya rivers) and also beyond the Syr Darya and in Semirechye (though some scholars have placed them in Turkmenistan or linked them to the Massagetae); and (3) the western Saka, whom the Greeks

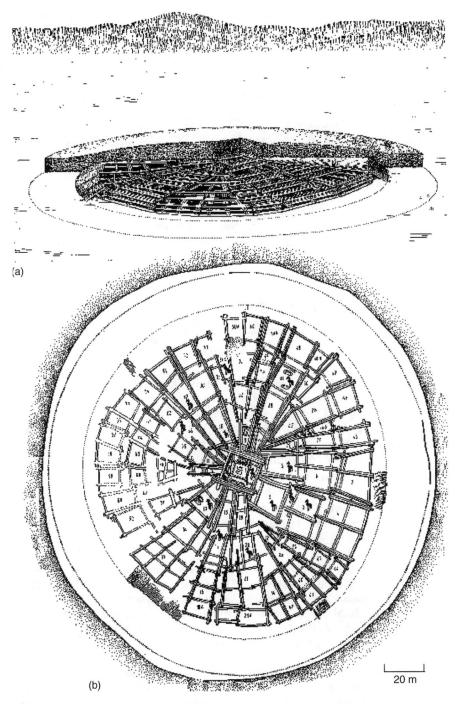

(a)

(b)

20 m

Figure 6.4 Arzhan: a royal tomb from the eighth century BCE, reproduced from
Jeannine Davis-Kimball, V. A. Bashilov et al., *Nomads of the Eurasian Steppes in the
Early Iron Age* (Center for the Study of Eurasian Nomads, Berkeley, Cal.: Zinat
Press, 1995).

Map 6.1 Central Asia in the first millennium BCE.

referred to as Scythians.[17] The *Apasiakoi* ('marsh' or 'water' Saka) of the Syr Darya delta were sedentizing pastoralists who also engaged in irrigation agriculture, fishing and crafts. Some may even have founded large towns, such as the fortified settlement of Chirik-Rabat, on a now dry bed of the Syr Darya, deep in the Kyzylkum desert, which contains evidence of fishing and farming as well as pastoralism.[18] In the delta of the Syr Darya, there is a vast cemetery associated with the Tagisken culture. This contains burials from the tenth to the fifth century BCE.[19]

> Here, on the picturesque banks of the river, majestic tombs once rose, the largest of which, with a diameter of about 25 m, consisted of a cylindrical structure made of rectangular sun-baked bricks. Inside was a rectangular burial chamber, while the cylindrical structure itself was surrounded by a ring wall leaving a passage 2 m wide between the two. The chamber contained over a hundred bronze nails which were apparently used to hold up the rugs that lined the walls.[20]

Though most of the tombs have been looted, what remains suggests that these communities had access to great wealth. S. P. Tolstov claimed that this was a royal burial ground of a group of semi-sedentary Saka known as the Sakaravaks, who may be the same as the 'Saka Haumavarga'. Their culture and way of life are clearly derived from the steppe bronze traditions, but also show influences from the towns of the Oxus civilization.[21]

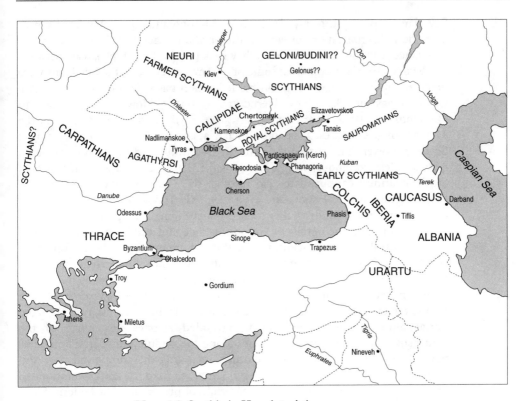

Map 6.2 Scythia in Herodotus' time.

In the Pontic region, there is evidence of increased mobilization from at least the eighth century. The oldest written references to pastoralists in this region occur in Homer.[22] In the *Iliad*, there are references to 'horse-milkers' and 'milk-drinkers' living north of the Thracians, while the *Odyssey* refers to the sunless lands of the Cimmerians who 'live in Perpetual Mist' near the frontier of the world. These accounts presumably derive from Greek traders who sailed the Black Sea. Written sources, from Assyria to Greece, mention violent pastoralist invasions of Iran and Mesopotamia from the north in the eighth and seventh centuries. Assyrian records record the invasions of two warlike peoples, the Gimmirrai, or Cimmerians, and the Ashguzai or Scythians. Both groups seem to have spoken Iranian languages ancestral to modern Ossetian.

It is possible that the mobile pastoralism of the Cimmerians evolved within the more sedentary 'Srubnaya' or 'Timber-Grave' cultures of the second millennium.[23] However, the tribes known in Greek sources as 'Scythians' probably came from Central Asia. According to Herodotus (4.11–12), Scythian tribes entered the Pontic steppes under pressure from the Massagetae. The Scythians, in turn, drove out the Cimmerians, who by this time dominated a huge Pontic empire from the Don to the Danube, probably from a base in the Kerch' peninsula. Some of the Cimmerians fled through the Caucasus and raided Anatolia and northern Mesopotamia for some 20 years. From the 670s,

Scythians, too, began to invade northern Mesopotamia, probably from a base in modern Azerbaijan or perhaps, in the northern Caucasus. Here, sometimes in alliance with Cimmerian groups, they took part in the complex wars between Media and Assyria. For at least some of the seventh century, the Scythians were organized into a powerful supra-tribal federation based in modern Azerbaijan, whose kings are listed by Herodotus (1:03).[24] However, according to Herodotus (1:106), about 28 years after the Scythian conquest of Media, the Median king, Cyaxares, massacred their leaders at a banquet, and destroyed Scythian power. The surviving Scythians fled north and began to establish a new, and less ambitious, empire north of the Black Sea. For a decade or two, Scythian armies continued to raid through the Caucasus and into the Near East, reaching into Palestine, and even Egypt (Herodotus, 1.104–5).[25] In 612, under a king called Madyes, they sacked Nineveh, in alliance with Media.

Though not all the details of Herodotus' account can be trusted, much of it is plausible. Seventh-century Scythian kurgans have been found in Azerbaijan; there are contemporary fortifications near modern Darband on the Caspian shores; and Scythian three-sided bronze arrowheads have been found in Mesopotamia, Syria and Egypt.[26] The archaeology of the North Pontic region also fits neatly into such an account. From c.650, rich nomadic burial mounds appear both in the wooded steppes just north of the Caucasus, and in the wooded steppes along the middle Dnieper. These contain all the hallmarks of Scythic culture, including the compound bow and quivers full of three-sided arrows, Scythian horse harness, and decorations in the Scythian animal style. Yet the material culture of the first regions occupied by these pastoralist invaders also retains elements derived from the earlier Srubnaya cultures. This pattern suggests the establishment of pastoralist hegemony over largely sedentary populations previously ruled by Cimmerians. Groups of Scythians may also have settled as far afield as the inner Carpathians, and even between the Volga and Kama rivers. Finally, early Scythian remains from the north Caucasus, also reflect the time they spent in Mesopotamia. For example, Soviet archaeologists have found the remains of a Scythian temple built in Iranian style.[27]

Though the equipment of early Scythian kurgans clearly belongs to the pastoralist world, decades of rule in northern Mesopotamia may explain why the Scythians who settled north of the Black Sea occupied not the deep steppe, but wooded steppelands already settled by farming populations. Before 500 BCE, there is hardly any sign of settlement in the deep steppes just north of the Black Sea. Apparently, the early Scythians chose to settle as pastoralist rulers of farming populations rather than as self-sufficient pastoralists.

After the constant nomadism and the military emergencies of the seventh century, the Scythians slowly established a more stable system. Many continued to live as mobile pastoralists, but some became more sedentary and even merged with local farming populations. Even pastoralist elites probably spent increasing periods in the towns and settlements of the lands they now ruled.[28] Eventually, the great confederations of the nomadic era fragmented. There is no sign of a single, overarching system of rule. Instead, there probably existed several regional tribal alliances, each of which took tributes from

Figure 6.5 'Scythian' art, reproduced from Jeannine Davis-Kimball, V. A. Bashilov et al., *Nomads of the Eurasian Steppes in the Early Iron Age* (Center for the Study of Eurasian Nomads, Berkeley, Cal.: Zinat Press, 1995).

local farming populations. We know of only one occasion, when Darius invaded Scythia from the Danube in *c*.514 BCE, when several groups formed a single supra-tribal defensive alliance.[29]

From *c*.500 BCE, there are indications of new upheavals in the Scythian system, caused by renewed migrations from the central steppes. Greek sources describe the new arrivals as 'Scythian' which suggests that their culture was similar to that of the groups already settled in the region, though they maintained a more mobile pastoralism. By the middle of the fifth century, a new regional system had emerged. Its most striking feature is the appearance of large numbers of pastoralist burials in the true steppes. When Herodotus visited Olbia in c.450, there were large populations of mobile pastoralists in the steppes particularly along the lower Dnieper, north of the Sea of Azov, and in the Don delta.[30] Ordinary Scythian pastoralists engaged in regular migrations, such as those described by Strabo, from winter camps in the 'marsh-meadows' of the Black Sea coast, to summer camps in the deep steppe.[31] Slowly, there emerged the Scythia portrayed by Herodotus, which was dominated by mobile pastoralists, based in the Pontic steppes, and taking tributes both from farming communities to their west and north and from Greek colonies. Such relations persisted well into the third century BCE. According to a decree issued by the city of Olbia at that time:

> We have had to send "gifts" not only to the king, but also to those close to him. In addition, special contributions were demanded when Saitafarn [whose identity is not clear] passed by the town; and if he was not satisfied with their size, then he threatened us with war.[32]

As stability returned, trade flourished. The many rich burials of the lower Dnieper region show that pastoralist elites grew very rich from the fifth century. Artisan production increased in Scythian towns such as Kamenskoe on the Dnieper, or Elizavetovskoe in the delta of the Don or Nadlimanskoe in the Dniester estuary. It may be this wealth that eventually allowed the appearance of a large, but unstable political system in the fourth century, under a king called Atheas. According to Strabo, Atheas united all the Scythian tribes from the Danube to the Don. The Dnieper city of Kamenskoe may have been his capital. In 346, his forces defeated a Macedonian army which may have been led by the young Alexander, but in 339 BCE, the Scythian armies were defeated just south of the Danube and Atheas died at the age of 90.[33]

In the third century, Scythian tribes came under pressure once again from groups to their east. Recent archaeological evidence has demonstrated the arrival of new groups of pastoralists in the Volga/Don steppes at c.400 BCE.[34] Greek writers described the newcomers as 'Sarmatians', a generic label that includes many different groups, such as the Roxolani, Aorsi and Iazyges. There was no single invasion of the Pontic steppes but many separate incursions by different tribes, over many decades. Some groups, such as the Aorsi, had lived in the Kazakh steppes for centuries before being driven west. Others may have come from the more sedentary tribes of Central Asia along the Syr Darya. The Sarmatians do not appear to have created a unified state, or even a unified cultural zone. Only occasionally were there large-scale military invasions, though these could sometimes be devastating. Diodorus of Sicily reported in the first century BCE that Sarmatian invaders 'ravaged a large part of Scythia and, destroying utterly all whom they subdued, they turned most of the land into a desert.'[35] During this period, the tribal elites who built the great complexes of royal tombs along the lower Dnieper vanished, and so did many small, unfortified settlements in the steppes. The steppes were now dominated by various Sarmatian groups, which, by the first century CE had come under the domination of a group known as the 'Alans'.[36]

Though Sarmatian tribes from the east, and Thracian tribes from the west had destroyed Scythian power in the Pontic steppes, several smaller, largely sedentary, Scythian kingdoms survived on the lower Danube, and also in Crimea, where rising sea levels narrowed the Perekop isthmus, and made it particularly easy to keep out invaders. These Scythian kingdoms lasted until the third century CE, when they were overthrown by Gothic invaders. They formed small but powerful states based on agriculture and pastoralism, with fortified settlements and small towns, whose elites continued to live a semi-nomadic life.[37] These mini-Scythias set a pattern by which pastoral nomadic tribes, driven west across the Pontic steppes, eventually washed up, transformed into farmers and traders, in Crimea, Moldova, Hungary, and the Balkans, their pastoralist traditions preserved only in the lifeways of their aristocracies.

URBANIZATION ALONG THE SOUTHERN BORDERLANDS

In Khorezm, in lands settled by Saka tribes, there appear the first signs of urbanization, accompanied by a rapid expansion and improvement of irrigation systems. Large, artificial canals, substantial fortified towns, and perhaps even early state systems appear from the seventh and sixth centuries BCE. This was a strikingly 'militarized' urbanization. The fortified towns of Khorezm, such as the fourth- to first-century site of Koy-krylgan-kala, had sophisticated defensive systems including projecting bastions and carefully planned arrow slits. Statues and reliefs reveal a prosperous aristocratic culture, whose statuary and wine-making suggest Mediterranean influences. It was in this period that Khorezm became what it was to remain until modern times: a highly urbanized yet vulnerable outpost of urban civilization in the Inner Eurasian steppes. Like the semi-urbanised societies of the Pontic region, it was overrun by new waves of settlers from the steppes in the third and second centuries BCE.[38]

The first substantial settlement in Afrasiab, the old town of Samarkand, appeared between the sixth and fourth centuries BCE. By the fourth century, Samarkand consisted of a central fortress with its own walls, a larger, densely settled town surrounded by perhaps 12 kilometres of fortifications, and irrigated farmlands and villages beyond the walls. Alexander's Roman biographer, Quintus Curtius reports that the rulers of Samarkand kept huge game parks with 'noble wild beasts, confined in great woods and parks. For this purpose they choose extensive forest made attractive by perennial springs; they surround the woods with walls and have towers as stands for the hunters.'[39]

Along the Kopet Dag, there was a revival of urbanization after the decline of the 'Oxus' civilization in the late second millennium. Renewed urbanization was made possible by the building of irrigation systems more extensive than any that had existed in the region before. In the Misrian plain of eastern Turkmenistan, near the south-eastern corner of the Caspian, the Dahistan sites of the late second or early first millennia BCE, contain irrigation canals as long as 50 or 60 km, 5–8 metres wide, up to 2.7 m. deep, with many secondary and tertiary channels leading off them. In Khorezm, long main canals replace the small, less ramified systems typical of the second millennium. Their appearance represents a significant advance in irrigation techniques.[40] Similar systems of irrigation appeared in this period throughout Central Asia, in the Murgab, in Bactria, along the Zerafshan and in the Amu Darya Delta.

The extensive fortifications of the early Scythic era suggest great instability. From late in the second millennium, there appear large *qala*, with fortified centres. In the Dahistan culture, some *qala* were more than 100 acres in extent, much larger than the forts of the 'Oxus' civilization.[41] The Dahistan culture seems to have been a militaristic class society, based on agriculture and pastoralism. The major site of Yaz-depe, in south-east Turkmenistan, occupied 40 acres and had a central citadel 12 m height.[42]

Such settlements were to become typical of Central Asia, which emerged in the first millennium as a region of small fortified city-states whose relative isolation prevented the emergence of large empires, leaving each city vulnerable to attacks from neighbours, from pastoralists or from the armies of Outer Eurasia.

The militarization of the early Scythic era may even be reflected in religion, for it was during this period that Zoroastrianism crystallized from the religious traditions of the second millennium. Though Mary Boyce has argued forcefully that Zoroaster lived towards the end of the second millennium, many authorities have dated him to the sixth century BCE.[43] Like Muhammad, Zoroaster had close links with both the pastoralist and the sedentary worlds, though his power base was probably in the city states of Central Asia. The *Gathas*, the oldest Avestan scriptures, which are normally attributed to Zoroaster himself, contain no reference to agriculture, but many references to the herding of cattle. This suggests that he lived in a frontier land of sedentary pastoralists. Like Muhammad, Zoroaster heard the voice of God (Ahura Mazda), and fought to defend his revelation. Zoroaster's early military successes owed much to his first sponsor, a king called Vistaspa. The Zoroastrian scriptures contained in the *Avesta*, described the nomadic 'Turas' as eternal enemies of sedentary 'Iran'.[44] This polarity became a central theme of Central Asian literature, receiving its classic expression in the *Shah-Name* of Firdausi, written in the tenth century CE. The dualism of Zoroastrianism is also reflected in its theology, which portrays a universe dominated by conflict between Ahura Mazda and the spirit of evil, Ahriman. Eventually, however, it held that the principle of good would win and those who had obeyed the good would be resurrected.[45] Many elements of Zoroastrian ritual were already present in the cities of the second millennium. Zoroaster himself was essentially a reformer and purifier of the older *Avestan* tradition, who helped elevate the status of a supreme deity, Ahura Mazda, linked, historically with the Indian gods Mithra and Varuna.

It is tempting to see the elevation of Ahura Mazda over other gods as a symbolic reflection of early attempts at state formation, for the essence of his reform was the unification of a large and complex society of gods under a single benevolent god, Ahura Mazda, in opposition to his enemy, Angra Mainyu (Ahriman).[46] However, the pastoralist imagery of the *Gathas* suggests that, even if the religion crystallized in a region of city-states such as Khorezm or Bactria, its royal sponsors were of pastoralist origin.

During the first millennium, urbanization also expanded in Sinkiang and along the northern shores of the Black Sea. Evidence on the Tarim basin is extremely scanty. There were certainly agricultural communities here early in the second millennium, but the first definite evidence of towns appears only during the first millennium. The inhabitants of these communities were probably Indo-European speaking 'Saka' peoples from Central Asia.

Around the Black Sea, the history of urbanization can be traced both in the archaeological evidence and in literary sources. As the Scythians established themselves north of the Black Sea, Greek colonists began to settle in trading colonies around the northern shores. Greek interest in the region may date back as far as 1000 BC, when Greek ships in search of iron first sailed the southern shores of the Black Sea. Here, they discovered seas rich in fish, and lands with towns whose people were interested in Greek trade goods.[47]

The first permanent settlements of Greeks in the Black Sea were probably fishing colonies of Milesian sailors, rather like the first European settlements in Newfoundland. In the seventh century, 'factories' or trading bases were founded, probably by individual merchants. The oldest was probably at Berezan on the Don.[48] The first true colonies, such as the Milesian colony of Olbia, on the right side of the Bug delta, or Panticapaeum, controlling the straits into the Sea of Azov, were founded early in the sixth century. Greek sources described such settlements as formal colonies, but, as David Braund has argued, these accounts probably oversimplify a complex process. There already existed towns and trade systems along the Black Sea shores, and the people of Colchis made pottery on the wheel, produced wine, and worked metal well before the Greeks arrived.[49] Greek colonists, like European colonists in North America, had to find their own place in already established local systems.

> As usual in antiquity, ... interaction was an intensely personal affair: this was not the anonymous market-place of advanced capitalism, but a process of exchange articulated by and within human relations that were more than economic in the modern sense. In this pre-capitalist, pre-monetary exchange, personal relations were formed and developed, possibly entailing relationships between the communities of the principals. Although evidence is not available, it seems most likely that arrangements to marry and to settle in a new environment had their genesis in precisely such exchange.[50]

Towns also appeared further north in the wooded steppes, which had been farmed since the time of the Tripolye culture. Herodotus identifies groups of agricultural or semi-agricultural peoples, who 'sow and eat grain and onions, garlic, lentils, and millet' (Herodotus, IV:17). These lived mainly in the wooded steppes of Ukraine and the north Caucasus, though there were smaller populations of 'farming scythians' in Crimea and around the major Greek colonies. These communities also included craft workers and metal-workers. Some pastoralists may also have engaged in semi-nomadic farming in the steppes.[51]

On purely ecological grounds, it seems likely that the farming populations may have been quite large, probably larger than those of Scythian pastoralists. Though pastoralism dominated the political and military life of Scythia, demo-graphically, the Scythian system was dominated by farming and trade. Some agriculturalists may have been ethnically 'Scythian' (Herodotus, IV:18). Sedentism was particularly widespread from the fourth century, particularly in the eastern parts of Crimea, but also near the mouth of the Dniester. There also appear many smaller farming settlements along the lower Dnieper and some of the minor rivers leading into the steppes.[52] Around the Greek colonies there appeared populations of commercial farmers (Herodotus, IV:17) who supplied nearby cities and even parts of mainland Greece.

Many farming settlements in Scythia were large enough to be described as towns, and at least 100 fortified townships or *gorodishche* have been found in the forest steppes.[53] Some may have begun as the capitals of local agrarian chieftains, while others formed from the winter camps of pastoralist rulers, or from the artisan and commercial activities associated with regional trade net-works. Herodotus (4:108) described the town of Gelonus, which several modern researchers have linked to the site of Bel'sk on the river Vorskla.[54] His account suggests a pattern that can also be found in Khorezm, of pas-toralist domination over quite large agrarian settlements.

> The Budini are a great and numerous nation, with very blue eyes and red hair. They have a city among them, built of wood, and it is called Gelonus. Each side of the wall of it is thirty stades, and the wall is high and made of wood, and of wood, too, are the houses and the holy places. For there are holy places there belonging to the Greek gods and furnished out in Greek fashion, with images and shrines and altars made of wood; and they celebrate a festival to Dionysus every third year and perform the revels. For the Geloni are anciently Greeks who moved away from their trading posts and settled among the Budini, and the language that they speak is partly Scythian and partly Greek. The Budini and Geloni do not speak the same language at all, nor is their way of life the same [4:109]. The Budini are the true natives of the country and are nomads.... The Geloni work the soil, eat grain, and cultivate gardens; neither in shape nor in coloring are they like the Budini.

The Budini were attracted to Gelonus for its furs as well as its agriculture, for the local peoples took 'otters and beavers and certain other square-faced animals, whose skins are used for the fringes of mantles, and the testicles of them are useful for the cure of troubles of the womb' (Herodotus, 4:109).

The largest example of a Scythian 'town' in the steppe zone is Kamenskoe on the River Dnieper, the only Scythian urban settlement excavated in detail. Like most other steppe townships, it appeared in the fourth-century, perhaps in response to renewed invasions from the east. Fourth-century Kamenskoe occupied $c.12\,\text{km}^2$, was surrounded by extensive fortifications, and contained a citadel in its south western corner. As we have seen, it may have been the capital of the fourth-century ruler, King Atheas.[55] The presence of tentlike dwellings settled into earthen foundations in Nadlimanskoe, a Scythian town in the Dniester estuary, may illustrate how pastoralists began to establish durable winter dwellings, which eventually turned into towns. Though it may have begun as a fortified winter camp, Kamenskoe eventually became a great metalworking centre, whose products were exported to the steppes and to Greek cities of the Black Sea coast. Iron was mined and worked near Kamenskoe, for iron ore lay close to the surface, not far away in modern Krivoy Rog, and Scythian methods of tomb construction gave them the skills necessary to mine it.[56]

The role of pastoralists in the creation of steppeland towns can be seen most clearly in the case of Elizavetovskoye, in the Don delta. The oldest remains on the site of Elisavetovskoye belong to the sixth and fifth century, when it seems that Scythians had a winter camp at which they traded with Greeks, probably from Crimean Bosporus. The Scythian winter camp then became a permanent settlement and in the fourth century it grew into the 'largest barbarian marketplace of the entire Northern Pontic area.'[57] By late in the fourth century, Elisavetovskoye had become a Scythian town with administrative and religious functions. Finally, in the third century, there appeared a substantial Greek colony founded by the Bosporan kingdom.

LIFEWAYS AND POLITICS

LIFEWAYS

The literary evidence of the first millennium allows us, for the first time, to describe in some detail how pastoralists lived. Until the twentieth century, it was widely believed that the anthropological writings of Herodotus could not be trusted. However, archaeological work in this century has shown that his descriptions of the 'Scythic' culture of the Pontic region, which were based in part on a trip to Olbia in $c.450$ BCE, are remarkably precise. Perhaps the most astonishing confirmation of Herodotus' essential accuracy comes from the fifth- or fourth-century Pazyryk tombs in the Altai mountains. Here, semi-sedentary pastoralists buried their dead in highland tombs whose contents were subsequently flooded and frozen as a result of the activities of grave robbers. As a result, both flesh and textiles have been preserved, so that archaeologists have found the typical symbols of Scythic culture on textiles and tattoes, as well as in the details of horse burials. They have even observed ritual details known previously only from Herodotus, such as the skull found in one of the Pazyryk tombs, which had been scalped in exactly the way Herodotus describes.[58] Such research has shown that Herodotus is, for the most part, trustworthy in his anthropology. It also shows that many aspects of the culture he describes could be found as Far East as the Altai. The following account of Scythic lifeways refers mainly to the pastoralists of the Pontic steppes, though much of it probably applies to pastoralists of Central Asia as well.

There were, of course, many different types of pastoralism. Pure nomadism was probably uncommon in the Pontic steppes, where many pastoralists travelled with their herds in summer and occupied semi-permanent settlements for much of the winter. In the Caspian steppes to the east, pastoralists were probably more nomadic, travelling, like later Kazakh pastoralists, in large groups from winter camps along the Syr Darya to summer camps sometimes hundreds of kilometres to the north near the southern borders of Siberia. In the Caucasus or the mountain regions of Central Asia, pastoralists practised forms of transhumance, combined, sometimes, with simple forms of agriculture, much as they did in the early twentieth century. In hillier areas, pastoralists migrated vertically rather than horizontally, following the spring by moving slowly up the mountain slopes in the first half of the year, and then fleeing the winter as they moved down again in the second half.[59]

The diets of Scythian pastoralists, like those of modern Inner Eurasian pastoralists, were based on the meat and the fermented milk of their sheep, goats, cattle and horses, as well as on hunted animals. Amongst the Pazyryk tombs, archaeologists have found animal bones, cheese (kept, as amongst modern pastoralists, in leather bags), and vessels once filled with milk.[60] Ordinary Scythians kept the large-headed tough steppe ponies known from Mongolian times, though wealthier Scythians sometimes kept larger, more delicate breeds similar to the famed horses of Ferghana. Horses were the main prestige animals, though they were also used for their milk and their flesh. Particularly near towns, large cattle were an important part of pastoralist herds, used for their milk, their meat and their traction power. However, sheep travelled better in the steppes. The sheep of the Pazyryk settlements were of the fat-tailed variety still found in Central Asia.[61] The small number of finds of wild animal bones in Scythian settlements suggests that hunting was not a primary source of food, and was practised mainly as a form of military exercise.[62]

Like most early pastoralists of Inner Eurasia, Scythian pastoralists lived in the dome-shaped, felt-covered tents known in Chinese sources as *qionglu*.[63] Unlike the collapsible yurts and *gers* that appear for the first time from *c.*500 CE, these had to be carried on wagons. The Greek writer known as 'pseudo-Hippocrates', wrote of the wagons in which most Scythians lived:

> These are very small with four wheels. Others with six wheels are covered with felt; such wagons are employed like houses, some with two, some with three sections, and provide shelter from rain and wind. To these wagons they harness two or three pairs of hornless oxen. The women and children live in these wagons, but the men always remain on horseback.[64]

Herodotus described ordinary pastoralists as the 'eight-legged', because they owned a pair of oxen and a cart.[65] Of the highly nomadic Scythians of his day, he wrote: 'this people has no cities or settled forts; they carry their houses with them and shoot with bows from horseback; they live off herds of cattle, not from tillage, and their dwellings are on their wagons' (IV:46). Felt, mentioned in Herodotus' account, was a basic material for the making of dwellings throughout the pastoralist world. It was made from fibres of fur or hair, pounded together until they formed a strong material with exceptional qualities as an insulator.[66]

Scythians, like many other Inner Eurasian pastoralists, avoided water. Instead, they cleaned or ritually purified themselves in portable steam baths (Herodotus, IV:73–5). These consisted of tents made from woollen mats stretched over three poles tied at the top to make a tripod. Inside, they made a pit, in which they placed red-hot stones. On these they threw water and hemp seeds, which created a powerful and intoxicating steam bath. According to Herodotus: 'The Scythians in their delight at the steam bath howl loudly. This indeed serves them instead of a bath, as they never let water near their bodies at all' (IV:75). Herodotus adds that the women sometimes gave themselves mud baths with added cypress, cedar and frankincense. Tents and bags of hemp found in the Pazyryk tombs show the accuracy of Herodotus' account.[67]

Within families, there was a clear division of labour by gender. Women controlled what went on in the dwellings, while men controlled the large domestic animals, and fought. When Darius invaded the Pontic region in 514 BCE, Scythian leaders sent their wagons, with their women and children and most of their flocks, off to the north (IV:121). However, in an emergency, women also had to be able to undertake traditionally male tasks, and even to fight. This suggests, as Jacobson has argued, that in Scythic cultures, the normal division of roles by gender did not necessarily imply a corresponding hierarchy of status. Ctesias wrote of the Central Asian Saka that: 'in general [Saka] women are courageous and help the men in the dangers of war'.[68] This may explain the large number of stories about female warriors or 'Amazons' amongst Inner Eurasian pastoralists. Herotodus reported that the Sauromatian tribes, east of the Don, claimed to be descendants of Scythian men who had intermarried with Amazons. He added that, 'the women of the Sauromatians follow their old way of life; they go on horseback, hunting with their men and without them, and they go to the war, too, and wear the same dress as the men do' (IV:116). Herodotus was even told that no Sauromatian woman could marry until she had killed an enemy (IV:17).

Archaeological evidence supports such accounts. From the Altai to the Black Sea, female burials contained almost as much weaponry as male burials. Recent excavations at Pokrovka in north-west Kazakhstan, have revealed many burials of high status women with swords, daggers and arrows.[69] In Sauromatian graves, armed women account for 20 per cent of all known burials with arms, and in some groups of tombs, burials of women warriors occupy the central position and contain the richest goods. Even amongst the Scythians, there are many burials of women with entire sets of weapons, including arrows, spears and swords. The most striking burial of this kind

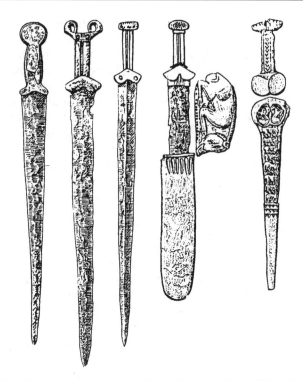

Figure 6.6 Scythian swords, reproduced from Jeannine Davis-Kimball, V. A. Bashilov et al., *Nomads of the Eurasian Steppes in the Early Iron Age* (Center for the Study of Eurasian Nomads, Berkeley, Cal.: Zinat Press, 1995).

belongs to the late fourth century and comes from the village of Sladkovskii, between the Don and the northern Donets.[70] Here, an adult woman was buried with a complete set of arms and armour: an iron spear, a second iron blade half a metre long, an iron sword 73 cm long, with a bronze hilt, and a quiver with iron and bronze arrowheads. There are ethnographic parallels in other pastoralist societies, which suggests that the stories about Amazons reflect, in mythological form, a gender division of labour which was widespread in pastoralist societies.[71] However, there is no good evidence for the existence of armies made up exclusively of women warriors.

For men, and sometimes for women, war was the key to prestige and honour. While successful management of one's herds ensured bare survival, and fortunate marriages created useful connections, success in battle promised wealth, status and power. At annual festivals in the Pontic steppes, regional leaders offered wine to those who had killed enemies in the last year, while those who had not killed were shamed and could drink no wine[72] (IV:66). Herodotus, who also came from a society that admired warfare, conveys starkly the militaristic tone of this world.

> When a Scythian kills his first man, he drinks his blood; of all those he kills in battle he carries the heads to the king. When he has brought in a head, he takes

a share of whatever loot they have obtained, but without bringing a head he has none. The warrior scalps the head thus: he cuts it in a circle round the ears and, taking the head in his hands, shakes it loose. Then he cleans out the flesh with the rib of an ox and kneads the skin with his hands. When he has softened it all, he has got himself, as it were, a napkin. He hangs the napkin from the bridle of the horse he rides himself and takes great pride in it. The man who has most skins as napkins is judged the greatest man among these people. Many of them also make garments to wear, out of the scalps, stitching them together like the usual coats of skin. Many Scythians also take the right hands of their enemies, when dead, and stripping the skin off, nails and all, make of them coverings for their arrow quivers. ...Many of them, too, flay whole men and, stretching the skins upon a frame, carry them round on their horses. (4:64)

The most prized trophies were the heads of defeated enemies. Commonly, a warrior would turn the head of particularly eminent victims into a drinking cup, by sawing the skull below the eyebrows, and gilding the upper part or covering it with hide. Heroes displayed such trophies with pride (4:65). In Bel'sk, archaeologists have discovered a workshop which seems to have specialized in the making of cups from human skulls.[73] Occasionally, those defeated in battle ended up as human sacrifices. According to Herodotus, one in a hundred captives were sacrificed to the god of war, who was represented by a huge sword. The victims had wine poured over their heads, before their throats were cut and their blood was poured over the sword/god (4:62). Often their right arms were severed once they were dead, presumably to prevent their souls from engaging in combat.

The military tactics of the Scythians depended on their mobility, their skill with the composite bow, and their ability to coordinate their actions. Traps, ambushes and harrassment, the techniques of modern guerilla armies, were natural to people used to hunting animals as well as humans, and they used such methods effectively in the campaign against Darius in 514. Scythian warriors kept their compound bows, together with supplies of arrows, in a specially designed case, known to the Greeks as a *gorytus*. They carried files with which they made their arrows razor-sharp before use, and often they attached thorns, which caught in the victim's flesh, or dipped their arrows in poisons made from adder's venom or hemlock. These techniques ensured a painful death even from light wounds.[74]

Where pastoralists were more sedentary, their military methods were closer to those of the agrarian world. Indeed, it may have been familiarity with the military tactics of central Asian pastoralists that encouraged Darius to invade the Pontic steppes. The Massagetae, though described by Herodotus as mobile pastoralists (1:216), certainly carried on irrigation agriculture in some regions along the Syr Darya, and even settled in towns. Their armies defeated Cyrus in *c*.529, using both infantry and cavalry, and armed with battle-axes and spears as well as bows.[75] Their military tactics were also typical of the agrarian world as is shown by Herodotus' account of the final battle of Cyrus' Central Asian campaign.

Of all the battles that were fought among the barbarians, I judge this to have been the severest,...First, they say, the two sides remained at a distance from one another and shot arrows, and afterwards, when all their missiles were spent, they fought hand to hand with spears and daggers. Long they remained fighting in close combat, and neither side would flee. But finally the Massagetae got the upper hand. (1:214)

The Massagetae used metal armour, including coats of iron mail and helmets, as did the Sarmatians of the Pontic region. Wealthier Scythians may also have used armour from as early as the sixth century BCE. Many Massagetean horses had breastplates of bronze, while their own weapons were made of bronze, but decorated with gold. The use of light bone armour was an old tradition in the steppes, probably dating to the second millennium BCE.[76] Pausanias described how pastoral nomads made bone armour from the hooves of mares, splitting them, then arranging them like 'the scales of a dragon', before sewing them with animal sinews into breastplates. Though weaker than metal armour, bone armour was light and cheap, and

Plate 6.3 Warrior on the Golden Comb (© Society for Co-operation in Russian and Soviet Studies).

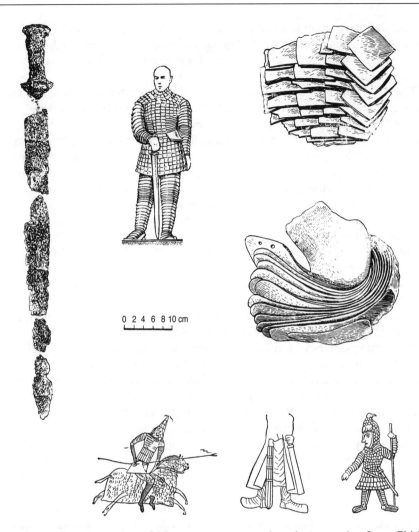

Figure 6.7 Reconstruction of Massagetean armour based on remains from Chirik-Rabat, reproduced from S. P. Tolstov *Po drevnim del'tam Oksa i Yaksarta*, (Moscow; Izd-vo vostochnoi literatury, 1962).

gave protection against most arrows and even against sword-thrusts.[77] The use of metal armour, at least by wealthier pastoralists, may have been a response to the improved compound bows of the Scythic era. The Romans called these heavy steppe cavalry *cataphractarii*. They were the earliest proto-types of the medieval European knight. The effectiveness of the early *cataphractarii* was limited, however, by the lack of stirrups, so that they gripped their horses precariously with their knees. This prevented them from wearing the heaviest types of metal armour, and made it relatively easy to throw them from their mounts. Besides, in the second century CE, Alans (probably descendants of the Massagetae) began to use Hunnic bows with stiffened end

147

pieces, that gave them enough power to penetrate early forms of armour. As a result, the tactics of the Massagetae and the Sarmatians died out once more on the steppelands, well before they began to transform warfare in medieval Europe.[78]

The appearance of armoured cavalry with heavier horses was a recurrent feature of steppe history at least from the first millennium. Lattimore notes that in steppe societies there was a characteristic 'alternation between elite, aristocratic, heavy-armed cavalry in small numbers and the light cavalry of mounted archers who represented a total mobilization of the manpower of a tribe or people, as in the time of Chinghis Khan'.[79] Light cavalry arise naturally out of steppeland life, and can fight over vast distances by using their tough steppe ponies in relays. However, heavily armed cavalry require large horses that need to be stall-fed, and probably need to be stabled in winter, so they can exist only in areas where some agriculture is practised. Usually, only wealthy pastoralists could afford to keep stronger breeds of stall-fed horses, so that the appearance of heavy cavalry probably signals a growth in material inequalities. Where we find heavily armed cavalry on the steppes, we can already suspect we are dealing with semi-agricultural societies, with a reasonably steep hierarchy of wealth and power, and perhaps, as with some of the Sarmatian tribes, with semi-urbanized peoples as well.[80]

Descriptions of Scythian religion reflect the diversity of the lands they occupied. The agricultural communities of the wooded steppes had ancient religious traditions, reflected in the building of monumental centres in towns such as Bel'sk, in which offerings of animals or produce were burnt for gods of the sun and fertility. Presumably, though we cannot be sure, such rituals involved elements of shamanism and of ancestor worship. Like most steppe religions, that of the Scythians was 'ethnic', for its details linked it to a particular political or social grouping. However, it shared many general features with other steppe religions, including: 'polytheism, the belief in a supreme deity, an armed equestrian deity, the veneration of Heaven, Earth, Water and Fire, the worship of ancestors, meditation in the form of shamanistic practices, both human and domestic animal sacrifice, etc'.[81] Scythian religious ideas also reflected wider influences, from Central Asia, northern Mesopotamia and the Greek world.[82] Herodotus' accounts suggest that the Scythians he encountered had incorporated many Greek gods into their pantheon, though it may be that Herodotus was using Greek names for Scythian gods (IV:302). Herodotus singled out as particularly important the practice of sacrificing animals, and sometimes humans, to Ares, who was represented by a large iron sword (IV:62). The hierarchical tribal structures of Scythian pastoralists are reflected in a powerful cult of ancestor gods from whom living rulers claimed descent.

The political functions of Scythian religion also appear in the role of the hereditary priests known as *enarei*. *Enarei* prophesied with the use of bundles of willow rods which they laid on the ground one by one, or they split the bark of lime trees and prophesied as they unwove the fibres of the bark. Like some Chukchi or Central Asian shamans, or like the *berdache* of some North American peoples, the male *enarei* often dressed in women's clothes.[83] They could be powerful political actors. When chiefs fell sick, they would summon *enarei* to identify who had caused the sickness. The priests would identify the culprit and that person, in turn, could ask other *enarei* to deny his guilt. Eventually, either the first accused would be executed, or, if most other *enarei* accepted his innocence, the original priests would be killed, by placing them in a wagon which was set on fire (IV:68). The brutality of the punishment suggests the political sensitivity of the work of the *enarei*.

Did distinctive religious traditions imply a distinctive sense of 'Scythian' ethnicity? The problem of ethnicity in non-literate societies is extremely complex. Modern forms of ethnicity, which in principle link each political unit with a particular sense of ethnic identity, offer misleading models for most pre-modern societies. Where political power is multi-layered, personal and unstable, and individuals are linked by many different, sometimes conflicting, ties of language, kinship, patronage and politics, ethnicity is hard to pin down. Some anthropologists have argued that in pre-modern societies there existed no enduring ethnicities apart from the pragmatic and often temporary choices made by individuals and groups. However, this is going too far. The many identities available in Inner Eurasia, though multiple and overlapping, could sometimes be experienced as objective realities that bound individuals and groups together. This sense of an external identity was embodied in powerful symbols of allegiance to individuals, dynasties, gods, and sometimes even vaguer group identities. For example, Herodotus describes Scythian origin myths that he encountered in Olbia, and these suggest the existence of at least some sense of a shared past (IV:5–7). He also tells two stories of Hellenized Scythians who were murdered for betraying Scythian customs (IV:76–80). The difficulty for the historian is to treat ethnicity in a balanced way. In the pastoralist world, the sense of identity could be extremely powerful, but it was also multiple and complex, varying from individual to individual, and depending on circumstance, rank, gender and kinship. This means that it is normally inappropriate to treat ethnonyms such as 'Scythian', as more than one of several available identities at any given moment. Nor is it possible to assume that coherent archaeological complexes represent coherent ethnic identities. Like most ethnic labels, the name 'Scythian' refers to a cluster of tribal groups whose leaders could, on occasion, combine behind powerful leaders, though their strongest identities were usually to more localized groupings. This, as we will see over and over again, was how ethnicity normally worked in the steppes.[84]

STATE FORMATION IN THE STEPPES?

The royal tombs scattered throughout the Inner Eurasian steppes in the first millennium show clearly that pastoralist societies could mobilize powerful confederations, and that their leaders acquired some of the elements of state power.[85] Despite their limitations, the political systems established by pastoralist leaders in the Pontic steppes could be extremely powerful and remarkably durable. In Scythia, the most powerful groups were the ruling clans that Herodotus described as the 'Royal Scythians' (IV:20). After 500 BCE, there appear several spectacular complexes of royal tombs, the most impressive of which are along the lower Dnieper. The tombs of some leaders are spectacularly rich. According to Herodotus, as many as 50 slaves were sometimes strangled and buried along with their royal masters, as well as whole herds of horses (IV:72). Recent excavations at the fifth- to fourth-century site of Chertomlyk, one of the two or three largest Scythian burial mounds, show that he did not exaggerate.[86] Other kurgans of the fourth and third centuries show equally steep gradations of wealth. In the Tolstaya Mogila tomb there is evidence of a huge funeral feast for over 1000 people. While aristocratic kurgans contain gold and silver work, some ordinary tombs made by Greek artisans, presumably to Scythian orders, contain no signs of luxury. The art work of the richer tombs also suggests a considerable cultural gulf, for many Scythian aristocrats became partly Hellenized.[87]

How, precisely, were such political systems created? And how did they function? Answering these questions is tricky because the evidence is so thin, and because existing theories of statehood were designed to explain statehood in the very different environments of the agrarian world. However, when combined with modern studies, the evidence is enough to suggest how political power was mobilized in the steppes.

Like many early states, the first statelike formations in the Inner Eurasian steppes were really more or less stable tribal alliances. Established groupings by family, clan or tribe survived, but above them there emerged supra-tribal dynasties, which could co-ordinate the activities and the economic and military resources of many smaller groups. So dazzling were the achievements of these ruling dynasties that the impression is often created, both in the epic oral literature, and the written records of contemporaries and historians, that they obliterated the lesser groupings. In reality, statelike structures in the steppes normally constituted only a precarious superstructure beneath which traditional lifeways, groupings and alliances survived, becoming visible again only on the collapse of the great ruling dynasties. More powerful state structures with significant bureaucratic structures and the ability to significantly reshape the groups they ruled probably did not appear in the steppes before the Hsiung-nu empire of the second century BCE. In the Scythic world, there appeared powerful ruling dynasties, and some took significant steps towards statehood, but none were sufficiently bureaucratized or durable to be regarded as true states.

We have seen already (ch. 4) that military threats could trigger the formation of large military alliances in the pastoralist world. Herodotus' account of the great war of the Scythian tribes with Darius in 514 BCE, shows how a large, multi-tribal army emerged through negotiation between different tribal leaders.[88] Faced with the threat of Darius' huge army (IV:87), 'The Scythians reasoned that they were not able to resist Darius' army in a straight fight on their own, and so they sent messengers to their neighbours' (IV:102). In response to the Scythian request to ally against the Persians, some neighbours agreed, while others refused (IV:119). As they retreated before Darius' huge army, the allied forces deliberately led their opponents through the lands of those tribes who had refused to join them. 'If they would not enter the war against the Persians voluntarily, said the Scythians, let them do so against their will.' There is no sign that the alliance survived Darius' retreat, after an unsuccessful campaign lasting only a few months.

Though forming such alliances was not difficult in an emergency, turning them into durable political systems was much more difficult. This was particularly true in the pastoralist world, where hierarchies of power, wealth and status were often shallow and unstable. The trick was to mobilize substantial material and symbolic resources, and use them to sustain the hierchies that emerged in periods of crisis. Wealth or prestige goods could be redistributed in ways that enhanced the ruler's prestige, paid for personal retinues that could enforce the leader's will, and locked lesser pastoralist leaders into enduring alliances.

However, mobile pastoralist societies produced only limited surpluses of any kind, so surpluses had to be mobilized from outside the pastoralist world. This is why durable political systems in the steppes always rested on relations of exchange or tribute-taking with neighbouring societies that produced more substantial or more valuable surpluses.[89] The exact mechanisms of state-formation varied depending on the types of tributes that different pastoralists could exact, and that, in turn, reflected the ecology of the regions they controlled. But all pastoralist states mobilized substantial wealth from non-pastoralist neighbours.

In the first millennium, we can observe such processes most clearly in Scythia and, later, in Mongolia (see ch. 8). Throughout the first millennium, Scythian leaders took resources from neighbouring agrarian communities by force or through trade. The earliest statelike entity of the Scythians, formed in the seventh century and based in modern Azerbaijan, depended largely on the war booty secured by raids into Assyria and Mesopotamia. However, once driven out of Mesopotamia, Scythian leaders had to rely on the more meagre resources they could extract from other pastoralists, or from farming communities of the wooded steppes or from the Greek trading towns of the Black Sea. The meagreness of these resources explains, in part, why pastoralist states in this region tended to be weaker than those that emerged later in the eastern steppes.[90] We hear of no great expansionist empires in the region, nor of durable imperial dynasties.

Despite this, pastoralist leaders did exact resources from their neighbours and some sustained a level of grandeur that Herodotus, at least felt worthy of the label, 'Basileus'. Relations between pastoralists and farming communities were unambiguous. The appearance of a string of fortified settlements along the southern borders of the Ukrainian wooded steppes late in the seventh century suggests that local rulers tried to resist Scythian incursions, though without success. Strabo wrote: 'The nomads...conduct wars for tribute. Having made land available to those wishing to engage in agriculture, they content themselves with the receipt of an agreed and moderate tribute, not for the sake of profit, but to satisfy their own everyday needs; but if the tribute-payers do not pay, they will engage in war with them.'[91] Tributes could include levies of troops as well as the collection of grain or other supplies. Scythian overlords also demanded contributions to celebrate the funerals of kings or chieftains. Amongst less well defended farming communities, tribute exaction could be a violent and brutal business. In the first century CE Ovid wrote that, as soon as the Danube was covered in ice:

> The enemy, mighty with his horses and his swiftly flying arrows, lays waste the countryside far and wide...Few are there who venture to till the land, and those who do, unhappy men, must plough with one hand and hold their weapon in the other. The shepherd wears a helmet as he plays his pipes, and the timorous sheep fear war more than the wolf.[92]

On the other hand, there may have been periods when the payment of Scythian tributes was not particularly burdensome, and had little impact on traditional lifeways.[93]

Over time, trade became as important as tribute. Gradually, the political and military power of Scythian leaders, and the commercial power of the Greek city states linked the various communities of Scythia into a single economic and cultural system. Early Scythian settlers acquired most of their ceramics and metal goods from the artisans of agricultural townships, either in the form of tributes or in exchange for pastoralist products. Regional artisans in centres such as Bel'sk imported their raw materials from the Caucasus, the southern Urals, and even, perhaps, from Kazakhstan.[94] Herodotus' account hints at the existence of extensive exchange networks reaching into the Urals and the central steppes (IV:24). Presumably the Scythians, like later pastoralist rulers of the Pontic steppes, tapped the commercial wealth passing through their lands by levying 'protection' rents. We know that Scythians sometimes traded furs to the urban communities to their south. We can presume, on the basis of later analogies, that these came from hunting societies of north Russia and the Urals, and were taken either as a form of tribute, or in return for Mediterranean goods traded through cities such as Bel'sk or Elizavetovskoe. According to Herodotus, Scythian traders exchanged goods with distant communities using local interpreters.[95] Perhaps these networks reached as far as the Altai, where the presence of sable fur clothing and even gold in the wealthier Pazyryk tombs, suggests the existence of a flourishing trade through this part of what Rubinson has called the 'fur routes', linking Siberia with China, from at least the fifth century BCE.[96] The importance of the Kerch' peninsula to both Greeks and Scythians suggests that trade routes passing along the Don towards the Volga, the Urals and Kazakhstan were already a lucrative source of commercial revenues. Haussig argues that a 'northern' Silk Road existed from at least the time of the Scythians, and that it reached as far as Kansu. This is probably an exaggeration, as the absence of significant amounts of goods from Central Asia indicates only occasional contacts with central or eastern Asia.[97]

Perhaps because they had relatively easy access to the pottery and metal goods produced in agricultural communities, there is little sign of metal work or pottery amongst nomadic Scythian communities; most of the ceramics and metal goods in early Scythian tombs were imported from agrarian regions, in a pattern of exchange already familiar in the fourth millennium BCE.[98]

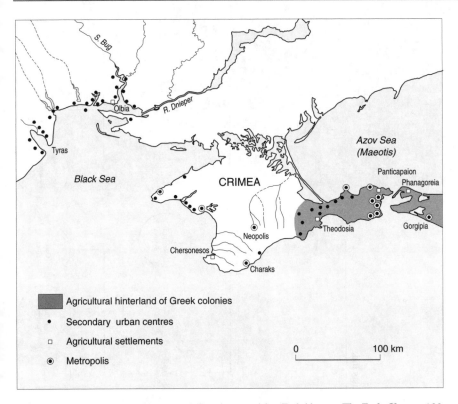

Map 6.3 Greek colonies of the north Pontic area. After Dolukhanov *The Early Slavs*, p.130

However, by the time of Herodotus, Scythian towns such as Kamenskoe and Elizavetovskoe had developed as important artisan and trade centres in their own right.

With the appearance of Greek city states, these systems of exchange linking hunter-gatherers, agriculturalists and pastoralists, began to reach into the Mediterranean as well. From the sixth century, Scythians began to import Greek prestige goods such as olive oil or wines in amphora, as well as vases, and metalwork in bronze, silver and gold. Before the late fifth century, Scythian trade was as much with the Persian as with the Mediterranean world, for up to the middle of the fifth century, Athens seems to have conceded to Persia control of the Black Sea and its trade. However, from the time of Pericles, Athenian influence increased in the Black Sea, and by 425 some 50 Black Sea cities were paying tributes to Athens, which were collected by Athenian warships. By Xenophon's time, most cities along the northern shores of Anatolia were Greek in orientation, whatever the ethnic origins of their populations.[99]

In the fourth century, precious goods produced to the orders of Scythian rulers, mainly in Greek cities of the Black Sea, but also in the Mediterranean, appear in colossal quantities in Scythian tombs. By the late fifth century, Greek vases begin to appear even in the tombs of ordinary Scythians. In return, Scythia supplied grain, above all to the trading cities of the

Table 6.1 Chart of regional and 'world systems'

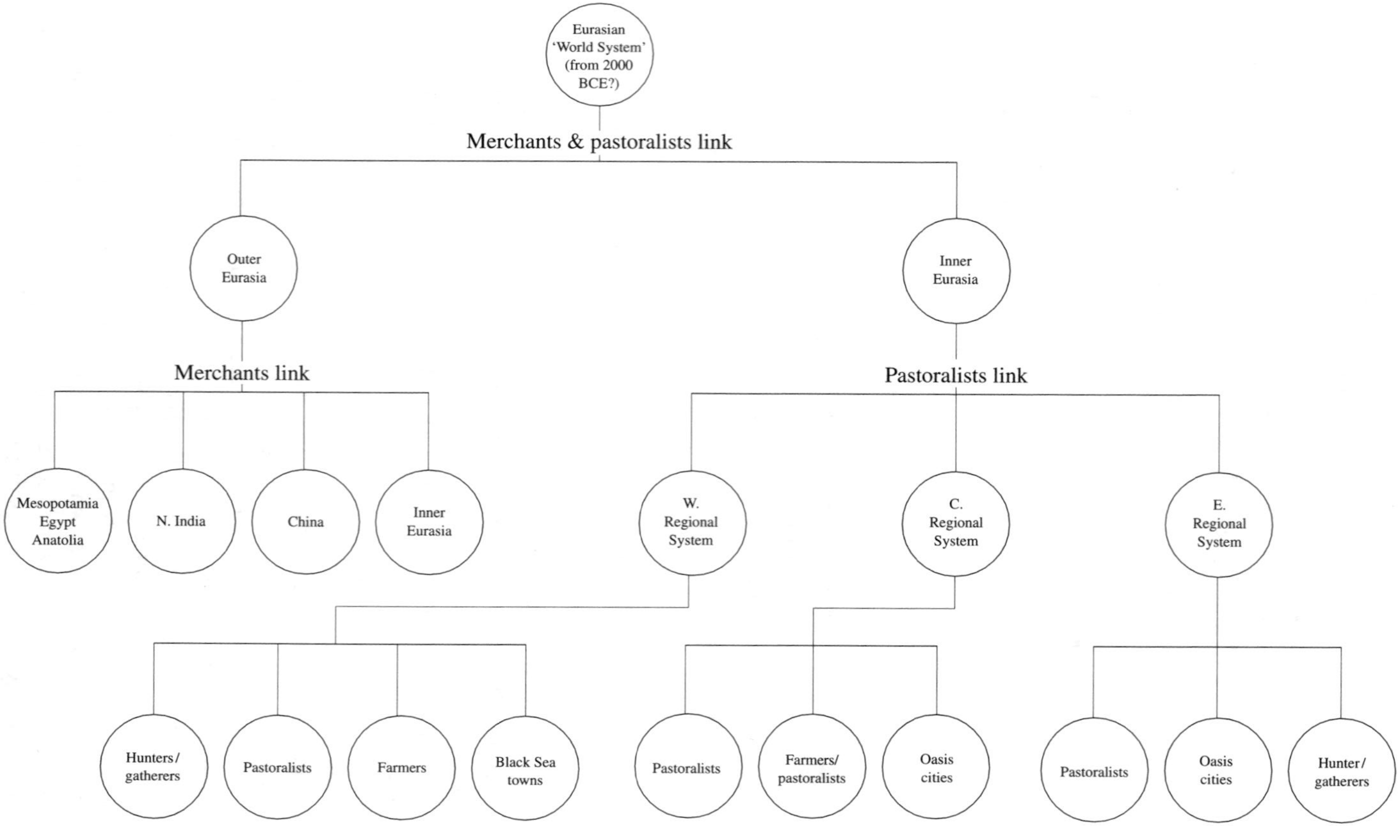

Bosporus. Though we do not know the details of this trade, it seems clear that Scythian chiefs acted as middlemen, exacting grain in the form of tributes, and then exchanging it for the luxury goods of the Greek Black Sea cities. Though grain was by far the most important Scythian export, other goods were also exported, including furs, fish, livestock produce and cattle, honey, wax and even slaves. Slaves were often captured in local conflicts, but were of little direct use to nomadic pastoralists, so they were generally traded on to merchants from the Mediterranean who specialized in artisan or warrior slaves. Slaves with Scythian names begin to appear in the Mediterranean from as early as the sixth century.[100]

Scythians also had services to sell, particularly military services. Frequently, they served as mercenaries in return for cash payments or prestige goods. Scythians supplied contingents to the armies of Cyrus as he fought Saka tribes of Central Asia late in the sixth century. Scythians also fought with the Persians at Marathon or on the flanks of the army of Darius III at Gaugamela, in 331 BCE. Finally, Scythian warriors acted as garrison troops within the Achaemenid empire.[101]

Such exchanges ensured that, despite the ecological, linguistic and cultural differences of the various communities of Scythia, there began to emerge a distinctive Pontic culture, which was the creation of Greek colonists and indigenous farming populations as well as of the dominant Scythian pastoralists. The penetration of Greek wares into the steppes and the towns and villages of the wooded steppes, and even into the forests of Russia and the Urals, brought remote communities into commercial contact with the Greek world. The return of Scythian mercenaries, some of whom may have lived for years in the Mediterranean, undoubtedly planted many elements of Greek thought and culture deep within Scythian society.[102]

The eclecticism of Scythian culture was particularly evident in the neighbourhood of Greek cities such as Olbia or Panticapaeum, where there began to emerge a syncretic world that was neither Scythian nor Greek. Using illustrations from a tomb of the first century CE, Rostovtzeff offers a fascinating reconstruction of the life of a gentleman of Scythian Crimea.

> The dead man, armed, and followed by a retainer, is riding towards his family residence, a tent of true nomadic type. His household, wife, children, and servants, are assembled in the tent and beside it, under the shade of a single tree; beside the tree is his long spear, and his quiver hangs from a branch. The interpretation is easy: the gentleman is a landed proprietor, who spends most of his time in town: in summer, during the harvest season, he goes out to the steppes, armed, and accompanied by armed servants; taking his family with him. He supervises the work in the fields, and defends his labourers and harvesters from the attacks of neighbours who live beyond the fortified lines: Taurians from the mountains, ferocious foot-soldiers; Scythians from the plains, horsemen and landowners. Who knows? perhaps he raids a little himself. Fights between neighbours are often represented in Panticapaean tomb-paintings of the first or second century BC. We see the Panticapaean chief, followed by his little army, battling with a black-bearded Taurian or with shag-haired Scythians. ...When he moves house, he uses heavy wagons to transport his tent, his furniture, and his family.[103]

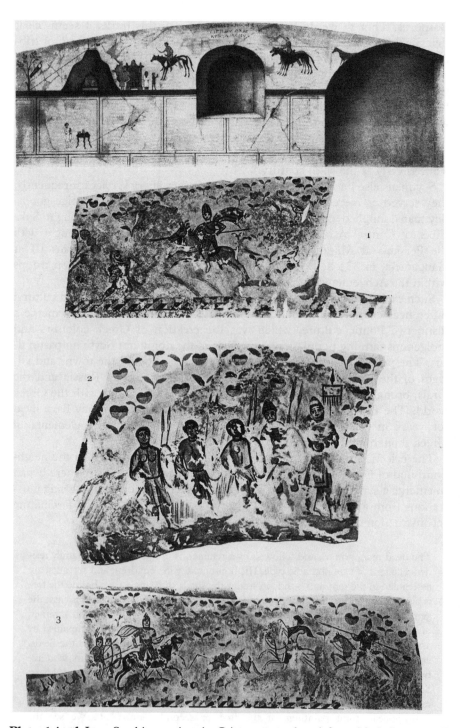

Plate 6.4a–d Late Scythian society in Crimea, reproduced from M. I. Rostovtzeff *Iranians and Greeks in South Russia* (Oxford: Oxford University Press, 1922). Photograph courtesy of the Bodleian Library.

Rostovtzeff's imaginary reconstruction is a reminder that, despite its dominant role in Inner Eurasian history, pastoralism never existed in 'pure' forms. It always interacted with other ecological adaptations, and there existed many intermediate lifeways.

NOTES

1 N. A. Bokovenko, 'History of studies and the main problems in the archaeology of southern Siberia during the Scythian period' in Davis-Kimball, ed., *Nomads* (pp. 255–61), p. 256.
2 See, e.g., Khazanov, *Nomads*, p. 95; Barfield, *The Nomadic Alternative*, pp. 132–4; and see V. A. Bashilov and L. T. Yablonsky, Introduction, in Davis-Kimball, ed., *Nomads* (pp. xi–xiv), p. xii.
3 This is the conclusion of most Soviet studies; for a good survey, see Jacobson, *Burial Ritual*, pp. 2–5; and see Bashilov and Yablonsky, Introduction, in Davis-Kimball, ed., *Nomads*, p. xiii.
4 Khazanov, *Nomads*, p. 95; L. T. Yablonsky, 'Some ethnogenetical hypotheses' in Davis-Kimball, ed., *Nomads* (pp. 241–52), pp. 242–3.
5 Rudenko, *Frozen Tombs*, translator's intro., p. xxvi; on the horse trade on the Chinese border, see Jagchid and Symons, *Peace, War and Trade*, pp. 8–10, 189; on the horse trade between Inner and Outer Eurasia, see Denis Sinor, 'Horse and pasture'; see also Golden, *Introduction*, p. 9.
6 Pulleyblank, 'Why Tocharians?', pp. 418–19; on the evolution of compound bows, McEwen, Miller and Bergman, 'Early bow design and construction', p. 55.
7 On the first four elements, Watson, *Cultural Frontiers*, p. 109, and see p. 113; on the last three items, see Bashilov and Yablonsky, Introduction, in Davis-Kimball, ed., *Nomads*, p. xiii and 195; on the importance of Siberian influences, see Esther Jacobson, 'Symbolic structures as indicators of the cultural ecology of the early nomads', in Seaman, ed., *Foundations of Empire*, pp. 1–25; see A. Askarov, V. Volkov and N. Ser-Odjav, 'Pastoral and nomadic tribes' in *HCCA*, 1: 467–70 for a description of the 'deer-stones', with designs in the 'Scythian' style, which appear from the Crimea to Eastern Mongolia, and N. A. Bokovenko, 'Tuva during the Scythian period' and V. V. Volkov, 'Early nomads of Mongolia', in Davis-Kimball, ed., *Nomads* (pp. 265–83 and pp. 319–33), pp. 271–2, 325–32.
8 Quintus Curtius, VII.8.30, Loeb edition, 2: 205–7. The translator, Rolfe, assumes the 'Tanais' is the Syr Darya, but the Don seems more likely. Briant, *Etat et pasteurs*, p. 183, notes that there is confusion between the Don and the Amu Darya in many Greco-Roman texts. The strength of ethnic and cultural ties between Saka and Scythian groups is emphasized in Klyashtornyi and Sultanov, *Kazakhstan*, pp. 31–48.
9 Chang, *Archaeology*, 3rd edn, pp. 392, 394; Prusek, *Chinese Statelets*, pp. 101, 119, 130, 134, 224; Chang, *Archaeology*, 3rd edn, pp. 391–4; Golden, *Introduction*, p. 43; Ssu-Ma Ch'ien, *Records*, 1: 74; Waldron, *The Great Wall*, p. 38; N. Ishjamts, 'Nomads in eastern Central Asia', in *HCCA* (pp. 151–69), 2:151.
10 Di Cosmo, 'Ancient Inner Asian Nomads', p. 1100 and see p. 1098, which stresses the survival of farming communities; Chang, *Archaeology*, 3rd edn, p. 391.
11 See, e.g., Altheim, *Attila*, pp. 19ff., and Khazanov, *Nomads*, p. 96; on the adoption of pastoralist military techniques and clothing, Ssu-ma Ch'ien, *Records*, 2:159.

12 Ishjamts, in *HCCA*, 2:152.

13 Askarov, Volkov and Ser-Odjav, 'Pastoral and nomadic tribes', in *HCCA*, 1:466–7; and di Cosmo, 'Ancient Inner Asian Nomads', p. 1099.

14 A. Abeketov and H. Yusupov, 'Ancient Iranian nomads in western Central Asia', in *HCCA* (pp. 23–33), 2:26–9; and see V. Semenov and K. Chugunov, 'New evidence of the Scythian-type culture of Tuva', p. 321, according to which dendrochronological dates give 745±40 BCE; on the labour involved in building it, N. A. Bokovenko, 'Tuva during the Scythian period', in Davis-Kimball, ed., *Nomads*, p. 265.

15 N. A. Bokovenko, 'History of the studies and the main problems in the archaeology of southern Siberia during the Scythian period', in Davis-Kimball, ed., *Nomads*, p. 260, on the wider significance of the Arzhan tomb, and see also N. A. Bokovenko, 'Tuva during the Scythian period', pp. 265–71; see also Semenov and Chugunov, 'New Evidence', p. 322, and see 315–17; under the Hsiung-nu, the seat of honour below the Shan-yü was on the ruler's left, facing north; Ssu-ma Ch'ien, *Records*, 2:164.

16 Bokovenko, 'Tuva during the Scythian period', in Davis-Kimball, ed., *Nomads*, pp. 280–1.

17 Abetekov and Yusupov, 'Ancient Iranian nomads' in *HCCA*, 2:23–4; and see the discussion in Vogelsang, *Rise and Organisation*, pp. 108–9 and 113–16, 131–2; V. I. Sarianidi, in *Ancient Civilizations*, Dec. 1995, p. 301, argues that 'Haomavarga' means 'those Scythians who made Haoma', i.e. 'Soma', thereby linking them with early forms of Zoroastrian rituals; see also L. T. Yablonsky, 'Some ethnogenetical hypotheses' in Davis-Kimball, ed., *Nomads*, pp. 250–1; and P'iankov, 'The Ethnic History of the Sakas'.

18 Abetekov and Yusupov, 'Ancient Iranian nomads', in *HCCA*, 2:30; Briant, *État et pasteurs*, p. 223.

19 Tolstov, *Po drevnim del'tam*, pp. 80–6, 137, 139, 154.

20 Masson and Sarianidi, *Central Asia*, p. 166. On the Tagisken culture, see also A. Askarov, 'The beginning of the Iron Age in Transoxania' *HCCA* (pp. 441–58), 1:444–6.

21 Tolstov, *Po drevnim del'tam*, p. 86, and pp. 182–4.

22 Moravcsik, *Byzantinoturkica*, 1:39; refs to *Iliad* XIII, 3–8 and *Odyssey*, XI, 14–19.

23 Dolukhanov, *Early Slavs*, p. 118.

24 Khazanov, 'The Early State', p. 427; on the possibility that their base was in the north Caucasus, see V. G. Petrenko, 'Scythian culture in the north Caucasus' in Davis-Kimball, ed., *Nomads* (pp. 5–22), p. 9.

25 On the attack on Palestine, see Jeremiah, 5:15–18, which refers to 'a mighty nation, . . . an ancient nation, a nation whose language thou knowest not . . .; their quiver is as an open sepulchre, they are all mighty men. And they shall eat up thine harvest, and thy bread, . . . they shall eat up thy flocks and thine herds; . . . they shall impoverish thy fenced cities'.

26 A. I. Melyukova, 'The Scythians and Sarmatians', in *CHEIA* (pp. 97–117), pp. 99–100; for the archaeological evidence of their passage past Darband, see Braund, *Georgia in Antiquity*, p. 45–6, and Melyukova, *Stepi evropeiskoi chasti SSSR*, p. 34; Vogelsang has argued that they conquered from south of the Caspian sea and merged with the Median elites; see Vogelsang, *Rise and Organisation*, pp. 214–15.

27 V. G. Petrenko, 'Scythian culture in the north Caucasus', and A. I. Melyukova, 'Scythians of southeastern Europe' (pp. 27–61), in Davis-Kimball, ed., *Nomads*,

pp. 18, 31–2; see also Marčenko and Vinogradov, 'The Scythian period', p. 806; Melyukova, *Stepi evropeiskoi chasti*, pp. 48–9.

28 Marčenko and Vinogradov, 'The Scythian period', p. 806.

29 Darius' campaign is described in Herodotus IV:1, 46, 83–7, 89, 92, 93, 97–8, 102, 118–43; and in Ctesias (fragments 13, 20–21), and Strabo (VII, 3, 14). According to Strabo, Darius' army turned back only 15 days' march north-east of the Danube, before even reaching the Dniester.

30 Melyukova, *Stepi evropeiskoi chasti*, p. 40; I have followed the periodization of Marčenko and Vinogradov, 'The Scythian period'; see p. 808.

31 Khazanov, *Nomads*, p. 51, citing Strabo, VII.3.17.

32 Cited in Khazanov, *Sotsial'naya istoriya*, 157.

33 Dolukhanov, *Early Slavs*, p. 120; Melyukova, *Stepi evropeiskoi chasti*, p. 35; Melyukova, 'Scythians of southeastern Europe', in Davis-Kimball, ed., *Nomads*, p. 29.

34 M. G. Moshkova, 'Brief review of the history of the Sauromatian and Sarmatian tribes', in Davis-Kimball, ed., *Nomads*, pp. 85–9.

35 Diodorus, 2.43, cited in E. I. Lubo-Lesnichenko, 'The Huns 3rd century BC–6th century AD', in Basilov, ed., *Nomads of Eurasia* (pp. 41–53), p. 41; see also Sulimirski, *The Sarmatians*, p. 18; Tolstov, *Po drevnim del'tam*, p. 186; Y. A. Zadneprovskiy, 'The nomads of northern Central Asia after the invasion of Alexander', in *HCCA* (pp. 457–72), 2:465–6.

36 M. G. Moshkova, 'Brief review' in Davis-Kimball, ed., *Nomads*, pp. 87–9, 150; Marčenko and Vinogradov, 'The Scythian period', p. 811.

37 Melyukova, 'The Scythians', in *CHEIA*, p. 107; V. S. Olkhovsky, 'Scythian culture in Crimea' in Davis-Kimball, ed., *Nomads*, pp. 72–3; see also Khazanov, 'Early state', p. 427; on the slow intermingling of Scythian and Sarmatian peoples from the fifth century, see Sulimirski, *The Sarmatians*, p. 100–11.

38 Tolstov, *Po drevnim del'tam*, p. 128, and see pp. 89ff., 123–7; also see N. N. Negmatov, 'States in north-western Central Asia' in *HCCA* (pp. 441–56), 2:446–9; and Yablonsky, 'Some ethnogenetical hypotheses', in Davis-Kimball, ed., *Nomads*, pp. 251–2.

39 Loeb edn, 2:235, from Q.C. VIII.i.11–13; the remains of frescoes from Afrasiab suggest the accuracy of this report; on the early history of Afrasiab, see *Ocherki istorii SSSR: pervoobshchinnyi stroi*, p. 242; Shishkina, 'Ancient Samarkand', pp. 86–9; and Gafurov, *Tadzhiki*, 1989, 1:95–6.

40 Askarov, 'The beginning of the Iron Age in Transoxania', in *HCCA*, 1:454–5.

41 The largest in Margiana, at Gonur, covered *c*.22 hectares. Lamberg-Karlovsky, 'The Bronze Age *khanates*', p. 403.

42 Masson and Sarianidi, *Central Asia*, p. 160.

43 According to Boyce, *History*, 1:189–90; but other sources have dated him to the sixth century BCE, partly on the basis of their identification of Cyrus with Zoroaster's patron, Vistaspa; Boyce, *History*, 2:68–9.

44 Abetekov and Yusupov, 'Ancient Iranian Nomads', in *HCCA*, 2:23; Boyce, *History*, 1:184–8, and see 1:4, 13–14, 17, 104–7; the *Avesta* was not fixed in writing until the sixth century CE, ibid., 1:20.

45 This eschatology, involving a final judgement, the defeat of evil, resurrection and eternal life, became a central idea in the monotheistic religions of the Mediterranean world; Boyce, *History*, 1:246.

46 Boyce, *History*, 1:192–3; the problem of an early Central Asian state is discussed clearly in Gafurov, *Tadzhiki*, 1989, 1:71–4; Frye is sceptical about the existence of anything tighter than a loose confederation of city-states (*History of Ancient*

Iran, p. 62); but Gardiner-Garden takes the idea of a pre-Achaemenid Bactrian state more seriously (*Ktesias*, pp. 6–8).

47 Rostovtzeff, *Iranians and Greeks*, pp. 61–2.

48 Tret'yakov and Mongait, eds, *Ocherki istorii SSSR: pervoobshchinnyi stroi*, p. 323; and see Rostovtzeff, *Iranians and Greeks*, p. 63.

49 Braund, *Georgia in Antiquity*, pp. 89–90; see also Marčenko and Vinogradov, 'The Scythian period, p. 806; on Olbia, see *Ocherki istorii SSSR: pervoobshchinnyi stroi*, pp. 326–32.

50 Braund, *Georgia in Antiquity*, p. 86.

51 di Cosmo, 'Ancient Inner Asian nomads', pp. 1110–11.

52 Melyukova, 'The Scythians', in *CHEIA*, p. 104.

53 Rolle, *Scythians*, p. 117.

54 Haussig, *Geschichte Zentralasiens…in vorislamischer Zeit*, p. 32 places it on the Volga, though Herodotus' claim (4:123) that Darius sacked the town suggests it was much further west. See Melyukova, *Stepi evropeiskoi chasti*, pp. 47–8 on the Budini and the controversy over the site of Gelonus.

55 Khazanov, 'Early State', p. 429; and see Melyukova, 'The Scythians', in *CHEIA*, p. 104. L. Pavlinskaya describes the kingdom of Atheas as 'the first nomadic state in history' in Basilov ed., 'Scythians and Sakians 8th–3rd centuries BC', in *Nomads of Eurasia* (pp. 19–39), p. 27.

56 Rolle, *Scythians*, p. 121; and see Melyukova, *Stepi evropeiskoi chasti*, pp. 52–3.

57 M. Yu. Treister, 'Archaeological news from the northern Pontic region', in *Ancient Civilizations from Scythia to Siberia*, 1: 1 (1994:2–39); p. 32.

58 Rudenko, *Frozen Tombs*, p. 221; Herodotus, IV, 64; Rudenko's book is still the fundamental source on the Pazyryk tombs, but excavations continue in the area to the present day; there is a good, brief, description in N. A. Bokovenko, 'Scythian cultures in the Altai mountains', in Davis-Kimball, ed., *Nomads* (pp. 285–97), pp. 288–92.

59 There is a superb description of the many types of pastoralism in modern and ancient Central Asia in Boris A. Litvinskii, 'The ecology of the ancient nomads of Soviet Central Asia and Kazakhstan', in Seaman, ed., *Ecology and Empire*, pp. 61–72; and see the equally vivid account of early modern Kazakh migrations in Klyashtornyi and Sultanov, *Kazakhstan*, pp. 328–34.

60 Rudenko, *Frozen Tombs*, p. 60.

61 Gryaznov, *Civilization of Southern Siberia*, p. 155; Rudenko, *Frozen Tombs*, p. 57; on horse breeds see Melyukova, *Stepi evropeiskoi chasti*, p. 114; Sinor, 'Horse and Pasture' on the nature of steppe ponies; Barclay, *Role of the Horse*, p. 87; and Azzarolli, *Early History*, pp. 69–70.

62 Melyukova, *Stepi evropeiskoi chasti*, pp. 114–15; Herodotus noted that the Scythians never used pig, and archaeological evidence supports this claim, IV:63.

63 See M. V. Kriukov and V. P. Kurylev, 'The origins of the yurt: Evidence from Chinese sources of the third century BC. to the thirteenth century A.D.', in Seaman, ed., *Foundations of Empire*, pp. 143–56.

64 Cited in Rudenko, *Frozen Tombs*, p. 62, and Melyukova, in *Stepi evropeiskoi chasti*, p. 113, from pseudo-Hippocrates, 'On wind, water and places', p. 25.

65 Khazanov, *Sotsial'naya istoriya*, p. 164–6.

66 Rhoads Murphey, 'An ecological history of Central Asian nomadism', in Seaman, ed., *Ecology and Empire* (pp. 41–58), pp. 47–8.

67 Rolle, *Scythians*, p. 94.

68 Cited in Rudenko, *Frozen Tombs*, p. 212; Ctesias was a physician at the Achaemenid court, who wrote a history of Persia of which fragments have

survived, on whom, see Vogelsang, *Rise and Organisation*, pp. 210–14 and Gardiner-Garden, *Ktesias*; on the gender division of labour see also Jacobson, *Burial Rituals*, p. 16 and Melyukova, 'The Scythians', in *CHEIA*, p. 106.

69 Davis-Kimball, 'Warrior women', p. 45; and see Davis-Kimball and Yablonsky, *Kurgans*.
70 Smirnov, 'Une "Amazone" du IVe siècle,' pp. 121–41; see also Melyukova, 'The Scythians', in *CHEIA*, p. 112; Dolukhanov, *Early Slavs*, p. 123.
71 Smirnov, 'Une "Amazone" du IVe siècle'.
72 On the term '*archai*', which, in this context, could be translated as 'chief' or 'governor', see Khazanov, *Sotsial'naya istoriya*, pp. 120–1; amongst the Hsiung-nu, after a battle, those with enemy captives or the heads of enemies killed received a cup of wine; Ssu-ma Ch'ien, *Records*, p. 165.
73 Rolle, *Scythians*, p. 83.
74 Ibid., p. 65.
75 Sulimirski, *The Sarmatians*, 29, 81; T. Sulimirski, 'The Scythians', in *The Cambridge History of Iran* vol. 2, Cambridge: Cambridge University Press, 1985, pp. 149–99, points out that some Scythians also used armour, but not saddles, or stirrups; on irrigation agriculture, see Tolstov, *Po drevnim del'tam*, pp. 80–6, 136.
76 Maenchen-Helfen, *World of the Huns*, pp. 242–7; and see Abetekov and Yusupov, 'Ancient Iranian nomads', in *HCCA*, 2:30; and Rolle, *Scythians*, p. 67.
77 Cited in Maenchen-Helfen, *World of the Huns*, p. 242; see pp. 241–50 for a good discussion of armour on the steppes.
78 Sulimirski, *The Sarmatians*, 32; McEwen, et al., 'Early Bow Design', p. 56; on the stirrup, Barclay, *The Role of the Horse*, pp. 40–1.
79 O. Lattimore, *Nomads and Commissars: Mongolia Revisited*, New York: Oxford University Press, 1962, p. 41.
80 Ibid., pp. 41–2.
81 Khazanov, 'The Spread of world religions', p. 12.
82 Herodotus' account is in IV, 5–11, 36, 59–63, 67–73, 76; see also Melyukova, *Stepi evropeiskoi chasti*, pp. 68, 122.
83 Vitebsky, *The Shaman*, p. 93.
84 There is a very good discussion of the problem of ethnicity in tribal societies in Heather, *The Goths*, pp. 3–7.
85 The best description of Scythian tombs is in Rolle, *Scythians*.
86 Herodotus, *Histories*, IV:71, 72 describes a royal burial; on Chertomlyk, see E. V. Chernenko, 'Investigations of the Scythian tumuli in the Northern Pontic Steppe', in *Ancient Civilizations from Scythia to Siberia*, 1 (1) (1994):45–53, p. 47-8; see also: Alekseev, Murzin, and Rolle, *Chertomlyk*.
87 Melyukova, 'The Scythians', in *CHEIA*, pp. 105–6; on Tolstaya Mogila, see Rolle, *Scythians*, pp. 34–5.
88 Briant, *Etat et pasteurs*, p. 195, argues that the real date is 513; in 519 Darius campaigned more successfully against the Saka in Central Asia, and captured their king, Skunkha. Briant adds that B. A. Rybakov has shown the accuracy of Herodotus' account in his: *Gerodotova Skifiya*, Moscow, 1979. However, the *Cambridge Ancient History*, 1980, vol. IV, pp. 234ff. is more sceptical.
89 See, e.g., W. Irons, 'Political stratification among pastoral nomads', in *Pastoral Production and Society* (pp. 361–74); p. 362; Khazanov, *Nomads*, p. 3, argues that all nomadic societies (i.e. pastoral nomads) depend on outside societies. However this is strictly true only of pastoral nomadic states.
90 See Golden, 'The Qipcaqs of Medieval Eurasia', in Seaman and Marks, eds, *Rulers from the Steppe*.

91 Cited in Khazanov, *Sotsial'naya istoriya*, p. 156; on Scythian forts, see Melyukova, *Stepi evropeiskoi chasti*, p. 68.

92 From *Tristia ex Ponto*, cited in Gryaznov, *Civilization of Southern Siberia*, p. 132.

93 Sulimirski argues this was true of the early rule of the Scyths before the fifth century; 'The Scythians', in *Cambridge History of Iran*, p. 154.

94 Melyukova, *Stepi evropeiskoi chasti*, pp. 115–16.

95 Ibid., p. 120; see Herodotus, IV:24 for Herodotus' description of this trade route.

96 Rudenko, *Frozen Tombs*, p. 223. In the Altai there was too little pasture for horses to be the main item of trade. In the steppes, though, horses probably acted as a form of currency. On the 'fur route', see Rubinson, 'A reconsideration of Pazyryk', in Seaman, ed., *Foundations of Empire*, pp. 68–76.

97 Haussig, *Geschichte Zentralasiens ... in vorislamischer Zeit*; and see Melyukova, *Stepi evropeiskoi chasti*, p. 120.

98 Melyukova, *Stepi evropeiskoi chasti*, p. 115.

99 Braund, *Georgia in Antiquity*, pp. 126–7 and 132–5, and see pp. 123–5; as Braund points out, evidence of trade with Persia suggests that Athens before the late fifth century was not as dependent on Ukrainian grain as has sometimes been supposed; see, also, P. D. A. Garnsey, 'Grain for Athens', in P. A. Cartledge and F. D. Harvey, eds, *Crux: Essays in Greek History Presented to G.E.M. de Ste. Croix*, Exeter, 1985, pp. 62–75; see also Melyukova, *Stepi evropeiskoi chasti*, p. 117.

100 Melyukova, *Stepi evropeiskoi chasti*, pp. 118–20; Khazanov, *Sotsial'naya istoriya*, pp. 137–40.

101 Briant, *Etat et pasteurs*, p. 198.

102 Haussig, *Geschichte Zentralasiens ... in vorislamischer Zeit*, pp. 41–8, argues that this may have been a very important route for the penetration of Greek culture in Scythia.

103 Rostovtzeff, *Iranians and Greeks*, pp. 160–1.

FURTHER READING

For the first time, written sources now become available. The most important early sources on Inner Eurasia are Herodotus, and Ssu-ma Ch'ien. On the archaeology of the Scythia era, See *HCCA*, vol. 2; Rudenko, *The Frozen Tombs*; Rolle, *World of the Scythians*; Artamanov, *Kimmeritsy i skify*; Gryaznov, *Civilization of Southern Siberia*; Davis-Kimball, ed., *Nomads*; and studies by Melyukova. The origin of the Scythian compound bow is discussed in McEwen, et al., 'Early Bow Design'. On the eastern region, see Watson, *Cultural Frontiers*; *Journal of Indo-European Studies*, vol. 23, nos 3 and 4 (1995); Prusek, *Chinese Statelets*; Chang, *Archaeology of Ancient China*. On Central Asia, see Briant, *Etat et pasteurs* and *L'Asie centrale*; Tolstov, *Po drevnim del'-tam*; and *HCCA* vol. 2. On the Pontic steppes, see works by Melyukova, the foremost modern Soviet specialist on the Scythians. Also valuable are Khazanov, *Sotsial'naya istoriya*; and the brief survey in Dolukhanov, *Early Slavs*. There are more popular accounts, with illustrations, in Rice, *The Scythians*; and Phillips, *The Royal Hordes*. Despite its age, Rostovtzeff's *Iranians and Greeks* is still valuable. Kursat-Ahlers, *Zur frühen Staatenbildung*; Khazanov, 'The Early State among the Scythians'; Krader, 'The Origin of the State'; and Christian, 'State Formation in the Steppes', are just part of the large literature on state formation in the pastoralist world. On early Georgia, see Braund, *Georgia in Antiquity*. On the Silk Roads, Haussig's *Geschichte Zentralasiens ... in vorislamischer Zeit*, is full of intriguing ideas and hypotheses but not always reliable. On the Sarmatians, the standard history is Sulimirski, *The Sarmatians*, but see also the recent archaeological work summarized in Davis-Kimball, *Nomads of the Eurasian Steppes*. On Amazons, see Davis-Kimball, 'Warrior Women of the Eurasian Steppes'; Smirnov, 'Une "Amazon"'; and the dismissive account in Blok, *The Early Amazons*. On religion, see Boyce, *Zoroastrians*, and *A History of Zoroastrianism*; and Khazanov, 'The Spread of World Religions'.

[7] OUTER EURASIAN INVASIONS AND THEIR AFTERMATH

T<small>HE</small> threat posed by militarized pastoralists to agrarian lands in Outer Eurasia, and the growing wealth of some of the Inner Eurasian borderlands during the first millennium, provoked some of the earliest attempts by agrarian states to create empires that included parts of Inner Eurasia. Written evidence now lets us document in some detail the impact on Central Asia and neighbouring regions of these early attempts at imperial conquest, which prefigured the later attempts by Sassanian Iran, the Islamic caliphate, and Han and T'ang China.

OUTER EURASIAN INVASIONS: SIXTH TO THIRD CENTURIES BCE

ACHAEMENIDS

The first great Iranian empires, those of the Medes and the Persian Achaemenids, were founded by peoples whose ancestors had probably invaded Iran from the Inner Eurasian steppes at the end of the second millennium BCE. The depiction of short swords (*akinakes*), Scythian three-sided arrows, and costumes with trousers, on Median reliefs, shows continuing links with the steppes.[1] So, in a sense, Achaemenid attempts to conquer parts of Central Asia represent a reconquest of an original Iranian homeland.

The imperial history of the Medes and Persians dates from the mid-seventh century, when the Medes rebelled against their Assyrian overlords. However, the empire they created owed so much to Scythian and Saka mercenaries and allies that it can be thought of as a product of the type of pastoralist invasions that had occurred earlier, in the second millennium, and were to occur again, five centuries later, under the Parthians, and one and a half millennia later under the Saljuks. Between 653 and 624, Scythian tribes ruled over the Medes and may even have merged with Median elites.[2] However, Median tribes reestablished their independence in 624 under King Cyaxares, who expelled the Scythians after massacring their leaders, and turned Media into a major power, with a capital in Ecbatana (modern Hamadan). In 612 BCE, in alliance with Scythians, the Medes destroyed the Assyrian capital of Nineveh

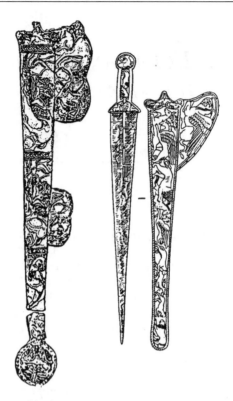

Figure 7.1 Scythian *akinakes*, reproduced from Jeannine Davis-Kimball, V. A. Bashilov et al., *Nomads of the Eurasian Steppes in the Early Iron Age* (Center for the Study of Eurasian Nomads, Berkeley, cal.: Press, 1995).

and seized much of northern Mesopotamia. They may also have captured the regions of southern Turkmenistan, later known as Parthia.[3]

Between 553 and 550, Cyrus II (r. 559–529), a leader of the Persian Achaemenid family, overthrew Astyages, the ruler of the Medes, assumed the Median title of 'Great King, King of Kings, King of the Lands', and conquered Mesopotamia, Parthia and Anatolia. The rich trading cities of southern Central Asia soon attracted Cyrus' attention. Cyrus probably inherited Parthia from the Medians. By 539, he had conquered Bactria and much of Sogdia. He then established a line of fortresses which included the fortress of Kyreshkata, or 'Cyropolis', on the Syr Darya (modern Ura-tyube). In 529, he decided to assert his authority over the Massagetae of the Uzbek steppes, between the deltas of the Amu Darya and Syr Darya.[4] Herodotus' description of this fatal last campaign, gives some fascinating glimpses into this frontier world (1:201–16). The death of the Massagetean supra-tribal ruler or 'king', left his wife, Tomyris, as ruler just before Cyrus invaded their lands. According to Herodotus, Cyrus prepared for his campaign by building a number of border forts, and building rafts for the crossing of the Araxes (which may well refer, here, to the Amu Darya).[5] Nevertheless, Cyrus agreed to enter Massagetean lands in peace and negotiate a new relationship with the Massagetae. However, on the suggestion of Croesus, king of Lydia, he set a trap (Herodotus 1:127). Exploiting Massagetian unfamiliarity with the wealth of Persia, he left a huge banquet, guarded only by weak troops. When the Massageteans had seized the banquet and become drunk, Cyrus' Medean soldiers slaughtered a third of them as they slept. They also captured the queen's son, Spargapises, who took his own life at the first opportunity. Tomyris warned that if Cyrus did not leave immediately, 'I swear by the sun, the lord of the Massagetae, that, for all your insatiability of blood, I will give you your fill of it' (1:212–3). Cyrus fell during the battle that followed, and (according to Herodotus' account) Tomyris fulfilled her terrible threat by fixing his head to an animal skin full of blood.[6]

Cyrus' successors, Cambyses (r. 529–522), and Darius I (r. 521–486), restored Achaemenid power in much of southern Central Asia. Indeed, Darius himself had close ties with Bactria, and his parents may have been both Bactrians and Zoroastrians. Darius also established Achaemenid authority over the Saka tribes that threatened the Khorasan road connecting central Persia with Bactria and the north-eastern provinces.[7] Under the date, 519 BCE, Darius recorded in the Bisutun inscriptions that:

> I marched with my army to the land of Saka. Thereupon the Saka who wore pointed caps, came out to join battle. When I came to the river [Amu Darya?], I crossed with the whole army to the other side. Thereupon I smote part of the Saka exceedingly, and the other (part) was captured...Their leader, by name Skunkha, was taken prisoner and led to me. Then I appointed another leader (for them), as was my wish. Thereupon the land became mine.[8]

Achaemenid power now reached as far as the Syr Darya and even into the Turkmen steppes which Cyrus had failed to conquer. Parthia, Khorezm, Sogdia and Bactria certainly paid tributes, and many of the region's pastoralists also accepted Iranian suzerainty. Central Asian soldiers fought in Achaemenid armies throughout the Persian empire, and their composite bows became one of the army's chief weapons. Terracotta figures of Central Asian soldiers, wearing the pointed hoods and narrow trousers of the Saka, have been found at sites throughout the Achaemenid empire, even as far away as Egypt.[9]

What was the impact on Central Asia of its incorporation within the Achaemenid empire? Historians have alternated between seeing the Achaemenid empire as a unitary system with strong central control, and a much looser hierarchy of already established regional kings ruled over by a remote 'King of Kings'. Recent scholarship stresses the looseness of imperial rule and the extent to which traditional rulers maintained their authority under Achaemenid suzerainty. After the initial conquest, the authority of the empire in the provinces depended mainly on the loyalty of local rulers.[10] According to Staviskij's account of Achaemenid rule in Bactria:

> When Alexander arrived, and probably even earlier, Achaemenid power did not rest so much on local garrisons and a Persian administration as on the loyalty of

Plate 7.1 Persepolis rock carvings, (© The Ancient Art and Architecture Collection).

a local aristocracy. This loyalty depended, it seems, not only on the power and authority of Achaemenid power, but equally on the interest that members of local nobilities had in belonging to this great and powerful state.[11]

Vogelsang has also argued that pastoralist Saka were never just subjects of the empire, but acted as vital 'middlemen' in managing the lands of southern Central Asia. The Imperial title of 'King of Kings' was, as this suggests, a precise description of the nature of Achaemenid power.

> The picture which begins to appear of the basic structure of Persian dominance of Eastern Iran, and perhaps of the Achaemenid empire as a whole, is a careful balance between gift-giving and gift-taking; the distribution of subsidies, and the taking of taxes, tribute and booty. Such a balance was not only sought for by the Persians, but also by their subjects, and these in turn by their subjects, etc. At the top of the pyramid, cooperation was extensive, and the Medes and Scythians/Sakas constituted the most loyal subjects of the Persians, because their leaders had most to lose if and when the system collapsed.[12]

The reforms of Darius I in 518 BCE created 20 different provinces, each headed by a satrap and a separate military commander. Herodotus' list of the tributes paid by each satrapy shows the very considerable wealth of the empire's Central Asian provinces. Bactria, the twelfth satrapy, paid 360 talents (or c.10 tonnes of silver); the fifteenth satrapy of the Saka and Caspii paid 250 talents, and the sixteenth satrapy, which included Khorezm and Sogdia, paid 300 (3:93). To put these figures in perspective, Babylon and Syria, the richest provinces, paid 1000 talents, while Egypt paid 700 and the trading provinces of Phoenicia, Palestine and Cyprus paid 350 talents. Some of this wealth was turned into coins, the first to circulate in Central Asia. According to Herodotus (3:117), control of Central Asia's canals was one key to Achaemenid power. Officials sometimes closed irrigation canals to force local communities to pay taxes. The empire as a whole was run from a central bureaucracy in Susa, and the system was supervised by an extensive network of police spies.

The relative peace established by the Achaemenids, as well as official road-building and support for agriculture, stimulated trade throughout the empire, and helped link Inner Eurasian trading networks more closely with those of Iran, Mesopotamia and the Mediterranean. Khorezmian turquoise appears in Persia, while Achaemenid goods appear deep in the steppes, including a pile carpet preserved in the Pazyryk tombs in the Altai.[13] The administration of the empire also encouraged travel between the different regions by officials, which probably led to the emergence of a syncretic Achaemenid culture among elites, whatever their origin. The Achaemenids also transplanted whole communities as a form of punishment, like the Assyrians. These included the earliest communities of Greeks to be settled in Central Asia. Beyond the satrapies there were regions loosely allied to the empire, such as the Massagetean and Saka tribes of the Syr Darya.[14]

The Persians were probably the first to introduce writing into Central Asia. The Aramaic script used by Persian officials later provided the basis for the regional written languages of Parthia, Sogdia and Khorezm, all of which were closely related to Persian.[15] The Persians also established an efficient post-horse service for the transmission of official mail. On the other hand, the adoption of Zoroastrianism as Persia's official religion late in the sixth century shows that Central Asia also had a significant cultural influence on the imperial heartland. It is probable that Zoroastrianism had gradually entered western Iran along trade routes from Central Asia, in the centuries before the Achaemenids. Members of the Achaemenid family may have taken it up as early as 600, for from that time on, Avestan names such as Vistaspa and Atossa are found within the royal family.[16]

Though the city-states of Central Asia probably gained much through their incorporation in the Achaemenid empire, as central power waned, local rulers eventually asserted their independence. By c.400 BCE, Khorezm and maybe parts of Sogdia had freed themselves from Achaemenid control, while Bactria was often in a state of revolt. The relative independence of these Central Asian satrapies probably explains their fierce resistance to the conquests of Alexander.[17] Indeed, not until the Arabic conquests of the seventh century CE was so large an area of Central Asia to be incorporated again into a durable world empire.

MACEDONIANS

Exactly two centuries after Cyrus' death, Alexander of Macedon reconquered much of southern Central Asia, in a campaign similar to that of Cyrus. Alexander entered Bactria in 329. Opposing him were loose alliances that included both pastoralists and regional rulers or *dihqans*. At first, his opponents were led by Darius' former satrap, Bessus of Bactria, who had Darius murdered in Hecatompylus (modern Shahr-i Qumis), before proclaiming himself Darius' successor. Bessus had led the most effective units of Darius' army at Gaugemela (331). His troops consisted of armoured Saka cavalry from Bactria and Sogdia, and he managed to lead most away from the defeat without great loss. He was supported by Spitamenes of Sogdia, and also expected help from Khorezm, from the Parthian Dahae, from the Sogdian Saka, from Kashmir, and from Saka tribes from beyond the Syr Darya. However, much of this support did not materialize, and Bessus managed to mobilize only c.7000 cavalry, far too few to challenge Alexander directly.[18] So he crossed the Amu Darya and destroyed its bridges.

Alexander pursued him, leading his army across the terrible stretch of desert between the Bactrian capital of Bactra, and modern Tirmidh, before crossing the Amu Darya on inflated hide rafts. Almost immediately, Bessus' allies sued for peace, and surrendered Bessus, who was led, naked and in chains, to Hecatompylus. He was scourged, his nose and ears were cut off, and he was executed in accordance with the gruesome penalties customary under the Achaemenids for pretenders to the throne.[19]

Bactria and much of Sogdia now accepted Alexander's suzerainty. However, like Cyrus before him, Alexander decided to challenge the pastoralist tribes of the Syr Darya, whose many fortified settlements along the

Syr Darya and in its delta had acted as bases for invasions of Iran since Cyrus' time and even earlier. This decision provoked a widespread uprising which was suppressed only after two years hard campaigning.[20] From the satrapal palace at Maracanda (Samarkand), Alexander marched to the Syr Darya. Here, he began to build a fortified town, Alexander Eschate (modern Khodjend). This provoked resistance throughout Ferghana and amongst the pastoralists north of the Syr Darya. Alexander defeated a pastoralist army north of the river, captured several fortress towns that had risen against him (their mud brick walls could not stand up to Macedonian siegecraft), and, like Chinggis Khan 1500 years later, massacred their men and enslaved their women and children. Meanwhile, Sogdia had risen in his rear, and massacred a garrison of Macedonians, inflicting the worst defeat of Alexander's career. He now embarked on one of his hardest campaigns. After wintering in Bactra (or perhaps in Nautaca, modern Shahrisabs), he spent a year and a half reducing the fortified *qala* and towns of Sogdia one by one, beginning in the Hissar mountains and then moving along the Zerafshan, perhaps reaching even as far as Merv. He began settling Greek soldiers in garrisons, many of which eventually turned into Greek towns. He also recruited local soldiers, and trained them in the Macedonian style of fighting in phalanxes.[21]

Alexander's campaign was helped by the divisions endemic in the region. The ruler of Khorezm, Pharasmanes, sent a delegation claiming that Alexander's enemies lacked the support of most Scythians.[22] In 328, according to Arrian, Alexander received a further offer of alliance, this time from the brother and successor of the Saka king who had died in the meantime. This proposed to seal an alliance with marriages between Alexander and his followers, and the daughters of Saka leaders. As this piece of diplomacy shows, war in frontier zones consisted as much of the rearrangement of allegiances as it did of direct military confrontation. Gift-giving and marriage were as important as warfare in the power politics of Central Asia. Eventually, Spitamenes was murdered by Massagetian allies who decided that their best option was to negotiate with Alexander before he invaded their lands. Alexander, too, shifted from suppression to conciliation. In early 327, he married a Bactrian princess, Roxana, the daughter of another Sogdian opponent, Oxyartes.[23]

The immediate impact of the Macedonian conquest was limited to those regions which were sacked by Alexander's armies. While Alexander was present in the region, it made sense to acknowledge his authority, and send him tributes and troops. But after he left to campaign in India, his authority proved even more fragile than that of the Achaemenids. As he lay dying in Babylon, in 323, he learned of a rebellion against him in Bactria. Bactria was reconquered in *c.*305 BCE by Seleucus (311–281 BCE). However, Seleucus and his successor, Antiochus I (r. 281–261), failed to establish Seleucid authority over Transoxiana or Khorezm, despite mounting two vast campaigns into the steppes in response to steppe invasions in *c.*281.[24] Within half a century the Seleucids had also lost Parthia and Bactria. Tarn wrote that, unlike the Roman empire, which he compared to a vertebrate animal, that of the Seleucids 'resembled rather a crustacean, not growing from any solid core but encased in an outer shell; the empire was a framework which covered a multitude of peoples and languages and cities. ... Even before the final dissolution, any satrapy could easily set up for itself... without endangering the life of the rest.'[25] In this, the Seleucid empire was similar to that of the Achaemenids, and set a pattern that was to prove common in the region.

However, culturally and economically, Alexander's invasion had a huge impact on Central Asia through the foundation of new cities, the acceleration of commerce, and the introduction of Greek populations and culture. Alexander did even more than the Achaemenids to link western Central Asia with the civilizations of the Mediterranean. He also extended Iranian influences further into the steppelands north and east of the Syr Darya. Alexander's defeat of the Saka at the Syr Darya frontier, the first ever suffered by northern pastoralists at the hands of an Outer Eurasian power, probably led to more direct relations between Persia and the lands beyond the Syr Darya, whereas previously, relations had been mediated by Bactria.[26] However, Alexander never made the mistake of invading the steppelands proper. Instead, he concentrated on controlling the wealthy, urbanized oases of Sogdia and Bactria.

In some areas, the Macedonian conquest caused much damage. Samarkand was largely destroyed by Alexander's armies, and may have lost its former cultural and economic power for some decades. However, Alexander also founded new towns, such as Merv in the Margiana oasis. Here, as conquest turned into settlement, Alexander began the construction of defensive walls similar to those being built at the same time along China's northern borders. Soon, Merv was surrounded by long walls to keep out pastoralist armies, in what Barthold calls 'the first construction of this type in Central Asia.'[27] Such walls were to become a key institution of Inner Eurasian history, and they mark a significant increase in the scale of defensive efforts against pastoralists. Under the Seleucids, Merv's walls were extended to about 250 km.[28]

By settling many newly founded cities with Macedonians, and establishing a unified political and cultural zone reaching from Greece to the Pamirs, Alexander also created closer ties with the commercial world of the Mediterranean. Arrian reported that Alexander planted colonies of 13,500 soldiers in the Amu Darya valley, and many retired soldiers also remained behind in the newly founded towns. Though some rebelled after Alexander's death and tried to return home, many more remained in the region. Their presence laid the foundations for Greek culture in the region, and their newly created towns stimulated trade and urbanization. Power, too, seems to have remained in the hands of Greek commanders after Alexander's death. Many established themselves as local rulers, and some even issued their own coinage. Under Selucus and his successors, new towns were formed, money was minted in the region, and there was a fresh wave of colonization.[29]

Excavations at Ai Khanum (the modern name literally means 'my wife, the moon') on the Afghan side of the Amu Darya, have shown the splendour of some of these cities, and their odd mixture of Greek and local influences in building, religion, language and lifestyles.[30] Ai Khanum was probably founded by Alexander during his pacification campaign of 328, though there were already irrigation works on the site before its conversion into a polis. It is one of the best preserved of all Greco-Bactrian sites, as it was never occupied again after the Greeks abandoned it. Its function was originally military, to protect the plains of the Amu Darya valley. Its wealth came from irrigation farming in the nearby plains, and the mining of lapis lazuli, gold, copper, iron and precious stones.[31] Built on a natural fortress, it had an acropolis, a palace, a mint, a gymnasium, aristocratic residential quarters, and temples. Its theatre is larger than any other Greek theatre known in Asia, and only slightly smaller than the theatre of Epidaurus, but the presence of royal boxes shows the more hierarchical structure of Bactrian Greek society. Names found on the site show clearly the presence of settlers who came originally from Greece, and probably lived off land grants near the city, as well as of indigenous Bactrians with Iranian names.[32]

Greek settlers identified local gods with Greek gods. As Tarn writes: 'in a polytheistic society you naturally worshipped the god who knew the way of the land.'[33] Thus, they took the Zoroastrian deity, Ahura Mazda, as a form of Zeus, and the god, Mithra as a form of Apollo. Elsewhere, local deities, often the deities of a particular town, entered Greek pantheons, and some Greeks began to worship Indian gods. Numismatic and archaeological evidence shows that the religions of Greco-Bactria were also influenced by Buddhism, which was introduced as early as the third century BCE.[34]

Other Seleucid measures, such as the introduction of a new calendar, and new regulations on banking, stimulated trade and travel, and encouraged intellectual exchanges throughout the empire. Seleucus himself was greatly interested in his Central Asian provinces. He had married a Bactrian princess, Apama, the daughter of Spitamenes, and their son, Antiochus, became viceroy of Bactria for a time. The great wealth of the irrigated oases along the Amu Darya and the Zerafshan, the metals and precious stones of the mountain regions, and their position as a bulwark against the steppe nomads, made them a vital part of the Seleucid empire.[35]

FRONTIER EMPIRES

The Seleucids lost their grip on Central Asia by the middle of the third century. In their place, local dynasties emerged. Two of these, the Greco-Bactrian and Parthian dynasties, used the legal and bureaucratic structures created during two centuries of colonization to build up powerful regional empires, the first of this kind to appear in Central Asia.

The way Seleucid control broke down in this region was dictated by geography, and similar to the breakdown of Achaemenid power two centuries before. As central power relaxed, there emerged local contests for power, in which there were two main types of players: governors appointed from the imperial centre, and pastoralist leaders keen to assert their own authority. This pattern persisted during many centuries. So did another pattern: the

Plate 7.2 Greco-Bactrian coins, reproduced by courtesy of the Trustees of the British Museum.

fragmentation of power along fault lines that separated Eastern Iran, Bactria and Sogdia into three distinct regions. The most important dividing lines were the Central Iranian deserts along the western borders of Bactria, and the Amu Darya river.

THE GRECO-BACTRIAN KINGDOM: c.238–c.140 BCE

In the middle of the third century, the Seleucid governor of Bactria, Diodotus, founded what is known as the 'Greco-Bactrian' kingdom. At first, Diodotus struck coins with the name of the Seleucid monarch, Antiochus II, but after Antiochus' death in c.246, Diodotus' coins began to describe him as 'king'.[36] In c.238, he formally seceded from the Seleucid empire.[37]

Graeco-Bactrian control was firmest in Bactria itself and much looser, if it existed at all, in Sogdia, Khorezm and Ferghana, despite Strabo's claims that the kingdom included much of this area. The Greco-Bactrians may have exercised some control in the Tarim basin, though it is unlikely that Greek armies ever entered that region. In about 230 BCE, Diodotus' son, Diodotus II, was overthrown by one of his satraps, a Greek settler called Euthydemus, who ruled for 40 years until his death in c.190 BCE. During Euthydemus' rule, the Seleucid ruler, Antiochus III, made a further attempt to reassert Seleucid control over the region in c.207–206 BCE, during a two-year siege of Bactria.[38] According to Polybius, Euthydemus secured a lasting peace treaty by pointing out that masses of barbarians were waiting in the north to invade both kingdoms. The warning was appropriate, for both Euthydemus and Antiochus were the leaders of Hellenized elites ruling populations which, by language, culture, and tradition were closely related to the steppe pastoralists of Sogdia and the Turkmen steppes.[39]

Though its officials were literate, very little written evidence has survived about Greco-Bactrian society, and even archaeological evidence is thin, so that most of our evidence for the history of the kingdom comes from numismatics. As a result, the chronology of Greco-Bactrian history remains obscure. Nevertheless, the archaeological and numismatic evidence is enough to show that it was, as Frye writes, 'one of the great Hellenistic kingdoms, together with the Seleucids and Ptolemies.'[40]

Bactria, with its agricultural wealth boosted by improvements to its irrigation systems, was the heart of the kingdom, and Bactra was probably its first capital. It was also here that there were the largest Greek populations, and that Greek language, culture and art had their greatest impact. Ai Khanum may well have been a second capital, given the splendour of its palace; indeed it may have been the capital that one of the last Greco-Bactrian kings, Eucratides (r. second quarter or middle of second century) named Eucratidia.[41]

The distribution of Greco-Bactrian coinage and the presence of Greco-Bactrian imports from other regions suggests that there were extensive trade contacts with north-west India and Seleucid Iran, but contacts with the Mediterranean and China were limited. The Aristotelian philosopher,

Clearchus, who travelled to India to investigate religious practices, visited Ai Khanum, and left behind a copy of the Greek aphorisms from the Delphi temple but this was one of the last contacts with the Greek homeland. The most important caravan route of the period, described in Isidore of Charax' 'Parthian Stations', began in the Ganges valley, crossed the Punjab through Taxila, crossed the Hindu Kush into Bactria, and then went west towards Ecbatana or Anatolia, while another route remained south of the Hindu Kush. Using this second route, Greco-Bactrian traders could sometimes get around Parthia by sending goods down the Indus to Barygaza (modern Broach), and then, by sea to Mesopotamia.[42]

After c.180, Demetrius I, taking advantage of the collapse of the Mauryan empire in northern India, extended Greco-Bactrian power south into Gandhara and northern India and Pakistan, where there were already many immigrants from Central Asia. On his return to Bactria, he left his two main generals, Apollodorus (perhaps a younger brother) and Menander (a Greek settler) in charge of the Indian provinces.[43] In Bactria, Demetrius was defeated by Eucratides, who had been sent to reconquer Greco-Bactria by his relative, the Seleucid ruler, Antiochus IV. As a result, Menander set up as an independent ruler in northern India in the middle of the second century, where he ruled a predominantly Indian population under a small Greek elite, from a capital near modern Sialkot. Sanskrit references, including a grammatical exercise in Patanjali's Sanskrit grammar, refer to Yavana (Greek) military power in the region, and other sources suggest that Greek armies under Menander may have ruled from Barygaza in the West, to Magadha in the Ganges valley. It is possible that Menander converted to Buddhism; indeed a famous Pali Buddhist text, the 'Milinda Pañha' consists of a dialogue between Milinda/Menander and a Buddhist monk, Nagasena. Eucratides attempted, but failed to reestablish Bactrian power over northern India and eventually died fighting a Parthian invasion of Bactria.[44]

As its centre of gravity shifted southwards, Greco-Bactrian power crumbled in the north. In c.140–130 BCE, after existing for just over a century, the Greco-Bactrian kingdom collapsed under pressure from Saka tribes driven south by Yüeh-chih pastoralists from the eastern steppes (see chs 8 and 9).[45] The decline seems to have been gradual, as there is no sign of serious damage to Bactria's major cities. The abandonment of Ai Khanum, in c.145 BCE, may mark one pastoralist assault, but by then the western provinces had already been lost to Parthia. Though several Greek kingdoms survived south of the Hindu Kush until the end of the first century BCE, the last Greek ruler of Bactria was probably Heliocles (c.145–130 BCE).[46] In c.129–128 BCE, the Chinese ambassador, Chang Ch'ien, found the Yüeh-chih settled in Sogdia, on the northern banks of the Amu Darya and already exerting some control even over Bactria, on its southern shores. He described Bactria as a region of many small principalities with weak armies.[47]

The fall of Greek Bactria occurred just before the opening up of the Silk Roads under the Han, which is why Barthold describes this event as, 'the first event of world history recorded both in Western (Greek) and Far-Eastern (Chinese) sources.'[48] From this time until the seventh century CE,

Chinese sources are the most important written sources on the history of Central Asia, as much of Central Asia now drifted out of the orbit of Mesopotamian civilization and culture.

THE PARTHIAN EMPIRE: *C.*238 BCE–*C.*226 CE

The decline of the Greco-Bactrian Empire marked the ebb of a long period of Outer Eurasian expansion within the Inner Eurasian borderlands. One of the main rivals of the Greco-Bactrian kingdom, the Parthian empire, represented a very different type of state that was to become more common during the next millennium: an agrarian state with a ruling dynasty from the Inner Eurasian steppes.[49]

In *c.*245 BCE, Andragoras, the satrap of the province of Parthia, asserted his independence from the Seleucid empire. However, in 238, Andragoras faced an invasion from pastoralists known as the 'Parni'. Their powerful army, like that of the Massagetae in the Achaemenid era, included infantry, as well as both heavy and light cavalry. The Parni had moved into southern Turkmenistan early in the third century, and were a branch of the larger group of Saka tribes known as the 'Dahae'.[50] Leading the Parni was an energetic leader called Arsaces (r. 238?–217?). Though a shadowy figure in the sources, Wolski has argued that the reverence given to him by his successors suggests that he was a military and political genius of the type of other pastoralist leaders such as Chinggis Khan. Coins from his reign show him as 'a Scythian warrior, bow in hand'.[51] The Parni may have been driven south by even more powerful enemies in the steppes of Khorezm. If so, what Andragoras experienced as a pastoralist invasion was, from the point of view of the Parni, an armed retreat. Arsaces defeated and killed Andragoras, and, after conquering Parthia and Hyrcania, established a capital at Nisa, near modern Ashkhabad. However, he and his successors continued to use Seleucid coinage for almost a century, which suggests that they accepted at least the nominal authority of the Seleucids. The site of Nisa has been excavated by Soviet archaeologists. It contains a large fortress, a fire temple, and extensive wine cellars. It also contains many documents written on clay fragments in Aramaic script but in the Parthian language, and these give some insight into the workings of the Parthian regional bureaucracy and tax collecting system.[52]

At first, the Parthian hold on Parthia and Hyrcania was fragile, threatened both by the Seleucids in the south and other pastoralists to the north. In *c.*228, Seleucus II may have briefly driven Arsaces out of Parthia into the Turkmen steppes, but Arsaces seems to have returned quite soon.[53] In *c.*208, Antiochus III reconquered Hyrcania from Arsaces' son, Arsaces II (r. 217?–191?), but soon made peace, and formalized the relationship of dependence.[54]

It was Mithridates I (*c.*171–138) who transformed the regional state of the Arsacids into a great empire. The Roman defeat of the Seleucids at the battle of Magnesia, in 192 BCE, permanently weakened the Seleucids, and soon after, Mithridates conquered most of the Seleucid empire. By 148 he controlled Media and in 141 he conquered Babylonia. He may have done so with the help of Saka pastoralists from the Turkmen steppes, whom he later settled in the province of Sakastan (later Seistan).[55] In the east, the Parthians took Margiana from Greco-Bactria, and the last Seleucid resistance was crushed in 129 BCE by Mithridates' son, Phratres II (r. 138–128). After conquering Babylon, Mithridates began to issue coins of his own, describing himself as 'great king', in imitation of his Achaemeid predecessors. These show him as an Iranian emperor, and suggest the extent to which the Arsacids attempted to identify with the sedentary traditions of the Achaemenids rather than the pastoralist traditions of their Parni ancestors.[56] The imperial Parthian dynasty he created was to last for another four centuries, and to be Rome's major rival in the east until it collapsed in 224 CE. However, even under Mithridates, the Parthian empire remained almost as 'segmentary' as most pastoralist federations. The Arsacids ruled a federation of kingdoms, not a unitary empire.

Their polity was a complex symbiosis of pastoralist and agrarian traditions, and divisions between these different worlds affected its political, cultural and religious life. Much of Parthia's fighting power came from the pastoralist, or semi-pastoralist, eastern regions. Indeed, Tarn argued that Parthia was really a dual system, ruled in the west by the Arsacids, while in the east, the dominant dynasty was that of the Suren.[57] The Suren owed their power to the role they had played in defeating Saka and Massagetaen invasions which had destroyed the Greco-Bactrian kingdom, and nearly destroyed the Parthian empire between 130 and 124 BCE. It was also a Suren prince who defeated the Romans at Carrhae (53 BCE), using a regional army from Seistan, consisting mainly of 10,000 of his own cavalry and subjects. The Suren army included heavy cavalry, in which both the men and horses wore iron mail. They rode without stirrups, using powerful warhorses specially bred in the steppes of Media. However, like all Parthian armies, that of the Suren also included light cavalry, who displayed the tactical flexibility of traditional pastoralist armies.[58]

The Arsacids never created a bureaucracy as unified as that of Rome, and it took great skill to forge any kind of unity from the diverse territories they ruled. The frequency with which the Arsacids moved from capital to capital, from Nisa in Margiana to Hecatompylus in Hyrcania, from Ecbatana to Ctesiphon on the Euphrates, reflects the absence of a clear bureaucratic centre. The Arsacid dynasty seems not even to have had its own army (though it presumably had some troops of its own), but had to rely mainly on the armies of regional satraps or aristocratic families such as the Suren.[59] The ruling class of the 'azat' or 'free' was a powerful, and relatively independent group of sub-kings and princes, who were descendants of Parni chiefs, and leaders of Parthia's cavalry armies.[60] Below them was a large class of ordinary Parni pastoralists, who dominated the light cavalry. The religious traditions of Central Asia shaped the ideologies of Parthia, as Zoroastrianism spread slowly amongst Parthian elites. Zoroastrian symbols such as fire altars began to appear on coins, and the Zoroastrian book of holy writings, the *Avesta*, was probably codified under the Arsacids.[61] But even Zoroastrianism failed to create a strong sense of Parthian unity.

Though the early Arsacids deliberately maintained Achaemenid rather than Greek traditions, the economic, demographic, and political centre of the Parthian empire lay in the rich, Hellenized cities of Babylonia. Here, local elites whose incomes derived from trade or irrigation farming, had little sympathy with the pastoralist traditions of the Arsacids. In the cities of Babylon, the closest cultural, commercial and diplomatic ties were with Rome. The Arsacids distrusted the Hellenistic cities of Mesopotamia, and installed Arsacid governors with Parthian garrisons.[62] However, they understood the importance of agriculture and trade, particularly international trade and did nothing to discourage the extensive trades with the Mediterranean, passing mainly through Palmyra in northern Syria, and with the Caucasus and northern India. Parthia established diplomatic contact with both Rome and China under Mithridates II (123–87). Indeed, it has been suggested that it was Parthian silks, received as gifts from Han ambassadors, that first introduced silk to Rome, probably late in the first century BCE.[63] The Arsacids and the cities of Mesopotamia shared a common interest in monopolizing trade along the newly established trade routes by preventing direct contact between Chinese and Roman merchants and diplomats. The *Hou Han Shu* recorded that: 'The kings of Ta Ch'in (Rome) always desired to send embassies to China, but the Parthians wished to carry trade with Ta Ch'in in Chinese silks and therefore cut them off from communication.'[64] On the whole, Parthian attempts to control the trade of the Silk Roads between China and the Mediterranean was a success. Numismatists have found hardly any Roman coins east of Parthia before the Byzantine period.[65] On the other hand, there are signs that the Parthian boycott may have encouraged attempts to bypass it by developing sea routes from Egypt to Barygaza in India, and even to the Chinese coast.[66]

Archaeological excavations show that, at least during the early centuries of Parthian rule, irrigation agriculture flourished. Cereal production expanded, and so did vineyards and technical crops such as cotton and sesame. There was also much trade with cattle-raising pastoralists on the empire's northern borders.[67] Carpet-making and metalwork flourished, particularly in the armour-making centre of Margiana.

After several centuries, the loose imperialism of Parthia began to unravel under the stress of military conflicts with steppe pastoralists and the Roman empire. There were massive Saka invasions in *c.*130 BCE, and invasions of Alan tribes from the Caucasus in 72 CE and again in 135–6. The Saka invasions of 130 BCE began when Phratres II hired a Saka army to help defeat the Seleucids, but refused to pay them because they arrived too late. The Saka demanded payment anyway, and when their demands were not met began sacking Parthia itself, starting a new war in which the Parthian monarch was killed.[68] In the second and third centuries CE, conflicts with Rome were frequent and eventually unsustainable. Like the Median rulers 700 years before, the declining Arsacid dynasty was eventually overthrown by a regional ruler from the southern province of Persia. Ardashir founded the Sassanian dynasty in *c.*226 CE, and named it after his grandfather, Sasan.[69] According to the Arabic historian, al-Tabari, Ardashir personally killed the last Arsacid,

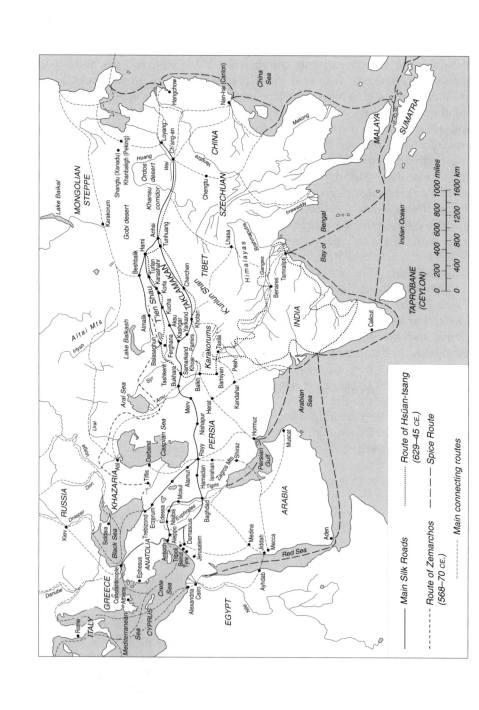

Main Silk Roads   ⋯⋯⋯⋯ Route of Hsüan-tsang
                                        (629–45 CE.)

Route of Zemarchos   – – – Spice Route
(568–70 CE.)

                                    ⋯⋯⋯⋯ Main connecting routes

| 0 | 200 | 400 | 600 | 800 | 1000 miles |
| 0 | 400 | 800 | 1200 | 1600 km | |

Artabanus, at the climax of the final battle fought near modern Bulgayagan, between Isfahan and Nihawand.[70]

In its loose political structures, and its internal divisions between pastoralist and agrarian populations, Parthia symbolizes well the type of symbiotic state that was to be created many times by successful pastoralist invaders of the agricultural lands of north China, Afghanistan, Iran and the Balkans. Only in its remarkable longevity was it unusual.

In another way, too, the Parthian empire illustrates an enduring pattern, only hinted at in the earlier history of the Central Asian borderlands. Here, the fact that strips of steppeland reached deep into modern Afghanistan and Iran, and even into Anatolia, lured pastoralist armies deep into these regions of Outer Eurasia. Frequently, they established powerful Outer Eurasian states that slowly shifted their ecological foundations from the steppes into the sown lands. Eventually, they became more or less traditional agrarian empires, distinctive only in the attachment of their ruling elites to the traditions, the symbols and the paraphernalia of a pastoralist past. While the second millennium invasions of northern India, and the early history of the Medes and Persians, anticipated this pattern, it was to appear again in the history of the Hephthalite and Kusana empires, the Saljuk and Ottoman empires, and the Moghul empires of northern India.

NOTES

1 Vogelsang, *Rise and Organisation*, pp. 142 and 175.
2 Ibid., pp. 215, 305.
3 Dandamayev, in *HCCA*, 2:38; Vogelsang, *Rise and Organisation*, p. 176.
4 M. A. Dandamayev, *Political History*, p. 66, and see p. 33.
5 On Herodotus' confused use of this name, see Vogelsang, *Rise and Organisation*, p. 183; and Yablonsky, in Davis-Kimball, ed., *Nomads*, p. 251.
6 Other accounts of Cyrus' death differ in details, though all place his death in East Iran; see Vogelsang, *Rise and Organisation*, pp. 187–9 and Dandamaev, *Political History*, pp. 66–8; according to Ctesias' account, Cyrus died of wounds in a later steppe campaign; see Gardiner-Garden, *Ktesias*, pp. 17–20.
7 Vogelsang, *Rise and Organisation*, p. 131–2; on Darius' links with Bactria see Holt, *Alexander*, p. 39; Boyce, *History*, 2:68–9, points out that Darius' father was named after Zoroaster's patron, Vistaspa.
8 Cited in Dandamaev, *Political History*, p. 136.
9 Dandamaev, 'Media and Achaemenid Iran' (pp. 35–65), in *HCCA*, 2:45.
10 See the discussion in Vogelsang, *Rise and Organisation*, Introduction.
11 Staviskij, *La Bactriane*, p. 25.
12 Vogelsang, *Rise and Organisation*, p. 244 and see p. 18.
13 Dandamaev, 'Media and Achaemenid Iran' (pp. 35–65), in *HCCA*, 2:55.
14 Arrian described the Scythians who opposed Alexander's invasion as 'not subject to Bessus [the satrap of Bactria] but...in alliance with Darius'; cited in A. H. Dani and P. Bernard, 'Alexander and his successors in Central Asia', *HCCA* (pp. 67–97), 2:67; on the earliest communities of Greeks in Central Asia, see Frye, *Heritage of Central Asia*, p. 90 and Gardiner-Garden, *Ktesias*, p. 4.

15 Dandamayev, 'Media and Achaemenid Iran', in *HCCA*, 2:47–8, 55.

16 Boyce, *History*, 2:7–8, 41.

17 Frye, *History of Ancient Iran*, p. 141.

18 Bosworth, *Conquest and empire*, pp. 107, 76–7; Briant, *Etat et pasteurs*, pp. 207–10.

19 Bosworth, *Conquest and empire*, p. 108.

20 This is Holt's interpretation, see *Alexander*, pp. 55–60.

21 Bosworth, *Conquest and empire*, pp. 117, and see 109–10; Holt, *Alexander*, p. 66 on his wintering at Nautaca; p. 62, on the garrisoning of Merv, and see p. 56.

22 Briant, *Etat et pasteurs*, p. 224; Vogelsang, *Rise and Organisation*, p. 235 argues that any ruler of Khorezm must have been accustomed to dealings with the Persian satrap of Bactra, so that in sending a delegation to Alexander in Bactra he was probably following established protocol.

23 Dani and Bernard, 'Alexdander and his successors in Central Asia', in *HCCA*, 2:72.

24 Wolski, *L'Empire des Arsacides*, p. 26.

25 Tarn, *Greeks*, p. 4.

26 Briant, *Etat et pasteurs*, p. 231.

27 Barthold, 'A short history of Turkestan', in *Four Studies on Central Asia* (pp. 1–68), 1:3–4, and see 5–6.

28 Parts of this wall have been excavated, Dani and Bernard, 'Alexander and his successors', in *HCCA*, 2:91; on walls as a major institution from China to Scotland, see Lattimore, *Inner Asian Frontiers*, 2nd edn, xlv and xliv.

29 *Ocherki istorii SSSR: pervoobshchinnyi stroi*, p. 265; and see Dani and Bernard, 'Alexander and his successors', in *HCCA*, 2:88–9.

30 See P. Bernard, 'An ancient Greek city in Central Asia', see also Litvinskii and Pichikian, 'The Hellenistic architecture and art of the Temple of the Oxus', on another important Hellenistic site at Takht-e Sangin.

31 Rapin, 'Greeks in Afghanistan: Ai Khanum', in Descoeudres, ed., *Greek Colonists*, p. 331; and see P. Bernard, 'The Greek kingdoms of Central Asia', in *HCCA* (pp. 99–129), 2:104; Holt, *Alexander*, p. 62.

32 Bernard, 'Greek kingdoms', in *HCCA*, 2:105, 112.

33 Tarn, *Greeks*, p. 68.

34 Bernard, 'Greek kingdoms', in *HCCA*, 2:116–17; J. Harmatta, et al., 'Religions in the Kushan empire' in *HCCA* (pp. 313–29), 2:314.

35 Dani and Bernard, 'Alexander and his successors', in *HCCA*, 2:91; and see Frye, *History of Ancient Iran*, p. 167.

36 Dani and Bernard, 'Alexander and his successors', in *HCCA*, 2:95.

37 Wolski, *L'Empire des Arsacides*, p. 200.

38 Gardiner-Garden, *Apollodorus*, p. 21; according to some accounts, Euthydemus was co-leader, with Diodotus, of the original secession, ibid., pp. 11, 23–9; see also Tarn, *Greeks*, p. 82; Golden, *Introduction*, p. 48; Bernard, 'Greek kingdoms', in *HCCA*, 2:100; *Cambridge History of Iran*, 3(1), pp. 239–40.

39 Staviskij, *La Bactriane*, p. 28, stresses the cultural gulf between rulers and people in Greco-Bactria; Polybius' comments from K. Enoki, G. A. Koshelenko and Z. Haidary, 'The Yüeh-chih and their migrations', in *HCCA* (pp. 171–89), 2:179.

40 Frye, *History of Ancient Iran*, p. 179. On the confused issue of the date of separation from the Seleucid empire, see Ibid., pp. 179–80.

41 Bernard, 'An Ancient Greek City in Central Asia', and Bernard, 'Greek kingdoms', in *HCCA*, 2:100, 110.

42 Haussig, *Geschichte Zentralasiens... in vorislamischer Zeit*, p. 128; and see Dani and Bernard, 'Alexander and his successors', in *HCCA*, 2:92; Bernard, in *HCCA*, 2:107, 125; Isidore of Charax, *Parthian Stations*; though dated to *c.*0 CE, its information probably comes from the reign of Mithridates II (r. 123–87 BCE); Wolski, *L'Empire des Arsacides*, p. 13.

43 Tarn, *Greeks*, pp. 166–7; Bernard, 'Greek kingdoms', in *HCCA*, 4:98–9.

44 Tarn, *Greeks*, p. 219, and see pp. 247, 258, and p. 226, which gives dates of Menander's reign from 167–150/45; see also Puri, *Buddhism in Central Asia*, p. 19; and Bernard, 'Greek kingdoms', in *HCCA*, 2:101.

45 Enoki, Koshelenko and Haidary, 'The Yüeh-chih', in *HCCA*, 2:178, and Puri, *Buddhism in Central Asia*, p. 191, the Yüeh-chih invaded later; the earliest invaders were Saka displaced by the Yüeh-chih and later driven further south into India.

46 Bernard, 'Greek kingdoms', in *HCCA*, 2:103; Frye, *History of Ancient Iran*, p. 193.

47 Bernard, 'Greek kingdoms', in *HCCA*, 2:103; and see Gardiner-Garden, *Apollodorus*, pp. 49–50.

48 Barthold, 'A short history of Turkestan', in *Four Studies on Central Asia*, 1:4.

49 Our knowledge of the Arsacid or Parthian empire remains both thin and biased, as there are no indigenous literary sources and little epigraphic or numismatic material, particularly for the early period; for the early dynastic history, I have relied on the reconstruction of Wolski, *L'Empire des Arsacides*, who gives a chronology on pp. 200–1.

50 Colledge, *Parthians*, p. 25; Wolski, *L'Empire des Arsacides*, p. 101.

51 Wolski, *L'Empire des Arsacides*, p. 69, and see pp. 49, and 52–7.

52 Colledge, *Parthians*, p. 27; Gafurov, *Tadzhiki*, 1:150–4.

53 Wolski, *L'Empire des Arsacides*, p. 68.

54 Colledge, *Parthia*, p. 27; Wolski, *L'Empire des Arsacides*, p. 64.

55 According to Tarn, *Greeks*, pp. 222–3.

56 Wolski, *L'Empire des Arsacides*, p. 97; Colledge, *Parthians*, p. 29.

57 Tarn, *Greeks*, p. 204, and see pp. 222–4 for their role in defeating invading Saka tribes; Wolski, *L'Empire des Arsacides*, p. 90, accepts a similar theory; on the Suren, see also Colledge, *Parthians*, p. 31–2.

58 Colledge, *Parthians*, pp. 40–1, 61–2, 65; and Wolski, *L'Empire des Arsacides*, p. 113.

59 Wolski, *L'Empire des Arsacides*, p. 115; Colledge, *Parthians*, pp. 62, 67.

60 G. A. Koshelenko and V. N. Pilipko, 'Parthia', in *HCCA* (pp. 131–50), 2:144–5.

61 Ibid., p. 149.

62 Wolski, *L'Empire des Arsacides*, pp. 106–7.

63 Yü, *Trade and Expansion*, p. 165; on Parthian trade networks, see also Colledge, *Parthians*, pp. 32–4; and Koshelenko, and Pilipko, 'Parthia', in *HCCA*, 2:137–9.

64 Cited in Yü, *Trade and Expansion*, p. 156.

65 Koshelenko and Pilipko, 'Parthia', in *HCCA*, 2:246; and Colledge, *Parthians*, p. 80.

66 See Yü, *Trade and Expansion*, pp. 157, 172–6.

67 Koshelenko and Pilipko, 'Parthia', in *HCCA*, 2:136–7.

68 Colledge, *Parthians*, pp. 52, 166; Koshelenko and Pilipko, 'Parthia', *HCCA*, 2:133, 181–2, 457; Gafurov, *Tadzhiki*, 1:161–2.

69 Colledge, *Parthians*, p. 173; the date 226 is from Wolski, *L'Empire des Arsacides*, p. 195.

70 Lieu, *Manichaeism*, p. 5.

FURTHER READING

Once again *HCCA*, vol. 2 is invaluable, but so, for Central Asia is the *Cambridge History of Iran*. There is a huge literature on the Achaemenids. Particularly valuable for this study have been works by Vogelsang, *The Rise and Organization of the Achaemenid empire*; Frye, *History of Ancient Iran*; Briant, *Darius* and *L'Asie centrale*; and Dandamaev, *A Political History*; as well as essays by Gardiner-Garden. On the Macedonians in Central Asia, See Bosworth, *Conquest and empire*; Holt, *Alexander the Great and Bactria*; and Briant, *Etat et pasteurs*. On the Greco-Bactrians, Tarn, *The Greeks in Bactria*, is still fundamental, despite its age; but see also Staviskij, *La Bactriane*; and Bernard, 'An ancient Greek city', and Bernard 'The Greek kingdoms of Central Asia', in *HCCA* 2:99–129; and Litvinskii and Pichikian, 'The Hellenistic architecture and art of the Temple of the Oxus'. On the Parthians, there are useful surveys in Debevoise, *A Political History of Parthia*; and Colledge, *The Parthians*, but Wolski, *L'Empire des Arsacides*, is more up to date. On trade routes, see Haussig, *Geschichte Zentralasiens...in vorislamischer Zeit*; Yü *Trade and Expansion*; and Schoff, trans., *Parthian Stations*.

[8]   *THE HSIUNG-NU EMPIRE*

I<small>N</small> the second century BCE, the formation of a great pastoralist empire in the eastern steppes started a new migratory pulse that was felt in the Inner Eurasian steppes for more than half a millennium. The rise and fall of the Hsiung-nu empire affected the whole of Inner Eurasia. Indirectly, it also shaped the destiny of agricultural empires from China to Rome.

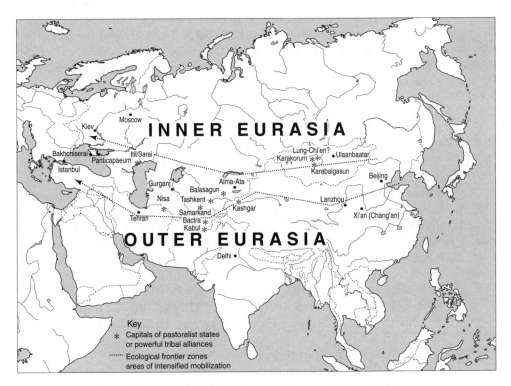

Map 8.1 Pastoralist states of Inner Eurasia: 200 BCE–1800 CE.

CREATION OF THE HSIUNG-NU EMPIRE: 200–133 BCE

ORIGINS OF THE HSIUNG-NU EMPIRE

By the fifth century BCE, Chinese officials knew of several powerful groups of pastoralists to their north. They used the generic term, 'Hu' to refer to these horseriding barbarians, who were so different from the agricultural barbarians with which they had long familiarity. By 300 BCE, there were three large pastoralist associations north of China, whose stability suggests that they were well on the way to becoming true pastoralist states. One group, the Hsiung-nu, was based in the Ordos region, in the northern loop of the Huang He.[1] The Tung-hu (or 'Eastern barbarians') dominated eastern Mongolia, while the Indo-European speaking Yüeh-chih dominated Kansu.

Like the word, 'Scythian', and many other steppe ethnonyms that appear in written sources, the term, 'Hsiung-nu' is used both of a particular tribal group with its own language and traditions, and, in a generic sense, of a large and varied group of tribes, often with a single overall leader. Though most tribes described as 'Hsiung-nu' shared a similar lifeway, strongly influenced by the Scythic cultures of the central and western steppes, they were not all Hsiung-nu in language or even physical anthropology. Chinese sources even record a Hsiung-nu tribe of the fourth century BCE whose men had large noses and red beards. Presumably, like the Yüeh-chih tribes of Kansu, these groups spoke a form of Indo-European. Yet it is unlikely that the ruling clans of the Hsiung-nu were Europoid in language or anthropological origins. Unfortunately, we know very little about the Hsiung-nu language. However, most scholars believe that the core tribes spoke early forms of Turkic or Mongolian, for the two language groups were closer 2000 years ago than they are today.[2] To the west, the tribes known in Chinese sources as the Ting-ling and later as T'ieh-le (and linked to the Turkic Oghur) may have spoken early forms of Turkic.[3]

By the middle of the third century, Hsiung-nu tribes formed a powerful tribal association with an established royal clan, the Lüan-ti, and a leader known as the *shan-yü*. However, they were coming under increasing pressure from expansionist Chinese states. In 214 BCE, emperor Shih-huang-ti, the founder of the first unified Chinese empire, drove the Hsiung-nu north from their traditional homelands in the Ordos.[4] This devastating blow should have destroyed the Hsiung-nu as a political force. They were now the weakest of the three major pastoralist federations to China's north. Indeed, Tumen, their *shan-yü*, was forced to send his eldest son, Motun, as a hostage to the Yüeh-chih. However, four years later, in 210 BCE, the Ch'in emperor died and his dynasty collapsed. This allowed the Hsiung-nu to reoccupy the Ordos region. Then Tumen's son and successor, Motun, began to turn the Hsiung-nu into a great imperial power.

Ssu-ma Ch'ien's eerie and violent account of how Motun built up his power contains legendary motifs, but also tells us much about the process of state-building in the steppes. According to Ssu-ma Ch'ien, Tumen disliked Motun, and wanted a younger son to succeed him. So he attacked the Yüeh-chih even though they held Motun hostage, in the expectation that this would ensure his son's death.[5] However, Motun survived in heroic style by escaping on a stolen horse. After Motun's return, Tumen had to give him the military rank appropriate for the heir-apparent, that of commander of 10,000 horse. Motun used his new position to build up a disciplined personal army, which he eventually used to seize power.

> Mo-tun had some arrows made that whistled in flight and used them to drill his troops in shooting from horseback.[6] 'Shoot wherever you see my whistling arrow strike!', he ordered, 'and anyone who fails to shoot will be cut down!' Then he went out hunting for birds and animals, and if any of his men failed to shoot at what he himself had shot at, he cut them down on the spot. After this, he shot a whistling arrow at one of his best horses. Some of his men hung back and did not dare shoot at the horse, whereupon Mo-tun at once executed them. A little later he took an arrow and shot at his favorite wife. Again some of his men shrank back in terror and failed to discharge their arrows, and again he executed them on the spot. Finally he went out hunting with his men and shot a whistling arrow at one of his father's finest horses. All his followers promptly discharged their arrows in the same direction, and Mo-tun knew that at last they could be trusted. Accompanying his father, the *shan-yü* T'ou-man, on a hunting expedition, he shot a whistling arrow at his father and every one of his followers aimed their arrows in the same direction and shot the *shan-yü* dead. Then Mo-tun executed his stepmother, his younger brother, and all the high officials of the nation who refused to take orders from him, and set himself up as the new *shan-yü*.[7]

Motun assumed the title of *shan-yü* in 209 BCE and held it until his death in 174. Using the power of his highly disciplined personal retinue, as well as tribal levies which accepted his legitimacy as the *shan-yü*, Motun began to extend his power beyond the Hsiung-nu heartland.

He began by attacking the other great tribal confederations. The Tung-hu, in eastern Mongolia, tested the authority of the new *shan-yü*, by demanding gifts. Motun granted their requests until they overreached themselves by demanding Hsiung-nu lands in the Gobi. With his disciplined armies, he caught the Tung-hu unprepared, killed many of their men, took their women and children prisoner, and captured their herds. In rituals that the Scythians would have appreciated, Motun executed the Tung-hu leader, and had a ritual drinking cup made from his skull. This was lovingly preserved by successive *shan-yü* and used on special ceremonial occasions. After destroying the Tung-hu, Motun turned on the Yüeh-chih to his west, and seized back from them traditional Hsiung-nu lands along the western loop of the Huang He. His power now reached to the Han defensive lines that crossed the Ordos. He extended it to the north by defeating several groups of pastoralists and hunter-gatherers in southern Siberia.[8] Domination of the north Mongolian borderlands gave the Hsiung-nu access to the furs and other goods of the Siberian forest lands and also to the metals of the Mongolian Altai. Victories in the Mongolian steppes, the forest lands to the north, and the borderlands

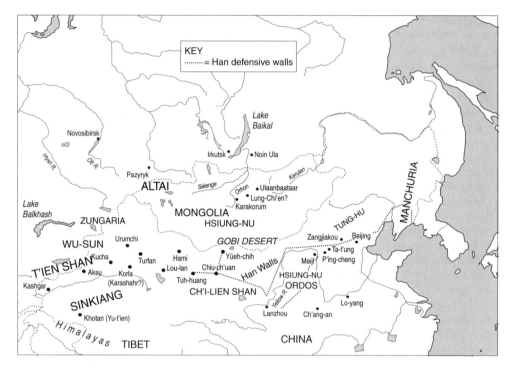

Map 8.2 The Hsiung-nu empire.

of the Ordos and eastern Kansu, built up Motun's authority, wealth and prestige so that: 'the nobles and high ministers of the Hsiung-nu were all won over by Motun, considering him a truly worthy leader.'[9]

These conquests gave Motun access to considerable wealth.[10] However, none of the lands Motun now controlled could provide the large flows of goods necessary to fund a durable pastoralist state. To do that, he had to tap the vast wealth of China. Fortunately, the weakness of the newly established Han dynasty eased his task. In 201, the first Han emperor, Kao-tsu (206–195), responded to Hsiung-nu raids into North China by launching an attack on Motun's capital in the north of modern Shansi province. The campaign was a disaster. The severe cold of the steppes north of the Chinese walls killed or crippled up to a third of Kao-tsu's vast army. The remnants were ambushed when they thought they were pursuing a weak and demoralized enemy. The Han emperor found himself besieged at P'ing-ch'eng (modern Pinglucheng, *c.*150 k. west of Ta-t'ung) for seven days, and had to negotiate humiliating terms before escaping ingloriously from the Hsiung-nu trap.

In 198, Kao-tsu negotiated the first of the so-called *ho-ch'in* treaties. The Chinese agreed to supply regular gifts of silk, wine, grain and other goods; they offered a royal princess in marriage to the *shan-yü*; and they agreed to treat the Hsiung-nu as diplomatic equals. In addition, they formally surrendered control of the northern Ordos beyond the Ch'in defensive walls.

In return, the Hsiung-nu undertook not to invade Han territory. The relationship established in 198 lasted for over 60 years. As Thomas Barfield has shown, the system of *ho-ch'in* treaties, though never perfect, offered much to both sides.[11] For the Chinese, it bought relative stability along their northern borders for, at least in principle, Chinese support made Motun and his successors powerful enough to control most pastoralists of the Mongolian steppes. For the Hsiung-nu elite, the system provided a stable flow of prestige goods, collected from the whole of China and concentrated through the powerful fiscal bureaucracy of the Han. It was the redistribution of this wealth that tied lesser tribal leaders into the Hsiung-nu system and sustained the prestige of the *shan-yü*. Motun could also use this wealth to maintain a loyal 'service' nobility, whose members owed their position to ability and service rather than birth. These were the 'Ku-tu-hou'; they included his personal bodyguard.[12]

Later in his reign, Motun took one more expansionist step. In 175 BCE, he sent an army west under his son, the 'Wise King of the Right', to destroy the Yüeh-chih. According to his own account in a letter to emperor Wen, the army 'succeeded in wiping out the Yüeh-chih, slaughtering or forcing to submission every member of the tribe. In addition [it] conquered the Lou-lan, Wu-sun, and Hu-chieh tribes, as well as the twenty-six states nearby, so that all of them have become a part of the Hsiung-nu nation.'[13] Control of the wealthy oasis city-states of Kansu and Sinkiang allowed the Hsiung-nu to establish contacts of trade and even tribute with rulers in Ferghana and Sogdia. Though the wealth exacted from the 'western regions' was not as great as that exacted from China, these conquests undoubtedly enhanced the *shan-yü*'s wealth, prestige, and power. At Motun's death in 174 BCE, his empire reached from Manchuria, through Sinkiang and into eastern Central Asia.

HSIUNG-NU LIFEWAYS

At the heart of the system created by Motun were the pastoralist tribes who dominated it. These shared in the Scythic culture common to most Inner Eurasian pastoralists in the first millennium BCE.

In much of Mongolia, there existed a largely nomadic style of pastoralism. In times of peace, Hsiung-nu pastoralists lived in small camping groups, following seasonal migrations. Most lived like their Scythian counterparts in wagons that carried domed tents.[14] Ssu-ma Ch'ien writes:

> They move about in search of water and pasture and have no walled cities or fixed dwellings, nor do they engage in any kind of agriculture. Their lands, however, are divided into regions under the control of various leaders.[15]

The most important animals (the five *mal* of modern Mongolia) were the horse, cattle, camel, sheep and goats. The horse was the animal of prestige, and crucial for warfare and travel, though in more arid regions camels or cattle were the main form of transport. Bactrian camels or oxen (or yaks in mountainous regions) hauled tents between campsites. Sheep and goats

Figure 8.1 Rock carving from Kizil-Kaya, southern Siberia, probably of Hunnic life, second or third centuries CE. Drawing by Jon Wilsher, reproduced from E. D. Phillips *The Royal Hordes* (London: Thames and Hudson, 1965).

provided wool, but all the animals provided meat and milk. Milk was drunk fermented, like modern *koumiss*. Animal dung or *argal* was an important fuel in the steppes where there was little wood. The harsh winters of Mongolia, in which temperatures can drop to −40°C, meant that in spring all livestock were weak, and if there were late frosts (the much feared *dzud*), they could die in huge numbers. Spring was therefore a bad time for warfare, as it was throughout the Inner Eurasian steppes. However, autumn was a good time, as animals were fit and well-fed, and the peasants of agricultural lands were bringing in their harvest.[16]

Migration patterns were undoubtedly similar to those practised in recent centuries. The shortest migrations were in hilly regions such as the Hangai mountains, where different types of pasture could be found close together. In such regions, modern pastoralists rarely travel more than 30 km during the year. Migration routes were longer in steppe zones such as the Gobi, where families might have to move 10 or 12 times a year between isolated water sources, in migrations extending up to 120 or more km. Summer camps were generally on high ground, where there were cool breezes, while winter camps were in protected regions with reduced snow cover, in mountain basins or on the southern side of hills.[17]

Hsiung-nu men were as preoccupied with war as Scythian men. In battle, they used improved complex bows that could penetrate armour.[18] They also used swords and spears. Like the Massagetae and Sarmatians, some of the wealthier Hsiung-nu warriors used armour, probably of bone or leather, but sometimes of bronze. Excavations at Noin-Ula in northern Mongolia, show that they may have used early forms of stirrups as well as saddles with pommels.[19] The Hsiung-nu used all the traditional tactics of pastoralist warriors, including feigned retreats, sudden surprise attacks, and constant harassment of weakened opponents. However, under Motun's leadership, the Hsiung-nu also displayed exceptional discipline. In battle, their generals used whistling arrows to communicate with each other.[20]

Neither crafts nor farming were unknown on the steppes, despite the claims of most contemporary accounts.[21] The felt rugs found in the Noin-Ula excavations are similar to those made in nineteenth-century Tuva, as are many of the wooden implements and leather-making tools found at other sites. Research into the chemical composition of fine iron and bronze objects of the Hsiung-nu period shows that most were made by steppe artisans, who carried their equipment as they migrated. Indeed, iron goods were common throughout the steppes by the fourth century BCE. Nevertheless, pastoralists near farming lands often found it easier and more 'cost-effective' to acquire manufactured goods from their neighbours either by raiding or trading.[22]

By the second century BCE, there were few farming communities in the steppes, but farming never vanished entirely. Some farming may have been semi-nomadic, and based on the use of simple wooden implements which have rarely survived in the archaeological record. However, in some regions, farmers used iron ploughshares hauled by domestic livestock. Elsewhere, there existed settled fortified communities of pastoralists, who also engaged in hunting and farming.[23] Some regions, particularly hillier regions in the Orkhon valley, enjoyed fertile soils and rivers that could be used for irrigation farming. Here, Motun and his successors deliberately planted farming communities, often near major winter camps. The remains of about 20 settlements of this kind have been excavated in recent years. The Ivolga site, c.16 kilometres south of modern Ulan-ude, was established during Motun's early campaigns into north Mongolia. It may have been an indigenous settlement, conquered by the Hsiung-nu and used as a frontier garrison from which tributes were collected from forest tribes. However, its inhabitants, consisting of captured Han farmers, Hsiung-nu soldiers, and local people, had to provide their own food. So the settlement contained permanent houses and workshops, and its people grew millet, barley, and wheat, smelted iron and bronze, and made tools, weapons, household goods, jewellery and pottery. Some of its houses had heating systems carried through ducts under the floors.[24]

Some pastoralists, particularly those furthest from farming lands, may have practised simple forms of irrigation farming. The Soviet anthropologist, Vainshtein, has described the role of farming amongst pastoralists of modern Tuva, who practised irrigation farming, using simple ditches from streams. Here, men returned to work their fields several times a year from migration routes which covered only small distances. This may have been a common pattern in the Inner Eurasian steppes, particularly in remote areas distant from systems of exchange with agrarian societies.[25] In some regions, as we have seen, local sedentary populations farmed for survival. However, the 'farming Hsiung-nu' were far less important demographically and economically than the farming Scythians and produced little surplus wealth.

The most important farming regions under Hsiung-nu control were in the oasis settlements of modern Kansu and Sinkiang. These were the lands Motun had captured from the Yüeh-chih. Our first detailed descriptions of this region come from the first century BCE, after the Han dynasty had taken it from the Hsiung-nu. In the oases of the 'western regions', the Han found over 30 'Walled City-States', including Turfan, Lou-lan, Karashahr, Kucha, Aksu, Kashgar, Yarkand and Khotan.[26] In the far west, there were peoples speaking Iranian languages and with cultures similar to those of the Central Asian Saka. In the Ili valley, the lands of the Wu-sun, there is evidence of fortified settlements and irrigation agriculture. Here, as in the Turfan region, people probably spoke languages close to the ancient Saka languages or to some form of Tocharian.[27] The size of these cities varied from c.80,000 (Kucha) to less than 200. Most were walled, and their people practised irrigation agriculture. In arid regions, such as Shan-shan (Lou-lan, near Lob Nor), pastoralism was important. Many cities in Sinkiang produced fine woollen, linen, cotton and silk textiles, which were greatly valued in China. Metalwork, in particular arms-making, was also highly developed. Chinese goods such as silk, linen, paper and lacquerware were imported to the western regions. In return, they sent textiles, horses, grapes, alfalfa and jade to China.[28]

The oasis cities of Kansu and Sinkiang, like those of southern Central Asia, or the Black Sea cities, were prosperous but weak. This inhibited the formation of powerful local states, and made the region tempting prey either for neighbouring pastoralists or agrarian empires. As the *Han-shu* puts it: 'The various states of the Western Regions each have their rulers and their chiefs. Their large bodies of armed men are separated and weak, with no means of united control.'[29]

STATE BUILDING IN THE MONGOLIAN STEPPES

Building a pastoralist state from these very different communities meant exacting tributes and controlling trade networks. Prestige goods were of particular importance in state building, for most subsistence goods could be supplied within the pastoralist community or from the small agricultural communities dotted throughout the steppes.[30]

For almost a century, the Hsiung-nu *shan-yü* demanded and received tributes from the defeated Tung-hu, in the form of cattle, horses, sheep and furs. They also exacted tributes from the semi-nomadic Wu-sun, former tributaries of the Hsiung-nu who had occupied former Saka lands in Zungaria after driving the remnants of the Yüeh-chih out of the region. However, pastoralist communities generated few surpluses, and produced few prestige goods. Siberian tribes also yielded valuable, but limited tributes, mainly in the form of furs.[31]

More important as sources of tribute were the oasis city states of Kansu and Sinkiang. The Hsiung-nu appointed a special 'Commandant of Slaves', based in Karashahr, who extracted large tributes from the city states, mainly in the form of horses, livestock and textiles.[32] Like the Han after them, they probably took hostages from the ruling families of these cities. By the middle of the second century, the Hsiung-nu even exacted tributes from parts of eastern Central Asia such as Ferghana, for the earliest Chinese envoys to the region found that the Hsiung-nu were feared and respected here: 'whenever a Hsiung-nu envoy appeared in the region carrying credentials from the *shan-yü*, he was escorted from state to state and provided with food, and no one dared to detain him or cause him any difficulty.'[33]

The Hsiung-nu engaged directly in trade, sending many of the goods they received in Chinese tribute through Zungaria to Central Asia, from where some goods travelled on to the Mediterranean and Mesopotamia. First-century BCE tombs from the later Hsiung-nu capital of Noin-ula on the Tola river, suggest the extent of Hsiung-nu control over these trades. They contain 'wool fabrics, tapestries, and embroideries brought to north Mongolia from Sogdiana, Greek Bactria, and Syria. From the Han empire to the south a huge quantity of various kinds of silk cloth, embroideries, quilted silk, and lacquerware and bronze jewelry came to the Hun headquarters.'[34]

Though significant, the wealth of the western regions was nothing to that of China. So, unlike Scythia or southern Central Asia, where pastoralist leaders could extract substantial amounts of wealth from local farming or trading populations, in the eastern zone, creating a pastoralist state meant tapping the wealth of a powerful and dangerous agrarian empire. Doing this was the key to Motun's success, and that of his successors.

The Hsiung-nu extracted resources from China through a complex amalgam of commerce, extortion, bluff, gift-giving and diplomacy. At the most violent end of the spectrum lay the booty raid. Though never a basis for stable relations, this was always available as a threat or a last resort, or as the gambit of ambitious regional leaders. So familiar was the booty raid that Chinese officials created detailed typologies. *Lüeh-pien* meant looting border areas; *k'uo-pien* meant a border encroachment; *ju-k'uo* was an invasion; *ta-ju* a great invasion; *shen-ju* a deep invasion and *ta-chü ju-k'uo* a large-scale invasion. Small-scale raids could be launched at any season. Larger invasions were more profitable in autumn when horses were well-fed, and farmers were in the fields, rather than behind city walls.[35] However, the booty raid was destructive, and in warfare as in disease, excessive virulence may destroy the prey. This was a strategy to be used sparingly, or by leaders unsure of their future and not thinking far ahead. Leaders who aimed at more sustainable flows of wealth, had to use subtler methods.

Thomas Barfield has argued, convincingly, that conquest was not the best way of tapping China's immense wealth, for it merely forced conquerors to set up new fiscal systems.[36] Motun's method of dealing with China, which Barfield has called the 'Outer Frontier Strategy', was to threaten destructive raids, in order to exact resources as a sort of protection rent. In this way, the Chinese bureaucracy bore the costs of collection and transportation, and even, in the case of government-owned enterprises such as silk factories, of production.[37] A Chinese eunuch, Chung-hsing Shuo, who fled to the Hsiung-nu, described the strategy bluntly to Chinese envoys:

> Just make sure that the silks and grainstuffs you bring the Hsiung-nu are the right measure and quality, that's all. ...If the goods you deliver are up to measure and good quality, all right. But if there is any deficiency or the quality is no good, then when the autumn harvest comes we will take our horses and trample all over your crops![38]

An odd consequence of this strategy was that the Hsiung-nu and the Han ended up relying on each other. Macro-parasites, like micro-parasites, have to protect their hosts.[39] A system of regularized exchanges first appeared after the *ho-ch'in* treaty of 198 BCE. During the next 60 years, the treaties were renegotiated ten times. Through them, the Hsiung-nu, with a population of no more than a million, tapped the wealth of an agrarian empire 50 times as large.

In return, the Han gained limited influence in the steppes. Chinese officials hoped that Chinese luxury goods would eventually undermine the independence of their pastoralist opponents. They referred hopefully to the 'five baits'. These were: '1. elaborate clothes and carriages to corrupt their eyes; 2. fine food to corrupt their mouths; 3. music to corrupt their ears; 4. lofty buildings, granaries, and slaves to corrupt their stomachs; 5. gifts and favours for Hsiung-nu who surrendered.'[40] Pastoralists were well aware of the dangers posed by Chinese luxury goods. Excessive dependence on Chinese goods was bound to undermine the militaristic culture of the steppes and create new forms of economic and political dependence. As Chung-hsing Shuo commented:

> when you get any of the Han silks, put them on and try riding your horses through brush and brambles! In no time your robes and leggings will be torn to shreds and everyone will see that silks are no match for the utility and excellence of felt and leather garments. Likewise when you get any of the Han foodstuffs, throw them away so that people can see that they are not as practical or tasty as milk and kumiss![41]

To the Hsiung-nu, commercial exchanges were as important as tributes or gifts. They needed prestige goods to sustain their own power, while in times of difficulty, they needed foodstuffs as well. Chinese merchants were also very interested in trade with the Hsiung-nu. They bought livestock, furs (exacted by the Hsiung-nu as tributes from the north), and the precious stones and textiles the Hsiung-nu took from the western regions. A Chinese source lists the main Chinese imports. They included mules, donkeys, camels and horses, as well as sable, fox, badger and marmot furs, steppeland carpets and precious stones such as jade. Chinese garrison soldiers also engaged in trade with neighbouring pastoralists. However, Chinese governments were usually less enthusiastic about cross-border trade and actively banned trade in strategic goods such as weapons or iron.[42] When short of horses for warfare or transportation, Chinese governments reluctantly supported cross-border trade. But usually, they saw it as a dangerous drain on Chinese wealth. So it was usually pastoralists who demanded the opening of border markets, sometimes with the support of local Chinese merchants or other petty traders.[43] When forced to trade, Chinese officials tried to turn trade to diplomatic and military advantage. When emperor Wen Ti (180–157) first allowed border markets, an adviser told him:

> It is the border markets [*kuan-shih*] which the Hsiung-nu need most badly, and they have sought desperately to obtain them from us, even resorting to force. I urge your majesty to send envoys with lavish gifts to make peace with [the Hsiung-nu], using this opportunity to inform them of our decision, made not without reluctance, to grant their request of establishing large-sized border markets. Upon the return of our envoys we should immediately open up many [markets] in locations of strategic importance. In each of these market places sufficient military forces must be stationed for [our] self-protection. Every large border market should include shops which specialize in selling raw meat, wine, cooked rice, and delicious barbecues. All the shops must be of a size capable of serving one or two hundred people. In this way our markets beneath the Great Wall will surely swarm with the Hsiung-nu. ... When the Hsiung-nu have developed a craving for our rice, stew, barbecues, and wine, this will have become their fatal weakness.[44]

However, border markets also created problems for the Chinese. Chinese traders often outwitted commercially naive pastoralists, as well as their own officials, so that violence, corruption and smuggling were rife.[45]

There was an important symbolic aspect to cross-border exchanges, for negotiations over symbolism reflected hard-headed assessments of the balance of prestige and power. For much of the second century, Chinese diplomats treated the Hsiung-nu as equals. The emperor Wen-ti conceded that north of the Great Wall, the Hsiung-nu *shan-yü* enjoyed Heaven's mandate. Marriage alliances were a vital aspect of the symbolic relationship.[46] In worlds saturated with the idiom of kinship, marriage was a powerful way of stabilizing relationships between clans, tribes and states. For steppe rulers marriages with Chinese rulers conferred great prestige. They also had a long history. Indeed, the carriage found in the fifth- or fourth-century BCE Pazyryk tombs may have been part of the dowry of a Chinese princess.[47] Emperor Kao-tsu granted Motun a royal bride, in the hope that a son-in-law and perhaps later a grandson would be easier to control than an alien pastoralist emperor. As an official argued: 'who ever heard of a grandson trying to treat his grandfather as an equal? Thus your soldiers need fight no battles, and yet the Hsiung-nu will gradually become your subjects.'[48]

The sending of a royal daughter as a bride to a steppeland ruler was also a form of hostage-giving, and even of trade. For Chinese officials, the brides were pawns in a diplomatic game, while pastoralists were as interested in the dowries, gifts, titles and trade opportunities that came with them.[49]

Marriage was often a relatively cheap form of diplomacy. As an official of the T'ang dynasty argued in 814 CE, when the Uighurs controlled Mongolia, a marriage might cost the revenue from one large region, but a military campaign involving, perhaps 30,000 infantry and 5000 cavalry, would cost much more.[50] The interests of the poor women traded in this way counted for little. Liu Xijun, whom the Chinese married off to the aged ruler of the Wu-Sun, in Zungaria, late in the second century, is reputed to have written a poem that conveys the heartache felt by the victims of this ancient trade, which left aristocratic Chinese ladies to live out their lives in tatty splendour in the steppes.

> My family sent me off to be married on the other side of heaven. They sent me
> a long way to a strange land, to the king of Wu-sun. A domed lodging is my
> dwelling place, with walls made of felt. Meat is my food, with fermented milk
> as the sauce. I live with constant thoughts of my home, my heart is full of
> sorrow; I wish I were a golden swan, returning to my home country.[51]

Taken together, the symbolic and material exchanges of the *ho-ch'in* system, as well as the lesser revenues from Kansu and Sinkiang, provided the wealth and prestige that allowed Hsiung-nu elites to maintain their authority and prestige throughout the steppes. Using this wealth, successive *shan-yüs* created a disciplined army and a bureaucratized system of government based on Chinese models.

Chinese sources refer to 24 leading 'ministers', of which the four most important were the 'Worthy King of the Left' (or eastern region), the 'Luli king of the Left', the 'Worthy King of the Right' (or western region) and the 'Luli king of the Right', each of which had its own governmental bureaucracy. These four positions were, in effect, governorships of the empire's four quarters, and they were usually held by brothers or sons of the ruling *shan-yü*. The 'Worthy king of the left' was the senior position, usually held by the heir-apparent. Within each quarter, different tribes had their own recognized territories.[52] Such divisions, beginning with the fundamental division into 'left' and 'right' (eastern and western) sections, were to reappear in many pastoralist empires, and they probably reflect little more than a formalization of existing tribal hierarchies and territories. According to Ssu-ma Ch'ien, many of these positions were hereditary, which suggests that even Motun had little success in breaking the regional power of great regional chiefs.

However, Motun did make sure that regional rulers were well aware of his power. His first capital was in northern Shansi province, but the later Hsiung-nu capital was at 'Lung–Ch'ien', 'the Dragon Site', in the Hangai mountains west of modern Ulaanbataar, and not far from the later Mongol capital of Karakorum. Like the Versailles of Louis XVI, this ceremonial centre helped forge a wider sense of unity from disparate ethnic and social elements. Motun summoned tribal leaders to his capital three times a year. At these gatherings there were games, like the modern Naadam festival, and the unity of the broader alliance system was reaffirmed. Such meetings also allowed for a rudimentary census of people and livestock, an administrative device introduced by Chung-hsing Shuo.[53] Administering the Hsiung-nu empire required a minimum of literacy in a previously illiterate world. Some Hsiung-nu officials certainly learnt literacy, while officials such as Chung-hsing Shuo brought their bureaucratic and diplomatic skills with them. We should not be surprised, therefore, that there is some evidence of a distinctive Hsiung-nu writing system, for runes similar to those of the later Orkhon Türk script have been found in Noin-Ula and other burial sites.[54]

We know little of Hsiung-nu religion, and what we know suggests that, like Scythian religion, it had strong political overtones, and was actively used to support the legitimacy of Hsiung-nu elites. It was probably an amalgam of many different influences, including forms of shamanism (there is what looks like a shamanic headdress in the Noin-Ula tombs), the practice of animal sacrifices, particularly of horses, forms of ancestor worship, Zoroastrian influences from Central Asia and influences from China. Motun himself prayed to the Sun each morning and to the Moon each evening, and he also conducted annual sacrifices with other tribal leaders.[55]

> In the first month of the year the various leaders come together in a small meeting at the *shan-yü*'s court to perform sacrifices, and in the fifth month a great meeting is held at Lung-ch'eng at which sacrifices are conducted to the Hsiung-nu ancestors, Heaven and Earth, and the gods and spirits.[56]

In 121 BCE, there is a fascinating reference in the *Shih chi* to the Chinese capture of 'the golden man which he [a Hsiung-nu *shan-yü*] used in worshipping Heaven'. This may have been a Buddhist image, in which case, it constitutes the earliest reference to Buddhism in Mongolia or, indeed, anywhere in China.[57] There are signs of the increasing importance of gods of the heavens (*tngri*), that were to be so important in later Mongolian religion, and of which the highest was the *köke tngri*, or eternal heaven.[58] The traditional title of *shan-yü* already implied the blessing of Heaven, for its full version, 'T'ang-li-ku't'u Shan yü', meant 'Great Son of Heaven'. This is one of many examples of Chinese religious influences. Like the Chinese, the Hsiung-nu consulted shamans before military expeditions, and, like Chinese soothsayers, they read the crack marks that appeared on burnt shoulder bones.[59]

THE HAN COUNTER-OFFENSIVE AND HSIUNG-NU DECLINE: 133 BCE–220 CE

THE HAN COUNTER-OFFENSIVE

By the reign of the great Han emperor, Wu-ti (141–87 BCE), the *ho-ch'in* system was beginning to break down. It had long been criticized by Chinese officials, and despite its cost, conflicts had become endemic along China's northern borders. In 133 BCE, after a prolonged debate, Wu-ti decided that the system was too expensive, too humiliating and too ineffective to continue. Instead, he decided to crush the Hsiung-nu, and launched an all-out offensive which was to last for several decades.

As his adviser, An-kuo, told him, the risks were great. Campaigning in the steppes posed huge logistical problems for Chinese armies. It was reckoned that each Chinese soldier needed 18 bushels of dried rice for a 300-day march, and this had to be carried by oxen, who required an extra 20 bushels each, and could not survive more than 100 days in desert country.[60] Weather was another problem. Chinese armies were equipped neither for the extreme heat of the desert summers nor for their winters. For these reasons, it was not reckoned possible for a Chinese army to survive more than 100 days in Hsiung-nu territory. Further, civilians in China's northern provinces suffered from the obligation of supplying the army with food and clothing.

Wu-ti launched his campaigns with an unsuccessful attempt to lead the Hsiung-nu armies into a trap, in order to destroy them at one blow.[61] The failure of this attempt condemned both sides to prolonged and expensive warfare. From 129 BCE, Wu-ti sent a series of armies deep into the Hsiung-nu steppes. After the campaigns of 127 BCE, the Hsiung-nu lost control of the Ordos region, and the Chinese government began to set up irrigation works and to garrison even some lands north of the Huang He. Though expensive, these early campaigns had enough success to persuade some pastoralist groups to secede from the Hsiung-nu as early as 121 BCE.[62] However, as long as the Hsiung-nu stayed north of the Gobi, it seemed that Han armies could not reach them. In 119 BCE, Wu-ti decided to send two armies north of the Gobi from northern Shansi, under experienced frontier generals, Wei Ch'ing and his nephew, the young cavalry general, Ho Ch'ü-ping.

> They agreed... to fatten the horses on grain and send out a force of a hundred thousand cavalry, along with a hundred and forty thousand horses to carry baggage and other equipment (this in addition to the horses provided for transporting provisions).[63]

Both armies succeeded in crushing large Hsiung-nu armies, and Wei Ch'ing sacked Lung-Ch'ien. The Hsiung-nu *shan-yü*, I-ch'ih-hsia (126–114), was driven north of Lung-Ch'ien as far as Lake Baikal with the remnants of his armies. Here, he settled in the city of Noin-Ula. The centre of gravity of Hsiung-nu power now began to shift northwards and westwards. While their eastern wing controlled lands north of Yün-chung province (near modern Baotou on the north-eastern corner of the loop of the Yellow River), their right wing held lands to the north of modern Kansu province.[64]

The change of policy was costly for the Chinese as well. Indeed, it was to pay for Wu-ti's campaigns that the Chinese government introduced for the first time state monopolies on the trade in salt, iron and liquor, as well as a range of other goods.[65] However, despite its cost, Wu-ti's campaigns had greatly weakened the Hsiung-nu system, territorially, militarily and economically. The end of the treaty system had also deprived the Hsiung-nu *shan-yü*s of the flows of tribute on which much of their power depended.

Wu-ti dealt the Hsiung-nu a second blow by challenging their power in Sinkiang. As early as 139 BCE, even before he attacked the Hsiung-nu directly, Wu-ti tried to outflank the Hsiung-nu by sending an envoy, Chang Ch'ien, to contact those sections of the Yüeh-chih who had migrated westwards after being defeated by the Hsiung-nu.[66] The mission was extremely dangerous, as the Hsiung-nu still controlled the Kansu corridor through which it would have to travel. Chang Ch'ien set out with a Hsiung-nu slave, Kan-fu, and an embassy of 100 men, but was captured in the Kansu corridor and held for 10 years. Eventually, with Kan-fu and a Hsiung-nu bride, he escaped and travelled on through modern Sinkiang to the kingdom of Ta-yüan (Ferghana) in Central Asia. With help from the ruler of Ta-yüan, he travelled on to the kingdom of the Yüeh-chih, now settled in Sogdia, just north of Ta Hsia [Bactria]. He returned to China around the southern route through the Tarim basin, was captured once more by the Hsiung-nu, but escaped again after another year of captivity. In 125 BCE, 13 years after he had left, he returned to China with only his wife and his slave.

Chang Ch'ien's trip was an event of great significance in the history of Han China, the Hsiung-nu and even Eurasia as a whole, for it marks the beginning of the first successful attempts by China to establish official diplomatic and commercial links with Central Asia. In his report to Wu-ti, Chang Ch'ien described the walled cities of Ferghana, the region's famous wines and its 'heavenly' horses that seemed to sweat blood; as well as the lands of Sogdia, with their city states ruled now by the pastoralist Yüeh-chih.[67] He also passed on descriptions of other lands, including India, Parthia, Mesopotamia, and the pastoralist kingdoms of K'ang-chü (Tashkent?) and Yen-ts'ai, which was probably based near the mouth of the Syr Darya on the Aral Sea.

Knowledge of the wealthy lands of Central Asia encouraged Wu-ti to attempt to establish Chinese suzerainty over them. He was particularly interested in the possibility of securing the strong Ferghana horses as an alternative to the Mongolian ponies used by the Chinese cavalry, and supplied by the Hsiung-nu.[68] In 121 BCE, the Hun-yeh king, the regional Hsiung-nu commander of the Kansu corridor, surrendered to the Han after repeated defeats at the hands of Ho Ch'ü-ping. The Han now secured permanent control of the Kansu corridor, which opened for the first time a secure pathway towards the west. In 104 BCE, the Chinese government set up a new administrative district at Chiu-ch'üan, and soon after, another at Tun-huang. They also built forts and defensive walls as far as Tun-huang, and started settling Chinese farmers in the Kansu oases, and even, perhaps, as far west as Turfan (Ku-shih).[69]

In 117 BCE, Chang Ch'ien, though now in disgrace for his failures in a campaign of 122 BCE against the Hsiung-nu, was given a chance to redeem himself by leading a second expedition westwards. The main object of this expedition was to establish contact with the Wu-sun, whose fortified capital was at Ch'ih-ku, in the basin of Lake Issyk Kul in modern Kyrgyzstan. The Wu-sun were probably an Iranian-speaking people, possibly ancestors of the later Alans/As and modern Ossetians. Their ruler and founder, the K'un-mo, had been a vassal of the Hsiung-nu before occupying his current lands, but had asserted his independence 'and refused any longer to journey to the meetings of the Hsiung-nu court', presumably because of their recent defeats at the hands of the Han.[70] Having failed earlier to make allies of the Yüeh-chih,

Chang Ch'ien's aim this time was to persuade the Wu-sun to move into the Kansu region as loyal vassals of the Han. In return, he was to offer the K'un-mo a Chinese bride. Chang Ch'ien set off with 300 attendants, many thousands of cattle and sheep, and precious gifts of gold and silk. Sending some of his men to make contact with the kingdoms he had visited or heard of further west, he opened negotiations with the Wu-sun before returning to China. Though his negotiations failed, the Wu-sun sent a return delegation to China. This was so impressed with China's wealth, that the two powers negotiated an alliance that lasted for much of the next century.

This was merely the first of a large number of embassies and trade missions sent to the west. In return, foreign envoys from as far afield as Parthia, returned to the Han capital, where they were entertained lavishly by the emperor. While many of the goods exchanged along these routes should count as gifts or diplomatic presents, most of the envoys also traded on their account, so there was some genuine trade. Ssu-ma Ch'ien commented that most of the envoys were from poor families, and 'handled the government gifts and goods that were entrusted to them as though they were private property and looked for opportunities to buy goods at a cheap price in the foreign countries and make a profit on their return to China'. As a result, these expeditions turned the 'Silk Roads', for the first time, into a major international trade route, linking eastern, central and western Eurasia into a single system of regular commercial exchanges by land.[71] Silk dominated these trade routes because of its unique combination of lightness, low bulk and high value. However, it was never the only commodity to travel these routes. Extensive finds of Chinese coins and other objects in Central Asia show the size of this trade, as do finds of Sogdian documents in Tun-huang.[72]

However, Wu-ti was interested in more than commercial contacts with Central Asia. In 104 BCE, he sent an army under Li Kuang-li, to conquer Erh-shih, the capital of Ferghana, in response to the murder of some Chinese envoys. However, the expedition failed through lack of supplies from local populations. Supplied with massive reinforcements, Li Kuang-li was sent off again in 102 BCE, and this time managed to lead an army to Ferghana. Members of this expedition defeated the ruler of Ferghana and brought back grapevines, and war horses, as well as a promise to send more horses as annual tribute.[73]

Li Kuang-li's victory greatly enhanced the prestige of the Han throughout the Western regions, and local leaders began sending envoys with gifts. However, controlling the western regions was never easy and Han power was greatest in the Tarim basin and weakest north of the T'ien shan. Many local states found themselves caught unhappily between the Han and Hsiung-nu empires, which is why so few were willing to help Li Kuang-li's first expedition to Ferghana. Hsiung-nu tributes were burdensome, but so was the task of feeding and providing for the many embassies travelling to and from China. Lou-lan, in Lob Nor, accepted Han suzerainty in 108 BCE, but continued to send hostages to the Hsiung-nu and, occasionally, harrassed Han officials. Only in 77 BCE was a pro-Han ruler installed after the murder of his predecessor by local agents.[74] In 71 BCE, Han and Wu-sun forces together

Plate 8.1 Remains of a Han beacon tower.

defeated the Hsiung-nu, and for a time the son of the Wu-sun *K'un-mo* ruled much of the Tarim basin from Yarkand. From 59 until the end of the reign of Wang Mang (*c*.9–23 CE), the Chinese ruled the 'western provinces' through specially appointed 'protectors-general', based in Wu-lei, to the west of Karashahr. Much of our knowledge of Sinkiang in the Han era comes from the reports of these officials. The situation of local protectors-general was delicate, for they had to rely mainly on troops recruited from the local population.[75] For these reasons, they sought and acquired detailed knowledge of local populations, supplies and the distances from town to town. Han China controlled the city states of Kansu and southern Sinkiang either through agreements with their rulers (backed up by taking members of their families as 'attendant sons' to China) or by planting garrisons of Chinese soldiers (*t'un-t'ien*), who brought their families with them, and were usually expected to be self-sufficient. In some cases, China even sent prisoners to the western region as labourers.[76] The Han also built defensive walls in the region. Some, with their beacon towers (from which fire signals could be sent from tower to tower as far as Ch'ang-an), can still be seen today. The system of walls and towers extended from the Jade Gate west of Tun-huang, through Lop Nor and to Kucha. The Chinese extended and improved irrigation works to support their colonies, and may even have introduced *karez* irrigation tunnels into the Turfan region. They also introduced iron-working to the western regions.[77]

After the death of the usurper, Wang Mang, in 23 CE, China lost control of Sinkiang, where, for a time, influence was shared by the Hsiung-nu and a Wu-sun state based on Yarkand. However, after 73 CE, Pan Ch'ao, brother of the historian, Pan Ku, led an army that restored Han control of Sinkiang. Direct Han control of the western regions lasted only until 107–19 CE, but Han influence persisted much longer.[78]

DECLINE OF THE HSIUNG-NU EMPIRE

The victories of Wu-ti weakened the Hsiung-nu militarily, prised away many of their major allies, such as the Wu-sun, and deprived them of the regular flow of tributes from China and the western regions on which their power had been based. Inevitably, the economic, military and diplomatic decline of the Hsiung-nu leaders encouraged internal divisions.

For almost 150 years, the succession from one *shan-yü* to another was remarkably smooth. But in 60 BCE, there began the first of several civil wars over the succession.[79] Eventually, one of the contenders in these complex and violent struggles took the calculated step of accepting symbolic subordination to China in return for protection. Ever since the Hsiung-nu defeat of 119 BCE, Chinese governments had demanded formal recognition of Chinese suzerainty and the sending of hostages as a condition for negotiations. Successive *shan-yü*s had rejected these terms until in 54 BCE, Hu-han-yeh, the *shan-yü* of a southern group of Hsiung-nu tribes, led his followers to the Great Wall frontier, where they asked the Han emperor Hsüan-ti (r. 73–49 BCE) for protection in return for accepting Han suzerainty. The following year, Hu-han-yeh sent a son as hostage to Ch'ang-an, and in 51 and 49 BCE he personally visited the emperor and paid homage.

The decision to submit was preceded by a vigorous debate amongst the Hsiung-nu leaders. One group argued that accepting Chinese terms would betray the Hsiung-nu's reputation for courage, make them into a laughing stock, and destroy their claim to be the 'head of all nations'.[80] Others argued that:

> the Hsiung-nu have gradually been whittled down and can never gain their former status. Although we exhaust ourselves in that endeavour we can never find a day's repose. Now if we submit to China, our nation will be preserved in peace; but if we refuse to submit we are running into perdition.[81]

The decision of the southern Hsiung-nu created a new, subordinate relationship with China, often described as the 'tributary' system. It had three main elements: (1) the payment of homage to the Chinese emperor; (2) the sending of royal hostages; and (3) the payment of tributes.[82] Barfield has described the new relationship as the 'Inner Frontier strategy'. Under this strategy, leaders of one side in a steppe civil war sought out Chinese support in return for symbolic subordination, while retaining considerable autonomy. From the Chinese point of view, the 'Inner Frontier strategy' was merely an early stage in the digestion of one more barbarian people. In later stages, such people could pass through various administrative relationships, leading eventually to full incorporation within the empire. However, as Barfield points out, the 'Inner Frontier strategy' could often prove very successful for pastoralist leaders, allowing them to rebuild their power and reunify the steppes.[83]

It certainly worked well for Hu-han-yeh. The Chinese emperor accepted his offer of suzerainty, but was careful not to demand too much, as he understood that China had much to gain from allying with a powerful steppe leader who could control the frontier tribes. China granted the southern *shan-yü* a status of relative equality, below the emperor, but above all Chinese nobles.[84] He was formally allowed to remain as ruler of his people, a status granted to barbarians on the frontiers with Rome only after the battle of Adrianople in 378 CE. When Hu-han-yeh came to the capital in 51 BCE, he was not made to kowtow to the emperor, but was loaded with gifts of gold, silk, clothing and rice, while his people were promised protection and supplies of grain, as well as access to border markets. In successive years, the size of the gifts increased, and the Chinese also supported the southern Hsiung-nu in times of famine.[85] Chinese material and diplomatic support enabled Hu-han-yeh to establish his authority over the southern Hsiung-nu, now living in the Ordos and the lands just north of the Huang He.

Hu-han-yeh's brother and rival, the northern *shan-yü*, Chih-chih, tried to negotiate a similar relationship with China. However, China now had little reason to care what happened deep in the steppes, and relations with China broke down in 45 BCE when Chih-chih killed a Chinese envoy. Chih-chih fled west to northern Sinkiang, where he allied with the K'ang-chü federation, attacked the Wu-sun, and eventually seized much of Ferghana. In 42 BCE, a Chinese army with barbarian troops, acting on the initiative of its leader, the 'Protector General' of the western region, Ch'en T'ang, entered Sogdia and killed Chih-chih. His armies may have included Roman soldiers captured by Parthia at the battle of Carrhae in 53 BCE, and transferred east to serve as Hsiung-nu mercenaries.[86]

With his rival dead, Hu-han-yeh and his followers reoccupied the steppelands of Outer Mongolia. Here, Chinese diplomats persuaded Hu-han-yeh to swear a solemn pact of peace, marked by a toast from the drinking cup made 150 years earlier from the skull of the defeated chief of the Yüeh-chih. The frontier now lay, once again, along the line of the Great Wall. In 33 BCE Hu-han-yeh visited Ch'ang-an once again, and received a wife, Wang Zhaojun, from the imperial harem. For almost 50 years, she helped maintain a relatively peaceful relationship between China and the Hsiung-nu.[87]

The new relationship proved durable, and very advantageous to the Hsiung-nu leaders. In return for the modest symbolic price of fealty, the Hsiung-nu leaders managed, once again, to control a flow of resources large enough to stabilize their authority over large areas of the steppes. Indeed, in time the flow of wealth increased until the Chinese government began to

dread the visits of Hsiung-nu delegations, as their size, and the cost of enter-
taining them steadily rose. It is extremely difficult to estimate the real burden
of such payments for the Chinese government, but Yü argues that, under the
later Han, annual payments to all barbarian peoples amounted to c.7 per cent
of government revenue.[88]

The relationship negotiated by Hu-han-yeh lasted until the reign of Wang
Mang. After the fall of the former Han dynasty, the Hsiung-nu leaders briefly
reasserted their independence, reestablished control over the Ordos and
northern Shansi, and even intervened in north China. In 44 CE, as emperor
Guang Wu-Ti (r. 25–57) established the Later Han dynasty, with its new
capital at Lo-yang, Hsiung-nu raids reached the Wei valley. Hu-han-yeh's
son, *shan-yü* Yu (r. 18–46 CE) now controlled an empire as large and as
independent as that of Motun.

However, *shan-yü* Yu failed to establish a durable version of the 'Outer
Frontier Strategy', and during the period of famine and civil war that followed his death in 46 CE, Hsiung-nu power collapsed. There now emerged a
permanent split between northern branches of the Hsiung-nu, committed to
the steppes, and southern branches committed to a closer relationship with
China. A southern group, led by *shan-yü* Pi (r. 48–56 CE), sent a delegation
to Lo-yang in 47, presenting a map of Hsiung-nu lands, and asking permission to be 'attached to the Inner'.[89] The Han agreed, and *shan-yü* Pi, with
40–50,000 soldiers, and a total population of two or three times as many,
moved into parts of the Ordos and Shansi province south of the walls. These
became the 'southern Hsiung-nu', and for them, the 'Inner Frontier strategy'
became a permanent relationship. The position of the southern Hsiung-nu
within the empire's defensive borders enabled them to negotiate with, and
receive gifts from, the Han, despite their relative weakness. Though Pi had to
kowtow to the Han emperor, and to settle at Meiji (modern Fugu), in the
north-western loop of the Yellow river, his authority revived, aided by
the generous gifts of the Han, and their decision to abandon direct control
of the north-western segment of the Ordos.[90] The sharp decline in Chinese
populations in the north, as a result of the civil wars after the fall of Wang
Mang, meant that the establishment of a buffer state made sense for the
Later Han.[91]

Though Hsiung-nu people and lifeways had been re-established from Ta-
t'ung to the western Ordos, as in the days of Motun, the southern Hsiung-nu
were still vassals of the Han. Indeed, their *shan-yü* was supervised by a
Chinese 'household emissary' who acted much like the British Resident to an
Indian court.[92] In 78 BCE, Wu-huan tribes, originally from the Khingan mountains, but long settled near the trading centre of Zhangjiakou, attacked the one
fixed target presented by steppe peoples, the tombs of their dead leaders.[93]
Other, more successful, attacks followed, from the Wu-sun in the west and the
Ting-ling tribes from the Baikal region. By the middle of the second century,
the effective authority of the *shan-yü* had almost vanished, the Hsiung-nu
polity no longer existed even in the south, and Mongolia became, once again,
a region of purely tribal politics. The last *shan-yü* died in c.220, as the Han
dynasty ended, a captive, like the last Han emperor, of the warlord, Tsao Tsao.

The power of the Northern Hsiung-nu, under Hu-han-yeh's grandson, P'u-nu (r. 46–83), had collapsed even earlier, as the flow of tribute dried up and subordinate tribes of Wu-huan and Hsien-pi defected. The end came after the death of P'u-nu in c.83 CE, and the severing of Hsiung-nu supplies of grain from Sinkiang by the victories of Pan Ch'ao. The Hsien-pi killed P'u-nu's successor in 87, skinned his body and took the skin as a trophy, before seizing much of Mongolia.[94] Many northern Hsiung-nu migrated south. Finally, an alliance of Chinese, Hsien-pi and southern Hsiung-nu advanced into Mongolia, assembled at Zhuoye Mountain, and destroyed the northern Hsiung-nu in 89 CE at Jiluo Mountain, 150 k further to the north-west. The Chinese army continued its advance and burned Lung-Ch'ien, while the northern *shan-yü* retreated to the west. During the next 50 years, Hsien-pi tribes took control of much of Mongolia.[95]

As Hsiung-nu authority collapsed, regional tribal leaders regained the independence they had lost in the era of Motun. Some pastoralists drifted south where they became Hsien-pi, while others headed west to the Ili valley, south of Lake Balkhash. Early in the second century, some of these western Hsiung-nu moved further west, following the migration of the earlier Yüeh-chih, into the lands along the Syr Darya.[96] These refugees, after considerable mixing with local populations, were eventually to play a significant role further west, where historians knew them as the 'Huns'. The first western notice of the Huns, in 160, places them near the Aral sea, while Ptolemy's geography claimed that some Hunnic groups had reached the Black Sea.[97] However, most of these Hunnic remnants remained in the Urals region for another 200 years before their descendants invaded the Ukrainian steppes late in the fourth century.

The westward migration of the Huns was part of a wider process of 'Turkicization' of the Inner Eurasian steppes. First in western Mongolia and Zungaria, then in the Kazakh steppes, and finally in southern Central Asia and the western steppes, Iranian-speaking pastoralists were supplanted by groups speaking early forms of Turkic or Mongolian. By 500 CE, Turkic languages dominated the central and western steppes, and by 1000 CE, they dominated much of southern Central Asia as well. In this way, the collapse of Hsiung-nu power reverberated throughout the steppelands of Inner Eurasia.

NOTES

1 Ssu-ma Ch'ien first mentions them in the year 318 BC see *The Grand Scribe's Records*, 1:112; he claimed they were descended from a ruler of the Hsia dynasty; see Ssu-ma Ch'ien, *Records*, 2:155 and 163; see also Prusek, *Chinese Statelets*, p. 224.
2 Jagdid and Hyer, *Mongolia's Culture and Society*, p. 206; Janhunen, *Manchuria*, p. 189, suggests that they spoke an early form of Bulgaric Turkic, while their eastern neighbours, the Hsien-pi and Wu-huan, spoke early forms of Mongolian.
3 See Golden, *Introduction*, pp. 93–5; they probably occupied a region extending from Lake Baikal to the Minusinsk basin, and may have been represented by the Tagar culture of the seventh to third centuries BCE.

4 N. Ishjamts, 'Nomads in eastern Central Asia', in *HCCA*, 2:163; de Crespigny, *Northern Frontier*, p. 177.

5 Ssu-ma Ch'ien, *Records*, 2:160–1.

6 On whistling arrows, see Vainshtein, *Nomads of South Siberia*, pp. 170–1. Such arrows have been found in Hsiung-nu and Turkic graves, and were also used by the Mongols. Attached to their shafts were bone spheres with perforations which made a whistling noise. In hunting, they were used to scare hiding animals into leaving their refuge, to scare high-flying birds into flying lower, or to scare larger animals into freezing. Once flushed out, the hunter could shoot their prey with normal arrows. The sound of hundreds of whistling arrows was also used to terrify and demoralize enemy troops, as well as to show where soldiers should fire. See Klyashtornyi and Sultanov, *Kazakhstan*, p. 57, and the illustrations in Phillips, *The Mongols*, p. 44.

7 Ssu-ma Ch'ien, *Records*, 2:161.

8 Ibid., 2:161–5.

9 Ibid., 2:165; on conquests to the north, see Golden, *Introduction*, p. 61.

10 A fact ignored in much of the literature, but emphasized in di Cosmo, 'Ancient Inner Asian Nomads'.

11 Barfield, *Perilous frontier*, ch. 2; and see Ying-shih Yü, 'The Hsiung-nu', in *CHEIA* (pp. 118–49), p. 122; and de Crespigny, *Northern Frontiers*, p. 29.

12 Ishjamts, 'Nomads in eastern Central Asia', in *HCCA*, 2:158.

13 Ssu-ma Ch'ien, *Records*, 2:168.

14 Ishjamts, 'Nomads in eastern Central Asia', in *HCCA*, 2:158, 164; on p. 169 there is a terracotta model of a Hsien-pi ox-drawn wagon.

15 Ssu-ma Ch'ien, 2:155; the 110th ch. of the *Shih chi* is on the Hsiung-nu.

16 Jagchid and Hyer, *Mongolia's Culture*, pp. 20–2; in the tenth century, CE, a Byzantine emperor, Leo VI, advised attacking pastoralists in February, 'when their horses are weakened by the hardships of winter.' Thompson, *Attila*, rev. edn, p. 61.

17 Jagchid and Hyer, *Mongolia's Culture*, p. 26; Vainshtein, *Nomads*, gives superb accounts of particular migration routes; and see Novgorodova, *Drevnyaya Mongoliya*, p. 26.

18 See McEwen, et al., 'Early bow design and construction', pp. 55–6.

19 Ishjamts, 'Nomads in eastern Central Asia', in *HCCA*, 2:160; but see Barclay, *Role of the Horse*, p. 114, which claims that true stirrups first appeared, probably in China, between the second and fifth centuries CE; on armour, Maenchen-Helfen, *World of the Huns*, p. 247.

20 According to Altheim, *Attila*, p. 21.

21 di Cosmo, 'Ancient Inner Asian nomads', passim.

22 Jagchid and Symons, *Peace, War and Trade*, p. 2; on Hsiung-nu crafts, see Vainshtein, *Nomads of South Siberia*, pp. 199–200; on the Noin-Ula excavations, and for pictures of these felt carpets, see Ishjamts, 'Nomads in eastern Central Asia', in *HCCA*, 2:152, 159–63; on Noin-Ula, see Rudenko, *Kul'tura khunnov*.

23 di Cosmo, 'Ancient Inner Asian nomads', pp. 1100–3, 1115.

24 Phillips, *The Royal Hordes*, p. 120 and see Kiselev, ed., *Drevnemongol'skie goroda*; see also the comments in Humphrey, Introduction to Vainshtein, *Nomads of South Siberia*, p. 14; on Ivolga, see Lubo-Lesnichenko, 'The Huns', in Basilov, ed., *Nomads of Eurasia*, p. 50; Davydova, *Ivolginskii kompleks*, pp. 6, 83–4; di Cosmo, 'Ancient Inner Asian Nomads', p. 1115.

25 Caroline Humphrey, Introduction to Vainshtein, *Nomads of South Siberia*, p. 15: 'Thus, paradoxically, it was amongst the most "barbaric" of the nomads that

agriculture and irrigation construction were most in evidence.' She argues, also, that the same applies to crafts, which were most developed furthest from civilization; ibid, p. 17; see also p. 13, and Ch. 4, and pp. 83–94; and see di Cosmo, 'Ancient Inner Asian nomads', p. 1100.

26 Ma Yong and Sun Yutang, 'The western regions under the Hsiung-nu and the Han', in *HCCA* (pp. 227–46), 2:227. The often cited figure of 36 states is purely symbolic. Hulsewe, *China in Central Asia*, p. 71.

27 J. Harmatta, Conclusion, in *HCCA* (pp. 485–92), 2:488; di Cosmo, 'Ancient Inner Asian nomads', p. 1108.

28 Ma Yong and Sun Yutang, 'The western regions', in *HCCA*, 2:229–34; p. 230 includes a good description of the village site of Niya; see also di Cosmo, 'Ancient Inner Asian nomads', pp. 1106–7; Hulsewe, *China in Central Asia*, p. 73.

29 Hulsewe, *China in Central Asia*, pp. 202–3; Waldron, *The Great Wall*, p. 62.

30 di Cosmo, 'Ancient Inner Asian nomads', pp. 112–14.

31 On these subordinate tributary relationships, see Barfield, *Perilous Frontier*, pp. 48–9; there is a good, brief survey of Han relations with the Wu-sun, in Hulsewe, *China in Central Asia*, pp. 43–4; and see Zürcher, 'The Yüeh-chih', p. 360 for some relevant passages from the *Han Shu* 96A.14b; see also de Crespigny, *Northern Frontiers*, p. 368.

32 Ma Yong and Sun Yutang, 'The western regions', in *HCCA*, 2:228; and Hulsewe, *China in Central Asia*, pp. 73 and 203; there are detailed descriptions of most of these states in the *Han-shu*, translated in Hulsewe, ibid.; as Khazanov points out, pastoral nomads often thought of agriculturalists as 'slaves', because they were immobile and weak; *Nomads*, p. 160.

33 Ssu-ma Ch'ien, *Records*, 2:279.

34 Lubo-Lesnichenko, 'The Huns', in Basilov, ed., *Nomads of Eurasia*, p. 47; and see Phillips, *The Royal Hordes*, pp. 114–20. The Hsiung-nu moved their capital here in 119 BCE, after being defeated by Han armies; Watson, *Cultural Frontiers*, p. 125.

35 Jagchid and Symons, *Peace, War, and Trade*, pp. 24–5.

36 This is the basic idea of Barfield's *Perilous Frontier*.

37 Yü, *Trade and Expansion*, p. 28.

38 Ssu-ma Ch'ien, *Records*, 2:172.

39 The metaphor is taken from W. H. McNeill's *Pursuit of Power*.

40 Barfield, *Perilous Frontier*, p. 51.

41 Ssu-ma Ch'ien, *Records*, 2:170.

42 Yü, *Trade and Expansion*, pp. 117–32, and see pp. 97–8, and 191 ('Discourses on salt and iron').

43 Jagchid and Symons, *Peace, War, and Trade*, p. 13; Rossabi, *China and Inner Asia*, p. 82 argues that Chinese claims that exchanges consisted of tribute, not trade, are ingenuous, and not to be taken too seriously.

44 Cited in Ying-Shih Yü, 'The Hsiung-nu', in *CHEIA*, p. 124.

45 Jagchid and Symons, *Peace, War, and Trade*, pp. 182ff, on smuggling and the chaos of the borderlands.

46 Indeed, Jagchid and Symons describe marriage, trade and war as the three main elements in the relation between China and northern barbarians; *Peace, War, and Trade*, p. 1, and ch. 5; on the concession of diplomatic equality, see ibid., p. 65.

47 Rudenko, *Frozen Tombs*, p. 191; similar carriages have been found in China from the warlord period, and there are descriptions of similar vehicles in accounts of campaigns against northern tribes as early as the ninth century BC, and in accounts of gifts to northern tribes; ibid., 192.

48 Ssu-ma Ch'ien, *Records*, 1:289.
49 Jagchid and Symons, *Peace, War, and Trade*, p. 141; Hulsewe, *China in Central Asia*, Intro, pp. 60–1.
50 MacKerras, *Uighur Empire*, 1972 edn, p. 113.
51 Hearing of the poem, emperor Wu-Ti was touched, and regularly sent her gifts, but Liu Xijun died in the lands of the Wu-sun; Hulsewe, *China in Central Asia*, pp. 148–9.
52 Ssu-ma Ch'ien, *Records*, 2:163; de Crespigny, *Northern Frontiers*, pp. 176–7.
53 Ssu-ma Ch'ien, *Records*, 2:164, 170; Barfield, *Perilous Frontier*, p. 53, gives an example of the diplomatic subtleties Chung taught the Hsiung-nu.
54 Ishjamts, 'Nomads in eastern Central Asia', in *HCCA*, 2:165–7, on the 'Hu' script.
55 Ssu-ma Ch'ien, *Records*, 2:164; Heissig, *Religions of Mongolia*, pp. 4–5; Ishjamts, 'Nomads in eastern Central Asia', in *HCCA*, 2:164–5.
56 Ssu-ma Ch'ien, *Records*, 2:164; Jagdid and Hyer, *Mongolia's Culture*, pp. 120–1, add that in Manchu times, meetings of banners (*khushighu*), and the *oboo* festivals that survive into this century, and include sporting contests, continue these traditions.
57 Ssu-ma Ch'ien, *Records*, 2:180; but Zürcher, *The Buddhist Conquest*, 1:21, and Ch'en, *Buddhism in China*, pp. 28–9, doubt that this was a Buddhist image.
58 Heissig, *The Religions of Mongolia*, pp. 4–6; Pulleyblank argues that tengri may be a loan word from the Chinese word for heaven, once pronounced 'chengli'; 'Why Tocharians?', p. 420.
59 Ishjamts, in *HCCA*, 2:165; according to Kürsat-Ahlers, the first part of the full title of the Hsiung-nu leader comes from the word, tengri; see *Zur frühen Staatenbildung*, p. 266.
60 Ying-Shih Yü, 'The Hsiung-nu', in *CHEIA*, p. 130; see Jagchid and Symons, *Peace, War, and Trade*, p. 53, for the writings of Yen Yu, a general of the early first century CE, who makes these points and may be Ying-Shih Yü's source, and p. 60 for An-kuo's advice.
61 Ssu-ma Ch'ien, *Records*, 2:136–7.
62 Ibid., 2:181, and see 2:178, 183.
63 Ibid., 2:182.
64 Ibid., 2:187, and see 2:195, 185; on Noin-Ula, see Ying-Shih Yü, 'The Hsiung-nu', in *CHEIA*, p. 129.
65 Yü, *Trade and Expansion*, p. 17.
66 Ssu-ma Ch'ien's account of this embassy is in the *Shih chih*, ch. 123; see also ch. 96 of the *Han-shu*, in Hulsewe, *China in Central Asia*.
67 The sweating of blood was caused by a parasite that can still be found in Central Asia; it caused bleeding which, when mixed with sweat in summer months created a pink colour; Barclay, *Role of the Horse*, p. 48.
68 Barclay, *Role of the Horse*, p. 48; and see Ssu-ma Ch'ien, *Records*, 2:269–70.
69 On Ku-shih, Ssu-ma Ch'ien, *Records*, 2:277; see also ibid., 2:204–5, 271; Ma Yong and Sun Yutang, 'The western regions', in *HCCA*, 2:228; Hulsewe, *China in Central Asia*, pp. 75–6; de Crespigny, *Northern Frontiers*, pp. 7–10; Sir Aurel Stein was the first modern expert to prove that the Han walls reached as far as Lob Nor; see *On Ancient Central Asian Tracks*.
70 Ssu-ma Ch'ien, *Records*, 2:272; on the Indo-European links of the Wu-sun, see Frye, *Heritage of Central Asia*, p. 165.
71 However, sea routes probably carried more goods between China and the Mediterranean in the classical era; Adshead, *China in World History*, pp. 23–4; see also Ssu-ma Ch'ien, *Records*, 2:276–9.

72 *Ocherki istorii SSSR*, 1:546; one of the Sogdian documents is illustrated on p. 552.

73 The successful campaign is described in *Han-shu*, ch. 61, Hulsewe, *China in Central Asia*, pp. 228–36; Li Kuang-Li died in 90 BC, killed by the Hsiung-nu after they defeated him; Ehr-shih was probably medieval Sutrishna, between Khojend and Samarkand; see Hulsewe, *China in Central Asia*, pp. 75–6; and see Ssu-ma Ch'ien, *Records*, 2:282–7 on these expeditions.

74 Hulsewe, *China in Central Asia*, Introduction, p. 46, 76, and pp. 87–9 on the unenviable situation of such petty states; see also Yü, *Trade and Expansion*, pp. 145–7.

75 Hulsewe, *China in Central Asia*, pp. 64–6, 164; Y. A. Zadneprovskiy, 'The nomads of northern Central Asia after the invasion of Alexander', in *HCCA* (pp. 457–72), 2:460–1.

76 Hulsewe, *China in Central Asia*, p. 63; Lattimore, *Pivot of Asia*, p. 8; and see Ssu-ma Ch'ien, *Records*, 2:185, 264; Ma Yong and Sun Yutang, 'The western regions', in *HCCA*, 2:239–43; and see Yü, *Trade and Expansion*, pp. 147–50.

77 Yü, *Trade and Expansion*, p. 169; Ma Yong and Sun Yutang, 'The western regions', in *HCCA*, 2:242.

78 Yü, *Trade and Expansion*, pp. 150; de Crespigny, *Northern Frontiers*, p. 258.

79 Barfield, *Perilous Frontier*, pp. 60–1.

80 Cited in Ibid., p. 62.

81 Ibid.

82 Yü, *Trade and Expansion*, pp. 38, 43.

83 Barfield, *Perilous Frontier*, p. 63ff; and see Yü, *Trade and Expansion*, pp. 70–8.

84 On this debate, see Tinios, *Pan Ku*, pp. 55–8.

85 Barfield, *Perilous Frontier*, p. 64.

86 Ishjamts, 'Nomads in eastern Central Asia', in *HCCA*, 2:164; see Dubs, *A Roman City in Ancient China*, however Yü, *Trade and Expansion*, pp. 89–91, is sceptical of Dubs's claim that Roman mercenaries were settled in a city of their own in Kansu, after 36 BCE.

87 On her role, see de Crespigny, *Northern Frontiers*, p. 189ff.; see also ibid., p. 188.

88 Yü, *Trade and Expansion*, p. 64; between 51 BCE and 1 BCE, the amount of silk fabric given in 'gifts' rose from 8,000 pieces to 30,000 pieces; Barfield, *Perilous Frontier*, p. 65.

89 Honey, *Medieval Hsiung-nu*, p. 1.

90 On this decision, which meant abandoning the 'forward' policy of the Ch'in and of Wu-ti, see de Crespigny, *Northern Frontiers*, pp. 30–1; see also Ying-Shih Yü, 'The Hsiung-nu', in *CHEIA*, p. 143.

91 de Crespigny, *Northern Frontiers*, pp. 243–6, on the sharp decline in Chinese settlement of the Ordos region and northern Shaanxi.

92 De Crespigny, *Northern Frontiers*, pp. 238.

93 Barfield, *Perilous Frontier*, p. 59; note the similarity with the advice the Scythian king sarcastically offered to Darius in 513/19 BCE; on Wu-huan settlement near Zhangjiakou, de Crespigny, *Northern Frontiers*, p. 37.

94 De Crespigny, *Northern Frontiers*, pp. 294–5; Barfield, *Perilous Frontier*, p. 77.

95 De Crespigny, *Northern Frontiers*, pp. 269–71, 304.

96 This final collapse is described in Ying-Shih Yü, 'The Hsiung-nu', in *CHEIA*, p. 147–9; Zadneprovskiy, 'The nomads of northern Central Asia', in *HCCA*, 2:469.

97 Artamonov, *Istoriya khazar*, p. 42.

FURTHER READING

On the Hsiung-nu empire, the fundamental primary source is Ssu-ma Ch'ien. There is no thorough modern history of the Hsiung-nu. Gumilev's, study, *Khunnu*, comes closest, and includes a good historiographical discussion, but it is dated. As if in compensation, there are many good brief accounts of Hsiung-nu history or lifeways. These include the relevant sections of *HCCA*, vol. 2; *CHEIA*; *The Cambridge History of China*; Barfield, *Perilous Frontier*; Altheim, ATTILA; Golden, *Introduction to the History of the Turkic Peoples*; Phillips, *Royal Hordes*; and Kürsat-Ahlers *Zur frühen Staatenbildung.* On relations with China, see Barfield, *Perilous Frontier*; Jagchid and Symons, *Peace, War, and Trade*; de Crespigny, *Northern Frontiers*; Tinios, *Pan Ku*; and Yü, *Trade and Expansion*. Yü's book is also good on the rise of the Silk Roads, as is Hulsewe, *China in Central Asia*, the best source on the 'western regions'. On the archaeology and ecology of the Hsiung-nu, see di Cosmo, 'Ancient Inner Asian nomads'; Vainshtein, *Nomads of South Siberia*; Davydova, *Ivolginskii kompleks*; and Lubo-Lesnichenko, 'The Huns', in Basilov, ed., *Nomads of Eurasia*. On religion, see Heissig, *Religions of Mongolia*; on lifeways of the eastern steppes, see Jagchid and Hyer, *Mongolia's Culture*.

[9] 'BARBARIAN' INVASIONS BEFORE 500 CE

M OTUN's achievement, in creating a stable relationship of political and military equality between a steppe empire and a neighbouring agrarian empire, was remarkable and unusual. More often, less powerful and less stable systems dominated the borderlands between Inner and Outer Eurasia. Weaker systems made for a complex, and often violent politics of invasion and counter-invasion. Periodically, pastoralist groups, caught between expansionist neighbours in the steppes and agrarian empires to the south, took their chances in the agrarian world, invading where they found regional defences weakest. Most had little success. However some, like the Parthians, the Yüeh-chih and the Turkic T'o-pa, succeeded so spectacularly that they established new ruling dynasties in the Outer Eurasian borderlands.

At least on a small scale, conflicts of this kind had occurred since the fourth millennium. However, we cannot describe them in any detail before the early centuries of the modern era. The era known to historians of western Eurasia as the era of 'barbarian invasions', was a period of intensified border conflict from China through Central Asia to the Caucasus and the Balkans. Its most striking feature is the failure of Outer Eurasian Empires to mount effective counter-invasions. Though no great steppe empires emerged for several centuries, the political and military initiative throughout the borderlands lay with ambitious pastoralist leaders from Inner Eurasia. This chapter will describe the turbulent politics of the borderlands in the Hunnic era.

CENTRAL ASIA: 50 BCE–500 CE

In the first centuries of the contemporary era, pastoralist migrations driven by the expansionism of the Hsiung-nu dominated the history of Central Asia. There were probably many invasions of this kind across the Central Asian borders. However, those we know most about were the few that achieved enduring success by creating ruling dynasties in the borderlands of modern Iran and Afghanistan. The pastoralist dynasties that managed to do this, the Kusanas and Hephthalites in Afghanistan and northern India, were recapitulating the history of earlier invasions, such as those of the ancestors of the Medes and later the Parthians.

Map 9.1   The Balkans in the Hunnic era.

THE KUSANA: *c.*50–250 CE

The founders of the Kusana empire were descendants of the Yüeh-chih. The Yüeh-chih probably spoke an Indo-European language of some kind, and their ancestors may have settled in Kansu as early as the second millennium BCE. Indeed, if they spoke the early Indo-European language known as Tocharian, their ancestors may have arrived there as early as 2500 BCE. On the other hand, the Yüeh-chih may have been an eastern branch of the Saka, perhaps closely related to the peoples who built the tombs of Pazyryk.[1] Before their defeats by the Hsiung-nu, early in the second century, they had dominated the oasis cities of Kansu and northern Sinkiang, so they understood the blend of pastoralism and oasis agriculture that was characteristic of southern Central Asia.

Within a few years of Motun's death in 174 BCE, his son and successor killed the Yüeh-chih leader, turned his skull into a drinking cup, and forced his followers to flee westwards under the leadership of his son. There followed a 30-year migration through largely hostile lands, during which the Yüeh-chih mingled with other groups. Some Yüeh-chih settled in the Turfan region. Others headed for Zungaria, where they encountered the Wu-sun. In 133–29, the Wu-sun expelled the Yüeh-chih from the Semirechye. In the Tashkent region, the surviving Yüeh-chih and their followers encountered another emergent pastoralist state that Chinese sources called the K'ang-chü. The K'ang-chü confederation was built on the wealth of the fortified cities along the Syr Darya and may have survived until the fifth century CE. Like so many later political systems in this region, it was probably ruled by pastoralist elites, but included many towns and farming communities. Archaeological evidence suggests that its influence was greatest along the trade routes leading towards the Aral Sea, and further West, through Sarmatian lands towards the south Urals. The western parts of this 'Northern Route', between the Aral and Caspian seas, was controlled by tribes referred to as Yen-ts'ai, who probably included Sarmatian tribes such as the Alans.[2] Perhaps because of the strength of the K'ang-chü and their neighbours, the Yüeh-chih had to head south, through Ferghana, into Sogdia. In c.130 BCE, they drove Saka pastoralists out of Sogdia and seized their grazing lands. Driven south by the Yüeh-chih, Saka migrants, in their turn, invaded the lands to their south. They destroyed Greco-Bactria and nearly destroyed the young Parthian empire as well, an episode which conveys well the nature of the domino effect which operated across the steppelands.[3]

Wu-ti's envoy, Chang Ch'ien, visited Sogdia in 128 BCE, within two or three years of the Yüeh-chih conquest. He found that the Yüeh-chih still lived a nomadic life, and reported, with conventional exaggeration, that they could field an army of 100,000 mounted archers. In Sogdia, the Yüeh-chih had found lands even richer than those of Kansu. Here, for a time, their migrations ended. Archaeological evidence shows that they were careful not to ruin the prosperous irrigation cities and trade networks of Sogdia and Bactria. They probably settled in the fertile pasturelands between Sogdia's mercantile centres, contenting themselves with the exaction of tributes. The large amounts of town-made ceramics in Yüeh-chih tombs show that relations with the oasis cities of Sogdia were close. Both the archaeological and written evidence suggest that towns flourished under the Yüeh-chih.[4]

When Chiang Ch'ien visited, there was no overall ruler in Ta Hsia (Bactria). He reported that:

> Its people cultivate the land and have cities and houses. Their customs are like those of Ta-yüan [Ferghana]. It has no great ruler but only a number of petty chiefs ruling the various cities. The people are poor in the use of arms and afraid of battle, but they are clever at commerce. ... The population of the country is large, numbering some million or more persons.[5]

Chinese eagerness to establish diplomatic relations with the Yüeh-chih suggests that they already had a firm grip on Sogdia and northern Bactria. Like the Hsiung-nu, the Yüeh-chih seem to have had a political and ceremonial centre which maintained a sense of shared loyalties. This was probably at Khalchayan in the Surkhan Darya valley south of Samarkand. However, the Yüeh-chih were not united, but remained organized in five separate tribal groups or *yabghu*s.[6]

This loose system of regional statelets survived for almost 200 years, maintaining many of the cultural, political and commercial traditions of the Greco-Bactrian state, but under Yüeh-chih suzerainty.[7] In c.50 CE,

Plate 9.1   Headless statue of Vima (Takto?) Kadphises.

Kujula Kadphises, the leader of one of the Yüeh-chih *yabghu*s, the Kusana (Kuei-shuang in Chinese sources), defeated his four rivals and set up a unified empire based on Bactra. According to the *Hou-Han Shu* ('History of the Later Han'), he died at the age of 80, after which his son, now known to be Vima Takto, conquered large areas of northern India, probably towards the end of the first century. A headless statue of a Kusana ruler that survives in Mathura is probably a representation of Vima Takto, the first Kusana ruler to create a large empire in India. 'Since then,' notes the *Hou Han-shu*, 'the Yüeh-chih have been extremely rich and strong.'[8] These conquests, consolidated by Vima Takto's son, Vima Kadphises, gave the Kusana control of the important branch of the Silk Roads that led along the Indus valley to the port of Barygaza (modern Broach), from which ships could sail to Egypt, bypassing Parthia. By 100 CE, the Kusanas were probably trading along this route with the support of Roman traders, who were keen to avoid commercial dependence on Parthia. Roman coins were used along this route and Vima Kadphises imitated them on his own coinage.[9]

The Kusana empire reached the height of its power under Kaniska, the son of Vima Kadphises. There has long been debate about the dates of Kaniska's rule, which are the basis for Kusana chronology. Dates proposed for his accession have ranged over almost two centuries, from late in the first to late in the third century CE, but recent opinion suggests that he ruled towards the middle of the second century.[10] He and his successors, Huviska and Vasudeva I, are generally described as the 'Great Kusanas'. Their power was all the greater because it coincided with the declining years of the Parthian empire. The wide distribution of coins and inscriptions from Kaniska's reign, combined with other archaeological evidence, suggests that his empire included modern Tajikistan and parts of southern Turkmenistan and Kyrgyzstan, as well as most of Afghanistan and Pakistan, parts of northern and eastern India, and even some cities of the Tarim basin, including Kashgar, Yarkand and Khotan. However, it probably did not include Khorezm or all of Sogdia. As late as the third decade of the third century, a Chinese traveller in Indo-China remarked that the world was divided into three realms, each ruled by a 'son of heaven': China, Rome and the Kusana empire.[11]

Under Kaniska, the Kusana centre of gravity shifted into northern India. The capital moved from Bactra to Peshawar, or perhaps to Mathura on the river Yamuna.[12] Kaniska assumed divine status, as a *devaputra* ('son of God'), a title analogous to the Chinese imperial title of 'son of Heaven'. Despite these changes, pastoralist traditions retained at least a symbolic importance. A Chinese report written in the middle of the third century maintained that the Yüeh-chih were still 'skilled in the (use of) bows and horses'. On coins, Kaniska appears as 'a robust bearded figure with Central Asian peaked headdress and long boots and heavy coat', like traditional portraits of Saka pastoralists.[13]

Probably in the 230s, Ardashir, the founder of the Sassanian dynasty, conquered Margiana and Seistan. According to al-Tabari, the Kusana rulers accepted Sassanian suzerainty, and a later Kusana dynasty survived, as suzerains of the Sassanians, for much of the third century.[14] Like the Greco-Bactrians before them, the Kusanas had been pulled south by the wealth of northern India, and pushed south by military pressure from Iran and the Central Asian steppes.

The most striking feature of the Kusana empire is the variety of influences in its political system, its religion and its art. Not only were the Kusanas a pastoralist dynasty ruling an agrarian empire; they also maintained active trading and cultural contacts with Rome, Parthia, India and China. They used Indian titles, such as *maharaja rajatiraja* ('great king', 'king of kings'), as well as their Iranian and Greek equivalents (*saonano sao* and '*basileus basileon*), while Kaniska even used the Roman title, *kaisara*.[15] The later Kusana pantheon included steppeland Iranian deities, Greco-Bactrian and Zoroastrian deities, local deities and Buddhist gods and Bodhisattva, as well as being influenced by Jainism and Vishnuism. In Central Asia, all the great Eurasian religious traditions, Zoroastrianism, Hellenism, Christianity, Brahmanism, Buddhism, Confucianism, Taoism and later Manichaeism, were mixed in a cultural melting pot from which emerged new ideas, gods,

Plate 9.2 Headless statue of Kaniska I, Mathura.

Plate 9.3 Coin of Kaniska.

scriptures and images. Kusana art and writing are as eclectic as Kusana politics and religion. Archaeologists have found Greek statuary, Chinese lacquers, Indian carved ivory, as well as Egyptian glassware. The earliest evidence for a written form of the Bactrian language, using the Greek alphabet, comes from the reign of Vima Kadphises. This represents a revival of Iranian letters after the long period of Hellenism in Bactria. It was probably during this period, too, that Tocharian became an important written language.[16]

The Kusana empire played a particularly important role in the spread of Buddhism to Parthia, Central Asia and China. Bactria probably had contacts with Buddhism since the time of Ashoka in the third century, and certainly since the second century BCE, when the Greco-Bactrian kings, Demetrius and Menander both patronized the religion. There were certainly Buddhists amongst the Yüeh-chih by the first century CE, and the coinage of Kujula Kadphises shows clear Buddhist influence. Buddhism reached China some time between the first century BCE and the middle of the first century CE. The first Buddhist texts to reach China were a gift from the Yüeh-chih in about the year 2 BCE. In the first century CE, Buddhism spread to Parthia, Margiana

215

Plate 9.4 Kusana sanctuary at Surkh Kotal.

and Sogdia, almost certainly from the Kusana empire. In the second century, Buddhism spread rapidly in the Tarim basin, particularly in Kucha and Khotan, which had emerged, along with Kashgar in the West and Lou-lan in the East, as the area's dominant towns. It also began to spread in China in the time of Kaniska, for there are many records of Kusana or Kusana-trained Buddhist monks from Parthia, Sogdia, Bactria, India and the Tarim basin working and translating in Lo-yang from the second century CE. Kaniska himself is reputed to have convened the fourth great Buddhist Council, probably in Kashmir/Gandhara, and with his support, Buddhism spread throughout the Kusana empire.[17] By the fifth and sixth centuries, Buddhism was the dominant religion in Bactria and the Tarim basin, and the major towns all had large monasteries.

As Liu has shown, the close relationship between Buddhists and merchants along the trade routes between India, the Kusana Empire, and China had a significant impact on the evolution of Mahayana Buddhism. In particular, it encouraged the emergence of practices such as alms-giving, which made it easier for the wealthy to purchase their way to salvation, and for Bodhisattvas willing to accept precious gifts to transfer the merits they had accumulated, almost as if they were trade goods. Mahayana imagery from the Kusana period often described the Buddha as a sort of spiritual caravan leader, while Buddhist monasteries appeared at the nodal points of the trade routes between India and China, and some, such as Bamiyan, functioned as caravanserais. Kusana Buddhism may also have acquired a Zoroastrian overlay, particularly when taught by Buddhists of Parthian origin. For example, the Buddha 'Amithaba' or 'Infinite Light', is similar in many ways to the Zoroastrian Ahura Mazda.[18]

The social structure of the Kusana empire was variegated, with small villages and towns, large cities, areas of mobile pastoralism and isolated mountain communities. In towns and villages, aristocratic elites of *azatkar* owned the land, and acted as retainers of local and regional rulers. In the cities, the merchants, or *xvakar*, owned much property and exerted considerable influence. Below them were the craftsmen or *karikar*, as well as large numbers of dependents or slaves, who were used mainly in household service, particularly amongst the wealthy. While some land was undoubtedly held by local rulers or temples, much was held by lesser landowners and perhaps most was held collectively by commune-like villages, over which local *dihqans* held economic and legal rights.[19]

Political stability over a wide area, systematic royal support for irrigation, and flourishing trade networks, made the Kusana era one of great prosperity. Irrigation agriculture was the foundation of the empire's wealth in Central Asia. Large-scale irrigation systems were developed in new regions along the Zerafshan, near modern Tashkent, and along the Syr Darya. Indeed, it may be that the area irrigated along the lower Amu Darya and Syr Darya was greater than the area irrigated today, though there were fewer small feeder canals, so that irrigation was less intensive and supported smaller populations. Most impressive of all is the irrigation system of Khorezm, on the margins of the Kusana empire. The calculations of modern archaeologists suggest that at least 15,000 labourers worked for two months to dig the Kîrkkîz canal, while it took 6–7000 labourers each year just to keep the canal from silting up.[20] An earlier generation of Soviet scholars, committed to finding a 'slave mode of production' in Central Asia, saw such irrigation work as a product of slave labour. However, it now seems likely that most of the labour came from local village communities which benefited directly from the irrigation systems they built and maintained. To supervise this work, there existed in pre-Islamic Khorezm a special school of irrigation engineers, with mathematicians, map makers, astronomers and engineers. In some mountainous regions of Bactria, such as the Kopet Dag and the upper Zerafshan valley, water was carried through systems of underground *karez*, similar to those of the Turfan oasis today. Agricultural methods also improved, as more iron implements were used, and wooden ploughs with metal ploughshares replaced simple hoes. Crops included cereals, fruits and fodder crops such as lucerne, cotton and poppy. There may have been extensive commercial production of wines in Khorezm, Bukhara and Margiana, while horses were bred commercially, particularly in Ferghana.[21]

Peace, prosperity, supportive governments, ecological variety, and strategic location, encouraged population growth and stimulated trade. The number and variety of coins minted under the Kusana suggests the extent of monetary exchanges, while the large number of bronze coins suggests that most sections of the population used money. Caravan routes led through the K'ang-chü lands of Ferghana, the Chach (Tashkent) oasis, and the pastoralist regions north of the Syr Darya. Along these routes, the agricultural produce, textiles, handicrafts and weaponry of the agricultural zones were traded for the furs, skins, meat, fibres and livestock of the steppes. There was also trade with the Mediterranean, India and China. A Kusana embassy may have visited Rome in 99 CE, and many Roman coins have been found on Kusana territory. Trade between the Roman empire and the west coast of India, in particular the ports of Barbaricon and Barygaza, flourished from the time of the Emperor Augustus, as ships learned to make regular use of the monsoon winds, thereby avoiding the tolls imposed by the Parthian empire.[22] Sogdian merchants reached Alexandria in the west and Tun-huang in the east, and Sogdians often acted as guides for Silk Road caravans travelling through the Tarim basin. Along these networks, Kusana merchants established themselves as middlemen between China, Rome and India, trading in silk, spices, gems and even in the furs of the Urals region. Finds of coins, even in villages, show that monetary relations were widespread in Sogdia, Bactria and Gandhara, but less developed in Khorezm, Ferghana and Semirechye. In the mountainous eastern regions, gold, silver, iron, copper, rubies and lapis lazuli were mined. There was also an extensive exchange of peoples. In Khorezm in the late Kusana era there is evidence of the presence of Indian soldiers, who may even have founded a local dynasty in the third century CE.[23]

Like earlier empires in the region, the Kusana empire was really a federation of city-states, held together by a pastoralist dynasty and its armies. Under Kusana rule, towns flourished as never before, growing in numbers, in size, and in social complexity. Intensive building of temples in the Kusana period also increased the ideological and religious role of towns. The largest towns, such as Merv, Balkh, Termez and Afrasiab/Samarkand may have had populations as large as 50,000 people. Most Kusana towns were fortified, and each had its own palaces and local rulers. Most large towns had carefully built fortified walls, palaces for officials, as well as temples, workshops and houses. Each city had considerable populations of artisans and other urban workers. Handicrafts, including work in pottery, metal jewellery and weaponry, and textiles, were highly developed. Northern Indian cities were particularly prosperous. Some had carefully designed defensive systems, central palaces, areas of houses with shops in their lower stories, special areas for bazaars, parks, shrines and even lakes. Some even had underground sewerage systems. A northern Indian source describes a city of the Kusana era, with 'elephants, horses, chariots and pedestrians, with groups of handsome men and women; it was crowded with ordinary people, warriors, nobles, brahmans, merchants and workers' and a variety of ascetics.'[24] Visitors included Sakas, Bactrians and Chinese. Shops sold flowers, perfumes, jewellery; street hawkers sold herbs, fruits, fish and meat, while it was also possible to eat in restaurants, or to be entertained by actors, magicians, acrobats or wrestlers.

Though the Kusana dynasty had collapsed by the end of the third century, the complex cultural, political and economic mix of the regions it had ruled survived under later rulers.

SASSANIANS AND HEPTHALITES: 250 CE–550 CE

The Sassanian empire was more successful than the Parthian empire in stabilizing Iran's steppe borderlands. It controlled Margiana and parts of Bactria, but never controlled Sogdia and Ferghana, and exercised at best a loose and fluctuating suzerainty over Khorezm.

The Sassanians adopted a mainly defensive strategy towards the steppes. Merv, the centre of Margiana, was the military capital of the eastern provinces. The many inscriptions found in the town, in many different languages, show that it was also a vital trading entrepôt. By the fifth century, the Sassanians had constructed a huge system of fortifications, walls and forts, reaching some 200 kilometres from the Caspian sea, almost to Merv. West of the Caspian, in modern Azerbaijan, they built another system of fortifications to defend against invasions from the northern Caucasus, the route that Scythians had taken when invading Assyria, and through which Alan and Hunnic invaders attacked in the second and fourth centuries CE. The centre of this system was Darband, which had been the key to a similar defensive system even in the Scythian era. In the 560s, the greatest of Sassanian rulers, Khosrow I, rebuilt this system, with Byzantine help. Darband itself lay in a small pocket of fertile land, at a pass between the sea and the mountains. It was built between two parallel walls, that extended into the sea, where there was a harbour protected by a chain. There were towers along the walls, and where the wall met the mountains, there was a citadel. The wall continued for another 40 kilometres into the mountains, after which the line was defended by mountain forts.[25]

The Sassanians made no real attempt to conquer eastern central Asia. In Sogdia, as Kusana power declined, so did urban centres such as Samarkand. However, by the late fifth century, there re-emerged the same system of independent, but wealthy oasis city-states that Chang Ch'ien had observed late in the second century BCE. These were supported by irrigation agriculture, surrounded by the smaller fortified settlements of the nobility, the *dihqan*s, and traded with local pastoralists. The wealth and sophistication of urban life in Central Asia before the Islamic invasions is suggested by the astonishing wall paintings of Panjikent, *c.*40 miles east of Samarkand, which date from the sixth to eighth centuries. These show a very wealthy world of lords in their palaces or tents, or in hunting or battle scenes, many of which may derive from the oral traditions later recorded by Firdausi in the *Shah-name*. Sogdia's cities flourished from the wealth of the silk trade, and supported a powerful merchant class. According to contemporary accounts, merchants were often as powerful and wealthy as the *dihqan* class, and some lived, like the *dihqan*, in castles of their own.[26]

From the fourth century, Sogdia and Bactria, and perhaps parts of Khorezm, once again came under the suzerainty of a large empire founded, like the Kusana empire, by pastoralists fleeing the eastern steppes. In the middle of the fourth century, as some Hunnic groups headed for the western steppes, another loose alliance of tribes perhaps of Hsiung-nu origin, but probably mixed with Turkic and Iranian elements, began to raid the eastern borders of the Sassanian empire. Latin sources described them as Chionites, which is probably the same word as 'Hsiung-nu' or 'Hun'.[27]

By 350 CE, the Chionites controlled much of Sogdia, and in the next 50 years they also conquered Bactria and parts of northern India. For a time they were ruled by a dynasty known as the Kidarites from their founder. However, from *c.*466, they were ruled by a new steppe dynasty known as the

'Heftal', who drove their Kidarite rivals south into India. After conflicts with their former allies, the emerging Juan-juan federation of western Mongolia, they headed south like the Yüeh-chih 500 years before, and seized much of Bactria, eastern Sinkiang as far as Karashahr, and parts of northern India. In the late fifth century, the Heftal dynasty, now based in Bactria, with capitals near Herat and at Kunduz, east of Balkh, united the Chionite tribes into a large confederation as eclectic as the Kusana empire. The Hephthalites also took over the culture and written language of the Kusanas. By the sixth century, their elites were settling down, and many lived in cities. However, pastoralism remained important. The Chinese Buddhist, Sung Yün, who travelled through their lands in c.518, noted a type of transhumance: 'In the summer the people seek the cool of the mountains; in the winter they disperse themselves through the villages.' Though they were still illiterate, Sung Yün reported that they received tributes from 40 surrounding nations, from Persia to Khotan.[28]

The Hephthalites frequently raided Sassanian lands, and for several decades after 484 exacted tribute from them, while Sassanian leaders sometimes hired Hephthalite mercenaries or used them as allies in internal conflicts. In 484, the Hephthalites inflicted a serious defeat on the Sassanian empire and killed its emperor, Peroz I (459–84). A period of chaos and famine followed in Iran, in which the egalitarian reforming religion of Mazdakaizm flourished. Its sponsor, Kavad I (488–531), was overthrown in 496 and replaced by his brother. However, Kavad managed to escape and fled to the Hephthalites, whose ruler was his brother-in-law. In 499, with the support of a Hephthalite army, he returned to the throne. In 528, Kavad turned against Mazdakaizm, killing its leader and many of his followers. In the first half of the sixth century, he and his successor, the greatest of all Sassanian Emperors, Khosrow I Anushirvan (531–79), re-established Sassanian Iran as a great international power. In 557, Khosrow allied with a new steppe people, the Türk, and in the early 560s the allies destroyed the Hephthalite army and killed its leader. This marks the end of the Hephthalite empire, though Hephthalite populations survived in Tokharistan (Bactria) for many centuries, while small Hephthalite states survived in northern India.

The history of the Kusana and Hephthalite empires illustrates once again an enduring pattern in the Central Asian borderlands, which was dictated by the region's ecology. Both empires were established by pastoralists lured into the many regions of steppe scattered through eastern Persia and Bactria, and it was this that explains why they eventually established powerful Outer Eurasian empires.

THE WESTERN REGION: 200 CE–500 CE

The western borderlands between Inner and Outer Eurasia differed significantly from those of Central Asia and northern China. Unlike China or Iran, Rome faced agrarian barbarians along most of its northern borders, while its borders with the steppes were narrow and constricted. For Rome, Hungary and Romania played the role of the Ordos, and the Danube played a role similar to the Yellow River. East of the Carpathians, the Danube divided the Balkans from the Pontic steppes; while to the west it divided the steppes of eastern Hungary (the 'Alföld'), from the lusher plains of western Hungary. In 8 BCE, Tiberius secured Roman control of Pannonia, in western Hungary, and established a new *limes* or military frontier along the Danube. A century later, in *c*.105 CE, Trajan led an army into eastern Hungary and parts of Transylvania, where he created the new province of Dacia.

The narrowness of the ecological frontier on Rome's north-eastern borders made it difficult for pastoralist leaders to establish a regular system for the exploitation of the Roman Empire. However, it also meant that Rome had less experience than Chinese or Iranian dynasties of dealing with pastoralists. Since at least the Scythian era, pastoralists had sometimes formed loose systems of rule, both east and west of the Carpathians. However, in doing so, they had to compete with the agrarian 'barbarians' that dominated Rome's northern borders. During the era of the great invasions, Roman armies stationed along the Danube had to cope, first, with agrarian barbarians who migrated through western Inner Eurasia, and then with a series of devastating pastoralist invasions, beginning with those of the Huns in 376 CE.

GOTHS: *c*.200–370 CE

The Germanic peoples generally known as 'Goths', though not of Inner Eurasian origin, are of great significance in the history of Inner Eurasia, for their migrations into modern Belarus, Ukraine and Russia prefigure the emergence of Rus', the first great agrarian state of Inner Eurasia.

Like all tribal names, the word 'Goth' is convenient rather than precise. It was used of a number of peoples from northern Europe who began to migrate southward through eastern Europe towards the Danubian frontiers of the Roman empire from *c*.150 CE. Our knowledge of the early history of the Goths and related tribes depends largely on the *Getica*, a history of the Goths written in *c*.550 by a Gothic historian, Jordanes, living in Constantinople. Jordanes used sources compiled at the Ostrogothic court of northern Italy, some 30 years earlier, so his account is, at least in part, an attempt to provide a retrospective genealogy for the Ostrogothic rulers of Italy. There is much in it that is pure myth; nevertheless, archaeological research in eastern and central Europe has shown that his account preserves some important features of early Gothic history.[29]

The name, 'Goths' ('Gutones'), first occurs in the first century CE, in the writings of Tacitus. Tacitus placed the Goths in the north of modern Poland. They were one of several Germanic groups associated loosely with a distinctive archaeological culture, the 'Wielbark' culture. According to Jordanes, the Goths eventually migrated south under a leader called Filimer. As they crossed a great river (the Dnieper?), a bridge broke. Those who had already crossed conquered and settled southern Ukraine, the northern Caucasus, and the Crimea, forming the 'Ostrogoths', while those left behind moved south and settled just north of the Danube, where they formed the 'Visigoths'.

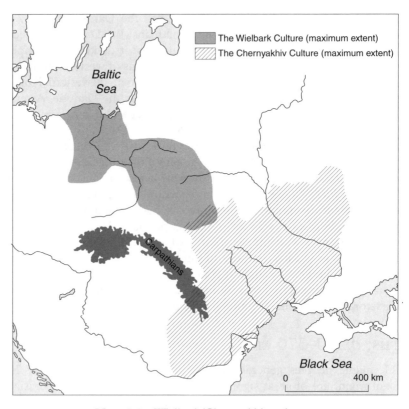

Map 9.2 Wielbark/Chernyakhiv cultures.

Both the archaeological and the literary evidence suggest that there were, indeed, large-scale, often warlike, migrations of Germanic groups southwards through central and eastern Europe from *c*.150 to *c*.230.[30] There is literary evidence of turbulence along the Danubian frontiers of Rome from *c*.166, and archaeological evidence of turbulence within the Wielbark culture. Most important of all, in the third century there appeared along the Pontic coast from the Danube to the Don, a new archaeological culture, the Chernyakhiv culture, which is clearly descended from the Wielbark culture. However, Jordanes' account of a single migration, from which there emerged two distinct groups, the Visigoths and Ostrogoths, is a projection into the past of the powerful Gothic dynasties of the sixth century. In reality, there were many separate migrations of different Germanic groups with different names. Some consisted of armed raiding parties of several hundred soldiers, while others were clearly systematic migrations in search of new lands, for they included women and children.[31]

From *c*.230, some of these groups began to mount large-scale raids into the Roman Empire. In 251, Gothic armies killed a Roman emperor, Decius, and destroyed an entire Roman army. The Danubian frontier had to be recaptured by Claudius II in 269. After 255, when Rome lost its Bosporan fleet, Gothic rulers controlled most of the Black Sea ports. In 267, a vast fleet of some 2000 ships led by Goths and Herulians, entered the Aegean and raided cities and monasteries on both the Greek and Asian coasts for two years. Several groups of soldiers were put ashore and left to fight their way home by land, though few survived to return.[32]

A new emperor, Aurelian, completed mopping-up operations in 271, and established almost a century of relative peace by surrendering control of Dacia to the western Goths in 275, as the later Han had surrendered control of the Ordos. After this, Gothic tribes began to occupy modern Romania and Hungary north and east of the Danube. In c.300, Diocletian stabilized the Pannonian frontier. The Danube became once more a great fortified line, like a fluvial Great Wall of China, and local towns profited from the trade of soldiers and garrison troops. The border attracted Gothic settlements because the best opportunities for trade were here, close to the Roman camps and border towns. Along the Danube, as along the Chinese Great Wall, there appeared frontier markets, favoured by local traders, but eyed suspiciously by imperial officials. The Romans built an extensive system of forts along the southern shores of the Danube; there were 34 in Scythia (Dobrudja) alone. Behind this line lay a series of linked towns, also fortified, but able to supply the front line. Further back there were large fortified towns such as Philippopolis, Serdica and Adrianople. Like the Chinese, the Romans negotiated with their barbarian neighbours, hired them as mercenaries (from as early as 208), reluctantly allowed them to trade in specially regulated border markets and, on occasion, paid tributes to Gothic chiefs in an attempt to prevent raiding.[33] As a result, despite their small numbers, the Goths drew Rome's armies and its governmental machinery towards the threatened frontiers like a magnet, until in the early fourth century, the capital itself shifted to Constantinople.

By this time, there had emerged just beyond the Roman frontiers, a series of frontier kingdoms, in which Gothic and allied elites ruled local populations of Slavs, Sarmatians and even Germanic peasants. The archaeological record of the Chernyakhiv culture shows a world of small, unfortified villages, with wooden buildings. Amongst them, there appeared local chiefs, who settled in fortified stockades with their families, retainers, servants and slaves.[34] Below the aristocratic stratum of lords, there existed amongst the westernmost Goths a category of free peasants organized in villages or *haims*. A golden charm necklace which has survived from Gothic Pannonia, and which may date from just after the Hunnic invasions of c.375, links 45 model objects which offer a fascinating insight into the world of Goths just settled within the frontier.[35] The objects include items of agricultural equipment, such as yokes, sickles, spades, shears, pruning saws, ploughs and mattocks; items of livestock management, such as sheep shears, and a currying comb; items of transportation such as the runners of a sled, a waggon-brake and wheelwright's tool, and a small boat; craft implements including chisels, tongs, hammers and anvils, and cobblers' tools; military equipment including tridents, shields, spears, knives and clubs; and domestic items such as ladders, a pouring spoon, a hook and knife. Woven through them all are vine leaves.

Plate 9.5 Gothic necklace from Szilàgysomlyó, reproduced from T. S. Burns, *History of the Ostrogoths* (Bloomington: Indiana University Press, 1984). The numbered items are 1. yoke; 2. anchor; 3. sickle; 4. vine framing shears; 5. decorated peg (?); 6. pruning saw; 7. file; 8. *vine leaf*; 9. hook; 10. hinged pruning shears; 11. fork-like tool (?); 12. knife; 13. plough; 14. plough brake; 15. *vine leaf*; 16. spear; 17. arrowhead; 18. club with head specially faceted in squares and triangles; 19. chisel; 20. peg (?); 21. spade; 22. *vine leaf*; 23. dagger or sword; 24. model hand; 25. narrow spoon; 26. shield with central boss; 27. trident; 28. hammer; 29. anvil; 30. *vine leaf*; 31. axe; 32. club, perhaps especially for slaughtering animals; 33. round currying comb; 34. mattock or hammer with hollowed blade; 35. sled runner; 36. pouring spoon with ringed handle; 37. *vine leaf*; 38. serrated sickle; 39. Vintager's knife; 40. blacksmith's chisel for horse hooves; 41. tongs; 42. hammer; 43. anvil; 44. sheep shears; 45. ladder; 46. and 47. cobbler tools; 48. hook on the end of a decorate plate; 49. decorated wheel-wright's tool; 50. wagon brake or another yoke.

Crafts practised in Chernyakhiv sites included pottery, carpentry and metalworking. There were many homespun and woven textiles. In one instance, a complete comb-making workshop has been found. Clearly, there was considerable craft specialization, which suggests a society 'at least one remove from local self-sufficiency'.[36] The presence of large numbers of Roman coins also suggests a partially monetized economy. Some coins may have been exchanged for trade goods, but Gothic soldiers in the Roman army also received cash wages. The large number of Roman amphorae shows the extent of trade with the Roman empire, while the main Gothic exports were probably captured slaves. In summary: 'the physical remains of the Sintana de Mures/Chernyakhiv Culture suggest an economy devoted largely to subsistence agriculture, but with some craft specialization and considerable trade with the Roman empire.'[37]

There has been much debate about the nature and extent of the Gothic kingdoms of the fourth century. There is literary evidence of at least two powerful Gothic kingdoms in the third quarter of the fourth century, one based on the Danube, the other further east. The Danubian kingdom was dominated by tribes known as 'Tervingi'. Its leader, Athaneric, described himself as a 'judge', rather than as a king, which suggests that he was a supra-tribal leader with limited authority over the individual tribes under his authority. However, we should not exaggerate his weakness, for his family ruled the Tervingi for almost 50 years. His power, and that of the Gothic elites he controlled, was based on his capacity to manage the complex and dangerous relationship with Constantinople. Tervingi fought in imperial armies, received imperial tributes, permitted the activities of Christian missions in the 340s, and their leaders were occasionally educated in Constantinople.[38] But they also had armies that could pose enough of a threat to encourage the payment of Roman subsidies. In 332, for example, the Emperor Constantine signed a treaty under which the Goths agreed to provide auxiliary troops in return for an annual payment and the opening of border trade at two fortified points on the Danube. This Gothic version of the *ho-ch'in* treaties negotiated by the Hsiung-nu lasted for over 30 years.[39] It ended in 367 when the Emperor Valens invaded the lands of the Tervingi in a war whose brutality was typical of such frontier conflicts. According to Zosimus, the Goths refused to meet Valens' invading army, so:

> he assembled all the servants and baggage attendants and promised to pay a fixed amount to anyone who brought in a barbarian's head. Excited by hope of profit, they all immediately entered the woods and marshes and killed anyone they found, receiving the agreed sum when they produced the heads of the slain. So many were destroyed in this way that the rest asked the emperor for peace.[40]

Further east, there was less opportunity to tap the wealth of Rome, and Gothic elites exploited the commercial and agrarian wealth of subordinate populations of farmers and traders as the Scythians and Sarmatians had done before them. Those Goths who settled in the Pontic region probably acquired many aspects of the traditional steppeland cultures. According to Wolfram, by the fourth century, 'the Scythization of the eastern Goths is completed: the armored lancer, who covered incredible distances and fought on horseback; the practice of hunting with falcons; shamanism; the adoption by the royal family of the Sassanian royal vestments; in short, the life-style of the Iranian-Turkish peoples of the steppe became part of the Gothic world.'[41]

Late in the fourth century, there is evidence of at least one powerful kingdom in the Pontic steppes. Ammianus, writing in 395, described the 'rich and extensive realm' of a Gothic group called the Greuthungi, whose leader was Ermanaric, 'a warlike king whose many heroic exploits had made him a terror to his neighbours'.[42] Jordanes' account, which relies heavily on Ammianus, can be interpreted to imply that Ermanaric ruled an empire reaching as far as the Urals and the Baltic. If so, it would have been an ephemeral predecessor to the later state of the Rus'. However, as Heather has argued, it is unlikely that an empire this extensive would have left so little trace in the written sources. The archaeology of the Chernyakhiv culture, suggests, instead, that there were as many as six separate fortified centres around the shores of the Black Sea, each of which may have been the capital of a powerful regional 'king'.[43] As in the Scythic period, these kingdoms probably took tributes from local peasantries, and taxed the trades passing through the northern silk roads or from the northern forests. As Wolfram has suggested, Jordanes' account of Ermanaric's bitter conflict for control of the lower Don may reflect attempts to control the trades through the 'Cimmerian Bosporus'.[44] It may be that Ermanaric claimed suzerainty over a number of semi-autonomous regional kingdoms in a loose political confederation similar to that of Athanaric. Such a confederation, like those of the Scythians and Sarmatians, would have combined considerable regional autonomy with the ability to mobilize rapidly in a crisis, and it might explain the claims Ammianus makes for Ermanaric's empire, despite its limited impact on Rome.

If this account is accurate, it suggests that the Goths, despite their agrarian background, created political systems typical of the Pontic steppes. These were based on the exploitation of local farming populations, and regional trade routes, but were never quite wealthy or powerful enough to extort the wealth of Rome as the Hsiung-nu had extorted the wealth of China. The great difference between the Goths and their pastoralist predecessors and successors was that the Goths were farmers, and if they failed to set up viable frontier states, they had the option of entering the agrarian world. After the disasters of 376, this was exactly what they did, with spectacular results.

HUNS: 370s–450s CE

The arrival of the 'Huns' in the 370s, transformed the situation along the western borderlands. For the first time in many centuries, the inhabitants of the Pontic region encountered a large pastoralist army in its most mobile and warlike phase. The terror that this first encounter generated amongst Goths and Romans still reverberates in the accounts of Ammianus or Jordanes.

Most modern historians accept that the 'Huns' were, in a loose sense, descendants of Hsiung-nu tribes who had migrated west after the collapse of the Hsiung-nu empire. However, the connection may be quite distant, and the Huns seem to have preserved no memory of their imperial antecedents in Mongolia. The name, 'Hun', certainly seems to be of Altaic origin (Turk. *kün*, meaning 'people', Mong. *kümün*, meaning 'man'). The few fragments of European Hunnic that survive show different linguistic elements, but Mongolian and Turkic seem to predominate. As Golden puts it: 'We do not possess an unbroken chain of evidence that directly links the Hsiung-nu to the Huns. But such a chain seems likely. The Hsiung-nu core (whether ethnic or political is unclear) remained, retaining its prestigious name while undergoing... ethnic and very likely linguistic changes.'[45]

After the collapse of the Hsiung-nu empires, many Hunnic groups mixed with Turkic, Ugric, Siberian and Iranian elements as they shifted westwards. This migration ended the ancient linguistic domination of the Kazakh steppes by speakers of Indo-European languages. There emerged in Kazakhstan a large, eclectic group of tribes mainly of Hunnic or Turkic origin, but with many other linguistic elements, and strongly influenced by Chinese, Iranian and Central Asian culture.[46] The earliest western report of those Hunnic groups who moved even further west places them between the Urals and the Aral Sea in *c*.160 CE. Here Hunnic tribes may have settled for over 200 years, long enough to lose all memory of their imperial past. In the middle of the fourth century some were driven even further west, perhaps by the growing power of the Juan-juan confederation, which had driven the Chionites into Central Asia in the same period.

After 360, Hunnic tribes crossed the Volga river and defeated the Alanic confederation of Sarmatian tribes, that dominated the eastern Pontic region. Once in control of the lands north of the Caucasus, the Huns, like the Scythians a millennium earlier, began to raid into northern Mesopotamia. There were huge Hunnic raids into the Sassanian empire in the 360s. In the 390s, there were massive Hunnic invasions of Syria and Mesopotamia, which may have been as destructive as the Scythian raids of the seventh century BCE. Many Huns settled permanently in the north Caucasus, where their descendants converted to Christianity in *c*.520.[47]

Other Hunnic tribes moved west. In *c*.375, an army of Huns, with Alan allies, crushed the empire of Ermanaric, and conquered the Pontic steppes. According to Ammianus, Ermanaric committed suicide.[48] His son died in battle, and his grandson, Vitheric, became leader of the demoralized Greuthungi. However, as he was a minor, it was two other leaders, Alatheus and Saphrax, who led a large contingent of Greuthungi west where they eventually settled in the Hungarian plain. Many eastern Goths clearly remained in the east under Hunnic suzerainty, for Gothic artefacts appear in the Pontic steppes throughout the next century. They undoubtedly paid tributes and served in Hunnic armies, but otherwise life may have continued much as before. Goths played an important part within the Hunnic confederation. Priscus reported that Attila's empire was led by Attila and his family, then by leading Hunnic nobles, and then by Gothic nobles.[49]

In Crimea, Gothic kingdoms survived for a long time, as Scythian kingdoms had before them.

In 376, under Hunnic pressure, many groups of Tervingi and Greuthungi sought permission to cross the Danube and settle in the Balkans. The scale of the crisis gave the Roman emperor, Valens, little choice. However, with much of his army fighting in Mesopotamia, he and his officials botched what turned into a huge and dangerous refugee crisis. Ammianus describes the desperate crossing of the Danube:

> Once the emperor's permission to cross the Danube and settle in parts of Thrace had been granted, the work of transportation went on night and day. The Goths embarked by troops on boats and rafts and canoes made from hollowed tree-trunks. The crowd was such that, though the river is the most dangerous in the world and was then swollen by frequent rains, a large number tried to swim and were drowned in their struggle against the force of the stream.[50]

The Roman armies failed to police the newly arrived Gothic contingents. Eventually, the corruption of Roman generals (Ammianus claims that local commanders sold dogs to the starving refugees in return for slaves), and their failure to provide food relief and to help the newly arrived Goths settle, led to a massive Gothic revolt within the Balkans. This culminated in the humiliating Roman defeat at the battle of Adrianople in 378 CE, when the emperor Valens was killed.[51]

After 376, the Huns emerged as the major power along Rome's Balkan frontiers. According to Ammianus, they had no overall leader when they first attacked eastern Europe. They probably lived in independent but allied tribes of several thousand people, each of which could probably field up to 1000 soldiers.[52] Ammianus' account, though stereotypical in some of its detail, suggests that in this period the Huns practised a highly nomadic form of pastoralism, which is exactly what we would expect during a period of mass migrations.

> They have no buildings to shelter them, but avoid anything of the kind as carefully as we avoid living in the neighbourhood of tombs; not so much as a hut thatched with reeds is to be found among them. They roam at large over mountains and forests, and are inured from the cradle to cold, hunger, and thirst. ... They wear garments of linen or of the skins of field-mice stitched together, and there is no difference between their clothing whether they are at home or abroad. Once they have put their necks into some dingy shirt they never take it off or change it till it rots and falls to pieces from incessant wear. ... [They] remain glued to their horses, hardy but ugly beasts, on which they sometimes sit like women to perform their everyday business. Buying or selling, eating or drinking, are all done by day or night on horseback, and they even bow forward over their beasts' narrow necks to enjoy a deep and dreamy sleep.[53]

They were, he wrote, hostile to agriculture or sedentism.

> None of them ploughs or ever touches a plough-handle. They have no fixed abode, no home or law or settled manner of life, but wander like refugees with

the wagons in which they live. In these their wives weave their filthy clothing, mate with their husbands, give birth to their children, and rear them to the age of puberty. No one if asked can tell where he comes from, having been conceived in one place, born somewhere else, and reared even further off.[54]

After their initial attacks, Hunnic tribes raided and probed along Rome's frontiers, but also proved willing to act in alliance with the Empire. For almost a quarter of a century, most were content to remain in the Pontic steppes. Then, in the first 20 years of the fifth century, groups of Huns began to move around the Carpathians and into modern Hungary.[55] As they consolidated their hold first on the Pontic and then the Hungarian steppes, they presumably settled into a pattern of semi-nomadic migrations. Clan and tribal groupings established regular migratory routes, new chiefly hierarchies emerged, and close relationships of trade or tribute-taking were established with subordinate agriculturalists and towns.[56] Regional Hunnic chiefs probably took over the trading and tributary systems of the Gothic kingdoms. They certainly showed great interest in cross-border trade, purchasing grain and weaponry from Rome. Hunnic elites were particularly interested in the prestige goods and coins they received in tribute, for these allowed them to purchase luxury goods that enhanced their status and influence amongst their own followers. Finds of Hunnic cauldrons along the Kama river, and Attila's gift of furs to visiting ambassadors, suggest that Hunnic tributary systems, like those of the Scythians, reached deep into the forest regions of western Inner Eurasia.[57]

The Huns soon adapted to the agrarian world of eastern Europe, and their own settlements became more sedentary. When he visited Attila's court in Hungary in 449, Priscus, our second major source on the Huns, described a world of pastoralist elites settled in pasturelands surrounded by farming regions. Priscus passed through many villages on his way to visit Attila. Eventually, he reached Attila's camp, which was a relatively permanent settlement in the middle of a treeless steppe in the Hungarian 'Alföld', probably east of the river Tisza. Priscus described it as 'a village, . . . like a great city, in which we found wooden walls made of smooth-shining boards, whose joints so counterfeited solidity that the union of the boards could scarcely be distinguished by close scrutiny. There you might see dining halls of large extent and porticoes planned with great beauty, while the courtyard was bounded by so vast a circuit that its very size showed it was the royal palace.'[58] Inside the palisade of Attila's palace were many circular wooden dwellings, modelled, presumably, on nomads' tents. Inside the hut of Attila's wife, Kreka, Priscus found a scene typical of many a wealthy pastoralist household, with the lady seated on felt mats, while her servants embroidered fine linen cloths. The wood for these royal palaces and their largely decorative palisades was all imported, as the nearby steppes were treeless. Nearby, was the house of Attila's lieutenant, Onegesius, which was distinguished by the presence of a stone bath-house, built from specially imported stone by an architect captured in Sirmium.[59] As Pletneva points out, the structure of Attila's steppe settlement, with its concentric squares, rectangles or circles, and the royal court at the very centre, was typical of many pastoral 'towns' that grew up around large winter camps.[60]

In the early fifth century, there emerged a more organized Hunnic polity. In 422, Hunnic tribes resumed large-scale attacks on the Balkans. In the 430s, these attacks were renewed under a leader called Rua, and his brothers, Mundiuch and Octar. In c.433, Rua demanded the return of Hunnic 'fugitives' from the Black Sea region, who were serving Constantinople. This suggests that Rua now claimed suzerainty over at least the western parts of the Pontic steppes. Indeed, Rua may have been the real founder of Hunnic power.[61] After invading Pannonia and Thrace, Rua concluded a treaty under which the Huns were to receive 350 pounds of gold a year.

Rua died in 432 or 433. To prevent a planned Hun attack on Roman territory, Emperor Theodosius II (408–50) raised the annual tribute to Rua's successors to 700 pounds of gold, and agreed to open border markets.[62] Enriched by the flow of Roman tributes, Rua's nephews, Bleda and Attila, sons of Mundiuch, maintained the authority he had established over both Hunnic and non-Hunnic tribes.[63] They spent the next years consolidating and extending their authority. Priscus refers to warfare in Scythia, and even to the possibility that the Huns extended their authority to the Baltic shores. In 433, Pannonia was surrendered once more to the Huns. In 441, when Constantinople's armies were engaged in North Africa and Syria, Hunnic armies invaded the Balkans, citing Constantinople's refusal to return 'fugitives' and failure to pay tributes in full. They devastated several major cities, including Sirmium and Singidunum (Belgrade), and left with huge amounts of booty and captives. In 443, Hunnic armies sacked the base of the Danube fleet at Ratiara, and the populous cities of Naissus and Serdica (Sofia) and crushed imperial armies in the Balkans. Travelling through Naissus six years later, Priscus found the river bank still covered with the bones of the dead.[64] Theodosius II had to negotiate humiliating terms to prevent the fall of Constantinople itself.

In c.445, Attila murdered his brother, Bleda. He became for eight years the sole leader of a Hunnic confederation that controlled much of modern Hungary and Romania, most of the steppelands north of the Black Sea, and even had considerable power in Germany and parts of Gaul. Attila's ambitions probably extended even further, for, according to Priscus, he intended, after subordinating the Romans, to turn on the Persians, following the route of earlier Hunnic armies through the Caucasus. As he built up his power, he showed extreme sensitivity to issues of honour and prestige, for these were important matters to a ruler whose diplomatic status did not yet match his real power. Priscus reports many incidents showing Attila's extreme interest in the return of fugitives who had betrayed him, and in the exact status and rank of diplomats sent to him from Constantinople.[65]

The brief glimpses of Attila contained in Priscus' account suggest that he wielded autocratic authority over his immediate followers. His power depended on the huge flows of revenues, through tributes, ransom payments and sheer booty, that Hunnic leaders had concentrated in their hands since the 420s. These he used to bind regional chiefs into loyal retinues. Under

Attila, powerful chieftains acted as members of their master's personal retinue, and were liable for any military or diplomatic service on which he might send them. The loyalty of Attila's retinues depended on his ability to reward them abundantly with the goods seized in imperial raids, with the prestige of noble rank, clothing and foodstuffs, and the privilege of going on embassies to Constantinople, during which they could expect to receive valuable gifts. As Thompson puts it: 'Attila's endless demands that Hun ambassadors should be received with "gifts" at Constantinople is not merely to be ascribed to a *politique de prestige* on his part...; it was a vital support of the social order then prevailing among the nomads.'[66] However, within their own tribal lands, there can be no doubt that such chieftains continued to wield great power, even if they were not Hunnic, for there is no sign of the existence of a central bureaucracy of any kind. At most, Attila enjoyed the services of Latin secretaries sent to him by his Roman ally, Aetius.[67]

In 447, Hunnic armies, with Gothic and Gepid allies, invaded the Balkans once more, and sacked large areas. Theodosius II had to raise the annual tribute to 2100 pounds of gold, to pay arrears of 6000 pounds immediately, and to evacuate a no man's land between the two powers. Though considerable sums, these tributes represented just over 2 per cent of the 270,000 pounds of gold received by the Empire each year in the fifth century. They were certainly not enough to bankrupt the empire, as Mommsen claimed.[68] They proved, however, that for a brief time, the Huns could play the 'Outer Frontier Strategy' in the west as their ancestors had played it in the far east. At his funeral, Attila's followers praised him, among other things, because he 'terrorized both empires of the Roman world after conquering their cities, and, placated by their entreaties that the rest might not be laid open to plunder, he accepted an annual tribute'.[69]

In 451, Attila led an army westwards to attack the Visigothic rulers of Gaul. Though Jordanes claimed the army numbered 500,000, in reality it was probably no larger than 100,000, the majority of whom were probably Goths. At the last minute, the western Roman emperor, Valentinian, decided to support his old enemies, the Visigoths, and Attila found himself facing a combined Visigothic and Roman army. His armies were defeated in June 450, during a momentous battle near Troyes, but allowed to escape east. In 452, Attila invaded Italy and destroyed many of the great cities of the north. This time, too, Attila turned back, probably because of an outbreak of plague, shortages of supplies in a land recently devastated by famine, and the fact that a Byzantine army had entered the Hunnic lands of Pannonia.[70] A year later, in 453, Attila was dead of a hemorrhage, and his empire began to unravel.

His followers gave him the funeral, or *strava*, of a great steppe ruler. According to Jordanes (who relied on Priscus here): 'His body was placed in the midst of the plain and laid in state in a silken tent as a sight for men's admiration. The best horsemen of the entire tribe of the Huns rode around in circles, after the manner of circus games, in the place to which he had been brought and told of his deeds in a funeral dirge.' His followers cut their faces as they rode around the grave, buried their chief with many precious objects, and then slaughtered those who had buried him to keep the burial site a secret.[71]

Attila's empire now fell apart, as his sons quarrelled over his inheritance. Unlike Motun, Attila had established no durable structures to hold the empire together. This may be partly because the Hungarian steppes can support smaller numbers of pastoralists, so that the Huns were greatly outnumbered by subject tribes. Or perhaps it was because he had less understanding than Motun of the importance of bureaucratic structures and rituals. With Attila's death, the flow of tributes and booty began to dry up, undermining the willingness of subordinate chieftains to follow new and untried leaders.[72] The Germanic tribes revolted; a Hunnic army led by some of Attila's sons was defeated in 454; and the Huns soon had to leave Hungary and flee to the Pontic steppes. Attila's empire broke into its many tribal segments. In 468, a mere 13 years after Attila's death, one of his sons, Dengizikh, demanded the opening of frontier markets along the Danube for Hunnic merchants, a sign, perhaps, of a serious shortage of prestige goods, weapons, and perhaps even foodstuffs. When the Byzantine government refused to reopen the markets, Dengizikh invaded but was defeated and killed, and his head was handed over to the imperial commander, Anagast, in Constantinople. Small, mixed groups described as Huns survived along the Danube frontiers for another decade or two, acting as mercenaries, petty raiders, or even settlers. But most 'Huns' returned to the Pontic steppes, where they merged with other pastoralist groups.[73]

Attila's career suggests that the 'Outer Frontier Strategy', worked so successfully by Motun, was harder to manage in the west. This was because of the remoteness of Rome, Constantinople and the empire's wealthier cities, the narrowness of the Balkan frontier, and the lack of good pasturelands west of the Carpathians.[74] Here, pastoralist rulers had to rely mainly on the wealth of local populations of farmers, forest-dwellers and pastoralists, while staying in the steppelands of Hungary or the Pontic steppes.

THE NORTH CHINESE BORDERLANDS AFTER THE HSIUNG-NU: 220–550 CE

Whereas the history of central and western Inner Eurasia in the early centuries of the modern era was driven by the migratory movements started by the Hsiung-nu, in the eastern steppes, pastoralists were sucked into a vacuum left by the collapse of empire on both sides of the great wall. There followed an extended period of complex politics conducted between weak and unstable political confederations until, in the sixth century, new imperial dynasties appeared in China and in the steppes.

After the fall of the Han, the eastern steppes were dominated by a series of weak tribal confederations, most of which adopted primitive strategies of raiding, so that conflict was endemic. However, as Thomas Barfield has shown, beneath the complex politics of the period it is possible to detect a pattern of events which tended, eventually, to restore political power both in

China and in the steppes. First, there appeared in the borderlands regional states ruled by pastoralists with some understanding of the agrarian world, as well as dynasties ruled by agrarian 'barbarians' similar to the Goths.[75] Manchuria played a crucial role at this stage, for its remoteness and ecological variety made it possible to experiment with symbiotic systems combining pastoralism and agriculture, in an environment of relative security. Eventually, as these polities began to depend more and more on the wealth of their Chinese populations, and the skills of their Chinese officials, they became Sinicized or were replaced by indigenous Chinese dynasties. As powerful new Chinese dynasties emerged, it became possible, once again, for powerful steppe leaders to contemplate some form of 'Outer Frontier' strategy.

THE NORTH CHINESE FRONTIER LANDS IN AN ERA OF ANARCHY

Chinese sources describe most of the tribes along the north Chinese borders after the collapse of the Hsiung-nu as Hsien-pi. The Hsien-pi tribes came from western Manchuria, and had once been part of the Tung-hu confederation over which Motun had his first great victory. However, the name certainly masks great ethnic and linguistic diversity and many Hsien-pi were probably Hsiung-nu under a new name. The language of the dominant Hsien-pi tribes was probably close to later Mongolian and Kitan.[76]

Though the Hsien-pi were more likely to practise agriculture than the Hsiung-nu, particularly near Manchuria, it is unlikely that their lifeways were very different from those of the Hsiung-nu era. Here is a Chinese description of the life of the Hsien-pi and the closely related Wu-huan:

> They are experts in riding and shooting and following the waters and grass to pasture their animals, and they have no definite place to live. They use yurts as their homes, and all the yurts point towards the east. They hunt birds and animals every day. They eat meat, drink milk, and wear wool and skins.... They depend on the Middle Kingdom for their supply of seed and grain. The *ta-jen* leaders are able to make bows, arrows, saddles and bridles, and to forge metals to make arms. They are able to dress hides, embroider, and weave woollen clothes.[77]

Though the Turkic title of 'kaghan' is first recorded amongst the Hsien-pi in the third century CE, they never formed a durable pastoral state.[78] This meant that Chinese officials had to deal with a multiplicity of local chiefs. As early as 49 CE, Han officials paid Hsien-pi chieftains bounties for the heads of northern Hsiung-nu. The Hsien-pi brought Hsiung-nu heads to markets in Liao-tung where they received gifts and cash. Many Hsien-pi tribes also received cash subsidies. After the defeat of the northern Hsiung-nu in 89 CE, many Hsiung-nu tribal leaders became Hsien-pi, and the Hsien-pi became the dominant peoples of Mongolia. However, the collapse of the northern Hsiung-nu deprived the Hsien-pi of the bounties on Hsiung-nu heads. As a result, Hsien-pi tribes began once more to raid northern China.[79]

Between 156 and 180, there did emerge a powerful Hsien-pi leader who might have founded a new state. His name was T'an-shih-huai. From a base north of Ta-t'ung, near modern Huade, T'an-shih-huai mounted annual raids into China, refused all offers of peace negotiations, defeated the largest Chinese army sent north since 89 CE in 177, and ended up controlling a federation that united all the lands once controlled by Motun. His influence reached from the Ussuri river to Zungaria and southern Siberia. However, the federation he created collapsed at his death in 180, like that of Attila in the far west almost three centuries later. As Barfield argues, this may have been because now there existed no large Chinese state powerful enough to establish a stable tributary relationship with steppe rulers.[80]

The civil wars of the period of Sixteen Kingdoms (301–439) led to a demographic collapse in north China. Ambitious pastoralist leaders along China's northern borders now found that, to extract tributes of any kind, they had to involve themselves directly in the governance of petty agricultural states. Sometimes they did so as frontier guards, similar to Roman *foederati*, or as mercenaries, invited in by rival Chinese groupings. In this way, partially Sinicized pastoralist tribes found themselves directly involved in the violent politics of north China.

In 304, remnants of the southern Hsiung-nu, now highly Sinicized, and at least partially sedentary, revolted and formed a new state within the old borders of China. Their leader, Liu Yüan (r. 304–10), revived the title of *shan-yü*, which had been abolished in 216. The new Hsiung-nu empire was an agrarian state ruled by highly Sinicized pastoralists, some of whom even began to consider themselves legitimate aspirants to the Imperial throne. The Hsiung-nu captured and destroyed the great imperial cities of Lo-yang (in 311) and Ch'ang-an (in 316), and executed the Chin emperors who ruled them. They now ruled most of northern China, forming the first barbarian dynasty to do so. They took the dynastic title of *Chao*. It is possible that their military success reflected, in part, the spread in Mongolia of the stirrup, which increased the effectiveness of armoured cavalry.[81]

As in most states of pastoralist origins, there soon emerged deep divisions over policy between those loyal to pastoralist traditions, and those who accepted Chinese traditions. Liu Yüan had been brought up as a hostage at the Chin court and naturally followed Chinese models of rule.[82] So did his son and heir, Liu Ts'ung (ruled 310–18). However, many Hsiung-nu were unhappy about such precedents, amongst them, Shih Le, the most successful of the Hsiung-nu generals. For Shih Le, the appropriate policy was to loot and raid northern China, and, if that meant clearing it of people, 'so much the better for Hsiung-nu horses.'[83] In 319, on the death of Liu Ts'ung, Shih Le, though not a descendant of Motun, proclaimed himself the first emperor of a new dynasty, the Later Chao (319–52). However, Shih Le's violent and predatory methods were so destructive that his 'empire' soon collapsed in bloody internal conflicts.

Meanwhile, Hsien-pi tribes in the Manchurian borderlands also began to create symbiotic polities combining agricultural and pastoralist elements. As Barfield has shown, these polities emerged in a distinctive sequence.[84] First, a pastoralist tribe would rule lands which included sedentary Chinese populations. Next, it would create separate administrative structures for its agricultural and pastoralist regions. Such structures gave leaders room to manoeuvre by building support in both spheres. When, eventually, such rulers conquered territory in the Chinese heartland, their dual administrative systems proved quite adequate for the two distinct tasks of conquest and administration. Their pastoral nomads provided the military strike force, while their farmers provided the fiscal wealth to support them. Like the Goths and other agrarian 'barbarians' in the far west, Manchurian dynasties were more able and more willing than pastoralist 'barbarians' to shift permanently, if necessary, into the agrarian world. While pastoralist armies raided northern China, Manchurian armies were more likely to settle permanently, which is why so many foreign dynasties in China came from Manchuria rather than the steppes.

The first symbiotic state of this kind in Manchuria emerged during the long reign of the Chinese educated Hsien-pi *shan-yü*, Mu-jung Hui (ruled 283–333). By the late third century, Hsien-pi tribes controlled extensive farming lands and cities in Manchuria. In 294, Mu-jung Hui founded a capital city in Manchuria. Here, he encouraged farming and silk-making, shifting, in this way, from predation to production. By 301 he was able to export grain to China. The agrarian sector of the economy was dominated by Chinese captives, and administered by Chinese officials. With their help Hui imposed greater discipline on his pastoralist army, and incorporated within it infantry, as well as siege warfare units.[85] His growing military power encouraged other Hsien-pi tribes to join him.

Hui's successor, Mu-jung Huang, proclaimed himself Emperor of a new dynasty in 337. The 'former Yen' dynasty (348–70) was the first of a series of Manchurian dynasties to rule northern China. Mu-jung Huang accepted the advice of Chinese advisers on the need to intensify agricultural production by planting refugees and prisoners on the land, and taking care of irrigation, even when this meant cutting into traditional grazing lands. His successor, Mu-jung Chün, took over the remnants of the Hsiung-nu Chao dynasty as it collapsed, and proclaimed himself Emperor of the Yen dynasty in 353.[86]

For the Yen as for the Chao, balancing the needs of their agricultural and pastoralist populations proved extremely difficult. The dynasty declined when, in Mu-jung P'ing, it was ruled by a leader who represented too effectively the predatory traditions of the past. The tribal elite consumed resources that should have been used to support the army, and the system collapsed in military defeat in 370.

EMERGING EMPIRES: T'O-PA/WEI (386–534) AND JUAN-JUAN (350–555)

The T'o-pa emerged as a significant political force in the third century CE, probably in eastern Inner Mongolia. In the fourth century, they formed the 'statelet' of Tai, in northern Shansi. Their language, like that of the Hsien-pi, seems to have been close to Mongol, but there were also Turkic-speaking elements amongst them, and eventually, their name (in its Turkic form of Tabgach) came to represent China in Turkic sources.[87]

Despite their pastoralist traditions, the T'o-pa inherited much of the administrative machinery and many of the officials of the highly Sinicized Yen dynasty, when T'o-pa Kui proclaimed himself the emperor of a new Wei dynasty in 396. Until 493, the T'o-pa, known to Chinese historians as the Northern Wei, ruled much of north China from P'ing-ch'eng near modern Ta-t'ung, not far from the first capital city of the Hsiung-nu. Under T'o-pa Tao (423–52), a contemporary of Attila, they captured Ch'ang-an in 430, and destroyed the Hsia dynasty, the last to be ruled by descendants of Motun. The T'o-pa also extended their control over the Wu-Sun of Zungaria, and over the Silk Roads of eastern Turkestan.[88] In 429, they temporarily drove the Juan-juan, who had emerged as a significant Mongolian power in the fourth century, well to the west. By 440, the Wei controlled all of northern China, much of Mongolia, and most of the 'western region' as well, but they never succeeded in conquering China south of the Yang-tse.

The emergence of a powerful dynasty in north China provided pastoralists with a new negotiating partner and encouraged the emergence of larger tribal systems in the steppes. Unfortunately for the Juan-juan, the T'o-pa, who were themselves of steppe origin, understood better than did most native Chinese dynasties how to deal with steppe armies. In particular, they proved expert at dividing steppe tribes through marriage alliances. They also understood that it was possible to fight them. As a T'o-pa general explained:

> In the summer their men and animals are scattered while in the autumn they all come together, their animals well fed. In the winter they change course and move south to plunder our frontiers. If we but come upon them by surprise [in the spring] with a great army and attack them, unprepared as they are, they will scatter in panic and flee. The stallions will be guarding their herds, and the mares will be chasing their foals, all fleeing in disorder. In a few days they will be unable to find grass or water, the men and animals will weaken, and we can bring about the enemy's sudden collapse.[89]

T'o-pa military strategy, like that of the Han Emperor, Wu-ti, depended on the maintenance of large cavalry armies, systematic disruption of the pastoralist economy, and a constant offensive that kept pastoralist opponents permanently off balance.

Towards the end of the fifth century, the Wei dynasty became more Sinicized. Under Yüan Hung-yen (471–99), T'o-pa language and customs were banned, and the capital was shifted from P'ing-ch'eng to Lo-yang in 493. Meanwhile, the growing influence of trade along the Silk Roads led to the adoption of Buddhism, a change that some historians have seen as part of a more general process of 'babarization' of Chinese elites.[90] The first historically attested Buddhist missionary to China was An Shih-kao, a Parthian prince, probably from Margiana, who became a Buddhist monk, with the name, Lokottama. He travelled to Lo-yang in c.140 CE, and taught and translated in the 'White Horse Monastery' until his death in 170. Under the late Han, and in the confused era after that collapse, Buddhism spread widely in both south and north China.[91] But not until the Wei dynasty did the religion acquire sustained official sponsorship. Outside modern Ta-t'ung, there are Buddhist caves mostly dug and decorated in the fifth century, and modelled on the fourth century caves of Tun-huang. The T'o-pa capital, P'ing-ch'eng, was dominated by a Buddhist monastery with a seven-storey stupa, built by the royal family in 476, and by the early sixth century, there may have been as many as 30,000 Buddhist monasteries in north China.[92] As the T'o-pa became more Chinese in culture and adopted Buddhism as their main religion, their handling of pastoralists became more defensive. The Wei began to build border defences and to pay tributes to pastoralists. In 494, the capital was relocated south to Lo-yang on the Yellow River. This deprived the border regions and their garrisons of the status, influence and supplies that had made them so effective.

These changes enhanced the potential bargaining power of the pastoralist Juan-juan. The linguistic and ethnic origins of the Juan-juan (Jou-jan? – even Chinese sources vary) are not clear, though their proper names seem neither Turkic nor Mongolian and may well derive from Siberian languages. Pulleyblank has suggested that they originated amongst the Wu-huan, who, in turn, may be linked with the Avar/Hun grouping of tribes from which the Hephthalites probably came.[93] The first Juan-juan confederation was established early in the fourth century, by a leader known as Mu-i-lu (r. 308–16), but it remained weak and divided for most of the century. In c.394, a leader called She-lun created a united empire and established his authority over most of the tribes of Mongolia. Avoiding direct confrontation with the Wei, he moved to northern Mongolia where he proclaimed himself kaghan of the steppe tribes, a project in which he was aided indirectly by the defeats the Wei inflicted on neighbouring tribes. T'o-pa power in China now left border tribes few of the many opportunities for manoeuvre that had existed for so long; and they had to choose either to accept subordination to the Wei or to join the Juan-juan. As Barfield puts it: 'The T'o-pa conquests... acted as the anvil against which the previously autonomous tribes were hammered into a steppe confederation by the Juan-juan.'[94] Under She-lun, who ruled from near Tun-huang, the Juan-juan empire reached from Turfan to northern Korea.[95]

Though defeated by the T'o-pa in 429 CE, the Juan-juan confederation revived quickly, and in the 430s they attacked the Kidara 'Huns' in Bactria, who may once have been their partners. A massive Wei invasion of Juan-juan lands in 458 forced the Juan-juan further west where they seized Turfan in 460. However, early in the sixth century, under their last great leader, A-na-kuei (520–52), they formed an alliance with their old enemies, the T'o-pa, just as the Wei dynasty was about to split into eastern and western wings. The Wei began paying the Jou-juan substantial tributes in return for military support, and in 526 the Wei emperor recognized the Juan-juan leader, A-nu-kuei as an equal.[96]

Juan-juan power was not particularly stable, but it was extensive. Their power was greatest in western Mongolia and northern Sinkiang, but they also exerted influence in eastern Mongolia and even, perhaps, in Central Asia through their links with the Hephthalites. In 534, the Wei empire split into eastern and western halves. The eastern Wei maintained an alliance with the Juan-juan, but in 545 the western Wei (534–57) formed an alliance with Bumin (T'u-men), a vassal of the Juan-juan and the future leader of the Türk.[97] The collapse of the Wei dynasties, and their successors, the Chou (557–81) and Ch'i (550–77), and of the Juan-juan (552) marked the end of a cycle of chaos and rebuilding under foreign dynasties. When a unified Chinese dynasty assumed power under the Sui in 581, they found in the steppes a powerful confederation, that of the Türk (552–640), ready to relaunch the imperial games first played with the Hsiung-nu 700 years before.

Beneath the complex details of the 'Hunnic' era, it is possible to see some enduring patterns in the relations between Inner and Outer Eurasia. In the Chinese borderlands, as in those of the far west, patterns of conflict were significantly different from those that appeared in the borderlands of Central Asia. In the eastern and western borderlands, the contrast between steppe-lands and agrarian lands was clearer than in Central Asia. Outside of Hungary, there was no significant area of steppe in eastern Europe, and the same was true south of the Ordos region in northern China. Here, therefore, pastoralist empires emerged, for the most part, along the borderlands. It was agrarian barbarians, from northern Europe or Manchuria, who settled deep inside the regions of agrarian civilization, and established new 'barbarian' dynasties and states. For pastoralists to cross to the other side of the ecological frontiers of Rome or China was a radical step, and it was usually easier to exploit societies on the other side of the frontier by remote control. That is why so few pastoralist empires actually created empires within the agrarian lands of north China or eastern Europe. Only in Central Asia did fingers of steppeland lead deep into Outer Eurasia, so only here was it common for pastoralists to create ruling dynasties in Outer Eurasia.

NOTES

1 This is the argument of K. Enoki, G. A. Koshelenko and Z. Haidary, 'The Yüeh-chih and their migrations', in *HCCA* (pp. 171–89), 2:174 and 178; see also ch. 5, and the special edition of *Indo-European Studies*, vol. 23, nos 3 and 4 (Fall/Winter, 1995), which is on the Tocharian problem.

2 On the Yen-ts'ai, Y. A. Zadneprovskiy, 'The nomads of northern Central Asia', in *HCCA*, 2:465–6; and Hulsewe, *China in Central Asia*, p. 129; on the K'ang-chü, Zadneprovskyi, in *HCCA*, 2:463 locates their capital at Tashkent; the K'ang-chü are described in the *Han-shu* (Hulsewe, *China in Central Asia*, pp. 123–31), but the same source (Ibid. p. 123) identifies K'ang-chü with the 'Stone country', which Hulsewe locates as Samarkand (and Golden, *Introduction*, p. 52, follows him), while Pulleyblank places their winter capital on the Syr Darya (Golden, *Introduction*, p. 125); see also Negmatov, in *HCCA*, 2:452–3, L. R. Kyzlasov, 'Northern nomads', in *HCCA*, 3:315–16; and Gafurov, *Tadzhiki*, 1:173–4; probably we should think of the K'ang-chü as based on the Saka settlements along the Syr Darya, with at least one capital near Tashkent, but with occasional control over the Zerafshan valley.

3   A. K. Narain, 'Indo-Europeans in Inner Asia', in *CHEIA* (pp. 151–76), p. 158; Chinese sources refer to the displaced peoples as Sakas; ibid., 173, and see Enoki, et al., 'The Yüeh-chih', in *HCCA*, 2:180–2; see also Tolstov, *Po drevnim del'tam*, p. 204; and P'iankov, 'The ethnic history of the Sakas', pp. 38–9.

4   Enoki, et al., 'The Yüeh-chih' in *HCCA*, 2:182–4; see also Hulsewe, *China in Central Asia*, p. 120.

5   Ssu-ma Ch'ien, *Records*, 2:269.

6   J. Harmatta et al., 'Religions in the Kushan empire', *HCCA* (pp. 313–29), 2:316; Frye, *History of Ancient Iran*, p. 251.

7   Frye, *Heritage of Central Asia*, p. 126.

8   Citations from the *Hou-Han Shu* from Zürcher, 'Yüeh-chih and Kaniska', p. 367; on Vima Takto, Joe Cribb, 'New Discoveries in Kushan Chronology', *Newsletter* of the Circle of Inner Asian Art, Edition 3, July 1996, pp. 1–2 describes the recently discovered Rabatak inscription, on which this chronology is based; see also Narain, 'Indo-Europeans in Inner Asia', in *CHEIA*, p. 159; B. N. Puri, 'The Kushans', in *HCCA* (pp. 247–63), 2:247; on the capital, Gibb, *Arab Conquests*, p. 8.

9   Puri, 'The Kushans', in *HCCA*, 2:257–8, and see 2:248–9, 254; on the importance of the monsoons for this trade route, see Haussig, *Geschichte Zentralasiens...in vorislamischer Zeit*, p. 128; see also Isidore of Charax, *Parthian Stations*, p. 19.

10 See Puri, 'The Kushans', in *HCCA*, 2:249–52; Harmatta gives 134 CE as the start of the Kaniska era, according to ibid., 2:253; this century-old controversy is surveyed in Gafurov, *Tadzhiki*, 1:178–84.

11 Staviskij, *La Bactriane*, p. 29; and see Narain, 'Indo-Europeans in Inner Asia', in *CHEIA*, p. 165; and see also Shishkina, 'Ancient Samarkand', p. 90

12 *Ocherki istorii SSSR: Pervobytno-obshchinnyi stroi*, p. 538; that Mathura became the capital is implied in Narain, 'Indo-Europeans in Inner Asia', in *CHEIA*, p. 169.

13 Narain, 'Indo-Europeans in Inner Asia', in *CHEIA*, p. 165; Narain (pp. 172–3) also mentions that the early Yüeh-chih kings seem to have practised deformation of the skull, which was a Sarmatian and Hunnic practice; on Kaniska's titles, Puri, 'The Kushans', in *HCCA*, 2:260–1; citations from the *Hou-Han Shu* from Zürcher, 'Yüeh-chih and Kaniska', p. 372, though it is possible that this report uses older information that had dated by the second century.

14 Puri, 'The Kushans', in *HCCA*, 2:255–6; Basham, ed., *Papers on the Date of Kanishka*, p. 391; N. N. Chegini and A. V. Nikitin, 'Sasanian Iran – economy, society, arts and crafts', in *HCCA* (pp. 35–76), 3:36–8, and A. H. Dani and B. A. Litvinsky, 'The Kushano-Sasanian kingdom', in *HCCA*, 3:103–18.

15 Harmatta et al., 'Religions in the Kushan empire', *HCCA*, 2:317; and Puri, 'Kushans', in *HCCA*, 2:261.

16 Narain, 'Indo-Europeans in Inner Asia', in *CHEIA*, pp. 167–8; J. Harmatta, 'Languages and literature in the Kushan empire', *HCCA* (pp. 417–40), 2:422; Liu, *Ancient India and Ancient China*, pp. 117–20.

17 Puri, *Buddhism*, pp. 37–8, 46–7, 90–101; Zürcher, *The Buddhist Conquest of China*, 1:23–38; Ch'en, *Buddhism in China*, pp. 18, 32–3; Zhang Guang-da, 'The city-states of the Tarim basin', in *HCCA* (pp. 281–301), 3:291–301.

18 Ch'en, *Buddhism in China*, pp. 15–16; on links with trade, see Liu, *Ancient India and Ancient China*, chs IV and V, particularly pp. 101–2, 107, 114–15.

19 A. R. Mukhamedjanov, 'Economy and social system in central Asia in the Kushan age', in *HCCA* (pp. 265–90), 2:289–90; and see B. A. Litvinsky and Zhang Guang-da, 'Central Asia, the crossroads of civilizations', in *HCCA* (pp. 473–90), 3:473–90; and Gafurov, *Tadzhiki*, 1:235–40, which illustrates the

difficulties Soviet historians faced in fitting Central Asia of this period into the Marxist 'slave mode'.

20 Mukhamedjanov, 'Economy and social system', in *HCCA*, 2:268–70 and 265; and see Tolstov, *Po drevnim del'tam*, pp. 94–5.

21 *Ocherki istorii SSSR: Pervobytno-obshchinnyi stroi*, p. 540; and see Mukhamedjanov, 'Economy and social system', in *HCCA*, 2:268–74; on the historiographical debate, see Gafurov, *Tadzhiki*, 1:224–30.

22 Liu, *Ancient India and Ancient China*, pp. 7–9; Gafurov, *Tadzhiki*, 1:205–7.

23 Tolstov, *Po drevnim del'tam*, p. 225; see also Narain, 'Indo-Europeans in Inner Asia', in *CHEIA*, p. 163; Golden, *Introduction*, p. 56; Mukhamedjanov, 'Economy and social system', in *HCCA*, 2:284–7; *Ocherki istorii SSSR: Pervobytno-obshchinnyi stroi*, pp. 539, 546.

24 Cited by B. A. Litvinsky, 'Cities and urban life in the Kushan kingdom', in *HCCA* (pp. 291–312), 2:303, and see 2:302, 309; see also Litvinskii in Gafurov, *Tadzhiki*, 1989, 2:351–2.

25 On this system of fortifications, probably built by Khosrow I, see Frye, *Golden Age of Persia*, pp. 13–15, and Frye, 'The Sasanian system of walls for defense', in *Islamic Iran and Central Asia*, III:12–13; see also Artamonov, *Istoriya khazar*, pp. 117–26, which includes a plan on p. 121; according to Novosel'tsev, *Khazarskoe gosudarstvo*, p. 101, recent excavations have shown fortifications here dating from the eighth to seventh centuries BCE; on Darband's history, see Bartol'd, *Sochineniya*, 3:419–30 and see Barthold, *A History of the Turkman People*, in *Four Studies* (pp. 75–170), p. 87.

26 Barthold, *Turkestan down to the Mongol Invasion*, p. 181, and p. xxix; on the decline of Samarkand before the late fifth century, see Shishkina, 'Ancient Samarkand', pp. 90–3; and B. I. Marshak, 'Sughd and adjacent regions', in *HCCA* (pp. 233–58), 3:233–58; Azarpay, *Sogdian Painting* and Belenitsky, *Central Asia*.

27 Chegini and Nikitin, 'Sasanian Iran', in *HCCA*, 3:38; on the complex debates over the origins of the Chionites, see Gafurov, *Tadzhiki*, 1:255–8.

28 Citations from Sung Yün from Beal, *Si-yu-ki: Buddhist Records*, I:xci; see also Menander, *The History*, p. 115; Frye, *Golden Age of Persia*, p. 38; Golden, *Introduction*, p. 80–2; according to al-Biruni, Kunduz was their capital, Vogelsang, *Rise and Organisation*, p. 62; see also E. V. Zemal, 'The Kidarite kingdom', in *HCCA*, 3:119–34, Litvinsky, 'The Hephthalite empire', in *HCCA*, 3:135–62, and Litvinsky and Zamir Safi, 'The later Hephthalites', in *HCCA*, 3:176–83; see also Chavannes, *Documents sur les Tou-Kiue*, pp. 224–6.

29 The best account of Gothic history is now Heather, *The Goths*; on Jordanes, see pp. 9–10.

30 See Jordanes, *The Gothic History*, pp. 57–8; also, Heather, *The Goths*, pp. 21–49; Wolfram, *History of the Goths*, pp. 12, 23; and Kazanski, *Les Goths*, pp. 19, 25.

31 Heather, *The Goths*, pp. 46–8.

32 Wolfram, *History of the Goths*, pp. 48, 51–5; Brown, *The Making of Late Antiquity*, pp. 22, 25.

33 Heather and Matthews, *The Goths*, p. 1, on Gothic mercenaries; and see Burns, *Barbarians*, pp. 19–20, 22, and map, p. 20; Burns, *History of the Ostrogoths*, pp. 32–4; Wolfram, *History of the Goths*, p. 56.

34 Wolfram, *History of the Goths*, p. 101; and Kazanski, *Les Goths*, p. 25; see also Heather and Matthews, *The Goths*, p. 98, and pp. 57–8 and 63.

35 Burns, *History of the Ostrogoths*, pp. 139–42, and pictures on pp. 140–1.

36 Heather and Matthews, *The Goths*, p. 90 and pp. 82–4; on combs, see Heather, *The Goths*, pp. 81–3.

37 Heather and Matthews, *The Goths*, p. 93, and see pp. 71, 91.
38 Heather, *The Goths*, pp. 60–2, and see p. 58.
39 Heather, *Goths and Romans*, p. 107; Wolfram, *History of the Goths*, p. 62.
40 Zosimus, *New History*, tr. Ridley, bk 4:11, p. 75.
41 Wolfram, *History of the Goths*, p. 115; on use of the term, 'Scythian', see p. 11.
42 Ammianus Marcellinus, *Later Roman Empire*, p. 415.
43 See, e.g., Burns, *History of the Ostrogoths*, p. 38; Jordanes, *The Gothic History*, pp. 84ff; Heather, *The Goths*, pp. 55–7 and see p. 53, for Jordanes' debt to Ammianus.
44 Wolfram, *History of the Goths*, pp. 87–8.
45 Golden, *Introduction*, pp. 87, and see p. 89; see also Golden, *Khazar Studies*, 1:28; Maenchen-Helfen, *World of the Huns*, insisted that there was no connection between the two, but most modern specialists are less sceptical.
46 Altheim, *Attila*, ch. 2; Golden, *Introduction*, p. 86; Bona, *Hunnenreich*, p. 29.
47 Golden, *Introduction*, pp. 107–8; Maenchen-Helfen, *World of the Huns*, pp. 43–4; and see Sinor, 'The Hun period', in *CHEIA* (pp. 177–205), p. 182; and Artamonov, *Istoriya khazar*, p. 53.
48 Ammianus, *Later Roman Empire*, 3.2, p. xxxi.
49 Burns, *History of the Ostrogoths*, pp. 46–7 and see pp. 53–5; and Bona, *Hunnenreich*, pp. 12–13.
50 Ammianus, *Later Roman Empire*, bk 31, section 4, p. 417.
51 See Burns, *History of the Ostrogoths*; on this critical period, Ammianus, *Later Roman Empire*, bk 31, sections 4 and 5, pp. 416–19; and Heather, *Goths and Romans*, pp. 128–35.
52 Thompson, *History of Attila and The Huns*, pp. 48–56; Ammianus, *Later Roman Empire*, p. 412; however, Bona, *Hunnenreich*, pp. 25–9, argues that Ammianus, who had no direct knowledge of the Huns, underestimates the power and sophistication of their political structures.
53 Ammianus, *Later Roman Empire*, pp. 411–12.
54 Ibid., p. 412.
55 Heather, *The Goths*, pp. 102–8.
56 Pletneva, *Kochevniki*, p. 44–5.
57 Bona, *Hunnenreich*, p. 40; and see Thompson, *The Huns*, pp. 177–82.
58 Cited by Jordanes, *The Gothic History*, p. 101; on the site of Attila's capital, see the discussion in Thompson, *The Huns*, pp. 276–7.
59 Gordon, ed., *Age of Attila*, p. 84, and see p. 90; almost 800 years later, the Franciscan missionary, William of Rubruck, was as surprised as Priscus to find European craftsmen in a barbarian capital.
60 Pletneva, *Kochevniki*, p. 45.
61 See, e.g., Thompson, *The Huns*, p. 227, but see also, pp. 84–5 on the limits of Hunnic control in the Pontic steppes; and see pp. 79–80; see also Sinor, 'The Hun period', in *CHEIA*, p. 187.
62 Sinor, 'The Hun period', in *CHEIA*, p. 187–8.
63 Attila's name may come from the Turkic word for the Volga, 'Itil' (Golden, *Introduction*, p. 90); if so, this may mean he began his career in the Pontic steppes.
64 Gordon, *Age of Attila*, p. 74; and see Thompson, *The Huns*, pp. 71, 84, 89.
65 See, e.g., Gordon, *Age of Attila*, p. 94; see also p. 91.
66 Thompson, *The Huns*, p. 192, and see pp. 178–9, 181–2, 187–9.
67 Ibid., pp. 122, 139.
68 Maenchen-Helfen, *World of the Huns*, p. 180, and see p. 182; and see Sinor, 'The Hun period', in *CHEIA*, p. 190; Thompson, *The Huns*, pp. 99–101.

69 Maenchen-Helfen, *World of the Huns*, p. 275; but (p. 276–7) he doubts the authenticity of the dirge which is from Jordanes.
70 Sinor, 'The Hun period', in *CHEIA*, p. 196; on the size of the Hunnic armies, Maenchen-Helfen, *World of the Huns*, p. 213.
71 Jordanes, *The Gothic History*, p. 124.
72 See the superb analysis in Thompson, *The Huns*, pp. 199–202, which is based, in turn, on the ideas of Lattimore; on the ecological aspects of the problem, Sinor, 'Horse and Pasture', pp. 182–3.
73 Golden, *Introduction*, p. 92.
74 Lindner, 'Nomadism, horses and huns', pp. 14–15 and Sinor, 'The Hun period', in *CHEIA*, p. 204.
75 Barfield, *Perilous frontier*, ch. 3.
76 Golden, *Introduction*, p. 69.
77 from the 'Book of Wei', cited in Jagchid and Symons, *Peace, War, and Trade*, p. 170.
78 Golden, *Introduction*, p. 71; there have been no completely successful attempts to trace the etymology of the term.
79 Barfield, *Perilous Frontier*, p. 86–8; it was traditional in the Chinese army to measure the success of a campaign by the number of heads brought back; Jagchid and Symons, *Peace, War, and Trade*, p. 178, point out that the need to fulfil quotas encouraged the Chinese to execute non-combatants.
80 Barfield, *Perilous Frontier*, p. 97, and see p. 89; there is a good account of his career in de Crespigny, *Northern Frontier*, pp. 330–42; and see Ishjamts, 'Nomads in eastern Central Asia', in *HCCA*, 2:156.
81 Honey, *Medieval Hsiung-Nu*, p. 7; Barfield, *Perilous Frontier*, p. 101.
82 On Liu Yüan, see Honey, *Medieval Hsiung-Nu*.
83 Barfield, *Perilous Frontier*, p. 103.
84 Ibid. pp. 104–5.
85 Barfield, *Perilous Frontier*, p. 107, and see pp. 98, 106, 111.
86 Ibid., p. 111.
87 This is Golden's conclusion; *Introduction*, p. 74.
88 Golden, *Introduction*, p. 75.
89 Cited in Barfield, *Perilous Frontier*, p. 122.
90 Golden, *Introduction*, p. 75; on 'barbarization', see Yü, *Trade and Expansion*, pp. 213–15.
91 According to legend, a white horse brought the first Buddhist texts to Lo-yang, Liu, *Ancient India and Ancient China*, p. 85; see also Zürcher, *The Buddhist Conquest of China*, 1:28–38; Zürcher, 'Yüeh-chih and Kaniska', p. 356; and see Puri, *Buddhism in Central Asia*, pp. 12 and 7; and Litvinsky, 'Outline History of Buddhism in Central Asia', in Gafurov, et al., *Kushan Studies in USSR*, p. 68; on Buddhism under the T'o-pa, see Ch'en, *Buddhism in China*, ch. 6.
92 Liu, *Ancient China and Ancient India*, pp. 145, 155.
93 Golden, *Introduction*, p. 76–7; Sinor, 'Establishment...of the Türk empire', in *CHEIA* (pp. 285–316), 291.
94 Barfield, *Perilous Frontier*, pp. 120, 122.
95 Chavannes, *Documents sur les Tou-Kiue*, p. 221, and Sinor, 'Establishment...of the Türk empire', in *CHEIA*, p. 293.
96 Barfield, *Perilous Frontier*, pp. 124–6; Jagchid and Symons, *Peace, War, and Trade*, pp. 170–1 describes one spectacular consignment of 'gifts' to the Juan-juan leader; on links with the Hephthalites and Avars, Golden, *Introduction*, pp. 76–8.
97 Golden, *Introduction*, p. 79.

FURTHER READING

HCCA, vols 2 and 3, and *CHEIA*, are valuable for many parts of this chapter. There is room for a book on the Yüeh-chih and the Kushan Empire, a crucial, but long-neglected problem in World history. The best recent surveys are in *HCCA*, vol. 2; *CHEIA*; Golden, *Introduction to the History of the Trukic Peoples*; and Frye, *Heritage of Central Asia*. Chinese sources on the Yüeh-chih are summarized in Zürcher, 'Yüeh-chih and Kaniska', and accessible in Hulsewe, *China in Central Asia*, while other Chinese sources on this period are available in Chavannes, *Documents sur les Tou-Kiue*, and Beal, *Si-Yu-ki*. On Buddhism in Central Asia, see Puri, *Buddhism*, and Litvinsky, 'Outline History of Buddhism'. On both trade routes and religious exchanges between India and China, see Liu, *Ancient India and Ancient China*. On Central Asia before Islam, see Barthold, *Turkestan*; Staviskij, *La Bactriane*; and Frye, *Golden Age of Persia*, and *Heritage of Central Asia*. On the Goths, the most recent studies include: Heather and Matthews, *The Goths*; Heather, *Goths and Romans*, and the same author's, *The Goths*; Kazanski, *Les Goths*; Wolfram, *History of the Goths*; and Burns, *History of the Ostrogoths*. The main primary sources are Ammianus Marcellinus and Jordanes, though both must be treated with caution. On the Huns, see Maenchen-Helfen, *World of the Huns*; Thompson, *A History of Attila and the Huns* (the revised edition includes an essay by Heather bringing it up to date); and Altheim, *Attila und die Hunnen*. Two brief surveys are Sinor, 'The Hun period', in *CHEIA*, pp. 177–205, and Sinor, 'The historical Attila'. On the archaeology of the Huns, see Bona, *Hunnenreich*. The main primary sources are Ammianus Marcellinus and Priscus. There are translations of Priscus' account of his embassy to Attila in Gordon, *Age of Attila*, and Blockley, *The Fragmentary Classicising Historians*. See also, Lindner, 'Nomadism, horses and Huns', and Sinor, 'Horse and pasture', on the ecological difficulties the Huns faced in Hungary. The most recent history of Byzantium is Treadgold, *A History of the Byzantine State and Society*. On the eastern steppes in this period, the best overview is in Barfield, *Perilous Frontier*. See also Jagchid and Symons, *Peace, War, and Trade*; Honey, *The Rise of the Medieval Hsiung-Nu*; and Golden, *Introduction to the History of the Turkic Peoples*.

Part IV

Turks, Mawara'n-Nahr and Rus':
500–1200

[10] TURKIC EMPIRES OF THE EAST

In the mid-sixth century, 750 years after the creation of the Hsiung-nu empire, a dynasty from the Altai region, ruling a confederation of mainly Turkic-speaking peoples, and building on the achievements of the Juan-juan, created a steppe empire that reached even further than that of the Hsiung-nu. The Türk empire broke up in less than a century, then reformed, then fell apart again into its tribal components. A successor empire, that of the Uighurs, collapsed a century later, in 840. The final collapse of these empires, like that of the Hsiung-nu, scattered fragments

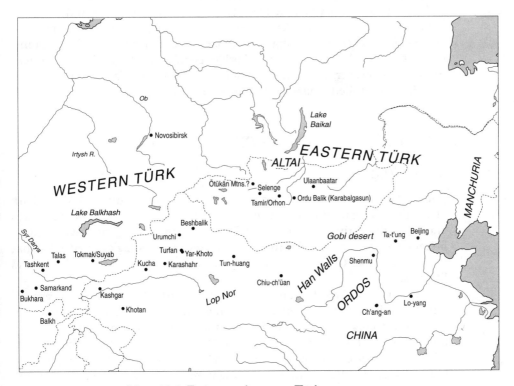

Map 10.1 Eastern and western Türks.

through the steppes and borderlands of southern Inner Eurasia, and reordered the politics, the demography and the culture of lands from Byzantium to Korea for several centuries.

THE TURKIC LANGUAGES

Most specialists agree that the Turkic and Mongolian languages constitute a distinct family within the larger, 'Altaic' group of languages, which includes Manchu/Tungusic, Korean and perhaps Japanese. Western Mongolian tribes, such as those referred to in Chinese sources of the Hsiung-nu era as 'Ting-ling', probably spoke early forms of Turkic, while eastern tribes, from the 'Tung-hu' or 'Hsien-pi' groups, probably spoke early forms of Mongolian. Gradually, it seems, the western dialects turned into ancient Turkic, while eastern dialects laid the foundations for Mongolian.[1]

The migrations that followed the break-up of the Hsiung-nu empire drew early Turkic speakers westwards. So there were probably many Turkic speakers within the Hephthalite and Hunnic confederations. From at least the time of Attila, we know that there were Turkic-speaking tribes in the Pontic steppes. These belonged to the 'Oghur' grouping, which probably migrated westwards from the Ting-ling/T'ieh-le tribes based north of Mongolia and in the Irtysh valley.[2] Today, Oghur Turkish survives only in modern Chuvash.

By the sixth century, Turkic dialects were already spoken from the Altai to the borders of Byzantium. As they spread, absorbing other peoples and new cultural influences, the groups that spoke these dialects created 'the ethnic foundation blocks for the later Turkic peoples of Central and Western Eurasia'.[3] However, it was the creation of a Turkic empire in the sixth century that established a distinctive 'Turkic' identity.

THE FIRST TÜRK EMPIRES: 552–630

THE TÜRK

Before the discovery and decipherment of the eighth-century Orkhon Türk inscriptions in the late nineteenth and early twentieth century, little was known of the early Türk empires.[4] However, since then, intensive study of literary sources (above all from China) and archaeological materials, has made it possible to construct a quite detailed account of their history and lifeways.

Many attempts have been made to identify 'Turks' before the sixth century, but the earliest clearly attested use of the ethnonym, 'Türk' (T'u-chüeh in Chinese), occurs in Chinese sources of the sixth century describing the creation of the first Türk empire.[5] Like the Hsiung-nu or Scythian empires, that of the Türk was ethnically and linguistically heterogenous. Its diverse origins are reflected in the contradictory origin myths contained in Turkic and Chinese sources. Early Chinese sources described the Türk as descendants of the Hsiung-nu, but this is at best a half-truth. That the Türk leaders were aware of some sort of cultural or political continuity with the Hsiung-nu is suggested by the importance they attached to the Tamir river, a western tributary of the Orkhon, and to the mountains of Ötükän, west of the Tamir, in the Hangai range. However, there is no sign of any dynastic links with the Hsiung-nu. On the contrary, origin myths suggest a clear genealogical break by deriving the Türk from the sole surviving member of a much older people. According to some legends, the ruling clan, the A-shih-na, was descended from a young boy whose tribe was destroyed by its neighbours. Though he was spared, his hands and feet were cut off. A she-wolf looked after him, and eventually, after fleeing to a cave in the Altai mountains, she bore and reared ten of his children. (The earliest of all Türk inscriptions, written in Sogdian in c.582, and found in Bugut in Mongolia in 1968, is accompanied by a representation of a wolf standing over a figure with no arms and legs.) It may be that we can identify the migration referred to in these legends, for, according to the historical Sui annals, in 439, after the T'o-pa conquest of eastern Kansu, a group of 500 families under a leader called A-shih-na fled to Kao-ch'ang (=Kocho, near Turfan). From there, they were driven north into the remote valleys of the eastern Altai, where they became metalworkers and subjects of the Juan-juan.[6] Perhaps, as Sinor has suggested, the 'caves' of these legends were the mines from which Turkic miners supplied A-shi-na metalworkers with their raw materials. The A-shih-na themselves may have spoken Hunnic, Hsien-pi or perhaps even Sogdian or Tocharian. However, the people they came to rule in the Altai spoke an eastern form of Turkic which eventually became the main language of the Türk empire.[7] Other origin myths refer to homelands north of the Hsiung-nu empire, or even to a homeland near the 'Western sea', which may reflect memories of participation in Hunnic migrations to the west.

Different myths probably derive from different components of the Türk association of tribes. Clearly, the 'Türk' were never just pastoralists, but drew on many different ecological traditions, from the metalworking traditions of the Altai, to the commercial and agrarian traditions of the Kansu corridor and the Turfan region. The achievement of the A-shih-na was to create a single political and cultural identity from these diverse traditions, and extend that identity to Mongolia in the east and the Caspian steppes in the west.

CREATION OF THE FIRST TÜRK EMPIRE: 552–81

In 534, the northern Wei (T'o-pa) dynasty divided into a western branch, based on Ch'ang-an (the western Wei, or Chou), and an eastern branch (the eastern Wei, or Ch'i), based on Lo-yang. The split created great instability along China's northern borders and opened new opportunities for frontier tribes of the Juan-juan federation.

According to the earliest Chinese references, the Türk appeared soon after this split as a powerful, if subordinate, group of tribes within the Juan-juan empire. They had a strong leader called T'u-men, who controlled the lands once ruled by the Yüeh-chih, from the Ordos to the Altai. Their armies used traditional steppe tactics, including ambushes, and rapid advances and retreats. For initial shock attacks, they had an aristocratic corps of heavy cavalry, known as 'wolves', who wore metal armour made by Türk metalworkers, and rode large, stall-fed horses.[8]

The first dated mention of the Türk occurs under the year 542. According to the historical Chou annals, for several years before this, the Türk had launched annual invasions of Shen-si province south of modern Shen-mu, as soon as the Yellow River froze over.[9] In 542, a new Chinese governor, Yü-Wen, tricked the Türk invaders into thinking that a huge Chinese army had been sent against them. In their disorderly retreat they left behind most of their booty, and their annual invasions ceased.

Clearly, the Türk were already a substantial force, for the local populations were used to hiding in fortified towns as soon as the Türk appeared. They must also have been relatively independent of their Juan-juan overlords, for in 545, their leader, T'u-men, tried to negotiate directly with the Western Wei for the purchase of silk. Western Wei officials took this as a sign of the growing power, maturity and commercial connections of the Türk, for T'u-men's request showed that his people were already trading goods from China to Central Asia.[10] Impressed by their power, the Western Wei began to see the Türk as potential allies against the Eastern Wei, who had close ties with the Juan-juan. In 545 the Western Wei sent an embassy to T'u-men. Leading the delegation was a Sogdian from the trading oasis of Chiu-ch'üan in Kansu province. Understanding that the embassy implied diplomatic recognition, T'u-men welcomed it, and sent a return embassy a year later.[11]

Soon after this, Türk armies suppressed a rebellion against the Juan-juan by a group of T'ieh-le tribes, who had formed a semi-autonomous empire (Kao-ch'e) in eastern Kazakhstan. However, instead of surrendering the defeated T'ieh-le to the Juan-juan, the Türk absorbed them within their own armies. With an enlarged army, T'u-men challenged the Juan-juan leader, A-na-kuei (520–52), by demanding a royal bride. A-na-kuei responded in insulting terms, describing T'u-men as his blacksmith and slave. In 551, T'u-men asked for, and received, a marriage alliance with the Western Wei. The next year, with a contingent of western Wei troops, he moved east and defeated the Juan-juan in Jehol province, north of modern Beijing. A-na-kuei committed suicide, leaving T'u-men the most powerful leader in the eastern steppes. T'u-men exchanged his former title of *yabghu* for the supreme title of *kaghan*, while his brother, Ishtemi (552–76), took the title of *yabghu*. In the Orkhon descriptions, written almost two hundred years later, the Türk of this period are called the 'Gök Türk'. The adjective, 'Gök' can be translated as 'blue', or 'heavenly', or even 'divine', and grants a semi-divine status to these founding figures.[12]

While T'u-men retained overall authority, and ruled the senior, eastern wing of the empire, from a base in the eastern Hangai mountains in Mongolia, Ishtemi ruled the western part of the empire from a winter camp near Karashahr. We can probably imagine these pastoralist capitals as large open areas covered with many felt tents, some of exceptional grandeur, and arranged in strict ceremonial order. The camps were probably large and permanent enough to attract small populations of farmers or farming pastoralists. The great ceremonial centres of the empire, the ancestral caves in the Altai, and the Ötükän mountains, lay between the winter camps of the two main leaders, so that contact between the empire's major centres was relatively easy.[13] The division of power survived T'u-men's death in 552, the succession and death of his first son, Kou-lo (553) the same year, and the succession of his second son, Muhan (r. 553–72). Ishtemi accepted Muhan's authority, apparently without question. A similar division between eastern and western wings had existed even earlier in the Juan-juan and Hsiung-nu empires, and it was probably a natural response to the severe logistical differences of ruling so large a territory without a developed bureaucracy.[14]

Muhan and Ishtemi now began hunting down the remnants of the Juan-juan and consolidating and expanding their empire. Muhan extended his power to Manchuria, where he defeated the Kitan. He also imposed his rule over the Kirghiz tribes in the Yenisei region to the north-west. He undoubtedly exacted tributes from the non-Turkic regions subject to him, but it was the wealth of China that was the key to Türk power. For almost 30 years, Muhan and his brother and successor, T'o-po (572–81), played the two states of north China against each other. They kept up the pressure with periodic booty raids, or by supporting one dynasty against the other.[15] For a time, they extracted from China huge amounts of silk and other luxury goods such as linens, gold, jade, vases, clothing, wine and ceremonial coaches, in return for steppe produce, of which the most important was horses. Under Muhan, the Chou dynasty sent 100,000 rolls of silk each year. In a desperate attempt to buy the allegiance of T'o-po, the eastern Wei (Ch'i) dynasty brought itself close to bankruptcy. Chinese luxury goods sustained the power of the Türk empire by providing the wealth that bound the alliance system together. The trade goods passed on to the western branch of the empire were used in diplomacy or trade with Iran and Byzantium. As Barfield writes: 'The silk trade was a major agent binding the Turkish empire together.[16]

Relations with the two dynasties of north China led to a degree of Sinicization. The Türk leaders negotiated marriage ties with both dynasties, and many Türks began to live in Ch'ang-an, particularly after the marriage of Muhan's daughter to the Chou emperor, Wu-ti, in 568. In Ch'ang-an, Türks lived in luxury, at the expense of the Chinese treasury, and many became Chinese in tastes and culture. Chinese culture also began to penetrate the steppes. T'o-po was attracted by Buddhism, the favoured religion of the Ch'i. With Ch'i help, he built Buddhist temples, had Buddhist scriptures translated into Turkish, and supported missionary activity amongst his people.[17]

In the western Türk empire, the great powers were more remote, and revenues had to be extracted through the manipulation of trade routes (with the help of Sogdian merchants) or by taking tributes from large numbers of petty local rulers. The western Türk never managed to extract more than token gifts from the great powers of Persia or Byzantium. At first, Ishtemi's forces moved west in pursuit of remnants of the Juan-juan empire. Although the details of this campaign are obscure, it seems likely that by 555, Ishtemi's power already reached to the Aral Sea. In about 558, he defeated the remnants of the Chionite Huns, who soon appeared in the Pontic steppes as 'Avars'. These victories extended his power to the Volga.[18] In 557, he concluded an alliance with the Sassanian emperor, Khosrow I, who married his daughter. In 562, the two armies attacked the Hephthalite empire. Türk armies took Chach (Tashkent) in 564, and the Hephthalites were finally crushed in 565 near Nesef (Karshi). A Türk/Sassanian border was established along the Amu Darya, and the A-shih-na became the new overlords of Central Asia east and north of the river. The new frontier survived despite a brief war between the two empires in 569, after Ishtemi demanded that Persia pay him the tributes they had once paid the Hephthalites.

Within 15 years, the A-shih-na had established Gök Türk suzerainty from the Volga to Manchuria, creating the first empire to dominate most of southern Inner Eurasia. With the capture of the North Caucasus in 567–71, and (with Utrighur help) of Bosporus (modern Kerch), in 576, the power of the Gök Türk reached to the Black Sea.[19] However, outside of western Mongolia, most of the peoples of the western empire were not, strictly, 'Türk'. Few identified their fate with that of the empire, so their loyalty had to be maintained through superior military force, and the redistribution of a steady flow of tributes and trade goods.

Almost two centuries later, the achievements of T'u-men and Ishtemi were celebrated in the Orkhon inscriptions, erected by the kaghans of the second Türk empire.

> When high above the blue sky and down below the brown earth had been created, betwixt the two were created the sons of men. And above the sons of men stood my ancestors, the kaghans Bumin [T'u-men] and Ishtemi. Having become the masters of the Türk people, they installed and ruled its empire and fixed the law of the country. Many were their enemies in the four corners of the world, but, leading campaigns against them, they subjugated and pacified many nations in the four corners of the world. They caused them to bow their heads and to bend their knees.[20]

This passage shows how little knowledge survived in the steppes of the Hsiung-nu empire. It also conveys well a heroic view of history which, though it may seem naive to a modern reader, was quite realistic in a world where the fortunes of each family, each camping group, and each clan depended mainly on the skill and good fortune of its leaders.[21] The success of the first Türk empire was due mainly to the political and military skills of T'u-men and Ishtemi, even though they built on foundations already laid by the Juan-juan.

POLITICAL, CULTURAL AND ECONOMIC ASPECTS

HOW DID THE NEW EMPIRE FUNCTION?

We have seen already that the material and cultural resources that sustained pastoralist empires had to come mainly from the agrarian world. Like the

Hsiung-nu, the Türk extracted resources both from the Chinese and from the commercial cities and towns of Central Asia. Until the establishment of the Sui dynasty in 581, the Türks, as the most formidable military force in the Chinese borderlands, were in an extremely good position to exact Chinese luxury goods through trade or in the form of gifts. In the West, trade was more important than tribute, and Ishtemi's diplomatic efforts were concerned as much with the silk trade as with territorial expansion. His commercial ambitions were sustained and guided by Sogdian traders with long experience of the trade's many nuances. As a Sui general complained: 'The Turks themselves are simple-minded and short-sighted and dissension can easily be roused among them. Unfortunately, many Sogdians live among them who are cunning and insidious; they teach and instruct the Turks.'[22] Sogdians had merchant communities along the entire length of the Silk Road, from at least the date of the 'Old Sogdian Letters', which were written in the early fourth century by Sogdians settled in Tun-huang. By the sixth century, Sogdian had become the main language of commerce along the eastern Silk Roads, and it soon became the lingua franca of the western Türk empire.[23]

Ishtemi's early contacts with Persia were shaped partly by a desire to control the trade routes through Hephthalite lands. Once the Hephthalites were defeated, commercial interests soon drove the allies apart, as the Sassanians, like the Parthians before them, preferred to restrict the flow of trade goods to Byzantium. A Sogdian merchant called Maniakh persuaded Ishtemi to send an embassy to Shah Khosrow requesting that Sogdian merchants be permitted to sell raw silk in Persia. Khosrow refused, and when a second Türk delegation arrived, he had its members poisoned. In 569, western Türk armies invaded across the Amu Darya, but made little progress against the great Sassanian system of fortifications based on Merv, and the two great powers made peace two years later, in 571. For several decades, the Amu Darya remained the border between the two empires. Another Türk attempt to conquer the Hephthalite lands beyond the Amu Darya in 588–9 and was crushed by a Sassanian army under Bahram Chobin, one of the folk heroes of middle Persian epic.[24]

On Maniakh's advice, Ishtemi now tried to open up the northern Silk Roads to Byzantium, which had fallen into disuse since the Hunnic invasions of the fourth century. This project threatened to break the Sassanian monopoly over the flow of resources to the Mediterranean, which had tightened with the Sassanian conquest of parts of the Arabian peninsula. For Sogdian merchants, the plan offered a way of bypassing the Jewish and Syrian rivals who controlled the routes through Syria. Western Türk embassies had visited Constantinople as early as 558 and again in 563. In 568, Maniakh led a third delegation, which carried a gift of raw silk, and a letter from Ishtemi.[25] Though the Byzantine emperor, Justin II, revealed that Byzantium could now produce its own silk, having smuggled silkworms from the east, he was clearly interested in the possibility of a military alliance with the Türk. In August 569, he sent a return embassy, led by a Byzantine official called Zemarkhos. This returned, a year later, with a caravan load of silks from the

Türk leader, Ishtemi. Though relations with Byzantium were never smooth (particularly after the Utrighurs, with Türk support, seized Bosporus in c.576), commerce between the two regions flourished as the northern Silk Road revived. Sogdian and Khorezmian merchants profited from control of the northern route, as did the cities of Crimea.[26]

These developments stimulated a revival of trade and of cultural contacts right across the Eurasian land mass. Samarkand became something of a boom town, and a potent symbol of the commercial alliance between Türks and Sogdians. As the capital of Sogdia, and the region's most powerful and influential city, the western Türk kaghans treated it with considerable respect. Its traditional ruling dynasty was left in power and kaghan Tardu even married his daughter to its ruler. The Chinese Buddhist, Hsüan-tsang, visited the town in 630, and wrote:

> Its capital was about 20 *li* in circuit, exceedingly strong and with a large population. The country was a great commercial entrepot, was very fertile, abounding in trees and flowers, and yielding many fine horses. Its inhabitants were skillful craftsmen, smart and energetic. All the Hu States regarded this country as their centre and made its social institutions their model. The king was a man of spirit and courage and was obeyed by the neighbouring states. He had a splendid army.[27]

As Beckwith has argued, 'that the silk routes remained in the hands of a people interested as much in trade as in warfare was of great import to the countries at the extremities of the trade routes as well as to those in between.'[28] The vigorous commercial contacts established by the Türk created a new 'world-system', linking the Mediterranean, the Near East, Persia, India and China. It also stimulated new trade networks through Khorezm and along the Volga river, which laid the foundations for the power of the Khazars and, later, the Viking Rus'. Further east, it enhanced the significance of the small oasis principality of Kao-ch'ang (Kocho, near Turfan).[29]

Administratively, the Türk empire was, like all pastoralist states, an 'imperial confederacy'. As Barfield has argued, such systems were

> autocratic and statelike in foreign affairs, but consultative and federally structured internally. They consisted of an administrative hierarchy with at least three levels: the imperial leader and his court, imperial governors appointed to oversee the component tribes within the empire, and indigenous tribal leaders.[30]

Though the sources are not entirely clear, we can be sure that the Türk kaghans, like Motun or Attila, had personal retinues. These probably included the heavily armoured knights known, totemically, as 'wolves', who formed the main strike force of the Türk armies. They had a special temple north of the Yellow River, where they gathered, fed their horses, and offered sacrifices before campaigning in north China.[31] Members of the royal family and regional chiefs were bound into the Türk system by the granting of gifts and a complex system of ranks and titles that borrowed freely from Sogdian and Chinese traditions. Those titles with the greatest prestige (*Shad*, *Yabghu* and *Tegin*) were held by members of the royal family, but lesser titles went to regional chiefs and officials.[32]

The Türk kaghans made conscious efforts to impress followers and outsiders with their wealth and splendour. At their winter camps, the two kaghans lived with their retinues in great splendour. In 569, the Byzantine ambassador, Zemarkhos, visited the winter camp of Ishtemi, at 'Golden Mountain', which was probably in the T'ien Shan mountains, north-west of Karashahr, though some scholars have placed it in the Türk homelands in the Altai. Zemarkhos was led before Ishtemi, who sat on a 'golden throne with two wheels, which could be drawn when necessary by one horse', in a tent with dyed silk hangings. The following day, he met Ishtemi in another dwelling, decorated with silk hangings and many statues. Here, 'Sizabul [Ishtemi] sat...on a couch made completely of gold. In the middle of the building were golden urns, water-sprinklers and also golden pitchers.'[33] The next day, the embassy was entertained in another dwelling, in which there was 'a couch of beaten gold which was supported by four golden peacocks. In front of this dwelling were drawn up over a wide area wagons containing many silver objects, dishes and bowls, and a large number of statues of animals, also of silver and in no way inferior to those which we make; so wealthy is the ruler of the Turks.'[34]

Like the Hsiung-nu, the Türk kaghans held annual gatherings of regional chiefs, which helped bind together the various groups that made up the empire. According to the Chou annals, 'Each year, the [eastern] kaghan led his chiefs to the ancestral caves [in the Altai] to offer sacrifices; in the fifth month, they gathered at the river Tamir to sacrifice to the God of the Heavens.'[35] These gatherings were great public festivals, like the modern Naadam festival or the classical Greek Olympic games. According to the Sui annals:

> the Türk slaughtered sheep and horses as sacrifices for the Heavens. The men played at dice, while the women played [a form of] football. They drank fermented mare's milk until they were drunk. Then they sang and cried out to each other.[36]

As long as the kaghans had the wealth and prestige to organize such gatherings and reward those who attended them, the unity of the empire's Türk core was likely to hold.

Holding the loyalty of non-Türk peoples was more difficult. Regional governors of various kinds controlled the provinces. By the reign of T'o-po, the empire's two halves were each split into four main sections, each ruled by a member of the royal family. Gumilev has suggested that there existed a system similar to that of Kievan Rus', under which members of the royal family moved by seniority from region to region. If so, this may have been a way of maintaining the power and unity of the A-shih-na dynasty, by rewarding loyalty within the family, and preventing the emergence of regional ties.[37]

Below the level of the royal family and the nobles or 'begs', it is possible to identify two more strata in ordinary Türk society: the pastoralists, whose young men fought in the Türk armies and were known as *er* or 'warriors', and those too poor to live as pastoralists. The poorer pastoralists often attached themselves to rich nobles as bodyguards or servants. However, those too poor to own horses were often settled as farmers in small villages. Such people lacked status as well as wealth in a society where the possession of wealth was seen as proof of valour and skill in arms. At the bottom of the Türk hierarchy were the slaves, usually war captives, and overwhelmingly female. (Male captives were often killed as they were regarded as more dangerous to their captors.) Their labour, and that of free Türk women, allowed the majority of Türk men to concentrate on warfare, while warfare, in turn, generated a steady supply of new captives/slaves. As the Orkhon inscriptions show, the Türk kaghans regarded the maintenance of this hierarchy as the key to the survival of the Türk people and state. Warfare was the foundation of the entire system, for it sustained the wealth and prestige of Türk nobles and warriors, and maintained a constant supply of slaves.[38]

The religious beliefs of the Türk varied greatly, and were influenced by several of the major religious traditions of China and Eurasia. However, most early Türk groups seem to have worshipped the Sky and the Earth, as well as a female deity of the household, known as Umay. Political ceremonials, which may show some Chinese influence, aimed at securing the blessing of the Heavens. Kaghans were treated as semi-divine figures, whose blood could not be shed, even when they were executed.[39] There are also clear shamanic elements in the rituals of enthronement of a new kaghan, with motifs of death, rebirth and distant journeyings.

> When a new ruler is chosen, the most senior amongst his retinue wrap him in a felt carpet [mimicking execution? DGC], and turn him around nine times. At each turn, his subjects bow down before him. Then he is helped on to a horse and allowed to ride. Then a silken scarf is put around his throat and is tightened until he is barely alive. Then it is loosened, and he is quickly asked: 'How many years will you be our kaghan?' As the kaghan is barely conscious, he cannot answer clearly, but they interpret his words as a sign of how long he will be in office.[40]

As Liu Mau-tsai has pointed out, this ceremony, so similar in many ways to the initiation of a shaman, suggests that there was a strong priestly element in the authority of a kaghan.[41] Indeed, the old Turkic word, *kam* (shaman), may be related to the word for 'blood' or 'lineage' (*kan*), and both meanings may be present in the earliest forms of the word, 'khan'.[42] Turkic shamans were particularly good at using special stones or *yat*s, to control the weather, often to gain a tactical advantage in battle. Other rituals suggest the importance of ancestor worship, while Türk origin myths hint at forms of totemism, in which wolves were particularly important. The seventh-century Byzantine writer, Theophylactus Simocattes, recorded that the Türks worshipped fire, as well as water and earth; that they had priests who foretold the future; and that they worshipped the god of the heavens above all.[43] In one of the earliest of all written descriptions of a shamanic trance, Menander recounts the purification ritual that Zemarkhos was forced to undergo when he first entered the Türk empire. The baggage of Zemarkhos' party was placed on the ground, and:

> They then began ringing a bell and beating a kind of drum over the baggage, whilst some ran round it carrying leaves of burning incense, flaming and crackling, and raged about like maniacs, gesticulating as if repelling evil spirits. Carrying on this exorcism of evil as they considered it, they made Zemarchus himself also pass through the fire.[44]

Close relations with China and Sogdia ensured that the culture of the Türk elites was pervaded with foreign influences. Most bureaucratic titles were borrowed. Sogdian traders also introduced writing systems. Two different writing systems appeared, both derived from Sogdian scripts, themselves ultimately of Aramaic origin. One was certainly in use by the late sixth century. The other, runic script, seems to have developed later (the first surviving example dates to the late seventh century), and many of the Orkhon runes were in fact carved by Chinese craftsmen.[45]

FRAGMENTATION AND DECLINE: 581–630

The Sinicization of parts of the Türk elite, a prolonged famine in the steppes, the emergence of a united Chinese dynasty, the Sui, in 581, and a succession crisis beginning with the death of T'o-po in the same year, combined to undermine the unity of the first Türk empire.

Leadership was crucial in the pastoralist world, and the decline of Türk power began with a succession dispute brought on because the most legitimate candidates for the kaghanate lacked the political and military skills needed to secure loyalty. Divisions at the top encouraged regional leaders, particularly those who did not belong to the ruling Türk tribes, to assert their independence, often with Chinese support. In this way, minor fissures widened into chasms that eventually destroyed the empire.

T'u-men and his brothers, Muhan and T'o-po, like Ishtemi and his son, Tardu (r. 576–603), in the west, had been strong and capable leaders. However, T'o-po's son, An-lo (581) was too pacific, and Muhan's son, Ta-lo-pien, was too combative to attract a strong and steady following. More capable were their cousins, She-tu (581–7) and Ch'u-lo-hu (588), whose claims to the throne were less direct. In his will, T'o-po passed the throne to Ta-lo-pien. However, at an assembly held in the Orkhon lands after T'o-po's death, She-tu and many others refused to accept Ta-lo-pien as kaghan because of his mother's low birth. Instead, they insisted that the throne go to An-lo. She-tu even threatened to leave the empire and defend the borders of his own lands 'with his sharp sword and his long spear'.[46] However, An-lo soon resigned from the leadership, and transferred power to She-tu, who was accepted as kaghan on the grounds that he was the 'wisest' of the sons of the first generation of kaghans.

The uncertain authority of the new kaghan was soon tested by the Sui emperor, Wen-ti (581–604). Less in need of Türk military support than his predecessors, Wen-ti stopped sending gifts to the Türks and expelled Türk residents of the capital, Ch'ang-an. Threatened with the loss of the Chinese 'gifts' and trade goods that had sustained Türk power, She-tu organized a huge raid into northern China in 582 with the support of the western kaghan, Tardu. Despite initial successes, in late 582, Tardu kaghan made a separate peace with the Chinese and withdrew his armies.

The Chinese now began to operate a systematic *Politik der Spaltung*.[47] A Chinese agent, Tsch'ang-sun Scheng, who had befriended She-tu before he became kaghan, and had spent some time among the Türk, understood well the personal and tribal conflicts within the Türk empire. On his advice, the Chinese government began to support She-tu's rivals within the royal family, and non-Türk tribes subordinate to the A-shih-na. In 584, fed by the Chinese with rumours of disloyalty within his own family, She-tu attacked the camp of Ta-lo-pien in 584 and killed his rival's mother. The attack provoked the first of many civil wars amongst the Türk. Ta-lo-pien fled to Tardu kaghan, taking several other Türk leaders with him, including She-tu's brother, Ch'u-lo-hu.[48] Tardu supplied them with a powerful new army, and Ta-lo-pien returned and attacked She-tu. In 584, both She-tu and Tardu offered to accept Chinese suzerainty in return for support, and the resumption of the exchanges of trade goods and gifts that were so vital for both kaghanates. After She-tu's death, in 587, his successor, Ch'u-lo-hu, briefly reunited the empire and crushed the still independent Ta-lo-pien, before turning on his former patron, Tardu. Ch'u-lo-hu was killed in battle with Tardu and the two wings of the empire began a new war that lasted until 593. Tardu now emerged as the most powerful figure in the empire. However, the kaghanal title was held by a son of She-tu, Yung-yü-lü, and he and Tardu had many old scores to settle.

The question that always faced ambitious, but weak leaders in the steppes was whether or not to play the China card, by accepting Chinese suzerainty in return for help against rivals. Rulers too weak to adopt what Barfield has called the 'Outer Frontier Strategy', could always consider the 'Inner Frontier Strategy' instead. Such manoeuvres created pro- and anti-China parties in the steppe, and Chinese diplomats exploited such divisions adroitly. Tsch'ang-sun Scheng, despatched to the steppes again in 594, gave his support to the new kaghan's cousin and rival, Jan-kan, who was too weak to pose a serious threat to China, but, if settled in north China, might provide a useful barrier against the Türk.[49] The offer to Jan-kan of a marriage alliance, and the many gifts that entailed, was enough to create a strong pro-Chinese party within the eastern kaghanate, but drove the new kaghan to ally more closely with Tardu. In 597, the Chinese helped Jan-kan settle, with his people, in the Ordos steppes.

The following year, the reformed Sui armies, now supported by Jan-kan and his followers, attacked Tardu and the eastern kaghan, Yung-yü-lü. Tardu's army was defeated, and Yung-yü-lü was murdered by agents recruited from the followers of Jan-kan. This left the Chinese puppet, Jan-kan, as the legitimate heir to the kaghanate.[50] Though still powerful, Tardu lacked legitimacy, and his reputation was tarnished by his defeat. Exploiting his weakness, the Chinese offered money and arms to subordinate tribes of northern Mongolia such as the T'ieh-le, and persuaded them to reject Tardu's authority. Tardu fled to the Tibetan Togon empire in modern Ch'ing Hai, where he was killed. His son, the kaghan of Bukhara, travelled to China in 604 to offer his submission but was arrested there. Meanwhile, the Chinese emperor declared Jan-kan the new Türk kaghan, and allowed him to return to the steppes. The T'ieh-le uprising ended with the withdrawal of Chinese support, but the western empire and the Tarim basin had been lost permanently to the eastern Türk kaghan, and in future, the T'ieh-le and the T'ang were frequently to ally against the Türk.[51]

I have analysed the breakdown of the first Türk empire in some detail, as it shows the mechanisms that led to the fragmentation of successive steppe empires. The Türk themselves were aware of many of the reasons for the breakdown of the first Türk empire. The Orkhon inscriptions offer a political and cultural analysis of the problem:

> the deeds of the younger brothers did not match those of the older brothers [T'u-men and Ishtemi], and the sons did not match the fathers, so, it seems, there appeared kaghans who were less able and lacked courage, and their officials were also less able and lacked courage. As a result of the falling away [literally 'lack of straightness'] of the rulers and the people, as a result of tale-bearers and the deceit of people from China, ... and also because the Chinese created conflicts between younger and older brothers and armed the people and rulers against each other, the Türk people fell into disarray.[52]

What this indigenous analysis misses is the economic aspect of the problem. Pastoral states were held together by the authority of strong leaders who dominated other groups of pastoralists and secured resources from the agrarian world. The slightest weakening of central authority – doubts about the legitimacy or the political and military skills of a new leader, or challenges from legitimate rivals – or a failure to maintain a steady flow of goods from outside, allowed cracks to appear in the system. These divided the ruling dynasties, and alienated subordinate tribes for whom the empire had always lacked legitimacy. As fissures appeared, rivals within the royal family challenged for power and sought allies among other tribal groups or amongst the Chinese. The penetration of Chinese money, luxury goods and culture made it particularly easy to form pro-Chinese factions. (According to a Chinese source, in 630 some 10,000 Türk families were living permanently in Ch'ang-an, and presumably they all had ties with families in the steppes.)[53] The segmentary structures of all pastoralist states meant that, when the unity of the central leadership broke down, they fragmented easily into their various components.

After 603, there were two distinct Türk empires, both of which accepted the nominal suzerainty of China. Both were powerful, but neither could match the power or prestige of the united empire they replaced. The eastern empire controlled Mongolia and parts of eastern Sinkiang. In much of this region, Türk tribes were the dominant ethnic and linguistic group, ruling a motley collection of T'ieh-le and Hsien-pi tribes. In the western empire,

Türk control was more indirect and mediated, to a greater extent by the influence of Sogdian merchants and advisers. The western empire also controlled large urban populations stretching from Tokharistan (Bactria) into modern Sinkiang. Here, 'The Turkic tribes were located at strategic points from which they could lash out at rebellious elements.'[54] From its base in the Semirechye region, the western empire controlled the central steppes and Sogdia, and much of the western Tarim basin from Karashahr to Kashgar.

For the next 30 years, the power of individual leaders waxed and waned erratically. The collapse of the Sui dynasty in 618, and the rise of the T'ang dynasty, shifted the balance of power temporarily in favour of the steppes again. Hsieh-li, kaghan of the eastern Türk (r. 620–34), returned to a strategy of raiding, but failed to establish a durable tributary relationship with the T'ang, and alienated many Türks by relying mainly on Chinese and Sogdian advisers. Between 627 and 629, appalling weather conditions caused severe livestock losses and famine, and brought his government near to collapse. In 630 a Chinese army captured him, and he died in captivity. His defeat ended the independent authority of the first eastern Türk empire. In its place there emerged several Turkic and non-Turkic tribal federations, all of which accepted Chinese suzerainty, and helped defend China's northern frontiers, in return for recognition, payment in kind, and a degree of independence.

In the west, the fall of Tardu led to a period of weakness and disunity. However, under kaghan Shih Kuei (611–18), central authority was restored from the Altai to the far west. Under his brother, T'ung yabghu kaghan (618–30), the western Türk flourished. T'ung yabghu kaghan reasserted his authority over the T'ieh-le tribes, helped the Byzantine emperor, Heraclius, in his wars in the Caucasus, maintained good relations with the T'ang, who promised him a daughter in marriage, and sent envoys known as *tudun*s to supervise the domains from which he took tribute.[55] He also conquered the former Hephthalite lands south of the Amu Darya. It was probably T'ung yabghu khaghan that the Chinese Buddhist pilgrim, Hsüan-tsang, saw in his full glory in 630, near the modern Kirghiz city of Tokmak, just months before the kaghan's death and the collapse of his empire. Hsüan-tsang met him and his entourage preparing for a royal hunt.

> The khan wore a green satin robe; his hair which was ten feet long was free: a band of white silk was wound round his forehead hanging down behind. The ministers of the presence ['ta-kuan', probably derived from 'tarkhan'], above 200 in number, all wearing embroidered robes and with plaited hair stood on his right and left. The rest of his military retinue clothed in fur, serge, and fine wool, the spears and standards and bows in order, and the riders of camels and horses stretched far away out of ken.[56]

Three days later, the kaghan returned from his hunt, and formally entertained the pilgrim with food and music in a tent with golden embroidery. He then provided him with an interpreter and letters of introduction to rulers from Semirechye to Kapitsa (near Kabul), all of whom owed the kaghan suzerainty.[57]

Within a few months of Hsüan-tsang's visit, T'ung yabghu kaghan was dead, murdered by his uncle, and a civil war began within the western empire. Much of its territory fell under Chinese control, and its last leader died fighting the Chinese in 659.[58] The western Türk empire fragmented into the so-called 'On Ok' or ten arrows, a loose confederation of ten tribes, divided into two groups of five tribes living on opposite sides of Lake Issyk-kul.

T'ang China now took the place of the western, as well as the eastern empire, claiming suzerainty over Inner Eurasia from Korea to Sinkiang and the Amu Darya. Under the second T'ang emperor, T'ai-tsung (626–49), China ruled both China and the Mongolian steppe. When the Chinese Buddhist Wang Hsüan-ts'e returned from his third mission to India in 661, he entered Chinese controlled territory in the Bactrian lands of Kapitsa.[59] The lands once ruled by the Türk were now governed once again by a number of unstable tribal federations, all of which accepted Chinese suzerainty and fought for the Chinese.[60]

THE SECOND TÜRK EMPIRE: 683–734

THE EASTERN STEPPES

Fifty years after the collapse of the eastern kaghanate, Kutlugh (i.e. 'the fortunate', also known as Elterish kaghan, 682–92), a disgruntled chief from the pastoralist enclaves of north China, left the Sinicized Türks of the northern Ordos, and returned with his supporters to the Mongolian steppes. Here, he assembled an army which reconquered most of the lands of the first eastern kaghanate between 687 and 691. He also imposed Türk suzerainty over other Turkic-speaking tribal groups, including the tokuz Oghuz and Karluk. The empire he created survived, despite occasional crises, for almost 60 years. Kutlugh's brother and successor, Mo-ch'o (Kapghan kaghan) ruled from 691 to 716. Kapghan kaghan established good relations with China, but spent much time in warfare with other steppe tribes, mainly Türks. He was succeeded, after a brief but vicious power struggle, by two sons of Kutlugh, Bilgä kaghan (Chinese, 'Mo-chi-lien', r. 716–34) and his younger brother Köl tegin, who was the real power behind the throne.[61]

The second kaghanate left extensive records of its own which allow us, for the first time, to hear how the leaders of a pastoralist state viewed the strategic and tactical problems they faced. The Orkhon inscriptions were carved in a runic script, by Chinese craftsmen, in stone monuments erected to Bilgä kaghan and Köl tegin, probably in the 730s. In form, they are a combination of political testament and political advice to a younger generation of rulers, like the twelfth-century will of the Russian prince, Vladimir Monomakh, or the manuals of advice that became so popular in the Islamic world.[62] They show that the rulers of the second kaghanate had a good knowledge of the history of the first kaghanate, a strong sense of the honour and distinctiveness of Türk identity, and a determination not to repeat the mistakes of their predecessors, or endure again the humiliation of subjection to the Chinese. Of his father, Köl tegin writes that he: 'organized those who had been deprived of their state, those who had been deprived of their kaghan, who had become slaves and servants, who had lost their Türk institutions'.[63]

The chief adviser and general of the kaghans from the time of Kutlugh to that of Bilgä kaghan was Tonyukuk, a Chinese-educated Türk of the A-shih-na clan. Indeed, Tonyukuk was probably the real political brain behind the second Türk empire for the runic inscriptions in his name insist that Kutlugh had little political or military judgement (literally, he 'couldn't distinguish between the fat and the thin bulls').[64] In other words, the second kaghanate was built on the basis of some astute Chinese statecraft. Tonyukuk argued forcibly for a return to traditional steppe ways, believing that the first Türk empire had fallen because its leaders had become too Chinese. When Bilgä-khan proposed building a walled city, with Buddhist and Taoist temples, Tonyukuk objected:

> The number of the Türk is small, only a hundredth of the population of the T'ang. That we can, nevertheless, resist the T'ang is thanks to the fact that we travel in search of grass and water, have no fixed settlements, and live from hunting. All our men are practised in war. When we are strong, we let our soldiers march off in search of plunder; when we are weak, we flee to the hills and forests and hide.[65]

If the Türk were to build cities and temples, he argued, these would provide fixed targets for China's huge armies, while their temples would undermine the military culture of Türk soldiers.

As Bilgä-khan explained, the best tactic for the Türk was to remain independent of the Chinese, both geographically and culturally, while extracting resources from them.

> The place from which the tribes can be [best] controlled is the Ötükän mountains. Having stayed in this place I came to an amiable agreement with the Chinese people. They [the Chinese] gave (us) gold, silver, and silk in abundance. The words of the Chinese people have always been sweet and the materials of the Chinese people have always been soft. Deceiving by means of their sweet words and soft materials the Chinese are said to cause remote peoples to come close in this manner. After such a people have settled close to them (the Chinese) are said to plan ill will there. ... Having been taken in by their sweet words and soft materials, you Turkish people were killed in great numbers. ... [But] if you stay in the land of the Ötükän and send caravans from there you will have no trouble. If you stay in the Ötükän mountains you will live forever dominating the tribes.[66]

This is as precise a description as one could wish of what Barfield has called the 'Outer Frontier Strategy'.

However, implementing such a strategy was never easy. The founders of the second Türk kaghanate were already Sinicized before returning to the steppes, which is why they were so sensitive to the danger of Chinese influence. Yet Chinese influence continued to penetrate the Mongolian heartlands. The very process of holding a coalition together by distributing Chinese luxury goods encouraged a taste for Chinese culture. Whenever conflicts broke out, within the royal family, or with subordinate tribes, there was a strong temptation for one side or the other to seek Chinese support. Tonyukuk's own protests against Chinese influences suggest that they remained significant in the second kaghanate.

On Bilgä kaghan's death by poison, in 734, the second Türk empire fell apart. In 744, the leader of a new steppe dynasty formed by a T'ieh-le tribe, the Uighurs, presented the Chinese emperor with the head of the last Türk kaghan. The T'ieh-le had long been under the heel of the Türk, their alliance with the Chinese was already at least a century old, and they had been relatively independent since about 716, so the T'ieh-le attack had been long in the making.[67] In symbolic revenge for two centuries of subordination, the Uighurs defaced the funeral monuments set up a decade before by the Türks. The second Türk kaghanate, like the first, had held together, despite occasional conflicts, under the rule of two generations of an extremely able ruling family. It fell apart, as internal conflicts allowed subordinate tribes to reassert their independence. By 745, the remnants of the Türks were being hunted down in the steppes. In that year, Po-beg, the widow of Bilgä-khan and the daughter of Tonyukuk, led a group of survivors to north China, where they surrendered, and agreed to serve as frontier troops.[68] Here they dissolved in the fluid ethnic and linguistic mix of the north Chinese borderlands, while tribes to the north and west who had once been their subjects assumed the Turkic ethnonym.

THE WESTERN STEPPES

In the lands of the western kaghanate, there survived regional tribal federations formed from remnants of the On Ok tribes. Normally, they accepted Chinese suzerainty, though this was contested in Central Asia by invaders from both Tibet and Arabia. Evidence from Panjikent, the best studied Sogdian town of this period, shows that Türk elites had developed close links with the major towns of Sogdia, occasionally settling in them as officials or even as rulers. These links survived during the early years of the Arabic invasions. Under khaghan Su-lu (717–38), a member of the Türgesh tribe, a loose alliance of Türk tribes held Islamic armies at bay until 737.

Su-lu ruled in the classical nomadic tradition of generosity. According to a T'ang history, 'every time he campaigned, he distributed among his generals, officers and members of his hordes all the booty he had taken. His subjects loved him and were entirely at his service.' He established marital alliances with the second eastern kaghanate and Tibet. Su-lu, like Ishtemi, knew how to impress foreign ambassadors. According to a tenth-century Arabic historian, al-Fakikh, early one morning, accompanied by ten riders, he took an Umayyad ambassador to a forest clearing at the top of a hill. As dawn broke, he ordered one of the riders to unfurl his flag. Immediately there appeared ten thousand armed riders in full body armour, cheering their leader. They fell into formation below Su-lu, who then ordered the other riders to unfurl their flags. As each flag was unfurled, ten thousand more riders appeared, until there stood before the kaghan 100,000 fully armed soldiers.[69]

His defeat at the hands of the Arabs, and his assassination in 737 or 738 mark the end of western Türk authority and also ended any chance of organized Türk resistance to the Arabs. The collapse led to new divisions between the On Ok tribes, and eventually to the infiltration of another group of tribes, the Karluks, who had been dispossessed of their lands by the Uighurs. Karluk defections to the Arabs were one of the main reasons for the Islamic victory over a Chinese army at the battle of Talas, in 751, and by 766, the Karluks controlled what remained of the western Türk lands, which they ruled from Suyab, near modern Tokmak.[70]

THE UIGHUR EMPIRE: 744–840

FOUNDATION OF THE UIGHUR EMPIRE

The Uighur empire was founded by a group of T'ieh-le tribes known as the Tokuz Oghuz ('the nine tribes'), who were dominated by the Uighurs. In 745, they overthrew the Türk empire and expelled their rivals, such as the Basmil and Karluk, to the west. The Uighur leader, Ku-li p'ei-lo, assumed the title of 'Kutlugh bilgä köl kaghan' (r. 744–7) and his clan, the Ya-lo-ko (Turk. Yaghlagar), became the Uighur royal family. Though the Uighurs were dominant, all nine T'ieh-le tribes retained important positions within the empire. These were reflected in the role of their leaders or representatives in court ceremonials, such as those associated with the reception of Chinese delegations. The Uighurs soon controlled most of the lands of the Hsiung-nu empire, from eastern Mongolia to the Altai mountains in the west, and the Gobi desert in the south. By 800, Uighur influence also reached west to Ferghana, and into the Tarim basin.[71]

As they consolidated their control over other steppe peoples, the Uighurs tried to preserve their traditional good relations with China. Ku-li accepted Chinese suzerainty, and his successor, Mo-yen-ch'o (747–59), sent annual embassies to Ch'ang-an, and received Chinese goods, in particular silk.[72] For a time, the Uighurs had little need to threaten China with booty raids, as legitimate trade and the gifts surrendered by weak Chinese governments keen to buy Uighur support, were sufficient to maintain the glory and power of the Uighur kaghans and that of their followers.

In return for Chinese goods, the Uighurs supplied horses, camels, yaks and hides to the Chinese. They also traded Siberian furs taken from subordinate tribes such as the Kirghiz. Uighur sables were particularly valued in China. The wide tributary networks of the Uighurs enabled them also to trade in other goods, including precious metals, precious stones such as jade and diamonds, textiles such as cotton and hemp and castoreum (a substance obtained from beavers and used as a perfume or medicine). Like the Türks, the Uighurs controlled the lucrative trade routes through the Kansu corridor, and for a time in the late eighth century, they charged heavy tolls on all travellers between Central Asia and China.[73] The Uighur kaghans used literate Sogdian traders as officials and advisers. Sogdian merchants accompanied Uighur diplomatic missions to China and became influential within China as silk traders and money lenders.

In general, the Uighurs were more open than the Türk to influences from the agrarian world. As soon as they had consolidated their grip on the steppes in the 750s under Mo-yen-ch'o, they began building cities with the help of Sogdian and Chinese artisans.[74] We know of at least two cities built in the 750s by Mo-yen-ch'o. One was built on the Selenga river. The other became the capital, Ordu Balik ('royal camp town', known from Chingissid times as Karabalgasun). As its name suggests, it began, like most steppe towns, as a royal encampment, in the Orkhon region, near the future Mongol capital of Karakorum.[75] Ordu Balik was larger and more significant economically than any previous steppe capitals, and it was supported by a hinterland of agricultural settlements. The Arab traveller, Tamim ibn Bahr, who probably visited it in 821, 'journeyed twenty days in steppes where there were springs and grass but no villages or towns: only the men of the relay service living in tents... And then, after that, he travelled twenty days among villages lying closely together and cultivated tracts... After all these days he arrived at the king's town [Ordu Balik].' He added that the town was 'a great town, rich in agriculture', surrounded by cultivated lands and by 'villages lying close together'. Archaeologists have found plentiful evidence of agriculture in the region, in the form of 'millstones, pestles and irrigation canals, and even evidence that grain, such as millet, was buried together with corpses'.[76] The crops grown were typical of Inner Asian oases: wheat, barley, millet, rice as well as fruits such as apples, apricots and gourds.

According to Tamim ibn Bahr, Ordu Balik was 'populous and thickly crowded and has markets and various trades.' At the time of his visit, it had twelve huge iron gates, and a walled palace in the centre, set on a mound and topped by a golden tent that could hold 100 people. The tent, which was clearly a potent symbol of kaghanal authority, may have been a gift from the Chinese as part of the marriage ceremony of the Chinese Princess T'ai-ho in 821.[77] Archaeologists have found evidence of handicrafts in the town, and the size of the surviving site ($c.7 \times 2.5$ km) makes it clear that it had a large population.[78] However, the existence of Ordu Balik does not necessarily imply widespread urbanization, and even during Tamim ibn Bahr's visit the town still had the slightly temporary appearance of a vast military camp. Most of its people probably lived in tents, though many tents may have been semi-permanent. It is probable that many of its inhabitants were not Uighurs.[79]

Their cautious approach to the Chinese, and their early interest in trade and urbanization suggests that the Uighur might have been content to use their armies to maintain their power in the steppes, while extracting resources from China through commerce rather than warfare. However, the breakdown of T'ang power in the 750s, after defeats at Talas (751), in Thailand (751) and Manchuria, and the outbreak of a rebellion led by the disgruntled T'ang general, An Lu-shan, in 755, tempted the Uighurs, too, to try more forcible ways of extracting resources from China. An Lu-shan soon controlled most of China's northern provinces and its best troops, and within months he had captured Lo-yang and was threatening Ch'ang-an. The Emperor abdicated and fled to Szechwan. In September 756, the Uighurs and Tibetans offered to help the new Emperor, who assembled an army that included Arabic and Khotanese contingents, as well as independent units of Uighurs and Tibetans. In return for his support, the Uighur kaghan demanded and received recognition of his diplomatic equality with the T'ang, and the promise of a royal Chinese bride. The new Chinese emperor ostentatiously treated the Uighur with great honour, for their armies were now the most important military force available to him. In 758, a Chinese embassy brought an imperial bride to kaghan Mo-yen-ch'o, whom they

Plate 10.1 Ninth-century Uighur wall painting from Bezeklik, (© Staatliche Museen zu Berlin-Preussischer Kulturbesitz. Museum für Indische Kunst).

found 'sitting in his tent dressed in a barbarian hat and an ochre robe. His insignia and body-guards were splendid and majestic.'[80] The kaghan distributed the gifts brought by the embassy (which included state seals, silk, gold and silver dishes, and other fabrics) 'down to the last one among his officials, chiefs, and others'.[81]

Together with the Emperor's new Arabic, Khotanese and Tibetan allies, the Uighurs defeated the rebels and reoccupied Ch'ang-an. In 757, the Uighur army took and looted Lo-yang, until they were bought off with 10,000 rolls of silk. The following year, Uighur armies crushed an uprising of the Kirghiz, on the northern borders of their empire. In 762, Mo-yen-ch'o's successor, I-ti-chien (759–79, called Mou-yü in the Chinese sources), helped crushed new uprisings in China. Uighur armies once more took Lo-yang and began to loot the old capital, burning down two temples in which many of the population were hiding, and killing or maiming thousands. According to one Chinese source, they caused such devastation that: 'Everybody was reduced to using paper for clothing, and there were even some who used the Classics for clothes'.[82]

The Uighurs now commanded Chinese wealth on a larger scale than any previous steppe empire, for, though they took booty from north China, they continued to receive Chinese gifts and trade goods. While they were on campaign, the Chinese supplied the Uighur armies with 20 cattle, 200 sheep and 4 hu (c.300 kg) of rice a day. Meanwhile, the Uighurs engaged in a sort of forced trade that has been described by two recent historians as 'a military visit to a Chinese bazaar'.[83] According to a Chinese dynastic history:

> The Uighurs, ...frequently used to send embassies with horses to trade at an agreed price for silken fabrics. Usually they came every year, trading one horse for forty pieces of silk. Every time they came they brought several tens of thousands of horses. ...The barbarians acquired silk insatiably and we were given useless horses.[84]

CONVERSION TO MANICHAEISM

The drawing of the Uighurs into Chinese internal politics after the An Lu-shan rebellion, had profound if unexpected consequences within the Uighur empire. After the second capture of Lo-yang in 762, the Uighur kaghan, I-ti-chien, stayed in the city for three months and got to know its large Manichean population. He then returned with a number of Sogdian Manicheans, converted to Manichaeism, and ordered his subjects to convert as well, dividing them into groups of ten, each responsible for the religious education of its own members.[85] The Uighurs were the only major power to convert, formally, to Manichaeism.

Before this century, our knowledge of Manichaeism, the 'Religion of Light', came mainly from hostile polemics. However, the discovery of many Manichean scriptures, mainly in the oases of Turfan and Tun-huang, has transformed our knowledge of its doctrines and history. The Prophet Mani

(216–*c*.274 CE) was born in the Parthian/Sassanian capital of Ctesiphon. His ideas were shaped by the Judaeo-Christian and Gnostic traditions of Sassanian Mesopotamia, but acquired Zoroastrian and even Buddhist elements after Mani travelled in India and Khorasan. Mani regarded himself as the last in a line of prophets beginning with Adam's son, Seth, and including Zoroaster, the Buddha and Jesus. Convinced that he could unite the revelations contained in other world religions, he encouraged missionary activity, modelling himself on the Apostle Paul.[86]

Mani saw history as a cosmic conflict between the forces of light and dark. Humans were caught up in the struggle as the element of light (the soul) fought with the element of darkness in which it was trapped (the material body). Mani's scriptures related the history of this epic contest in immense, and often lurid, detail, and he expected his followers to treat the fantastic details of this cosmological epic as literal, not metaphorical truths. Manichaeism's literalness, and its rich, and fantastic narrative detail, may explain why it proved so attractive in regions with polytheistic religions.[87] Manichaeism was hierarchical, dividing its followers into distinct groups, of which only the highest, the 'elect', had access to the religion's inner knowledge. The elect had to obey Manichaeism's strict commands to avoid killing of any kind, and to avoid animal-based foods.

Its hostility to violence, and its commitment to missionary activity gave Manichaeism a close and natural compatibility with merchants, and it spread easily along the Silk Roads. Merchants, who travelled widely and often spoke several languages, also made ideal apostles.[88] Manichaeism spread in Sogdia, even in Mani's lifetime, mainly through the work of his disciple, Mar Ammo. The beginning of persecution in Iran, at the time of Mani's own death in 274 or 276, sent a stream of refugees east, and Central Asia soon became the most important centre of the new religion. Sogdian merchants and apostles carried Manichaeism even further east into the Tarim basin and Sinkiang. By the seventh century, the Central Asian Manichean church had a certain autonomy, a large following, many monasteries, and a leader or *archegos* probably based at Yar-khoto (near Turfan). Islamic attacks from the middle of the seventh century, drove a new wave of Manichaean migrants eastward. Manichaeism reached China at the end of the seventh century but was confined, at first, to foreigners.[89]

Explaining the Uighur conversion to Manichaeism is not easy. We must not discount the possibility of genuine fervour. As Augustine's account of his years as a Manichean suggests, the initial appeal of the religion owed less to its mystical doctrines (which were known only to the elect), than to its vigorous polemics, its rich ritual life, and the close ties between its many cells.[90] According to a Chinese source, Jui-hsi, one of the Manichean priests brought back to Ordu Balik by I-ti-chien, 'was marvellously learned in the Doctrine of Light...and his eloquence was like a cascade. That is why he was able to initiate the Uighurs to the true religion'.[91] Perhaps, as Mackerras has suggested, I-ti-chien, like the Indian emperor, Ashoka, almost a 1000 years earlier, converted out of remorse at the cruelties his armies had inflicted, particularly in Lo-yang. Perhaps the beauty of Manichaeism's iconophilic

Plate 10.2 Wall painting from Kocho: Manichaean? priest and followers, (© Staatliche Museen zu Berlin-Preussischer Kulturbesitz. Museum für Indische Kunst).

manuscripts and its commitment to astrology were also important lures. Perhaps its strict hierarchy of 'elect' and 'auditors' appealed to the political instincts of the Uighur kaghan. Manichaeism may also have consolidated the Uighurs' existing commercial ties with Sogdian traders, and it certainly made Mongolia an important centre for Central Asian Manicheans. Finally, the adoption of a religion rejected in China may have shielded the Uighurs from excessive cultural dependence on China.[92]

I-ti-chien's attempt at forced conversion provoked discontent within the Uighur elite, and Manicheans complained of being attacked and even killed.[93] It is hard to believe that the ban on meat and fermented milk was taken seriously by pastoralists outside the city, but even in the capital, the new religion made slow headway. Anti-Manichaean feeling may explain the assassination of I-ti-chien and hundreds of other members of his family in 779 by his cousin and successor, Tun (779–89). Tun (Alp Kutlugh) appears to have led a broader reaction against Sogdian and agrarian influences.[94]

However, amongst Sogdian and Turkic trading communities along the main caravan routes to Central Asia, the attack on Manichaeism provoked several uprisings and led to a sharp decline in trade. Manichaean influence revived after Tun's death, and the emergence of a new royal dynasty, the Hsieh-tieh, in 795. Under the new dynasty, Manichaeism spread widely within the Uighur elites. There emerged a priesthood, who took the religion's prohibitions seriously, despite their imcompatibility with pastoralist customs and lifeways. Chinese officials reported that they 'drink water, eat strong vegetables [onions and garlic?], and abstain from fermented mare's milk'.[95] Such habits were so contrary to traditional Türk lifeways that it is tempting to see in them an aggressive and self-conscious rejection of pastoralist customs by Sinicized sections of the Uighur elites.

By the early ninth century, Manichaeism had spread widely within the empire's small urban population (much of which may have been Sogdian or at least non-Uighur), for a Chinese report of 813 notes that: 'Manicheans were trusted and respected among the Uighurs.' Tamim ibn Bahr reported that Manichaeism was the dominant religion in Ordu Balik when he visited the city.[96] The Uighur government also supported Manicheans beyond its domains, by encouraging the T'ang to build Manichean temples, and offering to protect Manicheans beyond its domains. The importance of Uighur protection was demonstrated by the savage persecution of Manichaeism that began in China after the collapse of the Uighur empire in 840. Just before the collapse of the empire, a Uighur kaghan threatened to kill all Muslims in his land to prevent a threatened persecution of Manicheans in Samarkand.[97] However, despite the enthusiastic support of the Uighur kaghans, Manichaeism put down shallow roots among ordinary Uighurs, for the Uighur kingdoms created in Sinkiang (at Beshbalik), and in Kansu after the collapse of the empire were as likely to be Buddhist as Manichean. In Turfan there emerged a Manichean Uighur government at Yar-Khoto, but even here most of the population was probably Buddhist or Nestorian.[98]

Along with Manichaeism, the Uighurs acquired a Sogdian script, which was later inherited by the Mongols and the Manchus. Literacy may have spread widely within the empire's towns, and it survived amongst Uighurs in the post-imperial age. The Soviet scholar, Tikhonov, has suggested that in the towns along the Silk Roads, up to a third of the population may have been literate.[99] Soon there emerged a rich Uighur literature, dominated by Manichean, Nestorian Christian and Buddhist influences.[100]

DECLINE AND FALL

Both contemporaries and later writers have blamed Manichaeism, with its pacific and ethical concerns, for the decline of Uighur military power, Gumilev even describing the spread of Manichaeism as 'a sort of suicide'.[101] The luxury and extravagance of the *kaghan's* court encouraged contemporaries in the belief that an ethical religion was likely to undermine the military virtues of a pastoralist society, as Tonyukuk had warned the Türk a century before. In reality, Manichaeism was a symptom rather than a cause, a sign of a deeper shift from military to commercial methods of exacting and controlling resources. Certainly, from the 780s, the Uighur elites became less interested in military virtues than their Türk predecessors, and more interested in a lifestyle of commerce, literacy and civilized luxury. Though there is no direct evidence, it is possible that they also began to use their commercial revenues to buy soldiers and generals. This suggests that the adoption of Manichaeism was a symptom of the gradual commercialization of the steppes during the long commercial boom of the late first millennium. Commercialization increased the economic, cultural, and personal links between the steppe and settled worlds, but also created new divisions within the steppes, between ordinary pastoralists and the increasingly 'urbanized' elites who ruled them. As Mackerras writes: 'Two quite distinct and utterly different societies grew up within the same empire. It became obvious with the passage of time that the two were politically, as well as socially, separate. The court's control outside the capital weakened, leaving opportunities for discontented local chiefs wide open.'[102] Besides, as Tonyukuk had warned a century before, urbanization created new dangers, for cities provided convenient military targets. The Kirghiz to the north had been in open rebellion since 821, and in 839 there was widespread famine and disease, combined with unusually heavy snows. In 840, a Kirghiz army led by a disgruntled Uighur chief, sacked Ordu Balik and destroyed the Uighur empire. The Chinese sources report, laconically, that 'The Uighurs scattered and fled all over the barbarian territory.'[103]

Uighur tribes set off in different directions, some to the west, some to Manchuria, some to the oases of Kansu or Sinkiang, such as Kao-cheng, where they formed a state in c.866.[104] Here, they found partial compensation for the loss of empire in their control of the vital trade routes between China and Central Asia. To China, they sent horses, jade, diamonds from the Middle East, high quality Siberian furs and other exotic goods (such as seal testicles, obtained from northern Siberia, and valued for their medical properties), in return for silk and other Chinese goods, which they traded west. In the tenth century, the Uighurs were supplying China with a variety of furs, including 'musk, as well as black, red, and striped foxes, furs of the grey squirrel, sable-marten, ermine (and) weasel'.[105] Their commercial power enabled the Uighurs to maintain close diplomatic ties with China in the tenth century. A Chinese official complained that the emperor Ming-tsung (r. 926–33):

bought all the horses without any differentiation and usually paid a much higher price than they were worth. [In addition], transportation and accommodation were also supplied [by the Court]. Those who approached the capital would be received by Ming-tsung in the palace and entertained with food and drink. After getting drunk they would sing one after the other in turn and talk about their customs in great enjoyment. When they left, they would again be richly rewarded.[106]

The Kirghiz, who brought down the Uighur empire, were also, like the Türk and Uighur, a confederation of Siberian, Mongolian and Turkic tribes under a Turkic ruling clan of T'ieh-le origin. However, they created neither a military nor a commercial empire in Mongolia.

Mongolia itself became a political vacuum, where Kitan tribes from Manchuria engaged in vigorous colonizing activities, setting up colonies and frontier posts settled by captives or Chinese settlers.[107] Though the details are obscure, these processes contributed to the linguistic and ethnic transformation of Mongolia into a Mongol-speaking rather than a Turkic-speaking land.

NOTES

1 Golden, *Introduction*, p. 19, and see pp. 16–18, 26–7, 61.
2 Golden, *Khazar Studies*, vol. 1, p. 43; and see *Introduction*, pp. 82, 89, 92–5, 97–106.
3 Golden, *Introduction*, p. 113.
4 Chavannes, *Documents*, p. 217; on the history of the runes and their decipherment, see the introduction to the Russian edition of the inscriptions, Malov, *Pamyatniki drevnetyurkskoi pis'mennosti*, pp. 11–14; English translations are available in Silay, ed., *Anthology of Turkish Literature*, pp. 1–20, and Tekin, *A Grammar of Orkhon Turkic*, pp. 261–95; there is a brief written survey of written scripts in Inner Asia in Sinor, *Inner Asia*, pp. 27–32.
5 Golden, *Introduction*, p. 116.
6 Liu Mau-tsai, *Die chinesischen Nachrichten*, 1:40, and see ibid., 1:5, and 2:806; it is tempting to identify Ötükän with modern Otgon Tenger, the highest mountain of the Hangai range, which lies *c.*100 km east of modern Uliastai, and 2–300 km north of the Mongolian Altai; see also Taşağıl, *Gök-Türkler*, p. 9; on the Bugut inscription, Klyashtornyi and Sultanov, *Kazakhstan*, p. 77.
7 Golden, *Introduction*, pp. 121, 126–7; Sinor, 'The historical role of the Türk empire', in 'Inner Asia and its Contacts with Medieval Europe', no. VII, p. 428; on the variety of linguistic influences in the Türk empires, see Sinor, 'The first Türk empire', in *HCCA* (pp. 327–35), 3:327–31.
8 Liu Mau-tsai, *Die chinesischen Nachrichten*, 1:9, and see ibid., 1:430–1; see also O. Lattimore, *Nomads and Commissars: Mongolia Revisited*, New York: Oxford University Press, 1962, p. 41; and Gumilev, *Drevnie tyurky*, pp. 65–7, and p. 140, where he suggests that heavy cavalry were used to break up opposing armies, who could then be destroyed by ordinary cavalry.
9 Liu Mau-tsai, *Die chinesischen Nachrichten*, 1:28–9.
10 Taşağıl makes this point, *Gök-Türkler*, pp. 15–16.
11 Liu Mau-tsai, *Die chinesischen Nachrichten*, 1:6–7.
12 Taşağıl, *Gök-Türkler*, p. 1; Malov, *Pamyatniki drevnetyurkskoi pis'mennosti*, p. 36, translates 'Gök Türk' as 'Blue Türk', which does not convey the sense of the original, that these were god-like founders of a people; on the complex system of titles amongst the Türk, see M. R. Drompp, 'Supernumerary Sovereigns: Superfluity and Mutability in the Elite Power Structures of the Early Türks (Tujue)', in Seaman, ed., *Rulers from the Steppe* (pp. 92–115), pp. 92ff.; see also Liu Mau-tsai, *Die chinesischen Nachrichten*, 1:7, and 2:492.
13 On the role of these centres, see Liu Mau-tsai, *Die chinesischen Nachrichten*, 1:10; see also ibid., 1:10, 2:500, 722; according to Taşağıl, *Gök-Türkler*, pp. 31, 106, an early ninth-century source puts Ishtemi's winter camp seven days north-west of Karashahr.

14 As Chinese sources pointed out; Chavannes, *Documents*, pp. 20 and 47.

15 Liu Mau-tsai, *Die chinesischen Nachrichten*, 1:433–41 lists and maps all known Türk raids into China; on the expansion of the empire to east and west, see the historical Chou annals, cited in ibid., 1:8.

16 Barfield, *Perilous Frontier*, p. 133; and see Golden, *Introduction*, p. 131.

17 Liu Mau-tsai, *Die chinesischen Nachrichten*, 1:461–2 and see 1:13.

18 Golden, *Khazar Studies*, 1:37; on the Avars, see *Menander*, pp. 45–9, 252–3; see also Gumilev, *Drevnie tyurki*, pp. 33–4.

19 Gumilev, *Drevnie tyurki*, pp. 47–51.

20 Cited in Sinor, 'Establishment... of the Türk empire', in *CHEIA*, p. 297; Malov, *Pamyatniki drevnetyurkskoi pis'mennosti*, p. 36.

21 As Liu Mau-tsai puts it: 'The strength of a kaghan was decisive for the fate of his state.'; *Die chinesischen Nachrichten*, 1:431.

22 Lieu, *Manichaeism*, p. 228.

23 Golden, *Introduction*, p. 145; Klyashtoryni and Sultanov, *Kazakhstan*, pp. 96–7; Gafurov, *Tadzhiki*, 1:206–8, 329–31.

24 Gumilev, *Drevnie tyurki*, pp. 46–7; J. Harmatta and B. A. Litvinsky, 'Tokharistan and Gandhara under western Türk rule (650–750)', in *HCCA* (pp. 367–401), 3:368–9; see also Blockley, ed., *Menander*, pp. 111, 113.

25 Blockley, ed., *Menander*, pp. 115–17; see also Lieu, *Manichaeism*, p. 97; Haussig, *Die Geschichte Zentralasiens... in vorislamischer Zeit*, pp. 165–6 stresses the importance of Sassanian conquests in Arabia, which enabled them to control all trade routes from India to the Mediterranean.

26 Drège and Bührer, *Silk Road Saga*, pp. 34–5; on the attack on Bosporus, see Gumilev, *Drevnie Tyurki*, 106–8; on Zemarkhos' mission, see below, and Blockley, ed., *Menander*, pp. 117–27; Zemarkhos' caravan carried much silk, and the Persians tried hard to prevent its return; Klyashtornyi and Sultanov, *Kazakhstan*, pp. 92–4.

27 Watters, *On Yuan Chwang's Travels*, I:94; see also Lieu, *Manichaeism*, p. 228 on Samarkand as a 'boom-town', and Marshak, 'Sughd and adjacent regions', in *HCCA*, 3:236–9.

28 Beckwith, *The Tibetan Empire*, p. 179 .

29 Gumilev, *Drevnie Tyurki*, 153–4; and see Beckwith, *The Tibetan Empire*, p. 178; on the history of Kocho/Kao-ch'ang, see Zhang Guang-da, 'Kocho', in *HCCA* (pp. 303–14), 3:303–14.

30 Barfield, *Perilous Frontier*, p. 8.

31 Liu Mau-tsai, *Die chinesischen Nachrichten*, 1:320, and see 1:9.

32 The Sui Annals reported that the 28 different classes of titles were all hereditary, which suggests the limits to which strictly bureaucratic principles applied; Liu Mau-tsai, *Die chinesischen Nachrichten*, 1:41.

33 *Menander*, p. 121, and see p. 119; on the site of 'Sizabul's' winter camp, see ibid., p. 264, and Taşağıl, *Gök-Türkler*, pp. 31, 106; and Chavannes, *Documents*, pp. 235–7; not all authors accept the identity of Sizabul with Ishtemi, see, e.g., Sinor, 'The first Türk empire', in *HCCA*, 3:333.

34 *Menander*, 121.

35 Liu Mau-tsai, *Die chinesischen Nachrichten*, 1:10, 2:500.

36 Ibid., 1:42.

37 Gumilev, *Drevnie tyurki*, pp. 56–9; and see *Menander*, p. 173.

38 The best short accounts of Türk social structure are in Klyashtornyi and Sultanov, *Kazakhstan*, pp. 138–50, and S. G. Klyashtornyi, 'The second Türk empire', in *HCCA* (pp. 335–47), 3:336–8.

39 Golden, *Introduction*, p. 147; the favoured method of executing royalty was to wrap them in a carpet and crush them to death; there is a good, brief, survey of Türk religious beliefs in Liu Mau-tsai, *Die chinesischen Nachrichten*, 1:458–63, and in Klyashtornyi and Sultanov, *Kazakhstan*, pp. 150–2; on the 'indigenous' religions of the Inner Eurasian steppes, see Khazanov, 'The spread of world religions', pp. 12–13.

40 Liu Mau-tsai, *Die chinesischen Nachrichten*, 1:8, from the Chou annals.

41 Liu Mau-tsai, *Die chinesischen Nachrichten*, 1:459–60.

42 Kürsat-Ahlers, *Zur frühen Staatenbildung*, p. 329, citing Togan, Z. V., *Umumi Türk Tarihine Giris* (Introduction to Türk history), vol. 1, Istanbul, 1946: Ismail Akgün Matbass..

43 Simocatta Theophylactus, *History*, p. 191; on the use of *yats*, see Boyle, *Mongol World Empire*, XXII, pp. 184–92.

44 Cited in Boyle, *Mongol world empire*, XXII, p. 183.

45 Golden, *Introduction*, pp. 151–2; Klyashtornyi and Sultanov, *Kazakhstan*, pp. 153–66.

46 Liu Mau-tsai, *Die chinesischen Nachrichten*, 1:44; see also Gumilev, *Drevnie tyurki*, ch. 9 on these succession disputes.

47 The phrase is Liu Mao-tsai's; see *Die chinesischen Nachrichten*, 1:396–8.

48 Ibid., 1:49; Tsch'ang-sun Scheng's biography is in ibid., 1:96–110.

49 Ibid., 1:103–4.

50 Gumilev, *Drevnie tyurki*, pp. 140–1.

51 Mackerras, *Uighur empire*, 1972 edn, p. 8.

52 Malov, *Pamyatniki drevnetyurkskoi pis'mennosti*, p. 37.

53 Liu Mau-tsai, *Die chinesischen Nachrichten*, 1:344.

54 Golden, *Introduction*, p. 134; the Western Türk controlled all the lands between Turfan and the Afghan kingdom of Kapitsa visited by the Chinese Buddhist pilgrim, Hsüan-tsang, in 630; Chavannes, *Documents*, p. 197; Klyashtornyi and Sultanov, *Kazakhstan*, pp. 96–7.

55 Golden, *Introduction*, p. 135; Klyashtornyi and Sultanov, *Kazakhstan*, pp. 94–5, claim that he personally took part in Heraclius' Caucasian campaign of 627–8, which is described in ch. 11.

56 Watters, *On Yuan Chwang's Travels*, I:74 and 77; and see Chavannes, *Documents*, p. 194, who cites Julien's translation.

57 Beal, *Life of Hiuen-tsiang*, p. 44; see also Watters, *On Yuang Chwang's Travels*, I:74–5.

58 On the decline of the western empire, see Sinor, 'Establishment... of the Türk empire', in *CHEIA*, pp. 309–10.

59 Chavannes, *Documents*, pp. 279–80; on T'ang and Tibetan rule over the 'Western regions', see Mu Shun-ying and Wang Yao, 'The Western Regions under the T'ang empire and the kingdom of Tibet', in *HCCA* (pp. 349–65), 3:349–65.

60 As they remembered, with bitterness later; the Orkhon inscription in honour of Köl tegin records: 'for fifty years they gave [the Chinese] their labour and strength'; Malov, *Pamyatniki drevnetyurkskoi pis'mennosti*, p. 37.

61 Sinor, 'Establishment... of the Türk empire', in *CHEIA*, p. 312; Klyashtornyi, 'The Second Türk Empire', in *HCCA*, 3:335–6, 339–40.

62 See the beginning of the short inscription in honour of Köl tegin, in Malov, *Pamyatniki drevnetyurkskoi pis'mennosti*, p. 33; on the role of Chinese craftsmen, ibid., p. 35: 'I... brought masters from the emperor of the Chinese, and ordered them to carve these inscriptions.'

63 Cited in Sinor, 'Establishment... of the Türk empire', in *CHEIA*, p. 311; Malov, *Pamyatniki drevnetyurkskoi pis'mennosti*, pp. 37–8.

64 Malov, *Pamyatniki drevnetyurkskoi pis'mennosti*, p. 65.

65 Liu Mau-tsai, *Die chinesischen Nachrichten*, 1:172–3.

66 Cited in Barfield, *Perilous Frontier*, 148; Malov, *Pamyatniki drevnetyurkskoi pis'mennosti*, pp. 34–5.

67 Mackerras, *Uighur Empire*, 1972 edn, p. 8; Sinor, 'Establishment... of the Türk empire', in *CHEIA*, p. 313.

68 Gumilev, *Drevnie Tyurki*, p. 365.

69 Klyashtornyi and Sultanov, *Kazakhstan*, pp. 101–2; on Türks in Panjikent, see B. A. Litvinskii, in Gafurov, *Tadzhiki*, 1989, 2:368.

70 Golden, *Introduction*, p. 141, and see pp. 190–1.

71 C. Mackerras, 'The Uighurs', in *CHEIA* (pp. 317–42), p. 322; see also Mackerras, *Uighur Empire*, 1972 edn, pp. 8–9, 55, 120; Golden, *Introduction*, p. 158.

72 Gumilev, *Drevnie Tyurki*, p. 370.

73 Mackerras, *Uighur Empire*, 1972 edn, p. 30; and see Golden, *Introduction*, pp. 170–1.

74 Gumilev, *Drevnie Tyurki*, p. 383; Mackerras, *Uighur Empire*, 1972 edn, p. 10, there are Sogdian design elements in many Uighur buildings; and p. 50, on the presence of Chinese artisans.

75 Mackerras, *Uighur Empire*, 1972 edn, pp. 9, 13.

76 Mackerras, 'The Uighurs', in *CHEIA*, 337; and see Vainshtein, *Nomads of South Siberia*, p. 146; the site was known in Mongol times, when Juvaini described 'the ruins of a town and a palace'; Juvaini, *History of the World-Conqueror*, 1:54; Tamim ibn Bahr cited from Minorsky, 'Tamim ibn Bahr's Journey', p. 283.

77 Mackerras, *Uighur Empire*, 1972 edn, p. 183; the Tibetan ruler had a similar tent, ibid., p. 183; Tamim ibn Bahr cited from Minorsky, 'Tamim ibn Bahr's journey', p. 283.

78 Minorsky, 'Tamim ibn Bahr's journey', p. 295.

79 Golden, *Introduction*, p. 175; and see Mackerras, 'The Uighurs', in *CHEIA*, p. 339; Minorsky, 'Tamim ibn Bahr's journey', p. 284.

80 Mackerras, *Uighur Empire*, 1972 edn, pp. 63, 65.

81 Ibid., p. 64.

82 Ibid., pp. 25, 76–7.

83 Jagchid and Symons, *Peace, War and Trade*, p. 74; and see Mackerras, *Uighur Empire*, 1972 edn, p. 57.

84 Mackerras, *Uighur Empire*, 1972 edn, p. 86.

85 Barfield, *Perilous Frontier*, 159; there is a brief discussion of the doctrines and history of Manichaeism, and of I-ti-chien's conversion in Mackerras, 'The Uighurs', in *CHEIA*, pp. 329–30.

86 Lieu, *Manichaeism*, p. 87–9; this is the best modern account of Manichaeism; see p. 69 on Manichaeism's Judaeo-Christian roots and pp. 7–32 on the 'Teachings of Mani'.

87 Ibid., pp. 31–2.

88 Ibid., p. 98–101; Weber has suggested that ethical religions, in general, have a natural attraction for merchants because of their concern for fair dealing; see Hodgson, *The Venture of Islam*, 1:133.

89 Lieu, *Manichaeism*, p. 230–2, and see pp. 109–12, 220, 228.

90 Ibid., p. 168ff.

91 Mackerras, 'Uighurs', in *CHEIA*, p. 330.

92 Golden, *Introduction*, p. 174; and see Lieu, *Manichaeism*, p. 175–7; Mackerras, *Uighur Empire*, 1972 edn, p. 26; and the analysis in Khazanov, 'The spread of world religions'.

93 Lieu, *Manichaeism*, p. 235.

94 Golden, *Introduction*, p. 160; Mackerras, *Uighur Empire*, 1972 edn, p. 10, 88–9, 152; and see Mackerras, 'The Uighurs', in *CHEIA*, p. 335.

95 Mackerras, *Uighur Empire*, 1972 edn, p. 109, and see p. 10; see also Mackerras, 'The Uighurs', in *CHEIA*, p. 333; Klyashtoryni and Sultanov, *Kazakhstan*, pp. 110–11.

96 Minorsky, 'Tamim ibn Bahr's journey', p. 283; and see Mackerras, 'The Uighurs', in *CHEIA*, p. 325.

97 Lieu, *Manichaeism*, p. 114; see also ibid., pp. 237–9; and Mackerras, *Uighur Empire*, 1972 edn, pp. 42–3, 168.

98 Lieu, *Manichaeism*, p. 240–2; Golden, *Introduction*, p. 175.

99 Golden, *Introduction*, p. 173; Klyashtornyi and Sultanov, *Kazakhstan*, p. 160.

100 Golden, *Introduction*, p. 173.

101 Gumilev, *Drevnie tyurki*, p. 423; a ninth-century Arabic writer, al-Jahiz, argued that conversion to Manichaeism led to Uighur military decline; Mackerras, 'Uighurs', in *CHEIA*, pp. 340–1.

102 Mackerras, 'The Uighurs', in *CHEIA*, p. 341.

103 Mackerras, *Uighur Empire*, 1972 edn, pp. 124–5.

104 See Gabain, *Das Leben*; and Minorsky, 'Tamim ibn Bahr's journey', p. 278.

105 *Hudud al-Alam*, written *c*.982, p. 94; and see Jagchid and Symons, *Peace, War, and Trade*, pp. 124, 168–9.

106 Jagchid and Symons, *Peace, War, and Trade*, p. 125.

107 Golden, *Introduction*, p. 186.

FURTHER READING

On the origins of the Türk, the best modern source is Golden, *Indroduction to the History of the Turkic Peoples*. Chinese sources are available in Liu, *Die chinesischen Nachrichten*; Chavannes, *Documents sur les Tou-Kiue*; Taşağıl, *Gök-Türkler*; Beal, *Si-yu-ki*, and *The Life of Hiuen-Tsiang*, and Watters, *On Yuan Chwang's Travels*. There are accessible modern accounts of the travels of Hsüan-tsang in Grousset, *In the Footsteps of the Buddha*, and Waley, *The Real Tripitika*. The Orkhon inscriptions are available in English translation in Silay, ed., *An Anthology of Turkish Literature*, Tekin, *A Grammer of Orkhon Turkic*, and in a Russian translation in Malov, *Pamyatniki drevnetyurkskoi pis'mennosti*. There is a unique Arabic account of the Uighur empire in Minorsky, 'Tamim ibn Bahr's journey'. The most important western sources on the early Türk are the summary of Zemarkhos' embassy in Menander's *History*; and the relevant passages in Simocatta Theophylactus, *History*. Gumilev's *Drevnie tyurki* is, like most of his works, very readable, but not always reliable. There are shorter surveys in Barfield, *Perilous Frontier*; *CHEIA*; Sinor, 'The historical role of the Türk empire'; Sinor and Klyashtornyi, 'The Türk empire', in *HCCA*, 3:327–48; Klyashtornyi and Sultanov, *Kazakhstan*, pp. 75–168; and Golden, *Introduction to the History of the Turkic Peoples*. There is also an interesting discussion in Kürsat-Ahlers, *Zur frühen Staatenbildung*. On the Uighur see Mackerras, *Uighur Empire*, and Sinor, Denis, 'The Uighur empire of Mongolia'. On Manichaeism, see Lieu, *Manichaeism*, and see also, Khazanov's analysis in 'The spread of world religions'. On the rise of Tibetan power, the most accessible source is Beckwith, *The Tibetan Empire*.

[11] TURKIC EMPIRES OF
WESTERN INNER EURASIA

Entanglement in the commercial and cultural networks of the Inner Eurasian borderlands could be both fruitful and dangerous for pastoralist rulers. By building commercial alliances, and borrowing from the cultural and religious traditions of the agrarian world, they could generate new types of power and new forms of legitimation. Yet influences from the agrarian world also threatened the military traditions of pastoralism. For local chieftains, used to a world of endemic feuding, the temptation to loot remained strong. However, casual raiding could undermine the commercial and political ties constructed by more far-sighted steppe leaders. Debates over these fundamental strategic choices divided even the most powerful pastoralist empires. Yet there was no way of avoiding them, for they arose from the very nature of state power in the steppes.

This chapter describes two very different steppe empires that emerged after the sixth century in the west of Inner Eurasia: the Avars, whose engagement with Outer Eurasian societies was, like that of the Huns, direct and brutal; and the Khazars, who, like the Uighurs, built a great commercial and political empire in the steppes and then converted to an Outer Eurasian religion, in this case, Judaism.

THE BYZANTINE FRONTIER AND THE AVARS:
c.560–630

THE BYZANTINE FRONTIER

From the middle of the fifth century, the steppes along Byzantium's Balkan borders were dominated by Turkic-speaking groups, many of whom had travelled west during the Hunnic migrations. Most belonged to the Oghur groupings known to the Chinese as T'ieh-le or Ting-ling. In the Pontic steppes, they mingled with remnants of the Huns, Iranian-speaking groups of Sarmatian or Alan origin, and Ugric-speaking groups from the Urals. Late fifth-century Byzantine sources refer to several distinct peoples, including Huns, Saraghur and Onoghur, and later Kutrighurs (between the Don and Dnieper), and Utrighur tribes (between the Don and the Volga). In 480, for

the first time, Byzantine sources mention 'Bulghars', or 'mixed' ones, an ethnonym that describes honestly what all these groups were in fact.[1]

Pressed from the east, the most westerly of these groups probed the
Byzantine borders, appearing as raiders, as mercenaries, as refugees, as
traders and occasionally as conquerors of the Danubian provinces or the
Balkans. Byzantium built and rebuilt its frontier fortifications. In 512,
emperor Anastasius (491–518) built the famous long walls defending
Byzantium. Procopius described a system of some 600 forts built or rebuilt
under Justinian (r. 527–65). The outer zone included a chain of forts and
fortified towns running from Belgrade along the southern shore of the
Danube to its mouth, following the ancient fortified lines of the Roman
empire.[2] Two more lines lay behind this outer frontier.

The trade routes through the Crimean Bosporus were one of the most vulnerable points in the Byzantine commercial system. Jordanes refers to a
group called the 'Altziagiri', north of Cherson, to whom merchants brought
the goods of Asia in the late fifth century, and to Onoghur trade in marten
skins, which suggests that the Onoghur controlled the trade routes to the
Urals.[3] Meanwhile, an independent Bosporan kingdom survived, based on
Kerch, where these trade routes reached the Black Sea. In the reign of Justin I
(518–27), Byzantium re-established its suzerainty over the Bosporan kingdom and its Turkic or Hunnic ruler, Grod, converted to Christianity.
Control of the Crimean Bosporus gave Byzantium leverage over the trade
with the Pontic steppes in which livestock produce was exchanged for the
wines, textiles, salt and craft goods of Crimea. Byzantium also demanded
that the Bosporus supply ships and naval equipment, so that control over the
Bosporus enhanced Byzantine naval power, as it had that of the Goths in the
fourth century. It also enhanced Byzantium's ideological influence, for
Bosporus became a Christian bishopric. From c.520 Christian missionaries
worked amongst Turkic/Hunnic tribes in the North Caucasus, preaching to
Christian captives and translating religious texts into local languages. Their
activities were supported by Christian towns of the Bosporan kingdom which
sent them wheat, wine, oil, linen and religious paraphernalia such as candles
and priestly robes.[4]

The mathematics of diplomacy, according to which the enemy of an
enemy is a friend, combined with Byzantium's long-standing interest in the
trade routes of the Azov region, ensured that Byzantium would normally
seek alliances with peoples of the eastern Pontic region against those closer
to its Danubian borders. Doing this depended on maintaining its precarious
foothold in the cities of south Crimea, of which Cherson was the most
important. In the tenth century, Constantine Porphyrogenitus described
vividly how such diplomacy worked. Byzantine negotiators were sent to
Cherson or any other agreed point on the Pontic coast. From there, they
arranged for a Pecheneg escort and took Pecheneg hostages, and then travelled into the steppes with carts full of gifts for local khans and their families
and allies. The key to successful diplomacy was to take plenty of gifts for, in
Constantine's words: 'these Pechenegs...are ravenous and keenly covetous
of articles rare among them, are shameless in their demands for generous

gifts, the hostages demanding this for themselves and that for their wives, and the escort something for their own trouble and some more for the wear and tear of their cattle.'[5]

In the late 550s, when the Utrighur controlled the eastern Pontic trade routes, Justinian managed to set them against their western neighbours, the Kutrighurs. The diplomatic manoeuvring involved was as brutal as that of the north Chinese borderlands. When Justinian first offered to subsidize Utrighur attacks on the Kutrighurs, the Utrighur leader, Sandilkh, replied that:

> utterly to destroy one's fellow tribesmen was unholy and altogether improper, 'For they not only speak our language, dwell in tents like us, dress like us and live like us, but they are our kin, even if they follow other leaders. Nevertheless, we shall deprive the Kutrigurs of their horses and take possession of them our-selves, so that without their mounts they will be unable to pillage the Romans.' This Justinian had asked him to do.[6]

Eventually, Byzantine gold overcame the scruples of the Utrighurs. They attacked the Kutrighurs, and released large numbers of Byzantine slaves. However, when they heard that Kutrighur refugees had been allowed to settle beyond the Danube as frontier guards, the Utrighurs complained bitterly.

> We live in huts in an infertile desert land, while these Kutrigurs can now eat as much bread as they like, get drunk as often as they like, and choose all sorts of special foods. They can also take baths, and wear gold ornaments; they wear delicate fabrics, dyed in many colours and coloured in gold.[7]

Both Byzantium and Sassanian Persia tried to exploit pastoralist allies, par-ticularly in the Caucasus. Here the main players in the sixth century were the Sabir tribes, who occupied the north Caucasus in c.515. The name 'Sabir', has been linked by some scholars with the name, 'Siberia' (where it may have been an alternative name for the Ugrian-speaking Mansi/Vogul), or even with the far-eastern Hsien-Pi. However, their language seems to have been Turkic. In all probability they represent a group of Turkic-speaking peoples who picked up Ugrian-speaking and Iranian-speaking tribes as they migrated west. According to Procopius, the Sabirs, though numerous, lacked perma-nent supra-tribal leaders, and never formed a durable confederation.[8]

Despite this, the services of the Sabirs were valued highly by both Byzantium and Persia, because they could field large armies, and had a repu-tation, unusual amongst pastoralists, for skill in siege warfare. However, they could be fickle allies, and frequently switched sides, depending on the size of the subsidies they were offered. Sometimes, different Sabir tribes found themselves in opposing armies. In 513, a Sabir army crossed the Caucasus and demanded that Persia offer them at least as much as Byzantium if they wanted to avoid an attack.[9] Proud of their pastoralist traditions, they said: 'We live by our weapons, the bow and the sword, and our strength comes from the meat we eat.' Two years later, they advertised their power in a huge raid south of the Caucasus, in which they attacked Iranian and Byzantine lands with scrupulous impartiality.

The Avars: c.560–630

In c.557, soon after the Utrighur attack on the Kutrighurs, a people who called themselves Avars, entered the western steppes. The Avars were probably remnants of the Juan-juan or Hephthalite empires fleeing from their Türk conquerors. Grave-finds in Hungary show that the aristocratic core of the Avar federation was of east Asian Hunnic origin, probably Mongol, though they had incorporated other tribal groupings in their migrations west. Oghuric Turkic was probably the lingua franca of their armies.[10]

In their origins and their subsequent history, the European Avars were similar to the Huns. In 558 they sent an embassy to Byzantium. Here is Obolensky's account of their reception by Justinian:

> [Constantinople's] citizens were accustomed to the sight of exotic barbarian envoys, yet the appearance of the Avars, with their long plaited hair hanging down their backs, and their swaggering behaviour, created a mild sensation. Their requests were the usual ones: precious gifts, an annual pension, and fertile lands on which to settle. The last request was ignored by the imperial government; nevertheless the Avars, placated by presents of gold-encrusted chains, saddles, bridles, couches and silken robes, concluded a treaty with the empire and promised to fight its enemies. Justinian could not but welcome this opportunity of securing an ally in the South Russian steppes, believing, as Menander saw it, that 'whether the Avars are victorious, or whether they are defeated, in either case the Romans will profit.'[11]

So striking were the Avar emissaries that Byzantine dandies began to imitate their 'Hunnic' hairstyle, by shaving their hair in front and tying the rest of their hair in long plaits.[12]

With Byzantine subsidies, the Avars brought under their control the Turkic and Iranian tribes of the Pontic steppes, from the Alans, to the Kutrighurs, Utrighurs and Sabirs, and prevented them from raiding Byzantine territory. However, relations with Byzantium soon soured, partly under pressure from the Türk, who regarded the Avars as fugitive slaves, resented their leader's use of the imperial title of 'kaghan', and demanded that Byzantium hand their leaders over. In 562, the Avar kaghan, Bayan, asked for permission to settle within the Empire. When the new emperor, Justin II (r. 565–78), pressured by the Türk, and determined to adopt a less conciliatory policy than his uncle, Justinian, rejected these advances, Avar-led armies began to raid the Danubian provinces. Soon, they had conquered the sedentary populations of proto-Slavs (Antes). In 565, Avar armies occupied the heartland of Attila's empire, in Pannonia, and from then on, there is little trace of them in the Pontic steppes.[13]

From Pannonia, the Avars, like the Huns before them, began to operate a European version of the 'Outer Frontier Strategy'. Reverting to the policies of Justinian, Tiberius (r. 578–82), agreed to pay the Avars 80,000 gold pieces a year and the Avars once again began to fight for the empire.[14] Despite this, they did nothing to discourage the Slavic invasions that began from *c.*576, driven by overpopulation, and Avar oppression. Slavic raids continued, sometimes with active Avar support, in the 580s and again at the beginning of the seventh century. During the reign of Emperor Maurice (r. 582–602), Slavs, sponsored by the Avars, began to settle the Balkans in large numbers. These massive invasions deprived Byzantium of most of its Balkan provinces, and permanently changed the ethnic and linguistic composition of the peninsula.[15]

In battle, the Avars made Slav soldiers advance first, yet they expected to take most of the booty. In 601, after a victory over Avar armies, Byzantine commanders found that only one fifth of their captives were Avars, while a half were Slavs and the rest were other barbarians, probably mainly Turkic. The dominance of the Avars over the Slavic Antes is shown in a famous description from Fredegar the Scholiast, who wrote that each winter they lived among the Antes, from whom they took tributes, including levies of women and children.[16] However, these same descriptions show that the Avars, whose own numbers were not large, were keen to maintain agricultural populations, from whom they could exact tributes.

The Byzantine military manual, the *Strategikon*, which is often attributed to Emperor Maurice, portrays the Avars as typical steppe warriors, though they seem to have relied more on armour than most pastoralist invaders, and were probably the first peoples to use stirrups in Europe. The use of stirrups, which may have originated amongst the Chinese, and been transmitted west by Türk pastoralists, had a huge impact on cavalry warfare, as it gave the rider a firmer seat, and a much greater capacity to sustain a shock.[17] It is not surprising, therefore, that Avar bows are larger than those of their predecessors, and that the straight swords typical ever since the Sarmatian era, begin to be replaced by one-sided swords with a slight curve, distant ancestors of the sabre, a weapon for cutting rather than stabbing. The two innovations belonged together, for to strike with the sabre it was necessary to stand in the stirrups.[18] Here is an account of Avar fighting methods and lifeways from the *Strategikon*:

> They are equipped with breast-plate, sword, bow and pikes; most of them carry two weapons in the battle, pikes on shoulder, bow in hand, using either of them as necessity requires. Not only they themselves are clad in armor, but also the breasts of the notabilities' horses are covered and protected by iron or felt coating. They are carefully trained in shooting with a bow, while riding a horse. They have a multitude of animals, both male and female with them, partly to secure the food supply, partly because their mass seems more impressive in that way. Unlike the Romans or Persians, they do not use fortified camps, but, dispersed in clans and tribes, they pasture their animals incessantly both summer and winter, until the day of the battle. Then they keep the necessary animals hamshackled near their tents, so they are kept and guarded till the moment of drawing up in battle formation. Assuming battle formation begins in the night.[19]

Relations between the Avars and Byzantium were not just military. Archaeological evidence from modern Hungary shows that there was much trade between Byzantium and the Avars in the seventh century. Byzantine artisans made goods especially for the Avar market, and imperial coins circulated amongst the Avars, who also had access to much of the wealth accumulated under Attila.[20]

The absence of large Avar cemeteries before 600 suggests that they were nomadic before that date. However, graveyards of the seventh century show that they began to occupy permanent winter quarters and to become semi-sedentary. Many graves contain sickles and axes and there are also signs of poultry farming. Despite this, the goods in the graves also show the continuing importance of pastoralism, and Avar settlements seem to have remained, mainly, in the better pasturelands of the Carpathian region.[21]

As the Avars became semi-sedentary, their power declined. Their grip on central Europe was broken in 623 by a Wendic uprising under a leader called Samo. In the Balkans, their power was broken in 626 when it seemed at its height, after an overambitious attack on Constantinople. In *c*.619, the Emperor Heraclius (r. 610–41), faced with a massive Sassanian invasion of Anatolia, personally negotiated with the Avar kaghan, offering large concessions in return for peace on his northern borders. Despite this, the Avars invaded the empire, reached Constantinople, and took almost 300,000 captives. Heraclius continued to pay tributes, now of 200,000 gold coins, and even sent as hostages the sons of some high-born families. In 626, with Persian armies on the Bosporan coast opposite Byzantium, the Avars invaded again at the head of an army of Slav, Bulghar and Gepid troops. On 29 July there began a famous ten-day siege. This was defeated through the strength of the imperial fleet, the inspiration of the Patriarch Sergius, and, according to the inhabitants of Constantinople, the intercession of the Holy Mother. A land assault by the kaghan's forces of some 80,000 was repulsed, and plans to link up with Persian troops across the Bosporus, and Slavic troops in *monoxyla* (dug-out canoes) were prevented by the navy which destroyed the Slav fleet. This humiliating defeat and the withdrawal of the Avar-led army ended Avar domination of the Balkan Slavs and Bulghars.[22]

The Avar defeat of 626 proved a turning point in the history of the eastern Mediterranean. The Avar empire was never as powerful again, though an Avar state survived in Pannonia, living off the booty of its imperial days, until it was finally crushed by the Franks in 796.

THE KHAZAR EMPIRE: 620s–965

While the Avar empire was formed by refugees from Türk power, that of the Khazars began as a province of the western Türk empire that became independent in the second quarter of the seventh century.

A CONQUEST STATE: 620s–750

The early Khazar empire included many different peoples of the North Caucasus and modern Daghestan. Its dynastic leaders probably came from the A-shih-na family of the western Türk. Most Khazar pastoralists were also probably of Turkic origin, though there were also Caucasian, Ugric and Iranian elements. Recent evidence suggests that the dominant language was an Oghur dialect.[23] Anthropologically and linguistically the Khazars were similar to the other Turkic peoples of the Pontic steppes. Anthropological remains, like those of the Hunnic and Avar empires, show a population with both Mongol and Europoid elements. 'The impression is that of an Inner Asian ruling stratum with its core tribes (often occupying key, strategic areas) ruling over a population that was significantly less Mongoloid in somatic type.'[24] The ethnonym, 'Khazar', emerged only in the late sixth century, with the appearance of a strong grouping of tribes, largely of Sabir origin, in Daghestan, within the western Turk empire.[25] They showed the same military prowess as the Sabir. However, under Türk leadership, they showed a greater capacity for political organization.

The Khazars first attracted outside attention as Caucasian allies of Byzantium. Their military commander, the *sad*, may have been Buri-sad, the nephew of the western Türk kaghan, T'ung yabghu kaghan (r. 619–30); while their overall ruler, the Khazar *yabghu*, may have been Buri-sad's father, Mo-ho sad, who returned from a Chinese embassy in 626.[26] In the 620s, presumably with the support of the kaghan of the western Türk, the Khazar *sad* led an attack south of the Caucasus from a base in Daghestan or the north Caucasus. In its geography and its targets, the Khazar attack is reminiscent of the Scythian raids of the seventh century BCE. The attack yielded so much booty in captives, livestock, and precious stones and textiles, that the *sad*'s father, the Yabghu khan, decided to join in a second attack.[27] The Khazar army invaded the lands south of Darband known as Albania. The following vivid if hostile and formulaic description, from a tenth-century Armenian history, describes the devastation inflicted on Darband in 627.

> Like waves in the sea, the Türks fell on the town of Chora [Darband] and destroyed it completely. Seeing the terrible threat posed by this vile, ugly, horde of attackers, with their slanting and lidless eyes, and their flowing hair, like that of women, the inhabitants were seized by terror. Especially terrifying were the archers, who were skilful and powerful, and rained arrows down like hail then, like savage wolves, shamelessly threw themselves on the people and mercilessly cut them down in the streets and squares of the town. They did not spare the beautiful or gentle, the young men or women; they did not even leave in peace the sick, the harmless, the maimed and the old. They did not even take pity on the children who hugged their slaughtered mothers, but sucked the children's blood like milk.[28]

After sacking Darband, the Khazar armies moved west to join emperor Heraclius, who was besieging Tiflis in Iberia, a region long disputed between Byzantium and Persia.[29] The Khazar leaders bowed to the Byzantine emperor, whose capital, Constantinople, had just been saved from the Avars. Heraclius feasted the Khazars, loaded them with presents, and promised his daughter in marriage to the Yabghu khan in return for a military alliance. The siege of Tiflis failed, and as the armies left, they were taunted by the defenders who painted caricatures of the emperor and the yabghu khan on huge pumpkins, which they publicly speared to pieces. Heraclius went on to conquer Syria, making peace with Persia in 628. In the same year, the Khazars stormed Tiflis successfully, put its inhabitants to the sword, and punished its Persian commanders for the insults they had suffered the previous year. The Yabghu khan had them blinded, then tortured them to death, skinned them, stuffed their skins with hay, and hung them above the city walls. Such brutalities were welcomed by the Christian Byzantines as well as by the (presumably) *tengri*-worshipping Khazars. Christian sources regarded the fate of the Persian commanders as God's just punishment for his enemies.[30]

In the same year, just a year after the sack of Darband, the Khazar *sad* invaded western Albania, in modern Karabakh. Here, the Christian bishop, Viro, saw the encampment of the Khazar army along the River Kura, near the Albanian capital, Partava.

> There, we saw them eating, squatting on their haunches like a caravan of camels, each with a bowl full of the meat of unclean animals. As well as their bowls and cups of salt water in which they dunked bits of meat when they ate, there were also silver goblets and dishes for eating, with golden engraving, which had been taken from Tiflis; there were also huge wooden drinking vessels in the shape of horns or gourds, from which they drank their brew. With their lips unwashed and covered in grease and fat, two or three would drink from the same goblet, drinking without any sense of restraint, filling their bellies with undiluted wine or camel or mare's milk, until they were like blown up winesacks. There were no cup-bearers or servants attending on them, even for the *sad*, around whom there was just a small forest of soldiers with their spears, who guarded his doors with their linked shields.[31]

The Khazar invasion of Albania caused a terrible famine, in which people were forced to eat leather and bark as well as the flesh of the dead. After the famine, the Khazars conducted a census of metalworkers as well as fishermen, and began taxing these trades, as well as taking the customary tributes formerly paid to Persia.[32]

Control of these wealthy lands in the Caucasus enhanced the influence and independence of the Khazar branch of the A-shih-na, just as the western Türk empire fell apart. Though the dynastic history of the region is obscure over the next 20 years, the Khazar polity was probably already quite independent.[33] When we next hear of Khazar rulers they are referred to as kaghans, which is strong evidence that they were of royal origin. The tenth-century *Hudud al-' alam*, whose third chapter is devoted to the Khazars, claims that their rulers belonged to the A-shih-na dynasty. So, by 650, a branch of the Türk royal family, with its Türk followers, was apparently ruling an independent Khazaria, dominated demographically and militarily by Khazar Turks.[34]

As the western Türk empire collapsed, there emerged a second successor state in the western Caucasus, dominated by Bulghar tribes. This state, 'Magna Bulgharia', dominated the Pontic steppes from the Kuban to the Dnieper, and controlled the crucial commercial routes through the north

Map 11.1 The Khazar empire.

eastern shores of the Black Sea. Its capital may have been Phanagoria, which had been the kernel of powerful regional states since Cimmerian times. Archaeological evidence suggests that its peoples migrated into the Kuban steppes during the summers, and returned to the shores to fish in winter and spring. Its leading clans probably belonged to the Tu-lu groupings who had opposed the A-shih-na clans throughout the Türk civil wars but it probably included Onoghur and other Oghuric elements as well.[35] Kubrat, its first independent ruler, was christened in *c.*619, and educated in Constantinople, where he became a close friend of the emperor Heraclius. In *c.*635, he rejected Avar overlordship and established an independent state, known in Greek sources as 'Great Bulgharia'. In *c.*670, Great Bulgharia was defeated by Khazar armies. Some of its tribes, under one of Kubrat's sons, Asparukh, moved west and entered the Balkans in *c.*679. Here, they settled, forming a Bulghar kaghanate which eventually became Slavic in language and (*c.*865) Christian in religion.[36] Other remnants of the Bulghar diaspora ended up in Italy, in Bavaria and in Hungary under the Avars, while considerable numbers remained in the Caucasus where they became subjects of the Khazars. Finally, some Bulghars headed north to the Volga-Kama region, where their descendants began to rule over local Finno-Ugrian peoples and established a powerful polity in the late ninth century.

With the defeat of 'Magna Bulgharia', Khazaria emerged as the major power in the Caucasus. About three centuries later, a Khazar ruler, Joseph, described this conquest as the point at which the Khazars first established themselves as a significant power, breaking out from their original homeland in modern Daghestan, and securing direct control of most of the north Caucasus.[37] Khazar forces probably pursued Asparukh's Bulghars west, extending Khazar authority to the northern Pontic steppes. The Khazars also gained influence in the trading cities of Crimea, and by early in the eighth century they had official representatives here. Their involvement in the restoration to power, and final removal from power of the Byzantine emperor Justinian II (r. 685–95, 705–11), during the first decade of the eighth century, consolidated their power in the eastern Crimea.[38]

Khazar military power was tempered during a series of wars with the emerging power of Islam. Arabic armies first attacked the Khazars through the Caucasus in 642, just ten years after the death of the prophet, and again in 652. In the second attack, an Arab army equipped with ballistae besieged the fortified Khazar capital of Belendjer in the north Caucasus, before being repelled by the Khazar armies. Though the victory enhanced the prestige of the Khazars, it owed much to geography. Armies invading through the Caucasus had to move with their supply columns either through the narrow strip of the Caspian coast past Darband (Arabic 'Bab al-Awab'), or through the Darial (Arabic 'Dar-i Alan') pass to the north of Tiflis, which classical writers knew as the 'Caspian gates'.[39] Both routes were difficult and exposed to attack from local populations and it is this, more than anything else that allowed Khazaria to remain outside the Islamic world, whilst much of Central Asia was being incorporated within it. Indeed, so good a defence were the Caucasus mountains that no empire to their south, not even that of Tamerlaine in the fourteenth century, ever succeeded in permanently conquering the lands to their north, with perhaps the one exception of the Scythians. It is, therefore, an exaggeration to claim that Khazar power alone checked the Islamic advance to the north of the Caucasus as the Franks checked their advance into Europe.[40]

In the 660s and 680s, the Khazars launched new booty raids south of the Caucasus.[41] From 713, Arabic armies made a second assault on the north Caucasus, as other Arabic armies began to occupy Sogdia. In 722 an Arabic army led by Jarrah ibn-Abdullah al-Hakami captured Belendjer, but then retreated south, fearing that its passage through the Caucasus would be cut by hostile peoples. In 730, an entire Muslim army, commanded by Jarrah, was destroyed by the Khazars at Ardabil, south of modern Azerbaijan, and Khazar troops advanced into Persia as far as Mosul. Seven years later, in 737, a massive Arab invasion, led by Marwan b. Muhammad (who was to become the last Umayyad caliph, ruling as Marwan II (744–50)), succeeded in bypassing the Khazar system of fortifications by attacking simultaneously along the coast and through the Darial pass.[42] It advanced through the north Caucasus and captured the new Khazar capital of Itil, in the Volga delta. Marwan's army pursued the Khazars north along the Volga, where he defeated the Khazars, and forced their kaghan to profess Islam. However, the long Arabic lines of communication, and the collapse of the Umayyad caliphate prevented the Muslims from gaining permanent control

of the Khazar lands. The conversion of the Khazar kaghan, and his subordination to the caliphate proved temporary.

By 750, the Khazar empire had emerged as a great international power,
controlling large, variegated populations and rich trade routes. Its rulers
enjoyed the prestige of a royal genealogy, while its armies had successfully
repelled the armies of Islam. Khazar control extended from the Kazakh
steppes north-west of Khorezm, through the Caucasus, and westwards to the
Dnieper and perhaps even the Danube. Northward, Khazar power reached
into the wooded lands of the Volga, the Don and the Dnieper. Though based
further east, the Khazars now controlled most of the lands once controlled
by the eastern Goths.

THE KHAZAR EMPIRE AT ITS HEIGHT

In the late eighth century, the economies of Byzantium and the Islamic world
revived after the military and economic disasters of the seventh century.
Khazar relations with the Islamic world improved after 750, for the Abbassid
caliphate proved less expansionist and more commercially-minded than
the Umayyad caliphate.[43] In 758, the second Abbasid caliph, al-Mansur,
instructed his governor in Armenia to marry a Khazar princess, having
decided that Armenia could not flourish without a firm peace with Khazaria.
The kaghan agreed to offer his daughter in marriage. Al-Tabari gives a
description of her magnificent journey south. The *khatun* travelled with a
huge following of attendants and slaves, vast herds of livestock, ten wagons
with tents of silk and floors covered in sables, and 20 wagons with gold and
silver vessels and other gifts from her dowry.[44]

In a more stable international environment, the Khazar rulers began to
exploit the human and material resources under their control more systematically, transforming an empire of conquest into a great commercial empire.
Originally, the resources of its pastoralist and agricultural populations provided Khazaria's subsistence base, while war booty sustained its political system. Gradually, however, its elites found other sources of wealth, and as they
did so, the nature of the empire began to change.

Unlike the Huns or the Avars, the ruling elites of the Khazars never abandoned their steppe homelands or lifeways, though many ordinary Khazars
probably did become sedentary farmers, particularly in Daghestan.[45] Their
original base in modern Daghestan was a region of great ecological variety,
similar in many ways to the Semirechye, with its rivers and lakes, and its fine
summer pastures in the mountains. The ecology of both regions encouraged
sedentization and urbanization. Amongst those who remained pastoralists, it
encouraged a semi-sedentary pastoralism characterized by short migrations.

In winter the [peoples of the north Caucasus] made maximum use of whatever
fodder was available in the steppes, and in spring herds were driven up into the
mountain pastures for the summer. In the winter pastures, along rivers and
streams, there appeared more or less permanent settlements, winter camps. In

summer, the old and weak, or those without enough stock or incapable even of hiring themselves out to richer neighbours, stayed in the winter camps. In order not to die of hunger, they began to take up agriculture and crafts. In this way there gradually appeared in the steppes villages with sedentary populations.[46]

Though the Khazar elites remained at least partly nomadic, many of the peoples they ruled were sedentary, and some lived in small towns. According to a contemporary account, the Khazar armies of the 620s included many different 'tribes and peoples, dwellers in the meadows and the hills, those living in towns or in the open, those who shave their heads [probably Bulghars] and those with braided hair [Türk]'.[47]

Agriculture had ancient roots in the north Caucasus and the southern Crimea. According to al-Mas'udi, in the north Caucasian kingdom of the Alans, settement was so dense that 'When the cocks crow [in one village] the answer comes from the other parts of the kingdom because the villages are intermingled and close together.'[48] Here agriculture, viticulture and fruit-growing flourished with the help of irrigation. In the steppes north of the Caucasus, settlement was thinner. However, in the eighth century, agricultural communities reappeared in the eastern Pontic and Don steppes, where they had largely disappeared since the Hunnic invasions. They also appeared even further north, in the wooded steppes of the middle Don where agriculture had never been significant.[49] Whether attracted by the relative peace established by the Khazar empire, or driven north by the wars with Islam of the early eighth century, these communities formed a distinctive culture known to archaeologists as the Saltovo-Mayatskii culture. The 400 or more sites of this culture extend from the upper reaches of the Donets and Don to eastern Crimea to the Kuban and the shores of the Caspian and along the Volga as far as modern Saratov.[50] The similarities of the many sites of the Saltovo-Mayatskii culture, despite clear evidence of different ethnic origins, also hint at the creation of a common Khazar culture, whose lingua franca was presumably Khazar Turkic. The appearance of inscriptions in Turkic runes, mostly about very ordinary topics and on objects of ordinary use, suggests widespread literacy, even in remote steppe communities or forts.[51] Further west, in Ukraine, the *pax khazarica* allowed intensive settlement by Slavic agriculturalists who occupied lands cleared by the Khazars of Bulghar-speaking pastoralists.

Towns grew up around fortified strongholds or the winter camps of pastoralist chieftains. The first Khazar capital, Belendjer, has been identified with a fortified site near the village of Chir-yurt in Daghestan, which controlled access to the fertile and densely settled valley of the Sulak river.[52] This was probably not founded by the Khazars for it seems to have been a part of the extensive system of fortifications built by the Sassanians against pastoralists such as the Sabirs and Khazars, and centred on Darband. Nevertheless, it was almost certainly founded originally by sedentizing pastoralists, for archaeological excavations have shown that many of Belendjer's dwellings were either yurts or designed in the form of yurts. During the Arabic attack of 722, its inhabitants defended it with a circle of 3000 linked wagons, in a formation similar to the traditional Turkic *kuren*. Surrounding it were many other fortified settlements whose origins may have been similar. There are also many small forts which, like the forts of ancient Bactria, were probably occupied by single aristocratic families.[53] The second Khazar capital, Samandar, at the site of Tarki near Mahachkala, was as good a natural fortress as Darband. It was for a long time the gathering point for Khazar troops heading south and it offered direct control of the flourishing land and sea trade routes along the western shores of the Caspian Sea. It remained a city of more or less permanent yurts in the seventh and eighth centuries. It was probably the main Khazar centre between the Islamic capture of Belendjer in the 720s, and Marwan's attack on Itil in 737.[54] By the tenth century it was more settled. According to al-Istakhri, it had 4000 vineyards and a largely Muslim population. It is possible that for a time the capital, and the name, Samandar, was moved to the much better defended inland site of Shelkovskoe on the river Terek.[55]

The third great Khazar capital, Itil, was in the delta of the Volga, somewhere north of modern Astrakhan, in what had been Burtas (Bashkir) lands. It began as a royal encampment, around which gathered a relatively permanent population of traders, craftsmen and farmers. Its history is apparent from its design: 'the fortifications of Itil, as in the Hunnic camp of Attila and the Bulgharian capital, Pliska, were concentric (with the khan's palace at the centre); indeed the plan of Itil, according to King Joseph, was "in the form of a circle".'[56] The Khazars probably began to use it as a capital later in the eighth century, though Itil developed as a flourishing commercial city only in the ninth century.[57]

> Atil [wrote al-Istakhri] is in two parts, one west of the river called Atil, which is the larger, and the other east of it. The king lives in the western part. ... The extent of this part in length is about a league. It is surrounded by a wall, though the buildings spread beyond. Their houses are felt tents except a small number built of clay. They have markets and baths. In the town are people of the Muslims, more than 10,000, it is said. They have about thirty mosques. The king's castle is at a distance from the river-bank and is of brick. No one else owns a brick building, the king not permitting anyone to build with brick.[58]

Early Itil, with its mainly felt dwellings, may have been semi-mobile, like nineteenth-century Ulaanbaatar, and this may explain the difficulty archaeologists have faced in locating its site.[59] According to al-Mas'udi, the king's palace was on an island in the Volga, and linked to one shore by a bridge of ships. The tenth-century Khazar king, Joseph, wrote that the royal quarter of the city, which the ruler occupied with his princes, slaves and servants, contained all the fields and vineyards needed to support the royal palace. Al-Istakhri claimed that the king's household included some 4000 people, and other leading figures may have had equally large households.[60]

Many occupants of Itil farmed and kept vineyards in the nearby steppes. King Joseph wrote: 'From the month of Nisan [April] we go out from the city, each man to his vineyard and to his field and to his tillage.' The

Khazars, he adds, went into the fine black-soil lands of the steppes, 'in joy and with songs'.[61] Crops included millet as well as rice. Fish was also important. Indeed, al-Istakhrii wrote that the Khazar diet consisted mainly of rice and fish, and the Soviet archaeologist, Pletneva, has argued that fish was a staple food of most pastoralists in this region.[62]

The Khazar rulers mobilized the wealth of the varied lands they controlled, using various methods on the spectrum from plunder to trade. Tributes were both a source of wealth and a sign of respect, but the authority to exact them had to be continually reasserted. As well as war booty, mining and metallurgy contributed to Khazar wealth from very early, for the Caucasus was one of the world's oldest metallurgical centres, and Khazar armies exacted tribute from this region from as early as 628. In the tenth century, the Khazar king, Joseph, exacted tributes from the Oghuz steppes west of Khorezm, from many cities of Crimea, from the lands of the Volga, including the Volga Bulghars, and from many Slavic tribes, as well as from the core territories of the north Caucasus.[63] We know from the Russian Primary Chronicle, that in the mid-ninth century, the Khazars collected 'a squirrel-skin and a beaver-skin from each hearth', from the Slavic tribes of the Polyanians (who occupied the lands around Kiev), the Severyans and the Vyatichians. Other goods entered Khazaria as tribute or trade-goods from the north. In the early tenth century, al-Istakhri reported that beaver skins, honey and wax came to Itil from Volga Bulgharia and Rus'. They also exacted tributes of furs, hides and honey from Volga Bulgharia and the lands along the Volga river system, and they may also have received slaves as a form of tribute. Most slaves traded south were 'idolators' according to al-Istakhri (i.e. not people 'of the book'), and probably came from pagan Rus', or the Finno-Ugric-speaking peoples of the woodlands, or from the steppes.[64]

The Khazars maintained their rights to tribute partly through periodic military tours and the taking of hostages, and partly by planting garrisons in subordinate lands. In the tenth century, ibn Fadlan reported that 25 separate peoples had to offer royal princesses as the khaghan's brides.[65] However, the taking of hostages naturally provoked hostility. In c.920, the attempt to take a second daughter of the Volga Bulghar kaghan induced him to seek help from the caliphate against the Khazars. In the late eighth and early ninth centuries, the Khazars built a network of forts along the Don and Donets to exploit the growing sedentary populations of the region, and the flourishing trades that passed northwards towards the Volga and the Baltic. Most were built from blocks of white limestone to a standard pattern, and sited on promontories overlooking river valleys. They acted, apparently, as winter bases for pastoralist armies that maintained Khazar authority and collected Khazar tributes. There may also have been Khazar forts as far afield as Kiev. Indeed, it is possible that Kiev was originally founded as a Khazar garrison. Kiev was a natural site for a garrison, as it controlled the lucrative trade routes to eastern Europe dominated by the Radanite Jews.[66]

The best known Khazar fort, at Sarkel on the Don, was built in c.840, with the help of Byzantine architects, probably to control Magyar pastoralists.

Sarkel also acted as a customs post, for it controlled the portage from the Volga to the Don. The site (excavated by the Soviet archaeologist, Artamonov, before it was flooded under the Tsimlyanskoe reservoir) was protected by the Don itself, then by a surrounding ditch, and finally by brick walls 3.75 metres thick, with huge towers at their corners.[67] The building techniques show that, though Byzantium offered architectural advice, the labour force was Khazar, and it was probably quite expert, for the Khazars had long experience of fort-building, and maintained much of the Sassanian system of fortifications scattered throughout Daghestan. Like many Khazar cities, what started out as a fortress soon became a small town, as settlements of farmers appeared, and the town's commerce expanded.[68] Sarkel's population belonged to two distinct types. One group represents local farming populations, who occupied semi-subterranean houses and used ceramics typical of the local 'Saltov' culture. The second group were pastoralists, who lived in mobile dwellings, with temporary brick fireplaces. They made up the fighting forces of the fortress. The artefacts of the first group, show many similarities with the mainly Bulghar cultures of the Don and the mainly Alan cultures of the north Caucasus. They probably represent syncretic Khazar or Bulghar populations, using Khazar as a lingua franca, while the culture of the second group seems clearly to be non-Khazar and probably represents Oghuz or Pecheneg Türks who served as mercenaries and auxiliaries.[69]

Tribute-collecting shaded imperceptibly into trade. Itil lay at the crossroads of two major trade routes. The first was a northern branch of the Silk Road, that led from the Syr Darya and Khorezm, around the north of the Caspian sea, through the Volga Delta and towards the cities of the Black Sea. The second connected the wealthy cities of Persia and Mesopotamia through the Caucasus, with the forest communities of the far north, the Baltic and northern Europe. Both routes flourished in the eighth and ninth centuries. This can be shown by an increase in the amount of silver found along them.[70]

The old trade routes between Persia and the forest lands of the middle Volga were clearly active in the sixth century, but declined during the seventh and early eighth centuries, partly because of the wars between Khazaria and the caliphate, and partly because of declining Byzantine and Sassanian demand for furs during the depression of the seventh and early eighth centuries. From the middle of the eighth century, trade revived along these routes. As early as 730, merchants from Khazaria appeared in Darband, while Darband merchants traded in Khazaria, paying a tithe for the privilege.[71] Merchants from Volga Bulgharia obtained furs from forest peoples to their north, in exchange for metal blades and harpoons which Islamic manufacturers prepared especially for the forest peoples. In the tenth century, al-Istakhrii reported that the Khazar king's revenues came from customs dues on trade by land and sea, as well as from tithes levied on trade goods and produce. According to the *Hudud al-' Alam*, 'the well-being and wealth of the king of the Khazars are mostly from the maritime customs.'[72] Khazar forts such as Kiev or Sarkel collected customs dues as well as tributes. Khazaria sent the goods it received as tributes or trade from the north on to the markets of the Caucasus, Khorezm, Khorasan and Constantinople, in return for textiles, luxury goods and large amounts of Islamic coinage, some of which it sent back to the north. Coins first begin to be used within Khazaria in the eighth century. Most were Arabic dirhams or Khazar imitations.[73] Though the Khazars mainly taxed the commerce of others, they may also have engaged directly in trade on their own account. It is possible, for example, that they controlled ships in the Caspian, the Black Sea, and along the Volga, despite al-Mas'udi's claim that they had no navy.[74]

Slowly, Khazar diplomacy began to reflect a growing dependence on commerce. Relations with Byzantium were dominated by competition for the trade routes from the Volga to the Sea of Azov and Crimea, and no permanent arrangement was ever reached. As early as the seventh century, the Khazars tried to replace Byzantium as suzerains over the northern and eastern shores of the Black Sea. Khazar boycotts sometimes deprived the Crimean towns of supplies of grain, forcing them to rely on supplies by sea or accept Khazar suzerainty. Meanwhile, both sides dabbled in the politics of the other. While in exile in the Crimea, the Byzantine emperor Justinian II (r. 685–95, 705–11), married the sister of the Khazar kaghan, and the kaghan himself visited Constantinople soon after Justinian's return to power.[75] By now, Khazaria controlled most Crimean ports, except for Cherson which they returned to Byzantium as an act of friendship. In 732, just after the great Khazar victory over the Arabs, Leo III, the 'Isaurian' (711–41), married his son to Chichek ('flower'?), the daughter of the Khazar kaghan. Their son, Leo IV, was known as 'the Khazar'. When Khazaria was at peace with the Muslim world, border conflicts in Crimea and Georgia easily led to conflict with Byzantium. Though Byzantium accepted Khazar suzerainty over much of Crimea in the eighth century, it simultaneously undermined that control by encouraging the spread of Christianity. In the late eighth century, the bishopric of Doros in Crimean Gothia, became briefly a metropolitan seat, supervising bishoprics in Crimea, Itil, Tamatarkha and other parts of Khazaria.[76]

Khazaria's trading contacts introduced large populations of Muslim traders (from both Khorezm and Persia) and Christians. Christianity had old roots in the region, for in Belendjer there are the remains of two Christian churches dating to the earliest years of Khazar rule. They probably reflect the spread of Christianity from Albania and Armenia.[77] There were also many Jews in Khazaria, particularly in Crimea and the north Caucasus. Some may have been refugees from the Sassanian persecutions of Mazdakaism early in the sixth century, while many more arrived during the first great Byzantine persecutions of Jews, under Heraclius, in 630–2, or the early eighth-century persecutions of Leo III. Radanite Jews were particularly important. Originally based in the Rhone valley, they controlled trade routes reaching from Europe to China, and trading in silk, furs, weapons, spices and slaves.[78] Jewish merchants were particularly important in towns such as Samander and Itil. Like Sogdians within the Türk empires, they were important and influential because of their trading connections and their literacy.

THE CONVERSION TO JUDAISM

A century after the Uighurs converted to Manichaeism, the Khazar kings and some of the leading Khazar families converted to Judaism. Khazar religious traditions, like those of other Turkic peoples, included the worship of *tengri*, as well as of natural forces such as fire. We know of these traditions both from literary sources and from the remains of Khazar religious sites.[79] These, and other religious traditions probably survived the conversion of the elites to Judaism, nevertheless, politically and diplomatically, the conversion to Judaism was a matter of immense importance.

The causes and timing of this momentous event remain obscure. There are hints in the Khazar records of a two-stage conversion, which has led some commentators to suggest that Judaism began to spread amongst the Khazar elites as early as the eighth century. Artamanov argued, for example, that Judaism began to spread in the 730s, after the invasion of Marwan, and was finally adopted as the official religion of the Khazars during a period of internal conflict late in the eighth or early in the ninth centuries. Simon Szyszman has argued in several works that the Khazar kings converted, not to Rabbinical Judaism, but to Karaism, as a result of the work of a Karaite missionary, Isaac Sangari, some time in the eighth century. However, the most recent account, which relies mainly on Khazar documents, suggests that the conversion was a simpler, and more rapid process, occurring in 861, perhaps as a result of a series of internal and external crises.[80] The so-called 'Genizah' letter, written in *c*.949, clearly preserves Khazar traditions. According to these, early Jewish settlers in Khazaria merged with the local population and lost most of their Jewish traditions. However, eventually a powerful Khazar military commander of Jewish origin, called Bulan, was persuaded by his wife, Sarah, to return to the Jewish religion, after which he took the Jewish name of 'Sabriel'. His conversion, and, perhaps, his active support of Judaism, provoked opposition within the Khazar elite, as a result of which, Bulan persuaded the Khazar kaghan to hold a formal disputation between representatives of different religions. Zuckerman argues that the story of a disputation can be taken quite literally, as it is confirmed by a Byzantine source, the *Life of Constantine*, which allows us to date the event precisely to 861. Constantine (St Cyril), the later creator of the first Cyrillic alphabet, learnt Khazar in Cherson before travelling to Itil in that year.[81]

Though Judaism spread within the Khazar elites and within the merchant community, it never spread widely amongst the Khazar population, and other religions, including Islam, Christianity and forms of traditional paganism, continued to thrive even in the tenth century. According to al-Istakhri: 'The smallest group is the Jews, most of them being Muslims and Christians, though the king and his court are Jews.' Ibn Rusta, who wrote in *c*.900, claimed that, though the rulers and elites adopted Judaism, most of the ordinary Khazars 'are of a faith similar to that of the Turks'. According to the Arab traveller, al-Mas'udi, in tenth-century Itil there were separate judges for the different religious groups, two for the Christian population, two for the Muslims, two for the Khazars (judging in accordance with the Torah) and one for the pagan population, the Rus' and *Saqaliba*. For the Muslim population there was a mosque and minaret in the eastern half of the city.[82]

After the conversion, there emerged a sort of dual kingship, as the power of the Khazar *kaghans* became more and symbolic, while real power fell into the hands of Jewish 'kings' or 'beks', descendants, apparently, of Bulan. By the late ninth century, military and political power was held by the *kaghan-bek* or *isha*, who handled day-to-day business and led the army. The 'great khaghan' became a purely sacral figure, isolated from the people, rarely appearing in public, and treated publicly as a near-god, though liable to be murdered if the fortunes of the polity declined. Those who approached him had to be purified by fire, and those who buried him were executed so that the site of his grave would remain secret.[83] Ibn Fadlan was told that the 'great kaghan' had 25 wives, each the daughter of a subordinate ruler, as well as 60 concubines, and each had a separate dwelling and was guarded by a eunuch. Ibn Rusta reported that: 'The power to command belongs to the Isha [bek], since in regard to control and the armies he is so placed that he does not have to care for anyone above him.'[84] In this way, military and sacral power were divided.

The conversion to Judaism may have narrowed the support basis of the Khazar rulers. The creation, probably in the same period, of a large, mercenary army, suggests declining support amongst the Turkic elites for the Khazar government, as it came to rely, increasingly, on its wealth rather than on more traditional ties of tribal loyalty. The use of mercenaries, like the use of foreign slave soldiers by the Abbasids from the early ninth century, suggests a decline in support amongst local aristocracies. By the early tenth century, the core of the Khazar standing army, which included some 12,000 soldiers, was recruited from Khorezmian Muslims, and their presence gave Islam a powerful voice in Khazarian affairs.[85] The army also included more traditional contingents of soldiers levied from the Khazar tribes. Al-Mas'udi noted that the Khazar kings were the only rulers of the region to have a standing army, though such armies were becoming the norm in the Islamic world.[86]

Though less Khazar, the army became more professional. Ibn Rusta, writing soon after 900, described its annual campaigns against the Turkic-speaking Pecheneg tribes who had entered the Pontic steppes late in the ninth century. 'When they go out in any direction, they do so armed in full array, with banners, spears, and strong coats of mail. He [the isha or bek] rides forth with 10,000 horsemen, of whom some are regular paid troops and others have been levied on the rich.'[87] At the end of a campaign, the Isha had first choice of booty, and the rest was divided amongst the troops. Pecheneg slaves were sold to Islamic countries.[88]

Government, too, became more professional as literacy spread in the ninth and tenth centuries. The letter of King Joseph refers to ancient genealogical texts, and in Crimea there are Khazar inscriptions in a runic script similar to the Orkhon Türk inscriptions. There may even have existed a cyrillic alphabet. After the conversion to Judaism, it is likely that Jewish writing, and the Jewish script became important not just for religious, but also for commercial and official purposes.[89]

In a distant echo of what had happened in the Uighur empire, and was also occurring amongst many Islamic states at the same time, legitimate authority and military authority became separated. Artamonov comments: 'Khazaria became a commercial city with a surrounding hinterland, and not a country with a capital.'[90]

CHALLENGES TO KHAZAR POWER

The Khazar empire remained a major international power until the middle of the tenth century. However, during the last century of its existence, there were many signs of fragility. The Khazars lost their ability to police the Pontic steppes, and also lost control of important sources of tribute. Both developments may reflect a shift in the government's support base away from the pastoralist Khazar elites and towards a narrower constituency dominated by merchants and Khazar adherents of Judaism.

In the lands between the Don and the Volga, there had long existed groups of Ugric speakers, strongly influenced by Turkic culture, who eventually were to form the core of the 'Magyar'. In the 820s and 830s, these groups became increasingly independent, and began attacking their Khazar overlords. They soon became independent of the Khazars, and were, for a time, the dominant force between the Don and the Danube.[91] It may have been the increased instability this caused in the steppes that persuaded Byzantium to send an architect to help Khazaria build the fort of Sarkel in 838. In the 890s, Pecheneg groups from the Kazakh steppes entered the Pontic steppes, driven west by neighbouring Oghuz, and breaching the cordon between the Pontic and Khazakh steppes created by the Khazars.[92] In c.895, they defeated the Maygars, who moved west of the Carpathians in c.898. In the almost deserted Hungarian basin, the Magyars formed a predatory state similar to that of the Huns and Avars. However, like the Bulghars, they eventually established a durable sedentary state, that of Hungary, in the late tenth century. In 1000 CE, under Istvan (Stephen), the Magyars converted to Christianity.

According to Gardizi, the Pechenegs were a numerous and wealthy people, with huge numbers of livestock, gold and silver utensils, fine weapons and battle horns made from the horns of bulls. A clear sign of the destructiveness of their invasions is the rapid decline of the 'Saltovo-Maitskii' culture after 890, and the abandonment of the white fortresses, which had been the keys to Khazar control of the lands between the Volga and the Dnieper.[93] By the middle of the tenth century, the Byzantine emperor, Constantine Porphyrogenitus (r. 913–59), regarded the Pechenegs, not the Khazars, as the dominant force in the Pontic steppes, despite the fact that the Pechenegs were divided into eight separate hordes, each with its own kaghan.[94] Like the Scythians, their kaghans occasionally met in gatherings at which they arranged military alliances, and these were powerful enough to overthrow Khazar suzerainty. From this time on, the Khazars lost control of the wealthy trade routes through the Pontic steppes. Sarkel now became a frontier fortress, and expanded in size and wealth through cross-border trade.[95]

The collapse of Khazar power in the Pontic steppes undermined Khazar authority elsewhere. By the early tenth century, the Oghuz tribes of the Kazakh steppes, the Bashkir tribes to the north of the Khazars, and even some of the Caucasian peoples of Khazaria, such as the newly Christianized Alans, were showing signs of impatience with Khazar suzerainty. Constantine Porphyrogenitus described how easy it now was for the Alans to cut the vital trade routes between Sarkel and Cherson.[96]

During the ninth century, there had emerged two more significant rivals to Khazar power within western Inner Eurasia. Closest to Itil was the emerging power of Volga Bulgharia. There is evidence of a Bulghar diaspora in the mid-Volga region from the late eighth century, but migrations continued, particularly in the middle of the ninth century, perhaps as a result of Magyar incursions. At some point, Bulghar elites began extracting tributes from the Slavic- and Ugric-speaking farming and woodland peoples of the region. This was an old pattern of relations in the region, for Sarmatian pastoralists had played a similar role as early as the third and second centuries BCE.[97] Early in the tenth century, the Volga Bulghars emerged as a significant commercial and military power, which accepted Khazar suzerainty, but with some reluctance.

Control of the trade routes along and parallel to the Volga was the basis of Volga Bulghar power. In the early tenth century, silver dirhams were so common that ibn Fadlan witnessed them being scattered over honoured guests at ceremonies.[98] From the middle of the tenth century, Volga Bulgharia began to mint its own dirhams, modelled on those of Samanid Central Asia. Much of the state's revenue came from trade, mainly in furs, for the rulers took a tithe on all trade passing through their lands. Ibn Fadlan, who visited in c.921, reported that the Bulghar kaghan personally checked on the payment of tithes by ships travelling through his realm.[99] Many of their furs, and other trade goods, then passed through Khazaria and the Oghuz lands of western Kazakhstan to Khorezm and on to the Islamic world. According to al-Muqaddasi, the goods traded in this way included:

> sable-skins, squirrel-skins, ermine-skins, marten, foxes, beavers, rabbits of all colors, goat-hides, wax, arrows, poplar wood, hats, fish-glue, fish-teeth, castoreum, yellow amber, *kimuxt* (a type of leather hide), Saqlab [Slav] slaves, sheep and cattle.[100]

The capital, Bulghar, was near modern Kazan. According to al-Muqaddasi, Bulghar could provide 20,000 horsemen.[101] It had a small artisan quarter, occupied by Slavic immigrants. Archaeologists have discovered evidence of at least 20 other towns in Volga Bulgharia, and many smaller settlements.[102] Most of the lands controlled by the Bulghar were wooded, with sedentary communities. According to ibn Rusta, who wrote early in the tenth century: 'They are a people who possess fields and agriculture and cultivate all (types of) grain: wheat, barley, millet and the like.' The main foodstuffs ibn Fadlan observed were millet and horse meat, as well as wheat and barley.[103]

Despite the agrarian basis of the lands they ruled, the Bulghar elites preserved the traditions of the steppes, for they regularly raided their southern neighbours, the 'Burdas' (Bashkirs), often taking captives as slaves. Ibn Rusta reported that they fought on horseback and demanded horses as tributes. According to ibn Fadlan, the Volga Bulghars lived in tents, though many of their subjects lived in wooden houses in the towns, in winter, and in tents in summer. The kaghan's tent was vast, capable of holding up to 1000 people, and was decorated with Armenian carpets and Byzantine brocades.[104]

In the early tenth century, the rulers of Volga Bulgharia still accepted Khazar suzerainty, and sent hostages to Itil. However, they were already trading directly with Samanid Central Asia, sending caravans to Khorezm along difficult routes that bypassed Itil and its customs officials. There is powerful evidence of the scale of this trade in the large numbers of Samanid dirhams that begin to appear in the Baltic in the tenth century. This route presumably deprived the Khazars of much of the wealth they had once levied on the trade along the Volga. Archaeological evidence shows that Islam began to spread amongst the Volga Bulghars from late in the ninth century, and when ibn Rusta wrote, early in the tenth century, he reported that most Volga Bulghars were Muslim, 'and in their settlements are mosques and Koranic schools; they have muezzins and imams'.[105] In c.920, a Bulghar kaghan sought the help of the caliphate in spreading Islam in his lands, and in defending them against the Khazars. The mission sent by the caliph, was described in extraordinary detail by one of its members, ibn Fadlan, whose account is the main literary source on the Volga Bulghars in this era. By c.950, the Bulgars were striking their own dirhams, which suggests that they no longer accepted Khazar suzerainty.[106]

More remote, but eventually more dangerous, was the power of Rus'. By 840, there is evidence of a Rus' kaghanate, probably based on the settlement of Gorodishche, near modern Novgorod. In 860, its leaders were powerful enough to launch a major attack on Constantinople, perhaps from ships that had travelled along the Volga or Don, through the territory of the Volga Bulghars and Khazars. Some time in the 20 years after 864, Rus' armies led a similar expedition to the Caspian, presumably with Khazar consent. Between 910 and 912, large Rus' armies travelled through Khazaria, probably from the Black Sea and Sarkel, and began to raid the Caspian sea, promising the Khazars a half of their booty.[107] According to al-Mas'udi, in c.912, the last of these expeditions was attacked by the largely Muslim population of Itil on its return from the Caspian, in revenge for the devastation it had caused to Muslim towns on the shores of the Caspian. Most of its members (30,000 men according to al-Mas'udi) were killed during a three-day battle in Itil, and the rest were slaughtered as they fled north through the lands of the Bashkir/Burtas and the Volga Bulghars.[108] This uprising suggests that the Jewish kings now had limited control even in Itil, their capital.

DECLINE AND FALL

Though Khazar control of the Volga trades was slipping, and they no longer controlled the Pontic steppes in the early tenth century, the Khazars still controlled the main trade routes from the Caspian to the Black Sea, and continued to exact tributes from many forest tribes. They may even have maintained a garrison at Kiev. They were still a major international power in the early tenth century, and both the Rus' and the Volga Bulghars probably accepted Khazar suzerainty. There is shadowy evidence of a period of warfare between Khazaria and Byzantium, in which the forces of Rus' and the Christianized Alan tribes of Khazaria were also engaged, for control of the trading ports of the eastern Pontic shores, such as Kerch.[109] On and off, this war may have lasted from the 920s until in 941 the Khazars repelled a Rus' attack on Kerch, and forced the Rus' troops to turn on Constantinople. Though Khazar armies probably held their own in these conflicts, in the letter of king Joseph, written in c.960, one can already detect a note of desperation: 'By the help of the Almighty I guard the mouth of the river and do not allow the Russians who come in ships to come by sea to go against the Arabs, nor any enemy by land to come to [Darband?]. I fight with them. If I allowed them for one hour, they would destroy all the country of the Arabs as far as Baghdad.'[110]

Joseph had good reason to be nervous. In 964–5, five years after he wrote, a Rus' army led by prince Svyatoslav defeated the Vyatichian tributaries of the Khazars along the Oka river, then sailed down the Volga, and defeated the Volga Bulghars. In 965, in alliance with Oghuz tribes from the Kazakh steppes, and perhaps also with the Pechenegs, his armies destroyed Itil and Samander, and Khazar power collapsed for good. Returning to Kiev via the Don, Svyatoslav destroyed the fortress of Sarkel and probably sacked Kerch.[111]

As Rus' power expanded, Slavic settlements spread in the lands of the Saltovo-Maitskii culture. Signs of this demographic shift are clearest at the site of Sarkel, where there appear typically Slavic semi-subterranean dwellings with brick stoves and moulded ceramics. By the next century, Sarkel (known in Slavic as 'Biela Vezha', White city) was a flourishing Slavic city, with developed handicrafts and extensive trade connections. However, by the twelfth century, it had been reclaimed by the steppes, and had become a winter camp of the Kipchak.[112] Further south, a Rus' principality emerged at Tmutorokan' early in the eleventh century, as Rus' princes asserted their authority over the trade routes that had once been the basis of Khazar commercial power. However, this, too, was lost to Rus' early in the twelfth century.[113]

Though a Rus' prince destroyed Khazaria, the polity he ruled owed much to Khazar commercial and political traditions. The debt has never been repaid, for modern Russian scholarship, partly under pressure from Stalinist censors, has generally refused to accept the role played by Khazaria in the creation of the medieval state of Rus'. Indeed, the greatest Soviet scholar of Khazaria, Artamonov, who was himself of Turkic descent, was forced to retract his earlier, positive assessment of Khazar influence on Rus', and argue in his *History of the Khazars*, that Russia took nothing of value from the Khazars.[114] Chapter 13 will show the profound impact of Khazaria on the early state of Rus'.

NOTES

1 P. B. Golden, 'The peoples of the south Russian steppes', in *CHEIA* (pp. 256–84), p. 258; and see Golden, *Introduction*, pp. 94–5, 103–4; Golden, *Khazar Studies*, 1:34; Moravcsik, *Byzantinoturcica*, pp. 65–7.

2 Obolensky, *Byzantine Commonwealth*, pp. 68–9; Artamonov, *Istoriya khazar*, p. 80.

3 Cited in Golden, *Introduction*, p. 98.

4 Artamonov, *Istoriya khazar*, pp. 92–4, and see 88–90; it may be that Grod was converted by this mission, which was led by a bishop, Kardost.

5 *Constantine Porphyrogenitus*, pp. 55–57; Noonan, 'Byzantium and the Khazars', pp. 118–20.

6 *Menander*, pp. 43, 45.

7 Cited in Artamonov, *Istoriya khazar*, p. 96.

8 Ibid., p. 74; and see Golden, *Introduction*, pp. 104–5; Artamonov, *Istoriya khazar*, ch. 3 is on the Sabirs.

9 Artamonov, *Istoriya khazar*, p. 70, and see p. 74; Golden, 'Peoples of the south Russian steppes', in *CHEIA*, pp. 259–60; Golden, *Introduction*, p. 105.

10 Golden, *Introduction*, pp. 109–10.

11 Obolensky, *Byzantine Commonwealth*, p. 72.

12 Artamonov, *Istoriya khazar*, p. 156, from the Chronicle of Feofan.

13 S. Szádeczky-Kardoss, 'Avars', in *CHEIA* (pp. 206–28), p. 207; Artamonov, *Istoriya Khazar*, p. 160; Gumilev, *Drevnie Tyurki*, p. 37, suggests that the Avars in these years acted as allies of Persia.

14 Szádeczky-Kardoss, 'Avars', in *CHEIA*, p. 208.

15 Obolensky, *Byzantine Commonwealth*, pp. 75–7.

16 Artamonov, *Istoriya khazar*, pp. 111–12; Szádeczky-Kardoss, 'Avars', in *CHEIA*, p. 212.

17 On the origins of the stirrup, Barclay, *Role of the Horse*, pp. 47, 113–14, and p. 98, which suggests that Avars began to use stirrups later than the sixth century; see also Szádeczky-Kardoss, 'Avars', in *CHEIA*, p. 211.

18 Pletneva, *Kochevniki srednevekov'ya*, p. 47; Artamonov, *Istoriya khazar*, p. 113.

19 Cited in Szádeczky-Kardoss, 'Avars', in *CHEIA*, p. 211.

20 Obolensky, *Byzantine Commonwealth*, p. 183.

21 Szádeczky-Kardoss, 'Avars', in *CHEIA*, p. 227.

22 Szádeczky-Kardoss, 'Avars', in *CHEIA*, pp. 212–14; See also Obolensky, *Byzantine Commonwealth*, pp. 78, 85.

23 Words in one of the few surviving Khazar documents, a letter from Kiev, seem to be Oghur, according to Golb and Pritsak, *Khazarian-Hebrew Documents*, p. 42; on Khazar origins, see Golden, *Introduction*, pp. 233–6; attempts have been made to show that they were of Iranian or Ugrian origin (Artamonov, *Istoriya khazar*, pp. 114ff. claims they were Turkicized Ugrians, like the Magyars), and these may contain some truth, for there were certainly people of Ugrian and Iranian descent within the grouping.

24 Golden, *Introduction*, p. 235.

25 Golden, *Introduction*, p. 236; and Artamonov, *Istoriya khazar*, p. 128; Pletneva, *Khazary*, 2nd edn, pp. 15–16.

26 Gumilev, *Drevnie Tyurki*, p. 159; Artamonov, *Istoriya khazar*, p. 146–7; Mo-ho-sad was in China from 618–626 and then vanishes from the Chinese records.

27 Artamonov, *Istoriya khazar*, p. 146; according to Klyashtornyi and Sultanov, *Kazakhstan*, pp. 94–5, it was the Western Türk kaghan, T'ung yabghu kaghan, who took part in these campaigns.

28 Cited from the Armenian *History of Albania* of Moisei Kagankatvatsi (which is based on the life of the Albanian bishop, Viro), from Artamonov, *Istoriya khazar*, p. 147.

29 On Iberia as a frontier region, see Braund, *Georgia in Antiquity*, ch. 7.

30 Artamonov, *Istoriya khazar*, pp. 148–50.

31 Cited from the *History of Albania*, in Artamonov, *Istoriya khazar*, pp. 151–2.

32 Artamonov, *Istoriya khazar*, p. 153.

33 Novosel'tsev, *Khazarskoe gosudarstvo*, p. 88, argues that, though they recognized the suzerainty of the western Türk, they were, in practice, independent from the 620s.

34 Artamonov, *Istoriya khazar*, p. 180, and see pp. 170–1.

35 Pletneva, *Kochevniki*, p. 48, and see pp. 20–1; on the Bulghars, see Golden, *Introduction*, pp. 103–4, 244–6.

36 Golden, 'The peoples of the south Russian steppes', in *CHEIA*, p. 262; and see Golden, *Introduction*, p. 245; Artamonov, *Istoriya khazar*, p. 161.

37 Pletneva, *Khazary*, 2nd edn, pp. 7, 21; on Joseph's letters, the only authentic Khazar source on Khazar history, see Pletneva, *Khazary*, pp. 5–13, or Kokovtsev, *Evreisko-khazarskaya perepiska*.

38 Pletneva, *Khazary*, 2nd edn, pp. 22–3; and see Golden, *Khazar Studies*, 1:60–1; on the relative autonomy of Khazar-controlled Crimea, see Artamonov, *Istoriya khazar*, pp. 252–8, and see ibid., p. 174.

39 These were the two easiest passes through the Caucasus but there were many more; see Braund, *Georgia in Antiquity*, p. 45.

40 Dunlop, for example, writes: 'Though the great mountain range would doubtless have caused the invaders from the south much difficulty in any case, sooner or later they would have overrun any but a strong and well-organized resistance. Such they appear to have met in the Khazars.' *History*, p. 46; Artamanov makes a similar point, *Istoriya khazar*, p. 224.

41 Artamonov, *Istoriya khazar*, p. 181.

42 Magomedov, *Obrazovanie*, p. 193; and see Dunlop, *History*, pp. 64–6, 69–71.

43 Golden, *Introduction*, p. 239.

44 al-Tabari, III: 647; cited in Dunlop, *History*, pp. 179–8; and see Artamonov, *Istoriya khazar*, p. 241.

45 Magomedov, *Obrazovanie*, p. 95.

46 Pletneva, *Khazary*, 2nd edn, p. 24.

47 Cited in Artamonov, *Istoriya khazar*, p. 146, from the *History of Albania*, which used contemporary sources, and see pp. 155–6; Bulghars often wore a single plait on a shaven head, a style later mimicked by prince Svyatoslav and the Cossacks of Ukraine.

48 Golden, *Khazar Studies*, 1:94.

49 Artamonov, *Istoriya khazar*, pp. 235ff; see also Mikheev, *Podon'e v sostave Khazarskogo kaganata*; Magomedov, *Obrazovanie*, pp. 97–8.

50 Pletneva, *Khazary*, 2nd edn, p. 41; the main archaeological survey of the culture is Pletneva's *Ot kochevii k gorodam*.

51 Pletneva, *Khazary*, 2nd edn, pp. 46, 48; Artamonov, *Istoriya khazar*, pp. 241, 293–4.

52 Magomedov, *Obrazovanie*, pp. 36, 49; and see the map in Dunlop, *History*, p. 88; Pritsak argues that it was at Semender on the River Terek; Pritsak, 'The Khazar kingdom's conversion to Judaism', in *Studies in Medieval Eurasian*

History, XI:262; Artamonov, *Istoriya khazar*, p. 399 places it near modern Bunaks in Daghestan; Pletneva, *Khazary*, 2nd edn, p. 25 places it further inland on the River Sulak.

53 Pletneva, *Khazary*, 2nd edn, pp. 28–9, and see pp. 25–7; Magomedov, *Obrazovanie*, pp. 28–34, 51, 95–6, 140, 146, 154; Artamonov, *Istoriya khazar*, p. 207.

54 According to Novosel'tsev, *Khazarskoe gosudarstvo*, p. 128; see also Pletneva, *Khazary*, 2nd edn, p. 28; Magomedov, *Obrazovanie*, pp. 54, 52–7, 183.

55 Magomedov, *Obrazovanie*, p. 59; this might account for differences in contemporary accounts of the location of Samandar; see also Dunlop, *History*, p. 95.

56 Pletneva, *Kochevniki*, p. 51.

57 Magomedov, *Obrazovanie*, p. 59.

58 Dunlop, *History*, pp. 91–2.

59 Golden, *Khazar Studies*, 1:106; it is also possible that the site lies under the shifting waters of the Volga delta.

60 Artamonov, *Istoriya khazar*, pp. 400–1, and see p. 394; see also Dunlop, *History*, p. 205.

61 Artamonov, *Istoriya khazar*, p. 398; Dunlop, *History*, p. 149.

62 Dunlop, *History*, p. 93, and see p. 225; see also Pletneva, cited in Golden, *Khazar Studies*, 1:103.

63 Artamonov, *Istoriya Khazar*, pp. 385–6; on taxation in 628, Dunlop, *History*, p. 30; and see Ibid., p. 227.

64 Dunlop, *History*, pp. 93, 96; ibn Fadlan, *Risala*, pp. 140–1.

65 Ibn Fadlan, *Risala*, p. 147; on ibn Fadlan's sources, see Dunlop, *History*, p. 109; in this customary way, a political relationship was represented symbolically as a relationship of kinship.

66 Curtin, *Cross-Cultural Trade*, p. 106; the main Arabic source is ibn Kurdadbeh; on the Khazar system of forts, see Franklin and Shepard, *Emergence of Rus*, pp. 95–6 and pp. 79–83; and Golb and Pritsak, *Khazarian-Hebrew Documents*, p. 44.

67 Artamonov, *Istoriya khazar*, p. 300; on Artamonov's excavations at Sarkel (now under the Tsimylanskii reservoir), see pp. 299ff.

68 Pletneva, *Khazary*, 2nd edn, pp. 52–4; Magomedov, *Obrazovanie*, pp. 125–45.

69 Artamonov, *Istoriya khazar*, pp. 312–13, and see pp. 307–8, 357.

70 Franklin and Shepard, *Emergence of Rus*, p. 8.

71 Ibid., pp. 7–10.

72 Golden, *Khazar Studies*, 1:67; al-Istakhrii cited in Dunlop, *History*, p. 93; on the Volga Bulghars, Janet Martin, *Treasure of the Land of Darkness*, p. 22.

73 Pletneva, *Khazary*, 2nd edn, pp. 56–7.

74 Dunlop, *History*, p. 229.

75 Ibid., pp. 171–2; Artamonov, *Istoriya khazar*, pp. 195–6; and see Noonan, 'Byzantium and the Khazars', for a general survey of relations with Byzantium.

76 Artamonov, *Istoriya khazar*, pp. 258–60 and see ch. 14; Golden, *Khazar Studies*, 1:65.

77 Magomedov, *Obrazovanie*, pp. 158, 166, 170.

78 On the Radanites, see L. Rabinowitz, *Jewish Merchant Adventurers: A Study of the Radanites*, London: Edward Goldston, 1948; on the extent of their trade networks, see Ibn Khurdadhbih's description, cited in Golden, *Khazar Studies*, 1:108–9.

79 Magomedov, *Obrazovanie*, pp. 155–8.

80 Zuckermann, 'On the date'; Artamonov, *Istoriya khazar*, p. 327, argues for a prolonged period of civil conflict in the early ninth century; see also Artamonov,

Istoriya khazar, pp. 275–6, who bases his claim in part on al-Mas'udi's claim that the conversion occurred during the reign of the caliph Haroun al-Rashid (r. 786–809); see also Szyszman, *Le Karaïsme*, p. 71; my thanks to Leonid Lavrin for this last reference.

81 Artamonov, *Istoriya khazar*, pp. 331ff; Zuckerman, 'On the date', pp. 243–4.

82 Ibn Fadlan, in ibn Fadlan, *Risala*, pp. 147–8; the minaret was destroyed by the Khazar king, on hearing of the destruction of a synagogue in the Islamic world; al-'Mas'udi cited from Pritsak, 'The Khazar kingdom's conversion to Judaism', p. 266; al-Istakhrii cited from Dunlop, *History*, p. 92; ibn Rusta from ibid., p. 104.

83 Ibn Fadlan, in ibn Fadlan, *Risala*, pp. 146–7; Golden, 'Peoples of the south Russian steppes', in *CHEIA*, p. 264, and see p. 270; Artamonov, *Istoriya khazar*, p. 410 notes the similarity with the sacral kingships of Frazer's 'Golden Bough'; the earliest evidence on this division is in al-Mas'udi, cited in Artamonov, *Istoriya khazar*, p. 275; Zuckerman, 'On the date', p. 252 suggests that *isha* may be a form of the Turkic title, *sad*.

84 Cited in Dunlop, *History*, p. 104; ibn Fadlan, *Risala*, p. 147.

85 Pritsak, 'The Khazar Kingdom's Conversion to Judaism', p. 265; see al-Mas'udi's description of the Muslim soldiers, cited in Dunlop, *History*, p. 206; but Artamonov, *Istoriya khazar*, pp. 316–17 argues that there is no sign of Muslim burial at Sarkel, so that the troops were probably Oghuz, though they may, of course, have come from Khorezm-controlled lands; Crone, *Slaves on Horses* has argued that the use of *mamluk* armies by the Abbasids reflects their lack of legitimacy amongst the populations they ruled, and much the same may be true of the Khazars as well.

86 Dunlop, *History*, p. 207.

87 Cited in ibid., p. 105.

88 Artamonov, *Istoriya khazar*, p. 352; Dunlop, *History*, p. 105.

89 Artamonov, *Istoriya khazar*, pp. 268–9; these western Türk runes have not yet been deciphered, see Klyashtornyi and Sultanov, *Kazakhstan*, p. 156.

90 Artamonov, *Istoriya khazar*, p. 414.

91 Sugar, *History of Hungary*, p. 9; on the complex problem of Magyar origins which has spawned a vast literature, see Golden, *Introduction*, pp. 258–62, and 'People of the south Russian steppe' in *CHEIA*; and Moravcsik, *Byzantinoturcica* 1:131–4.

92 Pletneva, *Polovtsy*, p. 10; Artamonov, *Istoriya khazar*, p. 298.

93 Artamonov, *Istoriya khazar*, p. 357, and see p. 350; Franklin and Shepard, *Emergence of Rus*, pp. 97–8; Golden, *Introduction*, pp. 264–70 is on the Pechenegs.

94 Golden, *Introduction*, p. 265; Constantine Porphyrogenitus, *De Administrando* 1:167–71.

95 Pletneva, *Polovtsy*, pp. 14–15, argues that from this time on, the Khazar empire was doomed; see also ibid., p. 17.

96 Constantine Porphyrogenitus, *De Administrando*, 1:65; and see al-Istakhri, cited in Dunlop, *History*, pp. 95–6.

97 Smirnov, *Volzhskie bulgary*, p. 11; Pletneva, *Stepi Evrazii*, p. 77; Golden, *Introduction*, pp. 253–8.

98 E.g. ibn Fadlan, in ibn Fadlan, *Risala*, pp. 131–2.

99 Cited in Franklin and Shepard, *Emergence of Rus*, p. 63; ibn Fadlan, *Risala*, pp. 140–1.

100 Cited in Golden, *Introduction*, p. 256.

01 Fedorov-Davydov, ed., *Gorod Bolgar*, pp. 3, 10.
02 Smirnov, 'Volzhskaya Bulgaria', pp. 209–10.
03 Ibn Fadlan, *Risala*, p. 136; ibn Rusta cited from Golden, *Introduction*, p. 254; on the dates of ibn Rusta's sources, see Dunlop, *History*, pp. 107–8.
04 Ibn Fadlan, *Risala*, p. 137; Golden, *Introduction*, p. 256.
05 Cited in Franklin and Shepard, *Emergence of Rus*, p. 62, and see pp. 63–4.
06 Noonan, 'Byzantium and the Khazars', p. 126.
07 Franklin and Shepard, *Emergence of Rus*, p. 88, and p. 56.
08 Artamonov, *Istoriya khazar*, p. 371.
09 Zuckerman, 'On the date', pp. 254–68 for a recent reconstruction of the murky diplomatic and military history of this era.
10 Cited in Dunlop, *History*, p. 240.
11 Artamonov, *Istoriya khazar*, p. 428; the above is Artamonov's hypothetical reconstruction of Svyatoslav's route; Pletneva, *Polovtsy*, p. 18 argues for the Pecheneg alliance.
12 Pletneva, *Polovtsy*, p. 98; Artamonov, *Istoriya khazar*, pp. 430 and 449.
13 Pletneva, *Polovtsy*, p. 99; Franklin and Shepard, *Emergence of Rus*, pp. 200–1.
14 Artamonov, M. I., *Ocherki drevneishei istorii Khazar*, Leningrad, 1936, and *Istoriya khazar*, Leningrad, 1962; see Anna Frenkel, 'The Jewish empire in the land of future Russia', p. 143.

FURTHER READING

On the western steppes after the Huns, there are good essays by Golden and Szádeczky-Kardoss, in *CHEIA*. See also Artamonov, *Istoriya Khazar*; Golden, *Khazar Studies*, and *Introduction to the History of the Turkic Peoples*; Pletneva, *Stepi Evrazii v epokhu srednevekov'ya*; and Moravscik, *Byzantinoturkica*. Obolensky, *Byzantine Commonwealth*, offers a Byzantine perspective, while Constantine Porphyrogenitus, *De Administrando*, gives a Byzantine perspective from the mid-tenth century. On the Khazars, Artamonov, *Istoriya Khazar*, remains fundamental, even though Artamonov was forced by Stalinist censors to modify the conclusions of an earlier study (*Ocherki drevneishei istorii Khazar*, Leningrad, 1936) to downplay the significance of the Khazars. (See Anna Frenkel, "The Jewish Empire in the Land of Future Russia'.) More recent Soviet studies are Pletneva, *Kochevniki srednevekov'ya*, and *Khazary*; Magomedov, *Obrazovanie*; and Novosel'tsev, *Khazarskoe gosudarstvo*. The standard western account is still Dunlop, *History of the Jewish Khazars*, while Noonan, 'Byzantium and the Khazars', surveys diplomatic relations with Byzantium. Koestler's *The Thirteenth Tribe*, is not reliable. The very small number of Khazarian documents, dating from the tenth century, are available in Kokovtsov, ed., *Evreisko-hazarskaya perepiska*, and Golb and Pritsak, *Khazarian-Hebrew Documents*. All the major sources discuss the Khazar conversion to Judaism, but see, in addition, Khazanov, 'The Spread of World Religions', which follows Artamonov's approach; Pritsak, 'The Khazar kingdom's conversion'; Szyszman, *Le Karaïsme*, which claims that the Khazars were Karaïte; and Zuckerman, 'On the date', which offers a new chronology and explanation. On Volga Bulgaria see Smirnov, *Volzhskie bulgary*, and 'Volzhskaya bulgariya'; Fedorov-Davydov, *Gorod Bolgar*; and ibn Fadlan, *Risala*; as well as the discussion in Golden, *Introduction to the History of the Turkic Peoples*. On trade routes through Khazaria, see Franklin and Shepard, *Emergence of Rus*.

[12] MAWARA'N-NAHR: ISLAMIC CIVILIZATION IN CENTRAL ASIA

In the second half of the first millennium, the rhythms of Central Asian history recapitulated those of the Scythic era. A period of pastoralist expansion (by Scythic Iranian-speakers in the first cycle, and Turkic-speakers in the second) was interrupted by invasions from Iran led by expansionist dynasties of pastoralist descent (Achaemenid in one case, Arabic in the other). Culturally, both cycles were marked by an increase in Outer European influences, Achaemenid, Greek and Buddhist in the earlier period, Arabic, Iranian and Islamic in the later. During the seventh century, Islamic Arabic armies invaded the lands of Transoxiana, which they called, 'Mawara'n-nahr', the 'land beyond the river'. In the eighth and ninth centuries, the riverine oases of Sogdia, Bactria and Khorezm were incorporated within the Islamic world, and Islam became, as it still is today, the basis of the region's culture, lifeways and politics. Eventually, the Abbasid caliphate fragmented, like the Seleucid Empire, into regional powers, some ruled by former governors of the empire, some by dynasties of steppe origin, some by local chiefly families, some by dynastic upstarts. In the tenth century, under the Samanids, a local dynasty that had absorbed the administrative and cultural traditions of Abbasid Iran, Central Asia became for a few decades the most prosperous and intellectually creative region of the Islamic world.

ISLAMIC CONQUEST: 650–900

BEFORE ISLAM

For several centuries before the arrival of Islam, Central Asia had been loosely incorporated within great empires whose centres lay elsewhere. The Sassanian empire had controlled the Merv region and the large eastern province of Khorasan. North and South of the Amu Darya, dynasties of pastoralist origin had exercized a more or less strict suzerainty over local dynasts since the collapse of the Seleucid empire. Since the decline of the Kusana empire in the third century, the Kidarite and then the Hephthalite empires had dominated much of Bactria and Sogdia, until the conquests of the first Türk empire in the middle of the sixth century.

Plate 12.1 Wall painting from Panjikent: 'The harp player', (© Society for Co-operation in Russian and Soviet Studies).

However, for most inhabitants of Central Asia, imperial rule was remote. It was felt through the demands of tax-collectors, or the passing of imperial armies, but otherwise had little impact on daily life. For the most part, farmers, merchants and *dihqans* adapted to the demands of distant emperors or khans without changing their traditional lifeways. The significant powers were the local rulers or *dihqans*. In cities such as Bukhara and Samarkand, or in regions such as Khorezm, these formed urban dynasties of their own, such as the *khudats* of Bukhara, who served as more or less nominal regional representatives of empire.[1] The political and economic centres of gravity of Central Asia were the Merv oasis in the west, the Balkh oasis south of the Amu Darya, the string of oases along the Zerafshan, including Samarkand and Bukhara, Khorezm to the south of the Aral Sea, and the oases along the Syr Darya from Ferghana to Chach (Tashkent) to the Aral Sea.

Local rulers tried to limit the amount of revenue passed on to imperial overlords, and to maximize the amounts they received themselves. Local pastoralist chiefs often ignored imperial authorities entirely. Rulers with some political skills and some confidence in the future, looked after the regional systems of agriculture and trade on which their prosperity depended. They maintained canals and *qanats*, protected their borders by establishing frontier garrisons, and built caravanserais for traders. As an eleventh-century prince of Tabaristan wrote in a book for his son:

> Make it your constant endeavour to improve cultivation and to govern well; for understand this truth: the kingdom can be held by the army, and the army by gold; and gold is acquired through agricultural development and agricultural development through justice and equity. Therefore be just and equitable.[2]

Less able or less far-sighted rulers devastated whole regions as their armies criss-crossed the region in search of easy booty, and its complex and fragile infrastructure of canals, towns and trade routes fell into disrepair.

It is not easy to detect long-term economic trends in this era, but Soviet studies of the irrigation systems of Khorezm have shown that there were many signs of decay in the fourth and fifth centuries. Then, from the seventh century, the irrigation systems begin to be extended and rebuilt in newer and more sophisticated ways. In particular, there appears a much denser, and more delicately adapted system of small canals. A more ramified system of canals could support larger populations, which presumably provided the demographic foundation for the emergence of strong local states. In Khorezm, at least, local rulers began to live in forts built at strategic points on these irrigation systems, which gave them great power over villages and towns downstream from them. Commercial wealth also expanded from the sixth century onwards throughout Central Asia. Growing wealth supported local commercial and aristocratic elites, as well as a multitude of regional rulers, and sustained a luxurious aristocratic life-style that can be seen in the murals of Panjikent which date from the sixth to the eighth centuries. Wealth and the patronage of the wealthy also nourished a flourishing and sophisticated secular and religious architecture, art and literature. Literacy spread videly in the towns (spelling and writing books for schoolchildren have been ound in Sogdia and the Tarim basin), and even into the steppes, while Buddhist monasteries from Bactria to Khotan to Tun-huang, and institutions uch as the astronomical observatories of Khorezm, maintained a level of cholarship as high as anywhere else in the world. Supporting the wealthy vas a large population of urban craft workers, petty traders and other workrs, whose cramped quarters have been excavated in Panjikent.[3]

Keeping order was a task shared by everyone. Most of the population, vhether pastoralists or irrigation farmers, kept arms and expected to use hem, so that it was always possible, in principle, to form an emergency army y drafting ordinary citizens.[4] However, most *dihqans* and local dynasts naintained their own retinues of professional soldiers, which they supported rom the revenues of taxation, trade or raiding. For the *dihqans*, living in forified manors, lavish hospitality was a way of maintaining regional networks f influence and patronage. Istakhri was astonished at the hospitable tradiions of the *dihqan* class, of which an extreme example was the Sogdian famy that prided itself on having kept its doors open for a century, feeding and odging each day between 100 and 200 travellers.[5] This was the level of poliics that shaped the daily life of villagers and townspeople in Khorezm, or astoralists along the Syr Darya, even if the wars of the great imperial powers ometimes turned their lifeways upside down. Most villagers lived in comnunities linked by the collaborative demands of irrigation agriculture, and he need to cope with the often oppressive fiscal demands of local landlords r *dihqans*, their regional overlords and their local officials and enforcers.

When Islamic armies first entered Central Asia in the middle of the sevnth century, within 20 years of the Prophet's death, they represented just ne more external threat. Yet within two centuries, Islam had transformed he cultural traditions of most settled regions of Central Asia, and was begining to transform the cultural life of pastoralist regions as well.

THE FIRST ISLAMIC INVASIONS: 650–750

The Prophet, Muhammad b. Abd Allah b. Abd al-Muttalib b. Hashim, was orn in the prosperous trading city of Mecca in c.570. He belonged to the Quraysh tribe, and spent his early life in Mecca or with Bedouin connections f his family in the desert. His early career was in trade, for the Quraysh were merging as the dominant force in the extensive trade networks focused on Mecca. In c.610, he began to receive the revelations that eventually made up he Qu'ran.[6]

In 622, Muhammad and his followers fled to Medina. This event, the *Hijra*, marks the beginning of the Islamic calendar. By the time of his death n 632, he and his followers had reconquered Mecca, and embarked on what roved an astonishing period of military expansion. Arabic armies with Bedouin cavalry destroyed Sassanian rule in its Iraqi heartland in 637. In 42, they defeated the last great Sassanian army at Nihawand in the Iranian lateau near modern Hamadan. The next year, Muslim armies conquered nuch of north-western Iran and Azerbaijan. Their astonishing military

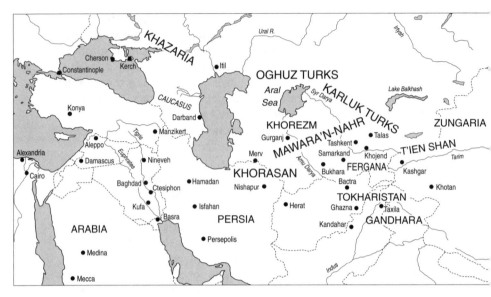

Map 12.1 Islamic civilization in Central Asia.

success owed something to Sassanian weakness after the victories of Heraclius, and something to the inspiration of their new religion. But they were also due, in part, to an important, if gradual, technological innovation: the evolution after 500 BCE of the North Arabian saddle. This made it possible to use camels in warfare, rather than just as pack-animals, and encouraged the evolution of a more militaristic culture amongst camel-herders based on the use of both camel and horse. In this way, camel-herders began to acquire some of the military advantages long enjoyed by horse-riding nomads of Inner Eurasia.[7]

The first attempts by Arabic armies to advance into Inner Eurasia, through the Caucasus, were checked by the Khazars in 653–5. Meanwhile, the last Sassanian leader, Yazdegird, fled, like Darius before Alexander, until he reached Merv, where he was murdered in 651. Islamic armies, now with large contingents of Syrian and even Sassanian soldiers, followed him into Central Asia in 651, and made Merv their base in the region, as the Sassanians had done before them. Yazdegird's son, Peroz, fled further east and died in China, where he had set up a government in exile. To hold the distant outpost of Merv, the Arabs settled some 50,000 Arab families in the oasis in 671. This was the largest group of Arab settlers outside of Arabia, and helps explain why Khorasan and Merv soon became important centres of Islamic military and cultural influence. By 730, most of the settlers had become farmers, and had put down strong roots in the Merv region.[8]

Almost immediately, Arabic armies crossed the Amu Darya into Mawara'n-nahr. Chinese sources record that Arabic armies first crossed the Amu Darya as early as 655. However, the early attacks were merely summer raids. Their aim was to take booty from the region's rich cities, to show that

the Arabs intended to protect Khorasan from nomadic incursions, and perhaps to secure control of the region's trade routes. Not until about 682 did
an Arabic army winter east of the Amu Darya.[9] Conquering Mawara'n-nahr
was much more difficult than conquering Persia, for, since the collapse of the
Western Türk empire, there was no single authority whose defeat entailed the
fall of all regional authorities. Instead, the Arabs encountered regional powers which, though divided and weak, were toughened by constant regional
warfare. Each city and each region had to be reduced separately. Early
attempts at conquest were also undermined by the confusion of the first two
Islamic civil wars, of 656–61 and 680–92.[10]

The first successful conqueror of Mawara'n-nahr was Qutayba b. Muslim.
Qutayba was appointed governor of Merv in c.705 by the sixth Umayyad
caliph, al-Walid (r. 705–15). The conquest required diplomatic skills to divide
his opponents, and financial skills to pay for his armies, as well as the purely
military skills of a decisive and energetic general. Exploiting local feuds,
Qutayba tried when possible to act as the ally of local leaders in disputes with
their rivals, and to fight in alliance with local armies which were often larger
than his own, Arabic armies. To finance his campaigns, he even borrowed
from Sogdian merchants. This policy of divide and rule worked in part
because there were no local traditions of unity in the face of such invasions.
According to al-Tabari, regional leaders met annually in Khorezm to coordinate resistance but the regularity of these meetings shows how little success
they had.[11] One by one, Qutayba conquered Bukhara, Balkh, Samarkand and
the larger towns of Khorezm and the Syr Darya. From conquered rulers
Qutayba demanded suzerainty as well as troops for future campaigns. Like the
Macedonians a millennium earlier, he settled garrison troops in the towns,
often clearing out whole quarters for the new settlers. In Bukhara he founded a
mosque, the first step in Bukhara's rise as a major centre of Islamic learning.[12]

The brutality of these early conflicts helped destroy the pre-Islamic culture
of the region, and many of its records. Tenth- and eleventh-century Persian
scholars such as Firdausi or al-Biruni tried to preserve some remnants of
Sassanian culture in Mawara'n-nahr, but despite their efforts, little has survived. Al-Biruni claimed that Qutayba had destroyed the ancient libraries of
Khorezm and killed most of its scholars. The early invasions were certainly
destructive. One of Qutayba's commanders in Khorezm removed the clothes
of his captives and let them freeze to death, while Qutayba himself massacred
all the men and enslaved the women and children of Paikend after it rose
against him. Qutayba's armies also took enormous amounts of booty, flood-
ing the slave markets of Kufa, Basra and Merv, and presumably lowering the
price and raising the demand for Central Asian slaves.[13]

In 715, after rising against the new caliph, Qutayba was murdered, while
campaigning in Ferghana, and the Arabs lost control of much of the region.
There followed a period of confused warfare in which Arabic governors fought
to re-establish their authority, sometimes against Arabic rivals. One early governor, Ashras b. Abdallah as-Sulami (727–9) tried to encourage conversion to
Islam by not levying tribute on converts, but only succeeded in provoking a
revolt amongst local Muslims and Arabs. Arabic governors also intervened in

local feuds, and tried to fight off intervention by Türgesh tribes from the Semirechye. Usually, the Arabic governors, based in Merv, allowed local rulers to remain in power, even if they appointed Arabic *walis* to supervise them.[14] In fact, they needed the skills and experience of indigenous ruling dynasties used to constant feuding, for during the eighth century, Mawara'n-nahr remained a frontier region. In the 720s, Arabic governors began to build *ribats*, or frontier forts with cavalry garrisons, directed mainly against nomadic incursions. These were often paid for out of private endowments, and many of the fighters who lived in them were religious volunteers, or *ghazis*.[15] Despite this, the Türgesh kaghan, Su-lu, defeated Arabic armies in 720 and 723, and became a major force in the region before his final defeat at the hands of Arabic armies in 737.

Beyond the Türgesh lay their nominal suzerains, the T'ang emperors of China. In desperation, local rulers sought Chinese help from as early as the time of Qutayba. The following petition to the Chinese emperor, sent in 718 by Ghourek, the ruler of Samarkand, conveys something of the flavour of this period of Islamic conquest:

> Your subject [Ghourek], like the grass and soil trampled by your horses for a million *li*, submits to the holy emperor who, by the grace of the Heavens, rules the entire world. The members of my family, and the various *Hou* kingdoms, have long been sincerely devoted to your great empire;... Now for 35 years [i.e. since the first major invasions of the early 680s] we have fought ceaselessly with the *Ta-che* [Arabic, 'Tajik'] brigands; each year we have sent large armies of foot soldiers and cavalry on campaign, without ever enjoying the good fortune of receiving soldiers sent to help us by your imperial kindness. For more than 6 years [since Qutayba's siege of Samarqand in 712], the general in command of the *Ta-che*, has come here at the head of a numerous army; we fought him and tried to defeat him, but many of our soldiers were killed or wounded; as the infantry and cavalry of the *Ta-che* were extremely numerous... I returned behind my walls to defend myself; the *Ta-che* then besieged the city, placing 300 ballistae against the walls and at three points they dug deep ditches, trying to destroy our kingdom.[16]

Ghourek asked for Chinese troops and sent gifts of a horse, a Persian camel and two mules, a meagre offering that shows how warfare had impoverished the great trading city of Samarkand. However, the T'ang dynasty could do little. To the north, they faced a revived Türk khanate. In Tibet, they faced a powerful empire that expanded at the same time as Islam, until, by the late seventh century and again in the late eighth century, it controlled the Tarim basin and the eastern sections of the Silk Roads, and had diplomatic relations with the caliphate, the Türks and China. Ghourek, like all local rulers, had to manoeuvre between various regional powers. He accepted Arab suzerainty at least twice in his career, though in 731 he was once again allied with the Türgesh against the Arabs.[17]

THE EARLY ABBASIDS: 750–850

By the middle of the eighth century, Mawara'n-nahr was the focus of complex international rivalries that stretched across the whole of Eurasia. The main participants in this eighth-century 'Great Game' were the armies of Islam, Tibet and T'ang China. Other regional powers were also engaged as allies or victims. The outcome of these conflicts was resolved by two major events that occurred around the year 750: the emergence of the Abbasid caliphate, and the Chinese defeat at the battle of Talas in 751.

The third great Islamic civil war lasted from 744–50. It ended in 750 when a Khorasani army, with large numbers of disgruntled Arab settlers from the Merv region, as well as contingents from Mawara'n-nahr, and led by a Persian, Abu Muslim, marched west, defeated the last Umayyad caliph, Marwan, in 750, and installed a new caliph from the Abbasid branch of the Prophet's family. Though the second Abbasid caliph, al-Mansur, had Abu Muslim murdered in 755, Khorasani influence on the Abbasid caliphate remained strong. For many years, Abbasid military power rested on Khorasani troops, and the garrison at the new capital of Baghdad was recruited mainly from Khorasan. At the same time, bureaucratic families from Central Asia, such as the Barmakids, a Persian family from the Balkh region, played a vital role in the early Abbasid bureaucracy. In other ways, too, the Abbasid caliphate was strongly influenced by Persian and Central Asian traditions. In 762, caliph al-Mansur founded a new capital, Baghdad, near the old Sassanian capital of Ctesiphon. As Central Asia became Islamic, Islam became more Persian.

The second decisive event was the battle of Talas in 751. The Abbasid caliphate resumed the assault on Mawara'n-nahr immediately after its establishment in 750. Abu Muslim's lieutenant, Ziyad b. Salih, suppressed rebellions in Bukhara and Samarkand with great bloodshed.[18] Meanwhile, Chinese victories over Tibet had weakened a major prospective rival of the Abbasids. As for China, though distance and geography had always made it difficult to control Central Asia directly, after the fall of the Türgesh, they made one more attempt at the direct control of Central Asia. In 749, a Chinese army led by a Korean, Kao-hsien-chih, appeared in Ferghana and claimed Chinese suzerainty over the region. Ziyad b. Salih marched against the Chinese army, and defeated it at Talas in July 751. The defeat ended Chinese ambitions west of the Tarim basin for almost a millennium.[19]

A revived caliphate, based on Khorasani armies, and free of the threat of Chinese or Tibetan rivalry, could now consolidate its control over Khorasan and Mawara'n-nahr. Only now did Islam begin to penetrate more deeply into the life of Central Asia's inhabitants. However, conversion was a slow process. As Adshead puts it, in Central Asia, Islam 'failed...as a tornado [but] succeeded as a glacier'.[20] Its uneven progress reflected the very different types of society that coexisted in the region. When Islam arrived in the seventh century, it encountered a confusing bazaar of religions. Zoroastrianism was common in Sogdia and Khorezm, and Buddhism in Bactria.[21] Christianity reached Margiana in the Sassanian period, as did Manichaeism. In the eighth century, under the Nestorian Catholicos, Timotheos (780–823), Nestorianism became a proselytizing religion in the region, while Judaism also had many adherents. Archaeological evidence shows that at Talas (modern Dzhambul) local populations professed

Zoroastrianism, Christianity and Buddhism as well as a local version of a Bacchic cult, a cult devoted to a fertility goddess, Anahit, and the traditional Turkic worship of the heavens, or Tengri. In the steppes and in villages, one could find shamanistic practices, while the Oghuz encountered by ibn Fadlan in 921 prayed to Tengri.[22] The variety of religions gave to the religious culture of Central Asia a certain anthropological relativism. Thus, a Nestorian work argued that, at the last coming, the Messiah would appear in different forms: 'To the Greeks he would appear as Zeus or Hermes, to the Jews as the Messiah, to the Magians as Pesiotan, to the Indians as Brahma and Buddha, to the Chaldaeans as Bel, to the Turks as Tengri, and to the Chinese as 'Gabour' (Parthian *bgpwhr*, 'Son of God' = Chinese *t'ien-tzu* 'Son of Heaven').'[23] Something of this variety survived in Central Asia even after the coming of Islam, but now it was variety within a single, unifying religion.

The first conversions to Islam took place in the major towns. Resistance often took the form of support for unofficial forms of Islam, such as early forms of Shi'ism. Some movements invoked the name of Abu Muslim, whose rebellion against the Umayyads had generated utopian hopes of egalitarian reforms. Between 776 and 783, much of Mawara'n-nahr was taken over by a rebel movement led by a certain Hashim b. Hakim, a former captain of Abu Muslim, who declared himself a prophet in the line of Adam, Noah, Abraham, Moses, Jesus, Muhammad and Abu Muslim. His teachings of social and material equality may owe something to the survival in Khorasan of Mazdakite ideas. In Arabic sources, he was known as al-Muqanna, the 'veiled one', because he wore a green veil, declaring that otherwise mortal eyes would be dazzled by the light from his face. (Enemies said the veil was to hide his deformities.) His main successes were in Kish (Shakhrisabs), Nesef (Karshi), and Bukhara. According to Narshakhi, he continued the old strategy of using Turkic pastoralists against Arabs. He 'invited the Turks and permitted them (to take) the life and possessions of the Muslims. Many troops came from Turkistan in the hope of plunder. They pillaged the districts and carried the women and children of Muslims into captivity and killed (others).'[24]

Despite such movements, by 850, most of the towns of Mawara'n-nahr were Muslim. The word 'Tajik', originally used of Arab settlers from the Tayy tribe in Iraq, was soon being used of all converts to Islam, whether Arab or Persian.[25] Though not persecuted, Zoroastrianism faded away as it lost elite sponsorship. After this first stage, in Mawara'n-nahr, as in Iran, the countryside fell to Islam between 850 and 950. By the mid-tenth century, the process was so nearly complete that 'Firdosi and other Iranian literary men or intellectuals felt the need to save something of the pre-Islamic legends and culture which had almost become extinct.'[26] The conversion of the steppes was a longer and more complex process which will be described later. Partly, this is because the Arabs preferred to live in the citied regions of the south. It was in the towns that there emerged the distinctive Central Asian Islamic culture that eventually began to permeate the steppes and to give the region a cultural unity that has persisted to the present day.[27]

Though Islam implied cultural incorporation within the Abbasid empire, the gradual fragmentation of the Abbasid empire ensured that politically, Khorasan remained relatively independent. Early in the 9th century, Khorasan provided, for the second time, the launching pad for a new caliph. caliph Haroun al-Rashid (r. 786–809) made detailed plans for the succession after his death, under which his elder son, Muhammad (later caliph al-'Amin) was to become caliph, while his younger son, Abd Allah (later caliph al-Ma'mun) was to rule Khorasan quite independently. In 809, Haroun died while in Khorasan to put down a rebellion in Samarkand. Abd Allah, who had accompanied him, began, with the help of his *wazir*, al-Fadl b. Sahl, to build local alliances in the region in preparation for the inevitable war over the succession. Khorasan made a good power base as its armies were still amongst the best in the caliphate, practised as they were in the harsh frontier war of the Central Asian borderlands. In 811, Abd Allah's brother sent a large army against him, supplied with a special silver chain with which to imprison the future al'Ma'mun.[28] However, the small Khorasani army, under a regional commander, Tahir b. al-Husayn, defeated the army of caliph al-'Amin. Formally, al-Ma'mun became caliph in 813, on the death of his brother. For a time, he contemplated making Merv his capital, but in 819, he returned to Baghdad, which remained the demographic, economic and political centre of the Abbasid empire.

In 821, Tahir was made the governor of Khorasan, and after his death in 822, the position passed on to his sons and grandsons until 873. Tahirid Khorasan, with its capital at Nishapur, was never truly independent, for the Tahirids accepted the suzerainty of the caliphate, continued to pass on tributes to Baghdad, issued coins in the name of the caliphate, and maintained a prominent position at its court.[29] However, within Khorasan, the Tahirids acted with great independence. In this way, there began a gradual fragmentation of power in the Abbasid domains as a whole, and Khorasan in particular.

Tahir's son, Abdallah (r. 822–44), was in some ways an ideal Islamic ruler. He was a strong governor, and maintained stability throughout Khorasan. He also showed exceptional concern for the fate and prosperity of the mass of the population. 'God', he said, 'feeds us by their hands, welcomes us through their mouths and forbids their ill treatment.'[30] He supported an extensive program of popular education. In Transoxiana, he encouraged the working out of basic principles for the control of waterways, and supported large irrigation projects, such as the building of a huge canal near modern Tashkent, a medieval precursor of the great canal of modern Ferghana. The Tahirids also mounted many successful slave-raiding expeditions far out into the Turkic steppes, and became important providers of slaves or *ghulams* for the *ghulam* armies which became important during the reign of caliph al-Mu-tasim (r. 833–42).[31] Though we know little of Tahirid rule, it is possible that it pioneered many of the methods of government adopted later in Khorasan and Mawara'n-nahr.

In 873, a new regional dynasty, of entirely non-aristocratic origin, the Saffarids, conquered Nishapur, and seized power from the Tahirids. The founder of the Saffarid dynasty was a copper-smith (*saffar*), Yaqub, from the turbulent, and bandit-ridden southern province of Seistan. Yaqub created a local army recruited in part from Kharijite *ghazis*, or 'warriors for the faith' in what was still an Islamic frontier land. Yaqub's power was never accepted by Baghdad, and rested directly on military force, so much of his wealth came from confiscations. In his life-style and manners, he remained a soldier all his life, 'wearing cotton garments, sitting on the bare ground, and sleeping with his head on his shield'.[32] He made an exception only for special occasions such as the reception of ambassadors, when he was surrounded by a bodyguard consisting of two contingents, each of 1000 men, chosen from his best soldiers.

Yaqub's brother and successor, Amr, achieved greater legitimacy by securing formal appointment as the caliph's viceroy in Khorasan. Amr also used more formal methods of rule. Some idea of the size of his court is conveyed by the remark of Nizam al-Mulk that: 'His humanity and magnanimity went so far that four hundred camels were required to transport his kitchen.'[33] The army was still the basis of the ruler's power, so paying the army was an important ritual, and in this, Amr imitated the rituals of the Sassanian shahs. A special official, called the *arid*, had responsibility for the issuing of pay every three months. At the sound of a drum, the soldiers assembled for their pay, and were called up, one by one, beginning with the ruler, Amr. After inspecting his horse and equipment, the *arid* nodded approval and handed over his pay. 'Amr placed the money in the leg of his boot and said: "God be praised, that He hath permitted me to serve faithfully the Commander of the Faithful, and had made me worthy of his favours." After this Amr took his seat on an eminence and watched the horsemen and infantry in turns present themselves before the *arid*, undergo the same close scrutiny, and receive their money.'[34]

By the time of Amr's defeat, in 900, at the hands of the Samanid rulers of Mawara'n-nahr, the Abbasid caliphate had lost all but nominal suzerainty over Khorasan and Mawara'n-nahr.

THE SAMANID RENAISSANCE OF THE TENTH CENTURY

Two conditions made for prosperity in Central Asia. First, strong government had to ensure that farmers and traders could do their work in safety and security. Second, there had to be governments that cared about the region, and did not tax it too heavily. These conditions were most likely to appear when there existed powerful regional governments. They were unlikely either under imperial governments that sucked out the region's wealth for the benefit of distant courts, or under weak local dynasties engaged in constant feuding and raiding. Central Asia achieved this ideal balance rarely. The Kusana empire was such a period, and so was the period of regional government that began as Abbasid power unravelled in the ninth and tenth centuries. The most important Central Asian dynasty of this era, and the one about which we have most information, is that of the Samanids, so we will describe Samanid Central Asia in some detail.

THE SAMANID DYNASTY

Before the Samanid period, the 'khudats', the traditional rulers of Bukhara, had retained some autonomy, despite accepting Islamic suzerainty. Usually, they maintained a villa in Merv, the first capital of Islamic Khorasan.[35] In 738, Saman-khudat, a Persian from the region of Balkh, and the ancestor of the Samanids, converted to Islam. Four of his grandsons were appointed as regional governors in Mawara'n-nahr in c.820. The governorships became hereditary under the Tahirids and in 875, after their fall, Nasr b. Ahmad was appointed governor of Mawara'n-nahr by caliph al-Mu'tamid. His brother and successor, Isma'il Samanid (r. 893–907), who had long been governor of Bukhara, was the real founder of the dynasty's fortune. After the death of his brother in 893, Isma'il Samanid was invested by the caliph as governor of Transoxiana. In the same year, he conquered the Talas region from the Karluk. In 900, he destroyed a Saffarid army and captured the Saffarid ruler, Amr, whom he sent to Baghdad, where Amr was executed two years later. After destroying Saffarid power, Isma'il Samanid was made governor of Khorasan as well as Transoxiana. He died in 907. His tomb in Bukhara is one of the few pre-Mongol buildings still to survive in the region.

While they accepted the position of *amirs*, or regional governors, under the caliph, the Samanids ruled Khorasan more independently than the Tahirids or Saffarids, for they seem never to have sent tribute to Baghdad. However, they preserved the administrative and bureaucratic structures of the caliphate. The ruler had autocratic power, in theory at least. In practice, his most important function was the choice and appointment of subordinate officials.[36] Like all pre-modern states, the Samanid state is best thought of as a federation rather than a unitary system. Regional dynasties held power in many of its provinces, including Seistan (Saffarids), Balkh, Ghazna, Khorezm and elsewhere; and, according to al-Muqaddasi, most sent presents to Bukhara rather than tribute. Power over the regions had to be constantly renegotiated. The Samanid rulers governed through a system which, like that of the Abbasids, was divided into two main structures: the military and ceremonial structures of the palace, the *dargah*, headed by the chief *hajib*; and the civilian and fiscal administration of the *diwan* or chancery, headed by the chief *wazir*.[37]

The Samanids were the first Central Asian rulers to rely mainly on armies of slaves or '*ghulam*' (literally 'boys'), mostly recruited from the steppes. Though the use of professional soldiers of slave origin was an established practice in Central Asia, the Abbasid caliphs began to use Turkic slave-soldiers from the time of al-Ma'mun's brother and successor, al-Mu'tasim (r. 833–42). Al-Mu'tasim formed a private army of 3–4000 slaves even before becoming caliph. These he purchased at first in the slave markets of Baghdad, but then from the Samanid governors of Transoxiana. However, the precedent had been set by his brother, al-Ma'mun, during the fourth civil war, in which he depended largely on troops from Khorasan, supported by units of Turkic slaves. *Ghulam* armies soon played so critical a role in the internal conflicts of the caliphate that what began as private retinues became the most important military units in the Islamic world. From the middle of the ninth century, slave soldiers remained the strike forces of Islamic armies in settled regions until modern times, and as their power rose, so that of the Abbasid dynasty declined.[38] Their emergence reflects the failure of Islamic conquest dynasties to find an enduring source of legitimation amongst the free populations they ruled, just as the use of eunuchs or slaves as officials in many other agrarian empires reflects a partial failure to establish a sense of legitimacy amongst the free population.[39]

The Samanid armies consisted both of Persian *dihqans*, who might bring dependents with them, and Turkic captives. However, like other Islamic rulers of the period, they relied increasingly on armies of professional *ghulam* soldiers, whose first loyalty was to the Samanid ruler. Slaves in general, and *ghulams* in particular, came mainly from the lands north of the Syr Darya. The trade was extremely profitable, and the Samanid rulers kept tight control over it. They controlled the border markets where slaves were traded; they licensed slave traders, and levied dues on all sales, which were collected by tax-farmers. They also established special training centres for slave recruits to the army. It was probably Isma'il Samanid who began the shift towards professional slave armies, for many of his campaigns were in Khorasan, where his armies could attract neither religious volunteers, nor gentry.[40]

For the slaves, military service opened up new career prospects, and some rose to giddy heights, for Islamic society lacked the sense of caste so strong in India or even in the Christian world. Nizam al-Mulk (1018–92), *wazir* of the Saljuk leader, Alp Arslan, describes the typical career path of a successful *ghulam* in the eleventh century, when the system had become even more highly institutionalized. His account is modelled on the career of Alp Tegin, the founder of the Ghaznavid dynasty.

> after a *ghulam* was bought, for one year he was commanded to serve on foot at a rider's stirrup, wearing a Zandaniji [cloth from a town near Bukhara] cloak and boots; and this *ghulam* was not allowed during his first year to ride a horse in private or in public, and if it was found out [that he had ridden] he was punished. When he had done one year's service with boots, the tent-leader spoke to the chamberlain and he informed the king; then they gave him a small Turkish horse, with a saddle covered in untanned leather and a bridle of plain leather strap. After serving for a year with a horse and whip, in his third year he was given a belt [and sword?] to gird on his waist. In the fourth year they gave him a quiver and bow-case which he fastened on when he mounted. In his fifth year he got a better saddle and a bridle with stars on it, together with a cloak and a club which he hung on the club-ring. In the sixth year he was made a cup-bearer or water-bearer and he hung a goblet from his waist. In the seventh year he was a robe-bearer. In the eighth year they gave him a single-apex, sixteen-peg tent and put three newly bought *ghulams* in his troop; they gave him the

title of tent-leader and dressed him in a black felt hat decorated with silver wire and a cloak made at Ganja. Every year they improved his uniform and embell-ishments and increased his rank and responsibility until he became a troop-leader, and so on until he became a chamberlain. When his suitability, skill and bravery became generally recognized and when he had performed some out-standing actions and been found to be considerate to his fellows and loyal to his master, then and only then, when he was thirty-five or forty years of age, did they make him an amir and appoint him to a province.[41]

Reliance on paid, professional armies had many consequences throughout the Islamic world. First, it led to a growing separation between the military and civilian populations, particularly after Nasr b. Ahmad's (r. 914–44) rejection of Sunni Islam towards the end of his reign. By the late tenth cen-tury, the Samanids had largely lost the support of nobles and clergy and were totally dependent on their *ghulam* armies. Secondly, it linked fiscal and mili-tary power together, for *ghulam* armies translated commercial and agrarian revenues directly into military power. Third, the practice created new dan-gers, for, while well-paid *ghulams* enhanced the power of their ruler, unpaid or disgruntled soldiers could, and frequently did, overthrow incompetent rulers, beginning with Isma'il Samanid's son and successor, Ahmad (r. 907–14). Finally, the use of paid armies reduced the importance of the traditional military class of *dihqans*, and made rulers less dependent than pre-viously on the support of the towns. Many *dihqans* left the fortified rural vil-las typical of pre-Samanid Mawara'n-nahr, and settled in the growing towns. As a result, Mawara'n-nahr ceased to be the land of rural forts it had been since at least the Scythic era.[42] However, while the power of the *dihqans* dwindled, that of the central rulers temporarily increased for now, for the first time, local rulers had large armies owing them personal loyalty. If they could manage their mercenary armies, the power and independence of local rulers was undoubtedly enhanced. The use of *ghulams* was analogous to the use of bodyguards or personal retinues in pastoralist states. It worked well in an era of conquest, when there was plenty of wealth to distribute. However, it was much harder to work such a system in an era of stability, when finances were tighter.[43]

Wazirs headed the civilian administration of the Samanids. They ruled through 10 or so *diwans* or 'bureaus'. Most *diwans* handled fiscal matters, though others looked after the lands of the royal family, or maintained order and justice in the towns, or spied on other officials, or managed the postal services maintained for government officials.[44] At provincial levels, there were similar, if less elaborate, bureaucracies, headed by regional *wazirs* known as *hakims*. However, many of these posts were hereditary, and those who held them often showed great independence from the Samanid centre in Bukhara.

The third significant group in Bukharan society was the town population, which controlled much of the region's commercial wealth. As Islam spread, the towns of Mawara'n-nahr came under the influence of local religious teachers or *faqihs*. Islamic religious leaders held an authority that has no real counterpart in Christian society, for it depended on a charisma and prestige that secular leaders were reluctant to challenge because they often lacked such legitimacy themselves. The judicial authority of the *qadis*, who gave their judgements outside the mosques, was particularly important. In Bukhara, from Samanid times, the most influential clerics, known in this period as *ustadh*, or 'leaders', belonged to the Hanafite school.[45] After the fall of the Samanids, they became a dominant force in Bukharan politics.

ECONOMIC AND COMMERCIAL EXPANSION

At least in the first half of the tenth century, competent and strong government from Bukhara created the preconditions for economic and commercial expansion. Indeed, Samanid Mawara'n-nahr became for a time a sort of economic and even cultural dynamo for the whole Islamic world.[46]

Bukhara's importance probably dates from the Hephthalite era, when it was first surrounded by walls, but its greatest era came under the Samanids, when it was the most important city of the Islamic world. In the eighth century, a second line of walls was built, which enclosed the markets as well as the ancient town centre, the *shahristan*. Each set of walls had eleven gates. Bukhara's local economy depended on a complex system of local waterways, almost all of which were artificial.[47] Al-Muqaddasi describes the canals of Bukhara in the Samanid era:

> The river enters the town on the Kallabadh side; here sluices are constructed, forming wide locks and built of timber. In the summer flood season one after another of the beams is removed according to the height of the water, so that the larger part goes into the locks, and then flows to Paykand; without this skillful arrangement the water would have reverted to the town. ... below the town are other sluices ... built in the same manner. The river cuts through the town, passes through the bazaars and disperses (in canals) along the streets. There are large open reservoirs in the town; on the edge are structures of planks with doors, which serve for ablutions.... The water is turbid and a lot of refuse is thrown into it.[48]

Bukhara was crowded and had a reputation for bad air and bad water. As in many of the cities of medieval Europe, urban growth was probably accompanied by the emergence of a population of urban poor, whose living conditions were appalling, and who, unlike the wealthy, had no chance to escape bad air and bad water by fleeing in summer to country estates.[49]

Samarkand was probably more salubrious than Bukhara. Medieval visitors reported that: 'a considerable part of the area was occupied by gardens, almost each house possessing one; in viewing the town from the summit of the citadel no buildings were to be seen because of the trees in the gardens.'[50] Khorezm also flourished; as a region of small villages and farms with fortified points dotted amongst them it was transformed into a land of large, wealthy, commercial towns. According to al-Muqaddasi, the Khorezmian capital, Kath, contained a magnificent mosque and a royal palace, and had many notable scholars and merchants. Its muezzins had no equal in the

Abbasid lands for 'beauty of voice, expressiveness in recitation, deportment, and learning'. Yet, he added:

> the town is constantly flooded by the river, and the inhabitants are moving (farther and farther) away from the bank. The town...contains many refuse drains, which everywhere overflow the high road. The inhabitants use the streets as latrines, and collect the filth in pits, whence it is subsequently carried out to the fields in sacks. On account of the enormous quantity of filth strangers can walk about the town only by daylight.[51]

Even the smaller towns of Khorezm, many no larger than villages, often had fortified walls, gates, drawbridges, bazaars, mosques and prisons. As throughout the pre-industrial world, the charity of the wealthy could do something to mitigate the worst poverty. In Khorezm, ibn Fadlan noted that in winter, beggars felt free to enter any house, to sit before the fire and ask for bread.[52]

Urban growth and the building of walls sharpened the division between urban and rural populations.[53] The towns depended largely on the produce of irrigation agriculture. But maintaining these systems was a costly and complex business. Dams had to be built and maintained, canals and underground *karez* had to be kept clear from silt, water pumps (driven by windmills or camels) and wells had to be built and maintained. The political, military and legal problems were even greater. The entire system had to be protected from destructive enemy attacks; the labour for maintenance work had to be mobilized; and someone had to regulate who got water, when, and in what quantities. Agriculture and the towns it sustained could thrive when governments were strong, well organized, and willing, in partnership with regional rulers and local landlords, to invest in and organize the labour levies necessary to maintain and protect waterways. However, urban wealth also depended on good relations with pastoralist communities through whose lands passed the caravans that generated so much of Central Asia's commercial wealth. This was particularly true of Khorezm, whose military security and commercial wealth depended entirely on the success of its dealings with pastoralists. Because of their special role in trade with the steppes and Siberia, Khorezmians could be found throughout Mawara'n-nahr and Khorasan, where they stood out because of their tall fur hats.[54]

From Khorezm, great caravans set out to the north-west towards the lands of the Khazars and the Volga Bulghars, or carried the goods of the steppes and northern forests towards Merv, Khorasan and Baghdad, or eastwards towards Samarkand or Tashkent or Ferghana, from where they were taken further east, usually by Sogdian merchants, to China. Particularly along the steppe frontiers of Tashkent or Khorezm or Merv, local rulers established and maintained caravanserais along all the major trade routes at intervals of 25–30 kilometres, which corresponded to a day's journey. Built of stone, and protected by small garrisons, they were situated near sources of water or where natural defences were good.[55] Often, they developed into small steppe towns, and some have survived to the present day. In the 1940s, the Soviet archaeologist Tolstov demonstrated the value of aerial photography by tracing the caravan routes between Gurganj (modern Kunya-Urgench) and the northern Caspian, along which there were still many stone caravanserais with stone-covered wells. The key role of Gurganj in trade with the steppes helps explain why it became the capital of Khorezm in the late tenth century.[56]

The organization of caravans depended on the administrative and financial expertise of local merchants, who had extensive connections and used letters of credit, for which merchants in other towns would issue cash. We know of at least one Khorezmian merchant who had workshops in Bulghar on the Volga, as well as Khorezm and Gujarat. The need to defend themselves and keep supplies for many weeks, ensured that caravans were often huge, like 'miniature towns on the move'.[57] In the writings of ibn Fadlan, who was sent by Caliph al-Muqtadir (r. 908–32) to the Volga Bulghars, we have a superb account of life on a caravan travelling through the Oghuz steppes in the early tenth century. Ibn-Fadlan travelled north from Gurganj in 922 towards the Ural river.[58] The caravan in which he travelled was exceptionally large, consisting of 3000 pack-animals and 5000 men. As Frye notes, the size of this caravan helps explain the size of the Khorezmian colony at Bulghar and the amount of Moslem coinage that turns up in northern Russia in this period. The caravan left on 3 March, and took about 70 days to cover some 1000 miles.[59] Ibn Fadlan and his companions prepared for the journey by taking local advice. They bought Turkish camels, skin boats made from camel hides for river crossings, and enough bread, millet and salt meat for the three month trip. They also bought warm clothing for the freezing desert nights: 'Each of us put on a jacket, over that a coat, over that a *tulup* [a fur coat], over that a *burka*, and a helmet of felt out of which only the two eyes could look, a simple pair of under-drawers and a lined pair, trousers over them and house shoes of *kaymhuht* and over these also another pair of boots. When one of us got on a camel, he could not move because of his clothes.'[60] Their trade goods consisted mainly of textiles and dried fruits, as well as gifts for the Oghuz and Pecheneg tribes through whose lands they would pass.

An immense variety of goods were traded through Mawara'n-nahr, literally from all parts of Eurasia. Cotton, for which the region was famous in the Samanid era, had been cultivated on a large-scale in the Merv oasis since at least the fifth century, well before the Islamic period.[61] But the cities of Transoxiana also exported an extraordinary range of other textiles, leather goods, furs, livestock produce, metalwork, precious stones, foodstuffs and other goods. Writing in about 985 CE, al-Muqaddasi offers a remarkable list of exports from the region:

> from Tirmidh, soap and asafoetida [a strong smelling herb]; from Bukhara, soft fabrics, prayer carpets, woven fabrics for covering the floors of inns, copper lamps, Tabari tissues, horse girths (which are woven in places of detention), Ushmuni fabrics [from the Egyptian town of Ushmunayn], grease, sheepskins, oil for anointing the head;... from Khorezmia, sables, miniver [a white fur], ermines, and the fur of steppe foxes, martens, foxes, beavers, spotted hares, and goats; also wax, arrows, birch bark, high fur caps, fish glue, fish teeth [perhaps walrus tusks], castoreum, amber, prepared horse hides, honey, hazel nuts, falcons, swords, armour, khalanj wood, Slavonic slaves, sheep and cattle. All these

came from Bulghar, but Khorezmia exported also grapes, many raisins, almond pastry, sesame, fabrics of striped cloth, carpets, blanket cloth, satin for royal gifts, coverings of mulham fabric, locks, Aranj fabrics [probably cottons], bows which only the strongest could bend, rakhbin (a kind of cheese), yeast, fish, boats (the latter also exported from Tirmidh). From Samarqand is exported silver-coloured fabrics (simgun) and Samarqandi stuffs, large copper vessels, artistic goblets, tents, stirrups bridle-heads, and straps;...from Shash [modern Tashkent],[62] high saddles of horse hide, quivers, tents, hides (imported from the Turks and tanned), cloaks, praying carpets, leather capes, linseed, fine bows, needles of poor quality, cotton for export to the Turks, and scissors; from Samarqand again, satin which is exported to the Turks, and red fabrics known by the name of mumarjal, Sinizi cloth [from the Fars region, though originally the flax for them came from Egypt], many silks and silken fabrics, hazel and other nuts; from Farghana and Isfijab, Turkish slaves, white fabrics, arms, swords, copper, iron; from Taraz (Talas) goatskins;.... There is nothing to equal the meats of Bukhara, and a kind of melon they have called ash-shaq (or ash-shaf), nor the bows of Khorezmia, the porcelain of Shash, and the paper of Samarqand.[63]

The scale of Central Asian trade reflected, in part, the huge demand generated by Baghdad, a city of between 300,000 and 500,000 in the ninth century, and one of the largest cities of the world. It had a huge appetite for textiles, slaves and furs, as well as sweeteners such as honey. Bukhara had a reputation for textiles; Ferghana for metal goods, particularly weapons, and the Zerafshan valley for cotton and silks. In Ferghana, oil was extracted partly for lighting, and partly for use in sieges; clay pipes filled with oil were hurled into besieged cities as incendiaries.[64] The region also exported gold, silver, mercury, tar, asbestos, turquoise, iron, copper and lead. Samarkand had become the main exporter of paper to the Islamic world since its craftsmen had learnt the art of paper-making from Chinese artisans captured at the battle of Talas. The Samanids also extracted silver from the mines of the Hindu Kush, until these were captured by the Karakhanids in c.983. In the ninth century, Khorezmian melons were packed in lead cases filled with snow and transported to the caliph's palace in Baghdad.[65]

CULTURAL RENAISSANCE

Strong government and commercial prosperity stimulated a cultural renaissance which made Mawara'n-nahr, for a time, the cultural, intellectual and scientific centre of Islam.

Prosperity, the presence of large numbers of Arabic settlers, and the privileged position of Khorasan and Mawara'n-nahr within the Abbasid empire, encouraged local elites to patronize writers and scholars, while the eclectic traditions of a frontier zone encouraged the exchange of ideas. As a result, Islamic culture blossomed in Samanid Mawara'n-nahr. As Islam spread, so did the languages of Islam. Arabic, the language of scholarship and theology throughout the Abbasid empire, spread in the east; indeed the geographer al-Muqaddasi (d. c.1000) claimed that the purest Arabic of his time was spoken in Khorasan. Arabic was also the official language of Samanid bureaucracy, even though Persian was the main language in towns and Sogdian, though dying out, was still spoken in many villages.[66] Persian flourished as well as Arabic, though in modified forms showing strong Arabic influence. Many people from the region, like al-Biruni (d. 1048), whose native language was Khorezmian, had to learn both Arabic and the new, Islamicized forms of Persian written in Arabic script.[67]

Under the Samanids, Bukhara attracted scholars from the whole Muslim world. It became, as one contemporary put it: 'the focus of splendour, the shrine of empire, the meeting place of the most unique intellects of the age, the horizon of the literary stars of the world and the fair of the greatest scholars of the period'.[68] Al-Biruni described the remarkable book bazaars of Bukhara.[69] Ibn Sina (Avicenna; 980–1037) used the library of the Samanid rulers of Bukhara.

> I entered a house with many chambers; in each chamber were coffers of books, piled up one upon another. In one chamber were Arabic books and books of poetry, in another books on law, and so on, in each chamber books on one of the sciences. I read a list of books of ancient authors and asked for those I needed. I saw books whose very names are unknown to many people; I have never seen such a collection of books either before or since. I read these books, profited by them, and learned the relative importance of each man in his own science.[70]

Scholars taught students in their own homes, or those of their patrons, or near the mosques. Such gatherings may have been the origin of the *madrasahs*, the Islamic precursors of the modern University, as special endowments or *waqf* were established to support scholars and provide them with lodging and libraries, usually near a mosque. It is even possible that *madrasahs* had far older antecedents in Central Asia, for their architecture suggests the importance of Buddhist influences.[71]

Encouraged by lavish patronage and the vigorous intellectual exchanges of the Samanid world, thinkers and writers from Khorasan and Mawara'n-nahr helped incorporate within Islamic thought the Hellenic and Persian traditions of Sassanian Persia. Abulqasim Firdausi (c.940–1020), who wrote the vast heroic epic, the *Shah-name*, was born in north-eastern Khorasan, near the modern city of Mashhad, and his great epic preserved much of the region's Sassanian culture. Its gods, Ormazd and Ahriman, and the endless conflicts between Iran and Turan (the lands north of the Amu Darya) reflect the dualism of Zoroastrianism. The epic's central hero, Rustam, belongs as much to the pastoralist as to the agrarian world, and its account of the past ends with the Arabic invasions. Central Asia also contributed much to Islamic philosophy and science, mainly through the work of Ibn Sina. Ibn Sina was born near Bukhara but lived in many different parts of Iran. He probably did more than any other Islamic thinker to incorporate the thinking of Aristotle within the Islamic tradition. Khorezmian scholars were particularly important. Here, the complex engineering demands of building and maintaining irrigation canals encouraged original work in mathematics.

Under caliph al-Ma'mun, Muhammad b. Musa al-Khwarazmi (d. *c.*850), pioneered the use of a place-value system of numerals in Muslim mathematics, building on both Sanskrit and Hellenic traditions. Also from Khorezm were the philosopher, al-Farabi (d. 950), who was born into a military Turkic family on the Syr Darya, and did much to reconcile Islamic theology with Hellenic metaphysics; and the polymath, al-Biruni (d. 1048), who wrote on mathematics, geography, astronomy and history. Poetry was one of the glories of the Samanid era, reaching its height in the work of the Samarkandi poet, Rudaki. Mawara'n-nahr also contributed much to the early history of Sufism, partly through the influence of local Buddhist and shamanistic traditions.[72]

Geographical literature flourished and has left us with detailed accounts of many of the great cities of the Muslim world, and of many of the regions with which it had contact. The discipline of geography was important for both commercial and administrative purposes, but was also valued for its sheer exoticism. Its great pioneer was al-Istakhri [d. 951], who came from Fars, but based his world geography on an earlier work by a geographer from Balkh, as well as on his own travels.[73] Muslim geography divided the world into seven main regions: the Arabic and Persian realms at the centre, the Christian world of 'Rum' to the north-west with the Franks on their outer fringe, and the Indian world to the east, and finally, sub-Saharan Africa, Turkic Central Asia and China to the Far East. As Hodgson points out, this was the most realistic world geography of any Eurasian civilization.[74]

By any standards, Samanid Mawara'n-nahr had become a major centre of the type of agrarian civilisation that dominated Outer Eurasia. In its political and economic structures, as in its religion and its literate culture, Mawara'n-nahr represented a significant advance of agrarian civilization into the borderlands of Inner Eurasia.

NOTES

1   On the Bukhara dynasty, see Narshakhi, *History of Bukhara.*
2   From the *Qabus-nama* of Kay-Ka'us b. Iskandar (ed. R. Levy, London, 1951), written in 1082–3, cited in Morgan, *Medieval Persia*, pp. 11–12.
3   Tolstov, *Po drevnim del'tam*, p. 251, and see pp. 248ff; Azarpay, G., *Sogdian Painting*, pp. 35–46 discusses dating; B. A. Litvinsky and Zhang Guang-da, 'Central Asia, the crossroads of civilizations', in *HCCA* (pp. 473–90), 3:488; P. G. Bulgakov, 'Al-Biruni on Khwarizm', in *HCCA* (pp. 222–31), 3:228; there is a lengthy account of Sogdia before the Arabic invasions in Gafurov, *Tadzhiki*, 1:313–65, which is updated by Litvinskii in Ibid. 2:362–8.
4   Frye, *Bukhara*, p. 73.
5   Cited in Bosworth, *Ghaznavids*, 2nd edn, p. 32.
6   Kennedy, *The Prophet*, p. 30.
7   Argued in Bulliett, *The Camel and the Wheel*, pp. 87–110; the Nabataean kingdom, based on Petra from the second century BCE, was probably the first society to demonstrate the military potential of the camel; ibid p. 91.
8   Lapidus, *History*, p. 48; and see Kennedy, *The Prophet*, p. 86.

9   Barthold, *Turkestan down to the Mongol Invasion*, p. 183, and see p. 6 on the earliest Chinese reports; see also Frye, *Golden Age of Persia*, p. 77.

10 Gibb, *Arab Conquests*, p. 23; and see Frye, *Golden Age of Persia*, p. 74.

11 Cited in Barthold, *Turkestan down to the Mongol Invasion*, pp. 183–4, and see p. 185; see also Frye, *Golden Age of Persia*, p. 98; Gibb, *Arab Conquests*, pp. 31–2.

12 Crone, *Slaves on Horses*, p. 76; see also Frye, *Bukhara*, p. 16; and Narshakhi, *History of Bukhara*, p. 48.

13 Frye, *Golden Age of Persia*, p. 95; al-Biruni is cited in ibid., p. 81; see also Frye, *Heritage of Central Asia*, p. 209.

14 Gibb, cited in Wheeler, *Modern History of Soviet Central Asia*, p. 21 and see Barthold, *Turkestan*, pp. 189–90; A. H. Jalilov, 'The Arab conquest of Transoxania', in *HCCA*, 3:456–65.

15 Paul, *The State and the Military*, p. 16; and see Barthold, *Turkestan*, p. 189.

16 Chavannes, *Documents*, pp. 204–5; Ghourek had been elected as ruler in 710 because his predecessor had made peace with Qutayba; Jalilov, 'The Arab conquest of Transoxania', in *HCCA*, 3:458.

17 Barthold, *Turkestan*, p. 190; on the role of Tibet, see Hoffman, 'Early and medieval Tibet', in *CHEIA* (pp. 371–99), pp. 381–2; and Beckwith, *The Tibetan Empire*, p. 137.

18 Beckwith, *The Tibetan Empire*, p. 137.

19 Barthold, *Turkestan*, pp. 195–6.

20 Adshead, *Central Asia in World History*, p. 45; on the Arab conquests, see Gibb, *Arab Conquests*, and Barthold, *Turkestan*.

21 Litvinskii, 'Outline history of Buddhism', p. 121; and see Frye, *Golden Age of Persia*, pp. 28–9.

22 Ibn Fadlan, *Risala*, pp. 125–6; see also, on the mixture of religions, Golden, 'The Karakhanids and early Islam', in *CHEIA* (pp. 343–70), pp. 344–5; and B. A. Litvinsky, M. H. Shah and R. S. Samghabadi 'The rise of Sassanian Iran', in *HCCA* (pp. 473–84), 2:483–4.

23 Lieu, *Manichaeism*, pp. 87–8.

24 Narshakhi, *History of Bukhara*, p. 68; see also, Barthold, *Turkestan*, p. 199.

25 Frye, *Golden Age of Persia*, p. 96; using the evidence of Iranian genealogies, Bulliet argued that in Iran, *c.*8 per cent of the population may have been Muslim in 750; *c.*40 per cent in 800; and 70–80 per cent by 900; cited in Kennedy, *The Prophet*, p. 202; on the derivation of 'Tajik', see Frye, *Heritage of Central Asia*, p. 214.

26 Frye, *Golden Age of Persia*, p. 141; on the decline of Zoroastrianism, see Morgan, *Medieval Persia*, p. 15.

27 Golden, 'The Karakhanids and early Islam', in *CHEIA*, p. 344.

28 Kennedy, *The Prophet*, p. 150, and see p. 146.

29 Ibid., p. 161, points out that much of the revenue from Khorasan sent to Baghdad may have been used to support the Tahirids.

30 Cited in Barthold, *Turkestan*, p. 213.

31 Golden, *Introduction*, p. 192; see also Frye, *Golden Age of Persia*, p. 190; and Barthold, *Turkestan*, p. 213.

32 Barthold, *Turkestan*, pp. 218–19.

33 Nizam al-Mulk, *The Book of Government*, p. 18.

34 Barthold, *Turkestan*, p. 221.

35 Frye, *Bukhara*, p. 30.

36 Barthold, *Turkestan*, p. 227 makes this obvious, but important point.

37 Ibid., p. 227; al-Muqaddasi cited from ibid., p. 233.

38 Crone, *Slaves on Horses*, p. 80, and see p. 78; see also Kennedy, *The Prophet*, pp. 158–9; and Paul, *The State and the Military*, pp. 8, 25; Frye argues (*Heritage of Central Asia*, pp. 195–6) that the pre-Islamic tradition of Central Asian merchants using slaves as guards is the source of the *ghulam* tradition throughout the Islamic world.
39 The basic argument of Crone's *Slaves on Horses*, pp. 80–1.
40 Paul, *The State and the Military*, pp. 24–5; see also Golden, *Introduction*, p. 193; Frye, *Bukhara*, p. 121.
41 Nizam al-Mulk, *The Book of Government*, pp. 103–4; and see Barthold, *Turkestan*, p. 227.
42 Frye, *Bukhara*, p. 91, and see pp. 150–1; see also Barthold, *Turkestan*, p. 240; and Paul, *The State and the Military*, pp. 21–2.
43 Paul, *The State and the Military*, pp. 27–8.
44 Narshakhi listed ten distinct *diwans* in Samanid Bukhara; Barthold, *Turkestan*, p. 229; there is a detailed account of Samanid bureaucracy in Ibid., pp. 226–34.
45 Barthold, *Turkestan*, p. 232; see also Frye, *Bukhara*, p. 75, and p. 123.
46 Argued in many works by Frye, such as *The Golden Age of Persia*.
47 Frye, *Bukhara*, p. 32, and see pp. 9–10, 30.
48 Barthold, *Turkestan*, pp. 103–4, citing al-Muqaddasi.
49 Frye, *Bukhara*, p. 93; Barthold, *Turkestan*, p. 112.
50 Barthold, *Turkestan*, p. 88.
51 Cited in Ibid., p. 145.
52 Ibn Fadlan, *Risala*, p. 124; and see Barthold, *Turkestan*, p. 148–9.
53 Frye, *Bukhara*, p. 154.
54 Barthold, *Turkestan*, p. 238; Bosworth stresses the importance of relations with pastoralists in *Ghaznavids*, 2nd edn, p. 259.
55 Frye, *Bukhara*, pp. 72–3.
56 Khazanov, *Nomads*, p. 206; and see Bosworth, *Ghaznavids*, 2nd edn, p. 215; and Tolstov, *Po drevnim del'tam*, p. 8 and elsewhere.
57 Frye, *Bukhara*, p. 72, and see p. 73.
58 Russian version in ibn Fadlan, *Risala*; see also the sections translated in Frye, 'Notes on the Risala of Ibn-Fadlan', in Frye, *Islamic Iran and Central Asia (7th–12th centuries)*, XXIX.
59 Frye, 'Notes on the Risala of ibn Fadlan', in Frye, *Islamic Iran and Central Asia (7th–12th centuries)*, XXIX, Frye's notes on pp. 30–31, and see ibid., p. 17.
60 Frye, 'Notes on the Risala', in Frye, *Islamic Iran*, XXIX:12; and ibn Fadlan, *Risala*, p. 124.
61 *Newsletter of the Circle of Inner Asian Art*, edn 2, April 1996, p. 3.
62 The province near modern Tashkent; its capital, Binkath, may have been on the site of modern Tashkent; Barthold, *Turkestan*, p. 171.
63 Cited in Barthold, *Turkestan*, pp. 235–6.
64 Frye, *Bukhara*, p. 70.
65 Barthold, *Turkestan*, pp. 236–7, and see p. 164.
66 Frye, *Bukhara*, pp. 44, 60; and see Frye, *Golden Age of Persia*, p. 171.
67 Frye, *Golden Age of Persia*, p. x.
68 Abu Mansur al-Tha'alibi, cited in Frye, *Bukhara*, p. 59.
69 Ibid., p. 58.
70 Barthold, *Turkestan*, pp. 9–10; the library burnt down soon after Avicenna's visit, and jealous rivals maintained he had burnt it down to deny them access to it.
71 Litvinskii, 'Outline history of Buddhism', pp. 123–30; see also Lapidus, *History*, p. 165; Frye, *Bukhara*, pp. 131–2, 189.

72 Frye, *Golden Age of Persia*, pp. 158–9; on science, see Frye, *Golden Age of Persia*, p. 162; Hodgson, *Venture of Islam*, 1:414–15; al-Khwarazmi's name gave English the word, 'algorithm', while his main book gave it the word, 'algebra'.

73 Hodgson, *Venture of Islam*, 1:456 includes a good discussion of Islamic geography and its place in Islamic *adab* or court culture; see also Barthold, 'Short History of Turkestan', in *Four Studies*, 1:13.

74 Hodgson, *Venture of Islam*, 1:457.

FURTHER READING

On Central Asia before and during the introduction of Islam, see: Barthold, *Turkestan*; Tolstov, *Po drevnim del'tam*; Frye, *Golden age of Persia*, and *Heritage of Central Asia*; Golden, *Introduction to the History of the Turkic Peoples*; and the relevant parts of the *Cambridge History of Iran* and the *Cambridge History of Islam*. See also Frye, *Bukhara*. On the appearance of Islam in Central Asia, see also Lapidus, *History*; Kennedy, *The Prophet*; Litvinsky, Jalilov and Kolesnikov, 'The Arab conquest' in *HCCA*, pp. 449–72; and Gibb, *Arab Conquests*. Important primary sources on Mawara'n-nahr include Narshaki, *History of Bukhara*; Nizam al-Mulk, *The Book of Government*; the *Hudud al-Alam*; and ibn Fadlan, *Risala*. On Mawara'n-nahr before 1000, see, in addition, the essays by Frye, in *Islamic Iran and Central Asia*; and two older studies: Hodgson, *Venture of Islam*, vol 1; and Barthold, *Four Studies*. The best single account of Samanid Mawara'n-nahr, is in Frye's *Golden Age of Persia*. On the emergence of slave armies, see Crone, *Slaves on Horses*; and Paul, *The State and the Military*. Paul's *Herrscher, Gemeinwesen, Vermittler* came out too late to be used for this book. There are good illustrations, in Rice, *Ancient Arts of Central Asia*.

[13] THE ORIGINS OF RUS'

In the far west of Inner Eurasia, communities based on rainfall agriculture had existed in the forest steppelands of modern Ukraine and Moldova since the Cucuteni-Tripolye cultures of the fourth millennium BCE.[1] However, for four millennia they had barely spread beyond the forest steppes. Though numerous and prosperous enough to interest potential tribute-takers from the Scythians to the Goths, the farming communities of the far west were too scattered to provide the foundations for an agrarian state.

From c.500 CE, the situation was transformed by a huge, centuries-long migration of farming populations from eastern Europe. Farming expanded in the old core areas of forest steppe from the Danube to the middle Dnieper. But it also spread into the zone of mixed deciduous and evergreen forest further north, and even eastwards to the edge of the Don steppes. By the tenth century, the expansion of rainfall agriculture had laid the demographic and economic foundations for an agrarian state. Meanwhile, the growing demographic and economic wealth of these lands attracted traders and tribute-takers from Scandinavia and the steppes. Together, woodland farming communities and tribute-taking outsiders formed the first agrarian states based north of the Pontic steppes. In the ninth century, there emerged two strong polities dominated by immigrants, but based in the wooded zone: the kaghanates of Rus' and Bulghar. Both borrowed their statecraft from the Khazars. In the tenth century, Rus' leaders moved south, established a new capital at Kiev, overthrew the Khazar empire and established the first major agrarian empire to appear in western Inner Eurasia.

The appearance of Rus' marks a major turning point in the history of Inner Eurasia. Rainfall agriculture, unlike the irrigation agriculture of Central Asia, was not confined to a few ecological hot spots. On the contrary, once it began to spread more widely in the forested region, it created a thickening and expanding network of settlements over a huge area. Though it took many centuries, the states that built on this economic and demographic foundation eventually conquered most of Inner Eurasia. In the history of Inner Eurasia, Rus' and its successor states represent the belated triumph of the agrarian neolithic. The geographer, Mackinder, was alert to the revolutionary historical significance of this change.

Map 13.1 The peoples of Rus'.

When the Russian Cossacks first policed the steppes at the close of the Middle Ages, a great revolution was effected, for the Tartars, like the Arabs, had lacked the necessary man-power upon which to found a lasting empire, but behind the Cossacks were the Russian plowmen.[2]

THE EXPANSION OF FARMING IN WESTERN INNER EURASIA

THE SPREAD OF AGRICULTURE

At the end of the first millennium BCE, commercial agriculture was practiced in Crimea to supply the cities of the Black Sea coast and for exports to the Mediterranean. To the north, pastoralists dominated the Pontic steppes, while the communities that Herodotus referred to as 'farming Scythians' lived along the river valleys and in the forest steppes of the old Tripolye heartland. The forested lands further north had long been an area of scattered communities of foragers who adopted some of the technologies of the neolithic, including pottery. From the second millennium BCE, there are signs of the spread of a type of forest pastoralism from central Europe, in a belt that stretched just north of the wooded steppes, from the Baltic to the middle Dnieper and the middle and upper Volga. This tradition is associated with the so-called 'corded ware' cultures. It combined foraging, fishing and livestock-breeding. From 1000 BCE, some woodland communities also began to practise swidden agriculture.[3] Swidden farmers cleared well drained slopes near rivers, burnt the felled trees and farmed in their ashes for three or four years before moving on. This extensive and nomadic form of agriculture could only support small populations, and population densities in such regions were little higher than those of foraging communities. So, even at the beginning of the contemporary era, farming communities of the woodlands were confined to the southern edge of the great Russian forests, depended on livestock-rearing as much as farming, and farmed without ploughs. Their villages formed a thin lacework of settlements spread along the region's river systems.

The densest populations of farmers could still be found further south in the Tripolye heartland, which had also been the heart of the Chernyakhiv cultures in the Gothic period. Written sources describe the presence of numerous small communities of farmers in the region. Tacitus, writing in the first century of the modern era, described the 'Venedi' of western Ukraine as a 'populous race' who occupied a 'great expanse of land.'[4] The names attributed to these populations suggest that most spoke or used early forms of Slavic, though amongst them there may also have been groups who spoke Sarmatian, Gothic or Turkic languages. These communities used plough agriculture, reared livestock and had trading and other contacts with the Mediterranean. Most settlements were unfortified, which suggests that they were used to the suzerainty of Gothic, Sarmatian or Turkic tribute-takers, though they occasionally used the woods and swamps as refuges.[5]

From c.500 CE, there are signs of new migrations into and beyond the wooded steppes. Most migrants probably spoke some form of proto-Slavic or used it as a lingua franca. The fact that the various Slavic languages were still quite uniform even in the eleventh century, suggests that these migrations began from a compact east European 'homeland', whose precise location remains uncertain.[6] In the sixth century, Jordanes described a large area of agrarian settlement in eastern Europe, dominated by a 'populous race' of Slavic speakers (Venethi), and reaching from the Carpathians to the middle Dnieper, and northwards to the Vistula. Their major tribes he named as the 'Sclaveni' (who almost certainly spoke Slavic languages) and the 'Anti' (many of whom may have been of Sarmatian or Alan origin).[7]

During the next three centuries, peasants migrated in small groups, usually settling near river banks. They moved towards the middle Dnieper, or northwards towards the Baltic coast. During the eighth century, some moved into the mixed forest zone, and also east of the Dnieper, and by the ninth century, Slavic migrants were even settling amongst the Finnic-speaking peoples of the Volga–Oka river basin.[8] The increasing importance of agriculture in the mixed forest zone from the ninth century is shown by the fact that, according to the Primary Chronicle, the Vyatichians, who lived near modern Moscow, paid tributes to the Khazars 'by the plough'. It is also demonstrated by the rise of the Volga Bulghar state, which was based, in part, on tributes collected from immigrant farmers. Other migrants colonized lands near the steppes protected after *c*.750 by the *pax khazarica*, the zone of orderly government established by the Khazars. Some Slavic migrants may even have settled in the Don steppes, in the region of the Saltovo-Maitskii cultures.[9]

In some cases, it may be possible, through a combination of literary and archaeological evidence, to trace the migrations of particular Slavic groupings. The 'Slovenian' tribes seem to have split into two groups, one of which migrated south, to form the core of the modern population of Slovenia, while another group migrated to the north-west where they settled near modern Novgorod. West of Novgorod, groups speaking Baltic languages colonized the Baltic coast and parts of modern Belarus. In the north-west, settlement was particularly dense in the fertile lands around the later cities of Novgorod and Pskov. However, in general, colonization of the lands east and north of Kiev was much slower than colonization of the old farming lands. By the seventh century, Slavic migrations had probably achieved their maximum extent to the west and south, but in the more thinly populated north and east, they continued for many centuries.[10]

We do not know the exact form these migrations took. New households may have cleared land close to established villages, leading to a slow, amoeba-like migration, household by household. Or whole communities may have migrated in a more deliberate way. Such migrations may have been as organized as the migrations described by Caesar in Gaul, in which whole communities picked a likely territory after sending out scouts, packed up their crops and belongings like nineteenth-century settlers in the American Midwest, and set off with their belongings in carts drawn by horse or oxen.[11] But almost everywhere they went, from the sixth to the tenth centuries, Slavic-speaking migrants built log-houses (*poluzemlyanki*) sunk 40–70 cm into the ground for greater warmth. Their houses were roughly square with sides of 3–4 metres, with roofs of earth and straw, and with stone stoves that were used for heating and cooking. Slavic dwellings were, as Goehrke puts it, 'modest, dark and sooty'. Only in the north, around Novgorod and Pskov, did Slavic migrants borrow the Finnic technique of building houses at ground level.[12]

Explaining these population movements is extremely difficult. How and why did farming communities manage to break out of the Tripolye heartlands to which they had been confined for four millennia? We have already discussed the difficulties of farming in the woodlands, with their relatively harsh climates and their poor woodland soils or podzols. What needs to be explained here is the chronology: how and why were these difficulties overcome after 500 CE? The best we can do at present is to identify three types of factor: changing technologies and the push and pull of economic and political changes.

In the first millennium, improved farming technologies created population pressure throughout the 'barbarian' lands just north of the Roman empire, as farmers adopted better ploughs, with iron ploughshares hauled by oxen or horses, or started sowing more wheat and rye.[13] Improved techniques spread into much of eastern Europe, including the old farming areas of Moldova and central Ukraine. Here the so-called 'Prague' cultures show the spread of plough agriculture and stock-rearing, using Roman techniques including systematic manuring and crop rotations. Further north, migrants used more extensive systems of cultivation, though a light 'scratch' plough (ralo) became common. An improved light plough with a metal share (sokha) began to appear towards the end of the millennium. The sokha was particularly well adapted to the stony, root-filled soils of newly colonized woodland regions, whose thin top soils lost fertility if ploughed too deeply. The heavy plough (plug) began to spread in the woodlands only in the eleventh to twelfth centuries and perhaps even later.[14]

In the old core areas, the main crops in the sixth and seventh centuries were still millet and also wheats and barleys. Oats became more common as a summer crop, while pulses and flax and fruit such as apples were also grown. Everywhere, livestock were important, including horse, cattle, sheep, goats and pigs. However, the key to successful colonization further north was probably the spread of winter ryes. In the ninth and tenth centuries, winter ryes begin to appear in the mixed forest zone. Rye was more reliable than wheat in the colder, northern parts of Rus', and its introduction permitted the use of more intensive and productive systems of crop rotation.[15] The introduction of rye stimulated population growth right across the northern half of Europe in the first millennium and eventually allowed the emergence of non-agricultural specialists, including artisans such as smiths, or regional chiefs with retinues who could provide a measure of defence. As populations grew, and new implements came into use, the number of blacksmiths and the quality of their work increased in the ninth century.[16] This was the first sign of an emerging division of labour within the farming communities of the mixed forest lands.

However, technological change alone will not explain the Slavic and Baltic migrations, for many of the technologies they introduced had existed for some time. Migrants were also pushed or pulled into the region by a number of other factors. The negative pressures include over-population in central and eastern Europe and pressure from pastoralists in South-Eastern Europe. The most spectacular early signs of over-population in eastern Europe appear in the sixth century when Slavic-speaking communities began to migrate in vast numbers into the Balkans. The fact that these migrations began before the arrival of the Avars in the 560s suggests that population pressure was already intense in eastern Europe. However, the fact that Slavic migrations intensified after the Avar conquest of Pannonia suggests that Avar oppression was also an important incentive to migrate. The Russian Primary Chronicle records that the Avars

> made war upon the Slavs, and harassed the Dulebians, who were themselves Slavs. They even did violence to the Dulebian women. When an Avar made a journey, he did not cause either a horse or a steer to be harnessed, but gave command instead that three or four or five women should be yoked to his cart and be made to draw him.

Migrants were pulled as well as pushed into the woodlands west of the Urals. Dolukhanov has pointed out that these migrations occurred during a period of climatic warming analogous to the Climatic Optimum of the fourth millennium BCE, when the Tripolye cultures first flourished. In the first millennium CE, climates in eastern Europe were probably as favourable for farming as they had been since the second millennium BCE. Average temperatures seem to have risen from c.300 BCE to c.1200 CE, while rainfall increased from c.500 CE.[18] The evidence on climatic change is still too thin to clinch such arguments, but they accord well with the chronology of settlement.

Two other factors also attracted migrants. The first was the *pax khazarica*. From c.750, this protected the lands close to the steppes along the Donets and Don, and drew migrants into lands long dominated by nomadic pastoralists. Second was the increase in commerce along the waterways of Rus'. This was also made possible in part by the stability of Khazar power. In addition, the demand for forest goods such as boats, timber, furs, wax and honey expanded, because of reviving demand from Europe, Byzantium and the Islamic world after the economic slump of the seventh century. From the late eighth century, the flow of Islamic silver dirhams through the Don–Donets systems northwards towards the Oka and Volga probably indicates that settlers willing to act as guides, guards or suppliers of furs were attracted to the area. Even ordinary Slavic settlements may have engaged in trade to some extent for, though most were self-sufficient even in the tenth century, they also produced saleable goods. Most households had access to honey, wax, furs and other goods, while in winter, they made and dyed linen or woollen cloths or made pottery or burnt charcoal or dug in local marshlands for pig-iron for their blacksmiths.[19]

The migrations of the second half of the first millennium transformed the linguistic and ecological map of western Inner Eurasia. By 900 CE, most inhabitants of the lands west of the Urals were probably Slavic- or Baltic-speaking farmers. Their settlements reached from the steppes to the northern *taiga*, though the demographic centre of gravity remained in the wooded steppelands near Kiev.[20] Apart from the band of oases that stretched from Merv to Tun-huang, the newly colonized lands of the west were now the most densely populated region of Inner Eurasia.[21]

POLITICAL STRUCTURES

The process of migration probably generated structures of leadership and tribal alliances more extensive than those of neighbouring foraging communities. However, Byzantine accounts of the sixth and seventh centuries suggest that leadership was weak, at least in those regions closest to Byzantium. According to the *Strategikon*, the Byzantine manual of strategy attributed to emperor Maurice, which appeared in c.600, the Slavs and Antes lacked systematic military and political organization, and 'can neither obey nor fight in formation'. The absence of strong leadership meant that local communities warred amongst themselves, and lacked discipline in open battle. Naturally, Byzantine governments encouraged such divisions. The *Strategikon* advised the making of selective alliances with particular Slavic tribes, so that they will 'not come under the power of a single leader'.[22] Its author clearly understood that any group that could impose some unity on these lands would prove a formidable rival.

The archaeology of the eighth century shows a world of small villages, with 4–10 or at most 20 houses, usually strung out in a line near a river. Most villages appear in clusters of 5–15 settlements roughly 5 kilometres apart, with larger gaps of 20 or 30 kilometres between clusters. The larger villages often contain a religious centre or a place of refuge or perhaps a smithy.[23] The Soviet historian, Froyanov, has suggested that each of these clusters, which may have included from a few hundred to a few thousand people each, represents a distinct tribe or *verv'*. In the eighth and ninth centuries, fortified settlements begin to appear, often on strategic positions overlooking river junctions, so that Scandinavian migrants of the tenth century called Rus' *Gardariki*, the land of forts. Many fortified settlements may have begun as the dwellings of tribal leaders. As populations and productivity grew, markets and artisan settlements appeared within or outside their earthen or wooden stockades, until they began to develop into small towns. Such sites spread along the valleys of the Dnieper, the Dniester and the Bug, and in the ninth century, they also spread further north.[24]

There are hints that more complex political structures appeared first in newly colonized lands east of the Dnieper, in regions controlled by the Khazars. In the late eighth century, while most settlements west of the Dnieper remained unfortified, those to the east were more likely to be founded on promontories overlooking river junctions or valleys, and to have earthen ramparts or even expensive wooden stockades. Here, there is evidence of wealthy individuals, who probably profited from the flow of silver dirhams through Khazar lands from the late eighth century. In these lands trade, however modest, provided the surplus wealth necessary for the emergence of small aristocratic elites of petty chiefs. Trade routes also attracted armed outsiders from both the steppes and the Baltic lands, so that these communities also had a greater need to defend themselves.[25]

The Russian *Primary Chronicle*, written mainly in the eleventh century, lists several large tribal groupings which had appeared by the ninth or tenth centuries. Most were probably Slavic-speaking, although some probably included Baltic- or Finnic-speakers. These groupings extended over large territories, and usually included at least one town as well as clusters of smaller settlements. They could mobilize troops for local conflicts, as we read in the Chronicle that some took tributes from their neighbours. There can be no doubt of the reality of these groups, for they are mentioned in several sources, and tenth-century evidence shows that some, such as the Drevlyane, probably had powerful leaders even in the ninth century.[26] Goehrke suggests that groupings such as the Drevlyanians or the Polyanians, who lived near Kiev:

> could surely provide defence against pastoral nomads, and also protection against Varangian booty raids and demands for tribute, and they were therefore politically [*herrschaftlich*] organised. In other words, they had sovereign rulers [*Fürsten*] who had retinues of warriors.[27]

This is probably overstated. Such groupings provided limited protection against external tribute-takers. Besides, the lack of unequivocal references to kingship in this period, or of clear evidence for royal capitals or even wealthy elites suggests that their leaders were still powerful regional chiefs, the managers of extensive but local alliance systems.

The political weakness of Slavic chiefs, even east of the Dnieper, reflect the fact that most of their wealth still came from subsistence farming, and their armed strength consisted mainly of tribal levies of farmers under local chiefs. The migrations of the eighth and ninth centuries provided abundant demographic raw material for state-building, but it was the appearance of outsiders specializing in trade and warfare that catalysed the formation of larger and more powerful state structures.

THE KAGHANATE OF 'RUS''

HISTORIOGRAPHICAL CONTROVERSIES

The fundamental written source for the early history of Rus', The Primary Chronicle has been reconstructed by modern scholars from material embedded in other surviving chronicles. It was compiled in the Pecherskii ('Caves') Monastery in Kiev, in the late eleventh century, some two centuries after the appearance of a Rus' state, and the versions that have survived were edited by Ryurikid princes in the early twelfth century, so it is as much a genealogical charter as a historical record.[28] As a result, it must be treated with some caution. Nevertheless, all attempts to reconstruct the early history of Rus' have to use it, and much of the material it contains can be shown to be accurate.

According to The Primary Chronicle, the first state of Rus' was formed in 862, when a diverse group of Finnic, Baltic, Slavic and Scandinavian communities in the Novgorod region invited three Viking chiefs, led by Ryurik, to be their prince. 'Our land is rich,' they said, 'but there is no order in it. Come to rule and reign over us.'[29] Meanwhile, a second group of Vikings, led by Askold and Dir, had conquered Kiev. In c.882, according to the Chronicle, Ryurik's successor, Oleg, conquered Kiev and created the first state to incorporate most of the woodlands between the Baltic and the Black Sea.

From at least the early eighteenth century, many historians have taken this account literally, and concluded that the first Rus' state was indeed created by Viking or 'Norman' mercenaries between 862 and 882, and took its name from the Finnic word for Swedes, Rotsi.[30] However, from the time of Lomonosov, in the mid-eighteenth century, there emerged an alternative, or 'anti-Normanist' position, which argued that the name, 'Rus'' was indigenous, and that it was Slavic tribes that did most of the work of state-formation in the region. In the twentieth century, the 'anti-Normanist' position became obligatory for Soviet historians, after Stalin rejected the Normanist position with its suggestion of Germanic conquest. Partly in reaction, most western historians adopted a Normanist position on the issue during the Cold War

Today, since the collapse of the Soviet Union, there is emerging a consensus that recognizes the importance of the Viking Rus', and the Viking origin of the ethnonym. However, it also recognizes the poly-ethnic nature of the state they created, and the crucial role of non-Viking groups in the formation and the linguistic and cultural evolution of Rus'.[31] What is still not adequately appreciated is the extent to which the earliest Rus' state was oriented towards the Khazars and Baghdad rather than towards Byzantium and the Christian world.

VIKING TRADERS AND TRIBUTE-TAKERS

The slaves, wax, honey and furs of the woodlands had attracted outsiders since at least the first millennium BCE, and probably much earlier. Most were willing to take what they wanted by force, but the vast distances they encountered, and the thinness of local populations often made trade an easier option. The expansion of farming undoubtedly stimulated trade in the woodlands, for it created new bases for supplies and repairs, and new internal markets. As a result, the commercial potential of the region grew rapidly, particularly from the eighth century, and so did its attraction for outside traders and would-be tribute-takers, including the Khazars and the Volga Bulghars.

In the eighth century, the growing wealth of the region began to attract Scandinavian traders as well. Their main commercial advantage was that they entered from the north-east, a thinly settled and weakly defended region close to the furs of the northern forests, and to areas of recent colonization beyond the reach of the Khazars or the Volga Bulghars. Here it was possible to levy tributes from local communities of foragers and farmers, and to control a vital segment of the trade route from the Baltic to Baghdad and Central Asia.

Recent numismatic and archaeological research has made it possible to estimate roughly how the volume of trade through the region fluctuated.[32] Finds of Sassanian and Byzantine silverware and Byzantine coins along the River Kama, dating from the sixth and early seventh centuries, and references in Jordanes to Swedish fur-traders, prove the existence of long-distance networks of exchange in the middle of the millennium. During the seventh and much of the eighth centuries, trade through the woodlands of Rus' declined, as a result of slackening demand from the depressed markets of Byzantium and Persia, and the conflicts between the Khazars and the Umayyad caliphate that periodically closed routes through the Caucasus. From the late eighth century, peace between the Khazars and the Abbasid caliphate, and renewed economic growth in the eastern Mediterranean, stimulated a revival of trade routes through the woodlands towards the Baltic and eastern Europe. The clearest sign of this revival is the appearance of silver dirhams in the north, from the end of the eighth century. Mapping of early finds suggests that silver dirhams travelled through the Caucasus, and then moved north and west along a number of routes, mainly through the Don and Donets river systems. The variety of routes suggests the existence of many local systems of exchange which swapped goods and coins in a relay of trade and tribute.[33]

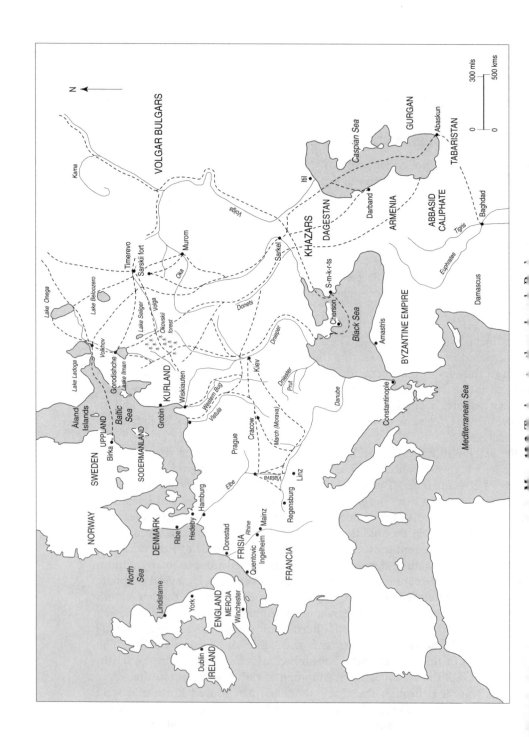

Abbasid dirhams, in turn, attracted Scandinavian traders in furs and slaves. Scandinavians had traded in the eastern Baltic since the iron age. As early as the sixth century, some may have travelled as far as Lake Ladoga in search of furs. A thirteenth-century Icelandic source, *Yngvar's Saga*, may preserve memories of the sort of world they entered. In one episode, the hero's son, Svein, encounters a group of natives along a river deep in Rus'.

One of the natives had a feather in his hand, and first he pointed up the stem of the feather, then the blade, which seemed to be a token of peace, so Svein responded with a hand-sign of peace too. The natives gathered under the lee-side of a cliff, offering various kinds of merchandise. Svein told his men they could go ashore, and they traded with the natives though neither side could understand what the other was saying.[34]

The sequel suggests how easily trade could turn into plunder.

Next day, Svein's men went ashore yet again to trade with the natives and for a while they exchanged goods, until one of the Russians [Vikings] tried to break an agreement he had just made to buy some furs. When the heathen lost his temper and punched him on the nose so that the blood poured onto the ground, the Russian drew his sword and sliced the heathen in two. At that the heathen people ran off shouting and screaming but in no time they gathered in what seemed an invincible army. But Svein told his men to arm themselves for war and march against the heathen, and in the fierce battle that followed the heathen, having no protective armour, fell in huge numbers. When they saw that they had lost the battle, the heathen ran, and Svein and his men won a great deal of plunder left behind by the others, which they carried down to the ships.[35]

In the seventh century, Scandinavians began to settle among the Finnic-speaking peoples of the eastern shores of the Baltic. But not until the late eighth century did they settle away from the Baltic coast. In the 750s, Vikings settled in Staraya Ladoga (Norse Aldeigjuborg) on the River Volkhov, just as the trading cities of Hedeby in Denmark and Birka in Sweden began to blossom. Staraya Ladoga controlled access by river to Lake Ladoga and the Baltic. It was probably part of a larger trade network which included Birka and Hedeby, functioning as a remote outpost of this system, a sort of eighth century Hudson's Bay settlement. It attracted native fur-traders and slavers, and offered in return manufactured goods from the Baltic, such as amber or glass beads. It sold some of its produce to traders from the south in return for Abbasid dirhams. There were boatyards to repair ships, workshops to modify or make simple trade goods such as beads, and also permanent dwellings, most of which are typically Scandinavian. The absence of fortifications before the mid-ninth century, and the small number of weapons in its cemeteries show that for a time the settlement was protected by its remoteness.[36]

Early in the ninth century, Viking traders probed south, founding new settlements on Lake Ilmen, at the southern end of the River Volkhov. The most important was a fortified settlement near modern Novgorod, known to archaeologists as 'Ryurikovo Gorodishche' or 'Riurik's town'. In the late ninth century, Gorodishche became an important trading emporium, and many Vikings settled here, as well as local Baltic-, Slavic- or Finnic-speaking people. Vikings also settled further south, perhaps amongst Slavic- or Finnic-speaking communities, at strategic centres near future towns such as Yaroslav. or Rostov or Smolensk.[37] Taken together, the fragmentary archaeological evidence suggests that by 850 Vikings had settled in a number of strategic settlements along the trade routes through the thinly populated mixed forest zone, sometimes in Viking colonies, sometimes amongst Baltic, Slavic or Finnic communities.

The existence of these colonies may explain the obscure references from c.840 to the existence of a 'kaghanate' of the Rus'. The earliest European reference comes from the *Annals of St Bertin*, and refers to a group of *Rhos* who visited Byzantium, and then tried to return home via Germany in c.838, rather than risk encounters with Magyars on the steppelands of southern Russia. The Frankish emperor, Louis the Pious, interrogated the *Rhos* somewhere near Mainz. He found that, though their leader was known as a *chacanus* (kagan), they were of Swedish origin.[38] It seems likely that their ruler was based in the group of Viking settlements along the River Volkhov, where the Russian chronicles place the first state of the Rus'. The most recent analysis of the kaghanate suggests that its capital was probably at Gorodishche. This may explain why ibn Rusta described the capital of the 'Rus' as 'an island around which is a lake', for the Scandinavian name for Gorodishche, 'Holmgarthr' literally means 'island compound'.[39] The fact that the Russian Primary Chonicle also locates the first Rus' capital at Novgorod offers further support for this hypothesis.

Our knowledge of the Rus' kaghanate is even more fragmentary than our knowledge of the Khazars and Volga Bulghars. However, a northern Rus' 'kaghanate' seems to have existed for at least 80 years, probably linking a loose federation of Viking settlements. It was able to field powerful armies that could cover large distances by land and sea; its wealth was based mainly on trade and plunder; and its political institutions were modelled on those of the Khazars.

One of the few contemporary accounts, that of ibn Rusta, written in around the 880s, gives a sense of the *condottiere* state of the Rus':

> They have a king who is called Khaqan Rus, and they make raids against Saqlaba [a term that may include woodland Slavs, Balts and Finno-Ugrians], sailing in ships in order to go out to them, and they take them prisoner and carry them off to Khazar and Bulkar [Bulghar] and trade with them there. They have no cultivated lands; they eat only what they carry off from the land of the Saqlaba. When a child is born to any man among them, he takes a drawn sword to the new-born child and places it between his hands and says to him: "I shall bequeath to thee no wealth and thou wilt have naught except what thou dost gain for thyself by this sword of thine." They have no landed property nor villages nor cultivated land; their only occupation is trading in sables and grey squirrel and other furs, and in these they trade and they take as the price gold and silver and secure it in their belts [or saddlebags].[40]

Archaeology confirms the impression that the Rus' were mainly interested in tribute-taking and trade. There are few signs of Rus' settling as farmers in the north. Settlements such as Staraya Ladoga or Gorodishche almost certainly had permanent colonies of Rus', but they were mainly there to service trade. Far more important were the transient populations of Scandinavian mercenaries and traders looking for business and employment. A thirteenth century Icelandic saga, Eymund's Saga, which refers to events of the eleventh century, describes the role that new Viking arrivals may have played in the Scandinavian settlements of the Rus' kaghanate. It tells how a Norwegian called Eymund sought fame and fortune by offering his services as a mercenary to 'King Jarisleif' of Novgorod.[41] He negotiated terms for himself and his followers with great care.

> 'Now, we're offering to take charge of the defences of the kingdom and become your hired soldiers, taking payment from you in gold, silver and fine clothes. Should you decide to give us a quick refusal and turn down our offer, we'll accept the same terms from another king.'[42]

Jarisleif asked for more precise terms, and was told:

> 'First of all, ... you're to provide us and all our troops with a great hall, and see to it that we'll never be without the very best of your provisions if we should want them. ... These men ... will be at your disposal, to go ahead of your troops in battle, in defence of the kingdom. You'll also pay every one of our soldiers an ounce in weight of silver, and to each Captain an additional half-ounce. ... We'll take payment in kind, beaver pelts and sable furs and other things readily available in your kingdom. ... And as long as there's plenty in the way of spoils you should be able to pay us out of that, but if we sit around doing nothing there'll be less pay.'[43]

It was probably men such as these who manned the large military expeditions mounted by the Rus' from at least as early as 860. In that year, a seaborne army of Rus' launched a fierce attack on Byzantium, which alerted Byzantium to the existence of a substantial military power in the north. In the next decade or two, there were equally large Rus' raids on the rich cities along the southern shores of the Caspian, probably launched with the permission of the Khazar *beks*. Such raids suggest that conventional trade was not generating enough wealth to support the Viking migrants who sought their fortune in the region. Perhaps, as Franklin and Shepard have suggested, the kaghanate of Rus' dealt with these dangerous fortune-seekers by sending them south. Certainly, there is evidence, both archaeological, and literary, that the Rus' kaghanate underwent periods of internal conflict. The chronicle accounts refer to the creation of independent Rus' polities, and the Arabic writer, al-Mas'udi, writes of Dir, the conqueror of Kiev that, though not a kaghan, he was the greatest of the Slav princes, and ruled huge and populous cities, that were visited by Muslim traders. There is archaeological evidence that Staraya Ladoga and Gorodishche were sacked in the 860s, while Ladoga acquired substantial fortifications for the first time in the mid-ninth century.[44] Taken together, these signs suggest the existence of a relatively unstable military elite, which was both strengthened and destabilized by the periodic arrival of new groups of fortune-seekers from Scandinavia.

However, the Rus' kaghanate clearly achieved a certain level of stability. By the middle of the ninth century, the Rus' were engaged in trade on a large scale, mainly along the Silver Road down to the Black Sea, where they had to pay tolls to Byzantine governors. From there they travelled into Khazaria where they paid tolls to the Khazars, and then on to the Caspian sea. Some went as far as Baghdad. According to the Arabic geographer, Ibn Khurdadhbih, even in the 840s:

> They bring furs of beavers and black foxes, as well as swords, from the most distant parts of the land of the Slavs to the Black Sea where the ruler of the Greeks collects the tithe [from their goods]. If they like, they go via the Slavic River [the Don] to Hamlih [on the Volga], a city of the Khazars, where the latter's ruler collects the tithe from them. Then they reach the Sea of Jurjan [the Caspian Sea] and land at the shore they like. Sometimes they bring their wares on camels from Jurjan to Baghdad, where Slavic eunuchs serve as interpreters for them. They profess to be Christians, and they pay [only] the head tax.[45]

By 900, the Rus' were sending large fleets down the Volga to the capital of the Volga Bulghars, probably from trading settlements such as Timerevo near modern Yaroslavl. Ibn Fadlan's account of Volga Bulgharia, written in 922, describes the Rus' soldier/traders who engaged in regular trade through Bulgharia, paying the Khazars a percentage of their profits. They had their own houses and warehouses, and traded in a wide range of goods including furs of many kinds (sable, squirrel, ermine, fox, marten and beaver) Frankish swords, wax, honey, amber, livestock produce such as hides, and slaves. Ibn Fadlan describes how, on arrival in Bulghar, the Rus' set up wooden totem poles with carved faces to which they sacrificed food, and prayed for success in finding rich buyers.[46]

Because of its orientation towards the trade routes from the Baltic to the Caucasus, the Rus' kaghanate was deeply influenced by Khazaria. The extent of this influence has been obscured by the Chronicle accounts which assume that Rus' had always been orientated towards Byzantium. In the Soviet period, Khazar influence was obscured by the anti-Semitism of Stalinist censors, who resisted the idea that early Rus' might have been influenced by a Jewish state. Steppe traditions were peculiarly evident in funeral rituals. Ibn Fadlan described a Viking funeral in which the dead chief was cremated in a tomb in his boat, which was drawn up on land. Before cremation, he was provided with food, wine, money, clothing and jewellery, and a slave girl, who volunteered to accompany him, was ritually murdered and cremated with him. The excavation of burial mounds from the towns of Rus' confirms the accuracy of this account. Many contain horses as well as slaughtered concubines and retainers.[47] Ibn Fadlan's account of the Rus' ruler suggests that he, like the Khazar kaghan by this time, was a purely ceremonial leader, while real power was held by a deputy. While the deputy 'commands the troops, attacks his enemies, and acts as his representative before his subjects', the kaghan himself 'has no other duties but to make love to his slave girls, drink, and give himself up to pleasure.'[48] Virtually a prisoner, the kaghan lived his life of sybaritic luxury surrounded by 400 retainers in a huge fortress, in a room decorated with precious cloths.

All in all, the fragmentary evidence on the kaghanate of the Rus' suggests that Viking traders and mercenaries had managed to create a moderately durable state, with a semi-sacred ruling dynasty like the Khazar kaghan, and a separate military leader like the Khazar *bek*. Like the Türk empire created by the A-shih-na dynasty, this based its power on a federation of elite warriors, funded by controlling trade routes between two large areas of agrarian civilization. Though they travelled by boat, the Vikings showed as great a flair for trade and booty as any pastoralist empire, and the relative poverty of their homelands gave them as great an incentive to raid richer lands. Pritsak has called the Vikings 'nomads of the sea', and the analogy is a good one, particularly in the era of the 'Rus kaghanate'.[49]

KIEVAN RUS'

THE MOVE TO KIEV

In the ninth and tenth centuries, Vikings who may or may not have been subjects of the Rus' kaghan, made several attempts to break the Khazar grip on the trade routes of the Volga and Dnieper. Between 860 and 880, Vikings launched raids down both the Dnieper and the Volga. In 910, apparently with the permission of the Khazar rulers, Rus' traders launched a huge booty raid on the Islamic coast of the southern Caspian.[50] However, on returning, most were massacred in Itil by the mainly Muslim soldiers of the Khazar army, and those who escaped were killed as they fled. More successful were attempts to bypass Itil, in which the Rus' may have cooperated with the Volga Bulghars. Ibn Fadlan's expedition reached Bulghar by a route that bypassed Itil, and the growing number of Samanid dirhams that turn up in Scandinavia from *c*.900 suggest that a lot of other caravans also took this route, which cut out the Khazar middleman.

In *c*.910, another large Rus' army launched at least one more attack down the Dnieper towards Byzantium. This time, they had more success than in 860, for in 911, a Rus' leader concluded a treaty regularizing trade relations with Byzantium. The Primary Chronicle claims that the expedition was led by a prince called Helgi/Oleg, whose position was perhaps analogous to that of the Khazar *bek*. He commanded a motley army of Vikings, Slavs and Finns.

Oleg sallied forth by horse and by ship, and the number of his vessels was two thousand. He arrived before Tsar'grad, but the Greeks fortified the strait and closed up the city. Oleg disembarked upon the shore, and ordered his soldiery to beach the ships. They waged war around the city, and accomplished much slaughter of the Greeks. ... Of the prisoners they captured, some they beheaded, some they tortured, some they shot, and still others they cast into the sea. The Russes inflicted many other woes upon the Greeks after the usual manner of soldiers.[51]

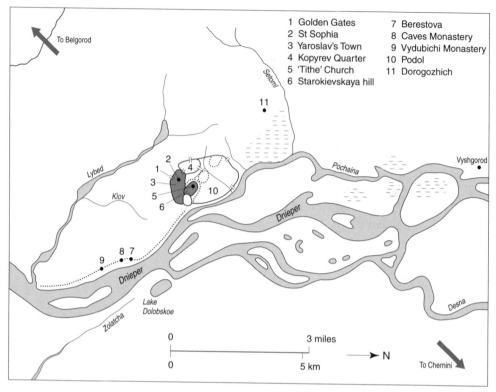

Map 13.3 Kiev and its environs. After Franklin and Shepard *The Emergence of Rus'*, p. 412.

The treaty concluded with Byzantium in 911 shows clearly the commercial and political ambitions of the new leaders of Rus'. According to the Chronicle, Oleg sought tribute, diplomatic recognition, trade rights for his merchants and also opportunities for members of his own retinue or *druzhina* to serve Byzantium as mercenaries. He demanded twelve *grivny* for every man in his fleet, and additional sums for the princes of specific cities. The commercial clauses in these treaties imply some commitment to a stable long-term relationship.[52] The Rus' demanded that their merchants be allowed to stay in Constantinople for periods as long as six months; that they be fed, housed and equipped for their return journey; and that they be allowed to trade without paying taxes.

The attack was probably launched from the Rus' kaghanate in the north. However, it showed an increasing interest in the trade routes leading from the Baltic to Byzantium, and this shift marked a slow, but significant reorientation in the interests and the international alignments of the Rus' kaghanate. There were several reasons for this growing interest in the Dnieper region. First, it was at the centre of one of the richest agricultural regions of eastern Europe, and had dense Slavic populations. Second, it controlled the lucrative land routes from central Europe to Khazaria. In addition, for armed traders willing to risk carrying their ships around the Dnieper rapids, where they were vulnerable to Pecheneg attacks, it also opened a direct trade route to Constantinople. Third, it was at the outer edges of the Khazar empire, and therefore less easily controlled by the Khazars. It is possible that the Khazars maintained a garrison in Kiev even in the late ninth century, but by 900, Viking settlement was beginning to undermine Khazar power along the Dnieper.[53] As Vikings began to settle along the middle and upper Dnieper, they began to take tributes from nearby tribes that had previously paid the Khazars, such as the Severyans and Radimichians. From 900, there is growing evidence of Viking settlement along the middle Dnieper. In Kiev, the *podol*, the trading port outside the original fortified area, expanded rapidly towards the end of the ninth century, as did the settlement of Gnezdovo, near modern Smolensk, which controlled the portages between the Dnieper and the river system of the north-west. Meanwhile, near Gorodishche, a new settlement was founded at what became the major city of Novgorod. The fact that the Chronicles portray Novgorod as the early capital of the northern Rus' suggests that it may have been created as a new and grander capital for the northern 'kaghan'. These changes suggest a new wave of Viking settlement in Rus', and the creation of a number of new centres of Viking power. They also suggest a realignment of Rus' interests away from Khazaria and towards Byzantium. This would give the later state of Rus' a very different cultural and economic orientation from that of the northern 'kaghanate'.[54]

By 940, the centre of gravity of Rus' power had shifted to Kiev. The Primary Chronicle maintains that Oleg conquered Kiev in 882 from local Viking rulers, Askold and Dir. However, the Chronicle's early chronology is notoriously unreliable and, as we have seen, ibn Fadlan, who visited Bulghar in 922, still seems to place the leader of the Rus' in the north. Besides, modern archaeology suggests that Kiev itself expanded rapidly only after 900. As a result, several recent scholars have proposed a revised chronology according to which Kiev did not become the capital of Rus' before the 930s.[55] The first clearly attested Ryurikid prince of Kiev, is Igor, who ruled in the 940s, perhaps with the support of Oleg. The fact that Oleg was not a Ryurikid suggests that he may have held a position similar to that of the Khazar *bek*, perhaps acting, also, as a regent during Igor's minority.

It is not clear how or when Igor established himself as an independent prince of Kiev. Perhaps the Chronicle account, which describes a northern conquest over a breakaway Viking polity based on Kiev, does capture the general trend of events even if it obscures the chronology. Perhaps it reflects the resumption of royal power by a vigorous young kaghan from his *bek*, Oleg. Whatever its cause, the move south created a much more powerful and unified state, based at the edge of the steppelands and controlling most of the lands from the Baltic to the Pontic steppes.

Kievan Rus' was soon embroiled in a complex four-cornered war with Byzantium, the Pechenegs and Khazaria. On the basis of Khazar documents, Zuckerman has suggested that a new phase of this conflict began in the early 940s, when a Rus' army, led by Helgi (Oleg?) attacked the Khazar-controlled Black Sea port of Samkerts/Phanagoria (later Tmutorokan').[56] Helgi was defeated by a Khazar army, and forced by the Khazars to launch a new attack on Byzantium, which he did in cooperation with his prince, Igor and a fleet of perhaps 1000 Rus' ships, as well as Pecheneg allies. When this attack failed, Igor returned to Kiev, while Helgi returned to Khazaria, and eventually died, an old man by now, seeking new conquests in the southern Caspian, and apparently rejected by the young prince Igor.

Depite this failure, Kievan Rus' soon emerged as a major international power. A few years later, in c.950, the Byzantine Emperor, Constantine Porphyrogenitus, wrote a famous description of Kievan Rus'.[57] The state he described was a loose federation of city-based princes from a single royal family. It was supported by a warrior elite that included Slavs and Finns as well as Vikings. It exacted tributes from semi-autonomous tribes, and also exploited the trade routes through the woodlands. He described in detail the methods of tribute-taking and trade that underpinned the system in the middle of the tenth century.

> When the month of November begins, their chiefs together with all the Russians at once leave Kiev and go off on the 'poliudia', which means 'rounds', that is, to the Slavonic regions of the Vervians and Drugovichians and Krivichians and Severians and the rest of the Slavs who are tributaries of the Russians. There they are maintained throughout the winter, but then once more, starting from the month of April, when the ice of the Dnieper river melts, they come back to Kiev.[58]

The goods collected for trade with Byzantium were dominated by the region's traditional exports of furs, wax, honey and slaves.[59]

To transport the goods they had collected on their rounds, the Rus' used the traditional Slavic dug-out canoes or *monoxyla*. These were prepared in Slavic villages during the winter. In spring, when the ice broke, their makers floated them down the Dnieper to Kiev, where they finished them and sold them to the Russians, who fitted them with tackle from older boats.[60] A Soviet historian has reconstructed how these boats were built:

> the trunk of a thick tree was first hollowed out with an axe and then trimmed with an adze. Then the log was steamed, and the sides distended to the required breadth; the bow and the stern were firmly tied to avoid any cracks; the process of stretching was consolidated by the insertion of thwarts made of stiff branches...Perhaps the tree was sometimes fitted out before being felled: in this case wedges were gradually driven ever deeper into the trunk; after two to five years the tree would fall, and the manufacture of the dug-out would be completed in the ordinary way. ...The size of these dug-outs varied considerably, from small canoes to enormous boats.[61]

Monoxyla were invaluable for navigation over a complex river system and could even be dragged across portages. They could also be quite large; sometimes their sides were built up to increase their carrying capacity, as in Cossack boats of the seventeeth century.[62] Once fitted out and loaded with cargo and men, the Rus' fleet set off for Constantinople in June. The most dangerous part of the journey began when they entered the steppelands just south of Kiev. Below modern Dnepropetrovsk, they came to a series of rapids whose dangers were increased by the presence of the Pechenegs, who had first entered the Pontic steppes at the end of the ninth century, and first clashed with the Rus' in 915.[63] The Rus' expeditions were most vulnerable as they dragged their boats, with their cargoes and enchained slaves, around the rapids. The dangers of this section of the route explain why the trade expeditions to Byzantium required such elaborate organization and defence.

During the rest of the tenth century, two main trends dominated the history of Kievan Rus': the need to consolidate around their new capital on the Dnieper, and further attempts to expand Kievan control to the south.

The fragility of the new system appeared as soon as Igor returned from the unsuccessful Byzantine campaign. To recoup his losses and pay his disgruntled retinue, Igor attempted in 945 to raise extra tributes from the neighbouring tribe of the Drevlyans. However, the Drevlyan leader, Mal, resisted these demands, and killed Igor.[64] Igor's wife, Olga, maintained the authority of Kiev during the minority of their son, Svyatoslav. She revenged herself on the Drevlyan, in a series of attacks described in gruesome detail in The Primary Chronicle. Later in her reign, Olga began to establish a more regular system of tax collection, backed up by an extensive system of regional fortifications. In the 950s, she also tried to negotiate a closer relationship with Byzantium. She travelled personally to Constantinople and eventually converted to Christianity.

Her son, Svyatoslav, became sole ruler sometime in the late 950s, and returned to a more aggressive strategy directed against both Khazaria and Byzantium. He ruled in the *condottiere* traditions of the Rus' kaghanate. According to the Chronicle:

> Upon his expeditions he carried with him neither wagons nor kettles, and boiled no meat, but cut off small strips of horseflesh, game, or beef, and ate it after roasting it on the coals. Nor did he have a tent, but he spread out a horse-blanket under him, and set his saddle under his head; and all his retinue did likewise.[65]

In 965, Svyatoslav led a campaign along the Volga river during which he forced the Vyatichians of the Oka river region to pay tribute to the Rus' rather than the Khazars. Then, in alliance with the Oghuz, he destroyed the Khazar empire, and sacked Itil, Samander and Sarkel. By the campaign's end, Rus' had replaced Khazaria as the dominant power in western Inner Eurasia. Svyatoslav may also have sacked Samkerts/Tmutorokan', thereby securing control of the vital trade routes through the Sea of Azov, however Rus' control of this region was not finally secured before 1016.

Soon after these victories, Svyatoslav agreed to a Byzantine request to attack Bulgharia. In *c*.968, with Pecheneg allies, he defeated Bulgharia. However, he was so impressed with the wealth of the lands he had conquered that he began to consider moving his own capital from Kiev to Pereslavl on the Danube. This plan, which would have entailed one more shift of the Rus' southwards, was thwarted when Svyatoslav was defeated by a Byzantine army in *c*.971. There is a superb Byzantine description of Svyatoslav, as he appeared during the peace negotiations with the Byzantine general and emperor, John Tzimiskes. It shows the extent to which some Rus' were still influenced by steppe manners and traditions.

> The emperor arrived at the bank of the Danube on horseback, wearing golden armour, accompanied by a large retinue of horse-men in brilliant attire. Sviatoslav crossed the river in a kind of Scythian boat; he handled the oar in the same way as his men. His appearance was as follows: he was of medium height – neither too tall, nor too short. He had bushy brows, blue eyes, and was snub-nosed; he shaved his beard but wore a long and bushy moustache. His head was shaven except for a lock of hair on one side as a sign of the nobility of his clan. His neck was thick, his shoulders broad, and his whole stature pretty fine. He seemed gloomy and savage. On one of his ears hung a golden ear-ring adorned with two pearls and a ruby set between them. His white garments were not distinguishable from those of his men except for cleanness.[66]

A year later, Byzantium set the Pechenegs on the retreating Rus'. A Pecheneg khan, Kurya, trapped and massacred Svyatoslav's forces as they forded the Dnieper cataracts, and made a gilded drinking cup from his skull. Kurya and his wife then drank a toast from the cup, and prayed for a son as brave as Svyatoslav.[67]

PRINCE VLADIMIR (980–1015) AND THE ADOPTION OF CHRISTIANITY

The civil war that broke out between Svyatoslav's sons showed how easily the federation of Kievan Rus' could have fragmented into a loose alliance of Viking-dominated city-states. However, in 980, Svyatoslav's younger son, Vladimir (r. 980–1015), marched on Kiev from Novgorod, with an army of recently recruited Scandinavian mercenaries, conquered the city, and reestablished a unified Rus' state based on Kiev.

With the support of his powerful retinue, Vladimir began to expand and strengthen his domains. In 985, after an inconclusive war with Volga Bulgharia, treaties between the two states established a stable relationship which left Rus' in control of the Dnieper routes and Volga Bulgharia in control of the Volga routes. To the south of Kiev, Vladimir constructed a huge system of fortifications known as the 'Snake Ramparts', extending for some 500 km, and including perhaps 100 forts or fortified settlements, as protection against the Pechenegs, who had killed his father. However, relations with the Pechenegs remained difficult and one occasion he even had to surrender his son, Svyatopolk, as a hostage. He also encouraged migration to the frontier regions of the south. Between 980 and 990, he captured Galicia and Volhynia from Poland, thereby establishing Rus' claims in eastern Europe that shaped the history of that region for many centuries.[68]

Vladimir's most significant achievement was the conversion of Rus' to Christianity. Conversion to Orthodoxy was the logical consequence of the realignment of Rus' away from the Islamic world or the now-vanished steppe polity of the Khazars. Christianity gave the Rus' state a new source of legitimacy, but one which, unlike the Judaism of the Khazars or the Manichaeism of the Uighurs, would sink deep roots amongst most sections of the population. Finally, it transformed the cultural life of Rus', providing it with a written culture and incorporating it in the wider cultural world of European Christianity.

The religions of pre-Christian Rus' combined the shamanistic practices of the forest world, with influences from the steppes, from Scandinavia and from Europe. In 911, the princes of Rus' swore to uphold the treaties they had negotiated with Byzantium on the name of two distinct deities, Perun (a Viking equivalent of Thor, the god of thunder, lightning, war and warriors, whose name may be related to old Iranian 'Farn') and Volos (a god of livestock). However, the major religions of Outer Eurasia had already begun to penetrate Rus'. Islam had made some inroads along the Volga trade routes, particularly after the conversion of the Volga Bulghars early in the tenth century. Under the Khazars, the city of Kiev may have been garrisoned by Islamic troops from Khorezm. Kiev also had a substantial population of Jewish Khazarian merchants in the tenth century.[69] There were also many Christians in Rus'. Ibn Khurdadbih wrote that even in the mid-ninth century, Rus' traders in Baghdad claimed to be Christians, while Patriarch Photius claimed that soon after the 860 raid, a delegation of Rus' appeared in Byzantium, accepted Christianity, and returned to their homeland with a Christian bishop and pastor. Princess Olga converted sometime between 946 and 960, probably in Constantinople and there was at least one Christian church in Kiev in her time.[70] Meanwhile, Christianity had also spread in the Baltic region, in Poland, whose king was baptised in 966, and elsewhere in eastern Europe. Svyatoslav's Balkan campaigns had also brought many Russians into contact with the Bulghars, who had adopted Christianity as early as 864.[71] By Vladimir's time, Christianity was familiar, even, perhaps, fashionable in some of the towns of Rus'.

However, Vladimir, like his father, Svyatoslav, or the Rus' traders seen by ibn Fadlan in Bulghar, 60 years earlier, was originally a devout pagan. According to the Chronicle, soon after taking power in Kiev, he 'placed idols on a hill outside the palace courtyard: wooden Perun, with silver head and golden beard, and Kh'rs, Dazh'bog, and Stribog, and Simar'gl, and Mokosh'. And they made an offering to them, calling them gods.'[72] This group of gods reflected the polyethnic cultural influences present in Rus', for it included Slavic gods of the sky and fertility (Stribog and Dazhd'bog); Iranian gods with similar functions (Khors and Simargl); a Finnic fertility goddess (Mokosh'); as well as Perun.[73] Vladimir also forced other cities, including Novgorod, to worship statues of Perun.

In c.988, Vladimir converted to Christianity. According to the Chronicle, Vladimir systematically compared the beliefs of Orthodox and Catholic Christians, of Muslims and Jews, and finally opted for Orthodox Christianity because of its tolerance of alcohol and the glory of its churches. In reality, diplomacy and trade counted for more than conviction.[74] In 987, the Byzantine emperor, Basil (r. 976–1025), faced with a Bulgharian army and a revolt in Anatolia, asked for Kievan military support. In return, Vladimir asked for the Empress's sister, Anna, as his bride, knowing, presumably, that this would entail conversion to Christianity. The Emperor was desperate enough to accept the offer, and in 988 Vladimir sent Kievan troops to support him. (These may have included some of the troublesome Varangian mercenaries who had helped Vladimir to the throne). The next year, Vladimir himself led an army to the Byzantine city of Cherson in Crimea. It is still not clear whether its aim was to crush the rebellion against Byzantium, or to force Basil to keep his promise.[75] Basil sent Anna to Cherson. She and Vladimir married, and Vladimir converted formally to Christianity.

Vladimir returned to Kiev with Byzantine priests and perhaps even a metropolitan bishop, and began to spread Christianity as eagerly as he had spread the worship of Perun eight years before. He destroyed and desecrated the great statue of Perun in Kiev, ordered the baptism of the entire population of Kiev and other major towns, and dedicated 10 per cent of all royal incomes to the support of the church. By 996, Kiev had several new churches, including the first great Orthodox church, the 'Church of the Tithe', which was built by Byzantine architects. This may have functioned as a royal residence for the Byzantine empress, Anna.[76] Bishoprics were also established in Belgorod, Novgorod, Chernigov and maybe Polotsk.

Over time, Christianity transformed the political and cultural life of Rus'. By creating a new identity, that of the *Pravoslavnye*, or 'Orthodox Christians', it gave to the Slavic, Finnic and Viking tribes and principalities of Rus' a new and more unified identity. As defenders of that identity and supporters of the Orthodox Church, the Ryurikid princes acquired a new and powerful form of legitimacy. This extended through all levels of society and turned the predatory *condottiere* state of the Rus' kaghanate into something more like a modern nation state.

NOTES

1 The archaeological evidence is surveyed in Gimbutas, *The Slavs*, Chs 1 and 2; for a more recent survey, see Dolukhanov, *Early Slavs*, Chs 4–7.
2 Mackinder, *Democratic Ideals*, p. 110.
3 Dolukhanov, *Early Slavs*, p. 114, and see pp. 82–91, and p. 133 for a summary of the situation in 0 BCE.
4 Cited in Vernadsky, *Ancient Russia*, p. 103; the earliest references to the Venedi all come from the beginning of the first millennium: they include Pliny, *Natural History*, IV:97, Ptolemy, *Geography*, III:5, 7, and Tacitus, *Germania*, XLVI; see Cross, and Sherbowitz-Wetzor, *Primary Chronicle*, p. 36.
5 Franklin and Shepard, *Emergence of Rus*, p. 72; and Mauricius, *Strategikon*, cited in Vernadsky, *Source book*, 1:8; on languages, see Dolukhanov, *Ancient Slavs*, p. 170.
6 Conte, *Les Slaves*, 30–1, points out that in the ninth century, the missionaries Kyril and Methodius felt it necessary to devise only one Cyrillic script; see Cross and Sherbowitz-Wetzor, *Primary Chronicle*, p. 62.
7 Jordanes, *The Gothic History*, pp. 59–60; and Goehrke, *Frühzeit*, pp. 6, 11–13; Vernadsky, *Source Book*, 1:8.

8 I. V. Dubov, 'The ethnic history of northeastern Rus'', cited in Kaiser and Marker, *Reinterpreting* (pp. 14–20), p. 17; see also Goehrke, *Frühzeit*, p. 112; Franklin and Shepard, *Emergence of Rus*, p. 73.

9 Franklin and Shepard, *Emergence of Rus*, p. 82; Primary Chronicle cited in Vernadsky, *Kievan Russia*, p. 101.

10 Conte, *Les Slaves*, p. 64, and see p. 50; see also Dolukhanov, *Early Slavs*, map, p. 161.

11 A suggestion of Kazanski, *Les Goths*, p. 29, citing Julius Caesar, *Gallic Wars*, I, 2–5.

12 Goehrke, *Frühzeit*, pp. 107–8.

13 Levasheva, 'Agriculture in Rus'', in Kaiser and Marker, *Reinterpreting*, p. 39; Goehrke, *Frühzeit*, p. 170.

14 Goehrke, *Frühzeit*, p. 111; see also V. P. Levasheva, 'Agriculture in Rus (fourth–thirteenth centuries)', in Kaiser and Marker *Reinterpreting* (pp. 39–44), pp. 39–41.

15 Dolukhanov, *Early Slavs*, p. 173; Goehrke, *Frühzeit*, p. 114, and see ibid., pp. 111–12.

16 Goehrke, *Frühzeit*, pp. 114–17.

17 Cross and Sherbowitz-Wetzor, *Primary Chronicle*, p. 55.

18 Dolukhanov, *Early Slavs*, p. 146, and see graph, ibid., p. 48.

19 Goehrke, *Frühzeit*, pp. 114–15, 171; on the role of silver, and on Slavic settlements on the borders with the steppes, Franklin and Shepard, *Emergence of Rus*, pp. 75–84.

20 Goehrke, *Frühzeit*, p. 173.

21 McEvedy and Jones estimate that some four million people lived west of the Urals by 1000 AD, making up over one half of the total population of Inner Eurasia at this time (*c.*7.6 million); *Atlas of World Population History*, pp. 78–82; however, most estimates of the populations of Kievan Rus' are higher; see, for example, the discussion in Vernadsky, *Kievan Rus'*, pp. 103–5.

22 Cited in I. D. Koval'chenko, ed., *Istochnikovedenie istorii SSSR*, 2nd edn, Moscow: Vysshaya shkola, 1986, p. 54; other citations from the *Strategikon* are from Vernadsky, *Source Book*, 1:8–9; on this source, see Moravcsik, *Byzantinoturcica* , 1:417–20.

23 Goehrke, *Frühzeit*, p. 110, and see p. 108; see also Froyanov, *Kievskaya Rus'*, 1974, pp. 16, 30; and B. A. Rybakov, 'Predposylki obrazovaniya drevnerusskogo gosudarstva', in *Ocherki istorii SSSR III–IX vv*, p. 852.

24 Constantine Porphyrogenitus, *De Administrando*, II:29; see also Tikhomirov, *Drevnerusskie goroda*; and Goehrke, *Frühzeit*, p. 171; for a more sceptical interpretation of these tribal units, see Franklin and Shepard, *Emergence of Rus*, p. 109.

25 Goehrke, *Frühzeit*, p. 109; Franklin and Shepard, *Emergence of Rus*, p. 75.

26 Goehrke, *Frühzeit*, p. 153; and see Cross and Sherbowitz-Wetzor, *Primary Chronicle*, p. 58; Froyanov, *Kievskaya Rus'*, 1980, p. 13.

27 Goehrke, *Frühzeit*, p. 171.

28 The account that follows is based on Serge A. Zenkovsky, *Medieval Russian Epics, Chronicles and Tales*, 43–4; and Aleshkovskii, *Povest' vremennykh let*; there is also a good account in Zuckermann, 'On the date', pp. 237–70, and 259–62.

29 Cited from Vernadsky, *Source Book*, 1:15; see Cross and Sherbowitz-Wetzor, *Primary Chronicle*, p. 59; note that 'Russians' appear both as inviters and as invitees, a clear sign of the ethnic mixing that had occurred by the late ninth century.

30 The best brief survey of these historiographical controversies is in Goehrke, *Frühzeit*, pp. 157–62.

31 Goehrke, *Frühzeit*, pp. 163-4, for a clear statement of this position.

32 The crucial research on this subject is that of T. Noonan; his work is summarized in Franklin and Shepard, *Emergence of Rus*.

33 Franklin and Shepard, *Emergence of Rus*, p. 27, and see ibid., pp. 7–8, 12, 25; see also Goehrke, *Frühzeit*, p. 122.

34 Palsson and Edwards, *Vikings in Russia*, p. 62; on early contacts between Scandinavians and Slavs, see Franklin and Shepard, *Emergence of Rus*, pp. 8–9.

35 Palsson and Edwards, *Vikings in Russia*, p. 62; though written by an author with no direct knowledge of Rus', *Yngvar's Saga* seems to refer to conditions in Rus' in the tenth and early eleventh centuries; ibid, p. 2.

36 Franklin and Shepard, *Emergence of Rus*, p. 19, and see pp. 12, 17, 20–1; Dolukhanov, *Early Slavs*, pp. 182–5, suggests that Staraya Ladoga was polyethnic from its earliest days.

37 The main sites here were Timerevo near modern Yaroslavl, and Gnezdovo, near modern Smolensk; both were clearly settled by Vikings towards the end of the century, but there are hints of settlement even earlier; Franklin and Shepard, *Emergence of Rus*, pp. 36, 101; on 'Gorodishche', see Franklin and Shepard, *Emergence of Rus*, p. 33; and Dolukhanov, *Early Slavs*, p. 187.

38 Jones, *History of the Vikings*, pp. 249–50; Vernadsky, *Source Book*, 1:11; there are only two other references to a Rus' kaghanate in Russian sources, one in the sermon 'On law and grace' of Metropolitan Ilarion (eleventh century), the other in the *Lay of Igor's Host* (Halperin, *Russia and the Golden Horde*, p. 12), but there are other references in Arabic sources.

39 Franklin and Shepard, *Emergence of Rus*, p. 40; ibid. pp. 31–41 discusses four possible sites: Sweden, Gorodishche, Rostov, and the Upper Volga; while Vernadsky, *Kievan Rus*, p. 174, proposes Tmutorokan' (modern Taman) on the straits of Kerch.

40 Vernadsky, *Source Book*, 1:9.

41 Palsson and Edwards, *Vikings in Russia*, p. 71; 'Yarisleif' is modelled on the eleventh-century Grand Prince, Yaroslav.

42 Ibid., p. 73.

43 Ibid.

44 Franklin and Shepard, *Emergence of Rus*, pp. 51–3, 55–6, 59; al-Mas'udi cited from Artamonov, *Istoriya khazar*, p. 368; the Chronicle gives 866 as the date for this expedition, and claims that it was launched from Kiev.

45 Cited in Vernadsky, *Source Book*, 1:9.

46 Ibn Fadlan, *Risala*, pp. 141–2; Jones, *A History of the Vikings*, 164, summarizing evidence from al-Mas'udi and al-Muqaddasi; Franklin and Shepard, *Emergence of Rus*, p. 67–8.

47 Jones, *History of the Vikings*, p. 256; ibn Fadlan's account is translated in Jones, *History of the Vikings*, pp. 425–30; and see Vernadsky, *Source Book*, 1:10, for a similar report from ibn Rusta, and al-Mas'udi's report that the Rus' women: 'desire to be burned with their husbands so as to follow them to paradise'.

48 Ibn Fadlan, *Risala*, p. 146.

49 Pritsak, *Origin of Rus'*, p. 16 and elsewhere.

50 Zuckerman, 'On the Date', p. 256.

51 Cross and Sherbowitz-Wetzor, *Primary Chronicle*, p. 64.

52 Ibid., pp. 64–9.

53 Pritsak argues that Kiev was a predominantly Khazar town until the 930s, see Golb and Pritsak, *Khazarian-Hebrew Documents*, p. 71.

54 Franklin and Shepard, *Emergence of Rus*, p. 126; on the growth of Kiev, see ibid., pp. 98–9.

55 See Zuckerman, 'On the Date', and Franklin and Shepard, *Emergence of Rus.*
56 Zuckermann, 'On the Date', pp. 256–9; Pletneva, *Polovtsy*, p. 15 suggests that the Pechenegs may have been allied to Oleg.
57 Constantine Porphyrogenitus, *De Administrando*, 1:18–20, 28; there is a good summary in Goehrke, *Frühzeit*, p. 157.
58 Constantine Porphyrogenitus, *De Administrando*, 1:63.
59 See the entry for 969 in Cross and Sherbowitz-Wetzor, *Primary Chronicle*, p. 86.
60 Constantine Porphyrogenitus, *De Administrando*, 2:57, 59; the word 'Rosia' for Russia first appears in the writings of Constantine, Ibid., 2:20; *Monoxyla* had long been used by the Slavonic tribes of Rus', Ibid., 2:23.
61 Cited in Constantine Porphyrogenitus, *De Administrando*, 2:36.
62 Ibid., 2:36.
63 Pletneva, *Polovtsy*, p. 15.
64 Byzantine writer, Leo Diaconus, records that he was tied to two trees, which were released and tore him in two; Fennell, *Russian Church*, p. 6.
65 Cross and Sherbowitz-Wetzor, *Primary Chronicle*, p. 84.
66 Vernadsky, *Origins of Russia*, pp. 276–7.
67 Pletneva, *Polovtsy*, p. 19; and see Cross and Sherbowitz-Wetzor, *Primary Chronicle*, p. 90.
68 On the early history of Galicia and Volhynia, see Subtelny, *Ukraine*, pp. 57–60; Franklin and Shepard, *Emergence of Rus*, p. 170–3 on Vladimir's fortifications; on relations with the Pechenegs, see Pletneva, *Polovtsy*, p. 21.
69 See Golb and Pritsak, *Khazarian-Hebrew Documents*, pp. xiii and 44, on the letter of Khazarian merchants found in the Genizah documents and dated from the early tenth century.
70 On the controversy over this episode, see Fennell, *Russian Church*, pp. 26–30; on the church, ibid., pp. 24–5; on the aftermath of the 860 raid, see ibn Khurdadbih, cited in Vernadsky, *Sourcebook*, 1:9, and Photius in Ibid., 1:12.
71 Fennell, *Russian Church*, p. 9.
72 I. Ia. Froyanov, A. Iu. Drovnichenko and Iu. V. Krivosheev, 'The Introduction of Christianity in Russia and the Pagan Tradition', in Balzer, ed., *Russian Traditional Culture*, pp. (3–15), p. 5; and Fennell, *Russian Church*, p. 33; these idols are similar to those observed by ibn Fadlan in Bulghar in *c*.922, ibn Fadlan, *Risala*, p. 142.
73 Martin, *History*, p. 6.
74 See the account in Fennell, *Russian Church*, Ch. 3.
75 See Franklin and Shepard, *Emergence of Rus*, pp. 162 for a summary of the controversy on this issue.
76 Ibid., pp. 164–5.

FURTHER READING

There is a huge literature on the early history of Rus. Good recent accounts of the prehistory include Goehrke, *Frühzeit* (which has a very useful discussion of sources on pp. 103–6); and Dolukhanov, *Early Slavs*. There is a brief collection of primary materials in Vernadsky, ed., *Source Book*. Other important primary sources include Cross and Sherbowitz-Wetzor, *The Russian Primary Chronicle*; Constantine Porphyrogenitus, *De Administrando Imperio*; ibn Fadlan, *Risala*; Palsson and Edwards, trans., *Vikings in Russia*; and the documents in Zenkovsky, *Medieval Russian Epics, Chronicles, and Tales*. A fine new history of early Rus', which makes thorough use of recent numismatic and archaeological research, is Franklin and Shepard, *Emergence of Rus*. This is particularly good on the importance of early trade networks. Also useful on this subject are Martin, *Treasure of the Land of Darkness*; and Boba, *Nomads, Northmen and Slavs*. Zuckerman, 'On the Date', offers an alternative reading of the chronicles of Rus'. There are many other histories of early Rus', including Vernadsky, *Ancient Russia, Kievan Russia*, and *The Origins of Russia*, which are still useful, though dated; Subtelny, *Ukraine*; Riasanovsky, *A History of Russia*; Froyanov's two volumes on *Kievskaya Rus'*; and the older Soviet classic, Grekov, *Kievskaya Rus'*. On the towns of Rus', the classic study is Tikhomirov, *Drevnerusskie goroda* (available in translation as *The Towns of Ancient Rus*). On the church, see Fennell, *A History of the Russian Church*. Two useful recent collections of essays are: Kaiser and Marker, *Reinterpreting Russian History*; and Balzer, *Russian Traditional Culture*. On the steppes, see Golden's essay 'Peoples of the South Russian Steppes', in *CHEIA*; Pletneva, *Polovtsy*, and *Stepi Evrazii*; and Akhinzhanov, *Kypchaki*.

[14] BEFORE THE MONGOLS: 1000–1220

At first sight, it might appear that by the end of the first millennium, the historical differences between Inner and Outer Eurasia had diminished. Inner Eurasia, like Outer Eurasia, now seemed to be dominated by urbanized agrarian regions with state-like structures, imperial religions and literate elites. Finally, it seemed, Inner Eurasia was succumbing to the agrarian neolithic revolution, with all its consequences.

Demographically, this impression is certainly accurate. Mawara'n-nahr and Rus' were now the regions of densest settlement, and most of Inner Eurasia's population lived here. Politically, too, these regions were more organized than the steppe. Powerful states had emerged in both Mawara'n-nahr and Rus', while the politics of the steppelands was more decentralized than at any time since the fifth century. There existed some powerful tribal confederations, but since the fall of the Uighur and Khazar empires no true pastoralist states had appeared.

Nevertheless, appearances are deceptive. The political and military structures of Mawara'n-nahr and Rus' turned out to be more fragile than they seemed, and the power of steppe peoples, from the Kipchak to the Saljuk, remained immense. Indeed, the rise of the Mongol empire in the thirteenth century showed that steppeland states, though difficult to form, could still dominate the agrarian regions of Inner Eurasia militarily and politically.

Ecologically, Mawara'n-nahr and Rus' were very different. Mawara'n-nahr was a region of scattered but densely populated oases that depended on irrigation agriculture. The large areas of arid steppe or desert that divided the major oases from each other, inhibited the formation of large and unified states in the region. Even in the Islamic period, when Mawara'n-nahr acquired for the first time a degree of cultural unity, stable regional states were rare. They appeared as a sort of transitional phase between periods of imperial rule from Iran, and periods of decentralization, in which power was held by shifting local alliances of urban and pastoralist elites. Despite the splendour of Samanid rule, state formation remained fragile and precarious in the agrarian lands of Mawara'n-nahr.

Rus', on the other hand, was a large zone of woodland settlements relying on rainfall agriculture. Here, there were large areas of contiguous agricultural settlements, which should have made it easier to create extensive and unified state structures. Yet the political structures of Rus' proved almost as fragile as those of Mawara'n-nahr, though for different reasons. In Rus', large agrarian populations had appeared only recently, so that state structures were raw and unstable, and lacked the ancient bureaucratic and legal traditions of Persia or China, or even Mawara'n-nahr.

Thus, ecology in one region and history in the other undermined the power of the major agrarian regions of Inner Eurasia. Besides, both Rus' and Mawara'n-nahr had long, exposed steppe frontiers and were more closely intertwined with the pastoralist world of the steppes than is often recognized. This unusual balance of power ensured that Inner Eurasian history would continue to move along different paths from that of Outer Eurasia.

THE STEPPELANDS

THE EASTERN AND CENTRAL STEPPES

North of China, the political centre of gravity shifted from Mongolia to Manchuria, a region, like Mawara'n-nahr, in which steppes, farming lands and mountain regions intertwined. From here, two local dynasties, the Kitan and the Jurchen, eventually conquered much of northern China, forming the Kitan 'Liao' dynasty (907–1125), and the Jurchen 'Chin' dynasty (1115–1234).[1] Oasis city-states, some ruled by Uighur or Tibetan dynasties, controlled the eastern end of the Silk Roads. The Mongolian steppes were dominated by regional groupings of pastoralists, none of which could seriously threaten northern China, or even control the eastern sections of the Silk Roads.

The most organized groups of pastoralists in the east lived in the lands once ruled by the Western Türk. In the ninth and tenth centuries, a Turkic people known as the Kimek ruled much of central, northern and western Kazakhstan from fortified towns and farming settlements in northern Kazakhstan and along the Irtysh river north-west of the Altai mountains. For much of the tenth century, their ruler assumed the title of 'khan'. Though the Kimek elites were pastoral nomads, the kaghanate was funded largely from the trade in Siberian sables to Muslim merchants in Mawara'n-nahr.[2] From c.766 the Karluk established a loose confederation centred on the Chu valley in the Semirechye, with Balasaghun and Talas as their main cities. Their leaders claimed descent from the A-shih-na. By the mid-ninth century the Karluks dominated the lands once held by the western Türk. After the defeat of the Uighurs, in 845, Karluk leaders, and other pastoralists may even have claimed the imperial title of 'kaghan', which began to suffer from a sort of titular inflation. By this time, the title existed in two distinct forms, the simpler, 'khan', and the more complex 'kaghan' which, according to al-Khwarazmi, meant 'a khan of khans, that is to say a leader of leaders, just as the Persians refer to a Shah-an-Shah'. By the late ninth century, the Karluk ruled most of the steppe tribes of eastern Kazakhstan. By the mid-tenth century, they claimed suzerainty over the Oghuz lands in the west, much of Sinkiang, and the Central Asian steppes as far as the Samanid empire, with Talas as a frontier town.[3]

In the steppes of western Kazakhstan, north and west of the Aral Sea, the dominant groupings by the eleventh century were Oghuz Turks. The Oghuz included both local groups, descended, perhaps from the ancient settlers of the Syr Darya region, and more recently arrived groups of Turkic-speakers.[4] Though they never formed a unified state, the Oghuz had an immense influence on the history of the central and western steppes. They controlled the northern branches of the Silk Roads that led around the Caspian and towards the Black Sea, and many of the trading towns on the lower Syr Darya. Indeed, by the eleventh century, some Oghuz had begun to settle down as farmers and traders. Their geographical position, and the military power of their many tribes, made them natural middlemen in relations between the city-states of Khorezm and Khazaria. One Oghuz group, known as the Saljuk, eventually conquered much of Mawara'n-nahr, Khorasan and even Mesopotamia. Their astonishing career is described later in this chapter.

We have some good contemporary accounts of life amongst the more nomadic Oghuz in the ninth and tenth centuries. In the ninth century, al-Yaqubi wrote:

> each [tribe] has a separate country and they war with one another. They have no permanent abodes nor fortified places. They dwell in the ribbed domes of the Turks. Its pegs are belts made from the skins of beasts and cows. Its cover is felt. They are the most clever people in making felt because they clothe themselves with it. There is no agriculture in Turkistan except for millet...Their food is mare's milk and they eat its flesh and most of what they eat is the flesh of wild game. There is little iron among them. They make their arrows from bones.[5]

Ibn Fadlan, who travelled among the Oghuz on his way to the Bulghars, has left a vivid description of their lifeways. Like most pastoralists, the Oghuz accepted the tradition known as the levirate: 'If a man dies who has a wife and sons, then the oldest of his sons marries his wife if she is not his mother.' He noted that the Oghuz, like the Scythians, feared water, and refused to wash, even to clean themselves from excrement, urine or sexual pollution. Their leaders adopted the Türk title of *yabghu*, while subordinate chiefs were known as 'tarkhans'. The most powerful *yabghu* was based at Yangikent on the lower Syr Darya, but he never controlled all the Oghuz tribes. According to a late tenth-century Samanid compilation, the *Hudud al-' Alam* ('Regions of the World'), 'Each of their tribes has a (separate) chief on account of their discords with each other.[6]

The Oghuz tribes often raided into Khazaria and Khorezm, taking their plunder and then retreating into the steppes. But they also traded with their sedentary neighbours. Like most pastoralists, their main trade goods were livestock (horses, cattle, camels and sheep), and livestock produce, including leather, meat and koumiss. They also traded in furs, in metals, and in craft products such as carpets, saddlery and weapons, as well as in slaves. According to the *Hudud*, they had many merchants. Ibn Fadlan noted the strong ties of credit, sponsorship and protection between Oghuz and Khorezmian merchants. Khorezmian merchants had to find sponsors amongst the Oghuz, who looked after them in the steppes. In return, Oghuz traders expected hospitality and help when in the towns of Khorezm. Close contacts with the Oghuz even affected urban life in Khorezm, for ibn Fadlan found that in some urban households, on cold nights, yurts were erected inside for extra warmth.[7]

Urban lifeways also influenced the steppes. Particularly striking is the slow spread of Islam amongst pastoralists along the borders of Mawara'n-nahr. Muslim merchants from Khorezm sought out Muslim partners in the steppes, or encouraged their trade partners to convert. Sometimes, they left agents behind in steppe settlements, and these built mosques, so that, by the tenth century, many settlements deep in the steppes already had their own mosques. The great wealth of Islamic merchants also lent Islam prestige in the steppes and encouraged conversion. Missionary activity was important, but much of this was informal, and dominated by the activities of Sufis. Sufis, whose teachings often included elements from other religions, including Buddhism, Christianity and Manichaeism, or even shamanistic practices of various kinds, found a readier hearing amongst pastoralists than more doctrinaire Muslims. Some pastoralists converted under more direct military and political pressure. In 893, Samanid armies conquered Talas, converted a Nestorian church into a mosque and tried to persuade the local chieftain to convert to Islam. Early in the tenth century, Oghuz and Karluk mercenaries serving Islamic rulers sometimes converted.[8] Finally, steppe leaders who converted in order to secure powerful allies in the towns of Mawara'n-nahr sometimes forced their followers to convert *en masse*.

In the mid-eleventh century, Turkic tribes known as the 'Kipchak' became the dominant grouping in the Kazakh and Pontic steppes. The Kipchak included the westernmost tribes of the Kimek kaghanate. Unlike the Kimek, they had retained their nomadic lifeways. By the early tenth century, they were already independent of the Kimek kaghanate, and a century later they began to move west, until they dominated the previously Oghuz steppes north and west of the Aral sea and began to enter the Pontic steppes. As a result, from the mid-eleventh century to the Mongol invasion in the mid-thirteenth century, Muslim writers called the entire area from the Altai to the Carpathians the 'Kipchak steppe' (Desht-i Kypchak). There may have emerged, briefly, a single Kipchak kaghanate. However, after 1130 this fragmented into several smaller groupings, one of which lay along the Syr-Darya river, where many Kipchak had their winter camps, and extended towards the Irtysh, while another lay west of the Aral sea, and a third lay to the northwest, in the Urals/Volga region. These regional divisions clearly had an ecological basis, for they reappeared within the Mongol successor states and amongst the Kazakh kaghanates.

What caused the pastoralist migrations of the tenth and particularly the mid-eleventh centuries remains obscure. However, they include the disruption caused by the breakdown of the Khazar empire, the emergence of the expansionist Kitan 'Liao' dynasty in Manchuria and northern China, and the Tangut state in Kansu, which forced many Mongolian peoples to move westwards, and expanding trade with the booming economies of Central Asia, which encouraged Central Asian pastoralists to expand their flocks and seek new pasture lands.[9]

THE PONTIC STEPPES

The Pontic steppes had long been a region of powerful, but loosely organized pastoralists. While the Khazars policed the region, no other significant pastoralist powers emerged. However, as Khazar power declined, new pastoralist groups began to threaten the agrarian lands of the Pontic region. The Magyars emerged as a significant force in the ninth century, and the Pechenegs from the end of the ninth century. In the middle of the eleventh century, the Kipchak displaced the Pechenegs and formed a ruling elite controlling remnant populations of Alans, Bulghars, Pechenegs and Oghuz. In the Pontic steppes they seem to have formed two, linked 'hordes'. One, based to the west of the Dnieper, was generally known as the Cuman. It included many Pecheneg and Oghuz, and its main language may have been Pecheneg. The tribes of the other group lived east of the Dnieper, and came to be known as the Polovtsy.[10]

Though first mentioned in the Rus' Chronicles under 1054, the Kipchak first attacked large areas of Rus' in 1062. For a time, they posed a very serious threat to the more southerly parts of Rus', and threatened to cut Kiev's commercial and cultural lifeline to Byzantium. Under strong leaders, Kipchak hordes could be powerful enough to mount periodic raids in search of booty and slaves, or to prevent settlement in valued pasture lands such as those just south of Kiev. They could even take fortified towns on occasion, though their main technique was the simple one of burning them with flaming arrows or with larger projectiles filled with burning oil. The following account, from the Laurentian chronicle, describes a devastating Kipchak raid of 1093, led by a Kipchak khan, Tugor khan. Its target was a town called Torchesk, some 65 kilometres south of Kiev, which was inhabited by *chernye klobuki*, sedentizing and often Christian pastoralists, often of Pecheneg or Oghuz origin. Since *c*.1080, the *chernye klobuki* had served Rus' as frontier guards, as the Southern Hsiung-nu had served the Later Han. Their town, Torchesk, was based on an old Scythian settlement, and its dwellings consisted mainly of yurts.[11] The passage conveys well both the ethnic complexity and the human tragedy of steppe warfare.

The Polovtsians [Kipchak] after seizing the town, burned it. They divided up the people and led them to their dwelling places, to their own relatives and kin. Many Christians suffered: miserable, tormented, numb from cold, from hunger and thirst, their cheeks sunken, their bodies blackened; in an unknown land, their tongues swollen, naked and bare-footed, their legs torn by thorns, they spoke to each other in tears, saying: 'I was from such a town', and 'I was from such a village', and so they spoke of their homelands with tears and sighs.[12]

To prevent prisoners from escaping, the Kipchak often crippled the males by slitting their heels and placing chopped horsehairs in the wounds so that the wounds kept chafing.

While some Rus' captives served Kipchak families as domestic slaves, most captives and livestock taken in such raids, as well as furs, were sold in the markets of Bulghar, Crimea, Kiev and Prague. For the Polovtsy, the Crimean cities of Korsun', which was controlled by Genovese merchants, and Tmutorokan' and Surozh' (Sudak), which were controlled by Byzantium, were the most important markets. From here the trade goods of the Mediterranean flowed back into the steppes, as they had since the Scythian period.[13]

Kipchak tribes did not simply raid Rus'. They also allied with Rus' princes, traded with them, and sometimes settled amongst them, like the Oghuz or Karluk in Mawara'n-nahr. Individual Kipchak warriors served in the retinues of Rus' princes while Kipchak slaves acted as servants or herdsmen. Exchanges of goods, and even of people encouraged the exchange of ideas, until, by the twelfth century, many Christians could be found amongst the Kipchak. Particularly from the middle of the twelfth century, political, dynastic and military relations often crossed ethnic, linguistic, ecological and denominational lines.[14] In the search for security and wealth, Kipchak chiefs allied with and intermarried with Ryurikid princes, and Ryurikid princes, in turn, engaged troops from the steppes to fight their civil wars. Intermarriage was a clear sign of the power and prestige of pastoralist hordes, so that princes of Rus' took wives from only the most powerful and threatening Kipchak hordes, and never did they willingly grant their daughters in marriage to Kipchak kaghans, a step which would have implied full diplomatic equality. The southern princes of Chernigov and Tmutorokan', formed long-standing alliances with Kipchak tribes, from the time of Oleg, son of Yaroslav's son, Svyatoslav.[15] In 1078, in alliance with a Kipchak army, he advanced from Tmutorokan' towards Chernigov to reclaim the patrimony of his father. In 1094, he drove Yaroslav's grandson, Vladimir Monomakh (d. 1125), out of Chernigov. Vladimir described how, with about 100 members of his *druzhina* and family, he was forced to retreat from the city, passing between lines of Kipchak, who 'licked their lips at us like wolves as they stood at the crossing and on the hills'.[16]

In 1113, a unified Rus' army under Monomakh inflicted a serious defeat on the Kipchak. Though Monomakh himself had often fought alongside Kipchak allies, in 1113, he led a united Kievan force deep into Kipchak territory, and won a major victory. Rejecting offers of peace, he executed twenty Kipchak chiefs, and ordered that Kipchak captives be hacked to death in retaliation for their many raids into Rus'.[17] For a time, these victories seriously weakened the Polovtsy. Rus' raids into the steppes, usually conducted in winter or spring when pastoralists were most vulnerable, and aimed at the taking of slaves and booty, as well as at frontier security, probably occurred more frequently than pastoralist raids into Rus'. For 30 years, the Polovtsy entered Rus' only at the invitation of Rus' princes; never again did they nomadize in the wooded steppes along the Donets river; and some groups

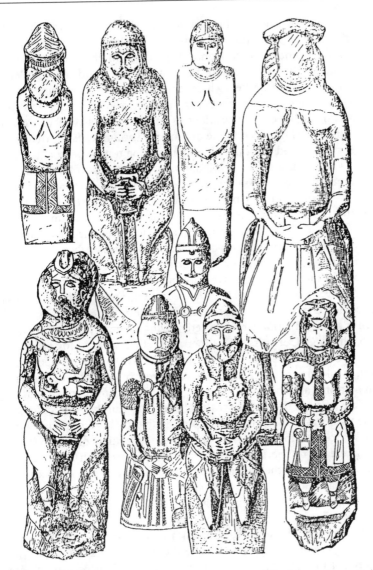

Figure 14.1 Polovtsy stone statues from the steppes, twelfth–thirteenth centuries CE, reproduced from S. A. Pletneva *Polovtsy*, (Moscow: Nauka, 1990).

even began to shift away from the increasingly dangerous frontier of Rus'. One group, led by Atrak, a son of the great Polovtsian kaghan, Sharukan, headed towards the north Caucasian steppes with 40,000 followers, and took service with the Georgian king, David. According to the poetic account in the Rus' chronicles, his brother, Syrchan, lured him home again by sending a bard who sang steppe ballads and gave him steppe herbs to remind him of his homeland. Eventually, he succumbed, declaring: 'It is surely better to leave one's bones at home than to find glory in foreign lands.'[18]

The successes of Rus' military campaigns of the early twelfth century led to a clarification of the situation along the borders. On the one hand, Rus' failed to hold outposts it had once held deep in the steppe. Early in the twelfth century, Rus' lost control of Tmutorokan', and also of Bela Vezha, the old Khazar fort of Sarkel, which now became a Polovtsian winter camp. Like Saksin, a steppe town probably on the site of the Khazar capital, Itil, such towns probably contained markets and bazaars, as well as Polovtsian or foreign artisans, who carved stone or wooden monuments, or made jewellery, weapons, saddles and armour. Like most steppe towns, they may have begun as large winter camps whose inhabitants, like (those of Saksin), dwelt in tents, sometimes protected by fortified walls, or gathered around more permanent towns founded by agriculturalists, such as Sarkel. On the Rus' side of the border, there emerged a fortified frontier region, similar to the Chinese 'Ordos'. This was occupied and defended, from about 1080, by semi-sedentary pastoralist allies of the Rus', in a western version of the 'Inner Frontier Strategy'.[19] Whatever their origins, most of these frontier pastoralists became known as 'chernye klobuki' (Turkic 'Karakalpaks' or 'black hats'). Many of the *chernye klobuki* became farmers, adopted Christianity, and accepted a more or less permanent position as frontier guards. The lifeways that emerged amongst these sedentizing frontier pastoralists anticipated those of the later Cossacks. 'The men were always ready for military expeditions, so that, in practice, the productive work was carried out by the women, while the male children were reared from childhood in a spirit of military daring and horsemanship.'[20] But, as in northern China, it proved impossible to close the border with the steppes entirely. Rus' cities continued to trade with steppe pastoralists, importing livestock (particularly horses) and livestock produce in return for luxury goods, which often appear in steppeland graves of the period. Frontier markets appeared like those of northern China, Ferghana, or the Balkan frontiers of Rome. And people, too, crossed the ecological frontier. In the Rus' chronicles, this is shown by the increasing number of Turkish names amongst the Rus', and of Slavic names in the steppes.[21]

By the late twelfth century, Kipchak military raids into Rus' were usually at the invitation of Rus' princes. While the descendants of Oleg Svyatoslavich often invited Polovtsy allies to support them, the descendants of Monomakh usually fought in alliance with the *chernye klobuki*.[22] Once invited into Rus', pastoralist armies were allowed to sack rival towns, and take away livestock and captives as compensation for their services. Sometimes, whole tribes arrived, with warriors, families, slaves and livestock; when this happened, farm lands were usually devastated by the pastoralist herds. For the small and relatively weak hordes of the twelfth-century steppelands, which seem to have numbered between 20,000 and 40,000 people (about one fifth of whom would have been warriors), such raids could be extremely profitable, and they were certainly less risky than uninvited raids which might unite all the princes of Rus' against the Kipchak.[23]

Why were steppe pastoralists generally so decentralized in the centuries after the fall of the Uighur and Khazar empires? Why do we see tribal or supra-tribal alliances, but no true pastoralist states? The question is important, for the political and military balance along all the Inner Eurasian borderlands depended to a considerable extent on the degree of political organization of pastoralists. To give just one illustration, Pletneva has estimated that in the twelfth century, there were between 500,000 and 600,000 pastoralists living in the Pontic steppes.[24] Assuming that one fifth of these were active warriors, a unified Polovtsian and Cuman army could have fielded an army of 50–60,000, which would have posed a massive threat to Rus'. The Mongol victories in the thirteenth century provide a spectacular illustration of the military power of unified pastoralist armies. Yet no armies of this kind emerged before the thirteenth century.

Unfortunately, explaining the level of political organization in the steppes is extremely difficult. It is tempting to see in the relative lack of political organization of the tenth to thirteenth centuries the end of a cycle that had begun with the creation of the Türk empire in the sixth century. Perhaps migrations into northern China, Mawara'n-nahr and Iran, or the Balkans and Hungary had reduced population pressure in the steppes. Or perhaps the answer is simpler, more personal and more naive: no new Motun or T'u-men appeared in the steppes before the end of the twelfth century.

RUS'

SOCIETY AND GOVERNMENT

By the death of Vladimir in 1015, Rus', with a population of 3 or 4 million, was the largest state in Europe and controlled an area of some 800,000 sq km.[25]

Vladimir's successor, Yaroslav (1019–54), came to the throne, like his father, after a bloody fratricidal war, in which his main base was the old capital of Novgorod. For over a decade after taking the throne, he had to share power with his brother, Mstislav, who was prince of Chernigov, and had conquered Tmutorokan' on the Crimean Bosporus. Indeed, it is possible that Mstislav held more real power than Yaroslav before his death in 1036. Under him, Chernigov emerged briefly as a serious rival to Kiev.

Despite these conflicts, Yaroslav's reign is usually regarded as the high point of Rus' power. His reputation rests, in part, on the positive reviews he received in The Primary Chronicle, which was based on chronicles that Yaroslav had probably vetted before his death.[26] Yaroslav extended Kievan control to the west, and towards the Baltic. Most important of all, in 1037 he achieved what seemed like a decisive victory over the Pecheneg tribes of the Pontic steppes, defeating them just outside Kiev, at the future site of the St Sophia cathedral. For some 25 years, Kiev enjoyed effective control over the steppes, creating the temporary illusion that agrarian Rus' had triumphed finally over the pastoralist societies to its south. Yaroslav also undertook institutional reforms that began the process of creating a more durable, less personal, state structure. He attempted to codify traditional law in the *Russkaya pravda* or 'Law of the Rus'', perhaps, initially, as an extension of the contracts princes had once negotiated with Viking mercenaries. He helped the church to emerge as a powerful, and central institution within the Kievan state, and Kiev itself became a city of churches. It was dominated by St Sophia, which was completed in 1047. Kiev's monasteries, particularly the Monastery of the Caves, dominated the church hierarchy, as only the monks, the 'black clergy', could become bishops.

Most of the people of Rus' still lived in small rural communities, and it was in the villages that most of its wealth was produced, as Soviet historians showed.[27] Peasants farmed the rich black soils of the wooded steppes with heavy ploughs of a type long familiar in the Mediterranean; in the mixed woodlands, lighter ploughs (*ralo*) predominated; while in the far north swidden systems were more common. In the villages, the household was the fundamental unit, while the village, or cluster of villages was analogous in its scale and some of its functions to the pastoralist 'reproductive group'. The peasant household, like the pastoralist family group, was a sort of business, in which men and women had different roles, but cooperation was essential for survival, and this undoubtedly implied a degree of mutual respect between men and women. However, the fact that the Rus' law code demanded twice as much blood-money for a murdered man as for a murdered woman, suggests that gender inequalities were as formalized as in the pastoralist world.[28]

The first rulers of Rus' had built their power on the systems of tribute and trade that converted surplus rural produce into cash and prestige goods with which they enhanced their own prestige and hired armed retinues. In the eleventh century, the relative (though not necessarily the absolute) importance of trade declined. On the one hand, the trade routes through the steppes were threatened by the Kipchak after 1060. On the other hand, princes and lords of Rus', whatever their ethnic origins, were now firmly established on the land. Most continued to live in towns, but they drew the foodstuffs, timber, and labour they needed for their own upkeep from dependent village communities, either in the form of dues or rents. The region that supported a prince was known as a 'living' or *zhizn'*, while leading nobles often received similar rights, under the name of *kormlenie*. As the Ryurikid system of rule stabilized, princes also began to issue laws, and to exact fines from offenders, and these payments for the maintenance of justice became a significant form of revenue in the eleventh century. Meanwhile, nobles began to take a direct interest in farming, particularly in horse-rearing, which was vital for a warrior elite that fought, like their pastoralist rivals, on horseback.[29] Trade retained its importance, but mainly as a source of religious or prestige goods.

These changes in the economic basis of Rus' illustrate the fundamental long-term advantage of the rulers of agrarian societies, in contrast to their pastoralist rivals. Agrarian elites did not have to depend exclusively on external sources of income for their wealth and power, for they could also rely on large surpluses generated by local populations of farmers.

In regions of densest settlement, the changing relationship between the peasants and the rulers of Rus' transformed independent peasant farmers subject to occasional forced tributes, into dependent peasants subject to regular exactions from distant landlords. It is doubtful that rural communities got much in return, perhaps occasional periods of stability, and access to some of the goods and opportunities that existed in the cities. Most peasants remained legally free, though there also existed a large class of slaves. However, the forms of legal and commercial dependence that appeared in the eleventh century laid the foundations for the harsher forms of dependence that evolved some centuries later in Muscovy.

Though most wealth was produced in the countryside, it was the towns that really flourished in Rus'. Most cities and towns remained small. However, Kiev expanded rapidly as a result of the building program launched by Yaroslav, with St Sophia at its heart. In the late eleventh century, Kiev became a commercial and craft centre for the trade networks of much of Rus'. Yet even Kiev, which became the largest city in Rus', probably had no more than 40,000 inhabitants at its height.[30] It consisted, like most of the larger cities, of a central fortified area on high ground, the home of its princes, with their palaces and churches; and an outer, suburban area by the river, where merchants and artisans lived. Here were the wharves which gave on to the river systems that linked the cities of Rus' into a single communications network. Few other cities had populations of more than a few thousand. Most were still overgrown, though fortified, villages with markets and churches, a few artisan workshops, and perhaps the fortified palace of a local prince. Townspeople still cultivated plots of land, usually beyond the city walls.[31]

Nevertheless, the towns dominated the political and cultural life of Kievan Rus'. By the middle of the eleventh century, Rus' was highly urbanized by the standards of contemporary Europe, with perhaps 13–15 per cent of the population living in its multiplying towns. The Soviet specialist, Tikhomirov, identified at least 225 urban settlements in eleventh-century sources, and the number may have risen to 300 by 1240.[32] Urbanization extended east as far as Volga Bulgharia, but no further, until you reached Zungaria. (In the thirteenth century, the Franciscan, William of Rubruck, noted as he travelled to Mongolia that Volga Bulgharia was 'the last region where there are towns'.)[33] As towns flourished, they attracted merchants from Scandinavia, Europe and the steppes, as well as large artisan populations. There were metalworkers, builders in both wood and stone, weavers, tanners, pottery makers, boatmakers, traders in timber, fish, honey and wax, and livestock produce, money changers, icon painters, as well as slaves and casual labourers.[34] The commercial power of the towns gave them considerable political power. The main power brokers lived here, the nobles or boyars, the warriors of the princely retinue or *druzhina*, leading church officials and the most powerful merchants. Political power was, therefore, based on the great towns. Indeed, Rus' was, really, a confederation of city-states. Each had its own prince, and each prince had his own retinue of cavalry warriors or boyars.

Princely *druzhiny* usually consisted of no more than 100 or so men, so they were too small to conduct major campaigns on their own. For major campaigns, the *druzhiny* were supplemented by recruits from the towns or pastoralist mercenaries. Major towns could often muster two to three thousand militia troops. Though urban militias were often of poor quality, this meant that a united Kievan Rus' could on occasion send armies of well over 10,000 men on foreign expeditions to the steppes or Constantinople. In defence, towns also expected to call upon ordinary citizens as well, though princes usually regarded such forces as cannon fodder. Town walls were vital to success in war, for siege-craft was underdeveloped in Rus and princely armies could rarely make an impression on a well fortified city. When the Mongol armies invaded in 1237, with their experienced and sophisticated siege trains, the cities of Rus' proved terribly vulnerable. However, it is possible to exaggerate the importance of warfare in Rus'. Despite the Chronicle accounts, which are full of wars, the amount of actual fighting that went on was limited. Like the knightly class of medieval Europe, the members of rival *druzhiny* understood each other, and had a common code of practice, that reflected a shared ethos and lifestyle. Often rival retinues faced off against each other, assessed each other's strengths and weaknesses, then negotiated or waited until one side had the prudence to withdraw.[35]

Politically, urban populations could be very influential. Town meetings or *veche*, often expelled unwanted rulers or invited rulers they preferred, sometimes under precise conditions, as if they were political and military mercenaries, hired on contract. Indeed, it may have been such occasions that persuaded the chroniclers to explain the foundation of the Ryurikid dynasty as a sort of contract. The Kievan *veche* often intervened in succession struggles. In 1068, it expelled Yaroslav's son, Izyaslav, while in 1113, it invited Vladimir Monomakh to become its prince. The leaders of Novgorod, whose mercantile wealth and distance from Kiev gave the town considerable independence, were particularly successful in limiting the power of their princes. Here, the office of town governor, or *posadnik*, became elective, and after 1136 Novgorodians generally chose which of the Ryurikid princes would rule them. Though firmly within the political networks of Kievan Rus', Novgorod played a role similar to that of the relatively independent commercial towns of the Hanseatic League, of which it was itself a member, or the commercial cities of Central Asia. By the eleventh century, it had a huge commercial empire, dominated by the rich fur-quarries of the north-east, but poor in agricultural produce, thinly populated and militarily weak. The princes of most other towns were more independent, but few could avoid some negotiation with the towns they ruled.

As Christianity spread, the towns became vital centres of culture and literacy. In the eleventh and twelfth centuries, hundreds, perhaps thousands of churches were built, and perhaps as many as 200 monasteries. Monasticism played a vital role in the 'high culture' of Rus', with the leading role being played by the Kiev Monastery of the Caves, founded in c.1054. Building on the traditions established by Abbot Feodosii of the Monastery of the Caves monasteries became the main providers of charity, along with private donors. Churches also enjoyed great political influence. Their support was vital to princely power, their officials were often high-born boyars, and many churches and monasteries also became substantial landholders.[36] In Rus' church and state formed closer relations than in the Islamic world, and both institutions benefited from the relationship.

Christianity gave Rus' a literate culture, but in doing so it made Rus' a cultural colony of Byzantium. The metropolitanate based in Kiev was known in Byzantium as the metropolitanate of 'Rhosia'. Of the 22 metropolitans who headed the church of Rus' before the Mongol invasion, 20 were Greek, selected and consecrated in Constantinople or Nicaea, and only two were Slavs; while most of the bishops were also Greeks. Conversion also encouraged closer cultural ties with Catholic Europe for, until the sack of Constantinople in 1204, the Orthodox church of Rus' showed little hostility to Catholicism.[37]

Orthodoxy gave Rus' a written language in Old Church Slavonic. Using this, Greek and Bulgharian clerics laid the foundations for a vigorous written culture. Though there was little direct interference from the patriarchate in Constantinople, the cultural impact of Byzantium was extensive. Yaroslav 'the Wise' was particularly renowned for his love and support of book-learning. However, his own books, like most of those copied in Kievan Rus', were not original works, but translations of Christian texts, mostly Greek.[38] Literacy distinguished the Christian from the pagan, because what the literate studied was the Bible, or translated works about the Bible. Rus' inherited from Byzantium a tradition of literacy that was conservative and religious and which almost totally ignored the Hellenistic traditions of the Eastern Mediterranean. The literature of Rus' includes: 'apocryphal literature, hagiography, *paterica*, homilies, historiography (the chronicles of John Malalas and George Hamartolus), secular tales (the exploits of Alexander of Macedon, Josephus Flavius's *History of the Jewish War*), natural history miscellanies (the *Hexaemera* – commentaries on the six days of Creation; the *Physiologus* – a treatise on animals, minerals and trees)'. Little of this work was original, but neither was most of the cultural output of the Islamic or Catholic world at that time. The most original work of the eleventh century, and the work that did most to give the literate society of Rus' a sense of its place in history, was the sermon of metropolitan Hilarion 'On Law and Grace', which placed the history of Rus' within a wider world history derived from the Christian scriptures.[39]

Literacy spread even amongst the laity. The number of writings, inscriptions and graffiti, on personal, business and religious matters, increased greatly, particularly in commercial Novgorod, in which there have been found many hundreds of birch-bark letters, almost 200 dated to before 1200. Similar letters have been found elsewhere, but they have been preserved best in Novgorod. However, literacy was rare in the villages.[40]

Christianity and literacy spread first in the urban areas of the south, but more slowly in the less urbanized lands further north. Most early bishoprics apart from Novgorod, were in the south, and burial rites suggest that this is also where Christianity spread most rapidly. In the north and in the countryside, traditional practices and beliefs survived much longer, sometimes into the twentieth century. The church fought hard against traditional forms of fortune telling, the worship of natural objects such as the sun, sky, lightning, trees, wells or hills, and the practice of shamanism or sorcery. It also opposed the work of rural healers who provided love potions or abortions.[41] The more puritanical clergy even opposed most popular entertainments. Under the entry for the year 1068, the Chronicle explains a Kipchak attack as punishment for the spread of various forms of devilry, including:

> trumpets and strolling players [or perhaps magicians? *skoromokhi*], *gusli* [stringed instruments] and *rusali* [festivals of remembrance for dead ancestors – revels]. For we see the pleasure grounds trampled bare and vast crowds of people on them, jostling one another, mounting spectacles invented by the devil – while the churches stand [empty]. When it is time for prayer, few are found in church. For this reason we are punished by God.[42]

In rural Rus', the theology of Orthodoxy counted for little. However, its images (permitted as a result of the failure in Byzantium of the iconoclastic movements of the eighth and early ninth centuries), its rituals, its festivals and prayers, when combined with traditional practices and beliefs, created a religious experience and a sense of identity that bound even the most remote villages into a wider cultural unity. In this way, Orthodoxy created a powerful popular basis for the legitimacy of the princes of Rus'.

In the tenth and early eleventh centuries, Rus' enjoyed a precarious unity imposed by a series of strong leaders from the Ryurikid dynasty. As in the pastoralist world, the ruling family treated Rus' as a sort of family firm. This meant that rules of succession within the ruling dynasty had a profound impact on political history. These rules were similar to those of the steppe for inheritance passed as easily from brothers to brothers as from brothers to sons. Uncertainties about succession inevitably created conflicts between different branches. These rivalries could be softened by granting junior members power over the regional principalities from which Rus' had been constructed. These they could treat either as the foundation for a hereditary domain, or as a springboard for promotion. However, no rules of succession succeeded in ending conflict. In practice, 'blood tanistry' was as important in Rus' as in the steppes. The nineteenth-century historian, Pogodin, calculated that civil war dominated 80 of the 170 years between the death of Grand Prince Yaroslav in 1054 and the Mongol invasion in 1237.[43]

At the top of the system, power remained personal. The prince of Kiev was referred to in Kievan graffiti both as a 'tsar' (from Caesar) and as a 'kaghan' and both titles probably suggest a semi-sacral status.[44] There was no formalized governmental bureaucracy beyond the retinue and household servants of the prince, and no independent statehood apart from the power of individual princes. Meetings, or *dumy*, of leading boyars, usually members of the *druzhina*, provided the ruler with advice, and a chance to build alliances with important nobles. As a result, the fate of Rus', like that of so many steppe empires, turned to a considerable extent on the family history of the royal dynasty. In his will, Yaroslav tried to create stable rules of succession by demanding that brothers and sons should inherit city-states by strict seniority, moving from city to city if necessary. For a time after his death different sons ruled in Kiev, Chernigov and Pereyaslavl in relative peace until the mid-1060s, when the system was destabilized by the beginning of Kipchak attacks from 1062, and attacks from a non-Ryurikid ruler, Vseslav of Polotsk, who tried to carve out a distinct northern empire in the lands once controlled by the kaghanate of Rus'. In Rus', as in the steppes, periodic attempts were made to resolve such conflicts, and these took the form of family 'conferences', of which the best known is the conference of Lyubech (1097). Here, the heirs of Yaroslav effectively divided the realm into distinct patrimonies. Like the *kuriltai* of the Mongols, these princely conferences affirmed the collegial, or familial nature of political power within the royal dynasty of the Ryurikids, but they had only a limited capacity to enforce unity as the dynasty itself expanded, as did the number of cities that needed princes or governors.

ECONOMIC AND POLITICAL CHANGES: TWELFTH AND THIRTEENTH CENTURIES

Under Vladimir Monomakh (d. 1125), a reunified Rus' attempted to achieve real military domination of the steppes. However, after his death, Rus' never again acted with such unity.[45] After the death of Vladimir Monomakh's son, Mstyslav, in 1132, Kiev was never again able to act as the capital of a united Rus'. The existence of the Ryurikid dynasty, and of a growing cultural unity based on the spread of Christianity and the Slavic language, ensured that the idea of a unified Rus' survived. However the reality did not. Part of the problem was the expansion of the Ryurikid dynasty itself. In the eleventh century, we can identify only about 20 or so Ryurikid princes, but by the end of the twelfth century, it is possible to identify up to 200, and as each branch of the family sought new lands to rule they created more and more regional principalities in a pattern of expansion and fragmentation that is familiar in pre-modern states.[46]

In practice, Rus' became a loose federation of city-states, unified in tradition, but no longer in reality. Meanwhile, the trade routes with Baghdad and Constantinople, which had made the fortunes of the Ryurikid family, declined. The Byzantine route lost much of its importance after the sack of Constantinople by the Crusaders in 1204. The rise of Baltic trades was only a partial compensation, and benefited mainly the northern city-states of Novgorod and Pskov, which now began to import German silver instead of the Central Asian dirhams which had originally made their fortunes.[47] Kipchak power in the steppes also deprived Kiev of any control over the Silk Roads through Crimea. At the end of the eleventh century, Tmutorokan' disappears from the Chronicle reports, and it may be that the commercial ports of the east Crimea had once again fallen into Byzantine hands.

However, it is inaccurate to see this simply as a period of political and commercial decline.[48] While international trade may have declined, the population of Rus' expanded and so did agricultural productivity and the number of towns. While the influence of Kiev declined in the twelfth century, that of many new regions increased, so that, in a sense, the fragmentation of Rus' was also a sign of expansion and change. Migrations continued to the north and east, into woodland regions still unpoliced in the eleventh century. Colonization raised agricultural production and increased populations in the northern regions. Peasants entered the lands of Finnic-speaking peoples clearing them with fire and axe and turning forest into farmland. The migrations occurred under growing pressure from the steppelands, increased demographic pressure in the Kievan heartlands, and, from the twelfth century, with the active support of powerful local rulers who provided protection against outside powers such as the Volga Bulghars. By 1200 the population of Rus' may have been twice that of 1000.

New power centres appeared as Kiev lost its hegemony. The most important were Vladimir-Suzdal' in the north-east and Galicia-Volhynia to the south-west of Kiev. The power of Vladimir-Suzdal' was based on the agricultural wealth of the *Vladimirskoe opolye*, a region of rich soils covering about 4000 km^2. But the wealth of the north depended, also, on demographic and military expansion into the fur-producing lands, control of which had long been disputed with the Bulghars. In the twelfth century, the princes of Vladimir-Suzdal' cut in on the lucrative Volga trade routes once shared between Novgorod and the Volga Bulghars. Novgorod still prospered from the sale of furs to the west. However, it was weakened by its reliance on grain supplies from other Rus' cities. Smolensk expanded rapidly in the twelfth century, partly by controlling the wealth that travelled over the river portages linking the northern river systems with those of the Dnieper. The expansion of northern towns, agriculture and trade attracted Ryurikid princes. The first northern prince to rule in Kiev was Yuri Dolgorukii (1154–7), prince of Suzdal', a son of Vladimir Monomakh, who had founded Vladimir in 1108. Yuri's son, Prince Andrei Bogolyubskii seized and sacked Kiev in 1169, but then transferred his capital to Vladimir. His son, Vsevolod III (1176–1212), who also ruled from Vladimir, was the first prince of Rus' to formally adopt the title of 'Grand Prince' and the last to exercise any form of suzerainty over the whole of Rus'. In the south-east, along the north-eastern slopes of the Carpathians, there emerged the powerful principality of Galicia-Volhynia. Galich on the River Dniester, which controlled the flourishing trade routes to the Danube and eastern Europe and the Balkans, first became a princely capital in *c*.1140. In 1199, Prince Roman Mstyslavich (1173–1205) united the principalities of Galicia and Volhynia. In 1203 he conquered Kiev itself. However, the great southern empire he established crumbled after his death in 1205, though it was temporarily reassembled by his son, Danylo (r. Volhynia 1223–64, and from 1238 in Galich as well). Under Danylo, Lvov was founded in 1256, and soon became the main commercial centre of the south-west.

By the late twelfth century, the most important principalities were, in the south-west, Galicia-Volhynia; in the south, Monomakh's old fief of Chernigov; to the north of Kiev, Smolensk; and, even further north, Novgorod; and, in the north-east, the region from which Muscovy was to emerge, the principality of Vladimir-Suzdal'. Smaller principalities, such as Ryazan, usually fell into the orbit of one of these larger principalities.

In the long run, political disunity exacted palpable human, cultural and economic costs as rival armies sacked neighbouring cities and destroyed the villages that supported their enemies. Kiev was sacked in 1169, and Kipchak armies sacked it again in 1184. In 1237, Chinggis Khan's grandson, Batu, was able to pick off the divided city-states of Rus' one by one, and to end the political independence of the east Slav lands for almost two centuries. Kiev was sacked again on 6 December, 1240, during the second phase of Batu's devastating invasion.

MAWARA'N-NAHR

In Rus' there emerged a reasonably clear border between the steppe and the farmlands. In Central Asia, the two were more closely intertwined. So were the cultural realms of oasis farmers and steppe pastoralists. Here, demographic pressure from the steppes led to a slow infiltration of Turkic-speaking pastoralists. Sometimes the process was piecemeal and gradual; sometimes it was militaristic and massive in scale.

The towns of Central Asia sucked in the marginal populations of the villages and the steppes, because of their high death rates, and the wealth and opportunities they offered.[49] The Samanid dynasty accelerated these processes as it came to rely more and more on armies of Turkic slaves. Eventually, the appearance of governments dominated by rulers of Turkic origin intensified the Turkicization of Central Asia.

It is difficult to track these demographic and linguistic changes in any detail. However, we can guess at their general shape. It is likely that Turkic languages first became dominant in the steppes between the major oases. Then, as Turkic governments arose, there appeared Turkic-speaking elites in the towns. Smaller farming villages were probably the last regions to become Turkic in speech and ethnic tradition. However, substantial Iranian-speaking populations have survived in the towns of Central Asia to the present-day, and in the mountainous areas of modern Tajikistan.

Much easier to track are the political changes that accompanied these linguistic changes. For a time, Samanid power prevented large-scale military incursions, though occasionally, the Samanids let whole tribes settle within Mawara'n-nahr, where they acted as frontier guards.[50] However, as Samanid power declined, increasing numbers of Turks began to settle not as individual migrants, or frontier guards or slave *ghulams*, but as the soldiers of conquering tribal armies. These processes led to the demographic and, by the eleventh century, the political domination of Mawara'n-nahr by Turkic-speakers. The Samanid dynasty was the last major Iranian-speaking dynasty to rule in Mawara'n-nahr. In 1000, it was replaced by two dynasties of Turkic origin.

Turkic migration into Central Asia from the tenth to the thirteenth centuries created a linguistic and ethnic balance that was to survive for many centuries. By the eleventh century, Central Asia had a Turkic military, Persian cultural traditions and an Arabic religion. According to an old Central Asian saying: 'To the Turks belongs the *imperium*, while to the Persians *magisterium* and to the Arabs *sacerdotum*.'[51]

THE GHAZNAVID AND KARAKHANID EMPIRES: 1000–70

The Ghaznavid and Karakhanid dynasties represent two quite distinctive types of Turkic polity.

The Ghaznavid empire was created by *ghulam* soldiers of the Samanids, and it largely preserved Samanid traditions and methods of rule. Its founder, Alp Tegin, was a *ghulam* who rose to be a commander or *hajib* in the Samanid army and played a vital role in the succession struggles of the early 960s. He was already a man of great wealth. According to Nizam al-Mulk, his lands included 500 villages, and in all the major Samanid cities he had 'houses, gardens, inns, bath-houses and farms'. He also owned 1 million sheep and over 100,000 horses, mules and camels.[52] In 961, he was appointed governor of Khorasan, but a year later he was dismissed. Rather than accept his fall, he led his soldiers to Ghazna in modern Afghanistan in 962, deposed the local ruler, and took his place. After his death, his successors accepted Samanid suzerainty, becoming, in theory, Samanid governors of Ghazna, though in practice they were independent rulers.

The real founder of Ghaznavid greatness, Sebük Tegin (r. 977–97), was also a *ghulam*. He was captured in the Chu valley, north-west of Issyk-kul, and sold to a slave-dealer in Chach. After a period of military training, he was sold at the slave markets of Nishapur to Alp Tegin, and rose rapidly through the ranks of the Ghaznavid army.[53] By his death, in 999, the Ghaznavid dynasty was already more powerful than the declining Samanid dynasty. Under Sebük Tegin's son, Mahmud (r. 997–1030), the Ghaznavid dynasty renounced Samanid suzerainty, secured the blessing of the caliphate, and became the most powerful state in the eastern Islamic world.

Though Turkic in origin and, apparently, in speech, Alp Tegin, Sebük Tegin and Mahmud were all thoroughly Persianized. Many of the scholars and writers of the Samanid court, including Firdausi and al-Biruni, transferred their allegiance to the magnificent court established by Mahmud at Ghazna. So did many Samanid officials. However, there were also significant differences between the two dynasties. Most important was the greater reliance of the Ghaznavids on their *ghulam* armies. This, in turn, explains why the Ghaznavids seemed more predatory than their predecessors, for maintaining large, professional armies was an expensive business. Consequently, the Ghaznavid rulers spent much time on campaign, travelling with their armies. Even the government's official papers were carried with the court on pack-animals, and lodged, along with the clerks who handled them, in specially erected tents. The army itself collected much of the money needed to support it, as well as many new slave recruits, on annual booty raids into northern India, which began the penetration of Islam into the Indian subcontinent. Conducted, in principle, as jihads, these campaigns won the Ghaznavids renown as *ghazis* or 'warriors for the faith'. However, they were, primarily, booty raids, similar in form and intent to the raids of the Kusana and the Hephthalites early in the first millennium. Despite the immense wealth collected during these raids, Ghaznavid taxation was heavy, and deeply resented, in Khorasan.[54] Though the blessing of the caliph, the power of Ghaznavid armies and the magnificence of their court ensured the Ghaznavid dynasty a certain legitimacy, they never created deeper bonds of loyalty that might have encouraged their subjects to defend them in a crisis.

In Transoxiana, the Samanids were replaced with a dynasty of a very different type, that of the Karakhanids. The Karakhanid royal family was probably of Karluk origin, from the region around Kashgar. Indeed, Pritsak has argued that their first leader can be identified with a Karluk leader of the mid-ninth century who claimed descent from the A-shih-na. Early in the tenth century, a Karakhanid leader based in Kashgar converted to Islam, probably under the influence of Sufi missionaries. By the middle of the century there is evidence of mass conversions amongst the local Turkish population.[55] As Karakhanid power expanded in the tenth century, they gradually took over many of the lands claimed by the Karluks. Their state, like the Türk empire, seems to have had two wings, an eastern (based originally in Balasaghun and then in Kashgar) and a western (based in Talas, then Samarkand), with the eastern dominant. The two halves corresponded, roughly, to eastern and western Turkestan. They became separate kaghanates in the eleventh century. In the tenth century, a still united Karakhanid empire came into conflict with Samanid power to the west and by the 970s the Karakhanids controlled parts of the Zerafshan valley, including the silver mines from which the Samanids had produced their silver dirhams.[56]

In 999, the Karakhanid leader, Nasr Ilig, conquered Bukhara. The Bukharan *ulama* persuaded its population not to resist the occupation, on the grounds that the conquerors were Muslims, a clear sign both of the growing power of the Islamic clergy, and of the gain in potential legitimacy available to those Turkic rulers who had converted.[57] In 1001, the Ghaznavid leader, Mahmud, and the Karakhanid leader, Nasr Ilig, negotiated a treaty that established the border of the two empires at the Amu Darya, thereby recreating the traditional division between Khorasan and Mawara'n-nahr.[58] From this date, Mawara'n-nahr was to be ruled by Turkic rulers until the late nineteenth century, except for two brief periods in the twelfth and thirteenth centuries (under the Karakitai and Mongols).

Culturally, as well as politically, the Karakhanids proved immensely significant. Mediating as they did between the pastoralist and urban worlds, their empire provided a natural setting for the emergence of the earliest secular literature in the Turkic language. The first Turkic book, a book of advice for rulers called *The Wisdom of Royal Glory*, was published under Karakhanid rule in Kashgar, in c.1069. The book consciously preserved Turkic traditions, citing the sayings of traditional Turkic rulers of Inner Eurasia, but weaving in Islamic themes with a strong Sufi influence. As the first surviving work of Turkish Islam, its significance is analogous in Turkic tradition to the *Shah-name* in Persian culture.[59]

Gardizi's magnificent description of a meeting between Mahmud and a later Karakhanid ruler, Yusuf Kadïr Khan in 1025, gives some idea of the wealth and grandeur of the Karakhanid and Ghaznavid empires. As the armies of the two rulers approached each other, south of Samarkand, Kadir Khan sent envoys requesting a meeting with Mahmud.

On coming within sight of each other they both dismounted; the Amir
Mahmud had previously given the Treasurer a precious stone wrapped in a
cloth and (at this point) he ordered it to be delivered to Qadir-Khan....The
next day the Amir Mahmud ordered a large tent of embroidered satin to
be pitched and everything to be prepared for an entertainment; (after this) he
invited Qadir-Khan through an envoy to be his guest. When Qadir-Khan
arrived Mahmud ordered the table to be spread as magnificently as possible;
the Amir Mahmud and the Khan sat at the same table. After the meal was
finished they went to the 'hall of gaiety'; it was splendidly adorned with rare
flowers, delicate fruits, precious stones, gold embroidered fabrics, crystal,
beautiful mirrors and (various) rare objects, so that Qadir-Khan could not
regain his composure. They remained seated for some time; Qadir-Khan drank
no wine, as it was not customary for the kings of Transoxania, especially the
Turkish kings, to do so. They listened to music for a little, then (Qadir-Khan)
rose. Thereupon the Amir Mahmud ordered presents worthy of him to be
brought, namely, gold and silver goblets, precious stones, rarities from
Baghdad, fine fabrics, costly weapons, valuable horses with gold bridles, sticks
studded with precious stones, ten female elephants with gold bridles and goads
studded with jewels; mules from Bardhaa [in Transcaucasia] with gold trappings, litters for journeys by mule with girths, gold and silver sticks and bells,
also litters of embroidered satin; valuable carpets, of Armenian work, as well as
uwaysi (?) and parti-coloured carpets; embroidered headbands; rose-coloured
stamped stuffs from Tabaristan; Indian swords, Qamari aloes [from Cambodia],
Maqasiri sandal wood, grey amber, she asses, skins of Barbary tigers, hunting
dogs, falcons and eagles trained to hunt cranes, antelopes and other game.
He took leave of Qadir-Khan with great ceremony, showed him many favours
and made him his excuses (for the insufficiency of his entertainment and
presents).[60]

After returning to his camp, Yusuf realized the extent to which he had been
outbid in the diplomacy of gift-giving by the more experienced Mahmud. In
panic, 'he ordered the Treasurer to open the doors of the Treasury, took
thence much money and sent it to Mahmud, together with the products of
Turkestan, namely fine horses with gold trappings, Turkish slaves with gold
belts and quivers, falcons and gerfalcons, sables, minever, ermines, black fox
and marten furs, vessels (i.e. leather bottles) of the skin of two sheep with
horns of the khutuww [probably walrus], Chinese satin and so forth.'[61] After
this, 'Both sovereigns parted entirely satisfied in peace and amity.'

The Karakhanid and Ghaznavid empires jockeyed for position for some
40 years. The annexation of Khorezm by Mahmud in 1016, and the succession struggles that plagued the Karakhanid dynasty seemed to ensure the
ultimate domination of the Ghaznavids. However, it was the Ghaznavids that
collapsed soonest, under the pressure of the frontier tribes they encountered
as a result of their expansion into Khorezm.

The Karakhanids proved slightly less oppressive as rulers, because, unlike
the Ghaznavids, who relied on professional armies that had to be paid every
three months, they relied to a much greater extent on levies of their pastoralist followers. The Karakhanids avoided interfering too directly in the government of Mawara'n-nahr, and left the Samanid bureaucracy largely in place

Like the Yüeh-chih a thousand years earlier, they preferred to maintain a traditional pastoralist lifestyle, camping in the pasturelands between the major cities. Shams al-Mulk, who ruled much of Mawara'n-nahr between 1073 and 1080, nomadized in the steppelands, and spent the winters with his army, near Bukhara. Here he ensured that his soldiers stayed mainly in their tents, and never stayed overnight in the towns, to prevent looting.[62]

THE SALJUKS: 1040–1170

In 1040, at Dandanaqan in the Khorezmian steppes near Merv, a large Ghaznavid army, which included Indian battle elephants, was defeated by an army of Oghuz pastoralists and *condottiere* known as the Saljuks after the grandfather of its two leaders, Toghrul and Chagrï.[63] The battle destroyed Ghaznavid power in Khorasan, though in Afghanistan and northern India, Ghaznavid dynasties survived until 1186. In a remarkable career which surprised themselves as much as their neighbours, the Saljuk leaders recapitulated the history of the Parthians, creating a great Iranian and Mesopotamian empire that transformed the history of the Middle East.

Like many other pastoralist dynasties that conquered the sedentary lands of Central Asia, the Saljuk came from the ecological borderlands along the Syr-Darya, and were already familiar with the urban and agrarian worlds to their south. By the early eleventh century, Oghuz tribes controlled many of the frontier towns along the lower Syr Darya, and many of the poorer pastoralists, known as *yatuk*, had settled down permanently as farmers or traders. Indeed, later in the eleventh century, Mahmud al-Kashgari described the lower Syr Darya as the 'land of the Oghuz towns'.[64] In 965, Oghuz tribes had taken part in the destruction of the Khazar polity, however, the power of the Rus' and the Pechenegs encouraged them to look south rather than westwards for expansionistic opportunities. At about this time, Saljuk, despite his lack of royal connections, emerged as a significant leader amongst the Oghuz. He may have served the Khazar at one time or even converted briefly to Judaism, for his sons were given Old Testament names.[65] In c.985 he converted to Islam under the influence of Sufis preaching along the lower Syr Darya. After this, he and his followers became involved in the complex wars between the Samanids and the rising powers of the Ghaznavids and Karakhanids. They served as mercenaries to both the Samanids and the Karakhanids. In return, the Saljuk were permitted to settle in Mawara'n-nahr or Khorezm.

The defeat at Dandanaqan came after several years of confused warfare during the reign of Mahmud of Ghazna's successor, Mas'ud (1030–41). Though the Saljuk armies had broken up in the last years of Mahmud's reign, in the mid-1030s they reformed in the south of modern Turkmenistan, under the experienced leadership of Saljuk's grandsons. Here, they were joined by large groups of Oghuz and Kipchak, driven south and west by the huge migratory currents of the mid-century. At first, the Saljuk leaders petitioned Sultan Mas'ud for permission to settle in return for military service, complaining that it was now impossible to live peacefully in their former homes in Khorezm and Mawar'n-nahr. Mas'ud turned down their request, and attempted to crush the Saljuk by force. However, the Ghaznavid armies proved too cumbersome to deal with the mobile forces of the Saljuks. Baihaqi, who travelled with Mas'ud's armies, wrote that, for the Oghuz:

> The steppe is father and mother. . . . Their camels can forage freely on herbage and find pasture over a wide distance, whereas we have to keep our camels tethered outside our tents, for they cannot be left to pasture outside the camp. That is the reason why they have no heavy baggage, so that they can come and go, whereas we have heavy baggage, and the need to look after it keeps us from going off to do other things.[66]

Ghaznavid armies had to stay close to supply points, usually towns or major forts and, as Khorasan suffered from the constant campaigns of Mas'ud's reign, the problem of supplies became acute, and the towns of Khorasan lost any enthusiasm they might once have felt for Ghaznavid rule.[67]

We have a superb eyewitness account of the entry of Saljuk forces into the Khorasani capital of Nishapur in May 1038, two years before the collapse of Ghaznavid power. It was written by a spy of Mas'ud's, and conveys vividly the conditions under which a desperate pastoralist army came to rule much of the Abbasid domains.[68] At first, an advance guard of 200 men appeared outside the town, advising it to surrender and accept Saljuk suzerainty. Remembering that Sultan Mahmud had once criticized the people of Balkh for not submitting to an enemy power, and causing the destruction of the town, the respected Qadi Sa'id advised submission. The town's religious leaders agreed to submit, but begged the Saljuks not to pillage the town, warning that: 'beyond this world lies another one, and like yourselves, Nishapur has seen much.' Ibrahim Yinal, Toghrul's brother, and the Saljuk commander, promised there would be no plundering, and a herald was sent around the markets to explain the situation. The next day, Ibrahim Yinal was received formally into the town.

> They laid out furnishings and carpets in the Khurramak Garden and prepared food and got ready to go out and meet [him]. . . . Half a farsakh from the city, Ibrahim appeared with two or three hundred horsemen, a banner, two beasts of burden, and with the whole group having a generally ragged and battered aspect. When the reception committee came up to him, [they saw that] he had a splendid horse; he had a pleasing face and manner of speaking which encouraged everyone. . . . An enormous crowd of people had turned out to watch; older men, who had only seen the [well-turned out] forces of Mahmud and Mas'ud, were secretly weeping, although outwardly smiling at the procession and concourse. Ibrahim dismounted at the Khurramak Garden, and they brought him large quantities of the food and refreshment which they had prepared for him. (p. 256)

On the Friday, the *khutba* was pronounced in the name of Toghrul, the Saljuk leader, which provoked some discontent among the crowd. About ten days later, Toghrul arrived with the Saljuk army.

> Toghrul was accompanied by 3000 horsemen, the majority of them wearing cuirasses. He himself had a strung bow over his arm, with three wooden arrows

fastened at his waist, and was fully armed. He wore a *mulham* tunic, a head-dress of *Tawwazi* cloth and felt boots. He installed himself in the garden at Shadyakh, as did as many as possible of his forces who could be contained there, the rest encamping round the perimeter of the garden. They brought there large quantities of food and refreshment which they had prepared and gave provisions to all the soldiers. (p. 256)

The following day, even the respected Qadi Sa'id, who had refused to meet the Saljuk advance guard, went to meet Toghrul. The Qadi addressed Toghrul with remarkable independence.

> Be circumspect, and fear God, His name is exalted. Render justice, and listen to those who have suffered tyranny and who are in wretched circumstances. Do not give free rein to this army of yours for them to wreak oppression, for an act of injustice is an inauspicious event. I am fulfilling my duty in coming to greet you, and I shall not come again because I am occupied in study, and apart from that, I do not give my attention to anything else. If you want to go back with a piece of wisdom, this advice of mine will be sufficient. (p. 256)

Toghrul replied respectfully, promising not to disturb the Qadi, and to accept his advice. He added: 'We [Saljuks] are new and strange [to all this] and do not know the usages of the Perso-Islamic tradition. The Qadi must not refuse sending advice to me in future' (p. 257). A local official who had supported the entry of the Saljuks, was made governor of the city.

Though Nishapur was not pillaged, it undoubtedly had to give tribute to the Saljuks though these were not necessarily as heavy as those levied by the Ghaznavids. More significant may have been the destruction caused to the fertile irrigated lands near the city by the Saljuk herds of sheep, horses and camels. According to a contemporary source, no region could support Toghrul's armies for more than a week without running out of supplies and food. But even this was probably no worse than the destruction caused in recent years by Ghaznavid armies. In the town of Baihaq, nothing was sown for seven years before 1038, except in gardens and orchards protected by the city's outer walls. Elsewhere, the value of land fell, ruining many *dihqan* families.[69]

By defeating Mas'ud in 1040, the Saljuks emerged as a major Islamic power. Toghrul had a throne erected on the battlefield of Dandanaqan, and pro-claimed himself *amir* of Khorasan. He then sent ambassadors to the Caliph, and to the Karakhanid rulers of Mawara'n-nahr and eastern Turkestan, to announce his accession. In 1042, the Saljuks conquered Khorezm, and in 1055, while Chagrï ruled Khorasan, Toghrul moved west, overthrew the Buyid dynasty, and conquered Baghdad. As Sunni Muslims, the Saljuks were welcomed by the caliph.

The Saljuks adapted rapidly to the new conditions under which they ruled. Soon, their armies, too, were recruited in part from *ghulams*, though they also used less disciplined tribal levies of Oghuz warriors seeking new pasture-lands in the regions now controlled by the Saljuk. Balancing these two constituencies was the major problem faced by the early Saljuk rulers, for,

while their political and military power derived originally from tribal supporters, the task of maintaining discipline, and limiting the destruction caused by
new settlers forced them to rely increasingly on expensive professional
bureaucrats and soldiers.[70] In 1071, Toghrul's successor, Chagri's son, Alp
Arslan (r. 1063–72), while pursuing Oghuz settlers into eastern Anatolia,
confronted and defeated a Byzantine army at Manzikert, and captured the
emperor, Romanos. Byzantium now lost eastern Anatolia for ever. The
Saljuks established a kingdom based on Konya, and large numbers of Turkic
pastoralists began to settle in the region.[71] The scale of these migrations,
which eventually transformed Anatolia into a Turkic-speaking region, indicates the extent of the demographic pressure created in the Inner Eurasian
steppes by the migratory movements of the eleventh century. But the battle
of Manzikert had an even more immediate significance, for it provoked the
series of European invasions known as the Crusades.

From steppe chieftains, the Saljuk had become the most important military power in the Islamic world. However, they recognized the symbolic
authority of the caliphate, and therefore assumed the title of Sultan, or
'power'.[72] In 1074, Saljuk armies conquered Transoxiana and took Bukhara
and Samarkand from the Karakhanids. In 1089, the eastern Karakhanid
kaghan accepted Saljuk overlordship and so, eventually, did the Ghaznavids.
The Saljuks now dominated Central Asia as well as Persia.

Under the strong rule of Toghrul Beg, Alp Arslan and Malikshah, the
Saljuk empire held together. With the help of the former Ghaznavid *wazir*,
Nizam al-Mulk, Alp Arslan and his successor, Malikshah (1072–92) created
government structures based on those of the Samanid polity. These were to
survive in the Persian world for many centuries.[73] With Nizam's encouragement, the Saljuks spread Sunni orthodoxy and suppressed Shi'a Islam, partly
by the founding of large numbers of *madrasahs*. Their Sunni orthodoxy
granted the Saljuks a legitimacy that their pastoralist origins might have
denied them in the Islamic world.

Like their predecessors, the Saljuks governed largely through already
established regional dynasties and bureaucracies, though some regions,
particularly the large cities, were also supervised by special appointees of the
Saljuk sultans.[74] At the centre of government was the Sultan's court, the
dargah, which controlled the Saljuk armies and tended to be itinerant.
Civilian government was headed by the various *diwans*, many of which stayed
in the Saljuk capitals of Nishapur, then Rayy, then Isfahan. However,
the head of the civilian administration, the *wazir*, usually travelled with the
court. As the government came to rely less on the military power of its tribal
levies it, too, faced the problem of paying for its bureaucracy and its armies.
The Saljuks resorted, increasingly, to a device that had been used before
them, but never to the same extent. This was the *iqta*, a temporary grant of
revenues from a region to a particular military or civilian official, similar, in
many ways, to the European 'fief', or the later Muscovite system of *kormlenie*.
The *iqta* was already a well-established device in the Islamic world. However,
the Saljuq, like other Central Asian pastoralists, had long familiarity with
arrangements under which powerful rulers granted pastoralists land in return

for military service, and this may help explain their enthusiastic adoption of the *iqta*.[75] The *iqta* provided a simple way of satisfying the demands and needs of the new, Saljuk elites, but in the long run it weakened the power of the centre for the powerful Turkic *muqta* who held *iqtas* often managed to turn them, in practice, into hereditary domains.

There has been much controversy over the extent of the destruction caused by the Saljuk invasions.[76] Saljuk armies caused immense destruction to some towns, while the entry of large numbers of pastoralists into the farmlands of Khorasan undermined the agricultural economy in some regions. Yet it is hard to detect clear signs of a general or long-term economic decline in Mawara'n-nahr in the eleventh and twelfth centuries, although Barthold and others have claimed to find evidence of urban decline during this period. On the other hand, there is also evidence of increased commercialization and urbanization; for example, the persistent shortage of good silver coinage from the late tenth century may reflect a steadily increasing demand for coinage, as well as a real shortage of silver.[77]

Saljuk power began to decline after the death of Malikshah (1092) and his great *wazir*, Nizam al-Mulk in the same year. Nizam was one of the first people to be assassinated by the Isma'ili sect of 'assassins', who had been established in Persia only two years before; they killed him in revenge for his persecution of Shi'ia Muslims.[78] However, the real causes of decline lay deeper, and reflected problems faced by all pastoralist empires. With the end of the period of conquest, less booty was available to reward pastoralist followers, and more resources had to be devoted to the agrarian and urban economy. As a result, local tribal, ethnic and regional loyalties reasserted themselves in new forms, sapping the power of the centre. Saljuk power declined in the west, though it was maintained in the east by Sanjar, who became governor of Khorasan in 1097, and then sultan of all the Saljuk in 1118. Sanjar based his power in Khorasan and made Merv his capital until his death in 1157. For a time, he claimed power over most of the lands of the Saljuk. However, his empire was weakened by his defeat in 1141 by the Karakitai, and finally destroyed when he was defeated and captured by Oghuz rebels in 1153.

THE KHOREZMSHAHS AND THE KARAKITAI: 1170–1220

In the twelfth century, Saljuk power in Central Asia was challenged, first by the Khorezmshahs, and then by the Karakitai.

The title of 'Khorezmshah' was old, probably pre-Islamic. However, since at least the Arabic conquest, Khorezm itself had been divided into two regions ruled, respectively from Kath and Urgench. In 996 a ruler from Urgench managed once again to reunite Khorezm politically, but it was soon incorporated within the rising Ghaznavid empire. Despite this, the power of the Khorezmshahs flourished under Ghaznavid rule, after the appointment of a powerful and relatively independent *ghulam* governor, Altuntash (1017–32). In 1097, the Saljuks appointed a new governor, Muhammad (1097–1127), son of the previous *ghulam* governor, Anushtegin.

Muhammad, who also received the title of Khorezmshah, became the founder of a remarkably successful dynasty, the Anushteginidy (1097–1231). He accepted Saljuk suzerainty, as did his son, Atsïz (r. 1127–56) for most of his reign, while after 1141 Atsïz paid tribute to the Karakitai. But in practice both ruled with considerable independence, and on several occasions, Atsïz formally rejected Saljuk rule. Under Atsïz, Khorezm expanded northwards, conquering Jand on the Syr-Darya and Mangishlak on the Caspian sea. In 1141, Atsïz was recognized as in independent sultan by the caliph, and began to mint gold coins in his own name. After the collapse of the Saljuk dynasty his son, Il Arslan (r. 1156–72), inherited one of the most powerful states in the eastern Islamic world. Economically speaking, the power of Khorezm rested on its control of the lucrative trade routes through Jand and the Kipchak steppes, that led to China, Siberia and the rising power of Rus'. As these routes all passed through Kipchak territory, the Khorezmshahs devoted much effort to the conquest of the trading towns along the lower Syr-Darya, and also established close military, commercial and even family ties with Kipchak leaders.'[79]

Since 1141, the main rival (and formal suzerain) of the Khorezmshahs had been the Karakitai (or 'Black Kitai') dynasty. This is known in Chinese sources as the 'Western Liao'. It was the first infidel dynasty to rule in Central Asia since the ninth century. The Karakitai dynasty was established by a member of the Chinese imperial dynasty of the Kitan, Yeh-lü Ta-shih, who led the remnants of the Kitan army west after their defeat by the Jurchen in 1124. His followers included representatives of many different tribal peoples, including Uighurs, but the Kitan themselves were probably Turkic- or Mongol-speaking.[80] By the end of 1129, Yeh-lü Ta-shih had conquered Kashgar and Khotan, creating the beginnings of a great empire in eastern Central Asia. Its centre was probably at Balasaghun in the Chu valley. Yeh-lü Ta-shih adopted the imperial title of *gür khan* or khan of khans. The Karakitai invaded Mawara'n-nahr in 1137. In 1141, in the battle of the Qatwan steppe, near Samarkand, the Gür Khan's armies defeated the Saljuk sultan, Sanjar. This victory probably gave rise to European legends of an anti-Muslim ruler in the east, known as Prester John. The Karakitai now ruled most of Sinkiang and Mawara'n-nahr. Like the Karakhanid, they remained largely nomadic, and were content to leave most local rulers in power, in return for tribute and formal submission.[81]

The Karakitai polity was complex, ethnically, linguistically and politically. Though Chinese was the main administrative language (and the language of its coinage), Persian and Uighur Turk were also used officially. Its populations included Buddhists, Christians, Muslims, and Manichaeans. Ethnically, it included Chinese, Uighurs, Kitan, Turks and Iranians, while ecologically it embraced steppes, mountains, deserts and oasis city-states. Its army, though originally of a Chinese type, gradually became a traditional steppe army, dominated by cavalry and organized according to a decimal system. This reflected the fact that the Kitan, even as rulers of northern China, had preserved their nomadic lifeways and traditions to an unusual degree.[82] Politically, the empire was loosely organized, content for the most part to take tributes from subordinate regions without rearranging them administratively.

The Karakitai victory in 1141 destroyed Saljuk power in Central Asia. After the Karakitai invasion, the Khorezmshahs paid tribute to the new rulers, but in practice ruled with great independence. Khorezmshah Tekesh (1172–1200), conquered Khorasan, and turned Khorezm into one of the great powers of the Islamic world. Tekesh's son, Ala ad-Din Muhammad, ruled from 1200 to 1220 before being defeated by the Mongols.[83]

In 1210, Muhammad's Khorezmian armies defeated the Karakitai army near Talas. For the first time, Khorezm was now free of all forms of suzerainty. In the same year, the Karakitai dynasty was overthrown by a coup led by a pastoralist chief from western Mongolia, the Naiman leader, Küchlüg. Muhammad himself was well aware of his new status, and began to call himself the 'second Alexander of Macedon'. In 1212, he captured and sacked Samarkand, which had resisted his authority, and then conquered the western regions of the Karakitai empire, sacking a number of cities along the Syr-Darya and in Ferghana. Within a few years, his authority was recognized from the Syr-Darya to Iraq.

Yet Muhammad's state was more fragile than anyone realized. The caliphate refused to accept his authority as secular leader of the Muslim world, and an attempt to conquer Baghdad in 1217 was a disastrous failure. His military power depended largely on Kipchak troops who were commanded by their own amirs and accompanied by their families. The loyalty of such allies was never certain. In Mawara'n-nahr, the brutality of his conquest ensured that he could count on little support there. Elsewhere, he had alienated local elites by removing traditional rulers and replacing them with members of his own family. Finally, his own authority was undermined by that of his mother, Terken khatun. According to an-Nasawi, the biographer of Muhammad's son, Jalal ad-Din, Muhammad obeyed his mother in all things, partly out of genuine affection, and partly 'because most government officials were from her people.' This caused great confusion, particularly after Muhammad moved his own residence to Samarkand, leaving his mother in control of Khorezm. Frequently, officials received decrees both from Muhammad and his mother, and usually they simply obeyed the decree with the latest date on it.[84]

In 1218, Mongol armies defeated and killed Küchlüg, who had alienated many of his subjects by persecuting Islam. Muhammad now found himself facing an enemy whose immense power no one in Mawara'n-nahr had yet appreciated.

NOTES

1 See H. Franke, 'The Forest Peoples', in *CHEIA* (pp. 400–23), ch. 15.
2 Golden, *Introduction*, pp. 204–5; Kumekov, *Gosudarstvo kimakov*, ch. 3 discusses economic and social structures, while pp. 115–22 discuss whether the Kimek created a true 'state'.

3 Golden, *Introduction*, p. 199, and see pp. 196–8; Golden, 'The Karakhanids', in *CHEIA*, pp. 350–1; ibn Fadlan, *Risala*, p. 129; al-Khwarazmi cited from Pletneva, *Polovtsy*, p. 31.
4 Tolstov, *Po drevnim del'tam*, p. 200; Agadzhanov, *Gosudarstvo Sel'dzhukidov*, p. 4.
5 cited in Golden, *Introduction*, pp. 195–6.
6 *Hudud al-'alam*, p. 101; ibn Fadlan, *Risala*, p. 126; Agadzhanov, *Gosudarstvo Sel'dzhukidov*, pp. 24–6.
7 ibn Fadlan, *Risala*, p. 124, and see pp. 126–7; see also *Hudud al-'alam*, pp. 100–1, and Agadzhanov, *Gosudarstvo Sel'dzhukidov*, pp. 159, 164–6.
8 Golden, 'The Karakhanids', in *CHEIA*, pp. 352–4; and see Golden, *Introduction*, p. 213.
9 On the origins and migrations of the Kipchak, see Klyashtornyi and Sultanov, *Kazakhstan*, pp. 116–38 and Akhinzhanov, *Kypchaki*, chs 1–3; on Kipchak lifeways and politics in the Kazakh steppes, see Akhinzhanov, *Kypchaki*, pp. 198–203, 230–2, and ch. 5; on the migratory movements of the mid-eleventh century, see Agadzhanov, *Gosudarstvo Sel'dzhukidov*, pp. 66–9.
10 Pletneva, *Polovtsy*, pp. 40, 101–2, and see pp. 29–30, 34.
11 Ibid., p. 80; and see Golden, 'Peoples of the south Russian steppes', in *CHEIA*, p. 277 on the *chernye klobuki*; on Tugor Khan, see Pletneva, *Polovtsy*, pp. 49, 136, and Noonan, 'Rus', Pechenegs, and Polovtsy', p. 303.
12 Vernadsky, *A Source Book*, 1:31; Torchesk ('Turk town') was *c.*65 miles south of Kiev.
13 Pletneva, *Polovtsy*, p. 120, and see p. 53; see also Conte, *Les Slaves*, p. 426.
14 Noonan, 'Rus', Pechenegs, and Polovtsy,' pp. 301–27.
15 Pletneva, *Polovtsy*, pp. 42–3, and see p. 104.
16 Franklin and Shepard, *Emergence of Rus*, p. 267.
17 Golden, 'The Qipcaqs of Medieval Eurasia', pp. 147–8.
18 Pletneva, *Polovtsy*, pp. 95–7, and see p. 109.
19 Franklin and Shepard, *Emergence of Rus*, pp. 326–7; Pletneva, *Polovtsy*, pp. 98–9, 116–7, 119, 122–4, 127; Akhinzhanov, *Kypchaki*, pp. 250–1.
20 Pletneva, *Polovtsy*, p. 83.
21 Ibid., p. 108.
22 Ibid., p. 106.
23 For some estimates of the size of tribal groups, see Pletneva, *Polovtsy*, p. 114–15; see also ibid., p. 106.
24 Pletneva, *Polovtsy*, p. 115.
25 Subtelny, *Ukraine*, p. 33.
26 Fennell, *Russian Church*, p. 12.
27 The classic Soviet demonstration of the importance of agriculture in Rus' is Grekov, *Kievskaya Rus'*.
28 Martin, *History*, p. 72; on plough types, see Dolukhanov, *Early Slavs*, p. 197; in the early modern period, under Kazakh customary law, the murderer of a man paid twice as much as the murderer of a woman, see Klyashtornyi and Sultanov, *Kazakhstan*, p. 318.
29 Froyanov, *Kievskaya Rus'*, 1974, 1:53–8; see also ibid., 1:63, 66–7; and see Martin, *History*, pp. 70–3; and Subtelny, *Ukraine*, p. 45.
30 Estimates range from 20,000 to 100,000; Franklin and Shepard, *Emergence of Rus*, p. 282; see also ibid., pp. 2, 13, 279, 287.
31 Froyanov, *Kievskaya Rus'*, 1980, p. 230, and see ibid., p. 227; see also Subtelny, *Ukraine*, p. 48.
32 Tikhomirov, *Drevnerusskie goroda*, pp. 39, 43; and see Subtelny, *Ukraine*, p. 48.

33 Dawson, *Mission to Asia*, p. 131.
34 See Vernadsky, *Kievan Russia*, ch. 5.
35 Franklin and Shepard, *Emergence of Rus*, pp. 195, 197–8.
36 On the last point there is no hard evidence of extensive landholdings, but Fennell argues that monasteries probably owned land; see Fennell, *Russian Church*, p. 72; on the role of the Monastery of the Caves, see ibid., pp. 64–8; and see also ibid., pp. 62–3.
37 Fennell, *Russian Church*, p. 103; and see ibid., pp. 46–7.
38 Ibid., pp. 105–6.
39 Franklin and Shepard, *Emergence of Rus*, pp. 213–4, and see p. 238; quotation from Fennell, *Russian Church*, pp. 106–7.
40 S. Franklin, 'Literacy in Kievan Rus'', in Kaiser and Marker, *Reinterpreting* (pp. 73–8), pp. 74, 78.
41 Fennell, *Russian Church*, p. 83; see also Moshe Lewin's 'Popular religion in twentieth-century Russia', in Lewin ed., *The Making of the Soviet System: Essays in the social History of Interwar Russia*, Methuen, London, 1985, pp. 57–71.
42 Fennell, *Russian Church*, p. 86.
43 Riasanovsky, *History of Russia*, 4th edn, p. 42.
44 Franklin and Shepard, *Emergence of Rus*, p. 215.
45 Golden, 'The Qipcaqs of Medieval Eurasia', pp. 147–8.
46 Franklin and Shepard, *Emergence of Rus*, p. 339.
47 Martin, *History*, p. 68.
48 This is argued forcefully in Franklin and Shepard, *Emergence of Rus*, e.g. p. 337.
49 Hodgson, *Venture*, 2:90 is good on the mechanisms of ethnic replacement in Central Asia.
50 Barthold, *Turkestan*, pp. 256–7.
51 Cited in Frye, *Bukhara*, p. 111.
52 Nizam al-Mulk, *Book of Government*, p. 110; his career has already been described in ch. 12.
53 Bosworth, *Ghaznavids*, 2nd edn, p. 40.
54 Bosworth, *Ghaznavids*, 2nd edn, p. 78, and see ibid., pp. 56, 91, 131; see also Agadzhanov, *Gosudarstvo Sel'dzhukidov*, pp. 28–39.
55 Golden, 'The Karakhanids', in *CHEIA*, pp. 357–8, and see pp. 354–6; and Klyashtornyi and Sultanov, *Kazakhstan*, pp. 112–4.
56 Frye, *Golden Age of Persia*, p. 205; Golden, *Introduction*, p. 215.
57 Hodgson, *Venture*, 2:120.
58 Golden, 'The Karakhanids', in *CHEIA*, p. 362.
59 As argued in Yusuf Khass Hajib, *Wisdom of Royal Glory*, p. 1; see also, ibid., pp. 9–10, 17–22.
60 Cited in Barthold, *Turkestan*, pp. 283–4.
61 Ibid., p. 284.
62 Ibid., p. 315; Frye, *Bukhara*, p. 175.
63 Bosworth, *Ghaznavids*, 2nd edn, p. 223 describes them as 'condottieri on the Islamic frontier, giving their services to whomever would promise them plunder and pasture land for their followers'; Frye, *Bukhara*, p. 186, also describes them as *condottieri*.
64 Bosworth, *Ghaznavids*, 2nd edn, p. 213; and see Agadzhanov, *Gosudarstvo Sel'dzhukidov*, pp. 19–26.
65 Golden, *Introduction*, p. 218; Artamonov, *Istoriya Khazar*, pp. 419–20; Dunlop, *Jewish Khazars*, pp. 258–61.
66 Cited in Bosworth, *Ghaznavids*, 2nd edn, p. 247.

67 Bosworth, *Ghaznavids*, 2nd edn, pp. 252–7.
68 Baihaqi's account is cited from Bosworth, *Ghaznavids*, 2nd edn, pp. 252–7.
69 Ibid., pp. 260–1, and see pp. 258–9.
70 Morgan, *Medieval Persia*, p. 29, and Agadzhanov, *Gosudarstvo Sel'dzhukidov*, pp. 79–91.
71 On the history of the Saljuks in Anatolia, see Tamara Talbot Rice, *The Seljuks*.
72 Morgan, *Medieval Persia*, p. 24; Golden, 'The Karakhanids', in *CHEIA*, p. 365.
73 Morgan, *Medieval Persia*, pp. 29 and 36–7.
74 On Saljuk government, see Morgan, *Medieval Persia*, ch. 4.
75 On the *iqta*, see Morgan, *Medieval Persia*, pp. 37–40; Agadzhanov, *Gosudarstvo Sel'dzhukidov*, pp. 76–9, 105–11.
76 See, e.g., Frye, *Golden Age of Persia*, pp. 169–70, on Saljuk destructiveness; for an account that stresses the smallness of Saljuk armies and the limits of their impact, see Morgan, *Medieval Persia*, pp. 32–3.
77 Barthold, *Turkestan*, p. 88; Frye, *Bukhara*, p. 152; Davidovich, *Denezhnoe khozyaistvo*, pp. 125–6; Buniyatov, *Gosudarstvo khorezmshakhov*, pp. 110–11.
78 Morgan, *Medieval Persia*, p. 32.
79 Buniyatov, *Gosudarstvo Khorezmshakhov*; Golden, 'The Karakhanids', in *CHEIA*, p. 369; Barthold, *Turkestan*, p. 233; Akhinzhanov, *Kypchaki*, ch. 4.
80 H. Franke, 'Forest Peoples', in *CHEIA* (pp. 400–23), p. 410.
81 Ibid., pp. 410–11; on Prester John, see de Rachewiltz, *Papal Envoys*, p. 3, and Gumilev, *Searches for an Imaginary Kingdom*.
82 Honey, *Stripping off Felt*, p. 11; on the Kitan polity, see Morgan, *The Mongols*, p. 49; one of the best accounts of the Karakitai is still in Barthold, *Turkestan down to the Mongol Invasion*, ch. 3.
83 Golden, 'The Karakhanids', in *CHEIA*, p. 369; Buniyatov, *Gosudarstvo Khorezmshakhov*.
84 Buniyatov, *Gosudarstvo Khorezmshakhov*, pp. 76–92, 128–9, 137.

FURTHER READING

On the world of the steppes, Ibn Fadlan, *Risala* offers the most vivid insight from this period. See also Pletneva, *Polovtsy*; Golden, *Introduction to the History of the Turkic Peoples*, the same author's essays in *CHEIA*, and also 'The Qipcaqs of Medieval Eurasia'; Akhinzhanov, *Kypchaki*; and Kumekov, *Gosudarstvo kimakov*. Noonan 'Rus', Pechenegs, and Polovsty' is good on the intertwining of pastoralist and agrarian politics.

On Rus', I have used, in addition to the sources listed under the previous chapter, Martin, *History of Medieval Russia*. On Mawara'n-nahr, important primary sources include the *Hudud al-'alam*; Nizam al-Mulk, *The Book of Government*; Yusuf Khass Hajib, *Wisdom of Royal Glory*; Bretschneider, *Medieval Researches*; and Juvaini, *The History of the World-Conqueror*. Useful secondary works include Barthold, *Turkestan*; Hodgson, *Venture*; Bosworth, *Ghaznavids*; Morgan, *Medieval Persia*; Agadzhanov, *Gosudarstvo Sel'dzhukidov*; Buniyatov, *Gosudarstvo Khorezmshakhov*; Frye, *Golden Age of Persia*; Gumilev, *Searches for an Imaginary Kingdom*; and Golden's essay on the Karakhanids, in *CHEIA*. The most recent Western study is Paul, *Herrscher, Gemeinwesen, Vermittler*.

PART V

The Mongol Empire: 1200–1260

[15] CHINGGIS KHAN

THE Mongol empire unified much of Inner Eurasia for a second time, creating a new political, military, economic and even epidemiological 'world system'. Its success seemed to demonstrate the enduring military superiority of pastoral nomadic societies over the agricultural societies of Inner Eurasia. Yet in retrospect, the Mongol empire appears as the last, spectacular, bloom of pastoralist power in Inner Eurasia. As it, and its successor states, declined from the fourteenth century, the balance of power within Inner Eurasia began to tip decisively in favour of the agricultural world, as it had much earlier in Outer Eurasia.

THE MONGOL EXPLOSION

For much of the twelfth century, Mongolia was a region of loose tribal confederations, like the Pontic steppes. In 1206, a leader of the Mongol group of tribes, Temüjin, was proclaimed the leader of all steppeland peoples, and adopted the title of 'Chinggis' or 'Universal' Khan. Having conquered the Mongolian steppes, his armies began to invade neighbouring sedentary lands. In 1207, they invaded the empire of the Tibetan and Buddhist Tanguts, or Hsia-hsia, who, with the Chin and Sung were one of dynasties that controlled China.[1] The Hsia-hsia controlled modern Kansu and Ninghsia, and held the eastern end of the Silk Roads. In 1211, Mongol armies invaded north China, capturing Beijing in 1215. In 1217, the Mongols turned west. They destroyed the Karakitai empire in modern Sinkiang, and in 1219 they entered Central Asia and destroyed the power of the Khorezmshah. In 1223, a Mongol army even entered the Pontic steppes and defeated an alliance of Rus' and Kipchak armies. Chinggis Khan's last campaign, which began in 1226 was directed, once more, at the Hsia-hsia empire, which it destroyed. The campaign ended in great bloodshed after Chinggis Khan's death in 1227.

At his death, Chinggis Khan controlled an empire as large as the first Türk empire of the sixth century.[2] However, unlike the Türk empires, that of the Mongols retained its expansionist momentum even after a generation of conquest. Under the rule of Chinggis Khan's third son, Ogodei (r. 1229–41),

Plate 15.1 Persian portrait of Chinggis Khan, (© Staatliche Museen zu Berlin-Presussischer Kulturbesitz. Museum für Indische Kunst).

new invasions were launched into China (in 1234) and into the western steppes and Rus' (in 1237). Batu, the son of Chinggis Khan's eldest son, Jochi, conquered Rus' in devastating campaigns between 1237 and 1240, led by Chinggis Khan's great general, Sübetei. Ogodei died in 1241, and was succeeded, after a complex power struggle, by his son, Güyük (r. 1246–8), who was succeeded, in turn, by his nephew, Mongke (r. 1251–59), in 1248. Under Mongke, the empire reached the height of its power. In 1252, Mongke sent his brother, Khubilai, to complete the conquest of southern China, a task finished only in 1279. In 1253, he sent another brother, Hulagu, westwards to conquer Persia and Mesopotamia. Hulagu's armies captured Baghdad and destroyed the remnants of the Abbasid caliphate in 1258. However, their defeat in 1260, at Ayn Jalut, in Syria, set a limit to Mongol power in Mesopotamia. After the death of Mongke, in 1259, the empire began to fragment, though for a time, his successor, Khubilai, claimed to rule an empire stretching from China to Syria.

Chapters 15 and 16 describe these astonishing conquests. They also attempt to convey something of the lifeways of Inner Eurasia during this era, for the successes of the Mongols attracted great interest throughout Eurasia, and generated a richer body of source materials than is available for the study of any earlier steppe empire.

BUILDING POWER IN THE STEPPES: THE PERIOD TO 1206

EXPLAINING THE 'MONGOL EXPLOSION'

It is tempting to seek large explanations for these vast events. It might be supposed, for example, that the Mongols rode to power on the crest of a Eurasia-wide commercial boom. Unfortunately, there is no evidence for such an expansion until *after* the creation of the Mongol empire. Several writers have attempted meteorological explanations of the Mongol explosion. Gareth Jenkins is the latest in a long tradition of writers to suggest that climatic change (in this case cooler, drier climates) may have encouraged military mobilization in the steppelands.[3] Such theories must always be taken seriously, but, as we have seen, they are extremely difficult to prove. Besides, they cannot fill the explanatory gap between military mobilization and the creation of a large pastoralist empire. Barfield's account of borderland politics encourages us to look for the emergence of a powerful Chinese dynasty, which might have forced pastoralist peoples to establish a more unified state. There did exist in north China, a Manchurian dynasty established by Jurchen peoples in 1125, and known as the 'Chin'. However, the Chin controlled only north-east China, while the Tanguts controlled Kansu, and the southern Sung dynasty controlled the lands below the Yang-tse.

We are left, therefore, with the simplest and most obvious explanation: the Mongol empire (like the Hsiung-nu and Türk empires) was created because of the exceptional military and political skills of an able and fortunate steppeland leader. Like it or not, this implies that the Mongol empire was a contingent event. Without Chinggis Khan, there would have been no Mongol empire. The element of contingency was built in to the very nature of steppeland politics, whose fluidity allowed able leaders to forge large and powerful pastoralist armies in a very brief time. However, Chinggis Khan took this familiar process further than any of his predecessors or successors. Chinggis Khan's role in the creation of the Mongol empire was so crucial that the following account will focus mainly on his career.

TEMÜJIN'S EARLY CAREER: BEFORE 1190

As a young man, Chinggis Khan was known as Temüjin. Temüjin established his power over the various peoples of Mongolia during several decades of vicious tribal conflict. Fortunately, we can describe this process in some detail for we have an account written from within the pastoralist world. The *Secret History of the Mongols* is an official chronicle of Chinggis Khan's reign. It is the first significant steppeland source to survive since the Orkhon inscriptions of the eighth century, and at present, 'the only existing history of a northern nomadic people written by themselves before the seventeenth century'.[4] According to its final paragraph, most of the *Secret History* (paras 1–268) was written in 1228, at the assembly or *kuriltai* that elected Chinggis Khan's son, Ogodei, as his successor. Its author was probably Chinggis Khan's adopted son, Shigi-khutugu.[5] It was, therefore, written by people with intimate knowledge of Chinggis Khan and his career. Its frequent criticisms of Chinggis Khan are reassuring for the modern historian, as they show that, though the Chronicle undoubtedly has a particular point of view, its author did not feel obliged to sanitize or glamourize its subject matter. Despite the many difficulties of using the *Secret History*, it remains the crucial source for the early history of the Mongol empire.

Temüjin, the young man who later became Chinggis Khan, was born in modern Kentei province, in about 1165. His father, Yesugei, belonged to the chiefly Borjigid lineage of a group of tribes known as Mongols.[6] Following an ancient steppe tradition, Temüjin's father named him after a man he had captured from the Tatars. The name seems to be related to the Orkhon-Turkish words, *temür* ('iron'), and the suffix, *jin* ('smith'), so the name literally means 'blacksmith'.[7]

Temüjin grew up in a Mongolia organized in loose tribal federations. The names of these federations – the Mongols, Tatars, Merkit, Kerait, Naiman and others – create the illusion of a federation of nations. In reality, like most steppeland tribal names, these names describe fragile and unstable alliance systems headed by local aristocratic or royal clans and including many heterogenous elements. The most important groupings in Temüjin's time were his own tribes, the Mongols, which may have been a part of the larger Tatar grouping, whose centre lay further east, near the Khingan mountains; the Turkic and partly Nestorian Kerait, based on the Orkhon river; the Naiman in western Mongolia, whose leading clans were probably Oghuz Turks and may also have been Nestorian; and the Merkit of the Baikal region.[8] Most of these peoples were pastoralists, but few were *just* pastoralists. Thus, the Merkit engaged in traditional forest activities such as fishing, hunting, reindeer-herding and the taking of furs; while the Kerait and Naiman, who had contact with the oases of Kansu, were probably familiar with the commerce of the Silk Roads, and may have included some agricultural populations. The groupings themselves were fluid. For most individuals, tribal and clan allegiances were far more important than the larger groupings, and individuals, households and clans moved easily from group to group as a result of warfare or marriage or ecological crises. None of the groups were monolithic in their ecological practices, their language, their loyalties or their religions.

According to the genealogies reproduced in the *Secret History*, the legendary ancestors of the Mongols had moved to the region of the Tola, Onon and Kerulen rivers, some time in the eighth century. They may have been forest peoples from the Amur region who migrated west and south along the Kerulen and Onon rivers, becoming pastoralists in the tenth to early eleventh centuries. The Mongolian scholar, U. Onon, suggests that the name 'Mongol' may derive from 'Onon gol' or 'Onon river'.[9] T'ang Chinese sources described the 'Meng-wu' as part of a large group of pastoralist tribes, related to the Hsien-pi, who shaved their heads, lived either in felt-covered huts or in tents carried on carts, and kept pigs and cattle rather than sheep. As E. D. Phillips has argued, 'This is surely a description of tribes from the forests who were only beginning to live as nomads and were poor and ill-equipped.'[10]

In the early twelfth century, Mongol leaders formed a powerful grouping within the wider Tatar world of east Mongolia. However, their power collapsed after they were defeated in the 1160s by Tatars, who had the backing of the Manchurian Chin dynasty. During Temüjin's childhood, the Mongols were weak, divided and vulnerable. They had noble lineages that claimed descent from a semi-mythical, wolflike founder, Burte-chino, but now such leaders enjoyed little more than the prestige of remembered authority. None held overall leadership of the Mongol tribes. Temüjin himself was of chiefly origin, for his father was the leader of the Tayichi'ud clans. At one time, Yesugei even had a strong enough following to restore to power a Kerait leader, To'oril, an event that was to prove of great importance to his son.[11] However, neither he, nor anyone else, could check the clan feuds that divided the Mongols. As Temüjin's shaman, Teb-tengri, put it:

before you were born the stars turned in the heavens. Everyone was feuding. Rather than sleep they robbed each other of their possessions. The earth and its crust had moved. The whole nation was in rebellion. Rather than rest they fought each other. In such a world one did not live as one wished, but rather in constant conflict. There was no respite, only battle. There was no affection, only mutual slaughter.[12]

The vicious conflicts of his childhood gave Temüjin a harsh political and military apprenticeship. Yesugei was poisoned by Tatars when Temüjin was only nine. His clan, the Tayichi'ud, immediately abandoned Yesugei's widow, Ho'elun Ujin, who came from another Mongol clan, the Onggirat. She and her children did not even receive help from Yesugei's brother, but lived as outcasts. There are times, we are told in the Secret History, when they lived by hunting, fishing and gathering along the banks of the Onon river. Ho'elun gathered wild pears and other fruits, dug up roots and wild garlic with a stick of juniper wood, and gathered elm seeds, while her boys caught fish using hooks made from needles. During this period of isolation and danger, relations within the family itself were far from happy. In c.1180, after a fight over fish they had caught, Temüjin and his brother Qasar murdered a third brother, Begter.[13]

Like Motun, Temüjin learnt, despite his high lineage, to depend on his own wits and the loyalties of trusted friends, rather than on the ties of kinship. In c.1180, he was captured and nearly murdered by members of his own Tayichi'ud clan. However, he persuaded the family guarding him to let him escape. Such stories suggest Temüjin's resourcefulness, and his remarkable capacity to attract friendship and loyalty. The Secret History tells another story which suggests the great importance he attached to personal loyalties. When robbers stole his household's horses, Temüjin pursued them. After several days, he met a young man, Bo'orcu, who was milking the mares of his father's herd. Bo'orcu had seen the thieves. He loaned Temüjin a fresh horse and, without even telling his father, joined Temüjin in his search. 'My friend,' he said, 'you've drained yourself in coming here. All men's sufferings are common. I will accompany you.'[14] After three days' riding, they found the encampment of robbers, stole back the horses, and escaped. When they returned to Bo'orcu's encampment, Temüjin offered some of his horses in thanks.

> Temüjin said, 'My friend, without you, how could I have recovered these horses? Let us divide them and you must tell me how many you will take.' But Bo'orchu said, 'I thought of you as a good friend when you (first) arrived exhausted, and I thought I could be of help to a good friend. I accompanied you (so) how can I think of taking this windfall? My father Naqu-bayyan is well known and I am Naqu-bayyan's only son. The (things) my father has obtained are more than enough for me. I will not take, (otherwise) the help I have given, what sort of help will it be? I will not take (them).'[15]

Bo'orcu became a lifelong friend and a member of Temüjin's household.

This episode provides a paradigm of what Temüjin understood by loyalty. Indeed, that may be precisely why such stories figure so prominently in the *Secret History*. Clan loyalties counted for so little in a period of anarchy, that politics turned largely on the capacity of potential leaders to attract personal retinues of loyal followers or *nöker*. In the Communist period, the word, *nöker*, was used to translate the Communist form of address, 'Comrade'. Like the *druzhinniki* of Rus', the *nöker* of a great leader were followers whose loyalty depended on friendship, fealty and contract rather than kinship. As a Soviet historian puts it: in an era of great confusion, 'the winner in the steppes was going to be, not the khan with the largest tribe, but the one with the largest and most loyal [retinue of] *nöker*.'[16]

Temüjin took the first step towards the recovery of his hereditary rights of leadership in *c*.1182, when he accepted the patronage of To'oril Khan, the leader of the Kerait tribes, and the former *anda*, or sworn brother of Temüjin's father. Of the relationship of *anda*, the *Secret History* reports: 'In earlier days, in the words of old men, it was said that, "Men who are sworn brothers (share) one life. They do not abandon each other but become protectors of that life."'[17] In 1182, Temüjin was probably about 16 years old, and already, by steppe tradition, an adult. Before his death, Yesugei had betrothed Temüjin to Börte, from the Onggirat tribe, and Temüjin had received as a dowry a black sable coat. He offered this, together with the services of his own tiny band of followers, to To'oril Khan. The gift, and To'oril's old ties to Yesugei, bound him to help Temüjin. Temüjin gained another influential friend in his own *anda*, Jamuqa. Temüjin and Jamuqa had sworn brotherhood as children, drinking gold dust together, and swapping blood and gifts. Since then, Jamuqa had acquired a substantial following.

Apart from these powerful friends, Temüjin's following consisted of no more than his immediate family of about ten people, including Bo'orcu, and Temüjin's servant, Jelme. In *c*.1183, Temüjin's new wife, Börte, was kidnapped by men of the Merkit tribe, in belated retaliation for the fact that Temüjin's father had kidnapped his wife, Ho'elun, from the Merkit. To'oril Khan, with 20,000 men, agreed to help Temüjin recover his wife, if Jamuqa agreed to help with his own 20,000 men. Jamuqa had reasons of his own for attacking the Merkits, as, according to Rashid al-Din, they had once held him captive. With his new allies, Temüjin attacked the Merkit and rescued Börte.[18]

This conflict was probably Temüjin's first experience of tribal warfare on a larger scale. It shows the great importance of honour and revenge in steppe warfare, for its aim was the recovery of Temüjin's wife, and it ended when that aim was achieved. It also shows the genocidal brutality of such conflicts in this period of anarchy. The victors destroyed the Merkit gers, killed many of the Merkit men, and enslaved their women and children. Finally, victory in such conflicts granted high prestige. This is illustrated by a curious episode that occurred just after the raid on the Merkit. In the Merkit camp, Temüjin's forces found Qo'aqchin, who was probably the mother of his half brother, Belgütei. When her son arrived with the victorious army she was ashamed, saying: 'I've been told that my sons have become qans and here am I, matched with a common man. How can I look into the faces of my sons now?'[19]

Victory, achieved with the support of powerful tribal leaders such as To'oril and Jamuqa, had transformed Temüjin's status. Temüjin himself recognized the debt he owed: 'After having gained the friendship of you both, Qan, my father, and Jamuqa, (my) sworn brother, my power has been increased by Heaven and Earth.'[20] Temüjin was now a chief, too, though the junior of To'oril Khan and probably even of Jamuqa.

For one and a half years, Temüjin and Jamuqa travelled together, with their followers, and Temüjin got used to his new chiefly status. This period ended with a strange episode that hints at an emerging rivalry between the two friends. One day, Jamuqa asked Temüjin whether they should camp at a site suitable for the horse-herders or the sheep-herders. Though puzzled, Temüjin chose to interpret the question as an implied slight, a suggestion, perhaps, that Jamuqa's status, like that of the horse-herder, was higher than that of Temüjin. Encouraged by his wife, Temüjin led his people away. As he travelled, he was joined by some of Jamuqa's people, a sign that he was acquiring a substantial reputation as a strong and generous leader. The Secret History attributes their desertion of Jamuqa to prophetic dreams.[21]

Towards the end of the decade, the leaders of the various clans that followed him, some probably senior in rank to him, agreed to elect him as khan.[22] The oath sworn to him by the chiefs who elected him shows clearly the relationship between booty and political leadership in the steppes. The chiefs promised to obey him in peace and war, and to give Temüjin all war booty, human, animal and material.

When you are made qan, we,
Galloping as a vanguard after many enemies,
Will bring in

> Girls and *qatun*s (i.e. ladies) of good complexion,
> Palace tents,
> Foreigners' *qatun*s and girls with beautiful cheeks,
> Geldings with fine rumps at a trot,
> And give them to you.[23]

As khan, Temüjin began to create around himself a large *keshig*, or house-hold. Eventually, this spawned the rudimentary bureaucracy of an embryonic pastoralist state. Temüjin built his *keshig* from a core of childhood followers and friends, appointing guards, military commanders (including Jelme's younger brother, the future general, Sübetei), cooks, builders of yurts and carts, and equerries. His cook promised him that

> (With) a two-year old wether [a castrated ram],
> I cook soup (and so)
> In the morning (you) will not lack,
> At night (you) will not be late.

The keeper of his carts promised that:

> I shall not let the suspension-strutted cart's
> Linchpin drop out.
> I shall not let the axled carts
> Fall to pieces on the broad road (highway).

His guards he instructed to 'Slice off the necks of the strong' and 'Empty the breasts of the arrogant!'[24] Finally, he appointed his oldest comrades, Bo'orcu and Jelme, as his senior commanders.

> When, apart from my shadow I had no friends,
> You became my shadows.
> You eased my mind,
> And in my mind you shall stay![25]

By now, Temüjin was one of the most powerful chiefs amongst the various Mongol tribes, with a following of about 30,000 warriors. Jamuqa may have been more powerful, but Temüjin's rising power made a showdown between the two former friends inevitable. In 1187 (Onon gives 1190), a fight between followers of Jamuqa and Temüjin led to a battle at Dalan-Baljut. According to the *Secret History*, each army numbered about 30,000 men. Temüjin was defeated and fled, and Jamuqa took a terrible revenge on those he suspected of treachery, boiling them alive in seventy cauldrons. The barbarity of this decision may explain why, despite his victory, many of Jamuqa's followers immediately went over to the defeated Temüjin.[26] There is a hint, in this episode, that Jamuqa was more inclined to take power for granted than Temüjin, who had more experience of destitution, and understood better the need to cultivate the loyalty of his followers.

TEMÜJIN BECOMES OVERALL LEADER OF THE MONGOLS: 1190–1206

In the early 1190s, we lose sight of Temüjin. It is possible that he spent some years in China, for he reappears in 1196 as an ally of the Chin dynasty in its wars against the Tatars. Meanwhile, Temüjin's ally, To'oril, had been forced into exile, and was returned to power with Temüjin's help. After Temüjin defeated the Tatars, the Chin granted both Temüjin and To'oril new titles, making To'oril the 'Ong Khan', or 'Overall Khan'. The Mongols and Keraits now replaced the Tatars as the most powerful tribes in the Mongolian steppes.

During this period, Temüjin also had to suppress a minor rebellion of members of the Jürkin clan, which was closely related to his own family. Temüjin executed the rebel leaders, despite a tradition that condemned the execution of members of one's own clan. Temüjin executed them by suffocation, to avoid dishonouring them by shedding their blood, and gave new positions to their now leaderless people. Some joined his bodyguard, becoming, in effect, hostages for the good behaviour of their relatives.[27] The methods used in quelling this rebellion were to prove typical of the ways Temüjin incorporated former enemy peoples into his growing army.

During the next few years, Temüjin, Jamuqa and To'oril fought a complex three-way war, whose chronology remains obscure. To'oril and Jamuqa were determined to check Temüjin's rising power, but neither acted decisively enough when they had the chance. In 1201, a motley coalition of clans from various tribes, including Mongols, Naiman, Merkit, Oirat, and even Temüjin's clan, the Tayichi'ud, chose Jamuqa as their 'Gür Khan', and agreed to attack Temüjin and the 'Ong Khan', To'oril. Once again, Jamuqa proved a less astute political and military organizer than Temüjin. Conflicts broke out amongst Jamuqa's allies, and as his armies fragmented, Temüjin attacked his old enemies, the Tayyichi'ut, and killed their leaders, 'the people of Tayyichi'ut bones... from their seed to their seed..., making them blow (in the wind) like ashes.'[28] Their followers he absorbed amongst his own following. A year later, after defeating the Tatars once again, Temüjin and his advisers took an equally decisive revenge on these former enemies as well, by executing all adult males, and distributing the rest as slaves.[29] Temüjin had destroyed the two main enemies of his childhood years, the Tayyichi'ut, and the far mightier Tatars.

The alliance between To'oril and Temüjin now broke up. Plans to marry Temüjin's eldest son, Jochi, to To'oril's daughter, aroused the jealousy of To'oril's son, Senggum, who persuaded his reluctant father to join forces with Jamuqa. In 1202, Temüjin was forced east to the borders of Manchuria, in a Mongolian equivalent of Mao tse Tung's Long March of 1934–5. So many of his followers deserted that, when they arrived at Lake Baljuna, only 4600 loyal troops remained. Here, according to Rashid al-Din, his followers took an oath of loyalty that was remembered many years later as a turning point in Mongolian history. Fortunately for Temüjin, the outcome of the Mongolian civil war now affected many powerful interests, not just within

Mongolia, but also in China and along the eastern ends of the Silk Roads. Temüjin probably found support not just from the Chin, but also amongst other groups, including Muslim merchants.[30]

Once again, Jamuqa proved unable to hold together a powerful alliance. Troops drifted away and the balance of power shifted back towards Temüjin. Eventually, Jamuqa fled west to the Naiman. In 1203, Temüjin defeated To'oril's armies, by attacking unexpectedly while they were feasting. To'oril himself was killed. A minor incident which was to prove very important was the granting of To'oril's younger niece, Sorqaqtani-beki, a Nestorian Christian, as wife to Temüjin's youngest son, Tolui. She proved an able politician, and it was partly through her skills that Tolui's line ended up dominating the empire after the death of Ogodei's son, Güyük, in 1248.[31] Her sons by Tolui were Mongke, Khubilai, Hulagu and Arik-Boke.

After defeating the Kerait, Temüjin became the most powerful leader in Mongolia. In 1204, he attacked the Naiman who had sheltered Jamuqa. His attack, in the foothills of the Altai mountains, succeeded partly because the Naiman leader, Tayang Khan, was old and indecisive, while his Naiman armies were ill-disciplined, and partly because Jamuqa and his Mongolian troops deserted the Naiman at the crucial moment.[32] Jamuqa fled north-west to Tuva. In 1205, his servants handed him over to Temüjin. Temüjin executed the servants for betraying their master. According to the *Secret History*, Jamuqa requested an honourable execution, without drawing blood, and Temüjin agreed to his old friend's request. However, according to another tradition, recorded in Rashid, Temüjin handed Jamuqa over to his cousin, who executed him by dismemberment.[33]

However, the Naiman Khan's son, Küchlüg, escaped with many Naiman troops to the west. In 1208, Temüjin's forces defeated them and drove them beyond the Irtysh into the Semirechye, from where they entered the empire of the Karakitai in Sinkiang. Küchlüg became an adviser to the Gür Khan of the Karakitai. In 1211, he seized power himself, and in 1213 became the last Karakitai Gür Khan. As he was a Nestorian Christian, and fought against the Islamic Khorezmshah, it may be, as Gumilev has argued, that his career generated a new cycle of Prester John legends.[34]

The defeat of the Naiman in 1204 left Temüjin with only a few loose ends to tie up. He crushed his ancient enemies, the Merkit, and dispersed the few survivors amongst his army, while the rest joined the Kipchak in the Kazakh steppes. In 1207, an expedition under Jochi secured the submission of many of the forest peoples of Southern Siberia, including the Oirat tribes later known as the Buriat.[35] In 1209, he received the submission of the Uighur court at Kao-ch'ang, near modern Turfan. The Uighur renounced their loyalty to the Karakitai, and were traditional enemies of the Hsia-hsia, so that this was a valuable diplomatic coup. The Karluk tribes also voluntarily accepted Mongol suzerainty. The Uighurs and Karluks were the first peoples outside the Mongolian sphere to submit to Temüjin, and their submission gave his empire security along its south-western borders. Effortlessly, the Mongols had secured control of the great trade routes that their Hsiung-nu predecessors had fought over for centuries.[36]

In 1206, at a great *kuriltai*, or assembly of steppe tribes, Temüjin was proclaimed the 'Universal Leader', or 'Chinggis Khan'. Onon argues that 'Chinggis Khan' was a new title created for Temüjin because the alternative, 'Gür Khan', had been held by Jamuqa. In Shamanist traditions, the Tengri were the spirits that ruled the Heavens, while the 'Chinggis' were those that ruled the land and the world below. His title made him, symbolically, the earthly counterpart of the Heavens. The blessing of Heaven was to become a central feature of Chinggissid symbolism.[37]

THE CREATION OF A NEW SOCIAL ORDER

As Chinggis Khan's career demonstrates, the most important single skill for an ambitious steppe leader was the ability to form and hold the allegiance of powerful followers, whether through generosity or terror. A leader who could do this could even survive the occasional military defeat. However, his career also showed that loyalty had to be based on ties more binding than those of kinship alone. Like Motun, Chinggis Khan largely bypassed the traditional ties of kinship and lineage, replacing them with new ties based on symbolic forms of kinship, on fealty and gift-exchange, and sometimes on bureaucratic ties of office and discipline.[38]

Chinggis Khan so distrusted ties of kinship that, over the years, he executed or threatened with execution about 12 of his closest male relatives. He preferred to rely on the support of loyal followers, bound to him through mutual benefit, service and sworn loyalty. The traditional relationships of this kind were those of *anda*, or blood-brothers, and those of *nöker*, or sworn followers. For Chinggis, the relationship of *nöker* was perhaps the most important of all, for he frequently executed the *nöker* of enemies who failed to serve their own leaders faithfully, while rewarding those who had fought loyally for their leaders even against him. However, there were other relationships of a similar kind, including relationships often interpreted as forms of domestic slavery but best thought of as relations of 'retainership' or 'vassalage'.[39]

Other forms of loyalty depended on mutual advantage or bureaucratic discipline. Like most successful military commanders, Chinggis Khan attracted the loyalty of ordinary soldiers by taking an interest in their welfare. He forbade officers to treat their soldiers badly, and insisted on them eating the same food as their soldiers. Both he and his son Ogodei made special efforts to raise funds and supplies for tribes in difficulties. Chinggis Khan certainly believed that his own life was little removed from that of his soldiers. Towards the end of his life, he wrote to the Taoist monk Ch'ang Ch'un: 'I am from the barbaric North...I wear the same clothing and eat the same food as the cowherds and horse-herders. We make the same sacrifices and we share our riches. I look upon the nation as a new-born child and I care for my soldiers as if they were my brothers.'[40]

Chinggis Khan, like all great steppe rulers, depended on the ability to distribute valued goods to powerful followers. This was one of the driving forces of Mongol expansion, for victories over agrarian lands generated huge flows of wealth which were used to enhance the wealth, prestige and power of the new Mongolian ruling elite. The scale of this redistributive process in the period after Chinggis Khan's death, can be gauged by John of Plano Carpini's remark that at the coronation of Güyük in 1246: 'there up on a hill a good distance away from the tents were stationed more than five hundred carts, which were all filled with gold and silver and silken garments, and these things were shared out among the Emperor and the chiefs. Each chief divided his share among his men, but according to his own good pleasure.'[41]

While generous to loyal followers, Chinggis Khan was pitiless to those who betrayed him. In 1217, he sent his best general, Sübetei, northwards to exterminate the remaining Merkit, in a final act of revenge for their attacks on him during his childhood. As Ratchnevsky points out, amongst the Mongols as in most tribal communities, revenge was regarded as a duty, not just a cruel pleasure. 'The idea of vengeance was the basis for the nomads' sense of justice; the duty to avenge was handed down from generation to generation.[42]

To consolidate these structures of loyalty, Chinggis Khan began, even before the *kuriltai* of 1206, to construct a rudimentary bureaucracy. While preparing for the final battle with Jamuqa, Chinggis Khan reorganized his own retinue, creating a strict decimal system, and a personal bodyguard. His *keshig*, or bodyguard, became the heart of the Mongolian governmental system. The *keshig* consisted mainly of sworn personal followers. At first, it included 70 day guards and 80 night guards, but by 1206 it included 10,000 men, or an entire *tumen*. Members of the imperial guard were mainly recruited from junior lines of other tribes (which made them, in effect, hostages). Members of the *keshig* outranked all normal army officers. The *keshig* also ran the royal court, so that it became 'the centre of the *ulus* – the "state on horseback" or nomadic empire – since it served to guard the person of the khan, to serve his royal yurts (*orda*), to aid in the formulation of policy, and to carry out any assigned course of action decided upon by the *kuriltai* or the khan.'[43] The role of the *keshig* survived under Chinggis Khan's sons and grandsons. Under Mongke:

> The imperial administration was...essentially an extension of the prince's household establishment in terms of organization, function, and personnel. It is for this reason that the Mongol Empire in general, and Mongke's reign in particular, have a pronounced patrimonial flavor.[44]

Within Chinggis Khan's army, the 95 commanders of 'thousands', the major military formations, included almost no close relatives of Chinggis Khan.[45] Most commanders were retainers, promoted for outstanding acts of loyalty or long service. These included childhood friends such as Bo'orchu, as well as the shepherds, Badai and Kishlik, who had saved Chinggis Khan's life in his wars with the Kerait.

Below the very highest level, Chinggis reorganized and reformed the Mongol army and Mongol society as a whole. Formally, the military system was based, like that of the Hsiung-nu, on units of ten, 100, 1000 and finally, the largest fighting unit of all, the *tumen*, of 10,000 soldiers. The decimal system was not new on the steppes. But Chinggis Khan implemented it more systematically than his predecessors, and in doing so completely reorganized the Mongolian ruling elite. Having destroyed much of the old steppe aristocracy, he used the decimal system to structure a new ruling elite, many of whose members lacked the traditional ties of lineage. Some tribes retained their traditional identities, surviving as separate 'thousands'. However, enemy tribes were scattered and distributed amongst different decimal units, within which old tribal loyalties counted for nothing. As Morgan puts it: Chingiz seems to have created what might be described as an artificial tribal system, in which old tribal loyalties were superseded by loyalty to the individual soldier's new military unit. Beyond that the Mongol royal house became the ultimate focus of obedience and allegiance.[46]

The leaders of the 'thousands' were Chinggis Khan's closest associates. They played the role that traditional chiefs might have played in a more traditional empire. The power of the 95 commanders that he appointed in 1206, and of the far fewer commanders of *tumen* (10,000s), supplanted that of traditional chiefs, as it was made illegal for soldiers or their families to leave the units to which they had been assigned. However, as the 'thousands' and *tumen* replaced traditional tribes, they also began to assume many of the functions and structures of tribes. The division of the army that took place after the 1206 *kuriltai* was really a reallocation of people. Chinggis Khan allotted particular pasture lands to each unit, and the new units soon created their own tribal loyalties and began to function as tribes. Often, the real size of decimal units was as variable as that of the tribes they replaced. The actual strength of *tumen*s was almost always less than 10,000, often less than 5000, and sometimes less than 1000. As a rule of thumb, the numbers of troops recorded in written sources can often be halved in order to estimate real numbers of troops. Rashid al-Din claimed that the Mongol army in 1227 probably included about 130,000 men. This is probably realistic, while estimates of numbers as large as 800,000 or more soldiers are gross exaggerations.[47]

Though in peace time the decimal system gradually reverted to a new form of tribalism, in war it provided a powerful way of enforcing military discipline. John of Plano Carpini described how the system worked when he visited Mongolia in the 1640s.

> When they are in battle, if one or two or three or even more out of a group of ten run away, all are put to death; and if a whole group of ten flees, the rest of the group of a hundred are all put to death, if they do not flee too. In a word, unless they retreat in a body, all who take flight are put to death. Likewise if one or two or more go forward boldly to the fight, then the rest of the ten are put to death if they do not follow and, if one or more of the ten are captured, their companions are put to death if they do not rescue them.[48]

The bureaucratization of warfare was influential in other areas as well. Mongol staff work and preparation for campaigns was meticulous. So was their intelligence, based on careful spying out of enemy strengths and weaknesses. As Allsen argues, what distinguished the Mongol armies was their capacity to coordinate large-scale manoeuvres, using couriers and special signal arrows, rather than relying simply on the bravery and skills of individual leaders.[49] These skills, logistical rather than military, were inculcated in the huge military exercises based on annual hunts. According to Juvaini Chinggis Khan

> paid great attention to the chase and used to say that the hunting of wild beasts was a proper occupation for the commanders of armies; and that instruction and training therein was incumbent on warriors and men-at-arms, [who should learn] how the huntsmen come up with the quarry, how they hunt it, in what manner they array themselves and after what fashion they surround it according as the party is great or small. For when the Mongols wish to go a-hunting, they first send out scouts to ascertain what kinds of game are available and whether it is scarce or abundant.[50]

In its equipment, tactics and strategies, the Mongol army was similar to earlier steppe armies. It, too, depended on the fact that pastoral lifeways provided a natural training for cavalry warfare, that all pastoralist men knew how to ride, to hunt, to use a compound bow with skill and accuracy, and all were toughened by the hard life of the steppe. These ordinary soldiers provided the bulk of the army. They were usually lightly armed and relied mainly on the bow. However, there also existed a core of more heavily armed cavalry, probably recruited from wealthier families who could afford better horses, armour and equipment, and who could mount direct cavalry charges.[51] Mongol commanders were skilful, and willing to improvise and to learn new techniques from foreign advisers. This was particularly true of siege tactics, which dominated warfare in the sedentary world, but had little place in steppe warfare. But the key to the success of the Mongol armies lay in structures of discipline, organization, and coordination that owed little to traditions of kinship.

Of course, ties of kinship did not vanish entirely in peace time or war, for kinship was the basic structuring principle of pastoralist society. Indeed, traditions of kinship survived alongside and within the new structures. Many of Chinggis Khan's own family, and many of their subordinates, ended up acquiring semi-hereditary power over regions, so that within a few generations, traditional forms of chieftainship re-appeared. Still, for several decades, as long as the central leadership had the energy and skill to make them work, the new social principles gave to Mongol society an extraordinary degree of unity and discipline.

Chinggis Khan also tried to create a formal system of written laws. Amongst those captured after the defeat of the Naiman in 1204, there was a literate official, Tata-tonga, who kept the official seals of the Naiman khan. The Naiman already had a script, based on that of the Uighur (itself derived from Sogdian and, ultimately, from Aramaic). It was probably Tata-tonga who persuaded Chinggis Khan to introduce the same script for the writing of Mongolian. He also convinced Chinggis Khan of the need for a more formal promulgation of laws, and the importance of written laws and seals. In 1206, Chinggis Khan made his adopted son, the Tatar orphan, Shigi-khutugu, a sort of keeper of the laws. He required Shigi-khutugu to list the lands and peoples allocated to various leaders, and to record legal decisions in a 'Blue Book'. The laws recorded in this way became the basis of the law code later known as the *Yasa*. The Blue Book itself has not survived, but it is possible to reconstruct many of its elements.[52]

CONQUERING SEDENTARY LANDS: 1206–27

After the *kuriltai* of 1206, Chinggis Khan began to launch military expeditions beyond the steppelands of Mongolia. Eventually, the wealth of the sedentary lands he conquered in China and Central Asia enabled him to transform a steppe empire into a world power.

What were his aims? Some have argued that China was always his main target.[53] Owen Lattimore argued that Chinggis Khan had a complex plan to conquer China while simultaneously keeping control of the steppes. However, as Morgan has pointed out, though this describes what happened, there is no evidence that this was *intended* to happen. Others have attributed to Chinggis Khan a systematic plan of world conquest. Certainly, this is how he understood his career towards the end of his life when he exhorted his descendants to: 'conquer the whole world and . . . live in peace with no people which has not freely submitted to them.'[54] However, there is no evidence that he had such plans when he first launched his great campaigns of conquest. In any case, as Thomas Barfield has argued, the Mongols, like most steppe leaders, were more interested in booty than in direct conquest. However, he argues, the attempt to extort tributes from China failed because the 'Chin' rulers refused to pay, which forced the Mongols to engage in a war of conquest.

> The Mongols' immense scale of killing in north China, their initial refusal to accept responsibility for government, and their frequent withdrawals from conquered cities and regions all point to an older pattern of nomadic warfare. The conquest of China was not a primary goal of the Mongols, but, ironically, simply a consequence of their having completely destroyed the Jurchen Chin regime which they had planned to extort.[55]

There is no need to posit a grand plan. Chinggis Khan's path to power generated its own momentum. His following was organized for war and sustained by the redistribution of war booty. Success expanded the size of his armies, as they incorporated defeated enemies. However, new armies had to be put to use and new followers had to be rewarded. As Morgan argues, if Chinggis Khan had not directed the energies of his armies outwards, they would have reverted, once again, to the steppe warfare that had devastated Mongolia for decades. War also justified new wars, for each created new

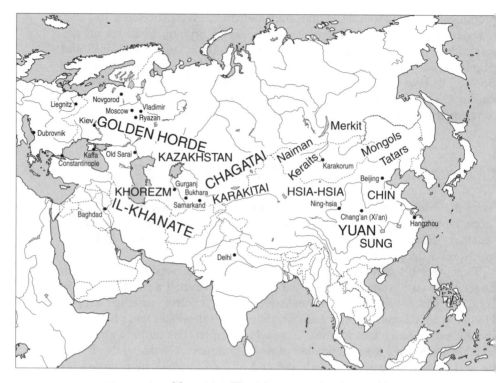

Map 15.1 The Mongol empire.

enemies and new threats.[56] Chinggis Khan had to take revenge on those who had betrayed him; and crush those who threatened his power or insulted his honour.

The same expansionist momentum persisted long after Chinggis's death. Even in the 1250s, 'Mongke's expansionist policy served as a rallying point for all of the Mongol leadership. Whatever their particular political and social orientation, or their personal attitude toward the accession of Mongke, they all were agreed upon one essential point: the principal and proper business of the Yeke Mongghol Ulus was conquest.'[57] This momentum allowed Chinggis and his successors to build a Eurasia-wide empire from a Mongolian base of probably no more than 700,000 people, whose resources consisted of little more than their herds of livestock.[58]

Each particular war of conquest also had its own, particular, logic. The first major attacks on the sedentary world, launched in 1209, were directed at the Hsia-hsia dynasty of north-west China. The Hsia-hsia empire was created in 1028 when Tibetan Tanguts destroyed the Uighur kingdom of Kan-chou.[59] To Chinggis Khan, it offered the nearest and weakest target amongst Mongolia's sedentary neighbours. It also controlled the wealthy Kansu oases, the key to the eastern end of the Silk Roads. Earlier attacks on Hsia-hsia in 1205 and 1207 were pure booty raids, and Mongol armies made no effort to take fortified cities. In 1209, Mongolian armies launched a more erious attack. Chinggis Khan led the campaign in person. However, the campaign showed the difficulties Mongol armies would face once they left the steppes. In particular, it showed how ill-equipped they were for siege warfare. Attempts to flood the Tangut capital, Zhongxing (modern Yinchuan), backfired, and flooded the Mongol camp instead. Despite this, the Tangut leader capitulated in 1210, and agreed to send large tributes of camels, woollen cloth, falcons and other goods. But he refused to send troops to join the Mongol army, on the grounds that his people were 'town-dwellers', and would not be able to endure the long marches of the Mongol army.[60] Chinggis Khan never forgave the Hsia-hsia for this refusal, and eventually exacted a terrible revenge.

North China offered a wealthier but more dangerous target. In invading it, Chinggis Khan was driven partly by bitter memories of past humiliations at the hands of the Chin. Besides, the Manchurian Chin dynasty was vulnerable, for it had many enemies amongst the Chinese and amongst non-Chinese groups such as the Kitan. Finally, north China was, as it had always been, the wealthiest and most promising source of tributes for an ambitious pastoralist leader. Refugees from China offered Chinggis Khan useful advice and encouraged him to attack. Mongolian armies attacked in 1211, and in 1215, they took the Chin capital of Zhongdu, near modern Beijing. They looted it for an entire month. After these initial victories, the Chin agreed, reluctantly, to pay tributes. The Chin leader gave a daughter in marriage to Chinggis, as well as horses, gold, and silk. The Mongol troops 'lading [their beasts with] satin and goods as many as they could carry, tied their burdens with silk and went away.'[61] However, the Chin paid their tributes reluctantly, and the Mongol armies returned to demand more. No stable peace was achieved, and gradually the campaigns turned into a war of siege and conquest.

In 1218, Chinggis turned west. His first western campaign was directed at an old enemy, the Naiman leader, Küchlüg, who now ruled the Karakitai empire. A force under Jebe defeated Küchlüg's armies near Kashgar, and killed Küchlüg. The local Muslim population received the Mongols as liberators, as Küchlüg had begun to persecute Islam.

Next year, the Mongols launched a campaign into Central Asia. There are many signs that Chinggis had not planned such a campaign, but preferred to establish a peaceful relationship with the Khorezmshah, Muhammad, in the hope of benefiting from an increase in trade between east and west. In 1218, there was an indecisive encounter between the armies of Jochi and the Khorezmshah, which did not lead to war. According to Rashid al-Din, Chinggis Khan wrote:

> Now that the frontier lands between us have been purged of the enemy and completely conquered and subjugated and neighbourly relations established between us, reason and magnanimity demand that we move along the road of peaceful accord. We should undertake to assist and support each other in times of need and to ensure the security of the caravan routes from disastrous incidents in order that merchants, on whose flourishing trade the welfare of the world depends, may move freely hither and thither.[62]

It is not clear how sincere these sentiments were. However, a series of diplomatic blunders on the part of the Khorezmshah and his officials ensured that the conflict, which might have occurred anyway, began sooner than necessary, and under conditions that favoured the Mongols. In 1219, Inal, the governor of the great trading city of Otrar, executed all the merchants and officials of a large mission sent by Chinggis Khan and seized their goods. Inal claimed (probably correctly) that many members of the mission were spies. Chinggis Khan sent a second embassy which demanded that Inal be punished and the trade goods be returned, along with an official apology. The Khorezmshah refused, in part because the governor was a nephew of his mother and a kinsman of many of his officials. Instead, he sanctioned what Inal had done, and executed all members of the second embassy. War was now inevitable.[63]

The Mongols held a special *kuriltai* before leaving on this, the most remote of their campaigns so far. At the *kuriltai*, Chinggis Khan declared Ogodei his heir. Apparently he saw Ogodei as a conciliator, and the person most likely to be able to resolve family disputes. Rashid al-Din wrote of Ogodei: 'He was famous for his intelligence, ability, judgement, counsel, firmness, dignity, and justice; but he was pleasure loving and a wine-bibber, and Chingiz-Khan sometimes used to rebuke and admonish him on that account.'[64] Chinggis Khan then assembled a large army, with troops from many different nations, including Han Chinese, Uighurs and Karluk. They headed west, hacking a path through the ice and snow of the high passes of the Altai before descending into the plains surrounding the Uighur city of Beshbalik.[65]

Like the Jurchen in north China, the Khorezmshah lacked the support of his own subjects, so the Mongols encountered a weak and divided enemy. Besides, Chinggis was as skillful as ever in exploiting divisions amongst his opponents, and in uniting his own, heterogenous, forces. For example, he deliberately circulated rumours suggesting that the Kipchak troops of the Khorezmshah's mother were planning to join the Mongol armies.[66] Mistrust of his own forces, and fear of the invaders led the Khorezmshah to avoid pitched battles. This gave the Mongols the military initiative, and the campaign turned into a series of sieges.

In the summer of 1219, near the River Irtysh, Chinggis Khan launched the campaign with a vast hunt. These huge *battue* hunts, which were a regular custom, could last for up to three months. Thousands of soldiers surrounded their quarry in a huge, but slowly contracting ring, at the centre of which they eventually slaughtered all but a few 'wounded and emaciated stragglers' who were let free. As Juvaini concludes: 'war – with its killing, counting of the slain and sparing of the survivors – is after the same fashion, and indeed analogous in every detail, because all that is left in the neighbourhood of the battlefield are a few broken-down wretches.'[67] Such hunts provided meat for the army, and, like modern war games, they provided training in coordinated manoeuvres, and helped generate a sense of unity within Chinggis Khan's heterogenous army.

Otrar fell in February 1220 after a siege lasting five months in which most of its population died. After the capitulation of Bukhara in the same month, its people were placed in front of the army in subsequent attacks. Bukhara itself was plundered and burnt to the ground. Then the Mongol army, 'as endless as the happenings of Time', in Juvaini's phrase, turned on the Sultan's homeland of Khorezm.[68] In the capital, Urgench, whose population put up fierce resistance, the craftsmen, women and children were enslaved, and the males were executed in batches of 24 to each Mongolian soldier. In 1222, the Taoist master, Ch'ang Ch'un, passed through Bactra, which had suffered similar treatment, and the only sound he could hear was the barking of dogs. The cities of Khorasan, including Merv and Nishapur, were destroyed with equal thoroughness by an army under Chinggis Khan's son, Tolui. In Merv, everyone was killed apart from a small number taken as artisans and slaves; local recruits as well as Mongol soldiers each had to execute several hundred people.[69] Nishapur suffered the same fate. Some 20 years later, the papal envoy, John of Plano Carpini, wrote:

> All those [the Mongols] take prisoner in battle they put to death unless they happen to want to keep some as slaves. They divide those who are to be killed among the captains of a hundred to be executed by them with a battle-axe; they in their turn divide them among the captives, giving each slave to kill ten or more or less as the officers think fit.[70]

The terror inspired by the Mongol armies may itself have contributed to their victories. A contemporary Muslim writer, Ibn al-Athir, writes: 'I have heard that one of them took a man captive, but had not with him any weapon wherewith to kill him; and he said to his prisoner, "Lay your head on the ground and do not move"; and he did so, and the Tartar went and fetched his sword and slew him therewith.[71]

Cities that did not resist were generally spared. And the destruction was concentrated in regions through which the main armies passed. Nevertheless, many of the worst affected regions took a whole generation to recover. In 1221, the Taoist master, Ch'ang Ch'un, arrived in Samarkand to find that its former population of 100,000 had been reduced to a quarter of that number. In Mawara'n-nahr, the devastation led to a profound economic collapse. Until about 1250, coins were minted only in Samarkand and Bukhara, which suggests that monetary exchanges almost ceased. In Samarkand, in the early 1230s, confidence in the local coinage was so low that coins were produced with the extraordinary warning that those who refused to accept them would be regarded as criminals. Evidence of a revival of monetary circulation and commerce in general begins to appear only in the 1250s. When Juvaini and the Chinese traveller, Ch'ang Te, visited in c.1260, they described Samarkand and Bukhara once again as flourishing cities.[72]

After the fall of Samarkand, the Khorezmshah fled, followed by Mongol armies, until he died on a remote island in the Caspian in January 1221. Meanwhile, guerilla attacks led by his son, Jalal al-Din, kept the Mongol armies busy in Bactria. In Bamiyan, Chinggis Khan ordered not merely the slaughter of the entire human population, but also, because his son Chaghatai had been wounded in the seige, all its animals as well.[73] In 1223, worried by the situation in Mongolia, Chinggis Khan decided to return. He reached the Irtysh in 1224 and entered Mongolia the following year.

Meanwhile, an army under Sübetei, that had been pursuing the Khorezmshah, passed through western Khorasan and Armenia and headed north past Darband, following the route of Scythian armies almost 2000 years before them and capturing the major towns as they went. In 1223, they entered the steppes north of the Caucasus. The Kipchak were apparently more alert to the danger this posed than the princes of Rus', and their khaghan, Kotyan, the father-in-law of prince Mstislav of Galicia, proposed an alliance, threatening: 'Today the Tartars [Mongols] have seized our land; tomorrow they will take yours.' An alliance of Rus' princes agreed to join with the Kipchak, but the Mongols defeated them at the River Kalka in the South Russian steppes. (Ironically, it may be that Sübetei himself was from the Uriangqai tribes who were Kipchak.) The Novgorod Chronicle recorded that 'for our sins, unknown tribes came, whom no one exactly knows, who they are, nor whence they came out, nor what their language is, nor of what race they are, nor what their faith is; but they call them Tartars.' According to another chronicle account, the defeated princes of Rus', including prince Mstislav of Kiev, were 'crushed beneath platforms placed over their bodies, on the top of which the Tatars celebrated their victory banquet.[74]

These campaigns gave the Mongols a firm grip on Central Asia, which now became part of the Mongol empire, politically, fiscally and militarily. However, the Mongol invasion left surprisingly little trace on the region ethnically. The main reason for this is that the number of Mongols in the armies of Chinggis Khan was actually small, for the Mongol army grew by incorporating the armies of those it defeated.[75] Most of its soldiers, in the Central Asian campaigns were Turkic rather than Mongol. As a result, the effect of the Mongol conquest was to increase the importance of the Turkic elements in Central Asian society.

The last campaign launched under Chinggis Khan's own leadership in 1226, aimed at the final subjection of Hsia-hsia. It ended soon after Chinggis's death in 1227. The initial aim of the campaign was to punish a region that had refused to accept full subordination to the Mongol Empire, and to enforce the payment of tributes demanded in earlier treaties. When Chinggis Khan died in August 1227, his army mourned him by launching a bloodbath. They slaughtered the entire population of Zhongxing city. They also killed anyone who encountered the funeral procession of the dead leader. It has been suggested that this slaughter, appalling even by Mongol standards, was intended, in part, to provide the soul of the dead khan with an escort of defeated enemies. It remains unclear where Chinggis Khan's remains were buried; perhaps in the Ordos region, or perhaps in Mongolia. His coffin was interred along with the corpses of 40 virgins and many choice horses.[76]

The succession was remarkably orderly, for Chinggis Khan had taken some care over the matter. As he lay dying, he made his many sons agree in writing to the succession of Ogodei. In the spring of 1228, a magnificent *kuriltai* was held on the Kerulen, to which came all the leading descendants of Chinggis Khan from their different 'hordes', and all his regional officials from all parts of the empire.[77] Amongst much feasting and discussion, they confirmed Ogodei's succession, without any serious dissent, and the empire was passed on to him intact. The smoothness of the transition allowed the Mongol empire to outlive its founder, for any divisions at this stage would certainly have caused its rapid dissolution. Chinggis Khan himself understood the danger perfectly well. Juvaini reports of him a story that other sources attribute to his ancestors:

> One day, at the time of his first rising to power...he drew an arrow from his quiver and gave it to [his sons]. Clearly it required no great strength to break it. He made the number two and so continued till there were fourteen, and even athletes were unable to break them. 'So it is,' he said, 'with my sons also. So long as they tread the path of regard one for another they shall be secure from the evils of events and shall be free to enjoy the fruits of their kingdom.'[78]

Apocryphal or not, this story conveys perfectly the crucial role of alliance-building in the construction of pastoralist states.

NOTES

1 On the Hsia-hsia, see Ruth Dunnell, 'The fall of the Xia empire: Sino-steppe relations in the late 12th–early 13th centuries', in Seaman and Marks, eds, *Rulers from the Steppe*, pp. 158–85.
2 The empire also owed much to Türk traditions; and many important Mongol worlds, including *ordu, tümen, khan, khatun, darkhan* and *ulus* are Turkic; Phillips, *Mongols*, p. 24.
3 Gareth Jenkins, 'A note on climatic cycles', pp. 217–26.
4 Jagchid and Hyer, *Mongolia's Culture and Society*, p. 213.
5 Ratchnevsky, *Genghis Khan*, p. xiv.
6 That there were hereditary ranks in Mongolian society is clear from section 21 of the *Secret History*, which distinguishes between lords and commoners, white bone or black bone lineages; Jagchid and Hyer, *Mongolia's Culture and Society*, p. 283; the date of Temüjin's birth, like so much in his biography before c.1196, is uncertain, and estimates range from 1155–67; Onon, *History and Life of Chinggis Khan*, gives 1162; for the sake of consistency I have used dates from Ratchnevsky, *Genghis Khan*; the whole problem is discussed in ibid., pp. 17–19.
7 Onon, *History and Life of Chinggis Khan*, p. 14, fn. 53; *demirci* is modern Turkish for 'blacksmith', from *demir*, iron; William of Rubruck claimed he had been a blacksmith.
8 See Ratchnevsky, *Genghis Khan*, ch. 1.
9 Onon, *History and Life of Chinggis Khan*, pp. xviii–xix, and see p. xi on their early migrations; according to Jagchid and Hyer, *Mongolia's Culture and Society*, p. 6, the name 'Mongol' or 'Meng-wu' first appeared in the T'ang period; see also Golden, *Introduction*, p. 284.
10 Phillips, *Mongols*, p. 24.
11 Ratchnevsky, *Genghis Khan*, p. 14; Onon, *History and Life of Chinggis Khan*, p. 65, para. 150.

12 Cited in Ratchnevsky, *Genghis Khan*, p. 12; from *Secret History*, para. 254.
13 Onon, *History and Life of Chinggis Khan*, pp. 21–2, para. 77; and see pp. 19–20, paras. 74–5 on their life in this period.
14 Ibid., p. 27 para. 90; on his earlier escape, see ibid., pp. 24–6, paras. 82–7.
15 Ibid., p. 28, para. 92.
16 Pletneva, *Kochevniki*. p. 116.
17 Onon, *History and Life of Chinggis Khan*, p. 42, para. 117.
18 Ibid., pp. 34–9, paras. 104–10, see also p. 32, para. 102; and see Ratchnevsky, *Genghis Khan*, p. 36.
19 Onon, *History and Life of Chinggis Khan*, p. 40–1, para. 112.
20 Onon, *History and Life of Chinggis Khan*, p. 41, para. 113.
21 Ibid., p. 45, para. 121, and see p. 43, para. 118.
22 Chinggis Khan claimed later that he had been quite willing to serve under someone else as khan; Onon, *History and Life of Chinggis Khan*, p. 86, para. 179; on the institution of 'khans' amongst the nobles, Jagchid and Hyer, *Mongolia's Culture and Society*, pp. 335–8.
23 Onon, *History and Life of Chinggis Khan*, p. 46, para. 123.
24 Ibid., p. 47, para. 124.
25 Ibid., p. 48, para. 125.
26 Ibid., p. 51, paras. 129–30.
27 Ibid., pp. 54–5, para. 137.
28 Ibid., p. 63, para. 148.
29 Ibid., p. 68, para. 154.
30 Ratchnevsky, *Genghis Khan*, pp. 72–3.
31 On her role, see Rossabi, *Khubilai Khan*, pp. 11–13.
32 Onon, *History and Life of Chinggis Khan*, p. 98, para. 195.
33 Ratchnevsky, *Genghis Khan*, pp. 87–8.
34 Gumilev, *Poiski*, pp. 135–6 and passim.
35 Onon, *History and Life of Chinggis Khan*, p. 133, para. 239.
36 On the important role of the Uighurs within the Mongol empire, see Allsen, 'The Yüan dynasty and the Uighurs of Turfan'.
37 Allsen, 'Changing forms of legitimation in Mongol Iran', in Seaman and Marks, eds, *Rulers from the Steppe*, p. 223; see also Onon, *History and Life of Chinggis Khan*, p. xviii.
38 Kürsat-Ahlers argues that this is true of most early states; *Zur frühen Staatenbildung*, p. 110.
39 Barfield, *Perilous Frontier*, pp. 192–4; Jagchid and Hyer, *Mongolia's Culture and Society*, p. 285; Lattimore also insists on the importance Chinggis Khan attributed to his *nöker*; see 'Inner Asian frontiers: defensive empires and conquest empires', in Lattimore, *Studies in Frontier History* (pp. 501–13), p. 507.
40 Ratchnevsky, *Genghis Khan*, p. 149, and see p. 148.
41 Dawson, *Mission to Asia*, p. 63.
42 Ratchnevsky, *Genghis Khan*, p. 151.
43 Jagchid and Hyer, *Mongolia's Culture and Society*, p. 343, and see p. 342–7 on the history of the institution; see also Barfield, *Perilous Frontier*, p. 196; and Onon, *History and Life of Chinggis Khan*, p. 95, paras. 191–2.
44 Allsen, *Mongol Imperialism*, p. 100.
45 Barfield, *Perilous Frontier*.
46 Morgan, *Mongols*, pp. 89–90; see also Khazanov, *Nomads*, pp. 237–8; there are parallels to this reorganization of ruling elites in Muscovite history, in particular during the *oprichnina* of Ivan the Terrible.

47 Morgan, *Mongols*, pp. 87–8; and see Vernadsky, *Mongols and Russia*, p. 119; Allsen, *Mongol Imperialism*, p. 193.

48 Dawson, *Mission to Asia*, p. 33.

49 Allsen, *Mongol Imperialism*, p. 6; on Mongol staff work, Jagchid and Hyer, *Mongolia's Culture and Society*, pp. 370–2.

50 Juvaini, *History of the World-Conqueror*, 1:27.

51 V. P. Alekseev, 'Some Aspects of the Study of Productive Factors in the Empire of Chenghiz Khan', in Seaman and Marks, eds, *Rulers from the Steppe* (pp. 186–98), p. 192.

52 Jagchid and Hyer, *Mongolia's Culture and Society*, p. 355; and see Onon, *History and Life of Chinggis Khan*, p. 112, para. 203; Ratchnevsky, *Genghis Khan*, p. 94.

53 This is argued, for example, in Morgan, *Mongols*, p. 14.

54 Ratchnevsky, *Genghis Khan*, p. 140; on Lattimore's views, see Morgan, *Mongols*, 73, who cites Lattimore, 'The geography of Chingis Khan', *Geographical Journal*, (1963) 129/1:6–7.

55 Barfield, *Perilous Frontier*, p. 197.

56 Morgan, *Mongols*, p. 63; and see Kürsat-Ahlers *Zur frühen Staatenbildung*, p. 108 on the capacity of wars to generate new wars.

57 Allsen, *Mongol Imperialism*, p. 79.

58 On the population figure, see Allsen, *Mongol Imperialism*, p. 5.

59 Haussig, *Geschichte Zentralasiens… in vorislamischer Zeit*, p. 260; and see Dunnell, 'The Fall of the Xia Empire'.

60 Ratchnevsky, *Genghis Khan*, p. 105; Onon, *History and Life of Chinggis Khan*, pp. 143–4 (para. 249), and 151 (para. 256), which describes how they refused to send troops to Central Asia; but Dunnell, 'The fall of the Xia empire', pp. 170–1 suggests that this was in reality an attempt to buy off demands for soldiers.

61 Cited in Barfield, *Perilous Frontier*, p. 200, from the *Secret History*; and see Morgan, *Mongols*, p. 66.

62 Cited in Ratchnevsky, *Genghis Khan*, p. 121.

63 Buniyatov, *Gosudarstvo Khorezmshakhov*, pp. 135–6.

64 Rashid al-Din Tabib, *Successors of Genghis Khan*, p. 17.

65 According to Yeh-lu Ch'u'ts'ai, who travelled with the army; Bretschneider, *Medieval Researches*, I:13–15.

66 Ratchnevsky, *Genghis Khan*, pp. 129–30.

67 Juvaini, *History of the World-Conqueror*, 1:29; there is a description of the huge battue hunts in ibid., 1:27–8.

68 Ibid., 1:124.

69 Ibid., 1:161–3; the local levies sometimes showed more enthusiasm for the work than Mongol soldiers; on the fate of Urgench, ibid., 1:127; Ch'ang Ch'un cited from Bretschneider, *Medieval Researches*, 1:93.

70 Dawson, *Mission to Asia*, pp. 37–8.

71 Boyle, *Mongol World Empire*, I:5.

72 Allsen, *Mongol Imperialism*, p. 89; Bretschneider, *Medieval Researches*, 1:131, and citation from Ch'ang Ch'un in ibid., 1:78; Juvaini, *History of the World-Conqueror*, 1:96; Morgan, *Mongols* (pp. 73–83) argues that contemporary accounts, mainly from the sedentary lands, exaggerated the devastation caused by the Mongols, however, Davidovich, *Denezhnoe khozyaistvo Srednei Azii v XIII veke*, pp. 129–35 offers powerful evidence for a prolonged period of commercial decline, at least in Mawara'n-nahr.

73 According to Juvaini, *History of the World-Conqueror*, 1:132–3.

74 From the 'Battle on the River Kalka', in Zenkovsky, *Medieval Russian Epics*, p. 195; Novgorod Chronicle cited in Morgan, *Mongols*, p. 136; on Sübetei's origins, M. G. Kramarovsky, 'The culture of the Golden Horde and the problem of the "Mongol Legacy"', in Seaman and Marks, eds, *Rulers from the Steppe*, (pp. 255–73), p. 255; Kotyan's remarks cited from Vernadsky, *Kievan Russia*, p. 237; there is a detailed account of the battle of the River Kalka in ibid., pp. 237–8.

75 Allsen, *Mongol Imperialism*, pp. 189–90; and see the calculations in Alexseev, 'Some Aspects of the Study of Productive Forces in the Empire of Chenghiz Khan'.

76 Ratchnevsky, *Genghis Khan*, p. 144: according to Juvaini, Ogodei sacrificed the 'moon-faced' virgins after the 1229 *kuriltai*; Juvaini, *History of the World Conqueror*, I:189; on the slaughter in Zhongxing city, Dunnell, 'The Fall of the Xia empire', p. 179.

77 Juvaini, *History of the World Conqueror*, 1:183–4 Rashid al-Din gives 1229; on Chinggis Khan's dying wish, Juvaini, *History of the World Conqueror*, 1:182–3.

78 Ibid., 2:593–4.

FURTHER READING

The best introductory history of the Mongol empire is Morgan, *The Mongols*, while Moses and Halkovic, *Introduction to Mongolian History and Culture*, is exactly what its title says it is. The best recent biography of Chinggis Khan is Ratchnevsky, *Genghis Khan*. The most important primary source is the contemporary account known as the *Secret History of the Mongols*, which I have used in the translation by Onon, *The History and Life of Chinggis Khan*. Juvaini, *History of the World-Conqueror*, is written by a contemporary who travelled in Mongolia and Central Asia and met many of the great figures of his time; while Dawson, *Mission to Asia*, includes accounts written by European travellers to the Mongol empire; and Bretschneider, *Medieval Researches* includes some Chinese sources. Dunnell, 'The fall of the Xia empire', is on the Hsia-hsia (Tangut) state, while Allsen, 'The Yüan dynasty and the Uighurs' is on the Uighur states of the Turfan region. Jenkins, 'A note on climatic cycles', offers a climatic explanation for the rise of Chinggis Khan. Boyle, *The Mongol World Empire*, is a collection of essays. See also Jagchid and Hyer, *Mongolia's Culture and Society*; Barfield, *The Perilous Frontier*; Sinor, 'On Mongol Strategy'; Vernadsky, *Mongols and Russia*; Phillips, *The Mongols*; and some of the essays in Seaman and Marks, eds, *Rulers from the Steppe*. Grousset's *The Empire of the Steppes* is dated. The Soviet novelist, V. G. Yan, produced a popular fictional history in his trilogy: *Chingiz-Khan, Batyi*, and *K 'poslednemu moryu'*. On religion, see Khazanov, 'The spread of world religions'; Thomas and Humphrey, *Shamanism, History and the State*; Heissig, *Religions of Mongolia*.

[16] THE MONGOL EMPIRE AND A NEW 'WORLD-SYSTEM'

RENEWED EXPANSION: 1227–60

Between 1227 and 1260, Chinggis Khan's successors launched new campaigns that turned their empire into the greatest contiguous land empire ever known. The north Chinese campaigns, already begun under Chinggis Khan, ended in 1234 with the final defeat of the Jurchen dynasty.

In 1235, a great *kuriltai* decided to launch an expedition to the west to conquer the lands allocated to Chinggis Khan's eldest son, Jochi. In 1236, 13 years after their first expedition to the Pontic steppes in 1223, Mongol armies headed west again. After immensely careful preparations, an army led by Jochi's son, Batu, commanded once again by Chinggis Khan's greatest general, Sübetei, and including two future great khans, Güyük and Mongke, entered the lands west of the Urals. It defeated a huge Kipchak army, and drove its survivors west. The Hungarian king Bela IV received a request from the Kipchak khagan Kotyan to let 40,000 of his people settle in Hungary in return for accepting Christianity. He agreed, and the nomads settled along the River Tisza, where they proved almost as troublesome as the Visigothic refugees who had fled from the Huns almost 900 years earlier. Meanwhile, the Mongols destroyed the kingdom of the Volga Bulghars and sacked their capital, Bulghar.[1] Then they entered Rus' in the winter of 1237–8. Winter was the best time to advance into the forest lands for rivers were frozen and goods could be hauled by sled. Besides, the Mongols and their horses were used to fighting in the cold. The campaign was brutal because most of the cities of Rus' refused to surrender, unaware, perhaps, of the skills of Mongol siege engineers. It began with the siege of Ryazan' in December. According to the Voskresensk chronicle:

> That same winter the godless Tatars, with their tsar Batu, came from the east to the land of Riazan', by forest ... and ... sent their emissaries ... to the Princes of Riazan', asking from them one-tenth of everything: of princes, of people, of horses.... And the princes replied: 'When we are gone, then all will be yours.' ... The princes of Riazan' sent to Prince Iurii of Vladimir, asking him to send help or to come himself; but Prince Iurii did not come himself nor did he heed the entreaty of the princes of Riazan', but rather he wished to defend himself separately. ... Then the foreigners besieged the town of Riazan', on

December 16, and surrounded it with a palisade; the prince of Riazan' shut himself up in the town with his people. The Tatars took the town of Riazan' on the twenty-first of the same month, and burned it all, and killed its prince, Iurii, and his princess, and seized the men, women, and children, and monks, nuns, and priests; some they struck down with swords, while others they shot with arrows and flung into the flames; still others they seized bound.... They delivered many holy churches to the flames, and burned monasteries and villages, and seized property, and then went on to Kolomna.[2]

Next the Mongols took Moscow, and then Vladimir. In Vladimir, the nobles and bishops took refuge in the Church of the Holy Virgin, which the Mongols burned to the ground. Pursuing grand prince Yuri II of Vladimir, who had escaped to the north-west, they took Suzdal and Tver. Yuri was killed in a battle at the River Sit'. In March, the Mongol forces entered the principality of Novgorod. However, with the spring thaw beginning, and supplies of food and fodder running low, the army returned south before taking Novgorod itself. They retreated by a direct route, avoiding the lands they had devastated on their way north, and foraging from estates and villages on their way.

Batu's armies spent two years in the steppes between the Don and Volga rivers, campaigning in the Caucasus, the Pontic steppes and the Chernigov region. In the autumn of 1240 they moved west. They captured and sacked Pereyaslav and Chernigov and in December, they destroyed the capital, Kiev. When John of Plano Carpini travelled through Kiev in 1246, he reported that 'we came across countless skulls and bones of dead men lying about on the ground. Kiev had been a very large and thickly populated town, but now it has been reduced almost to nothing, for there are at the present time scarce two hundred houses there and the inhabitants are kept in complete slavery.'[3] Batu's armies now split. One army headed through Poland towards Germany, where it defeated an army of Poles and Teutonic knights at Liegnitz in April 1241. The second army, pursuing the defeated khan of the Kipchak, invaded Hungary, and crushed the armies of King Bela IV at Mohi. Kaghan Kotyan of the Kipchak was murdered by a Hungarian mob on suspicion of being a Mongol spy. A year later, refugees travelled through a wasted land whose roads were so overgrown with weeds and thorns, that they had to navigate by the steeples of the villages through which they passed.[4] After Batu's armies had reunited, they rode across the frozen Danube, and while Batu's contingent headed for Bulgaria, a substantial force headed into Croatia and Dalmatia in pursuit of King Bela. Early in 1242, Batu learned of Ogodei's death.

Immediately, Batu led his armies back east. His decision marked a critical turning point in the history of Europe, for there is no sign that any force in Europe could have put up serious resistance to the Mongol armies. So the reasons for Batu's retreat are of some importance. The obvious reason is dynastic. During the Rus' campaign, Batu had quarreled with Ogodei's son, Güyük, and this threatened a serious dynastic crisis as soon as Ogodei died. Batu realized he could have little influence over the succession in Karakorum if he remained in distant Hungary. And this is the reason normally given for his retreat. This argument implies that Europe escaped the fate of China only through the accident of Ogodei's death. However, there was also a good strategic and ecological reason for retreating. Though the Hungarian steppes were good grazing lands, they were simply not large enough to support the vast Mongolian armies through a European campaign that might have lasted several years.[5] Of course, the Mongols faced similar difficulties in north China, but here they could always retreat and regroup in their Mongolian homelands which were only a month or two away. Besides, the Jurchen dynasty had so many internal enemies that the Mongols found many allies in their campaigns against it. Europe was different. Here, the Mongolian armies were many thousands of miles from their homeland, in lands without adequate pastures, and with no European allies. Besides, Europe consisted of many regional states. Unlike China, there was no Emperor whose defeat would mark a definitive end to the campaign. As David Morgan points out, the fact that the Mongols launched no new invasions of Europe suggests that they understood the difficulties such a campaign would present.[6] This explanation of Batu's retreat implies that the failure of the Mongols to conquer Europe owed more to geography and ecology than to the accident of Ogodei's death.

Batu retreated to the Kipchak steppe. Here, what seemed at first a temporary camp turned into a permanent base, as Batu laid the foundations for what was to prove the most durable of all Mongol polities, the 'Golden Horde', or the 'Khanate of Kipchak', as it was known to the Mongols.

After the death of Ogodei, there were no major campaigns of conquest for some ten years, due in part to the absence of strong central leadership. This period of uncertain leadership showed how easily the Mongol empire could have collapsed. Ogodei's son, Güyük, was elected Khan at a *kuriltai* in 1246, which Batu did not attend. However, Güyük died two years later, probably on the eve of launching an attack on Batu. Batu, now the senior Chingissid, negotiated for the election of Tolui's son, Mongke, at an informal *kuriltai* held in the eastern Kazakh steppes. However, Güyük's heirs opposed the decision and even attempted a half-hearted, and unsuccessful rebellion which was crushed ruthlessly. Mongke was formally elected khan only in 1251.

He soon launched new campaigns of conquest, partly to strengthen his own position, and partly because such campaigns were themselves a major foundation of central power. The third and fourth great campaigns undertaken by Chinggis Khan's successors, took their armies beyond the borders of Inner Eurasia. In 1252, Mongke sent his brother, Hulagu, into Persia. Hulagu's first mission was to crush the Shi'ite Ismailis, known as the Assassins. His second task was to secure the submission of the Abbasid caliphate. He left Mongolia in 1253, incorporating new units into his army as he moved through Central Asia. In 1256 he began the attack on the Ismailis, destroying their remote and superbly defended castles in Persia one by one. In 1258 he entered the lands of the caliphate. After a long siege, his troops sacked Baghdad, killing perhaps 200,000 of its people, including the last Abbassid caliph. In 1260, his armies invaded Syria. Here, there was a repeat of the events of 1241. News of the death of Mongke, combined with increasing difficulty in feeding the vast Mongolian cavalry armies, forced Hulagu to move north-west with much of his army. Later that year, the mainly Kipchak remains of his armies, commanded by a Nestorian Christian, Kit Buka, were defeated at the battle of Ayn Jalut by the forces of the Mameluke Sultan, Qutuz, whose forces were also mainly Kipchak, but also included Khorezmian soldiers.[7] Hulagu's retreat, like that of Batu 20 years before, proved permanent. The Mongols never occupied Syria, but they did create a new regional empire, the so-called 'Il-Khanate', in Persia and Iraq.

Khubilai and Mongke together launched the campaign for southern China in 1252. Their armies first conquered the lands to the east of Sung territory, but despite some early successes in the 1250s, the conquest was completed only in 1279. The conquest of China, begun in 1211, had taken the Mongols almost 70 years.

SUPPORTING THE ARMY: ADMINISTRATIVE AND POLITICAL STRUCTURES

Chinggis Khan's successors proved as skillful as he was at creating durable structures of rule that allowed a sustained mobilization of the empire's resources. Though they employed many experts from the sedentary world, the later Mongol rulers kept a firm grip on the process of state-building.

THE ARMY

Creating and supplying the armies that undertook these huge campaigns was itself a colossal undertaking. To a certain extent, the army supported itself. Under the decimal system, commanders of 1000s and 10,000s, like traditional chiefs, had their own grazing lands, from which they were expected to supply and support the households and families of their soldiers. Thus, the Franciscan missionary, William of Rubruck, who visited the court of Khan Mongke in the 1250s, reported that:

> Each captain, according to whether he has more or fewer men under him, knows the limits of his pasturage and where to feed his flocks in winter, summer, spring and autumn, for in winter they come down to the warmer districts in the south, in summer they go up to the cooler ones in the north.[8]

While the army was on the move, special officials, *yurtchi*, were responsible for allocating each unit to a particular camp site and area of pasture. However, the Mongols also planned carefully in advance. Before Hulagu headed west in 1252, Mongke sent out special officials to clear all livestock from the pastures along which the armies would travel, from Karakorum west. Local officials were ordered to prepare provisions and *koumiss* for the armies that were to pass through their lands, to clear away obstructions such as boulders from the route, and to build bridges.[9]

Co-ordinating the movements of different detachments was extremely complex, for, in order to find sufficient pastures, different units had to spread over large areas. Planning and scheduling in advance was extremely efficient, so that Mongol armies often met after months of separation on dates sometimes set over a year in advance.[10] Pastoralist lifeways themselves instilled some of the skills of logistics and scheduling necessary for a large campaign, for all pastoralists had to be able to schedule their migrations with some precision. Large-scale *battue* hunts also helped different units to coordinate their manoeuvres. The main object of the huge annual hunts, or *nerge*, was to maintain a vast but contracting ring of troops from which game could not escape. Foreign armies were often treated in the same way.[11] According to John of Plano Carpini,

> If it happens that the enemy fight well, the Tartars make a way of escape for them; then as soon as they begin to take flight and are separated from each other they fall upon them and more are slaughtered in flight than could be killed in battle. However, it should be known that, if they can avoid it, the Tartars do not like to fight hand to hand but they wound and kill men and horses with their arrows; they only come to close quarters when men and horses have been weakened by arrows.[12]

Their treatment of enemies and captives was as merciless as their treatment of game. John of Plano Carpini reported that, when besieging a town,

> they speak enticing words to the inhabitants making them many promises to induce them to surrender into their hands. If they do surrender to them, they say: "Come out, so that we may count you according to our custom," and when they come out, then they seek out the artificers among them and keep these, but the others, with the exception of those they wish to have as slaves, they kill with the axe.[13]

The Mongol armies were so large that tribal levies could not supply enough troops, particularly during major campaigns. Even Chinggis Khan had to incorporate defeated armies into his own to supplement recruitment from tribal levies. Ogodei established a more organized system of recruitment. He recruited from pastoralist societies (where recruitment was easy and almost total), and from sedentary societies (where it was more complex and could only be partial). Naturally, the Mongol armies themselves divided into pastoral nomadic cavalry and agriculture-based infantry. We know most about recruitment methods in Rus'. Here, regular recruitment probably did not begin until the completion of a census in the 1250s. After this, a pseudo-decimal system was introduced, with the creation of officials such as *temniki* (leaders of 10,000), or *sotskie* (leaders of one hundred).

Equipping these vast armies was also difficult. Most pastoralists brought their own weaponry with them. When John of Plano Carpini visited in the 1240s, Mongol soldiers had the following equipment:

> two or three bows, or at least one good one, three large quivers full of arrows, and axe and ropes for hauling engines of war. As for the wealthy, they have swords pointed at the end but sharp only on one side and somewhat curved, and they have a horse with armour; their legs also are covered and they have helmets and cuirasses. Some have cuirasses, and protection for their horses.[14]

Some had lances with hooks which they used to drag opponents from the saddle. Soldiers carried files for sharpening the edges of their arrows. The Mongol bow was composite, with an effective range of up to 300 yards, and required a pull of about 166 pounds. Recruits were told exactly what to bring with them to a campaign, down to 'banners, needles, ropes, mounts and pack animals', and if they missed anything at the regular equipment reviews, they were punished.[15]

MOBILIZING RESOURCES: TAXATION

Supplying these armies required a huge mobilizational effort. In the numbers involved and the distances covered, no armies before Napoleon's would match them again.[16] The most astonishing thing is that the Mongols managed not just to mobilize large pastoralist armies, but to mobilize huge infantry armies and siege-trains as well.

The formalization of this mobilizational effort appears most clearly in the regular censuses of the empire's resources. Steppe rulers had understood the importance of census-taking since at least the time of the Hsiung-nu. It was then, and remained, the key to successful mobilization for warfare. Chinese methods provided a model, and Chinese officials provided the expertise. The Mongols carried out censuses in north China in the mid-1230s. In 1252 Mongke launched a census of his entire empire, and recorded its results in special 'blue registers'. These listed households, just as traditional Mongol practice listed tents; however, the census-takers also listed land and resources in sedentary areas, as well as the number of adult males. Churches and their personnel were generally excluded, for the Mongols protected churches in most of their domains, which proved a powerful way of securing local submission. In Rus', for example, this policy helped secure the support of the church for the Mongol's ally, Alexander Nevskii (r. 1252–63).[17]

In Rus', there may have been two minor censuses immediately after the Mongol conquest, in the 1240s. Late in the decade, there are signs that Batu granted the lands west of the Volga to his eldest son, Sartak, who was probably a Christian. Sartak was preparing a more extensive census, with the cooperation of some Russian princes, when he died. The census finally began in 1254 in the Caucasus, and took some five years. It covered the lands of Rus', as well as other lands within Jochi's khanate, including the Kipchak steppe, Crimea and southern Siberia. We know most about the census in Novgorod, where Alexander Nevskii helped Mongol officials overcome local resistance. Censuses took place in winter, when they caused least disruption, and members of households were most likely to be at home.[18]

Having a clear idea of available resources was a matter of great importance. For example, when it became clear that Hulagu would need siege machinery for his Persian campaign, Mongke knew where to find it; and was able to sent 1000 Chinese artillery crews.[19]

> Troops for [Hulagu's] assault on the Assassins and Abbasids came from Mongolia, Turkestan, Iran, the Transcaucasus, and the Golden Horde. Food

to sustain these armies came from Armenia, Georgia and Central Asia. Technical specialists to operate the catapults and siege equipment were sent from China to undertake the difficult task of neutralizing the mountain strongholds of the Assassins and destroying the formidable fortifications of Baghdad.[20]

Accurate census information made it possible to create a regularized tax system to replace the ad hoc levies of the conquest period. The system was probably devised in the 1230s by the Sogdian Muslim merchant, Mahmud Yalavach, who had been made governor of Turkestan after the original Mongol conquest and later governed in Yüan China. His efforts laid the foundations of modernized tax systems throughout much of Inner Eurasia. Yalavach simplified the morass of existing systems, creating two main taxes, a poll tax (*qubchir*), and a tax on agricultural production (*qalan*). A further important tax was the *tamgha*, or tax on commerce. *Tamgha* was the Turkic word for a brand and was used, by extension, for the seal placed on taxed merchandise.[21] Monopolies, such as those on the salt produced in the Sea of Azov, offered another way of raising revenues.

As the amount of money in circulation increased during Mongke's reign, more taxes were probably collected in cash. The central government had good reason to favour cash taxes. They were easier to transport than contributions in kind, so that more could be dispatched to Karakorum, while less had to be left in the provinces. Besides, cash taxes were more flexible, and could be converted more easily into a wide range of goods and services. In the east, Chinese paper money circulated, perhaps as far as Zungaria. In Central Asia silver coins minted in Transoxania circulated widely, particularly after the systematic monetary reform carried out in the 1270s by Mas'ud Bek, the son of Mahmud Yalavach, which encouraged the minting of large amounts of good quality silver and gold coinage. In the Golden Horde, coins were minted in Volga Bulghar, from as early as 1250. However, in Rus', coins had not been used since the late eleventh century, and did not appear again until the fourteenth century. The taxes of Rus' were paid largely in furs, which acted as a pseudo-currency.[22]

Corvée was a further form of taxation imposed on all inhabitants of the empire, and exacted with similar efficiency. It was particularly important for the maintenance of the post-road system. The Mongols also had an eye for the talents of craftsmen, whether military (saddlers, bowmakers, engineers) or civilian, such as the silversmith, Mathew of Paris, whom William of Rubruck met in Karakorum.

As Mongol methods of mobilization became more systematic, the Mongols began to take more care to protect the productive capacity of the lands they ruled. They realized the short-sightedness of their destructive early campaigns under the influence of foreign advisers such as Mahmud Yalavach, or Ogodei's minister, Yeh-lu Ch'u-ts'ai. It is said that Yeh-lu Ch'u-ts'ai persuaded Ogodei not to lay waste to northern China, by explaining that the Mongols would raise far more revenue by taxing local farmers.[23]

Nevertheless, the early Mongolian campaigns had clearly undermined the productivity of the conquered lands. In China, populations shrank from *c.*100 million under the Sung and Chin to some 70 million in the 1290s; and the collapse was particularly spectacular in the north. In Iran, the Mongols helped ruin the ancient system of underground irrigation channels or *karez*. In Central Asia, simple neglect destroyed large parts of the irrigation system such as the canal system built in the Merv oasis by the Saljuk Sultan Sanjar, some 80 years earlier. In the agricultural lands of Semirechye, which were barely touched by Mongol armies, agriculture vanished probably because of a sharp increase in grazing by migrant Mongol pastoralists.[24]

By the 1250s, Mongol leaders understood that their own wealth and power depended on maintaining the productivity of both steppes and farm lands. Before launching his campaigns into Persia and China, Mongke tried to even out tax burdens, and limit the damage to productive capacity caused by military campaigns. Indeed, Allsen argues that, except for the sack of Baghdad, the campaigns of Mongke's time caused much less destruction than those of Chinggis Khan. Mongke also tried to restore production in devastated regions, such as Central Asia, apparently with some success. He was aided by the fact that the destruction was by no means universal, and many areas were flourishing within a few years of the conquests. However, some areas, such as the Chu valley of Semirechye, remained in ruins when William of Rubruck passed through them, as a result of deliberate decisions to set whole regions aside for pasture.[25]

The Mongols had always understood the value of trade. So it is hardly surprising that, under Mongol rule, trans-Eurasian trade flourished as never before. A number of merchants also rose extremely high in the Mongolian official hierarchy, the best known being Mahmud Yalavach.[26]

COMMUNICATIONS

The Mongol empire could not have been held together without an efficient system for transmitting orders and information. Under Ogodei, the Mongols built a more efficient post-horse system than any of their predecessors. The *yam* system, begun in 1234, established post-stations throughout the empire, roughly one day's ride apart, and ready to provide couriers with supplies and horses.[27] The post-houses also stimulated trade, for many functioned as caravanserais. Local army units maintained the post-stations, using resources taken, now on a more regular basis, from the local population. Travellers carrying the official authorization (the *paiza*, usually a wooden or metal inscribed tablet), automatically received fresh horses. Marco Polo saw the system at work in the 1270s.

> When one of the Great Khan's messengers sets out along any of these roads, he has only to go twenty-five miles and there he finds a posting station, which in their language is called *yam* and in our language may be rendered 'horse post'. At every post the messengers find a spacious and palatial hostelry for their lodging. These hostelries have splendid beds with rich coverlets of silk and all that befits an emissary of high rank.[28]

Marco Polo claimed that there were 10,000 of these posts, with at least 200,000 horses permanently ready for use. He claimed that it was possible, in extreme cases, to travel these routes at 200 or even 250 miles a day.[29]

> When a messenger wishes to travel at this speed and cover so many miles in a day, he carries a tablet with the sign of the gerfalcon as a token that he wishes to ride post haste. If there are two of them, they set out from the place where they are on two good horses, strongly built and swift runners. They tighten their belts and swathe their heads and off they go with all the speed they can muster, till they reach the next post-house twenty-five miles away. As they draw near they sound a sort of horn which is audible at a great distance, so that horses may be got ready for them. On arrival, they find two fresh horses, ready harnessed, fully rested, and in good running form. They mount there and then, without a moment's breathing-space, and are no sooner mounted than off they go again...in extreme urgency, they can achieve 300 miles. In such cases they ride all night long; and if there is no moon the men of the post run in front of them with torches as far as the next post. But they cannot ride as fast by night as by day, because they are delayed by the slower pace of the runners.[30]

A BUREAUCRACY

By the time of Mongke, there had emerged a central bureaucracy to administer the affairs of the empire. There were special offices in the capital, Karakorum, to deal with the affairs of the main khanates, and the most important local governors were often appointed jointly by Mongke and the regional khan. The main responsibility of these officials was to raise revenues. An order of Khubilai Khan from 1267 to the rulers of Annam, lists the obligations of local rulers.[31]

1 The ruler had to personally come to receive a charter;
2 relatives had to be left at the centre as hostages;
3 the population had to be registered;
4 army units had to be raised;
5 taxes had to be raised and sent to the centre;
6 a central official, under the name of *darughachi*, or some other title, would be sent in to supervize the mobilization of resources for the centre; and finally
7 a *yam*, or post-horse system had to be set up.

Equally important, there was an exchange of bureaucratic techniques and traditions throughout the empire. While Mahmud Yalavach may have introduced Central Asian bureaucratic and commercial techniques to China, Bolad (*c*.1240–1313), a Mongolian official with long experience in China, became a high-ranking official in the Il-Khanate from 1285 until his death, and played a significant role in its history. He was an important source of information for Rashid al-Din's histories, played a substantial military role, and advised on agronomy and other bureaucratic matters.[32]

All in all, the Mongols created bureaucratic structures that embraced much of Inner Eurasia, the Middle East and China, and left their mark on all the countries in which they appeared. Such unity was never to be achieved again after Mongke's death, from dysentery, in 1259, while campaigning in Szechwan.

THE CAPITAL

After the death of Chinggis Khan, the Mongol bureaucracy became too large to traipse around behind the great khan, and it settled in the capital city, Karakorum ('black rock'). There were few natural sites for cities in Mongolia. John of Plano Carpini wrote that: 'Not one hundredth part of the land is fertile, nor can it bear fruit unless it be irrigated by running water, and brooks and streams are few there, and rivers very rare. And so there are no towns or cities there with the exception of one which is said to be quite big and is called Caracarom.'[33] However, the valley of the River Orkhon had supported a degree of urbanization since the time of the Hsiung-nu empire. Chinggis Khan probably founded a temporary capital at Karakorum as early as 1220. Before that, it may have been a winter camp for the Kerait khans and perhaps even for Chinggis Khan. Chinese records noted the presence of many small winter camps with houses along the Kerulen river, and of agriculture and gardening in the Karakorum region. Most of these settlements depended on irrigation, as well as the presence of large pasture lands. However, according to Juvaini, agriculture appeared near Karakorum only during Ogodei's rule.[34]

Karakorum was built mainly by Khan Ogodei in the 1230s. It depended partly on irrigation agriculture from the River Orkhon just outside its walls. The Mongols also planted Chinese farmers here and in other regions. However, such towns could exist only as long as leaders made the political and economic effort necessary to maintain them. According to Rashid al-Din, Ogodei ordered that 500 wagons of food and drink should be sent to Karakorum every day. As Mongol leaders generally moved frequently with their large courts or *orda*s, their committment to such cities was always uncertain. Nevertheless, for a time, the city attracted large numbers of merchants to supply it. It also encouraged Mongolian aristocrats to take more interest in farming. According to William of Rubruck, many began to plant farming villages, mainly worked by captured peasants, particularly in the south of Mongolia.[35]

William of Rubruck was not impressed with Karakorum. He visited it only after several months with Mongke's court, and only when Mongke himself decided to visit his capital. With his royal patron, Louis of France, in mind, William of Rubruck wrote:

> not counting the Chan's palace, it is not as large as the village of Saint Denis, and the monastery of Saint Denis is worth ten times more than that palace. There are two districts there: the Saracens' quarter where the markets are, and many merchants flock thither on account of the court which is always near it and on account of the number of envoys. The other district is that of the Cathayans who are all craftsmen. Apart from these districts there are the large

palaces of the court scribes. There are twelve pagan temples belonging to the different nations, two mosques in which the law of Mahomet is proclaimed, and one church for the Christians at the far end of the town. The town is surrounded by a mud wall and has four gates. At the east gate are sold millet and other grain, which is however seldom brought there; at the west sheep and goats are sold; at the south oxen and carts; at the north horses.[36]

Mongke's palace stood near the city walls, and was surrounded by a wall of its own.[37] Here, the khan held gatherings of his nobles twice a year. Inside his palace, a captured French silversmith, William of Paris, had built a silver tree that spouted drinks of various kinds. The mound on which this palace stood can be seen today, just outside the walls of the monastery of Erdeni Juu, along with one of the stone turtles that once guarded it.

LIFEWAYS UNDER THE MONGOL EMPIRE

MATERIAL LIFE

Karakorum attracted many visitors during the thirteenth century, so, for the first time, we have numerous written sources on lifeways within a great steppe empire, as well as some archaeological evidence. The most vivid accounts of Mongol life in this period were written by Christian priests or monks sent to Mongolia as ambassadors and missionaries.[38] These accounts portray a world in which traditional pastoral lifeways coexisted with new, and exotic lifeways based on the sudden influx of wealth and ideas from the agrarian world into the Mongolian steppes. Almost as vivid is the description by the Taoist sage, Ch'ang Ch'un, of his journey from Beijing to the Kerulen and then through Mongolia to Central Asia, where he met Chinggis Khan. Cha'ng Ch'un's account conveys well the alpine landscapes of the Mongolian mountains, amongst which he encountered groups of nomadic pastoralists, who travelled in black wagons and lived in white tents. 'The people,' he wrote, 'are engaged in breeding cattle and hunting. They dress in furs and skins, and live upon milk and flesh-meat.'[39]

As this suggests, the dietary regime of most Mongols remained traditional. John of Plano Carpini noted the vital role of livestock produce, and the small amounts of food on which ordinary Mongols subsisted.

They have neither bread nor herbs nor vegetables nor anything else, nothing but meat, of which, however, they eat so little that other people would scarcely be able to exist on it.... They drink mare's milk in very great quantities if they have it; they also drink the milk of ewes, cows, goats and even camels. ...They boil millet in water and make it so thin that they cannot eat it but have to drink it. Each one of them drinks one or two cups in the morning and they eat nothing more during the day; in the evening, however, they are all given a little meat, and they drink the meat broth. But in the summer, seeing they have plenty of mare's milk, they seldom eat meat, unless it happens to be given to them or they catch some animal or bird when hunting.[40]

William of Rubruck reported that a single sheep could feed up to 50 men. Slaves 'fill their bellies with dirty water and are content with this'. When necessary, Mongols ate foods that disgusted European observers. John of Plano Carpini wrote that: 'they eat dogs, wolves, foxes and horses and, when driven by necessity, they feed on human flesh. . . . They eat the filth which comes away from mares when they bring forth foals. Nay, I have even seen them eating lice.'[41]

Milk was important, but it was rarely drunk fresh. William of Rubruck's description of how *koumiss* was made in the thirteenth century, could well have been written in modern Mongolia.

> Cosmos, that is mare's milk, is made in this way: . . . when they have collected a great quantity of milk, . . . they pour it into a large skin or bag and they begin churning it with a specially made stick which is as big as a man's head at its lower end, and hollowed out; and when they beat it quickly it begins to bubble like new wine and to turn sour and ferment, and they churn it until they can extract the butter. Then they taste it and when it is fairly pungent they drink it. As long as one is drinking, it bites the tongue like vinegar; when one stops, it leaves on the tongue the taste of milk of almonds and greatly delights the inner man; it even intoxicates those who have not a very good head. It also greatly provokes urine.[42]

William of Rubruck also describes 'milk wine' or 'caracosmos', which was made for 'the great lords' from mare's milk from which all solids had been removed. From the solids of milk, they made many different types of cheese. William of Rubruck added that 'They take the greatest care never to drink plain water.'[43]

In summer, the Mongols ate the flesh of animals that died naturally. Using the intestines of horses, they made sausages that impressed William of Rubruck; however most of the meat from slaughtered horses was preserved for the winter. Ordinary Mongols, like Chinggis Khan in his youth, sometimes hunted mice or marmots for food. Often, entire tribes conducted *battue* hunts for food.[44] Mongols also hunted with falcons and hawks.

Then, as now, nomadic Mongols lived mostly in mobile tents, or *ger*s, which John of Plano Carpini described in some detail:

> Their dwelling-places are round like tents and are made of twigs and slender sticks. At the top in the middle there is a round opening which lets in the light, and is also to enable the smoke to escape, for they always make their fire in the middle. Both the sides and the roof are covered with felt, and the doors also are made of felt. Some of these dwellings are large, others small, according to the importance or significance of the people; some can be speedily taken down and put up again and are carried on baggage animals; others cannot be taken down but are moved on carts. To carry them on a cart, for the smaller ones one is sufficient, for the larger ones three, four or even more according to the size. Wherever they go, be it to war or anywhere else, they always take their dwellings with them.[45]

Men and young women dressed in much the same way, and shared many of the same skills. John of Plano Carpini reported that young women rode as well as men, and for long stretches, and even carried and shot bows and arrows. However, married women dressed differently, the richer wives wearing fancy costumes and complex hats.[46]

Within the household, there was a clear division of labour. 'The men do not make anything at all, with the exception of arrows, and they also sometimes tend the flocks, but they hunt and practice archery, for they are all, big and little, excellent archers, and their children begin as soon as they are two or three years old to ride and manage horses and to gallop on them, and they are given bows to suit their stature and are taught to shoot; they are extremely agile and also intrepid.'[47] This description, by Friar John of Plano Carpini, probably exaggerates the idleness of ordinary male Mongols. William of Rubruck's account suggests that men had more to do than this.

> The men make bows and arrows, manufacture stirrups and bits and make saddles; they build the houses and carts, they look after the horses and milk the mares, churn the cosmos, that is the mares' milk, and make the skins in which it is kept, and they also look after the camels and load them.[48]

Only women made goods in cloth or leather. 'Their women make everything, leather garments, tunics, shoes, leggings and everything made of leather; they also drive the carts and repair them, they load the camels, and in all their tasks they are very swift and energetic.' It was probably women who made the large ox-hide containers that William of Rubruck saw, or the 'very nice shoes' made from horses' hides.'[49] William of Rubruck adds:

> It is the duty of the women to drive the carts, to load the houses on to them and to unload them, to milk the cows, to make the butter and *grut* [a form of cheese], to dress the skins and to sew them, which they do with thread made out of tendons. They split the tendons into very thin threads and then twist these into one long thread. They also sew shoes and socks and other garments.[50]

Matriarchs could be very powerful in steppe society, though they usually exercised their power from behind the throne. Foreign travellers noted that khans often received envoys with their wives seated behind them, which would have been unthinkable in China. The *Secret History* records several scenes in which Chinggis Khan's mother rebukes him severely. On one occasion, after he was supreme leader, and was threatening his brother, Kasar, she chased after him and disgraced him into pardoning his brother. In general, as in its account of Ho'elun's behaviour when her family was outcast, the *Secret History* shows a great willingness to treat the judgement, as well as the endurance and fortitude of woman with respect. Jagchid and Hyer argue that relations of rough gender equality could be found at all levels of society, and arose naturally from the isolated life of pastoralist families, which demanded close collaboration in domestic tasks.[51]

Class inequalities were limited in pastoral nomadic societies by the absence of large internal surpluses and a basic similarity of lifestyles. John of

Plano Carpini noted with surprise that: 'They all, the Emperor as well as the nobles and other men, sit at a fire made of the dung of oxen and horses.'[52] Nevertheless, there were ranks and hierarchies in Mongol society, and the gradients of wealth and rank steepened sharply during the imperial era. Most nobles lived in gers, but these varied greatly in size and magnificence. William of Rubruck saw gers up to 30 feet across. 'I have counted to one cart twenty-two oxen drawing one house, eleven in a row across the width of the cart, and the other eleven in front of them. The axle of the cart was as big as the mast of a ship, and a man stood at the door of the house on the cart, driving the oxen.'[53]

Great khans lived in huge pavilions that could hold many hundreds of people. The camp sites (orda) where many great nobles gathered, were like large towns. When Batu, the conqueror of Rus', camped, with his doorway facing south, his 26 wives each had a large tent, as well as tents for retainers, and as many as 200 carts each for their belongings. These camps were pitched in a strict order, which reflected the rules that applied within the gers of all Mongols. The more important (male) side was on the right (the west), and the junior side on the left, which reversed the symbolism of Hsiung-nu times. 'When they pitch their houses the chief wife places her dwelling at the extreme west end and after her the others according to their rank, so that the last wife will be at the far east end, and there will be the space of a stone's throw between the establishment of one wife and that of another. And so the orda of a rich Mongol will look like a large town and yet there will be very few men in it.'[54] William of Rubruck estimated that 500 heads of families travelled with Batu as he travelled south along the Volga. Allowing for family and servants, this must imply a migration of several thousand people. So large was this mobile city that, though a market accompanied the town, William of Rubruck could buy no food when he passed through, as the market was too far away.[55]

Inequalities were also apparent in clothing. While greater lords dressed in furs (some imported from as far afield as Rus'), and undergarments of silk, the poor used outer garments from the hides of dogs or goats, sometimes with linings of wool or cotton. For travelling through the Kazakh steppes in the winter of 1253–4, William of Rubruck was supplied with 'rough goat-skin garments, trousers of the same and boots or footwear made in [the Mongol] style, with felt socks and fur hoods also.'[56]

Despite these inequalities, even ordinary Mongolian herders benefitted in a modest way from the huge transfers of wealth that followed upon the Mongolian conquests. Most gained in status and material wealth, for they became, in some degree, the nobility of the Mongol empire. A thirteenth-century Chinese source notes that: 'Anciently, hides, wool and felt were all used in place of textiles. More recently, they use linen, silk, and golden silk.' It adds: 'There is no difference between the higher classes and the lower classes in design or style.' There was also growing interest in foreign styles, for the same source notes how common were the typically Chinese designs-based on the sun, the moon, dragons and the phoenix.[57]

Another measure of the benefits of empire for ordinary Mongolians was the widespread availability of slaves, generally prisoners of war. John of Plano Carpini was appalled at the way they were treated. Such captives:

> are never shown the respect that they [Tartars] enjoy but are treated as slaves and are sent into every kind of danger like other prisoners; they are first in battle and if a swamp or dangerous river has to be crossed, they have to try the passage first. They are also obliged to do all the work that has to be done and if they offend in any matter or do not obey a command they are flogged like donkeys. In short, it is little that they eat and little that they drink, and they are wretchedly clad, unless it happen that they can earn something as do the goldsmiths and other skilled craftsmen.... [Those] kept in their master's house as slaves are in a most unhappy condition. I saw them very often wearing leather trousers with the rest of the body naked in the extreme heat of the sun, and in winter they suffer from the intense cold. I saw some of the men who had lost toes and fingers owing to the great cold.[58]

The mechanisms through which Chinggis Khan created his empire ensured that the thirteenth century was a period of exceptional social mobility compared with other periods, such as the Manchu period, when there emerged stricter forms of hereditary nobility.[59] It was also a period of remarkable ethnic mixing. At Karakorum for the coronation of Khan Güyük, John of Plano Carpini saw people from most of the countries the Mongols had conquered, including China, Korea, Karakitai, other Tartar lands and Turk lands, Mesopotamia, the Balkans and the Caucasus, Rus', the cities of Central Asia ['Sarti'], Persia, and Siberian peoples such as the Mordvinians and Samoyeds. William of Rubruck and Plano Carpini were often made aware of the complex bazaar of customs and religions created by the Mongol conquests. While travelling along the Volga with the court of Batu, in August 1253, William of Rubruck met a Kipchak who greeted him with a 'Salvete Domini.' 'Surprised, I returned his salutation and asked who had taught him that greeting and he said he had been baptised in Hungary by our Friars who had taught it to him.'[60]

SPIRITUAL LIFE

Amongst the Mongols, traditional shamanistic practices and beliefs, of the type common in pastoralist societies, were widespread. Though based on oral traditions, these were surprisingly uniform over large areas. They were even quite institutionalized, and were organized, according to Heissig, 'in the fashion of a church'.[61] Jagchid and Hyer argue, plausibly, that the steppe landscapes, dominated by the land and the sky, naturally engendered religious beliefs dominated by the heavens. Mongol shamanism treated heaven (Tengri) as the supreme deity, with the earth as a subordinate, and female, partner. However, it also recognized the existence of local spirits. Shamans were believed to be able to contact both heaven and these lesser spirits.[62] Like most forms of shamanism, that of the Mongols was practical. Its aim was to secure help from the spirit world in this life, to cure disease, to ensure good fortune and abundance, and to foretell the future, rather than to save the soul. Its main elements were ancestor worship, the use of *onghot* dolls to represent ancestors or other protective spirits (*onghon*), the creation of small shrines or *obo* as dwellings for local spirits, the existence of male (*böge*) and female (*idughan*) shamans, who were sometimes also tribal leaders, and the worship of high places, of which the most important was the blue or eternal sky (*köke tngri, mongkë tngri*). William of Rubruck gives several examples of the important role played by soothsayers and shamans among the Mongols.[63] As under the Scythians, disasters or deaths were often blamed on the evil intent of sorcerers or others.

Mongol religion, like Mongol lifeways in general, was also shaped by the momentous changes of the imperial era. Even before Chinggis Khan, Mongolian social structures were hierarchical enough to exclude those of lower rank from sacrifices to Tengri. Amongst forest tribes such as the Oirats and Merkits, shamans were often chiefs.[64] Sometimes, rising chiefs competed with shamans or priests. As powerful political structures emerged, religious beliefs evolved with them. Powerful leaders tried hard to secure the visible approval of the gods. Sometimes this meant claiming or displaying shamanic or priestly power, or seeking other signs of heavenly approval. According to Juvaini, Chinggis Khan himself 'was versed in magic and deception, and some of the devils were his friends. From time to time he went into a trance, and in that state of unconsciousness the most various locutions came from this tongue... and devils who possessed him foretold his victories. The clothing that he put on [when he went into a trance] and that he wore during the first instance [trance] was packed away in a travelling trunk, and he usually carried it with him.'[65] Temüjin, as a skillful politician, sought prophecies, but also made them himself, and acquired a high reputation for such activities. He also checked the prophecies of others, presumably to distinguish between genuine prophecy and political manoeuvre. Some accounts describe Kökochu, the son of Yesugei's servant, Monglik, as a chief shaman, with the title of Teb-tengri, and interpret his rivalry with Temüjin as a conflict over shamanic powers, that ended only when Chinggis Khan had him executed in *c*.1210. However, Caroline Humphrey has argued that shamanic or inspirational practices were common amongst the warrior elite of the Mongols in this era, and could play a crucial role in political alliances and conflicts.[66]

By the time of Mongke, shamanic practices survived in family cults, but were being eclipsed by other forms of religious activity. Increasingly, religious practitioners became servants of the state, supervising rituals, and sometimes divining, but no longer directly entering into trances. The inspirational activities once widespread amongst elites, were transformed, professionalized, and incorporated within the state, or confined to marginal regions and private religious needs. The term, *bagshi*, presumably derived from the Indian, was used increasingly in Mongolian, from the time of Chinggis Khan, to refer to such 'official' shamans.[67]

The influence of Outer Eurasian religions had spread in Mongolia from well before the imperial period. The rulers of the Mongolian empire happily experimented with Buddhism, Nestorian Christianity, Islam, Taoism and Catholicism. Ogodei supported Buddhism and built Buddhist temples in Karakorum, as well as a huge stupa, which was completed only in 1256, just after the visit of William of Rubruck. William of Rubruck described 'pagan' [Buddhist] temples which, with their shaven-headed priests wearing saffron robes, observing vows of chastity, and chanting 'Om! Mani padme hum', sound remarkably like a modern Buddhist temple.[68] Mongke had a reputation for being interested in Christianity. However, the early Mongol leaders refused to commit themselves to a single religion, and had a well-deserved reputation for religious tolerance. Juvaini writes of Chinggis Khan that: 'he eschewed bigotry, and the preference of one faith to another and the placing of some above others; rather he honoured and respected the learned and pious of every sect, recognizing such conducts as the way to the Court of God.'[69] The tradition of tolerance survived at least to the time of Mongke. William of Rubruck writes that on Epiphany [January 6],

> Mangu Chan [Mongke] had made a great feast; and it is his custom to hold court on such days as his soothsayers tell him are feast days or the nestorian priests say are for some reason sacred. On these days the Christian priests come first with their paraphernalia, and they pray for him and bless his cup; when they retire the Saracen priests come and do likewise; they are followed by the pagan priests who do the same. The monk told me that the Chan only believes in the Christians; however, he wishes them all to come and pray for him. But he was lying, for he does not believe in any of them...; yet they all follow his court like flies honey, and he gives to them all and they all think they enjoy his special favour and they all prophesy good fortune for him.[70]

To make sure he covered all cosmological bases, Mongke also read animal bones. Bones were placed in a fire, and if they cracked in straight lines this was a sign of approval, while if they cracked crookedly, this meant avoiding plans already formulated.[71]

On occasions, the inclusiveness of official religion in this period has a remarkably modern quality. Mongke arranged for William of Rubruck to represent the Catholic faith at a debate attended also by Nestorian Christians, Muslims and Manichaeans. After the debate Mongke confessed to a rationalist deism that earned the admiration of Gibbon. 'We Mongols,' he said, 'believe that there is but one God, by Whom we live and by Whom we die and towards Him we have an upright heart.... But just as God gave different fingers to the hand so has He given different ways to men.'[72]

A MONGOLIAN WORLD SYSTEM?

At its height, the Mongolian empire was the largest land empire ever created. As a unified empire it lasted for half a century, but the shadow of Mongol unity survived for several decades more, and the empire's component parts survived as major states for much longer. As Morgan argues: 'The major difference between the Mongols and previous conquerors is that no other nomad empire had succeeded in holding both the Inner Asian steppe and the neighbouring sedentary lands simultaneously.'[73]

The Mongolian explosion marks a turning point in the history of Eurasia as a whole, for it realigned patterns of trade, diplomacy and politics for several centuries. For a time, it brought the different parts of Eurasia closer than they had ever been before. Though the Mongol conquests were destructive, they also created for some 75 years a huge zone of relative stability, which allowed for an intensified exchange of ideas, goods and people. These did much to stimulate the intellectual and commercial changes that eventually led to the emergence of the modern world.

> Venetian traders in Peking, Mongolian envoys in Bordeaux and Northampton, Genoese consuls in Tabriz, French craftsmen in Karakorum, Uighurs and Chinese motifs in Iranian art, Arabic tax officials in China and Mongolian law in Egypt; these all show that in the thirteenth century the world became smaller and better known.[74]

The Mongol conquests were the rivet that held together what Janet Abu-Lughod has called the 'world-system' of the thirteenth and early fourteenth centuries.[75] The journey from the Black Sea to Khanbalik (modern Beijing) was never easy, to be sure, even at the height of the Mongol Empire. Balducci Pegolotti's manual, written just before the Black Death, suggests that it took at least 300 days, but it was 'perfectly safe, whether by day or by night, according to what the merchants say who have used it'.[76] And for a merchant, that was the crucial thing. As a result of the Mongol conquests, Inner Eurasia, previously a region marginal to the histories of Outer Eurasia, became the centre of a single Eurasian system.

William McNeill has shown that the Mongol invasions also unified Eurasia epidemiologically, for they allowed the exchange of disease vectors throughout Eurasia. This had disastrous consequences for sedentary civilizations at both ends of the continent, for it was almost certainly the Mongol armies that, unwittingly, helped the rat populations of Asia to bring the plague bacillus both to China and to Europe. The ancient Silk Road had passed along the southern edges of the steppes, from oasis to oasis of the Central Asian deserts. However, under the Mongols, traffic increased along a more northerly route, which passed through the steppes themselves.[77] In areas where the plague bacillus had long been endemic, such as Yunnan and Burma, local customs had generally found ways of reducing its impact. However, large military movements, such as those of the Mongol armies, brought into infected regions people without local knowledge of how to avoid infection. It was this, argues McNeill, that accounts for the appearance of the plague bacillus for the first time amongst rodents of the Eurasian steppes. Chinese populations were probably infected in about 1330 for the first time. Then the disease spread along the east–west trade and communication routes of the Mongol empire. In 1346, a Mongol commander besieging the Crimean city of Caffa, catapulted diseased corpses into the city, and fleeing refugees carried it to Europe by boat.

In both its destructive and creative aspects, the Mongol Empire stands at the threshold of the modern world. It also marks the height of pastoralist power in Inner Eurasia. After the Mongols, no pastoralist state ever achieved power as extensive or durable as theirs. Though it was not obvious at the time, their empire marked the high water mark of pastoralist power in Eurasia.

NOTES

1   Soviet archaeologists found traces of this destructive campaign while excavating Bulghar; Fedorov-Davydov, *Gorod Bolgar*, p. 4; on the Kipchak flight to Hungary, see J. R. Sweeney, '"Spurred on by the fear of death"', pp. 39–40.
2   Cited from Vernadsky, *Source Book*, 1:45.
3   Dawson, *Mission to Asia*, pp. 29–30.
4   J. R. Sweeney, '"Spurred on by the fear of death"', p. 42; on the fate of the Kipchak in Hungary, see ibid., pp. 39–41.
5   Sinor, 'Horse and Pasture', in *Inner Asia and its Contacts...*, no. II.
6   Morgan discusses this issue in *Mongols*, pp. 140–1; the latest discussion is in Greg Rogers, 'An examination of historians' explanations for the Mongol withdrawal from east central Europe'.
7   On the diaspora of Khorezmian soldiers, see J. R. Sweeney, '"Spurred on by the fear of death"', p. 35.
8   Dawson, *Mission to Asia*, p. 94.
9   Juvaini, *History of the World-Conqueror*, 2:609–10; on Mongol military planning, see ibid., 2:608–10; and Sinor, 'Horse and pasture', p. 177; on the *yurtchi*, see Vernadsky, *Mongols and Russia*, p. 116.
10 Sinor, 'On Mongol strategy', in *Inner Asia and its Contacts*, no. VII.
11 Vernadsky, *Mongols and Russia*, p. 117; similar *battue* hunts, used both to train and provision an army before a major campaign, were organized by all the great steppe empires of the east, from at least the time of the Hsiung-nu, see Akhinzhanov, *Kypchaki*, pp. 254–5.
12 Dawson, *Mission to Asia*, p. 37.
13 Ibid., pp. 37–8.
14 Ibid., p. 33. And see Jagchid and Hyer, *Mongolia's Culture and Society*, p. 367.
15 Juvaini, *History of the World-Conqueror*, 1:30; on bows, Vernadsky, *Mongols and Russia*, p. 112; and see Dawson, *Mission to Asia*, pp. 35–8 for more on Mongol fighting equipment and methods.
16 Allsen, *Mongol Imperialism*, p. 225.
17 Ibid., p. 122, and see pp. 116, 120–1.
18 Ibid., pp. 136–7, 140–3.
19 Ibid., p. 202.
20 Ibid., pp. 219–20.
21 Ibid., p. 159; on Yalavach, ibid., pp. 147–8.
22 Ibid., p. 183, and see ibid., pp. 171–2, 180; on Bulghar, see Fedorov-Davydov, *Gorod Bolgar*, p. 5; on the numismatic evidence from Mawara'n-nahr, see Davidovich, *Denezhnoe khozyaistvo Srednei Azii*, pp. 121–51.
23 See I. de Rachewiltz, 'Yeh-lu Ch'u ts'ai', in A. F. Wright and D. Twitchett, eds, *Confucian Personalities*, Stanford: Stanford University Press 1962, pp. 189–216.
24 Khazanov, *Nomads*, p. 79; on destruction to the irrigation system, R. A. Pierce, *Russian Central Asia 1867–1914*, Berkeley: University of California Press, 1960,

p. 175; figures on the decline of Chinese populations can be found in Morgan, *Mongols*, p. 83.

25 Allsen, *Mongol Imperialism*, pp. 88–9.

26 Yalavach was merely the most successful of many Turks who rose high in the service of the Mongols; see de Rachewiltz, 'Turks in China under the Mongols'.

27 See the reference to the establishment of this system in Onon, *History and Life of Chinggis Khan*, pp. 170–1.

28 Marco Polo, *Travels*, pp. 150–1.

29 Ibid., pp. 154 and 151.

30 Ibid., pp. 154–5.

31 Based on Allsen, *Mongol Imperialism*, p. 114, and see pp. 100–4.

32 Allsen, 'Two cultural brokers of medieval Eurasia'.

33 Dawson, *Mission to Asia*, p. 5.

34 Juvaini, *History of the World-Conqueror*, 1:213; and see Pletneva, *Kochevniki*, p. 116; on Chinggis Khan's city, Rashid al-Din, *Successors of Genghis Khan*, p. 62, based on Marco Polo; on the archaeology of the Orkhon valley, Phillips, *Mongols*, pp. 94–103.

35 Dawson, *Mission to Asia*, p. 100; Rossabi, *Khubilai Khan*, p. 11; see also Rashid al-Din, *Successors of Genghis Khan*, pp. 62–3; on the planting of Chinese farmers, Vainshtein, *Nomads of South Siberia*, p. 146 and Lattimore, *Inner Asian Frontiers*, 2nd edn, p. 71.

36 Dawson, *Mission to Asia*, pp. 183–4.

37 Ibid., p. 175.

38 The best survey of these sources is in de Rachewiltz, *Papal Envoys*; on archaeological digs at Karakorum, see Phillips, *The Mongols*.

39 Bretschneider, *Medieval Researches*, 1:52.

40 Dawson, *Mission to Asia*, pp. 16–17.

41 Ibid., p. 16, and see pp. 98, 100.

42 Ibid., pp. 98–9.

43 Ibid., p. 99; equivalents of William of Rubruck's 'caracosmos' are made by Mongolian pastoralists today.

44 Dawson, *Mission to Asia*, pp. 100–1, and see p. 97; and Onon, *History and Life of Chinggis Khan*, p. 26, para 89.

45 John of Plano Carpini, in Dawson, *Mission to Asia*, p. 8.

46 William of Rubruck, Dawson, *Mission to Asia*, p. 102.

47 Dawson, *Mission to Asia*, p. 18; for a modern description of the division of labour, see Jagchid and Hyer, *Mongolia's Culture and Society*, p. 111: 'Men have comparatively more leisure than women in premodern nomadic society'.

48 Dawson, *Mission to Asia*, p. 103.

49 Ibid., p. 97; John of Plano Carpini cited from ibid., p. 18.

50 Dawson, *Mission to Asia*, p. 103.

51 Jagchid and Hyer, *Mongolia's Culture and Society*, pp. 94–5; they add that women's status declined in the eighteenth and nineteenth centuries under the Manchu; see also Onon, *History and Life of Chinggis Khan*, pp. 136–7, para 244.

52 Dawson, *Mission to Asia*, p. 5.

53 Ibid., p. 94.

54 William of Rubruck, in Dawson, *Mission to Asia*, p. 95.

55 Dawson, *Mission to Asia*, pp. 129–30.

56 Ibid., p. 130, and see p. 101.

57 Jagchid and Hyer, *Mongolia's Culture and Society*, p. 49.

58 Dawson, *Mission to Asia*, pp. 42–3.

59 Jagchid and Hyer, *Mongolia's Culture and Society*, p. 137.

60 Dawson, *Mission to Asia*, p. 130, and see p. 41.

61 Heissig, *Religions of Mongolia*, p. 2.

62 Jagchid and Hyer, *Mongolia's Culture and Society*, pp. 163–7.

63 Dawson, *Mission to Asia*, pp. 197–201; and see Heissig, *Religions of Mongolia*, ch. 2, as well as pp. 103–5 on *obo*, and also pp. 9–12.

64 Ratchnevsky, *Genghis Khan*, p. 96; and Humphrey, 'Shamanic Practices', p. 201, citing the *Secret History*, para. 70.

65 Cited in V. N. Basilov, 'The Scythian harp and the Kazakh kobyz: in search of historical connections', in Seaman and Marks, eds, *Foundations of Empire* (pp. 77–100), p. 94.

66 Humphrey, 'Shamanic practices', pp. 203–5; the conflict with Teb-tengri is discussed in Ratchnevsky, *Genghis Khan*, pp. 98–100; and see Onon, *History and Life of Chinggis Khan*, pp. 135–40, paras 244–6.

67 Humphrey, 'Shamanic practices', p. 206; see also ibid., pp. 207–8; on pp. 199, Humphrey distinguishes between a 'patriarchal' shamanism that supported clan and ancestral hierarchies, and a 'transformational' shamanism that dealt directly with the natural world; this is similar to Hamayon's distinction between 'hunting' and 'pastoral' shamanism, in the same volume, pp. 76–89.

68 Dawson, *Mission to Asia*, p. 139; on Ogodei's building, *Buddhism in Mongolia*, p. 15.

69 Juvaini, *History of the World Conqueror*, 1:26.

70 Dawson, *Mission to Asia*, p. 160.

71 Ibid., p. 164.

72 Ibid., p. 195, and see pp. 189–94, and 197.

73 Morgan, *Mongols*, p. 5.

74 Hambly, *Zentralasian*, p. 123.

75 Abu-Lughod, *Before European Hegemony*, p. 154.

76 Yule, *The Way Thither*, 2:292, cited in Abu-Lughod, 183.

77 McNeill, *Plagues and Peoples*, p. 143, and ch. 4 passim.

FURTHER READING

In addition to sources mentioned in the previous chapter, there are several works that focus on the Mongol empire after the death of Chinggis Khan. Rashid al-Din, *The Successors of Genghis Khan*, translates part of Rashid's World History. Allsen, *Mongol Imperialism* is on the structures of the Mongol Empire at its height. McNeill, *Plagues and Peoples* describes the epidemiological impact of the Mongol Empire; while Abu-Lughod, *Before European Hegemony*, argues that it created a new Eurasian 'world system'. Dawson, *Mission to Asia* contains accounts by westerners who travelled to the Mongol empire, a group described in some detail in de Rachewiltz, *Papal Envoys to the Great Khans*. Marco Polo's *Travels*, is from a slightly later period, the late thirteenth century. Rossabi, *Kubilai Khan*, is a biography of Chinggis Khan's grandson, who ruled China, and also employed Marco Polo. Martin, *Medieval Russia*, gives an up to date account of Rus' under Mongol control.

CONCLUSION

THIS volume has been about the lands at the heart of the Eurasian landmass up to the time of the Mongol empire. I hope it has persuaded the reader that Inner Eurasia does have a certain coherence, and that it is possible to write a coherent (though not an insulated) history of the region from the very earliest times.

I hope it has also persuaded the reader that the history of early Inner Eurasia is both interesting and important. It may now be worth stating the case for a distinctive history of Inner Eurasia more systematically.

For far too long, most historians have treated ancient Inner Eurasia as a realm marginal to the real concerns of history. That attitude has two main causes. First, the literate elites of the agrarian world, who produced most of the written sources used by modern historians, usually found the pastoralist or foraging lifeways of ancient Inner Eurasia unfamiliar, alien and threatening. Even the most sympathetic treated the peoples of Inner Eurasia as barbarians, and their histories as a sort of historiographical side road. Their attitude was encouraged by the second cause, the relative lack of written and even archaeological data left by most societies of ancient Inner Eurasia. In the twentieth century, specialists in many fields, linguists, archaeologists, anthropologists and some historians, have devoted immense effort to the task of assembling and using what data is available. Archaeology and anthropology in particular have produced much new information about pastoralist and foraging societies in general, and those of Inner Eurasia in particular. But most of the societies described in this volume remain on the margins of conventional historiography.

This is a shame and a mistake. I have tried to show that even those who take a conventional view of what is and is not important in history, should treat Inner Eurasia more seriously, for its societies had a profound impact on the agrarian civilizations of Outer Eurasia, which have been at the centre of most modern history writing. Inner Eurasia connected the different societies of Outer Eurasia from the stone age until recent times. And many important aspects of agrarian civilization in Eurasia derive from Inner Eurasia, or from attempts to deal with the societies of Inner Eurasia. The technologies and skills of pastoralism affected the military methods and even the dress of Outer Eurasia from at least the second millennium BCE. And the task of dealing with pastoralist military incursions had a profound impact on processes of state formation, particularly in northern China, Iran and Mesopotamia. The languages of much of Outer Eurasia, from Europe, through much of the Mediterranean world and as far as Iran, northern India and (for a time) much of Sinkiang, probably originated in Inner Eurasia. And, though this is harder to prove, it is likely that many elements in the religious practices of Outer Eurasia had Inner Eurasian roots.

To understand the role of Inner Eurasia is particularly important when considering the history of those agrarian societies that emerged within Inner Eurasia, in Central Asia and west of the Urals. The history of Central Asia and of Russia is deeply entangled with that of the pastoralist world of the steppes and the foraging world of the Inner Eurasian forest lands. Yet the extent of this influence has largely been ignored, particularly in the historiograhy of Russia.

The history of Inner Eurasia is also of significance in less direct ways. For those brought up in agrarian or industrial societies, early Inner Eurasia has much to teach just because its societies are so different. Here, politics, economics, ethics, family life and gender relations took quite distinctive forms, and studying those forms can enrich our own sense of the underlying principles of social organization, economic exchange, and ethical and spiritual life. Trying to make sense of that world is itself a worthwhile achievement, in so far as it may also help us make sense of our own world. There is no guarantee that this volume has escaped the many subtle and not so subtle biases that face a historian trying to understand Inner Eurasia, but the attempt must be made.

Finally, the history of Inner Eurasia is significant for its own sake, because it is the history of millions of men and women who, from the Stone Age to the present day, faced quite distinctive challenges and came up with quite distinct responses. Pastoralism and hunter-gathering lifeways contain rich and remarkably durable solutions to the basic problems faced by all humans. They are a remarkable part of the remarkable history of our own species of mammal.

The second volume of this history will describe the recent history of Inner Eurasia, from the Mongol era until the collapse of the Soviet Union in 1991. Its central theme will be the decline of pastoralist and foraging lifeways as they succumbed to the growing economic, demographic and military challenge of expansionist agrarian societies and then to the even more aggressive challenge of modern industrial societies. It will argue that the emergence of Soviet communism in the twentieth century can be seen, like the creation of the Mongol empire in the thirteenth century, as a final expression of the distinctiveness of Inner Eurasia's ecology, lifeways and history. Today, Inner Eurasian history, like that of every other region of the world, has joined the broader currents of world history, at a time when processes of globalization, both economic and technological, destroy the distinctiveness of region after region of the modern world.

CHRONOLOGY OF INNER EURASIAN HISTORY: *100,000 BP–1260 CE*

SUMMARY CHRONOLOGY

Ch. indicates the chapter in which this period is discussed

DATE	WEST		CENTRE		EAST	
	Forest	Steppe	Oases	Steppe	Steppe	Forest
100,000 BP–10,000 BP **(Palaeolithic)**	ch.2	ch.2	ch.2	→	←	ch.2
8000 BCE–6000 BCE **(Post-glacial)**	ch.3	→	→	←	←	ch.3
			+ Foraging societies of modern era			
6000–3000 BCE **(Neolithic)**	ch.4	ch.4	ch.4	ch.4	→	→
3000–1000 BCE **(Bronze Age)**	←	ch.5	ch.5	ch.5	→	→
1000–200 BCE **(Scythic era)**	ch.6	ch.6	ch.6 ch.7	ch.6 ch.7	→	→
200 BCE–500 CE **(Hunnic era)**	←	ch.9	← ch.9	← ↔	ch.8 ch.9	→
500 CE–1200 CE **(Turkic era)**	← ← ch.13 ch.14	← ch.11 → ch.14	← ch.12 ch.14	ch.10 → → ch.14	ch.10	→
1200 CE–1260 CE **(Mongol empire)**	←	← ch.16	← ch.16	← ch.16	ch.15 ch.16	→ →

DETAILED CHRONOLOGY

DATE	WEST	CENTRE	EAST
BP = Before Present			
Before 100,000		'lower palaeolithic'; occasional settlement during interglacials	
100,000–*c*.10,000		last ice age 'middle palaeolithic' = 100,000–40,000 Neanderthals in west and centre from *c*.90,000–*c*.35,000	
c.40,000–		←modern humans, revolution of 'upper palaeolithic'→ 'upper palaeolithic' = 40,000–10,000	
c.35,000–	Kostenki	Siberia colonized Malaya Siya	Siberia colonized
c.25,000	Byzovaya Dnieper basin sites Sunghir		Dyukhtai?
c.20,000		Antonova Gora	
c.20–16,000		←'Glacial Maximum'→	migrations to Americas?
c.14,000		Mal'ta site	
from *c*.12,000		interglacial climates	
BCE = Before Common Era			
10,000–*c*.6000		mesolithic cultures	
c.6000–2500 'Climatic optimum' Transition to neolithic		Hissar culture from *c*.6000–4000 Jeitun culture from *c*.6000	contacts with Americas
	Bug-Dniester cultures *c*.5500–4500 Dnieper-Don culture *c*.4500–3500	Kelteminar culture from *c*.5500–3500	farming, Kansu, from *c*.4500
c.4000– 'Secondary products revolution'	Tripolye/Cucuteni *c*.4500–3500 Usatovo *c*.3500–3000	Tedzhen delta, farming *c*.4500	
	Srednyi Stog/ Khvalynsk cultures: horse riding, early pastoralism	settlements in Zerafshan valley, horse riding north Kazakhstan?	
	First *kurgany c*.3500 nomadic pastoralism?		farming, Mongolia
c.3200–2500: Early Bronze Age	pit-grave culture; wheeled vehicles; pastoralist migrations?	urbanization, Central Asia (Namazga Depe IV); pastoralism, Afanasevo culture from *c*.2500	
c.1800–1600	pastoralist migrations?	pastoralist migrations? Sintashta; chariots	tundra cultures; pastoralism in steppes, Okunev culture; 'Seima-Turbino'
c.1800–1000: Late Bronze Age	steppe bronze cultures, timber-grave; 'corded ware' cultures in woodlands	steppe bronze cultures, Andronovo; Oxus civilization; Eurasian 'world system'?	
1300–1000			Karasuk culture

DATE	WEST	CENTRE	EAST
c.1200–800	pastoralist migrations?	pastoralist migrations?	pastoralist migrations?
9th–8th centuries	Scythic cultures; Cimmerians; Greek traders in Black Sea	Scythic cultures; Arzhan tomb	Scythic cultures; 823 pastoralists invade north China
7th century	Scythian invasions of Mesopotamia; first Greek towns by Black Sea	urbanization in Khorezm	
6th century		Afrasiyab; Zoroaster? c.550, Cyrus (r. 559–20)→ Achaemenid empire; c.539 conquers Bactria	
	c.514 Darius invades Scythia	c.529 Massagetae defeat Cyrus; Darius (r. 521–486) c.520 recovers Central Asia	
5th century	Herodotus visits Olbia c.450; royal tombs	Zoroastrianism in Achaemenid empire	
4th century	Sarmatians enter Pontic steppes; Kamenskoe founded	Pazyryk tombs, Altai?	pastoralist confederations north of China
	Scythian war v. Macedonia under Atheas 346–339	329–327 Alexander in Central Asia	military reforms of Emperor Wu-ling c.307
		c.305 Seleucus reconquers Central Asia	
3rd century		c.238–140 Greco-Bactrian kingdom;	221–06 Ch'in dynasty; 209–c.174
		c.238–CE 226 Parthian empire	Motun→Shan-yü, 206–8 former Han dynasty
2nd century		c.180, Greco-Bactrian invasions north India, Buddhist influences; Mithridates (r. 171–38) Parthia→Gt. Power	198 1st ho-ch'in treaty; 175 Yüeh-chih defeated
		c.130 Yüeh-chih expelled from Zungaria; c.140–130 Saka invade Bactria	Wu-ti (r. 141–87) attacks Hsiung-nu from 133
		c.129–8 Chang Ch'ien in Central Asia; 102 Han army enters Ferghana	139–25 Chang Ch'ien's 1st embassy; 121 Hsiung-nu lose Kansu; 119 Han armies→ Mongolia
1st century		53 battle of Carrhae	71 Han/Wu-sun defeat Hsiung-nu; 54 Hu-han-yeh→ Han suzerainty

DATE	WEST	CENTRE	EAST
CE = Common Era			
1st century		*c.*50–250 Kujula Kadphises→Kusana dynasty	23–220 later Han dynasty; 73 Han reconquest Tarim; 87 end of N. Hsiung-nu
2nd century	*c.*105 Trajan conquers Dacia	rule of Kaniska mid-century? Kusana conquer north India	156–80 T'an-shih-huai of Hsien-pi
		Huns nr Aral Sea *c.*160	Buddhism enters China
3rd century	from *c.*200 Goth migrations S.; *c.*275 Rome surrenders Dacia	226–642 Sassanian empire; Mani (216–*c.*274)	220 collapse of Later Han; death of last *Shan-yü*
4th century	to 375, Ostrogoth empire; 370 Hun invasions Pontic steppes; 378 battle Adrianople	*c.*350 Chionite Huns in Sogdia, Kidarite dynasty	304–52 Chao (Hsiung-nu); 348–70 Former Yen (Hsien-pi); 308–555 Juan-juan; 394 She-lun unifies Juan–juan
5th century	430's Rua leads Huns; Attila (r. 445–53)	*c.*430–565 Hephthalite empire	386–534 N. Wei (T'o-pa); –460 successful campaigns v. Juan–juan; 493 capital→ Lo-yang
6th century	515, Sabirs N. Caucasus; 550s Kutrighur/Utrighur wars; 565 Avars take Pannonia; 569–70 Zemarkhos to Türks; peasant migrations to Rus'	Khosrow I Anushirvan (r. 531–70); 565 Türk/Sassanian alliance destroys Hephthalites	T'u-men (d. 552) and Ishtemi (d. 576) found 1st Türk empire 552–630; 581–618 Sui dynasty; Türk empire splits
7th century	626 Avars besiege Constantinople; 628 Heraclius conquers Syria; 622 Hijra, 632 death of Prophet	618–30 T'ung yabghu Kaghan; 630 Hsüan-tsang visits Central Asia; 642 Moslem armies destroy Sassanian empire	618–907 T'ang dynasty
	620s–965 Khazar empire, 653–5 Muslims invade through Caucasus; 660s A-shih-na dynasty; 670 defeat Bulghars, who enter Balkans 679	655 Muslim armies enter Central Asia	683–734 2nd Türk empire
		Tibetan expansion	
8th century	737 Muslim invasion reaches Volga; 'Saltovo-Maitskii' cultures; 750 Vikings in Staraya Ladoga	*c.*705–15 Qutayba governs Central Asia; 750 Abbasid caliphate; 751 battle of Talas	730s Orkhon inscriptions; 744–840 Uighur empire; 755 An Lu-shan revolt; 762 – Manichaeism
		776–83 al-Muqanna; Haroun al-Rashid (r. 786–809)	

DATE	WEST	CENTRE	EAST
9th century	820s/30s, Magyars; 'Ryurikovo gorodishche', 840–*c*.920 Rus' khaganate?; 860 Rus' attack Byzantium; 861 or earlier Khazars→ Judaism; 890s Pechenegs defeat Magyars; Volga Bulghars	821–73 Tahirids *ghulam* armies 873–900 Saffarids Karluk confederation	840 Kirghiz overthrow Uighur empire
10th century	910–12 Rus' raid on Caspian; 921 Ibn Fadlan visits Volga Bulghars; 920–40 Khazar/Rus'/ Byzantine wars; by 940 Rus' shift to Kiev, Prince Igor	900 Isma'il Samanid (r. 893–907) defeats Saffarids; Firdausi (*c*.940–1020)	907–1125 Kitan 'Liao' dynasty
	c.960 letter of 'King Joseph'; 965 Svyatoslav destroys Khazars; Vladimir (980–1015), 988 Christianity	Oghuz Türk in steppes	
11th century	Yaroslav (1019–54); *c*.1050 Kipchak in Pontic steppes; *c*.1080 *Chernye klobuki*; 1097 Lyubech meeting;	997–1040 Ghaznavid empire; 999–1089 Karakhanid empire; 1040 Dandanaqan, Saljuks defeat Ghaznavids; 1055 Saljuks conquer Baghdad; 1071 battle Manzikert; 1074 conquer Transoxiana	990–1227 Tangut 'Hsia-hsia' dynasty
12th century	*c*.1113 Momomakh (d. 1125) defeats Kipchak; Yurii Dolgorukii (1154–7) of Vladimir-Suzdal'; Roman Mstyslavich (1173–1205) of Galicia-Volynia	1141 Karakitai defeat Saljuk leader, Sanjar at Qatwan steppe; rising power of Khorezmshahs	1125–1222 Jurchen 'Chin' dynasty; *c*.1165 birth of Temüjin; *c*.1184 attacks Merkit with Jamuqa and To'oril
13th century	1223 battle of Kalka; 1237 Batu invades Rus'; 1240 Kiev sacked, invasion of eastern Europe; 1242 Batu retreats to Volga, founds 'Golden Horde'	1210 Küchlüg rules Karakitai, 1218 killed by Mongols; 1220 Mongol invasion	1206 Temüjin elected 'Chinggis Khan'; 1215 Beijing captured; 1227 Chinggis Khan dies; 1222–1368 Mongol 'Yüan' dynasty; Ogodei (r. 1229–41); 1234 conquest of north China; 1235 decision to invade west; Mongke (r. 1251–9); 1253 invasion of Persia; 1258 destruction of caliphate; 1279 conquest south China

BIBLIOGRAPHY

T HIS is a list of most of the books and some articles that I have cited directly, or found helpful in researching for this book. The vast majority are in English. I hope it will provide a useful starting bibliography for readers new to the areas it covers. Included are mainly general studies of particular periods or topics, though there are also some more general reference works, and one or two bibliographical guides. Recent works receive priority. Older studies are included only if they have retained some value to the present day. Books and articles not listed in the Bibliography are cited in full when first mentioned in the footnotes.

ABBREVIATIONS

CHEIA = Denis Sinor, ed., *Cambridge History of Early Inner Asia*, Cambridge, Cambridge University Press, 1990.
HCCA = *History of the Civilizations of Central Asia*, 6 vols, UNESCO, Paris, 1992–

ENGLISH LANGUAGE SOURCES

Abu-Lughod, Janet L., *Before European Hegemony: The World System A.D. 1250–1350*, N.Y.: Oxford University Press, 1989.
Adshead, S. A. M., *Central Asia in World History*, Basingstoke: Macmillan, 1993.
Agadzhanov, S. G., Karryev, A., 'Some basic problems of the ethnogenesis of the Turkmen', in Weissleder, W., ed., *The Nomadic Alternative*, pp. 167–78.
Allsen, T., 'The Yüan dynasty and the Uighurs of Turfan in the 13th century', in Rossabi, ed., *China among Equals*, pp. 243–80.
Allsen, T. T., *Mongol Imperialism: the Policies of the Grand Qan Möngke in China, Russia, and the Islamic Lands, 1251–1259*, Berkeley: University of California Press, 1987.
Allsen, T. T., 'Two cultural brokers of medieval Eurasia: Bolad Aqa and Marco Polo', in M. Gervers and W. Schlepp, eds, *Nomadic Diplomacy*,

Destruction and Religion from the Pacific to the Adriatic, Toronto: Toronto Studies in Central and Inner Asia (1994), 1:63–78.

Ammianus Marcellinus, *The Later Roman Empire (AD 354–378),* trans. W. Hamilton, and intr., Wallace-Hadrill, Harmondsworth: Penguin, 1986.

Angel, L., 'Ecology and population in the eastern Mediterranean', *World Archaeology* (1972), 4:88–105.

Anthony, D. W., 'The "Kurgan culture", Indo-European origins and the domestication of the horse: a reconsideration', *Current Anthropology* (1986), 27:291–314.

Anthony, D. W., and Dorcas R. Brown, 'The origins of horseback riding', *Antiquity* (1991), 65(246):22–38.

Anthony, D. W., D. Y. Telegin and D. Brown, 'The origin of horseback riding', *Scientific American,* December 1991, pp. 44–48A.

Anthony, D. W., and N. B. Vinogradov, 'Birth of the chariot', in *Archaeology* (1995), 48(2):36–41.

Armstrong, Terence, *Russian Settlement in the North,* Cambridge: Cambridge University Press, 1965.

Azarpay, G., *Sogdian Painting,* Berkeley: University of California Press, 1981.

Azzaroli, A., *An Early History of Horsemanship,* Leiden: Brill, 1985.

Babur, *Babur-Nama,* ed. and trans. Annette Beveridge, London: Luzac, 1921.

Balzer, M. M., ed., *Shamanism: Soviet Studies of Traditional Religion in Siberia and Central Asia,* New York: M. E. Sharpe, 1990.

Balzer, M. M., ed., *Russian Traditional Culture: Religion, Gender, and Customary Law,* New York: M. E. Sharpe, 1992.

Barclay, H., *The Role of the Horse in Man's Culture,* London: J. A. Allen, 1980.

Barfield, Thomas J., *The Perilous Frontier: Nomadic Empires and China,* Oxford: Blackwell, 1989.

Barfield, Thomas J., *The Nomadic Alternative,* Englewood Cliffs: Prentice-Hall, 1993.

Barthold, V. V., *Four Studies on the History of Central Asia,* 3 vols, Leiden: Brill, 1956–62.

Barthold, W., *Turkestan down to the Mongol Invasion,* 4th edn, London, 1977, trans. T. Minorsky.

Basham, A. L., ed., *Papers on the Date of Kanishka,* Leiden: E. J. Brill, 1968.

Basilov, Vladimir N., ed., *Nomads of Eurasia,* trans. M. F. Zirin, Seattle and London: University of Washington Press, 1989.

Basilov, Vladimir N., 'Islamic shamanism among Central Asian peoples', *Diogenes* (1992), 158:5–18.

Bassin, Mark, 'Russia between Europe and Asia: the ideological construction of geographical space', *Slavic Review* (1991), 50(1):1–17.

Beal, S., trans., *Si-yu-ki; Buddhist Records of the Western World,* London: Kegan Paul, 1884; reprinted San Francisco, 1976, 2 vols in one.

Beal, S., trans., *The Life of Hiuen-Tsiang by the Shaman Hwui Li,* London: Kegan Paul, 1911.

Beckwith, Christopher I., *The Tibetan Empire in Central Asia: A History of the Struggle for Great Power among Tibetans, Turks, Arabs, and Chinese during the Early Middle Ages,* Princeton: Princeton University Press, 1987.

Belenitsky, A., *Central Asia*, Geneva: Nagel, 1968.

Bentley, Jerry H., *Old World Encounters: Cross-Cultural Contacts and Exchanges in Pre-Modern Times*, New York: Oxford University Press, 1993.

Bernard, Paul, 'An ancient Greek city in Central Asia', reprinted in *Scientific American*, special issue (1994), 5(1):66–75 (first printed, January, 1982).

Blockley, R. C., *The Fragmentary Classicising Historians of the Later Roman Empire. English Translations*, 2 vols, Liverpool: F. Cairns, 1983.

Blok, Josine H., *The Early Amazons: Modern and Ancient Perspectives on a Persistent Myth*, Leiden: E. J. Brill, 1995.

Boba, Imre, *Nomads, Northmen and Slavs: Eastern Europe in the Ninth Century*, The Hague: Mouton, 1967.

Bosworth, A. B., *Conquest and Empire: The Reign of Alexander the Great*, Melbourne: Cambridge University Press, 1988.

Bosworth, C. E., *The Ghaznavids*, Edinburgh: Edinburgh University Press, 1964; 2nd edn, Beirut: Librairie du Liban, 1973.

Bosworth, C. E., *The Medieval History of Iran, Afghanistan and Central Asia*, London: Variorum Reprints, 1977.

Boyce, Mary, *Zoroastrians, their Religious Beliefs and Practices*, London: Routledge and Kegan Paul, 1979.

Boyce, Mary, *A History of Zoroastrianism*, vol. I, *The Early Period*, Leiden: Brill, 1975, vol. 2, *Under the Achaemenians*, Leiden: Brill, 1982.

Boyle, J. A., *The Mongol World Empire, 1206–1370*, London: Variorum Revised Editions, 1977.

Braund, David, *Georgia in Antiquity: A History of Colchis and Transcaucasian Iberia*, Oxford: Clarendon Press, 1994.

Bregel, Yuri, ed., *Bibliography of Islamic Central Asia*, 3 vols, Bloomington: Indiana University Press, 1995.

Bregel, Yuri, *Notes on the Study of Central Asia*, Papers on Inner Asia, Bloomington: Indiana University Press, no. 28, 1996.

Bretschneider, E., *Medieval Researches from Eastern Asiatic Sources*, 2 vols, London: Trübner, 1898.

Brown, P., *The Making of Late Antiquity*, Cambridge, Mass.: Harvard University Press, 1993.

Buddhism in Mongolia, by Lamas of Gangdanthekchending Monastery, Ulan Bator, 1979.

Bulliet, Richard W., *The Camel and the Wheel*, Cambridge, Mass.: Harvard University Press, 1975.

Burns, Thomas S., *The Ostrogoths: Kingship and Society*, Historia Einzelschriften, no. 36, Wiesbaden: F. Steiner, 1980.

Burns, Thomas S., *A History of the Ostrogoths*, Bloomington: Indiana University Press, 1984.

Burns, Thomas S., *Barbarians within the Gates of Rome: A Study of Roman Military Policy and the Barbarians, 375–425 A.D.*, Bloomington: Indiana University Press, 1994.

Cable, Mildred with Francesca French, *The Gobi Desert*, London: Hodder, 1943.

Cambridge Encyclopedia of Archaeology, ed. Andrew Sherratt, Cambridge: Cambridge University Press, 1980.

Cambridge History of China, ed. D. Twitchett and J. K. Fairbank, Cambridge: Cambridge University Press, 1978–.

Cambridge History of Iran, vol. 4, *From the Arab Invasion to the Saljuqs*, ed. R. N. Frye, Cambridge: Cambridge University Press, 1975; vol. 5, *The Saljuq and Mongol Periods*, eds J. A. Boyle, Cambridge: Cambridge University Press, 1968; vol. 6, *The Timurid and Safavid Periods*, eds P. Jackson and L. Lockhart, Cambridge: Cambridge University Press, 1986.

Champion, T., C. Gamble, S. Shennan, A. Whittle, *Prehistoric Europe*, London: Academic Press, 1984.

Chang, Kwang-chih, *The Archaeology of Ancient China*, 3rd edn, New Haven and London: Yale University Press, 1977.

Chard, C. S., *Northeast Asia in Prehistory*, Madison: University of Wisconsin, 1974.

Chase-Dunn, Christopher, and T. Hall, eds, *Precapitalist core/periphery systems*, Boulder: Westview Press, 1990.

Ch'en, K. S., *Buddhism in China: A Historical Survey*, Princeton: Princeton University Press, 1964.

Chernykh, E. N., *Ancient Metallurgy in the USSR: The Early Metal Age*, Cambridge: Cambridge University Press, 1992.

Christian, David, '"Inner Eurasia" as a unit of world history', *Journal of World History* (1994), 5(2):6–36.

Christian, David, 'State formation in the steppes', in J. Perkins and J. Tampke, eds, *Europe: Prospects and Retrospects*, Sydney: South Highlands Press, 1996, pp. 243–58.

Claessen, J. M., ed., and P. Skalnik, *The Early State*, Mouton: The Hague, 1978.

Clarke, E. D., *Travels in Russia, Tartary and Turkey*, Edinburgh: n. p., 1839.

Clutton-Brock, J., ed., *The Walking Larder: Patterns of Domestication, Pastoralism and Predation*, London: Unwin Hyman, 1989.

Cohen, Ronald, and Elman R. Service, *The Origins of the State: The Anthropology of Political Evolution*, Philadelphia: Institute for the Study of Human Issues, 1978.

Colledge, M. A. R., *The Parthians*, London: Thames and Hudson, 1967.

Constantine Porphyrogenitus, De Administrando Imperio, Greek text ed. G. Moravcsik, trans. R. J. H. Jenkins, New edn, Washington, DC: Dumbarton Oaks Center for Byzantine Studies, 1967 (1st pub. 1949).

Constantine Porphyrogenitus, De Administrando Imperio, vol. II, Commentary, trans. R. J. H. Jenkins, University of London: Athlone Press, 1962.

Cribb, R. J., *Nomads in Archaeology*, Cambridge: Cambridge University Press, 1991.

Crone, Patricia, *Slaves on Horses*, Cambridge: Cambridge University Press, 1980.

Cross, S. H., and O. P. Sherbowitz-Wetzor, *The Russian Primary Chronicle: Laurentian Text*, Cambridge, Mass.: Medieval Academy of America, 1953.

Curtin, P. D., *Cross-Cultural Trade in World History*, Cambridge: Cambridge University Press, 1985.

Dandamaev, M. A., *A Political History of the Achaemenid Empire*, Leiden: Brill, 1989.

Dandamaev, M. A., and V. G. Lukonin, *Culture and Social Institutions of Ancient Iran*, Cambridge: Cambridge University Press, 1994.

Dani, A. H., and V. M. Masson, eds, *History of Civilizations of Central Asia: vol. 1 The Dawn of Civilization: earliest times to 700 B.C.*, Paris: Unesco Publishing, 1992 (*HCCA*, vol. 1).

Dankoff, R., ed., *Wisdom of Royal Glory (Kutadgu Bilig). A Turko-Islamic Mirror for Princes*, Chicago: University of Chicago, 1983 (and see Yusuf).

Davis-Kimball, Jeannine, and L. T. Yablonsky, *Kurgans on the Left Bank of the Ilek: Excavations at Pokrovka 1990–1992*, Kazakh/American Research Project, Berkeley: Zinat Press, 1995.

Davis-Kimball, Jeannine, Vladimir A. Bashilov, and Leonid T. Yablonsky, eds, *Nomads of the Eurasian Steppes in the Early Iron Age*, Center for the Study of Eurasian Nomads, Berkeley: Zinat Press, 1995.

Davis-Kimball, Jeannine, 'Warrior women of the Eurasian steppes', *Archaeology* (1997), 50(1):44–8.

Dawson, Christopher, ed., *Mission to Asia: Narratives and Letters of the Franciscan Missionaries in Mongolia and China in the Thirteenth and Fourteenth Centuries*, New York: Harper, 1966.

de Crespigny, Rafe, *Northern Frontier: The Policies and Strategy of the Later Han Empire*, Canberra: Australian National University, 1984.

De Rachewiltz, Igor, *Papal Envoys to the Great Khans*, London: Faber, 1971.

De Rachewiltz, I., 'Turks in China under the Mongols', in Rossabi, ed., *China among Equals*, pp. 281–310.

Debevoise, N., *A Political History of Parthia*, Chicago: University of Chicago Press, 1938.

Descoeudres, J.-P., ed., *Greek Colonists and Native Populations; Proceedings of the First Australian Congress of Classical Archaeology*, Oxford: Clarendon Press, 1990.

Dennell, Robin C., *European Economic Prehistory: A New Approach*, New York: Academic Press, 1983.

Dennett, Daniel C., *Kinds of Minds: Towards an Understanding of Consciousness*, London: Phoenix, 1996.

Dergachev, V., 'Neolithic and Bronze Age cultural communities of the steppe zone of the USSR', *Antiquity* (1989), 63(241):793–802.

di Cosmo, Nicola, 'Ancient Inner Asian Nomads: Their Economic Basis and Its Significance in Chinese History', *Journal of Asian Studies* (1994), 53(4):1092–1126.

Diószegi, V., and M. Hoppál, eds, *Shamanism in Siberia*, Budapest: Akademiai Kiado, 1978.

Dmytryshyn, B. et al., eds, *To Siberia and Russian America: Three Centuries of Russian Eastward Expansion: a Documentary Record*, 3 vols, Oregon: Oregon Historical Society Press, 1985–6.

Dolukhanov, P. M., *Ecology and Economy in Neolithic Eastern Europe*, London: Duckworth, 1979.

Dolukhanov, P. M., *The Early Slavs: Eastern Europe from the Initial Settlement to Kievan Rus'*, London: Longman, 1996.

Drège, J.-P., and E. M. Bührer, *The Silk Road Saga*, New York, Oxford: Facts on File, 1989.

Dubs, H. H., *A Roman City in Ancient China*, London, 1957.

Dunlop, D. M., *The History of the Jewish Khazars*, Princeton: Princeton University Press, 1954.

Dunnell, Ruth, 'Fall of the Xia Empire: Sino-Steppe relations in the late 12th–early 13th centuries', in Seaman and Marks, eds, *Rulers from the Steppe*, pp. 158–85.

Ehrenberg, M., *Women in Prehistory*, London: British Museum, 1989.

Eliade, Mircea, *Shamanism, Archaic Techniques of Ecstasy*, Princeton: Princeton University Press, 1974.

Elias, Norbert, *The Civilizing Process*, vol. 1: *The History of Manners*, Oxford: Blackwell, 1978; vol. 2: *State Formation and Civilization*, Oxford: Blackwell, 1982.

Fagan, Brian M., *The Journey from Eden: the Peopling of Our World*, London: Thames and Hudson, 1990.

Fagan, Brian M., *People of the Earth*, 7th edn, New York: Harper Collins, 1992.

Fennell, John, *The Crisis of Medieval Russia, 1220–1304*, London: Longman, 1983.

Fennell, John, *A History of the Russian Church to 1448*, London, New York: Longman, 1995.

Fletcher, J. F., 'Blood tanistry: authority and succession in the Ottoman, Indian, Muslim and later Chinese empires', in *The Conference for the Theory of Democracy and Popular Participation*, Bellagio, 1978.

Fletcher, J. F., 'Turco-Mongolian monarchic tradition in the Ottoman empire', *Harvard Ukrainian Studies* (1979–80), 3/4:236–51.

Fletcher, J. F., 'The Mongols: ecological and social perspectives,' *Harvard Journal of Asiatic Studies* (1986), 46/1:11–50, also available in Fletcher, *Studies on Chinese and Islamic Inner Asia*, Aldershot: Variorum, 1995, no. IX.

Fletcher, Joseph, F., *Studies on Chinese and Islamic Inner Asia*, Aldershot: Variorum, 1995.

Foley, R., *Humans before Humanity*, Oxford: Blackwell, 1995.

Forsyth, James, *A History of the Peoples of Siberia. Russia's North Asian Colony 1581–1990*, Cambridge: Cambridge University Press, 1992.

Francfort, H.-P., 'The Central Asian dimension of the symbolic system in Bactria and Margiana', *Antiquity* (1994), 68:406–18.

Frank, A. G., *The Centrality of Central Asia*, Amsterdam: Centre for Asian Studies, 1992.

Frank, A. G., and Barry K. Gills, eds, *The World System: From Five Hundred Years to Five Thousand*, London and New York: Routledge, 1992.

Franklin, Simon, and Jonathan Shepard, *The Emergence of Rus 750–1200*, London and New York: Longman, 1996.

Frenkel, Anna, 'The Jewish empire in the land of future Russia', in *Australian Journal of Jewish Studies* (1995), IX(1 and 2):142–70.

Frontier in Russian History, Russian History (1992), 19(1–4), Special edn.

Frye, Richard N., *Bukhara: The Medieval Achievement*, Norman: University of Oklahoma Press, 1965.

Frye, Richard N., *The Heritage of Persia*, New York: New American Library, 1966.

Frye, Richard N., *The Golden Age of Persia: Arabs in the East*, London: Weidenfeld and Nicolson, 1975.

Frye, Richard N., *Islamic Iran and Central Asia (7th–12th centuries)*, London: Variorum Reprints, 1979.

Frye, R. N., *The History of Ancient Iran*, Munich: Beck, 1984.

Frye, Richard N., *The Heritage of Central Asia: From Antiquity to the Turkish Expansion*, Princeton: Markus Wiener Publishers, 1996.

Gafurov, B., M. Asimov et al., eds, *Kushan Studies in USSR*, Calcutta: Indian Studies, 1970.

Gamble, Clive 'The mesolithic sandwich: ecological approaches and the archaeological record of the early postglacial,' in Zvelebil, ed., *Hunters in Transition*, 33–42.

Gamble, Clive, *The Palaeolithic Settlement of Europe*, Cambridge: Cambridge University Press, 1986.

Gamble, Clive, and Olga Soffer, eds, *The World at 18,000 BP*, 2 vols, London: Unwin Hyman, 1990.

Gamble, C., *The Timewalkers: The Prehistory of Global Colonization*, London: Penguin, 1993.

Gardiner-Garden, J. R., 'Chang Ch'ien and Central Asian ethnography', *Papers of Far Eastern History* (1986), 33:23–79.

Gardiner-Garden, J. R., *Apollodoros of Artemita and the Central Asian Skythians*, Papers on Inner Asia, Bloomington, Ind., no. 3, 1987.

Gardiner-Garden, J. R., *Greek Conceptions on Inner Asian Geography and Ethnography from Ephoros to Eratosthenes*, Papers on Inner Asia, Bloomington, Ind., no. 9, 1987.

Gardiner-Garden, J. R., *Herodotos' Contemporaries on Skythian Geography and Ethnography*, Papers on Inner Asia, Bloomington, Ind., no. 10, 1987.

Gardiner-Garden, J. R., *Ktesias on Early Central Asian History and Ethnography*, Papers on Inner Asia, Bloomington, Ind., no. 6, 1987.

Gellner, Ernest, ed., *Soviet and Western Anthropology*, London: Duckworth, 1980.

Gibb, H. A. R., *The Arab Conquests in Central Asia*, New York, 1970 (1st publ., London: Royal Asiatic Society: 1923).

Gimbutas, Marija, *The Slavs*, London: Thames and Hudson, 1971.

Gimbutas, Marija, *The Civilization of the Goddess: The World of Old Europe*, San Francisco: Harper and Row, 1991.

Golb, N., and O. Pritsak, *Khazarian-Hebrew Documents of the Tenth Century*, Ithaca: Cornell University Press, 1982.

Golden, Peter B., *Khazar Studies*, 2 vols, Budapest: Akademiai Kiado, 1980.

Golden, Peter, 'The Qipcaqs of medieval Eurasia', in Gary Seaman, ed., *Rulers from the Steppe: State Formation on the Eurasian Periphery*, pp. 186–204.

Golden, Peter B., *An Introduction to the History of the Turkic Peoples*, Wiesbaden: Harrassowitz, 1992.

Goldschmidt, Walter, 'A General Model for Pastoral Social Systems,' in L'Equipe écologie et anthropologie des sociétés pastorales, *Pastoral Production and Society*, Cambridge: Cambridge University Press, 1979, pp. 15–27.

Gordon, C. D., ed., *The Age of Attila: Fifth-Century Byzantium and the Barbarians*, Ann Arbor: University of Michigan, 1966.

Goudsblom, Johan, *Fire and Civilization*, Harmondsworth: Allen Lane, 1992.

Graburn, Nelson, H. H., and B. Stephen Strong, *Circumpolar Peoples: An Anthropological Perspectus*, Pacific Palisades, California, 1973.

Grousset, Rene, *In the Footsteps of the Buddha*, trans. M. Leon, 1st publ. London: G. Routledge, 1932.

Grousset, René, *L'Empire des steppes*, Paris: Payot, 1939; Eng. trans. Naomi Walford, *The Empire of the Steppes. A History of Central Asia*, New Brunswick: Rutgers, University Press, 1970.

Gryaznov, Mikhail, *The Ancient Civilization of Southern Siberia*, New York: Cowles, 1969.

Gumilev, L. N., *Searches for an Imaginary Kingdom: the Legend of the Kingdom of Prester John*, trans. R. E. F. Smith, Cambridge: Cambridge University Press, 1987.

Halperin, Charles J., 'George Vernadsky, Eurasianism, the Mongols and Russia', *Slavic Review* (1982), 41(3):477–93.

Halperin, Charles J., 'Russia and the steppe: George Vernadsky and Eurasianism', *Forschungen zur osteuropaischen Geschichte* (1984), 36: 55–194.

Halperin, Charles J., *Russia and the Golden Horde: the Mongol Impact on Medieval Russian History*, Bloomington: Indiana University Press, 1985; London: Tauris, 1987.

Halperin, C., *The Tatar Yoke*, Columbus, Ohio: Slavica, 1986.

Hamayon, R. N., 'Stakes of the game: life and death in Siberian Shamanism', *Diogenes* (1992), 158:69–86.

Hambly, Gavin, *Central Asia*, London: Weidenfeld and Nicolson, 1969 (English edn of Hambly, *Zentralasien*).

Harmatta, J., ed., *History of Civilizations of Central Asia:* Vol. 2: *The Development of Sedentary and Nomadic Civilizations: 700 B.C. to A.D. 250*, Paris: UNESCO Publishing, 1994 (*HCCA*, vol. 2).

Hauner, Milan, *What is Asia to Us? Russia's Asian Heartland Yesterday and Today*, London: Routledge, 1992.

Haxthausen, Baron A. von, *The Russian Empire: Its People, Institutions and Resources*, London, 1856, 2 vols, reprinted London: F. Cass, 1968.

Heather, P. J., *Goths and Romans 332–489*, Oxford: Clarendon Press, 1991.

Heather, Peter, *The Goths*, Oxford: Blackwell, 1997.

Heather, Peter, and John Matthews, *The Goths in the Fourth Century*, Liverpool: Liverpool University Press, 1991.

Heiser, Charles B., *Seed to Civilization: The Story of Food*, New Edition, Cambridge, Mass.: Harvard University Press, 1990 (first pub. 1973).

Heissig, W., *A Lost Civilization: The Mongols Rediscovered*, New York: Basic Books, 1966.

Heissig, W., *The Religions of Mongolia*, trans. Geoffrey Samuel, London: Routledge and Kegan Paul, 1980.

Herodotus (trans. David Grene), *The History*, Chicago: University of Chicago Press, 1987.

Hiebert, F. T., *Origins of the Bronze Age Oasis Civilization in Central Asia*, Cambridge, Mass.: Peabody Museum, 1994.

Hiebert, F. T., and C. C. Lamberg-Karlovsky, 'Central Asia and the Indo-Iranian borderlands', *Iran* (1992), 30:1–15.

History of the Civilizations of Central Asia, vol. 1, *The Dawn of Civilization: Earliest Times to 700 B.C.*, eds A. H. Dani and V. M. Masson, Paris: UNESCO, 1992; vol. 2, *The Development of Sedentary and Nomadic Civilizations: 700 B.C. to A.D. 250*, ed. J. Harmatta, Paris: UNESCO, 1994; vol. 3, *The Crossroads of Civilizations: A.D. 250 to 750*, eds A. Litvinsky, Zhang Guand-da and R. Shabani Samghabadi, London: UNESCO, 1996.

Hodgson, Marshall G. S., *The Venture of Islam*, 3 vols, Chicago: University of Chicago Press, 1974.

Hoffecker, J. F., 'Early upper palaeolithic sites of the European USSR', in J. F. Hoffecker and C. A. Wolf, eds, *The Early Upper Palaeolithic*, Oxford: British Archaeological Reports, no. 437, 1988, pp. 237–72.

Holt, Frank I., *Alexander the Great and Bactria. The Formation of a Greek Frontier in Central Asia*, Leiden: Brill, 1988.

Honey, David B., *The Rise of the Medieval Hsiung-Nu: The Biography of Liu-Yüan*, Papers on Inner Asia, Bloomington, Ind., no. 15, 1990.

Honey, David B., *Stripping off Felt and Fur: An Essay on Nomadic Sinification*, Papers on Inner Asia, Bloomington, Ind., no. 21, 1992.

Hopkirk, Peter, *Foreign Devils on the Silk Road*, Oxford: Oxford University Press, 1984.

Hoppal, M., ed., *Shamanism in Siberia*, Budapest: Akademiai Kiado, 1978.

Hudud al'Alam. 'The Regions of the World'. A Persian Geography. 372 A.H.–982 A.D., V. Minorsky, trans. and notes, V. V. Barthold, pref., London: Luzac, 1937.

Hulsewe, A. F. P., and M. A. N. Lowe, *China in Central Asia. The Early Stage: 125 BC–AD 25*, Leiden: Brill, 1979.

Humphrey, C., 'Theories of North Asian shamanism', in E. Gellner, ed., *Soviet and Western Anthropology*, pp. 243–54.

Humphrey, Caroline, 'Shamanic practices and the state in northern Asia: views from the center and periphery', in N. Thomas and C. Humphrey, eds, *Shamanism, History and the State*, pp. 191–228.

Huntington, Ellsworth, *The Pulse of Asia*, London: Constable, 1907.

Ibn Khaldûn, *An Introduction to History. The Muqaddimah*, 3 vols, trans. Franz Rosental, Princeton: Princeton University Press, 1967.

Isakov, A. I., 'Sarazm: An Agricultural Center of Ancient Sogdiana', in Litvinskii and Bromberg, *Archaeology and Art of Central Asia*, pp. 1–12.

Isidore of Charax, *Parthian Stations by Isidore of Charax*, trans. W. H. Schoff, Chicago: Ares, 1989.

Jacobson, E., *Burial Ritual, Gender and Status in South Siberia in the Late Bronze-Early Iron Age*, Papers on Inner Asia, no. 7, Bloomington: Ind., 1987.

Jagchid, S., and P. Hyer, *Mongolia's Culture and Society*, Boulder: Westview, 1979.

Jagchid, Sechin, and Van Jay Symons, *Peace, War, and Trade along the Great Wall*, Bloomington: Indiana University Press, 1989.

Janhunen, Juha, *Manchuria: An Ethnic History*, Helsinki: Finno-Ugrian Society, 1996.

Jenkins, Gareth, 'A Note on Climatic Cycles and the Rise of Chinggis Khan,' *Central Asiatic Journal* (1974), 18(4):217–26.

Jones, Gwyn, *A History of the Vikings*, 2nd edn, London: Oxford University Press, 1984.

Jordanes, *The Gothic History of Jordanes*, in English, by C. C. Mierow, Princeton, 1915; reprint, Cambridge: Cambridge University Press, 1966.

Juvaini, *The History of the World-Conqueror by 'Ala-al-Din Ara-Malik*, 2 vols, trans. from the text of Mirza Muhammad Qazvini by John Andrew Boyle, Manchester: Manchester University Press, 1958.

Kaiser, Daniel H., and Gary Marker, *Reinterpreting Russian History: Readings 860-1860s*, New York: Oxford University Press, 1994.

Kennedy, H, *The Prophet and the Age of the Caliphates: the Islamic Near East from the Sixth to the Eleventh Century*, London: Longman, 1986.

Khazanov, A. M., 'Some theoretical problems of the study of the early state', in Claessen and Skalnik, *The Early State*, 77–92.

Khazanov, A. M., 'The Early State Among the Scythians', in Claessen and Skalnik, *The Early State*, 425–39.

Khazanov, A. M., *Nomads and the Outside World*, 1st edn, Cambridge: Cambridge University Press, 1984; 2nd edn, Madison: University of Wisconsin Press, 1994.

Khazanov, A. M., 'The spread of world religions in medieval nomadic societies of the Eurasian steppes', in M. Gervers, and W. Schlepp, eds, *Nomadic Diplomacy, Destruction and Religion from the Pacific to the Adriatic*, Toronto: Toronto Studies in Central and Inner Asia no. 1, 1994, pp. 11–33.

Klausner, C. L., *The Seljuk Vizierate: A Study of Civil Administration*, Cambridge, Mass.: Harvard University Press, 1973.

Klein, R. G., *Ice Age Hunters of the Ukraine*, Chicago: University of Chicago, 1973.

Klein, R. G., 'Reconstructing how early people exploited animals: problems and prospects', in Nitecki and Nitecki, *Evolution of Human Hunting*, pp. 11–45.

Klein, R. G., *The Human Career*, Chicago: University of Chicago Press, 1989.

Koestler, Arthur, *The Thirteenth Tribe: The Khazar Empire and Its Heritage*, London: Hutchinson, 1977.

Kohl, P. L., 'The "world-economy" of West Asia in the third millennium BC', *South Asian Archaeology 1977*, Naples, 1979, pp. 55–85.

Kohl, P. L., ed., *The Bronze Age Civilization of Central Asia, Recent Soviet Discoveries*, Armonk, N.Y.: M. E. Sharpe, 1981.

Kohl, P. L., *Central Asia: Palaeolithic Beginnings to the Iron Age*, Paris: Editions Recherche sur les Civilisations, 1984.

Kohl, P. L., 'The ancient economy, transferable technologies and the Bronze Age world-system: a view from the northeastern frontier of the ancient Near East', in Michael Rowlands, Mogens Larsen and Kristian Kristiansen, eds, *Centre and Periphery in the Ancient World*, pp. 13–24.

Koromila, M., ed., *The Greeks in the Black Sea*, Athens: Panorama, 1991.

Kozlowski, Janusz K., and Stefan K. Kozlowski, 'Foragers of Central Europe and their acculturation,' in Zvelebil, *Hunters in Transition*, pp. 95–108.

Krader, L., *Formation of the State*, Englewood Cliffs: Prentice-Hall, 1968.

Krader, L., 'The origin of the state among the nomads of Asia', in Claessen and Skalnik, *The Early State*, pp. 93–107.

Kwanten, Luc, *Imperial Nomads: A History of Central Asia, 500-1500*, Philadelphia: University of Pennsylvania Press, 1979.

Lamberg-Karlovsky, C. C., 'The Bronze Age *khanates* of Central Asia', *Antiquity* (1994), 68:398–405.

Lamberg-Karlovsky, C. C., 'The Oxus Civilization: the Bronze Age of Central Asia', in (1994), *Antiquity*, 68:353–4.

Lambton, Ann K. S., *State and government in Medieval Islam*, Oxford: Oxford University Press, 1981.

Lapidus, I. M., *A History of Islamic Societies*, Cambridge: Cambridge University Press, 1988.

Larichev, V., U. Khol'ushkin, and I. Laricheva, 'Lower and middle pale-olithic of northern Asia: achievements, problems, and perspectives', *Journal of World Prehistory* (1987), 1(4):415–64.

Larichev, Vitaliy, 'The upper paleolithic of northern Asia', *Journal of World Prehistory* (1988), 2(4):359–96.

Lattimore, Owen, *Pivot of Asia. Sinkiang and the Inner Asian Frontiers of China and Russia*, Boston: Little, Brown, 1950.

Lattimore, Owen, *Inner Asian Frontiers of China*, 1st edn, New York: American Geographical Society of New York, 1940; 2nd edn, 1951, paper-back edn, Boston: Beacon Press 1962.

Lattimore, Owen, *Studies in Frontier History: Collected Papers 1928–1958*, London: Oxford University Press, 1962.

Leakey, R., *The Origin of Humankind*, London: Weidenfeld and Nicolson, 1994.

Lee, R. B. and DeVore, I., eds, *Man the Hunter*, Chicago: Aldine, 1968.

Lefébure, C., 'Introduction: the specificity of nomadic pastoral societies', in L'Équipe écologie et anthropologie des sociétés pastorales, *Pastoral Production and Society*, Cambridge: Cambridge University Press, 1979.

Legg, Stuart, *The Heartland*, London: Secker and Warburg, 1970.

Lewis, Archibald R., *Nomads and Crusaders, A.D. 1000–1368*, Bloomington: Indiana University Press, 1988.

Lieberman, Philip, 'The origins of some aspects of human language and cognition', in P. Mellars and C. Stringer, *The Human Revolution*, vol. 1, pp. 391–414.

Lieu, Samuel N. C., *Manichaeism in the Later Roman Empire and Medieval China*, 2nd edn, revised and expanded, Tübingen: Mohr, 1992.

Ligabue, G., and S. Salvatori, eds, *Bactria: An Ancient Civilization from the Sands of Afghanistan*, Venice: Erizzo, 1989.

Lindner, R. P., 'Nomadism, horses and Huns', *Past and Present* (1981), 92:3–19.

Lindner, R. P., 'What was a nomadic tribe?', *Comparative Studies in Society and History* (1982), 24(4):689–711.

Litvinskii, B. A., and C. A. Bromberg, *Archaeology and Art of Central Asia: Studies from the Former Soviet Union*, Bloomfield Hills, Michigan: Bulletin of the Asia Institute, 1996.

Litvinskii, B. A., and I. R. Pichikian, 'The Hellenistic architecture and art of the Temple of the Oxus', in Litvinskii and Bromberg, *Archaeology and Art of Central Asia*, pp. 47–66.

Litvinsky, B. A., 'Outline history of Buddhism in Central Asia', in B. Gafurov, M. Asimov et al., eds, *Kushan Studies in USSR*, Calcutta: Indian Studies, 1970, pp. 53–132.

Litvinsky, B. A., ed., *History of Civilizations of Central Asia: vol. III: The Crossroads of Civilizations: A.D. 250–750*, Paris: UNESCO, 1996 (*HCCA*, vol. 3).

Liu, Xinru, *Ancient India and Ancient China: Trade and Religious Exchanges, AD 1–600*, Delhi: Oxford University Press, 1990.

Mackerras, Colin, *The Uighur Empire According to the T'ang Dynastic Histories*, Canberra: Australian National University, 1972.

Mackinder, H. J., 'The geographical pivot of history', *Geographical Journal* (1904), 23:421–37, and discussion, 437–44.

Mackinder, Halford J., *Democratic Ideals and Reality*, with additional papers, ed. A. J. Pearce, New York: Norton, 1962.

Macquarie Illustrated World Atlas, Sydney: Macquarie Library, 1984.

Maenchen-Helfen, O. J., *The World of the Huns*, Berkeley: University of California Press, 1973.

Mair, Victor H., 'Mummies of the Tarim Basin', *Archaeology* (1995), 48(2):28–35.

Mair, Victor H., 'Prehistoric Caucasoid corpses of the Tarim Basin', *Journal of Indo-European Studies* (1995), 23(3 and 4):257–307.

Mallory, J. P., *In Search of the Indo-Europeans*, London: Thames and Hudson, 1989.

Mallory, J. P., 'Speculations on the Xinjiang mummies', *Journal of Indo-European Studies* (1995), 23(3 and 4):371–84.

Marčenko, K., and Y. Vinogradov, 'The Scythian period in the northern Black Sea region (750–250 BC)', *Antiquity* (1989), 63(241):803–813.

Martin, Janet, *Treasure of the Land of Darkness: The Fur Trade and its Significance for Medieval Russia*, Cambridge: Cambridge University Press, 1986.

Martin, Janet, *History of Medieval Russia*, Cambridge: Cambridge University Press, 1995.

Masson, V. M., and V. I. Sarianidi, *Central Asia, Turkmenia before the Achaemenids*, London: Thames and Hudson, 1972.

Matyushin, G. N., 'The mesolithic and neolithic in the southern Urals and Central Asia,' Zvelebil, ed., *Hunters in Transition*, pp. 133–50.

Maxwell, Moreau, S., *Prehistory of the Eastern Arctic*, New York: 1985.

McCrone, J., *The Ape that Spoke*, London: Macmillan, 1990.

McEvedy, C., and R. Jones, *Atlas of World Population History*, Harmondsworth: Penguin, 1978.

McEwen, Edward, Robert L. Miller, and Christopher A. Bergman, 'Early bow design and construction', *Scientific American* (June 1991), 264(6): 50–6.

McGovern, W. M., *The Early Empires of Central Asia: A Study of the Scythians and the Huns and the Part they Played in World History*, Chapel Hill: University of North Carolina Press, 1939.

McNeill, William H., *Europe's Steppe Frontier, 1500–1800*, Chicago: University of Chicago Press, 1964.

McNeill, W. H., *Plagues and Peoples*, Oxford: Blackwell, 1977.

McNeill, William H., *The Pursuit of Power: Technology, Armed Force, and Society since A.D. 1000*, Oxford: Blackwell, 1983.

Mellars, Paul and Christopher Stringer, eds, *The Human Revolution*, 2 vols, Edinburgh: Edinburgh University Press, 1989–90.

Menander, *The History of Menander the Guardsman*, trans. and ed. R. C. Blockley, Liverpool: F. Cairns, 1985.

Mennell, Stephen, *Norbert Elias: Civilization and the Human Self-Image*, Oxford: Blackwell, 1989.

Mielczarek, M., 'Remarks on the numismatic evidence for the northern Silk Route: the Sarmatians and the trade route linking the northern Black Sea area with Central Asia', in Tanabe, et al. eds, *Studies in Silk Road Coins and Culture*, pp. 131–48.

Minorsky, V., 'Tamim ibn Bahr's Journey to the Uyghurs', *Bulletin of the School of Oriental and African Studies*, University of London (1948), XII, pp. 275–305.

Morgan, David, *The Mongols*, Oxford: Blackwell, 1986.

Morgan, David, *Medieval Persia 1040–1797*, London: Longman, 1988.

Moses, Larry, and Stephen A. Halkovic, Jr, *Introduction to Mongolian History and Culture*, Bloomington: Indiana University Press, 1985.

Narain, A. K., 'On the 'first' Indo-Europeans: the Tokharian-Yuezhi and their Chinese homeland', Papers on Inner Asia, Bloomington, Ind., no. 2, 1987.

Narshakhi, *The History of Bukhara*, ed. and trans. Richard Frye, Cambridge, Mass.: Medieval Academy of America, 1954.

Newell, R. R., 'The post-glacial adaptations of the indigenous population of the Northwest European Plain,' in S. K. Kozlowski, ed., *The Mesolithic in Europe*, Warsaw: Warsaw University, 1973, pp. 399–440.

Nitecki, Matthew H., and Doris V. Nitecki, eds, *The Evolution of Human Hunting*, New York and London: Plenum Press, 1987.

Nizam al-Mulk, *The Book of Government, or Rules for Kings*, trans. H. Darke, London: Routledge and Kegan Paul, 1960.

Noonan, T., 'Byzantium and the Khazars: a special relationship?', in Shepard and Franklin, eds, *Byzantine Diplomacy*, Aldershot: Variorum, 1992, pp. 109–32.

Noonan, T. S., 'Rus', Pechenegs, and Polovtsy: economic interaction along the steppe frontier in the pre-Mongol era,' *Russian History* (1992), 19(1–4):301–27.

Obolensky, Dmitri, *The Byzantine Commonwealth: Eastern Europe 500–1453*, London: Weidenfeld and Nicolson, 1971.

Olschki, Leonard, *Marco Polo's Asia*, Berkeley: University of California Press, 1962.

Onon, Urgunge, *The History and Life of Chinggis Khan (The Secret History of the Mongols)*, Leiden: E. J. Brill, 1990.

Ostrowski, Donald, 'The Mongol origins of Muscovite political institutions', *Slavic Review* (1990), 49(4):525–42.

Palsson, H., and P. Edwards, trans. and intro., *Vikings in Russia: Yngvar's Saga and Eymund's Saga*, Edinburgh: Edinburgh University Press, 1989.

Pan Ku, *History of the Former Han Dynasty*, 3 vols, H. H. Dubs, London: Kegan Paul, 1938.

Parker, W. H., *An Historical Geography of Russia*, London: University of London, 1968.

Pastoral Production and Society, L'Equipe écologie et anthropologie des sociétés pastorales, Cambridge: Cambridge University Press, 1979.

Paul, Jürgen, *The State and the Military: The Samanid Case*, Papers on Inner Asia, Bloomington, Ind., no. 26, 1994.

Phillips, E. D., *The Royal Hordes: Nomad Peoples of the Steppes*, London: Thames and Hudson, 1965.

Phillips, E. D., *The Mongols*, London: Thames and Hudson, 1969.

P'iankov, I. V., 'The ethnic history of the Sakas', in Litvinskii and Bromberg, *Archaeology and Art of Central Asia*, pp. 37–46.

Piggott, S., *The Earliest Wheeled Transport*, London: Thames and Hudson, 1983.

Polo, Marco, *The Travels of Marco Polo*, trans. R. Latham, Harmondsworth: Penguin, 1928.

Portal, Roger, *The Slavs: A Cultural, Historical Survey of the Slavonic Peoples*, London: Weidenfeld and Nicolson, 1969.

Praslov, N. D., 'Late palaeolithic cultural adaptations to the natural environment on the Russian Plain', *Antiquity* (1989) 63:784–7.

Praslov, N. D., V. N. Stanko, Z. A. Abramova, I. V. Sapozhikov and I. A. Borzijak, 'The steppes in the late palaeolithic', *Antiquity* (1989), 63:784–92.

Pritsak, O., *Studies in Medieval Eurasian History*, London: Variorum, 1981.

Pritsak, O., 'The Khazar kingdom's conversion to Judaism', in Pritsak, *Studies in Medieval Eurasian History*, London: Variorum, 1981, no. X.

Pritsak, O., *The Origin of Rus'*, vol. 1, *Old Scandinavian Sources other than the Sagas*, Cambridge, Mass.: Harvard University Press, 1981.

Prusek, Jaroslav, *Chinese Statelets and the Northern Barbarians in the Period 1400–300 B.C.*, Prague: Academia, 1971.

Pulleyblank, E. G., 'Why Tocharians?', *Journal of Indo-European Studies* (1995), 23(3 and 4):415–30.

Puri, B. N., *Buddhism in Central Asia*, Delhi: Motilal Banarsidass, 1987.

P'yankova, L. 'Central Asia in the Bronze Age: sedentary and nomadic cultures', *Antiquity* (1994), 68:355–72.

Ranov, V. A., and R. S. Davis, 'Toward a new outline of the Soviet Central Asian paleolithic', *Current Anthropology* (1979), 20(2):249–70.

Rashid al-Din Tabib, *The Successors of Genghis Khan*, trans. J. A. Boyle, New York: Columbia University Press, 1971.

Ratchnevsky, Paul, *Genghis Khan: His Life and Legacy*, trans. T. N. Haining, Oxford: Blackwell, 1991.

Renfrew, Colin, *Archaeology and Language: The Puzzle of Indo-European Origins*, London: Penguin, 1989.

Renfrew, Colin, 'Before Babel: speculations on the origins of linguistic diversity', *Cambridge Archaeological Journal* (1991), 1(1):3–23.

Riasanovsky, Nicholas V. 'The emergence of Eurasianism,' *California Slavic Studies* (1967) 4:39–72.

Riasanovsky, Nicholas V., *A History of Russia*, 5th edn, New York: Oxford University Press, 1993.

Rice, Tamara Talbot, *The Scythians*, New York: Thames and Hudson, 3rd. edn, 1961.

Rice, Tamara Talbot, *The Seljuks in Asia Minor*, London: Thames and Hudson, 1961.

Rice, Tamara Talbot, *Ancient Arts of Central Asia*, London: Thames and Hudson, 1965.

Rogers, Greg, 'An examination of historians' explanations for the Mongol withdrawal from east Central Europe', in *East European Quarterly* (1996), XXX(1):3–26.

Rolle, Renate, *The World of the Scythians*, London: Batsford, 1989.

Rossabi, M., *China and Inner Asia from 1368 to the Present Day*, London: Thames and Hudson, 1975.

Rossabi, M., ed., *China among Equals: The Middle Kingdom and its Neighbors, 10th–14th Centuries*, Berkeley: University of California Press, 1983.

Rossabi, M., *Kubilai Khan: his Life and Times*, Berkeley: University of California Press, 1988.

Rossabi, M., 'The "decline" of the Central Asian caravan trade', in G. Seaman, ed., *Ecology and Empire. Nomads in the Cultural Evolution of the Old World*, pp. 81–102.

Rostovtzeff, Mikhail I., *Iranians and Greeks in South Russia*, Oxford: Clarendon Press, 1922.

Rowell, Stephen C., *Lithuania ascending: A Pagan Empire in East-Central Europe, 1295–1345*, Cambridge: Cambridge University Press, 1994.

Rowlands, Michael, Mogens Larsen and Kristian Kristiansen, eds, *Centre and Periphery in the Ancient World*, Cambridge: Cambridge University Press, 1987.

Rowley-Conwy, Peter, 'Between cave painters and crop planters: aspects of the temperate European mesolithic', Zvelebil, ed., *Hunters in Transition*, pp. 17–32.

Rudenko, Sergei, *The Frozen Tombs of Siberia: The Pazyryk Burials of Iron Age Horsemen*, trans. M. W. Thompson, Berkeley and Los Angeles: University of California Press, 1970.

Sabloff, Jeremy A., and C. C. Lamberg-Karlovsky, eds, *Ancient Civilization and Trade*, Albuquerque: University of New Mexico Press, 1975.

Sahlins, Marshall D., *Tribesmen*, Englewood Cliffs: Prentice-Hall, 1968.

Sarianidi, V. I., 'Aegean-Anatolian motifs in the glyptic art of Bactria and Margiana', in Litvinskii and Bromberg, *Archaeology and Art of Central Asia*, pp. 27–36.

Savinov, D., 'The Sayano-Altaic centre of early medieval cultures', *Antiquity* (1989), 63(241):814–826.

Seaman, Gary, ed., *Ecology and Empire: Nomads in the Cultural Evolution of the Old World*, vol. 1 of the Proceedings of the Soviet-American Academic Symposia in Conjunction with the Museum Exhibitions, *Nomads: Masters of the Eurasian Steppe*, Los Angeles: Ethnographics Press, University of S. California, 1989.

Seaman, Gary, and Daniel Marks, eds, *Rulers from the Steppe: State Formation on the Eurasian Periphery*, vol. 2 of the Proceedings of the Soviet-American Academic Symposia in Conjunction with the Museum Exhibitions, *Nomads: Masters of the Eurasian Steppe*, Los Angeles: Ethnographics Press, University of S. California, 1991.

Seaman, Gary, ed., *Foundations of Empire: Archeology and Art of the Eurasian Steppes*, vol. 3 of the Proceedings of the Soviet-American Academic Symposia in Conjunction with the Museum Exhibitions, *Nomads: Masters of the Eurasian Steppe*, Los Angeles: Ethnographics Press, University of S. California, 1991.

Seaman, Gary, and Jane Day, *Ancient Traditions: Shamanism in Central Asia and the Americas*, a further vol. in the series, Proceedings of the Soviet-American Academic Symposia in Conjunction with the Museum Exhibitions, *Nomads: Masters of the Eurasian Steppe*, University Press of Colorado, 1994.

Semenov V., and K. Chugunov, 'New evidence of the Scythian-type culture of Tuva', *Ancient Civilizations from Scythia to Siberia* (1995), 2(3):311–334.

Service, E. R., *Primitive Social Organization: an evolutionary perspective*, New York: Random House, 1962.

Shepard, J., and S. Franklin, eds, *Byzantine Diplomacy*, Aldershot: Variorum, 1992.

Sherratt, A., 'Plough and pastoralism: aspects of the secondary products revolution', in *Patterns of the Past*, eds I. Hodder, G. Isaac and N. Hammond, Cambridge: Cambridge University Press, 1981, pp. 261–305.

Shilov, V. P., 'The origins of migration and animal husbandry in the steppes of eastern Europe', in J. Clutton-Brock, ed., *The Walking Larder*, London: Unwin Hyman, 1989, pp. 119–26.

Shishkina, G. V., 'Ancient Samarkand: capital of Soghd', in Litvinskii and Bromberg, *Archaeology and Art of Central Asia*, pp. 81–99.

Silay, Kemal, ed., *An Anthology of Turkish Literature*, Bloomington: Indiana University Press, 1996.

Simocatta, Theophylactus, *The History of Theophylactus Simocatta*, trans. M. and M. Whitby, Oxford: Clarendon Press, 1986.

Sinor, Denis, 'The historical role of the Turk empire', 1st publ. 1953, reprinted in *Inner Asia and its Contacts with Medieval Europe*, no. VII.

Sinor, Denis, ed., *Orientalism and History*, 1st edn, Cambridge: Heffer, 1954; 2nd edn, Bloomington: Indiana University Press, 1970.

Sinor, Denis, ed., 'Central Eurasia', in *Inner Asia and its Contacts with Medieval Europe*, no. 1, reprinted from Sinor, ed., *Orientalism and History*, 2nd edn, pp. 93–119.

Sinor, Denis, *Inner Asia: History, Civilization, Languages: a Syllabus*, 2nd, rev. edn, Bloomington: Indiana University Press, 1971.

Sinor, Denis, 'Horse and pasture in Inner Asian history', 1st publ. 1972, reprinted in *Inner Asia and its Contacts with Medieval Europe*, no. II.

Sinor, Denis, 'On Mongol strategy', 1st publ. 1975, reprinted in *Inner Asia and its Contacts with Medieval Europe*, no. XVI.

Sinor, Denis, *Inner Asia and its Contacts with Medieval Europe*, London: Variorum, 1977.

Sinor, Denis, ed., *The Cambridge History of Early Inner Asia*, Cambridge: Cambridge University Press, 1990 (*CHEIA*).

Sinor, Denis, *Studies in Medieval Inner Asia*, Aldershot: Variorum, 1997.

Sinor, Denis, 'The historical Attila', in Sinor, *Studies in Medieval Inner Asia*, no. VII.

Sinor, Denis, 'The Uighur empire of Mongolia', in Sinor, *Studies in Medieval Inner Asia*, no. V.

Soffer, Olga, 'Patterns of intensification as seen from the upper paleolithic of the central Russian plain', in T. D. Price and J. A. Brown, eds, *Prehistoric Hunter-Gatherers: The Emergence of Cultural Complexity*, Orlando: Academic Press, 1985, pp. 235–70.

Soffer, Olga, *The Upper Palaeolithic of the Central Russian Plains*, Orlando: Academic Press, 1985.

Soffer, Olga, ed., *The Pleistocene Old World*, New York: Plenum Press, 1987.

Soffer, Olga, 'Upper palaeolithic connubia, refugia, and the archaeological record from Eastern Europe', in O. Soffer, ed., *The Pleistocene Old World*, pp. 333–48.

Soffer, Olga, 'Storage, sedentism, and the Eurasian palaeolithic record', *Antiquity* (1989), 63:719–32.

Soffer, Olga, 'The middle to upper palaeolithic transition on the Russian plain', in Paul Mellars and Christopher Stringer, eds, *The Human Revolution*, 714–42.

Soffer, O., and C. Gamble, eds, *From Kostenki to Clovis: Upper Paleolithic-Paleoindian Adaptations*, New York: Plenum, 1992.

Ssu-ma Ch'ien, *Records of the Grand Historian of China*, trans. Burton Watson, 2 vols, New York: Columbia University Press, 1961.

Ssu-ma Ch'ien, *The Grand Scribe's Records*, ed. William H. Nienhauser, Jr, vols 1 and 7, Bloomington: Indiana University Press, 1994.

Stavisky, B. Y., 'Central Asia in the Kushan period. Archaeological studies by Soviet scholars', in B. Gafurov et al., *Kushan Studies in USSR*, pp. 27–52.

Stein, M. A., *On Ancient Central-Asian Tracks*, Chicago: University of Chicago Press, 1964.

Stringer, C., and C. Gamble, *In Search of the Neanderthals: Solving the Puzzle of Human Origins*, London: Thames and Hudson, 1993.

Subtelny, Orest, *Ukraine: A History*, Toronto: Toronto University, 1988.

Sulimirski, T., *Prehistoric Russia*, London: J. Baker, 1970.

Sulimirski, T., *The Sarmatians*, London: Thames and Hudson, 1970.

Sweeney, J. R., '"Spurred on by the fear of death": refugees and displaced populations during the Mongol invasion of Hungary', in M. Gervers, and W. Schlepp, eds, *Nomadic Diplomacy, Destruction and Religion from the Pacific to the Adriatic*, Toronto: Toronto Studies in Central and Inner Asia no. 1, 1994, pp. 34–62.

Tanabe, K., J. Cribb and H. Wang, eds, *Studies in Silk Road Coins and Culture: Papers in Honour of Professor Ikuo Hirayama on his 65th Birthday*, Kamakura: Institute of Silk Road Studies, 1997.

Tarn, William W., *The Greeks in Bactria and India*, 2nd edn, Cambridge: Cambridge University Press, 1951.

Teggart, Frederick J., *Rome and China: A Study of Correlations in Historical Events*, Berkeley: University of California Press, 1939.

Tekin, Talat, *A Grammar of Orkhon Turkic*, Bloomington: Indiana University Press, 1968.

Telegin, D. Ya., *Dereivka*, Oxford: BAR International Series 287, 1986.

Thomas, N., and C. Humphrey, eds, *Shamanism, History and the State*, Ann Arbor: University of Michigan Press, 1994.

Thompson, E. A., *A History of Attila and the Huns*, 2nd edn, Oxford: Blackwell, 1996, with pref. and new bibl. by Heather (1st pub., Oxford: Clarendon Press, 1948).

Tikhomirov, M. N., *The Towns of Ancient Rus*, Moscow: Progress, 1959.

Tinios, Pantelis Ellis, *Pan Ku, the Hsiung-Nu and 'Han Shu' 94*, PhD, University of Michigan, 1988, University Microfilms, 1991.

Toynbee, Arnold J., *Constantine Porphyrogenitus and his World*, London: Oxford University Press, 1973.

Treadgold, Warren, *A History of the Byzantine State and Society*, Stanford: Stanford University Press, 1997.

Trubetzkoy, N. S., *The Legacy of Genghis Khan, and Other Essays on Russia's Identity*, ed. A. Liberman, Michigan Slavic Materials, 1992.

UNESCO, *History of Humanity: Scientific and Cultural Development*, vols 1–3, London: UNESCO, 1994–6.

Vainshtein, Sevyan, *Nomads of South Siberia: The Pastoral Economies of Tuva*, Cambridge: Cambridge University Press, 1980.

Vasiliev, A. A., *The Russian Attack on Constantinople in 860*, Cambridge, Mass.: Medieval Academy of America, 1946.

Vencl, Slavomil, 'The role of hunter-gathering populations in the transition to farming: a Central-European perspective,' Zvelebil, ed., *Hunters in Transition*, pp. 43–51.

Vernadsky, G. V., *Ancient Russia*, New Haven: Yale University Press, 1943.

Vernadsky, G. V., *Kievan Russia*, New Haven: Yale University Press, 1948.

Vernadsky, G. V., *The Mongols and Russia*, New Haven: Yale University Press, 1953.

Vernadsky, G. V., *The Origins of Russia*, Oxford: Clarendon Press, 1959.

Vernadsky, G. V., ed., *A Source Book for Russian History from Early Times to 1917*, 3 vols, New Haven: Yale University Press, 1972.

Vitebsky, Piers, *The Shaman*, Basingstoke: Macmillan, 1995.

Vogelsang, W. J., *The Rise and Organisation of the Achaemenid Empire: The Eastern Iranian Evidence*, Leiden: E. J. Brill, 1992.

Waldron, Arthur, *The Great Wall of China*, Cambridge: Cambridge University Press, 1990.

Waley, A., *The Real Tripitaka and other pieces*, London: Allen and Unwin, 1952.

Watson, W., *Cultural Frontiers in Ancient East Asia*, Edinburgh: Edinburgh University Press, 1971.

Watters, T., trans., *On Yuang Chwang's Travels in India 629–645 A.D.*, 2 vols, London: Royal Asiatic Society, 1904.

Weissleder, W., ed., *The Nomadic Alternative: Modes and Models of Interaction in the African-Asian Deserts and Steppes*, The Hague: Mouton, 1978.

Wenke, Robert J., *Patterns in Prehistory: Humankind's First Three Million Years*, 3rd edn, New York: Oxford University Press, 1991.

Wheeler, G., *The Modern History of Soviet Central Asia*, New York: Praeger, 1964.

Wolf, E. R., *Europe and the People without History*, Berkeley: University of California Press, 1982.

Wolfram, Herwig, *History of the Goths*, rev. edn, trans. from German by Thomas J. Dunlap, Berkeley: University of California Press, 1988.

Yule, Sir Henry, trans. and ed., *The Way Thither, Being a Collection of Medieval Notices of China*, 4 vols, London: Hakluyt Society, Series 2, vols 33, 37, 38, and 41 (1913, 1924, 1925, 1926).

Yusuf Khass Hajib, *Wisdom of Royal Glory*, ed. and trans. Robert Dankoff, Chicago: University of Chicago Press, 1983 (and see Dankoff).

Yü, Ying-shih *Trade and Expansion in Han China*, Berkeley and Los Angeles: University of California Press, 1967.

Zenkovsky, S. A., *Medieval Russian Epics, Chronicles and Tales*, New York: Dutton, 1963; rev. edn, New York: Penguin, 1974.

Zosimus, *New History*, trans. R. T. Ridley, Canberra: Australian Association for Byzantine Studies, 1982.

Zuckermann, Constantine, 'On the date of the Khazars' conversion to Judaism and the chronology of the kings of the Rus' Oleg and Igor', in *Revue des Etudes Byzantines* (1995), 53:237–70.

Zvelebil, Marek, ed., *Hunters in Transition: Mesolithic Societies of Temperate Eurasia and their Transition to Farming*, Cambridge: Cambridge University Press, 1986.

Zürcher, E., 'The Yüeh-chih and Kaniska in Chinese sources', in A. L. Basham, ed., *Papers on the Date of Kaniska*, Leiden: Brill, 1968, pp. 346–90.

Zürcher, E., *The Buddhist Conquest of China*, 2nd edn, 2 vols, Leiden: Brill, 1972.

SOURCES IN OTHER LANGUAGES

Abramova, Z. A., *Paleolit Eniseya. Afontovskaya kul'tura*, Novosibirsk: Nauka, 1979.

Agadzhanov, S. G., *Gosudarstvo Sel'dzhukidov i Srednyaya Aziya v XI–XII vv.*, Moscow: Institut vostokovedeniya, 1991.

Akhinzhanov, S. M., *Kypchaki v istorii srednevekovogo Kazakhstana*, Alma-Ata: Nauka Kazakhskoi SSR, 1989.

Aleshkovskii, M. Kh., *Povest' vremennykh let*, Moscow: Nauka, 1971.

Alekseev, A. Yu., V. Yu. Murzin, R. Rolle, *Chertomlyk. Skifskii tsarskii Kurgan. IV v. do n.e.*, Kiev: Naukova dumka, 1991.

Altheim, F., *Attilla und die Hunnen*, Baden-Baden: Verlag für Kunst und Wissenschaft, 1951.

Artamonov, M. I., *Ocherki drevneishei istorii Khazar*, Leningrad: Gos. sots.-ekon. izd-vo, 1936.

Artamonov, M. I., *Istoriya khazar*, Leningrad: Izd-vo gos. Ermitazha, 1962.

Artamonov, M. I., *Kimmeritsy i skify*, Leningrad: Nauka, 1974.

Bartol'd, V. V., *Akademik V. V. Bartol'd Sochineniya*, 10 vols, Moscow: Izd-vo vostochnoi literatury, 1963–76.

Bona, I., *Die Hunnenreich*, Stuttgart: Theiss, 1991.

Briant, P., *Etat et pasteurs au Moyen-Orient ancien*, Cambridge, Cambridge University Press, 1982.

Briant, P., *L'Asie centrale et les royaumes proche-orientaux du premier millénaire*, Paris: Editions Recherche sur les civilisations, 1984.

Briant, P., *Darius: Les Perses et l'Empire*, Paris: Gallimard, 1992.

Buniyatov, Z. M., *Gosudarstvo Khorezmshakhov-Anushteginidov 1097–1231*, Moscow: Nauka, 1986.

Chavannes, Edouard, *Documents sur les Tou-Kiue (Turcs) Occidenteaux, recueilli et commentés suivi de Notes Additionelles*, S.Pb., 1903–4; reprinted in one volume, Paris, 1941 and Taipei, 1969.

Chistyakov, O. I., ed., *Russkoe zakonodatel'stvo x–xx vekov v devyati tomakh*, Moscow: Yuridicheskaya literatura, 1984–.

Conte, Francis, *Les Slaves. Aux origines des civilisations d'Europe centrale et orientale*, Paris: Albin Michel, 1986.

David, T., 'Peuples mobiles de l'Eurasie: Contacts d'une périphérie "barbare" avec le monde "civilisé", à la fin de l'Age du Bronze et au 1er Age du Fer', *L'asie centrale et ses rapports avec les civilisations orientales, des origines à l'age du fer*, Mission Archéologique Française en Asie Centrale, tome 1, Paris, 1988, pp. 159–68.

Davidovich, E. A., *Denezhnoe khozyaistvo Srednei Azii posle mongol'skogo zavoevaniya i reforma Masud-beka (XIII v.)*, Moscow: Nauka, 1972.

Davydova, A. V., *Ivolginskii kompleks (gorodishche i mogil'nik)-pamyatnik khunnu v Zabaikal'e*, Leningrad: Izd-vo Leningradskogo universiteta, 1985.

Dikov, N. N., *Istoriya Chukotki s drevneishikh vremen do nashikh dnei*, Moscow: Mysl', 1989.

Drevneishie gosudarstva kavkaza i srednei Azii, Moscow: Nauka, 1985 (See Koshelenko, ed.).

Fedorov-Davydov, G. A., *Obshchestvennyi stroi Zolotoi Ordy*, Moscow: Izd-vo Moskovskogo universiteta, 1973.

Fedorov-Davydov, G. A., *Gorod Bolgar: ocherki istorii i kul'tury*, Moscow: Nauka, 1987.

Froyanov, I. Ya., *Kievskaya Rus'. Ocherki sotsial'no-ekonomicheskoi istorii*, Leningrad: Izd-vo Leningradskogo Universiteta, 1974.

Froyanov, I. Ya., *Kievskaya Rus'. Ocherki sotsial'no-politicheskoi istorii*, Leningrad: Izd-vo Leningradskogo Universiteta, 1980.

Gabain, Annemarie von, *Das uigurische Königreich von Chotscho 850–1250*, Berlin: Akademie-Verlag, 1961.

Gabain, Annemarie von, *Das Leben im uigurischen Königreich von Qoco (850–1250)*, Wiesbaden: Harrassowitz, 1973.

Gafurov, B. G. (ed. B. A. Litvinskii), *Tadzhiki: drevneishaya, drevnyaya i srednevekovaya istoriya*, 2 vols, Moscow: Nauka, 1972; 2nd Russian lang. edn, with minor corrections and extended essay by B. A. Litvinskii, Dushanbe: Irfon, 1989.

Goehrke, C., *Frühzeit des Ostslaven*, Darmstadt: Wissenschaftliche Buchgesellschaft, 1992.

Grekov, B. D., *Kievskaya Rus'*, in *Izbrannye trudy*, vol. II, Moscow: Izd-vo akademii nauk SSSR, 1959.

Gumilev, L. N., *Khunnu. Sredinnaya Aziya v drevnie vremena*, Moscow: Izd-vo vostochnoi literatury, 1960.

Gumilev, L. N., *Drevnie tyurki*, Moscow: Nauka, 1967.

Gumilev, L. N., *Poiski vymyshlennogo tsarstva (legenda o 'Gosudarstve presvitera Ioanna')*, Moscow: Nauka, 1970.

Gumilev, L. N., *Drevnyaya Rus' i velikaya step'*, Moscow, 1992.

Gumilev, L. N., *Ot Rusi k Rossii: Ocherki etnicheskoi istorii*, Moscow, 1992.

Hambis, L., ed., *L'Asie Centrale. Histoire et civilisation*, Paris, 1977.

Hambly, Gavin, *Zentralasien*, in Fischer, Weltgeschichte, vol. 16, Frankfurt: Fischer, 1966.

Haussig, H. W., *Die Geschichte Zentralasiens und der Seidenstrasse in vorislamischer Zeit*, Darmstadt: Wissenschaftliche Buchgesellschaft, 1983.

Haussig, H. W., *Die Geschichte Zentralasiens und der Seidenstrasse in Islamischer Zeit*, Darmstadt: Wissenschaftliche Buchgesellschaft, 1988.

Ibn Fadlan, *Risala*, in Kovalevskii, A. P. (facs. edn, trans.), *Kniga Akhmeda ibn Fadlana o ego puteshestvii na Volgu v 921–922 gg.*, Kharkov: Izd-vo gos. universiteta im. A. M. Gor'kogo, 1956.

Kazanski, M., *Les Goths (ier–viier siecles ap. J.-C.)*, Paris: Ed. Errance, 1991.

Khazanov, A. M., *Sotsial'naya istoriya skifov*, Moscow: Nauka, 1975.

Kiselev, S. V., *Drevnyaya istoriya yuzhnoy Sibiri*, 2nd edn, Moscow: Izd-vo akad. nauk SSSR, 1951.

Kiselev, S. V., ed., *Drevnemongol'skie goroda*, Moscow: Nauka, 1965.

Klyashtornyi, S. G., and T. I. Sultanov, *Kazakhstan: Letopis' trekh tysyachiletii*, Alma-Ata, 1992.

Klyuchevskii, V. O., *Sochineniya v devyati tomakh*, Moscow: Mysl', 1987–90.

Kohl, P. L., *L'Asie Centrale: dès origines à l'âge du Fer*, Paris: Editions Recherche sur les Civilisations, 1983.

Kokovtsov, P. V., *Evreisko-khazarskaya perepiska v X veke*, Leningrad: Izd-vo akad. nauk SSSR, 1932.

Kol'tsov, L. V., ed., *Mezolit SSSR*, Moscow: Nauka, 1989.

Koshelenko, G. A., ed., *Drevneyshiye gosudarstva Kavkaza i Srednei Azii*, Moscow: Nauka, 1985 (see *Drevneyshiye gosudarstva*).

Kumekov, B. E., *Gosudarstvo kimakov IX–XI vv. po arabskim istochnikam*, Alma-Ata: Nauka Kazakhskoi SSR, 1972.

Kürsat-Ahlers, Elçin, *Zur frühen Staatenbildung von Steppenvölkern*, Berlin: Duncker and Humblot, 1994.

Kuz'mina, E. E., *Drevneyshie skotovody ot Urala do Tyan-Shanya*, Frunze, 1986.

L'Asie Centrale et ses rapports avec les civilisations orientales des origines à l'age du fer, Mission Archéologique Française en Asie Centrale, tome 1, Paris: De Boccard, 1988.

Liu Mau-tsai, *Die chinesischen Nachrichten Zur Geschichte der Ost-Türken (T'u-küe)*, 2 vols, Wiesbaden: Harrassowitz, 1958.

Magomedov, M. G., *Obrazovanie Khazarskogo Kaganata*, Moscow: Nauka, 1983.

Malov, S. E., *Pamyatniki drevnetyurkskoi pis'mennosti*, Moscow/Leningrad: Izd-vo akad. nauk SSSR, 1951.

Mavrodina, R. M., 'Rus' i kochevniki', in V. V. Mavrodin et al., eds, *Sovetskaya istoriografiya Kievskoi Rusi*, Leningrad, 1973, pp. 210–21.

Mavrodina, R. M., *Kievskaya Rus' i kochevniki*, Leningrad: Nauka, 1983.

Melyukova, A. I., ed., *Stepi Evropeiskoi chasti SSSR v skifo-sarmatskoye vremya*, Moscow: Nauka, 1989.

Mikheev, V. K., *Podon'ye v sostave khazarskogo kaganata*, Khar'kov: Izd-vo pri Kharkovskom gos. universitete izdatel'skogo ob'edinenii 'Vyshcha shkola', 1985.

Moravcsik, Gyula, *Byzantinoturcica 1: Die Byzantinischen Quellen Der Geschichte der Türkvolker*, 3rd reprint (of 1958 edn), Leiden: Brill, 1983.

Muminova, I. M., ed., *Istoriya Khorezma s drevneishikh vremen do nashikh dnei*, Tashkent, 1976.

Novgorodova, N. A., *Drevnyaya Mongoliya*, Moscow: Nauka, 1988.

Novosel'tsev, A. P., *Khazarskoe gosudarstvo i ego rol' v istorii Vostochnoi Evropy i Kavkaza*, Moscow: Nauka, 1990.

Ocherki istorii SSSR, vol. 1, eds, P. N. Tret'yakov and A. L. Mongait, *Pervobytno-obshchinnyi stroi i drevneishie godusarstva na territorii SSSR*, Moscow: Izd-vo akad. nauk SSSR, 1956.

Paleolit SSSR ed. P. I. Borisovskii, Moscow: Nauka, 1984.

Paul, Juergen, *Herrscher, Gemeinwesen, Vermittler: Ostiran und Transoxanien in vormongolischer Zeit*, Beirut and Stuttgart: Franz Steiner, 1996.

Pletneva, S. A., *Ot kochevii k gorodam. Saltovo-Mayatskaya kul'tura*, Moscow: Nauka, 1967.

Pletneva, S. A., ed., *Stepi Evrazii v epokhu srednevekov'ya*, Moscow: Nauka, 1981.

Pletneva, S. A., *Kochevniki srednevekov'ya: poiski istoricheskikh zakonomernos-tei*, Moscow: Nauka, 1982.

Pletneva, S. A., *Khazary*, Moscow: Nauka, 1986.

Pletneva, S. A., *Polovtsy*, Moscow: Nauka, 1990.

Rudenko, S. I., *Kul'tura khunnov i noinulinskie kurgany*, Moscow-Leningrad, 1962.

Sarianidi, V. I., *Drevnosti stran Margush*, Ashkhabad: Ylym, 1990.

Sarianidi, V. I., *Drevnii Merv*, Moscow: 1993.

Sinor, Denis, *Introduction à l'étude de l'Eurasie Centrale*, Wiesbaden: Otto Harrassowitz, 1963.

Smirnov, A. P., *Volzhskie bulgary*, Moscow: 1951.

Smirnov, A. P., 'Volzhskaya Bolgariya', in Pletneva *Stepi Evrazii v epokhu srednevekov'ya*, pp. 208–12.

Smirnov, K. F., 'Une "Amazone" du IVe siècle avant n.e. sur le territoire du Don', *Dialogues d'histoire ancienne* (1982), 8:121–41.

Staviskij, B. Ja., *La Bactriane sous les Kushans: problèmes d'histoire et de culture*, trans. P. Bernard et al., Paris, 1986.

Sugar, P. F., *A History of Hungary*, London: Tauris, 1990.

Szyszman, Simon, *Le Karaïsme. Ses doctrines et son histoire*, Lausanne: L'Age d'homme, 1980.

Szyszman, Simon, *Les Karaïtes d'Europe*, Uppsala: University of Uppsala, 1989.

Taşağıl, Ahmet, *Gök-Türkler*, Ankara: 1995.

Tikhomirov, M. N., *Drevnerusskie goroda*, 2nd edn, Moscow: Izd-vo Moskovskogo universiteta, 1956.

Tolstov, S. P., *Drevnii Khorezm*, Moscow: Izd-vo Moskovskogo universiteta, 1948.

Tolstov, S. P., *Po drevnim deltam Oksa i Yaksarta*, Moscow: Izd-vo vostochnoi literatury, 1962.

Wolski, Jozef, *L'Empire des Arsacides*, Acta Iranica 32, Louvain: Peeters, 1993.

Yan, V. G., *Chingiz-Khan*, Moscow: 1939 (trans. as Ian, V., *Jenghiz-khan: a tale of 13th Century Asia*, London: Hutchinson, 1945); *Batyi*, Moscow: 1941 (trans. as Ian, V., *Batu-khan: a tale of the 13th Century*, London: Hutchinson, 1945); *K 'poslednemu moryu'*, Moscow: 1955 (a Soviet era trilogy of novels about the Mongol conquests).

INDEX

Abbasid caliphate, 287, 294, 297, 304, 310–11, 313–15, 321, 335, 370, 374–6, 378–9, 386, 411, 414
Abu Muslim, 311–12
Achaemenid dynasty, empire, 130, 155, 163–8, 169–71, 176–7, 304; *see also* Cambyses; Cyrus II; Darius I; Darius III
Adrianople, 201, 223, 228
Afanasevo culture, 101, 106
Afghanistan, 3, 13, 18, 26, 109, 112, 170, 179, 209, 213, 370, 373
Afrasiab, 137, 159; *see also* Samarkand
Africa, xix, 23–5, 30, 31, 38, 72, 323
agrarian 'barbarians' *see* Goths; Manchuria
agriculture/agriculturalists, xx, 69, 88, 353; in Central Asia, 70–4, 103–4, 109, 113, 115, 124, 137–40, 142, 167, 171, 173, 177, 217, 306–7, 314, 319, 353, 416; difficulties in Inner Eurasia, 5, 7–8, 10, 14, 69–70; in eastern Inner Eurasia, 80–1, 128, 189–90, 233–5, 265, 388, 416, 418; origins, xx, 69; and pastoralists, 83–6, 91, 94, 100, 103–4, 113, 115, 124, 132, 148, 189–90, 228–9, 251, 256, 265, 287–9, 291, 296, 360, 388, 416, 418; in western Inner Eurasia, 49–50, 74–80, 83–6, 94, 100, 103–4, 124, 134–6, 140, 151–2, 155, 190, 223–6, 281–2, 327–32, 353, 360, 362, 367–8; in woodlands, 12–13, 56, 368; *see also* Cututeni-Tripolye culture; hot spots; irrigation; neolithic; rainfall agriculture; 'secondary products revolution'; swidden farming
Ahura Mazda, 138–9, 171, 216; *see also* Zoroastrianism
Ai Khanum, 170–1, 173–4

akinakes, 127, 163–4
Ala ad-Din Muhammad (Khorezmshah), 379, 385, 394, 401–4
al-'Amin, caliph, 313
Alans, 137, 147, 177, 197, 211, 219, 227, 277, 280, 288, 291, 296, 298, 329, 357
Albania (in Caucasus), 283–4, 292
al-Biruni, 55, 309, 322–3, 370
Alexander Eschate (Khodjend), 169
Alexander Nevskii, 414
Alexander of Macedon, 128, 136–7, 165, 168–71, 308–9, 379
al-Istakhri, 289–91, 293, 307, 323
al-Khwarazmi, 323, 326, 354
alliances, 34, 88, 90, 102, 129, 135, 150–1, 169, 194, 405; *see also* tribes; supra-tribal associations; states; Temüjin
al-Ma'mun, caliph, 313, 315–16, 323
al-Mansur, caliph, 287, 311
al-Mas'udi, 288–9, 292–4, 297, 339
al-Muqaddasi, 296, 315, 318, 320–1
al-Muqanna, 312
al-Muqtadir (caliph), 320
al-Mu'tamid, caliph, 315
al-Mu-tasim, caliph, 313, 315
Alp Arslan (Saljuk), 316, 376
Alp Tegin (Ghaznavid), 316, 370
al-Tabari, 177, 213, 287, 309
Altai mountains, 13, 26, 101, 103, 106, 125, 128, 141–2, 152, 185, 247–51, 255, 264, 272, 354, 356, 394, 402
Altaic languages, xvii, 227, 248
Altuntash (Khorezmshah), 377
Altyn-depe, 108–10
Amazons, 143–4
amber, 41, 296, 320, 337, 340, 372
America, xx, 9, 17, 18, 23, 37, 52, 54, 58, 148
amirs, 315, 317, 372, 375, 379; *see also* governors
Ammianus Marcellinus, 226–8
Amr (Saffarid), 314–15

Amu Darya (Oxus) river, 34, 48, 72, 105, 110, 112, 115, 138, 164–5, 168, 170–1, 173–4, 217, 252–3, 260–1, 304, 306, 308–9, 371
A-na-kuei, kaghan, 237, 250
An Shih-kao, 236
Anatolia, 72, 77, 86, 134, 153, 164, 174, 179, 282, 376
ancestors, 148, 195, 256, 366, 424
anda, 390, 395
Andrei Bogolyubskii, prince, 368
Andronovo culture, 102–5, 107, 115
Angara river, 26, 51
animal-based foods, 15, 28–9, 32, 86
animals, xix–xx, 10, 23, 28–9
Antes, 280, 329, 332; *see also* Slavs
Antiochus I (Seleucid), 169, 171
Antiochus II (Seleucid), 173
Antiochus III (Seleucid), 173, 175
Antiochus IV (Seleucid), 174
Anushtegin (Khorezmshah), 377
Arabia, 72, 82, 263
Arabic conquest of Central Asia *see* Islamic invasions
Arabic language, 321–2
Arabs, 266–7, 286, 298, 304, 307–9, 311–12, 323, 369
Aral sea, 48, 203, 211, 227, 252, 306, 355–6
Aramaic, 167–8, 175, 257, 398
archaeology, xvii–xviii, 26, 30, 39, 52, 69, 90, 99–101, 104, 123–4, 134, 141, 143, 149, 170–1, 173, 175, 177, 211, 217, 222–3, 226, 248, 265, 281, 285, 288–90, 296, 330, 333, 335, 337–9, 343, 430
Arctic, xx, 3, 7, 10, 18, 29, 36–8, 47, 52–4, 56–8
Ardashir, 177, 213
aridity, xix, 5, 7–8, 10, 13, 23, 26, 28, 47, 87, 106, 110, 124
Arik-Boke, 394
aristocracies/elites, 137, 148, 150, 167, 187, 216, 223, 250, 255–6, 281, 294, 306, 362–4, 396–7, 405, 422; *see also* ruling clans